Handbook of
Counselling
Psychology

Praise for the book

This is an excellent text that encompasses the current state of the discipline of counselling psychology; it is an asset for students, practitioners and academics. One of the vital features is the first chapter that states central concepts about counselling psychology in context, and in so doing shows its firm philosophical roots where the emphasis is firmly based on 'being with' in the person–other relationship, as opposed to 'doing something to' the other.

The second edition is a developmental step forward for counselling psychology, where the discipline's stance on what constitutes science, inquiry and the nature of evidence-based practice is clearly outlined. The versatility of the text is illustrated by theoretical perspectives on practice; the framework of the life-span appreciates the developmental view where distress is seen as a part of human experience as opposed to pathology. These features contribute to a counselling psychology text that is essential reading material.

Professor Pam James
August 21st 2002

Handbook of
Counselling
Psychology

Second edition

Edited by Ray Woolfe
Windy Dryden
Sheelagh Strawbridge

SAGE Publications
London • Thousand Oaks • New Delhi

First edition published 1996, Reprinted 1997, 1998, 2001

Second edition published 2003

SAGE Publications Ltd
6 Bonhill Street
London EC2A 4PU

SAGE Publications Inc
2455 Teller Road
Thousand Oaks, California 91320

SAGE Publications India Pvt Ltd
B-42, Panchsheel Enclave
Post Box 4109
New Delhi 110 017

British Library Cataloguing in Publication data

A catalogue record for this book is available
from the British Library

ISBN 0 7619 7206 4
ISBN 0 7619 7207 2 (pbk)

Library of Congress Control Number: 2002108663

Typeset by C&M Digitals (P) Ltd., Chennai, India
Printed in Great Britain by The Cromwell Press Ltd, Trowbridge, Wiltshire

Contents

List of Figures

List of Tables

Notes on the Contributors

Chris Barker is a Senior Lecturer in Clinical Psychology at University College London. His research interests centre on the process of psychological helping in all its various manifestations, from the formalized settings of counselling, therapy and medical practice to the informal settings of helping in everyday relationships and in mutual support groups. He is a co-author of *Research Methods in Clinical Psychology* (2002).

Michael Barkham is Professor of Clinical and Counselling Psychology and Director of the Psychological Therapies Research Centre at the University of Leeds, and also Visiting Professor at the University of Northumbria at Newcastle. He has carried out various research trials into the processes and outcomes of psychological therapies. In addition, he has carried forward a research programme to help build a robust evidence base for the effectiveness of the psychological therapies in routine practice settings.

Simon Biggs is Professor of Social Gerontology at Keele University within the School of Social Relations. He is an executive member of the European Master's Programme in Gerontology and a Chartered Counselling Psychologist with particular interest in Jungian approaches to work with older adults. He has written widely in the areas of social policy, social theory, ageing studies and professional identity.

Robert Bor is a Consultant Psychologist at the Royal Free Hospital London in the Infection and Immunity Directorate. He is a Chartered Clinical, Counselling and Health Psychologist, Associated Fellow of the British Psychological Society and a UKCP Registered Systemic Psychotherapist. He was formerly Counselling Psychology Course Director in the Psychology Departments of City University, London and London Metropolitan University. He is now a Visiting Professor at City University and Emeritus Professor of Psychology at London Metropolitan University. He has a special interest in the impact of illness on families and close relationships. A Fellow of the Royal Aeronautical Society, he provides psychological counselling in the aerospace industry.

Michael Burton is now retired from his role as Director of Psychological and Counselling Services at the University of Sussex. He is a Chartered Counselling Psychologist and member of the Guild of Psychotherapists. He is currently in therapy (again!) exploring what lies beneath the manic defences of the last fifty years.

Cassie Cooper is a practising Kleinian-trained Psychoanalytic Psychotherapist and Counselling Psychologist, with a strong leaning towards Attachment Theory. She is a founder member and Fellow of the British Association for

Counselling and Psychotherapy and an active member of the UK Council for Psychotherapy. She is joint editor of the BPS *Psychotherapy Newsletter*. Formerly head of a university diploma course in counselling, she works as a psychotherapist, supervisor and examiner in London, besides acting as consultant to BBC Drama on counselling issues.

Roslyn Corney is Professor of Psychology at the University of Greenwich, Director of Research in the School of Social Sciences and Law, and Deputy Director (Research and Innovation) of One plus One. Her research has focused on the treatment of depression and anxiety in general practice, including the evaluation of counsellors attached to general practice. She has also conducted studies of help seeking, the use of formal and informal sources of help, psychosocial and psychosexual adjustment after surgery for cancer, GPs' attitudes to preventive medicine and patient satisfaction with medical care.

Adrian Coyle is Senior Lecturer and Research Tutor on the Practitioner Doctorate in Psychotherapeutic and Counselling Psychology in the Department of Psychology at the University of Surrey. His research and writing have addressed various issues within social psychology and lesbian and gay psychology (with a focus upon identity issues, psychological well-being and experiences of therapy) and qualitative research methods. He was co-editor (with Celia Kitzinger) of *Lesbian & Gay Psychology: New Perspectives* (2002).

Tom Davey is in private practice as an integrative psychotherapist and supervisor in Auckland, New Zealand.

Jim Downey is Consultant Clinical Psychologist and Head of the Child Clinical Psychology Specialty in Pembrokeshire and Derwen NHS Trust. He has worked in child and adolescent mental health services for nearly twenty years. He is particularly interested in Looked After Children and children diagnosed with a mental illness. He is committed to promoting a developmental perspective in services for troubled children. He represents child clinical psychology on the National Implementation Group developing CAMHS strategy in Wales.

Windy Dryden currently works at Goldsmiths College where he is Professor of Psychotherapeutic Studies as well as being the Programme Co-ordinator of the MSc in Rational Emotive Behaviour Therapy and the Diploma in Cognitive Approaches to Counselling and Psychotherapy. He is actively involved in the practice of REBT and in writing books on the subject for professionals and the general public.

Zack Eleftheriadou trained as a psychologist and a psychotherapist. She has a private practice in north London, and serves at the Medical Foundation for the Care of Victims of Torture, where she works with refugee children and their families. She has been a supervisor, trainer and consultant in the field of cross-cultural therapy for many years. She has published widely, including the book *Transcultural Counselling* (1994).

Alan Frankland is a Chartered Counselling Psychologist and Accredited Counsellor and Trainer. Formerly Principal Lecturer and Head of Counselling and Psychotherapy at Nottingham Trent University, he practises in Nottingham (APSI), is involved in training in England and France, and is BPS Registrar for Counselling Psychology. He is the co-author of a best-selling introductory text-book. He has been Chair of the Division of Counselling Psychology and on the BPS Board of Directors, and is a Fellow of the BACP.

Maria Gilbert is a chartered clinical psychologist, integrative psychotherapist, trainer and supervisor who has many years of experience in adult education, organizational consultancy and training and also maintains a private psycho-therapy and supervision practice. She is currently head of the integrative psychotherapy, integrative counselling psychology and psychotherapy, and super-vision courses at Metanoia Institute in West London. Her most recent publica-tion is *Psychotherapy Supervision* (2000), co-authored with Kenneth Evans.

Fiona Goudie is a Consultant Clinical Psychologist and has been Head of the Older Adult Psychology Division of Psychological Health, Sheffield since 1992. She is an honorary lecturer at Sheffield University. Recent research activity has been concerned with the impact of reminiscence on the quality of life of older people. Her clinical interests and publications focus on psychological therapies, depression and dementia. She co-edited *The Essential Dementia Care Handbook* (2002) with Graham Stokes.

Diane Hammersley is a Chartered Counselling Psychologist practising as a psychotherapist, supervisor, co-ordinator of training and trainer. Besides training teachers abroad she has run advanced training workshops for therapists. Author of *Counselling People on Prescribed Drugs* (1995), she specializes in addiction prob-lems. A former Chair of the Division of Counselling Psychology, she was a mem-ber of the Training Committee in Counselling Psychology and the division's Board of Examiners, of which she is Chair. She is interested in qualitative research.

Henry Hollanders lectures in the University of Manchester, where he directs the professional doctorate in counselling, supervises Ph.D. studies in the field of counselling and psychotherapy and supports the Master's and diploma programmes. He has had many years' experience as a practitioner and training consultant, having worked in medical, pastoral, educational and community settings. His integrative counselling practice is based in Pendle in Lancashire and in the city of Manchester.

Carolyn Kagan is Professor of Community Social Psychology at Manchester Metropolitan University. She is a Chartered Counselling Psychologist and qualified social worker and co-ordinates the first MSc in Community Psychology in the UK. She works particularly with vulnerable people, combining systems interventions with social action perspectives around individual, group and social change agendas with social justice at the core.

Jennifer M. Kidd is a Senior Lecturer in the Department of Organizational Psychology, Birkbeck College, University of London, and a Chartered Occupational Psychologist. Her main areas of research and publication are careers and career management, and her work focuses on the provision of informal career support in organizations and on the role of emotion in career development. She is co-editor of the *British Journal of Guidance and Counselling*.

Charles Legg is Senior Lecturer in Psychology at City University, London and specializes in the biological bases of behaviour which he approaches from a systems viewpoint. His current research is on appetites and food cravings. He has recently trained as a counsellor and is currently involved in synthesizing biological concepts within a systemic counselling framework, working with clients who are on weight-loss programmes.

John McLeod is Professor of Counselling at University of Abertay Dundee. His interests are in the relevance of research for practice, the social significance of counselling, and the development of narrative approaches. He is author of *An Introduction to Counselling* (third edition, 2003) and many other books and articles, and is editor of *Counselling and Psychotherapy Research*.

Martin Milton is Senior Lecturer and Course Director of the Practitioner Doctorate in Psychotherapeutic and Counselling Psychology at the University of Surrey. He is Consultant Counselling Psychologist and Registered Psychotherapist with the North East London Mental Health Trust. His research and writing embrace lesbian and gay affirmative psychology and psychotherapy, HIV-related psychotherapy and existential psychotherapy.

Vanja Orlans is a Chartered Counselling Psychologist, a Chartered Occupational Psychologist and a UKCP-registered psychotherapist. She is a director of the consultancy Psychology Matters and Course Co-ordinator of the MSc in Integrative Counselling Psychology and Psychotherapy at the Metanoia Institute, London. She has published on clinical and organizational matters, and is examiner for clinical training programmes in the UK and abroad. Her private practice includes counselling, psychotherapy, supervision and organizational consulting.

Stephen Palmer is Director of the Centre for Stress Management and Honorary Professor of Psychology at the City University, London. He is a Visiting Professor of Work Based Learning and Stress Management at the National Centre for Work Based Learning Partnerships at Middlesex University. He received the Counselling Psychology Award 2000 from the Division of Counselling Psychology of the British Psychological Society for his scientific and professional contribution to counselling psychology in Britain.

David Purves is a Principal Lecturer in Counselling Psychology at London Metropolitan University and a Chartered Counselling Psychologist and Psychotherapist. Forsaking a career as a professional diver, he gained his doctorate in experimental psychology from the University of Oxford in 1994, later retraining in counselling psychology. He now specializes in research on and the treatment of post-traumatic stress disorder. He has written and lectured extensively at home and abroad.

Peter J. Ross is a Chartered Counselling Psychologist and Chartered Occupational Psychologist. He is Director of the University of Reading Counselling Service, which offers counselling to university staff and students as well as occupational health support for staff and academic and cultural support for students. He has published extensively on belief systems; his main interest is depression and 'at risk' behaviour. He is a former Chair of the Heads of University Counselling Services.

John Rowan is the author of *The Reality Game* (second edition, 1998), *Ordinary Ecstasy* (third edition, 2001), *Healing the Male Psyche* (1997) and other books. He is on the editorial boards of *Self and Society*, the *Journal of Humanistic Psychology*, the *Transpersonal Psychology Review* and the *Counselling Psychology Review*. A founder member of the UK Association of Humanistic Psychology Practitioners, he is also a Fellow of the British Psychological Society and of the British Association for Counselling and Psychotherapy.

Michael J. Scott is the author of *Counselling for Post-traumatic Stress Disorder* (second edition, 2001), five other textbooks and numerous papers. He is an Honorary Research Associate in the Department of Psychology at the University of Manchester, where he teaches CBT on the Master's course. Recently he was a clinical supervisor and trainer in a controlled trial of cognitive therapy for substance abuse. He has a private practice which includes medico-legal work and is also consultant to a number of large organizations.

Carol Shillito-Clarke was one of the first people to be chartered as a Counselling Psychologist, in 1992. She is also a Fellow of the British Association for Counselling and Psychotherapy and is accredited by the BACP as both a Counsellor and a Supervisor. Since 1977 she has trained and worked as an integrative therapist, supervisor, trainer, lecturer and consultant in both the private and public sectors. She has a private practice in Warwick.

Diana Shmukler PhD is a Supervising and Teaching Transactional Analyst, Integrative Psychotherapist (UKCP), Clinical Psychologist (South Africa Medical and Dental Council), former Associate Professor of Applied Psychology (University of Witwatersrand, Johannesburg, South Africa), currently Visiting Professor of Psychotherapy (University of Derby). Diana is a member of the European Association of Integrative Psychotherapy. She teaches Integrative Therapy at Metanoia Institute in London as well as the Institute for Arts in

Therapy and Education. She has taught and run training workshops in South Africa, Australia, Holland, Austria as well as the United Kingdom.

Ernesto Spinelli is Professor of Psychotherapy, Counselling and Counselling Psychology and the Academic Dean of the School of Psychotherapy and Counselling at Regent's College, London. He is an internationally recognized exponent of existential psychotherapy whose many publications have been praised for their clarity and originality. He has served as Chair of the BPS Division of Counselling Psychology and in 2000 received the Division's Award for Outstanding Achievement in the Advancement of the Profession. His most recent book is *The Mirror and the Hammer* (2001).

Sheelagh Strawbridge is a Chartered Counselling Psychologist in independent practice. She has a background in university teaching on degree courses in social science and professional courses in counselling and social work. Her interest in ethical and socio-political issues in counselling/psychotherapy is reflected in her publications and her committee work for the BPS Division of Counselling Psychology. Among her publications is *Exploring Self and Society* (with Rosamund Billington and Jenny Hockey, 1998).

Eddy Street is a Chartered Clinical and Counselling Psychologist. He works as a Consultant Clinical Psychologist in the CAMH service of Cardiff and Vale NHS Trust and is Honorary Lecturer in the Department of Child Health, University of Wales College of Medicine. He has published widely on themes related to family therapy and is a past editor of the *Journal of Family Therapy*. His most recent book (with Mark Rivett) is *Family Therapy in Focus* (2003).

Léonie Sugarman is a Chartered Occupational Psychologist and author of *Life-Span Development: Frameworks, Accounts and Strategies* (second edition, 2001). She is Senior Lecturer in Psychology at St Martin's College, Lancaster, where she teaches on a range of professional and academic courses, including BSc (Hons) in Applied Psychology and a BACP accredited Dip (HE) in Person-Centred Counselling. She is a former Associate Editor of the *British Journal of Guidance and Counselling* and is currently Vice President of the British Association for Counselling and Psychotherapy.

Angela M. Taylor is Study Adviser at the University of Reading, where she is head of the Study Support Team. After work and research in neuropsychology at the National Hospital, Queen Square, she became a Chartered Psychologist and counsellor in further and higher education. Her research interests include specific learning difficulties, learning skills and strategies, and all aspects of adolescence. She is completing a book on counselling skills for youth workers and mentors.

Carol Tindall is a Senior Lecturer in Psychology at Manchester Metropolitan University and a part-time practising counsellor who has most recently worked with survivors of abuse. She teaches psychology and counselling on both undergraduate and postgraduate programmes, and is currently coordinator of the MSc in Psychology and Counselling at Manchester Metropolitan University. She has had many years' experience as a practitioner and in supervising BSc, MSc and PhD students in applied counselling psychology research.

Bill Wahl is a Chartered Counselling Psychologist and US Certified School Psychologist. On moving to England in 1995 he retrained as a Counselling Psychologist (independent route), principally studying with Petruska Clarkson at Physis, and spent five years with the North Devon Behaviour Support Team. Now staff psychologist for North Devon NHS Trust, he is involved with the BPS Counselling Psychology and Transpersonal Psychology sections; his principal interest is therapeutic integration.

David A. Winter is Professor of Clinical Psychology and Programme Director of the Doctorate in Clinical Psychology at the University of Hertfordshire and Head of Clinical Psychology Services for Barnet in Barnet, Enfield and Haringey Mental Health Trust. A past Chair of the BPS Psychotherapy section, he is a UKCP-registered Personal Construct Psychotherapist and has chaired the council's Experiential Constructivist section. He is the author of *Personal Construct Psychology in Clinical Practice* (1992) and over eighty other publications.

Ray Woolfe is a Chartered Counselling Psychologist, Psychoanalytic Psychotherapist and Accredited Counsellor. After a career as a university lecturer at the Open University and Keele he now has a private practice in psychology and psychotherapy in Manchester. He is Visiting Professor in Counselling Psychology at London Metropolitan University and a Fellow of BACP. In 2001 he received a special BPS Centenary Award for the Development of Counselling Psychology. Formerly Chair of the BPS Division of Counselling Psychology and Registrar of the Examination Board for the Diploma in Counselling Psychology, he is the author of many books and articles.

Preface

When the first edition of this book was published in 1994, counselling psychology was still in its infancy in Britain, having existed as a division of the British Psychological Society for only two years. At that time the discipline was still somewhat obsessively concerned with examining itself. This was reflected in the energy devoted to questions such as 'What is counselling psychology?' and 'How does it differ from cognate areas such as clinical psychology?' Attempts to answer such questions focused around topics such as working in different settings from other psychologists, employing different techniques, working with clients rather than patients, focusing on developmental issues as opposed to dealing with pathological conditions and emphasizing prevention rather than cure.

The somewhat introverted nature of this discussion was typical of a discipline trying to find its place within the larger psychological enterprise, and while these questions are still asked, they have ceased to dominate. Since those early days the discipline has come to have a more solid existence on the ground. A system has been established for accrediting training courses, and a number of such courses now exist, though located mainly in London or the south-east of England. In addition, there is now a well established professional qualifying route for independent trainees within the British Psychological Society.

Counselling psychology has become much more outward-looking, as is reflected in an increase in research output and publications and wider interest in the development of qualitative methodologies which are consistent with the humanist and subjectivist principles which underpin the discipline. In the early days it was difficult for newly qualified practitioners to gain employment outside private practice, but the situation has changed markedly, and increasingly counselling psychologists have found employment in a range of arenas such as the National Health Service, the prison service, industry and commerce, and many community settings.

The impact has been active and identifiable. For example, many psychology departments within the NHS now demonstrate a much greater acknowledgement of the centrality of the relationship between client and psychologist. It has provoked psychologists into thinking more broadly about their therapeutic work and questioning some of their assumptions, for example about the value placed upon subjectivity and objectivity and facilitating well-being as opposed to responding to sickness and pathology.

We believe the book reflects the changes which have occurred since the first edition and provides a comprehensive portrait of an established and outgoing discipline as it exists in the first decade of the new century. The first edition was well received and we have therefore seen no reason to amend the structure which characterized that volume. This involves a division into six parts. The first consists of a single chapter which sets the scene and examines the origins and philosophical basis of counselling psychology as it has developed in the United Kingdom.

Part II focuses upon methodology and contains three chapters on quantitative and qualitative research methods and upon evaluating practice. Michael Barkham alludes to some of the changes which have taken place when he refers to four research generations as opposed to the three described in the first edition.

Part III highlights practice and consists of nine chapters on individual paradigms and models. It contains a new chapter on transpersonal approaches. Developmental issues are of significant concern to counselling psychologists, and this theme is taken up in the Part IV, which examines different stages of the life course, detailing the psychological issues involved and the kinds of interventions made. The accounts link theory and practice , a focus which is maintained in the penultimate part.

Part V highlights some of the major themes and contexts with which counselling psychologists are engaged. The topics covered include primary care, cross-cultural care, family and couples, groups, career development work, the workplace, enhancing learning skills and stress management. Together these chapters provide an overview of key sectors in which counselling psychologists operate: health, education and work.

The final part is concerned with professional and ethical issues and looks ahead to developments over the next decade.

Overall, our view is that the book offers a detailed portrait of the history, philosophy, theory, methodology and practice of counselling psychology in Britain. We live in changing times, and psychology is not immune. It is possible that in the years ahead, with the growing emphasis on competences, we may move towards a more generalist, applied psychology. However, were this to happen our view is that counselling psychology would have a great deal to offer in shaping such developments. We hope and believe that this book will contribute to that end.

R.W.
W.D.
S.S.

Acknowledgements

The editors would like to acknowledge the efforts of all those people who have contributed to the development of counselling psychology in the twenty years since it first appeared in the United Kingdom as a section of the British Psychological Society. Some of them have written chapters for this book, but there are others too numerous to name without whom the discipline would not have flourished in the manner that it has.

The compilation of such a large project as this book owes much to the support and encouragement received from our editor at Sage, Alison Poyner, and her assistant Louise Wise.

Finally, please note that when case study material is used, all identifiable material has been removed and pseudonyms have been used to protect client anonymity.

Every effort has been made to trace all the copyright holders, but if any have been inadvertently overlooked the publishers will be pleased to make the necessary arrangement at the first opportunity.

Table 4.1   'Matrix of levels and quality areas involved in developing an audit' from J. Firth-Cozens (1993) *Audit in Mental Health Services*. Hove: Lawrence Erlbaum Associates.

Figure 4.2   'CORE System forms', with kind permission of CORE System Trustees.

Table 5.1   'Taxonomy of Defences' from J.C. Perry (1993) 'Defences and their effects', in N. Miller, L. Luborsky, J. Barber and J. Docherty, *Psychodynamic Treatment Research*. New York: Basic Books.

Table 5.2   'Results of Meta-Analysis' from E. Luborsky, B. Singer, B. Dickter and K.A. Schmidt (1993) 'The efficacy of dynamic psychotherapies', in N. Miller, L. Luborsky, J. Barber and J. Docherty, *Psychodynamic Treatment Research*. New York: Basic Books.

Table 7.2   'Model of Client Difficulties' from J.B. Persons (1989) *Cognitive Therapy in Practice: a Case Formulation Approach*. New York: Norton.

Part I
Setting the Scene

Chapter 1   Counselling Psychology in Context

1 Counselling Psychology in Context
SHEELAGH STRAWBRIDGE AND RAY WOOLFE

The nature and development of counselling psychology

Counselling psychology in the United Kingdom is of relatively recent origin. In 1982 the British Psychological Society established a Counselling Psychology Section and in 1989 it became a Special Group, a kind of half-way house between a scientific interest group and a professional body, with its own practice guidelines. In the same year the Society established a Diploma in Counselling Psychology, managed by a Board of Examiners, in order to provide a route to chartered status for trainees wishing to specialize in this area. In 1994 full divisional status was achieved, and psychologists with the Diploma or a Statement of Equivalence, gained through a grandparenting process, finally became eligible for chartered status. Thus, in the space of twelve years, counselling psychology established itself as a full profession of applied psychology in the United Kingdom alongside clinical, educational and occupational.

Of course counselling psychology has been recognized for a longer period in the United States. There is also a real sense of it being a contemporary representation of a much older tradition. For example, in the 1850s, Wilhelm Wundt argued that psychology is the science of consciousness. His research subjects were required to introspect their sensations and feelings, whilst William James suggested that the self is the product of the multiplicity of relationships that the person has with others. This early interest in consciousness and subjective experience was developed in continental Europe within the framework of phenomenology and existential phenomenology. However, until recently it was largely neglected in the United Kingdom and the United States, although it was pursued by symbolic interactionists such as George Herbert Meade, who pointed out that the self is not just constructed in a social context but has the capacity for self-reflection, or to be what Charles Cooley described as a 'looking-glass' self. Counselling psychology springs from and is inspired by the work of these thinkers and others like them who elevate understanding the subjective world of self and other into a primary position in psychology. It has a particularly strong connection with American humanistic and existential thinkers such as Abraham Maslow, Carl Rogers and Rollo May who also argued for the need to see human beings in a holistic manner, rather than as a collection of psychological parts, and grounded the practice of psychology in humanistic values. It is instructive, at this stage in our development, to return to earlier debates about science and values, and we shall do so briefly below.

Counselling as a practice has its origin in this American humanistic and existential psychology – indeed, the term 'counselling' is of American origin, reputedly coined by Rogers, who, lacking a medical qualification, was prevented from referring to his work as psychotherapy. British counselling psychology is, in turn, rooted in counselling. However, counselling (and psychotherapy), in Britain, largely developed separately, outside the profession of psychology, and counselling psychology represents a return to psychology initiated by psychologists trained in counselling and psychotherapy. As a developing branch of British psychology, it is committed to recognizing and establishing the value of the three major traditions in psychology, namely the phenomenological (including existential and humanistic) and psychoanalytic/psychodynamic traditions alongside the cognitive–behavioural tradition favoured by the mainstream of academic and applied psychologists. The histories are complex but we shall tease out further strands as part of this exercise in situating and exploring the identity of counselling psychology.

One question sometimes asked is how does counselling psychology differ in both its practice and research, if at all, from other psychological disciplines, particularly clinical psychology? Given the complexities of both histories and forms of practice, it is not easy to answer. However, some of the priorities in counselling psychology can be seen in the factors favourable to the recent growth of the discipline in Britain. Woolfe (1990) identified the following as of particular importance:

- An increasing awareness among many psychologists of the importance of the helping relationship as a significant variable in facilitating the therapeutic endeavour.
- A growing questioning of what is often described as the medical model of professional–client relationships and a move towards a more humanistic value base.
- A developing focus in the work of helpers on facilitating well-being as opposed to responding to sickness and pathology.

It is perhaps the focus on the quality of the relationship that is particularly significant, as there is growing awareness across a range of professions that helping involves more than the application of specific treatment regimes in a standardized fashion. Increasingly it is perceived as an interaction between two people in which a key factor is the quality of their relationship. There is widespread agreement that, whatever the skill, this is best employed within the framework of a relationship characterized by Rogers (1951) as containing the core personal dispositions of empathy, acceptance and congruence. The construct 'empathy' represents a particularly well researched domain, and Barkham (1988) has charted its continuing influence on psychologists over three decades.

We shall explore these themes further as well as a countervailing tendency that is, in part, connected with a number of more pragmatic factors also favouring the development of counselling psychology. These include recognition of the value of counselling as a framework for understanding and facilitating the work of organizations. The pace of change in organizations has led to a mushrooming of Employee Assistance Programmes and a demand for the services of psychologists with skills in both counselling and organizational dynamics. Another factor is the shortage of psychologists in mental health work. Psychology departments are increasingly responding by redefining themselves as clinical and counselling departments, with an emphasis on psychology as a facility for the community and a concern with the wider educative and preventive aspects of mental health. Such developments are, in themselves, in tune with the spirit and philosophy of counselling psychology. Nevertheless, in these contexts, the pressure on resources, coupled with a justifiable demand for accountability, favours a somewhat limited view of evidenced-based practice and a strong tendency to promote short-term problem or solution-focused work and standardized packaged or manualized 'treatments' to the exclusion of longer-term in-depth work.

Counselling psychology is currently experiencing a tension between these opposing tendencies, which we later characterize as between 'being-in-relation' and 'technical expertise'. We link the pressure towards technical expertise with a wider social process first described, and termed 'rationalization', by Max Weber. The tension is rooted in how we define science and the relationship between science and values which, in turn, is linked with long-standing intractable questions about human free will and the extent to which human behaviour is determined by internal and external causes. We can only outline some of the issues as we see them.

We attempt, in this chapter, to place counselling psychology in context but this is a complex task that includes a consideration of historical processes, social and political forces, philosophical ideas and changing contexts of employment. As therapists we know that mining aspects of history to make sense of current issues is a messy business, and no doubt, in what follows, there will be confusion and over-simplification. We are involved in a process and there is no 'high hard ground' on which to stand as detached observers. We are bog-hopping in Donald Schon's 'swampy lowlands' pictured below. Nevertheless, we are confident that our experience will connect with that of others who share the ongoing struggle to make the developing identity of counselling psychology a self-determining process.

Scientist-practitioners

We have noted that counselling psychology in Britain can in some ways be seen as a return of counselling to psychology. The former is rooted in humanistic and existential-phenomenological psychology in which the search for understanding and meaning is central and in which the focus is upon an engagement with subjective experience, values and beliefs. The latter (in the United Kingdom and United States) has emphasized its roots in experimental behavioural science. These two positions are enunciated respectively by Deurzen-Smith (1990) and Williams (1991). We shall argue that this dichotomy is not unbridgeable and that a great deal depends on what we mean by 'science' and the notion of the 'scientist-practitioner'. Far from being dismissive of the demand to justify practice on the basis of evidence, counselling psychology recognizes the importance of clear conceptual frameworks within which research can develop and practice can be evaluated. Nevertheless, it is in acknowledging the contribution of different traditions that the relationship between science and practice, the relationship between science and values and the nature of science itself have all become crucial issues in the developing identity of counselling psychologists. Much discussion has focused on the notion of the 'scientist-practitioner'.

Whilst the emphasis on psychological theory and research highlights differences between the training of counselling psychologists and that of many counsellors and psychotherapists it suggests a kinship between counselling and clinical psychologists that, though somewhat conflicted, is certainly perceived by both groups. They work with similar client groups and forms of distress and, increasingly, in 'clinical' situations defined in medical terms. In these contexts the powerful, natural science-based, biomedical tradition of psychiatry, with its discourse of psychopathology and 'mental illness', has held sway since the nineteenth century. In such settings, the effectiveness of the struggle to establish and maintain a distinctly psychological approach has been enhanced by the strong bias towards experimental behavioural science in psychology. All this adds attraction to the identity of 'scientist-practitioner', already established in clinical psychology and in counselling psychology in the United States, and which has gained favour in British counselling psychology. Nonetheless, although the term emphasizes the need to engage in on-going research and the role of the practitioner as producer, as well as user, of knowledge and understanding, resistance to research is displayed by many practitioners of clinical as well as counselling psychology. A variety of reasons may account for this (Pelling, 2000; Woolfe, 1996). However, whilst not discounting much useful research that has been and continues to be conducted within the framework of the dominant model of scientific research within psychology, a significant factor must be its increasingly recognized limitations, particularly from the point of view of practice.

Donald Schön, writing generally about professional practice, has famously described this dominant or 'technical rationality model' of science as painting a picture of:

> a high, hard ground overlooking a swamp. On the high ground, manageable problems lend themselves to solution through the application of research based theory and technique. In the swampy lowland, messy, confusing problems defy technical solution. ... [But] ... in the swamp lie the problems of greatest human concern. (Schön, 1987: 3)

In the swampy lowlands which are the 'indeterminate zones of practice' characterized by uncertainty, uniqueness and value conflict, the canons of technical rationality do not apply. Indeed, technical rationality is not only an inadequate model for practice, it contributes to professional incompetence by focusing on problem solving at the expense of the crucial task of problem setting. Schön finds that, rather than applying formal theory and research, successful practitioners learn from experience. Reflection-on-action, often with other practitioners, and reflection-in-action, the monitoring of practice in process, are the crucial factors in this learning and keep practitioners alive to the uniqueness and uncertainty of practice situations.

The stress on continuing supervision, in counselling psychology, acknowledges this reflective activity as central to good practice within the discipline. It is perhaps given insufficient consideration as a process within which knowledge is actively produced, and this is something that could be more explicitly recognized in the way practice experience is written up for publication. Nevertheless, there is a need, in addition, to develop a clearer view of the range of approaches to more formal research, appropriate to the discipline, which can underpin the claim on 'science' as the basis of practice. As Spinelli notes, whilst the juxtaposition of 'practitioner' and 'scientist' may well provide our profession with a distinct identity this will only become possible 'when we begin to clarify more adequately just what kind of "science" we espouse as a means of making sense of our practice-based interventions' (2001: 4). In this context, and following Elton Wilson and Barkham (1994), we are tempted to reverse the term to 'practitioner-scientist' to stress practice and practice-based research as well as movement away from the dominant or technical rationality model of science. At the very least we must address and seek to transcend the gulf that has existed between the dominant view of science as value-free and practice grounded in humanistic values and characterized by uncertainty and value conflict.

This is becoming more urgent as all psychologists are increasingly called upon to justify their practice on the basis of evidence and to demonstrate technical expertise in 'treating' definable 'conditions' and 'disorders'. In 'clinical' contexts it is difficult to resist the biomedical model, and this is extending outwards to other organizations (such as Employee Assistance Programme providers) offering therapeutic interventions in human distress. All this highlights the tension between the dominant model of science, favouring medical and behavioural models of practice, and the humanistic values-based practice stressed in counselling psychology. Economic forces, coupled with the demand to be scientific and deliver evidence-based practice, bring pressure to conform to the criteria of the dominant, if limited, model of science and by extension of evidence. Research is constrained by notions of good design often inappropriate to complex life situations (Spinelli, 2001: 5). There is an inbuilt bias towards the cognitive-behavioural tradition which best fits the model and can, therefore, make the strongest claim for a distinctively psychological form of clinical practice (see e.g. British Psychological Society, Division of Clinical Psychology, 2000). This is encouraged by the emphasis on efficacy studies, characterized by 'randomized control trials', though, as Seligman (1995) argues, these may not be the best way to evaluate the effectiveness of therapy. Moreover, exaggerated claims may be made about the significance of the results or the adequacy of the design (see e.g. debates initiated by Bolsover, 2001, and Holmes, 2002).

Nonetheless, in the absence of a strong and well defined alternative, the pressure is difficult to resist. So, if 'scientific' and 'evidence-based' are key terms in the claim of counselling psychologists to professional competence, it is imperative that we examine, re-examine and refine our own conception/s of 'science', 'research' and 'evidence' in order to avoid being drawn into established medicalized forms of practice and research which are limited in their application within our profession. A useful contribution to this exercise has been made by Corrie and

Callahan (2000) and, with similar intention, we will also revisit the dominant model from a somewhat different direction and reflect on some of the newer perspectives that are gaining in credibility.

Science and counselling psychology

There are a number of linked elements, in the dominant (technical rationality) view of scientific psychology, which are challenged by counselling psychology. These are the emphasis on:

- Value-free inquiry,
- The objective observation of behaviour,
- The detachment of the psychologist/observer,
- The measurability/quantifiability of data and the derivation of statistical laws,
- Prediction and control,
- The separation of 'pure' research from its applications in practice.

In contrast, counselling psychology emphasizes:

- The value basis of practice,
- Subjective experience, feelings and meanings,
- The empathic engagement of the psychologist with the world of the client,
- The acceptance of the subjective world of the client as meaningful and valid in its own terms,
- The need to negotiate between perceptions and world-views without assuming an objectively discoverable 'truth',
- The qualitative description of experience,
- The development of insight and increased capacity for choice,
- The primacy of practice in generating knowledge.

The dominant model developed from the 'Enlightenment', a new framework of ideas about nature, human beings and society originating in the mid eighteenth century and centred in France. This marked the beginning of 'the modern period' or 'modernity' and was characterized by its challenge to the traditional European world-view dominated by Christianity and the Church's authority. It insisted on reason and rationality as the basis of knowledge, and the model of scientific knowledge born in the 'scientific revolution' of the seventeenth century was promoted as the key to the expansion of all human knowledge. This belief in the power of science was coupled with equally strong belief in technological and social progress, which would itself be enhanced by the scientific understanding of human beings and the workings of human societies.

The model of science that developed was rooted in the philosophies of empiricism and positivism. It stressed that knowledge claims must be based on 'objectively observable facts' verifiable against sense experience. This was important, as it proposed a rational, empirically based, method of creating knowledge free from religious dogma and moral values rooted in theology. The Enlightenment project was extremely successful and the model of scientific knowledge at its heart became the yardstick against which all claims to rational knowledge were judged. Of course, the power of science is clear when we consider its enormous influence in our lives. It is, therefore, not surprising that the natural science model was pre-eminent in the development of modern psychology, which had its origins in the second half of the nineteenth century, as one of the disciplines aiming to apply scientific methods to the study of human beings. The emphasis on objectivity and observability favoured a focus on behaviour, rather than subjective experience, and it was assumed that there are discoverable laws that could constitute a body of knowledge allowing the prediction and control of human behaviour. Once discovered, these laws could be applied to the treatment of criminality and mental illness, the assessment of abilities and aptitudes, the education of children, the organization of the workplace and so on. The model is inherently deterministic and locates control outside the agency of those being controlled.

Nevertheless, from the earliest conceptions of social science and psychology, people have questioned the appropriateness of using the same methods to study both the natural and the human world. Such questioning characterized 'humanistic psychology', a self-defined tendency of North American psychology emerging around 1940. Carl Rogers and Abraham Maslow were key figures who, although originally seen as rebels, were highly regarded and were elected to the presidency of the American Psychological Association in 1947 and 1968 respectively. Humanistic psychology became the 'third force' in American psychology, challenging behaviourism and psychoanalysis, both seen as over-deterministic, as well as the biomedical model in psychiatry, where it forged links with radical psychiatry. A significant impact was also made in the field of human relations in industry. Its emphasis on free will and human potential became significant in the context of the civil rights movement and a general questioning of Western concepts of progress in the post-Holocaust world. The climate of protest against the worst excesses of technological society, the threat of nuclear war and Vietnam added momentum (Herman, 1992). Counselling was just one of a range of democratizing practices in humanistic psychology. As we have noted, it stressed the quality of the therapeutic relationship and emphasized both the validity of the subjective experience and the capacity for self-determination and personal responsibility of the person in the client role.

Whilst the ideas of humanistic psychology are peculiarly American, Rogers, Maslow and others were aware of their philosophical and methodological roots in, for example, the European phenomenological tradition. Rogers linked his own work with this tradition (e.g. Rogers, 1964) that dates back at least to the nineteenth century, by which time history, psychology, sociology, economics and social anthropology had all emerged as empirical disciplines. Claims were made that their subject matter is crucially different from that of the natural sciences and requires differing methods of study. In Britain, John Stuart Mill coined the term 'moral sciences' to distinguish this group of disciplines. They were termed *Geisteswissenschaften* in German and this later translated as 'human sciences'. Their distinctiveness was strongly argued by the German philosopher William Dilthey, who linked the notion of human science with a theory of understanding and significantly influenced the development of research into human consciousness, subjective experience, meaning and culture.

However, in Britain and America the natural science model, based in positivist-empiricist philosophy, predominated throughout the social sciences and psychology, at least until the 1960s. By that time the phenomenological tradition was enjoying a period of revitalization in the climate of political and intellectual upheaval in Europe, where it was posing a vigorous challenge to all over-deterministic conceptions of history, social structure, social processes and human behaviour. Marxists, confronting the realities of Stalinism, renewed their interest in the early, more humanist, writings of Karl Marx and made a significant contribution to this challenge. Consciousness and human agency were re-emphasized and the development of methods appropriate to the study of self-conscious, reflective and self-determining beings was enthusiastically undertaken. The range of rigorous, qualitative research methods now available owes much to this period. For the most part these have been more eagerly embraced and developed in sociology, anthropology and cultural studies than in psychology, although there are notable exceptions. Jerome Bruner, for instance, made his important distinction between 'paradigmatic' and 'narrative' knowing in the 1980s and drew the attention of at least some mainstream psychologists to the significance of stories in human experience (Bruner, 1986).

Humanistic values and human potential

We have stressed the centrality of values in humanistic psychology. These are closely connected with a human science as opposed to a natural science approach. This is because they are inseparable from a view of human beings as self-conscious and reflective, with the capacity for choice and personal responsibility, as opposed to being entirely determined by internal and external causes. Early debates throw light on current issues, and those between Rogers and Skinner are pertinent here (see e.g. Wann, 1964; Kirschenbaum and Henderson, 1990). Some of these debates and the implications of the emphasis on values are interestingly reflected in a series of papers by Patterson written between 1958 and 1997 (Patterson, 2000: 235–325). The humanistic perspective has a positive view of human beings as 'in the process of becoming', guided by a 'self-actualizing' tendency. 'Self-actualization' is a central value in humanistic psychology. It is understood not only as the potential driving development but also as a highly valued developmental goal. Maslow provided its most elaborated description, and Rogers's notion of a 'fully functioning person' is similar. This is someone who is open to experience and is not defensive, who lives existentially (constantly in process, flexible and adaptable) and whose locus of evaluation and control is internal (Patterson, 2000: 273). The natural science perspective, in contrast, is more strongly deterministic. It is concerned with prediction and control gained through an understanding of the causes of behaviour; for example, in reflexes and responses to stimuli and reinforcements in the environment. Patterson notes that this latter perspective is encouraged by the American philosophy of efficiency that requires results in the shortest time and which, in psychotherapy, leads to dissatisfaction with long and complex processes. In this we can observe one influence of American society on the social and psychological sciences.

It has been suggested (Deurzen-Smith, 1990) that the philosophical underpinnings of counselling psychology lie in 'the immense gap left open by a psychology too devoted to narrow scientific principles to pay proper attention to what it means to be human'. She contends that psychology has lost its ability to function as an art. If the object of counselling psychology is to help people live lives that are more fulfilled, one enters inevitably into the realms of morals and ideology, subjects which are the domain of philosophy rather than science. We have some sympathy with this but contend that counselling psychology is grounded in a human science perspective and that this offers a sound scientific approach that acknowledges the significance of philosophical and moral questions and values artistry in professional work. In our view, counselling psychology in Britain firmly espouses this position in claiming that it seeks to:

> engage with subjectivity and inter-subjectivity, values and feelings ... to know empathically and respect first person accounts as valid in their own terms ... and ... to elucidate, interpret and negotiate between perceptions and world views but not to assume the automatic superiority of any one way of experiencing, feeling, valuing and knowing. (British Psychological Society, 2000)

At the heart of this philosophy is a belief that the therapeutic relationship involves working towards an authentic meeting of equals and has the intention of enhancing the self-determination and fulfilment of potential of the person in the client role. This remains valid whatever the nature of the problems or distress presented, and an attitude emphasizing 'becoming what one is capable of becoming' or 'self-actualization' is adopted. This involves a holistic and developmental view of an individual's life, life-style and location in their life course. Duffy (1990) emphasizes the importance of the helper's mind-set, so that problems and crises are perceived not as evidence of pathology but in the context of coping with ordinary human experiences. So difficulties and distress are seen as part and parcel of the human condition and there is always potential for creative change and enhanced well-being even in the face of death. This is quite different from both the biomedical and the older behavioural models in which the focus is on 'illness', 'pathology', 'disorder' or 'maladaptive behaviour' and helpers are seen as emotionally distanced, employing standardized assessment and therapeutic techniques from a perspective external to clients' subjective worlds. Rather than expecting clients to submit compliantly to 'treatment' prescribed by professionals, counselling psychology advocates an interactive alternative that emphasizes the subjective experience of clients and the need for helpers to engage with them as collaborators, seeking to understand their inner worlds and constructions of reality. The notion of *doing something* to clients is replaced by that of *being with* clients. What Rogers described as the 'core conditions' of empathy, acceptance and authenticity are paramount whatever the therapeutic modality.

The centrality of this humanistic value system offers one answer to the question of how counselling psychology differs from medical and other psychological approaches. As Duffy (1990) points out, the difference lies not in the methods employed or the type of problem worked with but in the philosophical position from which they do it. As the focus shifts away from the application of specific treatment skills and what we do *to* clients to how we are *with* clients, the emphasis is on *being-in-relation* rather than *doing*. It follows from this that the self of the helper is acknowledged as an active ingredient in the helping process. Thus arguments about whether counselling psychologists employ a different range of skills from those employed by cognate groups such as clinical psychologists or work with different client groups, which dominated the early years of counselling psychology in this country, become redundant. What matters is the approach, attitude or intentionality that any psychologist brings to the helping relationship. This emphasis on the person of the therapist is not just a theoretical proposition. It involves understanding therapy as a shared exploration, a process of mutual discovery into which the helper brings his or her own personal emotional history and baggage. This recognizes our mutual humanity. Like our clients we are people, with issues and difficulties in our lives, and understanding how these impact upon relationships with clients demands a willingness to explore our own histories, attitudes and emotional defences. Hence there is a stress in training and practice on personal therapy as well as supervision.

Though counselling psychology is rooted in humanistic values and a human science perspective, we noted earlier that it is committed to recognizing and establishing the value of the three major traditions in psychology. The humanistic psychology of the early 1960s, whilst championing human subjectivity and free will, courted utopian ideas of democracy and human perfectibility. From a more existential viewpoint, May engaged Rogers in debate about the neglect of the human capacity for evil (see Kirschenbaum and Henderson, 1990) and, similarly, Spinelli contends that humanistic psychology adopts an over-optimistic view of human nature and human freedom as well as a specifically North American attitude emphasizing technique (1989: 159). Additionally, the emphasis on self-actualization can lead to neglect of the self-in-relation, and questions of responsibility to others, as well as neglect of the contributions of both cognitive-behavioural and psychoanalytical psychology to our understanding of the internal and external factors that undoubtedly shape us. This can lead to a 'victim-blaming' attitude that minimizes the impact of oppressive conditions in people's lives. We agree with Patterson (2000) that, in respect of control, the important issue is the *locus of control*, who does the controlling. The intention in counselling psychology is to increase the capacity for self-determination, and this can involve offering insights and techniques, from the rich traditions of psychoanalytic and cognitive-behavioural psychology, for clients to explore and utilize for themselves. This, however, raises complex theoretical and technical issues, and an important area of continuing debate is the possibility of integration in theory and practice (e.g. O'Brien and Houston, 2000; Palmer and Woolfe, 2000; Lapworth et al., 2001).

Structuralism, post-structuralism and postmodernism

The general humanism of the early 1960s became subject to critiques, which, among other things, reasserted the role of social structures in shaping human identities and human history. Although humanism was seen as over-emphasizing the responsibility of individuals for their own circumstances and life chances, the critiques shared its focus on meaning and consciousness. Termed 'structuralist', they drew upon structuralist linguistics, which defines languages as structured symbolic systems. Subjective consciousness, dependent upon language, was seen as fundamentally social and, hence, more obviously available for scientific study. Human action was construed as generated within symbolic meaning systems in which socio-political power is legitimated in ideologies. Marxist and feminist studies were particularly important in showing how these power relations are reproduced through the construction of personal identities (see e.g. Billington et al., 1998: 52–7). As the structures of language and ideology operate, as it were, beneath consciousness, social science renewed its interest in psychoanalytical studies, particularly through the work of Jacques Lacan, who, influenced by structuralist linguistics, claimed, 'the unconscious is structured like a language' (1977: 20). Language thus provided a key, unlocking possibilities for studying both conscious and unconscious meanings and motivations.

Structuralism in turn became a focus of critique, it was again over-deterministic. 'Post-structuralism' emerged and was related to a broader movement of ideas termed 'postmodernism'. We can here only sketch the significance of these complex and debatable ideas for the development of counselling psychology. Post-structuralism was first associated with a number of French thinkers, including Michel Foucault and Gilles Deleuze, who, critical of the Marxist belief in the rationality of the historical process, turned to Nietzsche for inspiration and eventually launched a general attack on all overarching conceptions of reason and truth, declaring them to be repressive. Like Max Weber, they argued that the world can never be grasped within a single unified theoretical system. Life is inherently multifarious and contradictory and all thinking and evaluation limited within perspectives. They maintained a view of the relation between language and consciousness similar to that of the structuralists, but rejected the conception of languages as large unified systems in favour of smaller systems or 'discourses' located in specific forms of social relationship.

A central concern of postmodern thinkers is the way grand theories and overarching systems of thought tend towards totalitarianism. When we think of Auschwitz, Stalinism, Khomeini and Afghanistan it is easy to see their point, and one positive influence has been in their stressing and valuing human difference. The danger, however, lies in an extreme relativism of standards of truth and value in which anything goes, might comes to mean right and consensus becomes a dangerously totalizing force. Influential thinkers such as Foucault and Jean-François Lyotard recognized this and struggled, in their later works, to move beyond the tendency to equate truth with power (e.g. Lyotard, 1979; Lyotard and Thebaud, 1979). Lyotard maintains a stance against overarching belief systems, which he calls the great 'meta-narratives' of the modern period, and seeks to identify the liberating potential in postmodernism. He says that the recognition of the varied forms of social life, its 'little narratives', is the first step because it implies a renunciation of terror. The second step is a principle limiting consensus. Social life is seen as governed by a multiplicity of 'little narratives' inherently open to challenge and cancellation, so postmodernism has the potential of liberating us from the terror consequent on the search for a totalizing meta-narrative.

Polkinghorne (1992) has drawn attention to the relevance of postmodern thinking for a practice-led model of psychology. He argues that the psychology of practice emerged under the shadow of academic psychology and that, whilst the former focused on the discovery of general laws of human behaviour, the latter focused on pragmatic action in the service of mental health and personal development. Finding academic psychology's model of knowledge of limited relevance in responding to clients, the psychology of practice developed its own body of knowledge consisting of a 'fragmented collection of discordant theories and techniques', based on actual interactions between practitioners and clients. Underlying the generation of knowledge through practice is an implicit epistemology that is postmodern in character. It assumes that: there is no firm foundation for establishing indubitable truth; bodies of knowledge consist of fragments of understanding, 'little narratives' rather than large, logically integrated systems; these fragments are constructed in cultures; and knowledge is tested pragmatically, by its usefulness. This sits easily alongside Schön's 'reflective practitioner' model and Polkinghorne too links his 'postmodern epistemology of practice' with a range of studies of the ways in which professionals in a variety of disciplines actually develop and apply knowledge in practice.

This brief account can only indicate the broad tendency of postmodern thinking and we can simply note its relationship with a range of approaches to the study of human beings gaining influence in psychology, such as social constructionism, discourse analysis, conversation analysis, deconstruction and critical psychology (see e.g. Fox and Prilleltensky, 1997; Smith et al., 1995). Alongside developments in phenomenological research and psychoanalysis, these approaches have, in recent years, contributed much to the study of social relationships, culture and ideology, subjectivity and meaning and conscious and unconscious processes, by rigorous qualitative methods. They have also put values and political critique back on the agenda and, as these methods and approaches owe much to studies in literature and criticism, they are indicative of some *rapprochement* between science and humanities/arts-based research. When we consider the approaches to practice and inquiry developed in counselling psychology we can find some strikingly postmodern characteristics. Its recognition of competing therapeutic theories and refusal to align itself with a single model indicates resistance to a meta-narrative, particularly that of the dominant model of scientific rationality. In its respect for the subjective truths expressed in the 'little narratives' of our individual lives, in its celebrating and valuing of difference, and in its espoused intent to 'empower', it has the potential to contribute to challenging oppression. More specifically, interest in narrative approaches to therapy and the significance of stories in human lives is developing rapidly and, as we can see, this emphasis on narrative is central in postmodern thinking.

Technical expertise and being-in-relation in the employment context

All in all, we live in exciting times for psychological practice and research in general, and for counselling psychology in particular. The technical rationality model of science is finally being seen as, at least, limited in its application, and with the rapid development of qualitative and more politically conscious forms of research we are in a position to espouse methods more adequate to the study of what we do in practice. There is no shortage of evidence of the significance of common factors across models of therapeutic practice, and among these the quality of the therapeutic relationship is emphasized as central to therapeutic success. Therapy depends first and foremost on 'being-in-relation', not on technical experts with toolbags of techniques for diagnosing and treating specific problems. We now have research methods appropriate to exploring and describing more systematically and in depth the nature of such human meeting and we should not forget that psychotherapy is, *in its very nature*, research or, as Miller Mair prefers, 'inquiry' (e.g. Mair, 1999).

If, in this way, we can see our way into radically amending the identity of 'scientist-practitioner' we must not lose sight of the fact that this is only part of the story. We noted how the natural science model, which claimed to be value-free, became the yardstick of rationality in general. This led to the neglect of other forms of reason such as those appropriate to ethical and political thought and action (see e.g. Shotter, 1993). In contrast, we have seen that the more modest postmodern emphasis, on 'little narratives', the context-bound nature of knowledge and on pragmatism or usefulness rather than truth, carries the danger of relativism and the association of truth with power. Hence Lyotard's concern to limit consensus. In the context of practice we have noted Schon's stress on how the limited applicability of technical rational knowledge brings into focus value conflicts and the unavoidable responsibility that we have to others. Many situations are vague and uncertain, decisions must be made, actions taken and accounted for. Social life is, in a real sense, radically open, and social and moral concepts are 'essentially contestable' (Gallie, 1956). Under these conditions values, not truth, must provide the guiding principles. So we must not lose sight of our humanistic values, and an adequate 'scientist-practitioner'/'practitioner-scientist' identity must embrace forms of ethical and political reason within its compass. In our view the development of the profession depends on this as much as on good science.

Given that this promises a way forward, it is helpful to examine the countervailing tendency to be pulled back into the technical rationality model of research and the medical model of practice. This can best be understood in the context of wider social and historical processes. We have linked the technical rationality model of science with the coming of 'modernity' and this can be seen as part of a more general process of 'rationalization' conceptualized by Max Weber in his seminal analyses of modernization (see e.g. Brubaker, 1984; Whimster and Lash, 1987). Rationalization involves the application of the criteria of rational decision making into increasing areas of social life and is closely associated with the rise of industrial capitalism. Its effect is to construct a complex 'iron cage' of bureaucratic rules and regulations geared to calculable economic efficiency. Productivity, coupled with scientific and technological progress, becomes an end in itself as opposed to a means whereby human needs may be satisfied. George Ritzer (1993) argues that the process of rationalization continues to intensify. He coined the term 'McDonaldization' to characterize the highly controlled, bureaucratic and dehumanized nature of contemporary, particularly American, social life. The fast-food restaurant, built on principles of efficiency, calculability, predictability and control, where quantity and standardization replace quality and variety as the indicators of value, serves as a metaphor for the general mania for efficiency. Increasing areas of social life are subject to McDonaldization through, for example, shopping malls, packaged holidays, hotel chains and digital television. Perhaps more seriously, areas such as education and medicine are subject to this process. The stress on grades and league tables in education focuses attention on what is quantifiable in the end product, rather than the quality of the experience, and health care is increasingly impersonal and technological. Ritzer (1998: 59–70) has also considered the organization and experience of work and linked his perspective with Harry Braverman's (1974) analysis of the labour process. He recognizes that the 'de-skilling' and degradation of labour are characteristic of rationalization. Work is highly routinized, thinking is reduced to a minimum and even social interactions (e.g. with customers) are scripted (see Hochschild, 1983). Higher-level skills (such as planning, creativity, critique and genuine human contact) are effectively excluded so that producers and, in the service industries, consumers are systematically disempowered.

Even this brief outline suggests insights into the labour market, dominated by medicine, into which counselling psychology is increasingly drawn. The de-skilling of work in general has broad political implications, to which we cannot here do justice, but it is of particular concern to a profession that defines its practice in terms of human relations. We might learn much from Michael Apple's (1985) analysis of education from this perspective, but for now we can only note some of the means whereby, in therapy, complexity is minimized, process is routinized and thinking and human contact are reduced, e.g. by: the strong emphasis on training in techniques (despite the significance of the therapeutic relationship); attempts to operationalize competences; the demand for quantification in efficacy studies (without due regard to the adequacy of the measures or the quality of the experience); the consequent stress on diagnosis and problem specification (as opposed to the subjective experience of distress); attempts to package delivery through therapy manuals; and the use of computers to deliver some such packages.

Medical settings

Recognition and employment in medical settings, alongside clinical psychologists, have been and continue to be a legitimate aspiration of counselling psychologists. Nonetheless, it is here where the power of technical rationality and the forces of rationalization are felt most strongly. Moreover, the professional alliance with medicine, whilst serving the quest for legitimacy, encourages a general tendency to adopt biomedical language and practices (e.g. psychopathological assessment categories) in non-medical settings, such as Employee Assistance Programmes. So counselling psychology can become an inadvertent vector for the spread of McDonaldization. It is important, therefore, to associate counselling psychology with existing challenges to the biomedical model of mental distress *within* medical settings.

The categories of 'illness' and 'disorder' that have been devised and articulated, for example in the *DSM* manuals, suggest that there exist objective states which are value-free, existing externally to the subjective world of the assessor, and which require specific treatments (but see Kutchins and Kirk, 1999). Psychologists have constructed a plethora of tests to measure such phenomena as 'depression', 'anxiety' and 'neuroticism'. These have made 'individuality ... amenable to scientific judgement' (Rose, 1990: 140) and led to a state of affairs in which decisions about the borderline between normality and abnormality have come to be defined in terms of position on a scale. Technical concepts such as 'neurotic' and 'psychotic' have gained wide legitimacy and entered everyday discourse. However, as the terms describing mental states become apparently ever more 'scientific', they are increasingly distanced from the language of those who experience these states and it becomes more difficult for the non-expert to challenge such 'expert diagnoses'.

Johnstone discusses the powerful cultural assumptions that go along with being diagnosed as ill. Drawing on the notion of the 'sick role' (Parsons, 1951), she summarizes these as follows:

1 You are supposed to be unable to recover by a conscious act of will. You are not responsible for your disability, and can't help it.
2 You are exempted from certain social obligations and commitments.
3 You are supposed to see being sick as an undesirable state, and want to get well.
4 You are seen as being in need of specialized help, which is obtained by becoming a patient. (2000: 40)

Pilgrim and Rogers (1996) offer a similar picture of what is involved in the role of patient from the viewpoint of the professional. This includes disregarding views which disagree with those of the professional and regarding patients as irrational and, therefore, incapable of giving valid views. If we pull all these images together, what we get is a picture of passive victims who must put themselves in the hands of omnipotent professionals whose role is to rescue. The model takes no account of the social, economic or political context in which the person exists, and variables such as gender, class and race are ignored.

Pilgrim and Bentall (1999) describe the philosophical basis of this position as 'medical naturalism' and it fits firmly into the natural science, technical rationality model. Its logic is that 'psychiatric nosology proceeds incrementally with a confidence that there exists a real and invariant external world of natural disease entities' (p. 261). The outcome of this model is a focus on classificatory systems, with the professional as diagnostician. They contrast this with a model that they describe as 'social constructionism' in which 'psychiatric diagnoses are studied as representations of a variegated and ultimately unknowable human condition' (p. 261). The outcome of this alternative way of looking at the world is that causal arguments about mental health or illness can be understood only by examining what mental health professionals actually do. As Szasz (1974: 21) in an early seminal work puts it, 'The question, What *is* mental illness? is shown to be inextricably tied to the question, What do psychiatrists *do*?' It is thus a by-product of the activity of mental health professionals (see Parker et al., 1995). Even more radically, 'the study of psychopathology itself is replaced by a study of the ways in which psychopathology is represented or socially constructed' (Pilgrim and Bentall, 1999: 261).

None of this seeks to question the reality or minimize the experience of psychological distress. What it does do is question the adequacy of the disease model and the psychopathological classifications it entails. As Hacking argues, classifications in human science are 'interactive'. People classified are treated differently by others and, crucially, they may understand how they are classified and 'rethink themselves accordingly' (1999: 108). Once we acknowledge that medical categorizations of 'mental illness' are permeated by socio-cultural values and processes (see Pilgrim, 1983; Parker et al., 1995), we can develop alternative discourses about psychological well-being and distress which encourage a recognition of the validity of sufferers' own experiences and perceptions. The individual can be seen as existing at the centre of a personal matrix in which biology, social structure and life events combine with developmental processes to present each individual, at any one time, with a unique set of challenges. The helper ceases to be an expert assessor and becomes a collaborator, developing with the client a formulation about the nature of the distress and an approach to its amelioration. While the medical model regards users as patients, Pilgrim and Rogers explore the implications of perceiving them as consumers or survivors, both of which are seen as more empowering positions; the former by acknowledging that people can make positive choices, the latter by rendering professional services as problematic. The development of survivor and self-advocacy discourses is already achieving some success through, for example, the Mental Health User Movement (Wallcroft and Michaelson, 2001).

Conclusion

We have sought, in this chapter, to explore and contextualize the developing identity of counselling psychology as a dynamic socio-historical process. We are ourselves involved in this process and the chapter is itself an intervention. In practice, we regularly confront the tension between being-in-relation and technical expertise and find ourselves reasserting the centrality of values and counselling psychology's emphasis on being, not doing (Woolfe, 2001).

Irrespective of the approach, research supports the stress on relationship in therapy and Rogers noted that therapeutic relationships are not substantially different *in kind* from those in our everyday lives (Strawbridge, 2000). Writing from a psychoanalytical perspective, Peter Lomas (1999) has expressed concerns, similar to our own, about the pull away from relationship into technical expertise and the 'retreat from the ordinary'. This seems particularly pertinent in a climate of 'McDonaldization' in which what is crucial in therapy is threatened by the same process that undermines the quality of ordinary human relationships and increases psychological distress.

Finally we have emphasized counselling psychology's recognition of significantly different traditions in psychology. This acknowledges the impossibility of theorizing 'reality' within a single 'meta-narrative'. It does not mean that anything goes, and we would not wish to minimize issues of integration. However, we believe it does carry the injunction to resist closure and dogmatism and to maintain open and inquiring minds, and a degree of humility in the face of complexity, that is in the spirit of genuine science.

References

Apple, M.W. (1985) *Education and Power*. London: Ark/Routledge.

Barkham, M. (1988) 'Empathy in counselling and psychotherapy: present status and future directions', *Counselling Psychology Quarterly*, 6 (1): 24–8.

Billington, R., Hockey, J. and Strawbridge, S. (1998) *Exploring Self and Society*. London: Macmillan.

Bolsover, N. (2001) Correspondence with Peter Kinderman, *Clinical Psychology*, 5 and 6. Leicester: British Psychological Society.

Braverman, H. (1974) *Labour and Monopoly Capitalism: the Degradation of Work in the Twentieth Century*. London: Monthly Review Press.

British Psychological Society (2000) *Regulations and Syllabus for the Diploma in Counselling Psychology*. Leicester: British Psychological Society.

British Psychological Society, Division of Clinical Psychology (2000) *Recent Advances in Understanding Mental Illness and Psychotic Experiences*. Leicester: British Psychological Society.

Brubaker, R. (1984) *The Limits of Rationality: an Essay on the Social and Moral Thought of Max Weber*. London: Allen & Unwin.

Bruner, J. (1986) *Actual Minds, Possible Worlds*. London: Harvard University Press.

Corrie, S. and Callahan, M.M. (2000) 'A review of the scientist-practitioner model: reflections on its potential contribution to counselling psychology within the context of current health care trends', *British Journal of Medical Psychology*, 73 (3): 413–27.

Deurzen-Smith, E. van (1990) 'Philosophical underpinnings of counselling psychology', *Counselling Psychology Review*, 5 (2): 8–12.

Duffy, M. (1990) 'Counselling psychology USA: patterns of continuity and change', *Counselling Psychology Review*, 5 (3): 9–18.

Elton Wilson, J. and Barkham, M. (1994) 'A practitioner-scientist approach to psychotherapy process and outcome research' in P. Clarkson and M. Pokorny (eds) *The Handbook of Psychotherapy*. London: Routledge.

Fox, D. and Prilleltensky, I. (eds) (1997) *Critical Psychology: an Introduction*. London: Sage.

Gallie, W.B. (1956) 'Essentially contested concepts' in *Proceedings of the Aristotelian Society*, 56, reprinted in M. Black (ed.) *The Importance of Language*. Englewood Cliffs, NJ: Prentice Hall (1962).

Hacking, I. (1999) *The Social Construction of What?* Cambridge MA and London: Harvard University Press.

Herman, E. (1992) 'Being and doing: humanistic psychology and the spirit of the 1960s' in B.L. Tischler (ed.) *Sights on the Sixties*. New Brunswick NJ: Rutgers University Press.

Hochschild, H.R. (1983) *The Managed Heart: Commercialization of Human Feeling*. London: University of California Press.

Holmes, J. (2002) 'All you need is cognitive behaviour therapy?' *British Medical Journal*, 324 (7332, Feburary): 288–94.

Johnstone, L. (2000) *Users and Abusers of Psychiatry*. London and Philadelphia: Routledge.

Kirschenbaum, H. and Henderson, V.L. (eds) (1990) *Carl Rogers: Dialogues*. London: Constable.

Kutchins, H. and Kirk, S.A. (1999) *Making us Crazy: DSM, the Psychiatric Bible, and the Creation of Mental Disorders*. London: Constable.

Lacan, J. (1977) *The Four Fundamental Concepts of Psycho-analysis*. London: Hogarth Press.

Lapworth, P., Sills, C. and Fish, S. (2001) *Integration in Counselling and Psychotherapy: Developing a Personal Approach*. London: Sage.

Lomas, P. (1999) *Doing Good: Psychotherapy out of its Depth*. Oxford: Oxford University Press.

Lyotard, J-F. (1979, trans. 1984) *The Postmodern Condition: a Report on Knowledge*. Manchester: Manchester University Press.

Lyotard, J-F. and Thebaud, J.L. (1979, trans. 1985) *Just Gaming*, Manchester: Manchester University Press.

Mair, M. (1999) 'Inquiry in conversation – questions, quests, search and research', *Psychotherapy Section Newsletter*, 25 (June): 2–15. BPS.

O'Brien, M. and Houston, G. (2000) *Integrative Therapy: a Practitioner's Guide*. London: Sage.

Palmer, S. and Woolfe, R. (eds) (2000) *Integrative and Eclectic Counselling and Psychotherapy*. London: Sage.

Parker, I., Georgaca, E., Harper, D., McLaughlin, T. and Stowell-Smith, M. (1995) *Deconstructing Psychopathology*. London: Sage.

Parsons, T. (1951) 'Illness and the role of the physician: a sociological perspective', *American Journal of Orthopsychiatry*, 21: 452–60.

Patterson, C.H. (2000) *Understanding Psychotherapy: Fifty Years of Client-centred Practice*. Ross on Wye: PCCS Books.

Pelling, N. (2000) 'Scientists versus practitioners: a growing dichotomy in need of integration', *Counselling Psychology Review*, 15 (4): 3–7.

Pilgrim, D. (ed.) (1983) *Psychology and Psychotherapy*, London: Routledge.

Pilgrim, D. and Bentall, R.P. (1999) 'The medicalisation of misery: a critical realist analysis of the concept of depression', *Journal of Mental Health*, 8 (3): 261–74.

Pilgrim, D. and Rogers, R. (1996) *A Sociology of Mental Health and Illness*. Buckingham: Open University Press.

Polkinghorne, D.E. (1992) 'Postmodern epistemology of practice' in S. Kvale (ed.) *Psychology and Postmodernism*. London: Sage.

Ritzer, G. (1993) *The McDonaldization of Society*. London: Pine Forge.

Ritzer, G. (1998) *The McDonaldization Thesis*. London: Sage.

Rogers, C. (1951) *Client-centred Therapy*, London: Constable.

Rogers, C. (1964) 'Towards a science of the person' in T.W. Wann (ed.) *Behaviorism and Phenomenology*. Chicago: University of Chicago Press.

Rose, N. (1990) *Governing the Soul*. London: Routledge.

Schön, D.A. (1987) *Educating the Reflective Practitioner*. London: Jossey Bass.

Seligman, M.E.P. (1995) 'The effectiveness of psychotherapy', *American Psychologist*, 50 (12): 965–74.

Shotter, J. (1993) 'Rhetoric and the roots of the homeless mind', *Theory, Culture and Society*, 10 (4): 41–62.

Smith, J.A., Harré, R. and Langenhove, L. van (eds) (1995) *Rethinking Psychology*. London: Sage.

Spinelli, E. (1989) *The Interpreted World*. London: Sage.

Spinelli, E. (2001) 'Counselling psychology: a hesitant hybrid or a tantalising innovation?' *Counselling Psychology Review*, 16 (3): 3–12.

Strawbridge, S. (2000) 'Carl Rogers: a personal reflection', *Psychologist*, 14 (4): 185.

Strawbridge, S. and Woolfe, R. (1996) 'Counselling psychology: a sociological perspective' in R. Woolfe and W. Dryden (eds) *Handbook of Counselling Psychology*. London: Sage.

Szasz, T. (1974) *The Myth of Mental Illness*. St Albans: Paladin.

Wallcraft, J. and Michaelson, J. (2001) 'Developing a survivor discourse to replace the "psychopathology" of breakdown and crisis', *Journal of Critical Psychology, Counselling and Psychotherapy*, 1 (4): 264–77.

Wann, T.W. (ed.) (1964) *Behaviorism and Phenomenology: Contrasting Bases for Modern Psychology*. Chicago: University of Chicago Press.

Whimster, S. and Lash, S. (eds) (1987) *Max Weber, Rationality and Modernity*. London: Allen & Unwin.

Williams, D. (1991) 'The philosophical underpinning of counselling psychology: a reply to van Deurzen-Smith', *Counselling Psychology Review*, 6 (3): 8–10.

Woolfe, R. (1990) 'Counselling psychology in Britain: an idea whose time has come', *Psychologist*, 3 (12): 531–5.

Woolfe, R. (2001) 'The helping process', *Psychologist*, 14 (7): 347.

Woolfe, R. (1996) 'The nature of counselling psychology' in R. Woolfe and W. Dryden (eds) *Handbook of Counselling Psychology*. London: Sage.

Woolfe, R. and Dryden, W. (eds) (1996) *Handbook of Counselling Psychology*. London: Sage.

Part II
Research and Evaluation

2

Quantitative Research on Psychotherapeutic Interventions: Methods and Findings across Four Research Generations
MICHAEL BARKHAM

The aim of this chapter is twofold. First, to set out various aspects of research methodology employed in quantitative research in the psychological therapies and counselling psychology. In this respect, it focuses on the literature pertaining to psychological interventions designed to ameliorate people's experiences of psychological distress. In so doing, it recognizes that focusing on this specific population comprises but one part of the span of counselling psychology activities where the superordinate focus is on maximising people's well-being. And, secondly, the chapter aims to provide a summary of substantive findings derived from the application of quantitative methodologies across four overlapping generations of research from the 1950s to the present. Again, in so doing it recognizes that the discipline of counselling psychology embraces all potential research methodologies. However, although the meaning of the term 'quantitative' research may appear obvious, it is useful to operationalize its use in this chapter. McLeod (1993) has drawn various distinctions between quantitative and qualitative approaches to research in counselling. In brief, quantitative research comprises the measurement and analysis of variables, using tests, rating scales and questionnaires which are, in turn, interpreted via statistical analyses of the data. Theoretically, quantitative research requires the researcher to be value-free, although, as indicated below, this may be problematic. This view of quantitative research incorporates group contrast, correlational, naturalistic and single-case studies. The inclusion of the latter is important in light of recent criticisms directed at the field of counselling psychology: 'Counseling psychology, a field that reveres the individual ... virtually eschews single-case designs, a research methodology that is explicitly intended for studying the individual' (Galassi and Gersh, 1993: 525).

Within counselling psychology, the superordinate research approach should be methodological pluralism, incorporating both qualitative and quantitative methodologies. The critical point for the researcher is to select the approach which is most appropriate to the question being asked. For instance, if a practitioner wishes to know which of two counselling orientations is more effective, then this might best be addressed using a group contrast design. However, as long as, for example, audio tapes are made of the counselling sessions, then this does not preclude subsequent analyses of the tapes using qualitative methods such as task analysis or discourse analysis. However, McLeod (1994) has argued that mainstream research may have been slow to adopt this pluralistic position, with the two approaches being used to 'complement' each other rather than being integrated into a study of human beings.

General caveats in research

Whether the approach is quantitative or qualitative, it is worth stating several central premises upon which any evaluation of research in counselling psychology should be based. First, all research in counselling psychology and psychotherapy is flawed: the very nature of the exercise does not enable the researcher to achieve a 'perfect' study. Research is the art of reaching a compromise without sacrificing the integrity of any particular study. This invariably involves balancing the demands of four forms of validity: internal, external, construct and statistical validity. Briefly, internal validity concerns the researcher's attempts to control the influence of competing variables which might affect the results of the study. Laboratory studies can achieve a high degree of internal validity whereas studies of counselling in naturalistic settings are more difficult. External validity concerns the researcher's attempts to ensure that the results of the study have meaning in the 'external' world. Here, naturalistic counselling achieves high external validity in contrast to laboratory studies. Construct validity involves ensuring that the phenomenon under investigation is what it purports to be. In other words, ensuring that what is being sampled or measured is the actual construct under investigation. Statistical conclusion validity requires certain elements to be present, including adequate sample size, heterogeneity of participants, etc. A range of 'threats' to each of these four types of validity can occur and these are well summarized by Shapiro (1996). Secondly, there is no such thing as a 'definitive' study. Some studies will be more conclusive than others, depending upon a range of factors, but any study will always leave some questions for further investigation. Thirdly, replication is a central tenet of science. Accordingly, in looking at findings arising from counselling psychology we need to determine the extent to which they have been replicated. The centrality of this tenet gives rise to this chapter focusing on 'substantive' findings – that is, those findings which have been replicated. However, in order to capture possible intriguing and novel findings, this chapter will also include findings which are sufficiently interesting to require replication. Fourthly, there needs to be a recognition that researchers have biases, stated or unstated. This may appear contrary to the notion of quantitative research, which many people perceive as 'objective'. However, researchers investigate processes which interest them and such particular interests may well lead them to make research decisions which other researchers with different perspectives would not make. In addition, decisions made during the analysis and interpretation of the data may all be influenced in subtle ways by the biases of the researchers. Accepting this view, it is logical that the content of this chapter reflects my own orientation towards research.

Structure of the chapter

In terms of adopting a strategy for presenting methodological issues and substantive findings, the chapter will progress by presenting research as comprising four successive but overlapping generations beginning with Eysenck's (1952) critique of psychotherapy. These four generations, which are detailed more fully later in the chapter, can be summarized as follows. Generation I spans the period 1950s to 1970s and addresses the outcome question 'Is psychotherapy effective?' and the process question 'Are there objective methods for evaluating process?' Generation II spans the period 1960s to 1980s and utilizes scientific rigour to address the outcome question 'Which psychotherapy is more effective?' and the process question 'What components are related to outcome?' Generation III spans the period 1970s to the present and addresses the outcome question 'How can we make treatments more cost-effective?' and the process question 'How does change occur?' Generation IV research spans the period from the mid-1980s until the present and addresses the question of the clinical significance of counselling and psychotherapy for the individual. Within each of these four generations, the literature is considered via a series of specific themes, using four subheadings: (1) context (Why is this theme salient?); (2) methodological issues (pertinent issues in designing research aimed to address this theme); (3) substantive research findings (findings which are robust or intriguing); and (4) comment (overall judgement and impact). In this way, it is hoped to cover a range of issues combining fundamental components of good research as well as salient findings.

What this chapter does not aim to do is to provide a comprehensive coverage of all aspects of research in counselling psychology. To do so would require a considerably larger text than space allows here. Texts which incorporate methodological issues include Bergin and Garfield's *Handbook of Psychotherapy and Behavior Change* (fourth edition, 1994a), which, in addition to reviewing specific content domains, contains chapters on methodology (Kazdin, 1994) and process and outcome measurement (Lambert and Hill, 1994). The fifth edition (Lambert, in press) contains chapters on process and outcome measurement (Lambert and Hill, in press), outcomes (Lambert and Ogles, in press) and process (Orlinsky et al., in press). Heppner et al.'s *Research Design in Counseling* (1999) provides a thorough grounding in all aspects of research methodology. This text also provides an appendix comprising eighteen frequently used process measures which is a useful resource. Wampold (2000) has written on outcomes in individual counselling and psychotherapy while Hill and Williams (2000) have summarized findings on the process of individual therapy. In addition, Hill (1991) has summarized a range of methodological issues relating to process research as well as a collection of work on methods and findings relating to process research (Hill, 2001). Other texts include the third edition of Brown and Lent's *Handbook of Counseling Psychology* (2000) which focuses on North American research and Clarkson's *Counselling Psychology: Integrating Theory, Research and Supervised Practice* (1998) which draws solely on UK work. An influential text emanating from the United Kingdom is Roth and Fonagy's *What Works for Whom? A critical review of psychotherapy research* (1996, in press). In terms of designing and implementing research activity there is Aveline and Shapiro's *Research Foundations for Psychotherapy Practice* (1995) together with two excellent and complementary texts on research methods:

Barker et al.'s *Research Methods in Clinical and Counselling Psychology* (1994; in press) and McLeod's *Doing Counselling Research* (1994; in press).

From time to time, there are also special sections in quality journals which address methodological issues (for example, *Journal of Counseling Psychology*: special sections on 'Quantitative foundations of counseling psychology', 1987, and 'Qualitative research in counseling process and outcome', 1994). More broadly, there are many scientific journals which report on studies carried out in the area of counselling psychology and cognate disciplines. The key American research journals include *The Counseling Psychologist, Journal of Counseling Psychology, Journal of Consulting and Clinical Psychology, Psychotherapy* and *Psychotherapy Research*. Key British research journals include the *British Journal of Guidance and Counselling, Clinical Psychology and Psychotherapy, Counselling Psychology Quarterly* and the *Counselling and Psychotherapy Research Journal* which is published under the auspices of the British Association for Counselling and Psychotherapy (BACP).

Prologue

Prior to 1952, the field of counselling psychology and psychotherapy research was developing fast from the impact of the Second World War. In the United States there was early process work into therapist techniques using verbal response mode systems. For example, Porter (1943a, b) worked in the area of counsellor and client behaviours and Snyder (1945) worked in a similar domain, finding evidence supporting the theory that client insights follow therapists' acceptance of client attitudes and feelings. Rogers's first major publication, *Counseling and Psychotherapy* (1942), appeared, followed later by *Client-centered Therapy* (1951), which set a clear research agenda, initiating a generation of process research developing objective methods of measuring events of recorded therapy sessions. In his book he moved away from specific therapist techniques towards the theory that therapists should possess an attitude enabling clients to address their particular psychological situation. This publication provided the basis for his subsequent theory on the necessary and sufficient conditions of therapy.

Generation I, 1950s to 1970s: outcome efficacy and measuring the facilitative conditions

The early thrust of process work outlined above was cut across by the publication of Eysenck's (1952) critique of the effectiveness of psychotherapy which resulted in a generation of research focusing on the issue of efficacy. As such, the overarching theme of this generation is one of 'justification' for the enterprise of psychological interventions.

Establishing the efficacy of counselling

Context

Eysenck (1952) claimed that approximately two-thirds of all people presenting with neurotic problems who received non-behavioural psychotherapy improved substantially within two years and that an equal proportion of people presenting with similar problems who had not received treatment also improved within the same time period. This spawned a generation of research focusing both on the reanalyses of the data used by Eysenck and on new studies. These new studies incorporated a range of methodological components, including 'control' groups and various statistical concepts, which resulted in the development of a procedure called meta-analysis. These three methodological issues, control groups, statistics and meta-analysis, are considered in the following section.

Methodological issues

Control groups

The first issue concerns the use of control groups. There are three basic designs used in psychotherapy research to address the question of efficacy. The most basic element is a design comprising a before-and-after counselling comparison (often termed a pre–post comparison). In the design, all clients enter the study, complete some outcome measure pre-counselling, and then complete the same measure again post-counselling. It would be hoped that the overall mean score for the group of clients on the measure showed an improvement. However, it might be that clients improved owing to events which occurred outside the counselling setting, or it may be that some would have improved in the course of time alone. These concerns led to designs which 'controlled' for such influences. The nature of the control condition can vary. At its most simple level, it involves using a parallel group of people, matched on major demographic and psychological variables, who are offered no counselling. To achieve this, clients are randomized to one of the two conditions so as to ensure that there are no systematic differences between the two groups at this stage. They complete similar measures at equivalent times, with the only difference being the treatment they receive. The post-treatment comparisons should be a reasonable test of the superiority or not of a psychological intervention over no intervention.

Ideally this would be true, but there are a number of problems with this assumption. First, if a client is told that they will be assigned to either a group receiving counselling or a group not receiving counselling, then finding that they are in the no-treatment group is likely to have a considerable effect on them (disappointment, for example). Hence, far from being assured that it is a 'no treatment' group, it is more likely to be experienced as a group who have been 'rejected' for treatment. Further, some clients in this position may act on their own accord and begin to discuss concerns with friends, that is, seek out natural support systems. The underlying point here is that a 'no treatment' group is not as simple to implement as it sounds and, more important, there are inadequacies in terms of what it is actually controlling which undermine the scientific yield of the design.

A refinement of the 'no treatment' control group arose with the 'wait list' control group in which clients in the experimental group received treatment while a comparison group of clients were placed on a waiting list. Only after the experimental group had completed treatment would the control group then receive some form of intervention. Importantly, the subsequent treatment offered to the 'wait list' group does not have to be similar to the experimental treatment. What is important from the design perspective is that they receive something, as the purpose of the comparison group is to control for the elapsed time of treatment in the experimental group rather than a direct comparison of the subsequent intervention. This means that the subsequent treatment they are offered may be less than optimal. Obviously, this condition has some merit over the no-treatment condition but care needs to be taken in how long clients will be on a wait list. This raises some ethical questions and it might be considered that the wait-list group should receive a condition deemed to be as effective as the experimental condition. This is a balance of ethical and scientific concerns. However, the researcher can deliver the treatment to the wait-list control group in the same form as to the original group. In this situation, the design becomes a switching replication wherein not only does the initial treatment group have a control group, but the situation is exactly reversed (that is, replicated) for the other group. Hence there is an in-built replication within the study.

A third design involves a 'placebo group'. This design aims to provide the non-experimental group with a control condition for what has been generally termed 'non-specific' or 'common' factors. In other words, the placebo group is receiving the general factors associated with receiving a treatment but not the technically specific ones. Unfortunately, the problems with placebo treatments are considerable and can be considered to fall into two groups. First, all the criticisms levelled at no-treatment and wait-list controls equally apply to placebo conditions. For example, no matter what the form of the placebo treatment, it is bound to be perceived by the recipients as something 'less' than the experimental treatment. Secondly, there are issues specific to placebo conditions regarding determining what it is that is being 'controlled'. Strictly speaking, the only placebo conditions which are valid are those which employ a 'component control condition' in which the placebo is designed specifically to exclude the component of the experimental condition which is of particular interest. They are, accordingly, extremely difficult to implement and account for a minority of placebo studies. In terms of the variety of control groups, it is worth considering the overall function of any control group. Historically, a great many studies of particular interventions required a control group in order to address the primary question of whether this particular intervention was better than no intervention. As scientific knowledge is built up, the position of control groups in general needs to be questioned. If, for example, the vast majority of studies (which are deemed to pass some threshold of design adequacy) show that providing clients with a psychological intervention is consistently better than offering them no intervention, then the role of a control group whose purpose is to test for the effects of elapsed time or spontaneous remission becomes increasingly dubious on both scientific and ethical grounds. The use of a control group should be specific to an issue to which either the scientific literature cannot provide an answer or which is sufficiently ambiguous to warrant the use of a control group.

Statistical concepts

Turning to the second methodological issue (i.e. statistical concepts), quantitative research has relied heavily upon the concept of statistical significance, which allows the researcher to be confident about attributing an association to something other than chance. However, Rosenthal and Rosnow (1991) have pointed out that the likelihood of obtaining a significant result is a function of both the sample size used and the size of the effect under investigation. Let us consider, first, sample size and, second, effect size.

In brief, any difference between two variables can be shown to be statistically significant given sufficient power (that is, numbers of subjects). For example, this can often be seen in research using very large samples where correlations of less than 0.20 are reported as statistically significant (although such a correlation would account for only 4 per cent of the variance). The power required to detect a difference is a function of the size of effect expected and whether the test is one- or two-tailed. The norm for requisite power is usually held to be of the order of 0.80 (that is, a four in five chance of detecting a difference if one is present). Differences may well be obtained with considerably less power, which may well attest to the robustness of the finding. But findings of no difference when power is low or sub-optimal always mean that the most parsimonious explanation for the null finding is low power: that is, that there was insufficient power in the design to detect the difference (which may actually have existed). While discussing the phenomenon of statistical power, it is also worth noting that increasing the number of clients in the study is not the only way of ensuring adequate power. In any design, the researcher is attempting to heighten the focus of the contrast being made, or, in other words, reduce the error variance. Hence, by ensuring that clients are homogeneous according to the variable of interest, ensuring that the form of counselling provided is delivered systematically, etc., all these will help reduce the amount of error in the study and increase the likelihood of it detecting a difference (if one is there).

The concept of an effect size (ES) introduces a metric for determining a measure of the magnitude of the relationship between independent and dependent variables, namely stating how effective a given treatment is. This is usually indexed by the following formula:

$$ES = (M_t - M_c)/\text{pooled SD}$$

where M_t is the mean score on a given measure of the treated group, M_c is the mean score of the control group and pooled SD is the standard deviation of the

Table 2.1   Guide to interpreting between-group effect sizes

Cohen's guidelines for interpreting effect size	Effect size (d)	% of people in control condition who are below the mean of people in the treated condition
No effect	0.0	0.50
	0.1	0.54
Small effect	0.2	0.58
	0.3	0.62
	0.4	0.66
Medium effect	0.5	0.69
	0.6	0.73
	0.7	0.76
Large effect	0.8	0.79
	0.9	0.82
	1.0	0.84

treated and control groups combined. Accordingly, an effect size of 1.0 indicates that the treated group is one standard deviation unit better than the control group at post-treatment. By referring to a table of the central distribution, we can determine that this improvement equates with 84 per cent. Hence 84 per cent of the treated group are better than the average non-treated client. Cohen (1977) has provided guidelines for interpreting ES differences where 0.20 is small, 0.50 is medium and 0.80 is large. In comparing a treatment with a no-treatment group, we would expect a large difference (ES of 0.80 or more). Effect sizes usually relate to comparisons between treated and untreated groups. As such, they are detecting quite large effects (that is, differences between treatment and no treatment). Accordingly, the number of clients required in each group to detect a difference need not be very large. ES differences can equally apply to comparisons between two active treatment groups, in which case they would be expected to be smaller (as both interventions are active). Table 2.1 presents a guide to interpreting effect sizes between two groups. Comparisons within the same group (i.e. pre-/post-therapy outcome comparisons) will, understandably, be larger and the same guidelines for interpreting effect sizes should not be used.

Meta-analysis

We now turn to the third methodological issue, meta-analysis, which incorporates many of the statistical issues described in this section. When reviewing the outcome literature, reviewers would be presented with outcomes from a range of studies which invariably might be contradictory. For example, some studies might support the effectiveness of a specific intervention while others might not. In addition, some results might derive from better-designed studies than others, leading to the question of whether they should receive more weight. Hence reviewing the cumulative literature has become increasingly difficult. One important procedure which has dominated the psychotherapeutic literature since 1977 has been 'meta-analysis'. In this procedure individual studies themselves become the data, with the aim of deriving a summary of the findings from all studies and taking into account specific features of the studies themselves. Hence a meta-analytical study of psychological interventions for family therapy might collect all empirical studies investigating this area and delineate the dimensions on which these studies should be evaluated. The distinctive features of meta-analysis compared with other review strategies are the quantitative representation of key research findings in the studies reviewed and the statistical analysis of the distribution of findings across studies and the relationship to study features. Thus, rather than reduce data to either 'for' or 'against' (that is to say, all-or-nothing categories), meta-analysis examines both the direction and the magnitude of the effects and arrives at an overall conclusion. Further, selection of the literature is done in a determined way which can be written down and replicated by another researcher. Hence it is far more systematic than simply scanning a range of journals. Although there are a wealth of methodological issues involved, the technique arrived at a time which enabled researchers to use individual studies in the service of marshalling a more comprehensive answer about the efficacy of psychological interventions.

Substantive findings

Prior to considering the wealth of data arising from this generation, it is appropriate to consider first the various reanalyses of the data upon which Eysenck (1952) based his critique of psychotherapy. Bergin and Lambert (1978) made a number of observations about the way Eysenck had analysed his data. For example, they noted that the most stringent improvement percentage was used for psychotherapy while the most generous was used for calculating spontaneous remission rates. Also, differing rates could be deduced, depending on the criterion used. In general, their view was that conclusions drawn from the studies used by Eysenck were suspect owing to their inherent limitations (not surprising, given their date). In looking at more recent data, Bergin and Lambert (1978) found the rate for spontaneous remission to be 43 per cent rather than 67 per cent. Importantly, these authors also noted the finding from outcome studies that substantial change generally occurs within the initial eight to ten sessions, considerably quicker than the two-year time frame of spontaneous remission. The response of researchers to Eysenck's critique was to incorporate a control group into the research design, and one exemplar design of Generation I is the study by Sloane et al., (1975). They contrasted psychodynamic versus behavioural treatments, each with an average fourteen-session duration of treatment, with a wait-list control group. The total sample size used for the analysis was ninety clients, with thirty clients randomly assigned to each of the three treatment conditions. The setting was a university psychiatric out-patient centre in which 54 per cent of the clients were students. The design used three experienced therapists in each of the two psychotherapy treatment conditions. The results using interview-based measures showed improvement in all three conditions but with the two active treatments being broadly similar and both superior to the wait-list condition. These gains were maintained at various follow-up intervals.

The findings from the Sloane et al. (1975) study are generally representative and were 'confirmed' several years later by the publication of the original meta-analytical study carried out by Smith and Glass (1977) and elaborated upon in their book *The Benefits of Psychotherapy* (Smith et al., 1980). The book provides a considered way through the claims and counter-claims of various researchers. They also provide a useful summary of the major reviews of this period (1961–75) prior to the use of meta-analysis. Stated as percentages of the number of studies reviewed, Eysenck (1961, 1966) found 0 per cent of studies supporting the efficacy of psychotherapy and Rachman (1971) found 4 per cent. By contrast, Bergin (1971) found 37 per cent, Meltzoff and Kornreich (1970) 80 per cent, and Luborsky et al. (1975) 78 per cent. In terms of the methods used by the reviewers as to studies they either included or excluded in their reviews owing to design flaws, Eysenck (1961, 1966) and Rachman (1971) excluded between 13 per cent and 74 per cent of studies while Bergin (1971) and Meltzoff and Kornreich (1970) excluded no studies. Given that many of the same studies were being sampled by the reviewers, Smith et al. (1980) noted how these findings 'illustrate the different results that arise from different methods for studying the same topic by means of a research review' (p. 23).

This 'variability' in summarizing research findings provided an excellent rationale for using meta-analytic techniques. Smith and Glass (1977) collated 475 controlled studies (that is to say, treatment versus no-treatment) across eighteen differing therapy types (including placebo treatment and undifferentiated counselling). The average effect size across all studies was 0.85, indicative of a large effect for psychotherapy over no psychotherapy, indicating that the average treated person was better off than 80 per cent of non-treated people. The effects ranged from small effect sizes (0.14 for reality therapy) to large ones (2.38 for cognitive therapies other than RET). The authors found little evidence of negative effects, with only 9 per cent of the measures being negative (that is, control groups were better than treated groups). In terms of overall efficacy, the subsequent refinements of meta-analytic procedures and greater specificity, as well as the inclusion of more recent and more accomplished studies, have not delivered substantially different results, with the effect sizes remaining relatively stable.

In subsequent years, beyond the time frame of Generation I, many further studies have been included in meta-analytic reviews addressing the issue of 'efficacy'. Lambert and Bergin state: 'There is now little doubt that psychological treatments are, overall and in general, beneficial, although it remains equally true that not everyone benefits to a satisfactory degree' (1994: 144). The most concise summary of findings derives from meta-analytic studies. In the area of depression, the number of studies (n) included in the meta-analysis and the effect sizes for three major meta-analytic reports are as follows: Nietzel et al. (1987), $n = 28$, ES = 0.71; Robinson et al. (1990), $n = 29$, ES = 0.84; Steinbrueck et al. (1983), $n = 56$, ES = 1.22.

In terms of more diverse presenting problems, Lambert and Bergin (1994) provide a summary table of thirty meta-analytic reviews covering a range of presenting problems and psychological interventions. Five studies (including that of Smith and Glass) are defined as 'mixed' and result in a large average effect size of 0.90. The range of other studies is so diverse as not to warrant categorizing. However, they show the smallest and largest effect sizes (excluding control conditions) to range from 0.00 (schizophrenia; Quality Assurance Project, 1984) to 1.30 (stuttering; Andrews et al., 1980). Using only those studies ($n = 25$) which report effect sizes, the median effect size was 0.76, which is approaching a large effect size. In terms of comparisons, an effect size of 0.67 is obtained from nine months of instruction in reading, while the effect sizes for antidepressants range from 0.40 to 0.81. Thus, as Lambert and Bergin (1994) argue, there appears to be evidence that psychological interventions are as effective as, if not more effective than, medication. Apparently contrary to these substantial effects, it has been claimed that counselling/psychotherapy accounts for only 10 per cent of the outcome variance. This might appear small. However, it needs to be realized that 10 per cent variance arises from a correlation of 0.32 between counselling/psychotherapy and outcome. This is appreciably greater than other established correlations in the field: for example, correlations of 0.03 for the effect of aspirin on heart attacks, and 0.07 for service in Vietnam and alcohol consumption.

An additional question which has been raised is whether counselling is more effective than a placebo? In response, a critical point, well summarized by Lambert and Bergin, is worthy of reiteration:

> In interpreting this [placebo] research, it is important to keep in mind that failure to find incremental effects (effects beyond those attributable to common factors) for a specific therapy does not mean that psychotherapy is ineffective. Rather it means that no effect has been demonstrated beyond the effects of the common factors. (1994: 149)

Lambert and Bergin (1994) provide a useful summary table of fifteen meta-analytic studies whereby three two-way comparisons are made: psychotherapy versus no treatment, placebo versus no treatment and psychotherapy versus placebo. The first of these comparisons produces a mean/median effect size of 0.82 (i.e. very similar to that stated in the previous section). The placebo versus no-treatment comparison produces a mean/median effect size of 0.42, while the placebo versus psychotherapy comparison produces a mean/median effect size of 0.48.

By way of comment on the use of placebo controls, Lambert and Bergin (1994) summarize:

> we have concluded that the typical placebo controls used in outcome studies are so conceptually and procedurally flawed that they have essentially failed in their purpose of helping to isolate the active therapeutic ingredients. It is time to discontinue placebo controls and design studies with more meaningful comparison groups. (1994: 152)

Comment

In terms of outcome, Generation I research clearly established the efficacy of psychotherapy and also provided the basis for investigating components of what might make therapy effective. With regard to the former, it might be assumed that this issue has now passed. However, two observations are worth noting. First, while the amount of research carried out has been phenomenal, Eysenck still maintained the validity of his argument in his later writing (for example, 1992). Secondly, with recent changes in the service provisions for psychotherapy and counselling services within the National Health Service in the United Kingdom, it has again become a major issue as various stakeholders in the provision of services have begun to require outcome criteria. Hence it is a generation of work which has come, to some extent, full circle as the demand to justify the impact of counselling and psychotherapy meets market forces. Hence, while Generation I research may have put increasing weight on ensuring internal validity, the question of external validity has now come to prominence.

Measuring the facilitative conditions

Context

The influence of Rogers was profound in Generation I's development of objective procedures for measuring the events of recorded therapy sessions. His influence has been noted as deriving from his 'respect for the scientific method and dedication to the objective study of the efficacy of his methods' (Hill and Corbett, 1993: 5). While there was a great surge of activity in pursuit of establishing the efficacy of psychotherapy, it was largely Rogers and his students who pursued research on the process of therapy. While the earlier process work had focused on verbal response modes as indicators of therapist techniques, process measures turned to the evaluation of Rogers's facilitative conditions.

However, there is an intriguing tension between the findings of the research presented above and the assumptions underlying the research on process during Generation I. In the first edition of the *Handbook of Psychotherapy and Behavior Change*, Truax and Mitchell (1971) reviewed research on therapists' interpersonal skills. The premise for their review of particular therapists' skills was based on one particular view of the general effectiveness of psychotherapy and counselling:

> After a careful review of the relevant research literature dealing with the effects of counseling and psychotherapy, Truax and Carkhuff (1967) concluded that unfortunately Eysenck was essentially correct in saying that the average counseling and psychotherapy, as it is currently practised, does not result in average client improvement greater than that observed in persons who receive no special counseling or psychotherapy treatment. (1967: 301)

Hence much of the subsequent process research was premised on the assumption that specific skills training on specific therapists' variables would enhance the effectiveness of therapy.

Methodological issues

Examples of observationally based measures developed by students and colleagues of Rogers included the Experiencing Scale (Klein et al., 1970), the Client Vocal Quality Classification Scale (Butler et al., 1962) and the Accurate Empathy Scale (AES; Truax, 1961). Self-report measures which were developed included the Barrett-Lennard Relationship Inventory (BLRI; Barrett-Lennard, 1962). The last two measures (that is, the AES and BLRI) can be seen as representative of the work in this research generation, and each provided a major tool for investigating the therapeutic relationship and its components which began in Generation I and spanned Generation II research (see below).

A standard approach adopted in Generation I research was to select particular 'sections' of a session either randomly or systematically. The latter approach might have involved selecting three five-minute segments (for example, minutes 15–19, 30–4 and 45–9). This would appear 'representative' of the session. However, most studies carried out in the 1960s employed random time samples from therapy sessions when investigating Rogerian conditions. This approach reflects Generation I research because it bears the hallmark of the uniformity myth (Kiesler, 1966) which supposes that there is little fluctuation across clients, therapists and (in relation to this issue) sessions. The strategy of using random time samples assumed that it did not matter what particular segment was selected: one segment was as good as another in terms of accessing a particular therapeutic process. Such an approach appeared to be 'approved' by Rogers (see Rogers et al., 1967), who argued that small samples (for example, three samples of two to five minutes in length) from any given interview were sufficient to provide a basis for investigating, for example, the construct of empathy.

During this period, considerable research efforts were spent on establishing the empirical basis for associating the facilitative conditions with outcome. However, many questions arose concerning the research methodologies used which served to undermine the validity of the findings themselves.

Substantive findings

Examples of research in this early phase include the work of Rogers and Dymond (1954), who found evidence supporting the view that a good outcome was associated with improvements in self-perceptions. Other research drew on the work of Whitehorn and Betz (e.g. 1954), who found, via a retrospective study of psychiatrists, that those who were successful in working with schizophrenic patients were warm and communicated with their patients in a personal manner. Similar findings arose from the various reports of the classic study of the therapeutic conditions with a group of schizophrenic patients carried out at the University of Wisconsin (e.g. Rogers et al., 1967). This study arose following publication of Rogers's (1957) paper on the necessary and sufficient conditions for change. The Wisconsin project was a major empirical investigation undertaken with schizophrenic clients (Rogers et al., 1967). At the same time, Truax and Carkhuff (1967) published a text which included Truax's own version of some of the Wisconsin data. There were other compendiums of research which combined 'positive' results with the development of work on the facilitative conditions (for example, Carkhuff and Berenson, 1967) as well as a major review in the first edition of the *Handbook of Psychotherapy and Behavior Change* (Truax and Mitchell, 1971). This later text marks a recognition of the fallacy of assuming uniformity. In discussing the domain of therapist variables and their role in understanding the process of psychotherapy, Truax and Mitchell (1971) stated: 'it quickly became apparent to us that we were assuming that such variables are unitary when, in fact, they are not'. They went on: 'just as therapists are not unitary, neither are specific therapist variables'. They concluded: 'Therefore, in our opinion, most if not all the research dealing with therapist characteristics needs to be re-done' (1971: 300).

Comment

One result of the research work of Generation I was to show how the 'complex personal phenomena of psychotherapy could be brought out of the private consulting room into the purview of scientific study without disrupting these phenomena beyond recognition' (Orlinsky and Russell, 1994). Hence there was a view that any aspect of the psychotherapeutic process could be measured. In terms of process findings the tone was decidedly optimistic, and some questions have been asked about the manner in which some of the research was carried out. Garfield and Bergin (1994) recount the issues surrounding the mysterious disappearance of the initial data organized by Truax in the Wisconsin project. The final publication was based on an entirely new set of ratings. Garfield and Bergin state that 'Since 1967, scholars have appeared to treat with caution any of the published reports by Truax (but not his co-authors) concerning the Wisconsin Schizophrenia Project data' (1994: 11–12).

Generation II, 1960s to 1980s: specificity in outcome and process research

Research characterizing Generation II began in large part as a search for greater specificity in response to what became known as the 'uniformity myth'. This myth reflected the held view that clients were thought to respond similarly to particular interventions. In other words, little attention was paid to differences across clients, therapists, therapies or across the course of therapy itself. In response to this situation, the archetypal question of this generation became encapsulated in Paul's litany: 'What treatment, by whom, is most effective for this individual with that specific problem, and under which set of circumstances?' (1967: 111). Clearly this was an important and logical step in research, as it sought to address the issue of what was the most effective treatment.

In terms of process, Rogers's theory and research work paid scant attention to differences among clients. The question of whether psychotherapy is effective was seen as simplistic (Krumboltz, 1966), while process and outcome were increasingly viewed as differing across clients, therapists and therapies (Kiesler, 1966). Generation II research gained ground in the 1960s and was dominant through the 1980s. Indeed, there is still a considerable output from this generation, given that some of the major outcome studies were designed and implemented in the early 1980s and publications were appearing in the 1990s. In both outcome and process research, the key theme in Generation II research was 'specificity'.

The comparative efficacy of differing approaches

Context

Once the general theme of determining the overall efficacy of psychotherapy was instigated, Paul's matrix of specifying the various components led researchers to focus most on the differing types of interventions. In addition, the 1960s saw the rapid development of behaviour therapy within the domain of clinical psychology and fed the logical question as to whether these newer therapies (or other brands of therapy) were more effective than, for example, the verbal (for example, dynamically oriented) therapies. The research carried out in response to this question raised a number of methodological issues relating to design, measures, analyses of outcome data and statistical concerns. Each of these will be addressed in the following section.

Methodological issues

Design
The design usually employed to address the above question is known as a 'comparative outcome' trial. In this situation, the main focus of interest is in comparing two (or more) active treatments. The advantages of the comparative outcome designs include their ability to ensure that any demand characteristics of the two or more conditions are broadly similar. Also, they are the best means of ensuring that the placebo effects are controlled in as much as they are present for both conditions. Hence the main difference between the two or more treatments should be restricted to technical differences between the conditions. However, while this is a persuasive argument and has been the rationale for a series of studies, it needs to be noted that other proponents of the quantitative approach firmly hold to the view that a control condition should be administered (e.g. Kazdin, 1994).

The studies in this generation should be relatively sophisticated, benefiting from the lessons learned in Generation I. To provide a sense of the complexities involved, the outline design from one major comparative outcome study is presented here. (The results of this study appear in the following section.) One of the largest RCTs to date is the National Institute of Mental Health Treatment of Depression Collaborative Research Program (NIMH TDCRP; Elkin, 1994; Elkin et al., 1989). The design comprised three research sites in which 250 clients were randomly assigned to the four treatment conditions. The four treatment conditions comprised the two psychotherapies which were of major interest – namely, cognitive-behavioural therapy (CBT) and interpersonal psychotherapy (IPT). In order to provide a standard reference condition, the third condition comprised imipramine plus clinical management (IMI-CM). Finally, a placebo condition (PLA-CM) was used primarily as a control for the drug condition but also as an imperfect control for the two psychotherapies. Among the features of the design, separate therapists were used in the two differing psychotherapies. This is termed 'nested', in which the therapists administer only one particular treatment rather than delivering all treatments. The particular treatments were documented in training manuals and the delivery of the treatments was investigated to check on therapists' adherence to the treatment protocols. This is an example of the research requiring a level of control and monitoring over the delivery of the therapy which would not normally take place in more naturalistic settings. It is also a procedure which may rest uncomfortably with the philosophy of counselling psychology.

Because both psychotherapies are active (that is to say, they would both be expected to have a positive impact on psychological functioning), the effect size is likely to be appreciably smaller than for a treatment versus no-treatment design (for example, between small and medium). Logically, then, the sample size required to detect any difference will be larger. Ironically, therefore, it can be seen that, in terms of resources required, it is much more difficult to carry out a contrast of two or more active treatments than it is to carry out a study using a control group (such as a wait-list control in which clients receive some subsequent treatment).

Measures

It is incumbent upon users to be informed about aspects concerning the psychometric properties of measures they use and to report this basic information when using it. Basic requirements include data pertaining to validity and reliability. In terms of perspectives, outcome can be evaluated from three sources: the client, the counsellor and a third party. In contrast to many other helping professions, counselling psychology should aspire to obtain clients' perspectives on the change they have experienced. In addition, measures are based on one of two central assumptions: nomothetic or idiographic. Nomothetic measures comprise items that are invariant and that have been standardized on large samples and invariably are accompanied by norms. Idiographic measures are derived from the client's unique frame of reference and are specific to the client, a perspective which is congruent with the central role of the individual within counselling psychology.

Substantive findings

Bergin and Garfield summarize Generation II studies as follows: 'We have to face the fact that in a majority of studies, different approaches to the same symptoms (depression for example) show little difference in efficacy' (1994b: 822). This is the view summarized by Stiles et al. (1986) in their question 'Are all psychotherapies equivalent?' They posited three ways in which to understand the supposed equivalence of outcomes. The first was methodological, in that equivalence could be achieved through lack of stringency in research methodology. The second argument concerned the possibility that differing therapies may be broadly equivalent owing to the overriding effects of common factors. The third argument revolved around the implementation of new research strategies to detect differences.

The NIMH TDCRP implicitly addressed the first of these through implementation of one of the most stringent research designs. Findings showed that clients in the IMI-CM condition were most improved, clients in the PLA-CM condition least improved, and clients in the two psychotherapy conditions in between but generally closer to the IMI-CM condition. However, the differences were not large. Indeed, there were no differences between the two psychotherapies or between either of them and the IMI-CM. Differences between the psychotherapies and the placebo condition showed only one instance of a trend towards lower scores for clients in the IPT condition as compared with PLA-CM and no significant or trend advantage to CBT compared with PLA-CM. Findings from a UK study comparing cognitive-behavioural (CB) with psychodynamic interpersonal (PI) therapy in two durations (eight sessions and sixteen sessions) showed only a small advantage to CB over PI on the Beck Depression Inventory (Beck et al., 1961) and not on any other measures (Shapiro et al., 1994). Hence the CB advantage was restricted to a single measure. However, there was a significant severity by duration interaction which showed that clients with high severity depression did significantly better in sixteen than in eight sessions. Findings at one-year follow-up showed that clients in the 8-PI condition did less well than clients in the other three conditions (Shapiro et al., 1995).

The most recent meta-analysis carried out by Wampold and colleagues (Wampold et al., 1997) reaffirmed the equivalence finding. Their study found that, under the most liberal assumptions, the largest extent of any true difference in effect size was in the region of 0.20, which is viewed as a 'small' effect. One important point to keep in mind is that such a finding arose from applying more rigorous procedures than previously employed. For example, it only included studies making a direct within-study comparison between contrasting treatments and therapies that were deemed '*bona fide*' (i.e. treatments had to be both credible and therapeutic).

These findings have confirmed the view that technically different therapies result in broadly similar outcomes, a conclusion referred to as the 'equivalence paradox' (Stiles et al., 1986). It is not disputed that there is often a reported advantage to one particular method of therapy (invariably cognitive behavioural), but what is important is that the size of this advantage is relatively small. How such a small advantage translates into clinical status or psychological health is unclear.

Comment

In some ways, it is difficult to be conclusive about this generation of research. Some might argue that little has been gained from it, seeing the failure to identify specific differential effects as a poor outcome for a generation's work. At one level this disappointment is understandable, especially given the huge financial cost of some of the studies. There is also the view that the full yield from the work of this generation has not been realized, as it is a legitimate argument that what is still required is further specificity. What is clear is that such specificity is unlikely to be derived from further large-scale studies of the kind described above. However, the importance of the finding of broad equivalence of outcomes despite technical diversity should not be lost. Neither should it be forgotten that while 'active' treatments have consistently outperformed 'placebo' treatments, the difference between the two conditions has often been arithmetical rather than statistically significant.

The contribution of the facilitative conditions to outcome

Context

Process research built its base on the 'recorded' session and, in Generation II, was dominated by the work carried out to investigate the 'facilitative' conditions (i.e. empathy, warmth and genuineness). This was a logical step deriving from a theoretical basis and employing observational and self-report measures.

Methodology

A profound difficulty associated with the process research in Generation I was the lack of replication of specific findings. This arose out of the growing search for specificity contrasting with the uniformity myth. Process research applied its newly found objectivism through the use of seemingly rigorous and appropriate research designs. While the prototypical research study in Generation I employed a random technique for sampling time periods, Generation II research moved towards employing the 'session'. This move arose from the debate as to whether therapist skills were stable across time. This point had been raised by Karl and Abeles (1969) who found that when tape recordings were sampled during any of the five ten-minute portions, there were significant differences across the segments on a sample of therapist measures. Similarly, Gurman (1973) had been critical of the single-segment sampling strategy. He sampled high and low facilitative therapists during the initial four-minute segments in each of the five consecutive ten-minute segments and found that, regardless of their absolute ratings, all therapists' relative levels of facilitative-ness varied both within and across sessions. Hence the facilitative conditions appeared not to be as consistent as Rogerian theory would have predicted. Such a position led to, for example, Gurman's (1973, 1977) 'empathic specificity hypothesis'. This hypothesis suggested that a therapist's overall facilitativeness is less predictive of treatment outcome than their level of functioning around particular issues which are more critical to the client.

Substantive findings

The core period for Generation II process research was the 1970s and there is a noticeable difference between Truax and Mitchell's (1971) review from the *Handbook* reported above and the Mitchell et al. (1977) chapter published in *Effective Psychotherapy: a Handbook of Research*. The authors of the latter text acknowledged that the former had focused too much on gross outcome and not sufficiently on the potential correlates between, for example, empathy and out-come. Hence they stated that 'demographic and process studies were ignored which might have answered the question "Which therapists, under what con-ditions, with which clients, in what kinds of specific predicaments, need to reach what levels of these interpersonal skills to effect what kinds of client changes?"' (1977: 482).

In contrast to the 1971 review, which implied that the facilitative condi-tions were both necessary and sufficient, and that they were relatively invariant, Mitchell et al. stated that 'the mass of data neither supports nor rejects the overriding influence of such variables as empathy' (1977: 483). They went on: 'their [the facilitative conditions] potency and generalizability are not as great as once thought' (p. 483). Hence, while the authors reported some studies which supported the positive role of the facilitative conditions to varying degrees, the majority of studies they reported showed little or no direct relationship between the facilitative conditions and outcome (e.g. Sloane et al., 1975).

Comment

While process research focused largely on the facilitative conditions, which in itself became the basis of subsequent research on the therapeutic alliance, it was, as Orlinsky and Russell (1994) observe, 'peculiarly flawed' to the extent that it had virtually ceased by the late 1970s. The 'conceptual critique' specifi-cally in relation to the facilitative conditions, combined with the increasing search for psychologically appropriate methods of investigating aspects of the therapeutic process, led to the demise of research in this area. In historical terms the absence of a research centre linked with Rogers assisted the demise. More generally, there was probably a move away from investigating 'common' factors and towards determining the more specific components of individual orientations.

Generation III, 1970s to 1990s: cost-effectiveness and change pathways

The research included in this third generation spans the period from the 1970s to the 1990s and incorporates what appear to be two quite diverse interests: cost-effectiveness and change mechanisms. However, these two areas can be seen to be natural developments arising from the previous two generations of research. Cost-effectiveness has become a central concern, partly driven by research interest alone but also by the interest of a variety of stakeholders. As such, it is a natural extension of the outcome research carried out in Generation I. The focus on change mechanisms reflects an extension to the issue of 'specificity' which was a feature of Generation II process research, although it may equally be construed as a reaction to it. It is an extension in terms of it retaining specificity as a hallmark but a reaction in terms of refocusing research on to the process of change.

The nature of 'integrative' therapy

Context

The context for considering integration arises partly as a corollary to the above findings on the broad equivalence of outcomes from differing therapies. It also arises from counsellors' aspirations not to be constrained by a single theoretical orientation. Also, a perception that counsellors have multiple skills feeds the notion that the skills from a range of therapies can be utilized in response to a client's presenting problems. Certainly, recent surveys of therapists' orientations show the majority of therapists to describe themselves as 'eclectic'. It is worth noting in passing that the term 'integration' is now used considerably more than the term 'eclectic'. For example, the revised edition of the *Handbook of Eclectic Psychotherapy* (Norcross, 1986) was entitled *Handbook of Psychotherapy Integration* (Norcross and Goldfried, 1992). Similarly, the *Journal of Integrative and Eclectic Psychotherapy* became the *Journal of Psychotherapy Integration*. In addition, there has been a round table entitled 'Research directions for psychotherapy integration' (Norcross, 1993) published in the latter journal.

Methodological issues

The methodological issues in evaluating integrative therapies reflect those discussed previously, as the design issues involved effectively treat 'integrative' therapy as just one more type of therapy. Perhaps most important, the central problem is conceptual in as much as whether an integrative therapy is actually integrative or whether it is simply another brand of therapy. For example, combinations of therapies should not be viewed as integrative. What differentiates a combined therapy from an integrative therapy is the presence of an overarching integrative theory which binds the various therapeutic approaches in terms of some higher-order theory or model.

Substantive findings

Brockman et al. (1987) compared cognitive-analytical therapy (CAT: Ryle, 1990) with short-term psychodynamic therapy. Specific advantages were found for CAT. However, these were found on CAT-specific measures. Comparisons of global measures showed no significant advantage to either condition. Shapiro et al. (1992) combined prescriptive (i.e. cognitive-behavioural) and exploratory (i.e. psychodynamic interpersonal) therapies by administering them within a session but alternating within certain constraints across the course of therapy in response to a match between client requirements and a particular overarching integrative model. The outcome of this single case was successful but requires replication. Overall, there is a dearth of direct evidence for the equivalence in efficacy, let alone superiority, of integrative therapies. Much of the argument in support of their use derives indirectly from the equivalence of outcomes. In addition, it is not clear that skills and expertise gained in one particular method of delivery transfer to a more integrated method without additional training.

Comment

The current interest in and articles emanating from this domain are consider-able, but it has not been shown that integrative therapies are 'superior' to single-brand therapies. It is likely that integrative therapies are more palatable to practitioners, but that is a clinical preference. Following a major workshop which focused on the research required to move this area forward, little empiri-cal work has been carried out (Wolfe and Goldfried, 1988). Indeed, consider-ably more work needs to be carried out in order to provide hard data on the comparative efficacy of integrative therapies.

The relative efficacy of long-term and short-term counselling

Context

The 'debate' between long and short-term counselling has gained a central focus recently, in particular among those stakeholders who have an interest in providing a cost-effective service. In addition, there has been increasing inter-est in the delivery of models of short-term counselling within primary care set-tings where the focus has been on identifying those people experiencing 'mild to moderate' problems and delivering time-limited interventions as an appro-priately matched response. While the previous question focused on the method of the intervention, this question focuses on the duration of the intervention.

Methodological issues

In determining how much of a given intervention should be delivered to a person let us first consider issues relating to open-ended versus time-limited interventions. There is, implicit in this comparison, the view that open-ended interventions will be of longer duration than time-limited interventions. However, this is not necessarily true. The vast majority of research studies investigating time-limited therapies employ durations of twelve, sixteen or twenty sessions. In many instances, any of these may actually be longer than an open-ended intervention, particularly if the average duration is held to be in the region of between five and seven sessions. Hence, if a time-limited intervention was compared with an open-ended condition, it is likely that clients in the time-limited condition would receive more therapy than those in the open-ended condition.

As with the previous questions, power (that is to say, the size of the study) is an issue. In the same way that large effects will be expected to arise from more contrasting conditions, so larger effects would be expected to occur from contrasting briefer with longer-duration interventions. Of course, the main problem relates to controlling for elapsed time. Any comparison must carry out assessments at similar points in time.

In terms of what has become known as the 'dose-effect' literature, an important point is to ensure that any client has a sufficient dose in order to be able to evaluate its effectiveness. This point is akin to that in psychopharmacology in which the effectiveness of any given medication can only be determined once it has been established that a sufficient dose has been taken. In other words, it needs to be established that, if no effect is obtained, it is not attributable to the fact that not enough was given to have an effect. This notion of 'dose' may appear overly medical and contrary to the philosophy of counselling psychology. However, it is an attempt to model the match between client need and service resources.

Substantive findings

The major finding relating to the dose-effect literature derives from a study carried out by Howard et al. (1986) which combined fifteen outcome studies over thirty years. These authors found that the percentage of clients showing measurable improvement following specified numbers of sessions was as follows: 24 per cent after a single session, 30 per cent after two sessions, 41 per cent after four sessions, 53 per cent after eight sessions, 62 per cent after thirteen sessions, 74 per cent after twenty six sessions, 83 per cent after fifty two sessions and 90 per cent after 104 sessions. This relationship between the number of sessions received by clients and the percentage of clients showing measurable improvement was best represented by a negatively accelerating curve. This means that, while the curve 'accelerates' (the percentage of clients improving gets higher as a result of more sessions), it does so 'negatively', in that the greatest improvement occurs early in therapy and there are diminishing returns thereafter such that smaller and smaller gains are made later on in therapy in response to the provision of more sessions. However, it is worth noting that almost half the studies (seven) had a median of fifteen or more sessions, considerably more that the often quoted averages (Taube et al., 1984). Further, the data set did not comprise cognitive-behavioural, cognitive or behaviour therapy orientations. The findings from Howard et al.'s (1986) work are interesting in how they have been used by people espousing differing viewpoints. Howard et al. (1986) obtained two dose-effect curves: one based on therapist ratings and one on client ratings. Defence of longer-term therapy has utilized the former curve. In contrast, data from the client ratings suggest greater improvements to be derived from the initial eight to ten sessions. Research on brief therapies has been summarized by Koss and Shiang (1994).

The issue of cost-effectiveness has been addressed in several studies in which very brief interventions have been devised (i.e. therapy is construed as assessment). One model delivers therapy in the form of two sessions one week apart and a third session three months later. This generic model of therapy, termed two-plus-one therapy, has been evaluated in a large randomized controlled trial (Barkham et al., 1999). A total of 116 clients experiencing a range of subsyndromal depression received two-plus-one sessions of either CB or PI therapy either immediately or after a four-week delay (the latter acting as a control condition). The initial advantage for patients in the immediate group disappeared once clients in the delayed condition received treatment (i.e. offering treatment immediately relieved distress quicker but the other clients 'caught up'). In terms of the comparative treatments, there were no significant differences in outcomes between CB and PI therapies at the end of treatment. However, at one-year follow-up there was a significant advantage to CBT on the Beck Depression Inventory. Other features of the reporting in this study – for example, utilizing reliable and clinically significant methods to show that approximately two-thirds of clients met such stringent criteria for change – reflect Generation IV research.

The focus on brief therapies has continued, with researchers investigating and reviewing the components that make brief therapies effective. Messer (2001) has reviewed components that contribute to making brief psychodynamic therapy time efficient, while McGinn and Sanderson (2001) have done likewise for cognitive behavioural therapy. Of particular note is a review by Elliott (2001) of brief experiential therapy. What is of interest is that this review attempts to re-establish the evidence base for experiential therapies. Elliott (2001) identified a sample of twenty eight studies comprising both controlled and comparative studies. The pre-/post-change effect size (i.e. within-group) was in the order of 1.1, with the effects consistent across the three main types of problems studied: neurotic problems (ES = 1.02), depression (ES = 1.61) and anxiety (ES = 1.16). When comparisons were made between treated and untreated clients, there was a large effect size (ES = 1.14). Comparisons between experiential and non-experiential therapies showed very little difference (ES = −0.04). These findings suggest there to be an increasing evidence base for brief experiential therapies, which has particular significance in that the outcome work on experiential therapies is closely linked with many of the principal process researchers emanating from Generation IV.

Comment

Findings indicate that for many clients the greater impact of counselling or therapy occurs during the initial time frame, with subsequent gains requiring more time. However, for many clients, especially those who have been severely harmed, effective therapeutic work may not be possible until considerable work has been carried out in establishing, for example, the therapeutic alliance. What this means is that there are clients for whom briefer therapies are appropriate and clients for whom longer therapies are appropriate. The issue is to determine what is best for each client. It is not necessarily true that more therapy is always the preferred option. Given limited resources, it is important to ensure that longer-term interventions are appropriately used and that they are evaluated in order to provide supporting evidence for their use.

The efficacy of counselling in primary care settings

Context

In recent years, particularly in the United Kingdom, there has been an increasing drive towards focusing on services which are delivered in primary care settings. This has, in large part, been due to government initiatives and the establishment of *bona fide* professional groups which offer counselling and psychological therapies specifically in primary care (e.g. Counsellors and Psychotherapists in Primary Care).

Methodological issues

This particular theme gives rise to a number of issues relating more to how the RCT method is applied in a particular service setting. For example, in terms of clients there is the issue of setting appropriate severity thresholds (i.e. not accepting clients who present with too high a level of distress). In terms of counsellors, there is the issue of utilizing *bona fide* primary care counsellors as opposed to, for example, clinical psychologists working in GP practices. This latter point bears upon the developing professionalization of primary care counsellors. In terms of strict methodological issues, it has highlighted the potential role of patient preference trials (see below) as a subtle variant on the RCT design. Although it requires more resources, it goes some way to bridging the gap between internal and external validity.

Substantive findings

The impetus behind establishing effective psychological interventions in primary care has seen several programmes of research. One programme of research combining the issues of brief interventions and cost issues set in primary care has been carried out by Mynors-Wallis and colleagues (Gath and

Mynors-Wallis, 1997; Mynors-Wallis, 1996). A series of studies have been carried out on problem-solving treatment (PST) and observations include that PST can be effectively delivered in primary care by a range of professionals (e.g. psychiatrists, nurses) but that it may be more expensive than the usual treatment (by general practitioners) in primary care as indicated by direct costs. However, when indirect savings are considered, greater cost savings are likely. A Cochrane review carried out by Rowland and colleagues (Bower et al., 2002; Rowland et al., 2000) found four randomized and controlled patient preference trials comparing *bona fide* counselling in primary care with usual GP care. Findings suggested that clients receiving counselling had significantly better psychological symptom levels after their counselling compared with those receiving standard GP care, as indicated by an ES difference of 0.30.

A large outcome study – the London–Manchester trial – has compared non-directive counselling, CBT and usual GP care for the presentation of depression in primary care and is an exemplar of the combination of efficacy (Ward et al., 2000) and cost-effectiveness (Bower et al., 2000) issues that are a hallmark of Generation III research. A total of 464 patients took part in this prospective controlled trial, which utilized both randomized and patient preference allocation arms. Hence patients who had a preference as to which treatment they preferred selected that treatment condition. Those who stated they had no preference were randomized to one of the three treatment conditions. A total of 137 patients selected their own treatment, 197 patients were randomly assigned to one of the three treatment conditions, and 130 were randomized to one of the two psychological therapies (in which patients received upwards of twelve sessions). At four months, patients in the two psychological therapies showed greater gains on the BDI than those randomized to usual GP care (even though all groups improved over time). But, interestingly, there were no significant differences between the two psychological therapies (i.e. non-directive counselling and CBT) at four months and no significant differences between all three conditions at twelve months. The additional cost-effectiveness analysis (Bower et al., 2000) showed that there were no significant differences in direct costs, production losses or societal costs between the three treatment conditions at either four or twelve months. Hence it was concluded that the two psychological interventions were significantly more cost-effective in the short term (i.e. at four months), as patients showed greater improvement at no additional cost. However, all cost and clinical differences disappeared at twelve months.

Comment

This area of research has grown significantly in recent years and there are an increasing number of studies investigating counselling in primary care settings (e.g. Bedi et al., 2000). Because of the key role played by primary care in the delivery of health care, such studies are very timely. As the body of evidence accumulates, research activity can move on to address service-level issues (e.g.

access and drop-out rates) and also process issues (e.g. questions of developing good client–practitioner working alliance).

Identifying the effective change pathways?

Context

Building on the developmental stages arising from Generations I and II, in which process work moved from the use of random segments (1960s) to whole sessions (1970s), Generation III process research continued by beginning a *rapprochement* between research and clinical practice. Many features help define one generation from another and one which defines Generation III process research is Bordin's (1979) classic article on the working alliance which became a central focus of research into common factors in place of the facilitative conditions.

Research methodology

Process research is time-consuming, as the data derive from what happens within sessions. The approach therefore requires the researcher to tap either some component of the session itself or to acquire some measure of the phenomenon under investigation after the session. The former strategy is greatly assisted by taking tape recordings of sessions. However, a great deal of research which focuses on in-session activities has derived from sessions selected from the course of therapy without regard to any sampling strategy. The two main options are selecting all sessions or using some theoretical rationale which is applied to determine which session (or part of a session) is to be sampled. The first strategy assumes that the researcher is interested in the course of a phenomenon across time. This is obviously a time-consuming approach but one which is central to understanding the process of change. For example, while there might be evidence that the therapeutic alliance is associated with outcome, researchers and practitioners may be most interested in how the therapeutic alliance is established and how it changes over time. The second strategy necessitates some rationale for selecting a particular session. (This strategy can obviously be used in addition to the first but not vice versa.) Staying with the therapeutic alliance as an example, the researcher may ask the client to identify a session in which he or she feels the therapist did something to enhance the client's feeling of having a good therapeutic alliance. The client might write something at the end of the session indicating what it was. Such 'events' could then be collected for a number of clients and the data analysed in a quantitative manner. The researcher could also combine the two approaches if, for example, they had a theory that the resolution of a ruptured alliance would lead to a good outcome. Here the researcher would want to select a session in which there was evidence of a rupture and then analyse the session, and subsequent sessions, as deemed necessary.

Research investigating what counselling psychologists say in sessions has employed a variety of procedures which invariably require coding taxonomies. One level of interest has refocused on verbal response modes (VRMs), of which there are many taxonomies. In an attempt to determine common ground, a comparison of six systems was carried out (Elliott et al., 1987). A degree of commonality was found among the various systems, with 'question', 'information', 'advisement', 'interpretation', 'reflection' and 'self-disclosure' common to all six systems and 'reassurance' and 'confrontation' common to four of the systems. Whatever the system used, the data (usually a transcript of the counselling session) must first be divided into meaningful units. Here important issues underlie what a unit is. Indeed, there are a whole range of units, from the 'sentence' to 'an event'. Of critical importance is that the units are reliably identified prior to using the rating system. As with all coding systems, a range of requirements is necessary. Units need to be operationally defined, independent coders trained with reported reliability statistics, multiple coders used (usually three) in which the tasks are completed independently and consideration is given to the need to randomize the order if necessary. A very useful and accessible account of the many problems encountered in carrying out process research is given in Hill (1991) and Lambert and Hill (1994) – the latter covers both process and outcome.

Two particular problems have been identified regarding the validity of process research: the violation of assumptions of statistical tests, and 'fishing and error rate' problems. The first problem relates to the issue of the independence (or non-independence) of data. For example, if VRM codings are obtained from a client, these codings are not independent of each other. This problem also pertains to research more generally. For example, if four counsellors each see ten clients, the pairing of those ten clients with the same counsellor does not make the dyads independent of each other. Hence the degrees of freedom may more appropriately be taken from the number of counsellors rather than from the number of clients. The second problem relates to error rate and is especially salient in process research. For example, Wampold and Poulin (1992) highlight this problem, citing a study by Hill and colleagues (Hill et al., 1988) which contained more than 300 statistical tests. We might expect fifteen of these (five in every 100) to occur by chance alone, hence leading to a number of findings which could be described as 'false positives'. Corrections need to be made when so many statistical tests are carried out. A further issue in process research involves attributing causality. Process research invariably lacks the degree of experimental manipulation seen in outcome studies, and researchers need to be careful with respect to cause-and-effect relationships.

Substantive findings

The review of process and outcome in psychotherapy by Orlinsky et al. (1994) summarized a wealth of material relating to possible effective pathways. They identified stability of treatment arrangements and counsellor adherence to a treatment model as showing promise. They identified 'patient suitability' and 'therapist skills' as particularly robust, with over two-thirds of studies in each of these areas reporting significant findings. In terms of therapeutic operations the authors summarized three areas: problem presentation; expert understanding; and therapist intervention. With regard to problem presentation, the cognitive and behavioural processes within the client's problem presentation are related to outcome. Findings on 'expert understanding' target client problems and client affective responses during sessions. In terms of therapist interventions, there appears to be substantial evidence supporting experiential confrontation as well as interpretations. In addition, paradoxical intention appears to show a consistent relationship with outcome. In terms of the therapeutic bond, this showed strong associations with outcome, especially when assessed from the client's perspective.

The use of VRMs in various research studies has shown that therapists use responses which are consistent with their theoretical orientation (Elliott et al., 1987). Relating VRMs to immediate outcomes (that is to say, in-session), a range of studies identified 'interpretation' (or responses closely allied to it) as being 'effective'. For example, O'Farrell et al. (1986) found interpretation to be related to a decrease in client problem description and an increase in experiencing and insight, while Barkham and Shapiro (1986) found 'exploration' (a response between interpretation and reflection) to be associated with client and helper experiences of perceived empathy. However, the role of therapist 'intentions' is just as important. Horvath et al. (1990) found clients' ability to identify the intention of the counsellor depended, in addition to other factors, upon the stage of therapy, with understanding increasing from initial to mid-therapy and then decreasing. Factors accounting for this may involve the intentions becoming more complex or tacit as therapy develops. The complex relationship between these factors (for example, response modes and intentions) is summarized by Sexton and Whiston (1994):

> Based on a variety of complex factors (experience, training, client behavior), counselors develop intentions or goals that guide their choices of intentions or response modes. After each counselor response, the client reacts (decodes, interprets and experiences) and responds. In response, the counselor develops an adjusted intention and subsequent response mode. Over time these patterns become stabilized in client and counselor expectations. (1994: 21)

However, it has been found that response modes account for very little of the outcome variance, even for immediate outcome. Hill reports that 'therapist intentions and client experiencing in the turn preceding the therapist intervention each contributed more to the variance than did response modes' (1990: 289). She cites her intensive analyses of eight single cases (Hill, 1989) in which she found that 'client personality, therapist orientation and personality, and adequate therapeutic relationship, and events external to therapy all influenced whether or not clients incorporated changes begun in therapy' (1990: 289).

Research into the effectiveness of interpretations has been summarized by Orlinsky et al. (1994). These authors cited a total of thirty eight findings from sixteen studies, of which twenty four findings were positively related to overall outcome, eleven showed no association, and three showed negative associations. Hence, while two–thirds of the findings showed a positive association between interpretation and outcome, inspection of their data (Orlinsky et al., 1994: 303), in which eleven studies yielded sufficient information for the reviewers to determine effect sizes, showed the average size of the effect to be small (ES = 0.21). Garfield (1990), albeit basing his views on a previous review (Orlinsky and Howard, 1986), when only half the reported findings supported the link with a positive outcome, was also somewhat sceptical. Research into the accuracy of therapist interpretations has been carried out by Crits-Christoph et al. (1988), who found that accuracy of interpretation was the best predictor of outcome. Rather surprisingly, it was not related to improvements in the therapeutic alliance. However, Garfield (1990) has offered some criticisms of this particular research: for example, the mean ratings of 'accuracy' ranged from 1.49 to 1.81 on a four-point scale, with anchor points of one ('no congruence') and four ('high congruence').

The 'events' paradigm has yielded findings which bridge the use of the quantitative and qualitative approaches. In terms of the most and least helpful events in therapy, clients have reported the most helpful impacts to be problem solution, awareness and reassurance (Llewelyn et al., 1988). The least helpful was reported to be 'unwanted thoughts'. This latter finding, while not surprising, raises the point that clients and therapists have differential perspectives, with the clients experiencing 'unwanted thoughts' as negative while therapists may well see them as a necessary stage for the client to progress through towards improved psychological health.

Comment

This area of research has combined much of the more 'technical' and quantitative research efforts. However, difficulties undoubtedly occur when evaluating specific techniques, and many researchers in this domain have contrasting views. For example, Garfield has stated that there is 'no truly strong support for the accuracy of interpretation as a process variable of importance ... the interpretation or explanation that is *accepted* by the patient is the one that may have some positive therapeutic impact' (1990: 276). Others, for example Silberschatz and Curtis (1986), argue that the interpretations that are important are those which are consistent with the client's unconscious plan for therapy rather than those relating, for example, to the transference. However, the story is incomplete, as much of this work so readily lends itself to further research using more qualitative methods. For example, investigations into the mechanism of insight in psychological therapies have been progressed by intensive qualitative study of insight events in both psychodynamic interpersonal and cognitive behavioural therapy (e.g. Elliott et al., 1994). It is an area where there is considerable merit in harnessing both quantitative and qualitative methods.

The debate concerning the respective roles and contributions of specific and common factors is still as much an issue as ever and has been referred to as 'the great psychotherapy debate' (see Wampold, 2001). Ahn and Wampold (2001) carried out a meta-analytic study to determine the extent to which proven psychological therapies (i.e. those that had shown themselves to be efficacious) produce client change via specific mechanisms as opposed to common factors. Importantly, the studies used were 'component' studies which involved comparisons between the treatment package and the treatment package without a theoretically important component. A total of twenty seven studies met the criterion for inclusion in the study and the results showed that the effect size for the difference between the two conditions (with component versus without the component) was not significantly different from zero. Further, the authors suggested that, because there was very little variance in the effect sizes, it was unlikely that important variables were moderating the effect sizes.

Establishing the role of the therapeutic alliance

Context

Process research has often been viewed as a dichotomy comprising common factors and specific techniques. As indicated above, research interest has moved from the facilitative conditions to investigating the therapeutic alliance. While the facilitative conditions have been viewed as a possible mechanism of change, the therapeutic alliance is best viewed as a mechanism which enables the client to remain in and comply with treatment (Bordin, 1979; Sexton and Whiston, 1994).

Methodological issues

This area of research has led to the development of a range of measures which tap the client–counsellor relationship. Primary candidates include the Working Alliance Inventory (WAI; Horvath and Greenberg, 1989) and the CALPAS (CALifornia Psychotherapy Alliance Scales, e.g. Gaston, 1991). However, different definitions have resulted in different measures of the alliance such that it is unclear whether any two measures are tapping the same phenomenon. There are also some quite important conceptual problems. One example is the potential confusion between items relating to the status of the client–therapist relationship with items asking about the client's progress in therapy. If an alliance measure asks a client about the latter, then this is tapping early outcome, and it would not be surprising to find positive associations between alliance and outcome. Another example concerns the extent to which items tap aspects of the client alone rather than the relationship between client and therapist. As client measures tend to be more highly correlated with outcome than therapist measures, it would not be surprising should a measure which taps more into the client's world rather than into the client–therapist relationship be highly correlated with outcome. Indeed, there are those who argue that the definition of the alliance should be limited to client contributions (e.g. Frieswyk et al., 1986) on the basis that this facilitates research. Others (e.g. Henry and Strupp, 1994) argue for an interpersonal approach. The point here is to ensure that any measure of the client–therapist relationship is tapping what it purports to measure. A thorough conceptual review of the client–counsellor relationship has been carried out by Gelso and Carter (1994), with replies by prominent researchers.

Substantive findings

Sexton and Whiston (1994) reviewed the research literature on the client–therapist relationship since 1985, using three domains: the 'real' relationship, the transference and the working alliance. Findings summarized here focus on the last of these: the working alliance. A meta-analytic review of twenty four studies (Horvath and Symonds, 1991) found that the working alliance was positively related to outcome and that client and observer ratings were better predictors of outcome than therapist ratings. However, the overall effect size only approached medium size and it appears that findings from individual studies are affected by such factors as when the alliance was assessed and the particular outcome index used. Overall, though, from the available evidence, it appears the therapeutic alliance may account for upwards of 45 per cent of outcome variance (Horvath and Greenberg, 1989).

The perspective taken by the rater influences the results, and it is invariably the client's ratings of the alliance that are most predictive of outcome. Further, if client change is the criterion for measuring outcome, then client ratings of process are the best judges. There is also evidence that clients have predispositions as to the quality of the alliance they might develop. Horvath and Greenberg (1994) cite work suggesting that clients who have difficulty in maintaining their social relationships or have experienced relatively poor family relationships prior to therapy are less likely to develop strong alliances. However, severity of presenting symptoms did not appear to impact on the quality of the alliance.

In terms of the temporal nature of the therapeutic alliance, research findings are equivocal, with some researchers (e.g. Eaton et al., 1988) finding that it is constant while others (e.g. Klee et al., 1990) have suggested the opposite. This is an area requiring further research, as it relates to the development and maintenance of the client–therapist relationship.

Comment

While there has been considerable effort in terms of measure development for the therapeutic alliance, there has been 'greater emphasis on interrater reliability and predictive validity and less emphasis on issues of dimensionality and convergent and discriminate validity' (Marmar, 1990). Thus it is not clear that equivalent emphasis has been placed on furthering our understanding of what are the actual components of this 'umbrella' concept.

Generation IV, mid-1980s onwards: the individual and meaningful change

Several events during the mid-1980s helped to define a fourth research generation. The first was the publication of Hill et al.'s (1983) single-case study in *Journal of Counseling Psychology*. The second was the use of new methodologies utilizing, for example, the 'events paradigm' (e.g. Barkham and Shapiro, 1986) and 'task analysis' (e.g. Rice and Greenberg, 1984). And the third was the publication of the procedures for determining the clinical significance of outcomes (Jacobson et al., 1984, 1986). As such, the research carried out in this fourth generation is characterized by a central focus on the individual (variously defined here in terms of both the client – user – and the counsellor) and on prioritizing the external validity derived from studying counselling in routine settings.

Determining the relevance of findings from efficacy studies to routine practice settings

Context

In previous research generations, large-scale research studies addressed questions about the 'efficacy' of a particular intervention as delivered under optimal conditions. The results of such studies formed the basis of 'evidence-based practice' (EBP), which is now required to substantiate the delivery of any psychological (or medical) intervention in service settings. As such, the EBP movement – which applies to all health-related professions – is now a central tenet of all health care delivery (see Parry, 2000). It is the basis upon which government health agencies make recommendations for treatment and is premised on the view that the gold standards of research methodology lie in randomized controlled trials (RCTs) and meta-analytic studies. The findings from these studies are then used to inform practice in routine settings. However, it is a questionable logic that findings derived from research studies carried out under optimal conditions should be adopted as policy and then directly transported 'down' into routine service settings. In contrast to the evidence-based paradigm, there has been an increased focus on how these findings relate to routine practice. This focus has culminated in the development of a complementary paradigm for accumulating and presenting evidence: 'practice-based evidence'. In this model, evidence is accumulated in routine practice settings in which practice can be defined as routine clinical treatment (RCT) and effectively built 'up' to derive an evidence base in which practitioners are partners (see Barkham and Mellor-Clark, 2000; Margison et al., 2000). Importantly, these two paradigms can inform each other, provided they are equally valued. This can also be seen to apply to process research, which is grounded in the day-to-day and moment-to-moment work of practitioners. Because each paradigm can be viewed as representing the constituencies of researcher and practitioner respectively, it is the combined yield of the two paradigms which will most likely yield an effective bridge between practice and research in the future.

Methodological issues

The development of practice-based evidence for counselling psychology rests upon the widening acceptance by practitioners of the potential utility of collecting routine process and outcome data to inform clinical practice and services. The move towards adopting outcome measures in routine practice settings has grown from developmental work on a range of different but related instruments. These include the Health of the Nation Outcome Scales (HoNOS; Wing et al., 1998); the Functional Analysis of Care Environments (FACE; Clifford, 1999), and the Clinical Outcomes in Routine Evaluation – Outcome Measure (CORE–OM; Evans et al., 2000, 2002). Between them, these measures cover the range of people presenting, from primary care settings to those deemed to be experiencing severe and enduring mental illness. The availability of these measures provides a real incentive for services to generate data that will inform their service and will, in turn, increasingly generate large data sets from which to investigate variables associated with outcomes. However, the question as to whether routine outcome measurement is feasible in the broad domain of mental health (including psychotherapy) remains to be addressed. Three criteria have been identified that outcome measures would have to meet. The measures would have to be (1) standardized, (2) acceptable to clinicians and (3) feasible for routine use (Thornicroft and Slade, 2000). Hence the agenda is very much slanted towards determining the effectiveness of psychological therapies. In addition, there needs to be a focus on investigating the process of change. In this respect, there are numerous well constructed and validated measures that tap a wide range of domains. (See chapter 17 in Heppner et al., 1999, for an excellent account of the issues in process design and examples of measures and procedures.)

Substantive findings

Shadish et al. (1997, 2000) addressed the key question of whether the findings from psychotherapy outcome studies were different as a function of their clinical representativeness. That is, are there outcome differences from studies spanning the continuum from efficacy to effectiveness? If no substantive differences are found, then this might help to allay concern that efficacy results are not transportable to routine clinical practice. And, indeed, the findings reported by Shadish (1997, 2000) provide support for this argument. Effect sizes from fifty six studies were categorized into three stages that increasingly represented routine clinical practice. There were no substantive differences in effect size as a function of clinical representativeness. This finding was replicated in a refinement of the earlier study (Shadish, 2000). Hence, this programme of work suggests that the concern about applying efficacy results to routine practice may be more apparent than real.

Comment

However, even if actual outcome results are similar, it still leaves the outcomes of routine settings as being determined by the results from efficacy studies. It is simply impossible for the efficacy paradigm to address the many questions that need to be asked and to deliver answers quickly enough in order to meet the needs of services and patients. Other outcome paradigms are needed, regardless of the transportability of efficacy results. Indeed, there have been calls for some radical reappraisals in how outcome research is carried out. In response, there has been proposed an integration initiative by the NIMH in an attempt to bridge the gap between efficacy and effectiveness research (Norquist et al., 1999). In effect, a new paradigm is proposed that would be inclusive of both experimental and observational data but which would require development of existing methods and new statistical techniques.

User perspectives

Context

In line with a whole range of social movements in the 1980s that began to focus on people as active users and consumers of services as opposed to passive recipients, there were increasing moves towards eliciting the views of clients as users or consumers of counselling and the psychological therapies. This opened the way for a new approach in research which aimed at sampling the views and opinions of everyday users of mental health services.

Substantive findings

Generation IV outcome research has developed both 'from' and 'in reaction to' the previous research generations. In the broadest sense, what is 'new' in Generation IV is the central focus on the user perspective and on prioritizing the external validity derived from studying routine settings. In terms of the former, a landmark but controversial study of psychotherapy even at the time of its publication was the Consumer Report Survey (*Consumer Reports*, 1995). *Consumer Reports* – the US equivalent of *Which?* magazine in the UK – carried out a survey of its readers who had experienced stress or other emotional problems at any time during the previous three years for which they had sought help from a range of support systems. Seligman (1995) reported the following key findings: (1) treatment by a health professional usually worked; (2) long-term therapy produced more improvement than short-term therapy; (3) there were no differences between psychotherapy alone and psychotherapy plus medication for any disorder; and (4) no specific modality of psychotherapy did any better than any other for any problem. His conclusions were that the findings confirmed the overall effectiveness of psychotherapy.

However, there was widespread criticism of the *Consumer Reports* focus on the small sample who actually responded to the mental health questions (around 4 per cent of the original sample), lack of a control group, paucity of information on a range of client, therapist and treatment variables, and lack of a reliable metric for summarizing therapeutic change (see *The American Psychologist*, October 1996, for detailed comments). Seligman viewed most of the criticisms as focusing on what the *Consumer Reports* might have done rather than on what it actually did within the financial and time constraints, and stated that 'this was first-rate journalism and credible science as well' (1995: 1086). However, some commentators have noted that the criticisms of the design noted above suggest that the *CR* survey is akin to a consumer satisfaction survey and should not be held up as an exemplar of effectiveness research (Nathan et al., 2000).

Comment

The *Consumer Reports* survey generated considerable debate which, in itself, is a positive outcome. Its real value probably lay in its challenge to the view that the RCT was the only method of obtaining robust evidence concerning the psychological therapies. However, its focus on 'satisfaction' places it apart from outcome research: satisfaction with services is a valuable component of any client's experience but it should not be equated with 'outcomes'. Clients may report high levels of satisfaction with a service but experience little or no change in the personal issues with which they initially presented.

Establishing whether improvements realized by clients are meaningful

Context

A recent trend has been to determine the clinical significance of a particular effect. This trend has arisen within the field of clinical psychology (Jacobson and Truax, 1991) but it should also be applicable to the field of counselling psychology. However, there are important caveats and these will be addressed before providing an example of clinical significance. Chapter 4 addresses this issue in greater detail.

Methodological

In relation to this issue, a principal driver for Generation IV has been the focus on establishing whether outcomes are meaningful. Jacobson et al. (1984, 1986, 1991) devised a heuristic to address two key questions. (1) Is the extent of client change reliable, given the change measure used? (2) What is the end state of the client in relation to any given population? Jacobson and Truax (1991) have summarized this work on determining reliable and clinically significant change and have provided three methods for calculating the index. The principle they use is movement by the client from one population (i.e. dysfunctional) to another (e.g. the general population, or non-distressed population). Of course, it is possible to determine membership of the 'normal' population only when normative data are available. In the absence of such data, movement to two standard deviations below the intake mean would signify 'clinical' change (i.e. belonging to a different population, although not necessarily a non-distressed population). This approach enables clinicians to identify individual clients who have met a specified criterion of improvement (e.g. Kendall et al., 1999; Kendall and Sheldrick, 2000). A review of the history, definitions and applications of clinical significance is provided by Ogles et al. (2001).

There are a number of caveats regarding clinical significance. First, there will be many who will argue against counselling psychology adopting a procedure termed 'clinical' significance. Although pedantic, there is a legitimate point: the same argument could be made by occupational psychologists. Hence there may well be a place for the term 'psychological significance', as that is what we are interested in (as opposed to statistical significance). Secondly, there needs to be a better means of appreciating the differing sizes of 'psychological' significance (in the same way as there are differing ranges of effect size). Importantly, counselling psychology addresses a range of issues, from those in which one would expect to obtain large effects to those where the effects may well be extremely small. The latter might apply in those cases where interventions are made within what is a normal population with the aim of improving psychological well-being. In cases of 'life enhancement' the effect will be small unless the measures used to tap the process are extremely sensitive to the phenomenon being measured.

Substantive findings

Given that this is a procedural matter, findings relating to these procedures are more of technical interest: it is their application which is interesting. Several studies have used such procedures or variants of them. For example, Barkham and Shapiro (1990) used them in a pilot study ($n = 12$) of brief counselling for job-related distress and found that, depending on the outcome measure used, between five and eight clients met the criteria for reliable and clinically significant change after only two sessions. Being able to state how many clients have reached a defined level of improvement makes results more tangible.

Similarly, various studies using components of the CORE system have indicated that, for example, approximately 80 per cent of clients referred to secondary care services scored above a predetermined clinical cut-off point prior to therapy, a figure which halved to approximately 40 per cent at discharge (Barkham et al., 2001). Another study carried out in primary care settings reported 58 per cent of clients showed both reliable and clinically significant change, with a further 17 per cent achieving reliable change (Mellor-Clark et al., 2001). Further research is required into determining the range of possible factors that influence outcomes in routine settings.

Comment

Within the counselling discipline, it has been suggested that researchers have been reluctant to adopt procedures for investigating clinical versus statistical significance (Heppner et al., 1999). However, the trend towards being able to say that a person now belongs to a normal population is a powerful one in terms of showing the effects of an intervention. While some counselling psychologists may find the notion of 'membership' of a population at odds with the discipline, it is important to appreciate that one strength of this approach is that it places the emphasis on the individual in the context of the group or population at large. This is in contrast to inferential statistics, in which the primary question being asked relates to the mean (average) of a group. However, parallel to the argument that methodological pluralism should be the aspiration, it would seem logical to embrace the same degree of pluralism in terms of analysing data. That is, researchers should consider the various ways of analysing and presenting data to ensure that the results are not biased towards one particular model or procedure of analysis.

The relation between measuring outcomes and therapeutic progress

Context

Generation IV research has built on these methodological developments, which have provided the means for better outcomes monitoring in practice settings.

Methodological issues

One component of this has been the recognition of an agreed core outcome battery – that is, an attempt to standardize the selection of outcome measures in order to facilitate increased comparisons across treatments, settings and services (Strupp et al., 1997). Lest it be thought that this was a new development, the idea of a 'core outcome battery' was first developed at a landmark conference in the 1970s (see Waskow and Parloff, 1975). But, whatever measure is selected, there is a considerable problem in collecting Time 2 data – that is, data at termination or discharge.

Substantive findings

Many clients terminate therapy unilaterally and it is difficult to obtain post-therapy data. Accordingly, monitoring outcomes is most likely to inform practice through the application of session-by-session tracking of individual patients in the context of empirically derived parameters that determine the range of response to particular interventions for particular diagnoses (e.g. Lutz et al., 1999). This 'patient-focused' outcome paradigm can provide individual dose-response curves to help inform individual case management and support clinical decision making in service of enhanced quality (e.g. Lambert, Hansen et al., 2001; Lueger et al., 2001). Systems have also been developed and validated for the early identification of 'signal' cases (e.g. Kordy et al., 2001). Evidence that outcome monitoring enhances clients' outcomes has been shown in a study evaluating the effects of providing practitioners with feedback on their clients' progress (Lambert, Whipple et al., 2001). Clients who were deemed not to be 'on track' in terms of expected outcome trajectories and whose therapists were provided with outcome feedback yielded a treatment ES advantage of 0.44 over an equivalent 'not on track' group whose therapists were not provided with outcome feedback. Although these results should be treated with caution – the authors note that the CIs for the size of treatment effect ranged from 'just above zero to more than .80' – there is a clear indication of the potential for a direct impact on clinical practice.

Comment

Findings from this area of research are embryonic. However, it raises many potential issues for practitioners. Data used to monitor a client's progress can equally be used to monitor the practitioner's performance. The desire to manage the performance of practitioners (as with any other professional) is understandable but fraught with problems. Considerable care needs to be taken in ensuring that the concerns of the client, the practitioner and the manager are each respected and that any monitoring system ensures a balance between these multiple stakeholders.

Focusing on the individual client

Context

At the beginning of this chapter reference was made to the relative paucity of single-case studies in counselling psychology, a discipline which purports to 'revere the individual'. Two publications (or series of publications) drew attention to the single case within counselling and psychotherapy: Hill et al. (1983) and Strupp's series of four individual case studies (1980a, b, c, d). More recently there has been a special section of the *Journal of Consulting and Clinical Psychology* (see Jones, 1993) devoted to single-case research in psychotherapy. While single-case methodology has applications across many disciplines (especially in more behaviourally oriented approaches), it might be expected that counselling psychology could frame a particularly human approach using this modality.

Methodological issues

Hill et al. (1983) presented four arguments justifying the use of single-case methodology. First, it describes more adequately what happens between counsellor and client; secondly, positive and negative outcomes can be understood in terms of process data; thirdly, both the client–counsellor relationship and the change process can be highlighted; fourthly, the outcome measures used can be specifically chosen, given the client's presenting problems. Kirschner et al. used a single-case approach in career counselling, stating, 'Case studies enable researchers to investigate the counselor–client interaction by allowing for the specification of techniques and the isolation of specific change mechanisms that might be unique to a specific dyad' (1994: 216). Many of the salient issues in using a single-case methodology both in process and in outcome work have been summarized by Hilliard (1993). Largely, the problems arise in non-behavioural interventions where the manipulations cannot be readily reversed (for example, a client cannot 'unlearn' an insight) and particular domains of functioning (cognitions and emotions, for example) are intrinsically interdependent. These give rise to problems of internal validity which are not easily addressed. Beyond these problems, there is the enduring issue of selection. Should the individual selected be an 'exemplar' of a particular process (such as a highly successful case), or should they be 'representative'? It probably happens that each is appropriate in differing situations. There is considerable merit in selecting, for example, a highly successful case if one has reason to suppose that putative processes will be more evident in good outcome cases (that is to say, good outcome cases are the place to be looking). However, if the presence of a process is hypothesized to be associated with a good outcome, it might then be appropriate to test for its absence in a poor outcome case. If it is also present in the poor outcome case to the same degree, then such a finding would argue against its having a specific role in facilitating good outcome. Selecting 'representative' cases might then be followed as a strategy to enhance generalizability of results.

Substantive findings

Given that this is a methodological approach, 'findings' has a rather different connotation. Since the publication of Hill et al. (1983) several further single cases have been published in the *Journal of Counseling Psychology*. For example, Kirschner et al. (1994) employed the single-case approach in career counselling. Findings indicated that the client found insight and challenge most helpful, suggesting that learning something new and having her perceptual world 'shaken up' was beneficial. Field et al. (1994) combined both quantitative and qualitative methodologies in an investigation of one particular model of the change process in a good outcome case (Stiles et al., 1990). Findings supported the theory that, in order to resolve a particular problematic experience, a client progresses through specific stages: in this particular case from vague awareness, through problem clarification, towards insight and application/working through.

Comment

High-quality research based on a single-case methodology is still the exception rather than the rule, supporting Galassi and Gersh's (1993) judgement that counselling psychology 'virtually eschews single-case designs'. There are obviously problems with the individual case study in terms of the extent to which internal validity can be assured. However, it is a challenge for counselling psychology research to devise and inform the scientific community regarding methods which are inherently rigorous but which allow greater consideration for the individual.

Conclusion and future generations

This chapter has provided an overview of key themes in the area of counselling psychology and cognate disciplines by placing them within a model of research 'generations'. While these generations can be placed in broad chronological and linear order, it is also apparent that for some areas of clinical practice there is a cyclical order, with some areas only now moving towards Generation I-type research. Hence these generations are conceptual and thematic and do not appear to have a definitive sell-by date. The cyclical phenomenon in which early issues are revisited by a new research generation or in which some political or social movement gives renewed salience to a paradigm from a prior research generation may suggest that there is a limit to the actual number of research generations. The accumulated evidence drawn from Generations I, II and III has provided a robust base for the broad activity of psychological therapies – and the evidence base is still growing. The hallmark of Generation IV research has been to move towards clinically meaningful research (process) and effectiveness in the field (outcome). In many ways this hallmark reflects both the reworkings of process work prior to Generation I (see prologue) and the outcome work comprising Generation I. Hence it may be useful in the future to reflect on developments and trends in the psychological therapies as reworkings of earlier research generations rather than construing them as genuinely 'new' generations.

Much of the material presented in this chapter derives from a traditional model of research, sometimes referred to as the 'medical' model, in which the focus is on identifying specific ingredients of therapies in pursuit of maximizing their effectiveness. This paradigm has been instrumental in building an evidence base from which national guidelines have been developed to help in the choice of psychological interventions for people presenting to psychological and counselling services (Department of Health, 2001; Rowland and Goss, 2000). However, even within this paradigm there is recognition of the contribution made to successful outcomes by 'common' factors. This has been the basis of the development of a 'contextual' model for understanding how clients change (see Wampold, 2001). Key components of this latter model comprise enabling clients to use their existing resources and providing them with a positive experience of the client-counsellor relationship (see Hubble et al., 1999). The increasing assimilation into the research community of the common factors model reflects both the weight of accumulated evidence and also recognition that the pursuit of 'technique' alone will not provide a rich and comprehensive basis for informing counselling practice. Similarly, such an approach places an emphasis on the role of the therapist as a person. From the perspective of continuing professional development, opening the counsellor to study would appear to be appropriate. Studies are still designed and powered primarily according to client numbers rather than based on practitioners. Methodologically, ignoring therapist effects will inflate any estimate of treatment effects. Therefore it is critical that the investigation of therapist effects becomes a central focus of research in the psychological therapies. Wampold (2001) has argued cogently for the 'therapy' to be replaced by the 'therapist' as the focus of future research. From a phenomenological perspective, counselling psychology – with its reflexive approach – should be one discipline to espouse this approach.

Overall, what might be considered to be the areas that will feature in future research generations? Hill and Corbett suggest an overall goal for process and outcome research in counselling psychology for the future: 'to develop new theories of therapy, to provide information for practitioners about how to intervene with clients at different points in therapy, and to develop training programs based on the empirical results of what works in therapy' (1993: 16). In addition, they identify a number of areas for development. First, to test the 'entire model ... of pretherapy characteristics ... process variables ... immediate outcome ... extratherapy variables ... and long-term outcome' (p. 16). Secondly, to address issues relating to 'timing, quality, and competence'. Thirdly, Hill and Corbett suggest that research should determine the effective components of therapy and then the treatment approach can be built (rather than vice versa, as is currently the case). Fourthly, the content of therapy work needs to be rekindled. These are huge and challenging tasks.

As a final comment, it is worth noting how much the present chapter, like those chapters in other texts on 'counselling' and 'counselling psychology', draws on the mainstream 'psychotherapy' literature. No single discipline (or professional division) has a monopoly of any one research tradition or scientific method – hence the commonality. However, it is also clear that commonality needs to be complemented with counselling psychology research building and extending specific research activities in the area of everyday/normal functioning and to utilize research approaches which harness its emphasis on the individual.

References

Ahn, H. and Wampold, B.E. (2001) 'Where oh where are the specific ingredients? A meta-analysis of components studies in counseling and psychotherapy', *Journal of Counseling Psychology*, 48: 251–7.

Andrews, G., Guitar, B. and Howie, P. (1980) 'Meta-analysis of the effects of stuttering treatment', *Journal of Speech and Hearing Disorders*, 45: 287–307.

Aveline, M. and Shapiro, D.A. (eds) (1995) *Research Foundations for Psychotherapy Practice*. Chichester: Wiley.

Barker, C., Pistrang, N. and Elliott, R. (1994) *Research Methods in Clinical and Counselling Psychology*. Chichester: Wiley.

Barker, C., Pistrang, N. and Elliott, R. (in press) *Research Methods in Clinical Psychology*, second edition. Chichester: Wiley.

Barkham, M. and Mellor-Clark, J. (2000) 'Rigour and relevance: practice-based evidence in the psychological therapies' in N. Rowland and S. Goss (eds) *Evidence-based Counselling and Psychological Therapies*. London: Routledge.

Barkham, M. and Shapiro, D.A. (1986) 'Counselor verbal response modes and experienced empathy', *Journal of Counseling Psychology*, 33: 3–10.

Barkham, M. and Shapiro, D.A. (1990) 'Brief prescriptive and exploratory therapy for job-related distress: a pilot study', *Counselling Psychology Quarterly*, 3: 133–47.

Barkham, M., Margison, F., Leach, C., Lucock, M., Mellor-Clark, J., Evans, C., Benson, L., Connell, J., Audin, K. and McGrath, G. (2001) 'Service profiling and outcomes benchmarking using the CORE-OM: towards practice-based evidence in the psychological therapies', *Journal of Consulting and Clinical Psychology*, 69: 184–96.

Barkham, M., Shapiro, D.A., Hardy, G.E. and Rees, A. (1999) 'Psychotherapy in two-plus-one sessions: outcomes of a randomized controlled trial of cognitive-behavioral and psychodynamic-interpersonal therapy for subsyndromal depression', *Journal of Consulting and Clinical Psychology*, 67: 201–11.

Barrett-Lennard, G.T. (1962) 'Dimensions of therapist response as causal factors in therapeutic change', *Psychological Monographs*, 76 (43, Whole No. 562).

Beck, A.T., Ward, C.H., Mendelson, M., Mock, J. and Erbaugh, J. (1961) 'Inventory for measuring depression', *Archives of General Psychiatry*, 4: 561–71.

Bedi, N., Chilvers, C., Churchill, R., Dewey, M., Duggan, C., Fielding, K., Gretton, V., Miller, P., Harrison, G., Lee, A. and Williams, I. (2000) 'Assessing effectiveness of treatment of depression in primary care: partially randomised preference trial', *British Journal of Psychiatry*, 177: 312–18.

Bergin, A.E. (1971) 'The evaluation of therapeutic outcomes', in A.E. Bergin and S.L. Garfield (eds) *Handbook of Psychotherapy and Behavior Change*. New York: Wiley.

Bergin, A.E. and Garfield, S.L. (eds) (1994a) *Handbook of Psychotherapy and Behavior Change*, fourth edition. New York: Wiley.

Bergin, A.E. and Garfield, S.L. (1994b) 'Overview, trends, and future issues' in A.E. Bergin and S.L. Garfield (eds) *Handbook of Psychotherapy and Behavior Change*, fourth edition. New York: Wiley.

Bergin, A.E. and Lambert, M.J. (1978) 'The evaluation of therapeutic outcome' in S.L. Garfield and A.E. Bergin (eds) *Handbook of Psychotherapy and Behavior Change*, second edition. New York: Wiley.

Bordin, E.S. (1979) 'The generalizability of the psychoanalytic concept of the working alliance', *Psychotherapy: Theory, Research and Practice*, 16: 252–60.

Bower, P., Byford, S., Sibbald, B., Ward, E., King, M., Lloyd, M. and Gabbay, M. (2000) 'Randomised controlled trial of non-directive counselling, cognitive-behavioural therapy, and usual general practitioner care for patients with depression, II. Cost effectiveness', *British Medical Journal*, 321: 1389–92.

Bower, P., Rowland, N., Mellor-Clark, J., Heywood, P., Godfrey, C. and Hardy, R. (2002) 'Effectiveness and cost effectiveness of counselling in primary care (Cochrane Review),' *The Cochrane Library*, Issue 2. Oxford: Update Software Ltd.

Brockman, B., Poynton, A., Ryle, A. and Watson, J.P. (1987) 'Effectiveness of time-limited therapy carried out by trainees: comparison of two methods', *British Journal of Psychiatry*, 151: 602–10.

Brown, S.D. and Lent, R.W. (eds) (2000) *Handbook of Counseling Psychology*, third edition. New York: Wiley.

Butler, E.R., Rice, L.N. and Wagstaff, A.K. (1962) 'On the definition of variables: an analogue of clinical analysis', in H.H. Strupp and L. Luborsky (eds), *Research in Psychotherapy*, II. Washington DC: American Psychological Association.

Carkhuff, R.R. and Berenson, B.G. (1967) *Beyond Counseling and Therapy*. New York: Holt Rinehart & Winston.

Clarkson, P. (1998) *Counselling Psychology: Integrating Theory, Research and Supervised Practice*. London: Routledge.

Clifford, P.I. (1999) 'The FACE recording and measurement system: a scientific approach to person-based information', *Bulletin of the Menninger Clinic*, 63: 305–31.

Cohen, J. (1977) *Statistical Power Analysis for the Behavioral Sciences*, second edition. Hillsdale NJ: Erlbaum.

Consumer Reports (1995) 'Mental health: does therapy help?', November, pp. 734–9.

Crits-Christoph, P., Cooper, A. and Luborsky, L. (1988) 'The accuracy of therapists' interpretations and the outcome of dynamic psychotherapy', *Journal of Consulting and Clinical Psychology*, 56: 490–5.

Department of Health (2001) *Treatment Choice in Psychological Therapies and Counselling: Evidence-based Clinical Practice Guideline*. London: Department of Health.

Eaton, T.T., Abeles, N. and Gutfreund, M.J. (1988) 'Therapeutic alliance and outcome: impact of treatment length and pretreatment symptomatology', *Psychotherapy*, 25: 536–42.

Elkin, I. (1994) 'The NIMH Treatment of Depression Collaborative Research Study' in A.E. Bergin and S.L. Garfield (eds) *Handbook of Psychotherapy and Behavior Change*, fourth edition. New York: Wiley.

Elkin, I., Shea, M.T., Watkins, J.T., Imber, S.D., Sotsky, S.M., Collins, J.F., Glass, D.R., Pilkonis, P.A., Leber, W.R., Docherty, J.P., Fiester, S.J. and Parloff, M.B. (1989) 'National Institute of Mental Health Treatment of Depression Collaborative Research Program: general effectiveness of treatment', *Archives of General Psychiatry*, 46: 971–82.

Elliott, R. (2001) 'Contemporary brief experiential psychotherapy', *Clinical Psychology: Science and Practice*, 8: 38–50.

Elliott, R., Hill, C.E., Stiles, W.B., Friedlander, M.L., Mahrer, A.R. and Margison, F.R. (1987) 'Primary therapist response modes: a comparison of six rating systems', *Journal of Consulting and Clinical Psychology*, 55: 218–23.

Elliott, R., Shapiro, D.A., Firth-Cozens, J., Stiles, W.B., Hardy, G.E., Llewelyn, S.P. and Margison, F. (1994) 'Insight in interpersonal-dynamic therapy: a comprehensive process analysis', *Journal of Counseling Psychology*, 41: 449–63.

Evans, C.E., Mellor-Clark, J., Margison, F., Barkham, M., Audin, K., Connell, J. and McGrath, G. (2000) 'Clinical outcomes in routine evaluation: the CORE Outcome Measure (CORE-OM)', *Journal of Mental Health*, 9: 247–55.

Evans, C., Connell, J., Barkham, M., Margison, F., Mellor-Clark, J., McGrath, G. and Audin, K. (2002) 'Towards a standardised brief outcome measure: psychometric properties and utility of the CORE-OM', *British Journal of Psychiatry*, 180: 51–60.

Eysenck, H.J. (1952) 'The effects of psychotherapy: an evaluation', *Journal of Consulting Psychology*, 16: 319–24.

Eysenck, H.J. (1961) 'The effects of psychotherapy' in H.J. Eysenck (ed.) *Handbook of Abnormal Psychology*. New York: Basic Books.

Eysenck, H.J. (1966) *The Effects of Psychotherapy*. New York: International Science Press.

Eysenck, H.J. (1992) 'The outcome problem in psychotherapy' in W. Dryden and C. Feltham (eds) *Psychotherapy and its Discontents*. Buckingham: Open University Press.

Field, S.D., Barkham, M., Shapiro, D.A. and Stiles, W.B. (1994) 'Assessment of assimilation in psychotherapy: a quantitative case study of problematic experiences with a significant other', *Journal of Counseling Psychology*, 41: 397–406.

Frieswyk, S.H., Allen, J.G., Colson, D.B., Coyne, L., Gabbard, G.O., Horowitz, L. and Newsom, G. (1986) 'Therapeutic alliance: its place as a process and outcome variable in dynamic psychotherapy research', *Journal of Consulting and Clinical Psychology*, 54: 32–8.

Galassi, J.P. and Gersh, T.L. (1993) 'Myths, misconceptions, and missed opportunity: single-case designs and counseling psychology', *Journal of Counseling Psychology*, 40: 525–31.

Garfield, S.L. (1990) 'Issues and methods in psychotherapy process research', *Journal of Consulting and Clinical Psychology*, 58: 273–80.

Garfield, S.L. and Bergin, A.E. (1994) 'Introduction and historical overview', in A.E. Bergin and S.L. Garfield (eds) *Handbook of Psychotherapy and Behavior Change*, fourth edition. New York: Wiley.

Gaston, L. (1991) 'Reliability and criterion-related validity of the California Psychotherapy Alliance Scales: patient version', *Psychological Assessment*, 3: 68–74.

Gath, D. and Mynors-Wallis, L. (1997) 'Problem-solving treatment in primary care' in D.M. Clark and C.G. Fairburn (eds) *Science and Practice of Cognitive Behaviour Therapy*. Oxford: Oxford University Press.

Gelso, C.J. and Carter, J.A. (1994) 'Components of the psychotherapy relationship: their interaction and unfolding during treatment', *Journal of Counseling Psychology*, 41: 296–306.

Gurman, A.S. (1973) 'Instability of therapeutic conditions in psychotherapy', *Journal of Counseling Psychology*, 20: 16–24.

Gurman, A.S. (1977) 'The patient's perception of the therapeutic relationship', in A.S. Gurman and A. Razin (eds) *Effective Psychotherapy: a Handbook of Research*. Oxford: Pergamon Press.

Henry, W.P. and Strupp, H.H. (1994) 'The therapeutic alliance as interpersonal process' in A.O. Horvath and L.S. Greenberg (eds) *The Working Alliance: Theory, Research, and Practice*. New York: Wiley.

Heppner, P.P., Kivlighan, D.M. and Wampold, B.E. (1999) *Research Design in Counseling* (second edition). Belmont CA: Brooks Cole Wadsworth.

Hill, C.E. (1989) *Therapist Techniques and Client Outcomes: Eight Cases of Brief Psychotherapy*. Newbury Park CA: Sage.

Hill, C.E. (1990) 'Exploratory in-session process research in individual psychotherapy: a review', *Journal of Consulting and Clinical Psychology*, 58: 288–94.

Hill, C.E. (1991) 'Almost everything you ever wanted to know about how to do process research on counseling and psychotherapy but didn't know who to ask' in C.E. Watkins Jr and L.J. Schneider (eds) *Research in Counseling*. Hillsdale NJ: Erlbaum.

Hill, C.E. (ed.) (2001) *Helping Skills: the Empirical Foundation*. Washington DC: American Psychological Association.

Hill, C.E. and Corbett, M. (1993) 'A perspective on the history of process and outcome research in counseling psychology', *Journal of Counseling Psychology*, 40: 3–24.

Hill, C.E. and Williams, E.N. (2000) 'The process of individual therapy' in S.D. Brown and R.W. Lent (eds) *Handbook of Counseling Psychology*, third edition. New York: Wiley.

Hill, C.E., Carter, J.A. and O'Farrell, M.K. (1983) 'A case study of the process and outcome of time-limited counseling', *Journal of Counseling Psychology*, 30: 3–18.

Hill, C.E., Helms, J.E., Tichenor, V., Spiegel, S.B., O'Grady, K.E. and Perry, E.S. (1988) 'Effects of therapist response modes in brief psychotherapy', *Journal of Counseling Psychology*, 35: 222–33.

Hilliard, R.B. (1993) 'Single-case methodology in psychotherapy process and outcome research', *Journal of Consulting and Clinical Psychology*, 61: 373–80.

Horvath, A.O. and Greenberg, L.S. (1989) 'Development and validation of the Working Alliance Inventory', *Journal of Counseling Psychology*, 36: 223–33.

Horvath, A.O. and Greenberg, L.S. (1994) (eds) *The Working Alliance: Theory, Research, and Practice*. New York: Wiley.

Horvath, A.O. and Symonds, D.B. (1991) 'Relation between working alliance and outcome in psychotherapy', *Journal of Counseling Psychology*, 38: 139–49.

Horvath, A.O., Marx, R.W. and Kamann, A.M. (1990) 'Thinking about thinking in therapy: an examination of clients' understanding of their therapists' intentions', *Journal of Consulting and Clinical Psychology*, 58: 614–21.

Howard, K.I., Kopta, S.M., Krause, M.S. and Orlinsky, D.E. (1986) 'The dose–effect relationship in psychotherapy', *American Psychologist*, 41: 159–64.

Hubble, M.A., Duncan, B.L. and Miller S.D. (1999) *The Heart and Soul of Change: What Works in Therapy*. Washington DC: American Psychological Association.

Jacobson, N.S. and Truax, P. (1991) 'Clinical significance: a statistical approach to defining meaningful change in psychotherapy research', *Journal of Consulting and Clinical Psychology*, 59: 12–19.

Jacobson, N.S., Follette, W.C. and Revenstorf, D. (1984) 'Psychotherapy outcome research: methods for reporting variability and evaluating clinical significance', *Behavior Therapy*, 15: 336–52.

Jacobson, N.S., Follette, W.C. and Revenstorf, D. (1986) 'Toward a standard definition of clinically significant change', *Behavior Therapy*, 17: 308–11.

Jones, E.E. (1993) 'Special section: single-case research in psychotherapy', *Journal of Consulting and Clinical Psychology*, 61: 371–430.

Karl, N.J. and Abeles, N. (1969) 'Psychotherapy process as a function of the time segment sampled', *Journal of Consulting and Clinical Psychology*, 33: 207–12.

Kazdin, A.E. (1994) 'Methodology, design, and evaluation in psychotherapy research' in A.E. Bergin and S.L. Garfield (eds) *Handbook of Psychotherapy and Behavior Change*, fourth edition. New York: Wiley.

Kendall, P.C. and Sheldrick, R.C. (2000) 'Normative data for normative comparisons', *Journal of Consulting and Clinical Psychology*, 68: 767–73.

Kendall, P.C., Marrs-Garcia, A., Nath, S.R. and Sheldrick, R.C. (1999) 'Normative comparisons for the evaluation of clinical significance', *Journal of Consulting and Clinical Psychology*, 67: 285–99.

Kiesler, D.J. (1966) 'Basic methodological issues implicit in psychotherapy research', *American Journal of Psychotherapy*, 20: 135–55.

Kirschner, T., Hoffman, M.A. and Hill, C.E. (1994) 'Case study of the process and outcome of career counseling', *Journal of Counseling Psychology*, 41: 216–26.

Klee, M.R., Abeles, N. and Muller, R.T. (1990) 'Therapeutic alliance: early indicators, course, and outcome', *Psychotherapy*, 27: 166–74.

Klein, M.H., Mathieu, P.L., Gendlin, E.T. and Kiesler, D.J. (1970) *The Experiencing Scale: a Research and Training Manual* I–II. Madison WI: Wisconsin Psychiatric Institute.

Kordy, H., Hannöver, W. and Richard, M. (2001) 'Computer-assisted feedback-driven quality management for psychotherapy: the Stuttgart–Heidelberg model', *Journal of Consulting and Clinical Psychology*, 69: 173–83.

Koss, M.P. and Shiang, J. (1994) 'Research on brief psychotherapy', in A.E. Bergin and S.L. Garfield (eds) *Handbook of Psychotherapy and Behavior Change*, fourth edition. New York: Wiley.

Krumboltz, J.D. (1966) *Revolution in Counseling: Implications of Behavioral Science*. Boston MA: Houghton Mifflin.

Lambert, M.J. (ed.) (in press) *Bergin and Garfield's Handbook of Psychotherapy and Behavior Change*, fifth edition. New York: Wiley.

Lambert, M.J. and Bergin, A.E. (1994) 'The effectiveness of psychotherapy' in A.E. Bergin and S.L. Garfield (eds) *Handbook of Psychotherapy and Behavior Change*, fourth edition. New York: Wiley.

Lambert, M.J. and Hill, C.E. (1994) 'Assessing psychotherapy outcomes and processes' in A.E. Bergin and S.L. Garfield (eds) *Handbook of Psychotherapy and Behavior Change*, fourth edition. New York: Wiley.

Lambert, M.J. and Hill, C.E. (in press) 'Assessing psychotherapy outcomes and processes', in M.J. Lambert (ed.) *Bergin and Garfield's Handbook of Psychotherapy and Behavior Change*, fifth edition. New York: Wiley.

Lambert, M.J. and Ogles, B.M. (in press) 'The efficacy and effectiveness of psychotherapy' in M.J. Lambert (ed.) *Bergin and Garfield's Handbook of Psychotherapy and Behavior Change*, fifth edition. New York: Wiley.

Lambert, M.J., Hansen, N.B. and Finch, A.E. (2001) 'Patient-focused research: using patient outcome data to enhance treatment effects', *Journal of Consulting and Clinical Psychology*, 69: 159–72.

Lambert, M.J., Whipple, J.L., Smart, D.W., Vermeersch, D.A., Nielsen, S.L. and Hawkins, E.J. (2001) 'The effects of providing therapists with feedback on patient progress during psychotherapy: are outcomes enhanced?' *Psychotherapy Research*, 11: 49–68.

Llewelyn, S.P., Elliott, R., Shapiro, D.A., Hardy, G.E. and Firth-Cozens, J. (1988) 'Client perceptions of significant events in prescriptive and exploratory periods of individual therapy', *British Journal of Clinical Psychology*, 27: 105–14.

Luborsky, L., Singer, B. and Luborsky, L. (1975) 'Comparative studies of psychotherapies: is it true that "everyone has won and all must have prizes"?' *Archives of General Psychiatry*, 32: 995–1008.

Lueger, R.J., Howard, K.I., Martinovitch, Z., Lutz, W. Anderson, E.E. and Grissom, G. (2001) 'Assessing treatment progress of individual patients using expected treatment response models', *Journal of Consulting and Clinical Psychology*, 69: 150–8.

Lutz, W., Martinovitch, Z. and Howard, K.I. (1999) 'Patient profiling: An application of random coefficient regression models to depicting the response of a patient to outpatient psychotherapy', *Journal of Consulting and Clinical Psychology*, 67: 571–7.

Margison, F., Barkham, M., Evans, C., McGrath, G., Mellor-Clark, J., Audin, K. and Connell, J. (2000) 'Measurement and psychotherapy: evidence-based practice and practice-based evidence', *British Journal of Psychiatry*, 177: 123–30.

Marmar, C.R. (1990) 'Psychotherapy process research: progress, dilemmas, and future directions', *Journal of Consulting and Clinical Psychology*, 58: 265–72.

McGinn, L.K. and Sanderson, W. (2001) 'What allows cognitive behavioral therapy to be brief: overview, efficiency, and crucial factors facilitating brief treatment', *Clinical Psychology: Science and Practice*, 8: 23–37.

McLeod, J. (1993) *An Introduction to Counselling*. Buckingham: Open University Press.

McLeod, J. (1994) *Doing Counselling Research*. London: Sage.

McLeod, J. (in press) *Doing Counselling Research*, second edition. London: Sage.

Mellor-Clark, J., Connell, J., Barkham, M. and Cummins, P. (2001) 'Counselling outcomes in primary health care: a CORE System data profile', *European Journal of Psychotherapy, Counselling and Health*, 4: 65–86.

Meltzoff, J. and Kornreich, M. (1970) *Research in Psychotherapy*. Chicago: Aldine.

Messer, S.B. (2001) 'What makes brief psychodynamic therapy time-efficient', *Clinical Psychology: Science and Practice*, 8: 5–22.

Mitchell, K., Bozarth, J.D. and Krauft, C.C. (1977) 'A reappraisal of the therapeutic effectiveness of accurate empathy, nonpossessive warmth, and genuineness' in A.S. Gurman and A. Razin (eds) *Effective Psychotherapy: a Handbook of Research*. Oxford: Pergamon Press.

Mynors-Wallis, L. (1996) 'Problem-solving treatment: Evidence for effectiveness and feasibility in primary care,' *International Journal of Psychiatry in Medicine*, 26: 249–62.

Nathan, P.E., Stuart, S.P. and Dolan, S.L. (2000) 'Research on psychotherapy efficacy and effectiveness: between Scylla and Charybdis?' *Psychological Bulletin*, 126: 964–81.

Nietzel, M.T., Russell, R.L., Hemmings, K.A. and Gretter, M.L. (1987) 'Clinical significance of psychotherapy for unipolar depression: a meta-analytic approach to social comparison', *Journal of Consulting and Clinical Psychology*, 55: 156–61.

Norcross, J. (ed.) (1986) *Handbook of Eclectic Psychotherapy*. New York: Brunner Mazel.

Norcross, J.C. (ed.) (1993) 'Research directions for psychotherapy integration: a round table', *Journal of Psychotherapy Integration*, 3: 91–131.

Norcross, J.C. and Goldfried, M.R. (eds) (1992) *Handbook of Psychotherapy Integration*. New York: Basic Books.

Norquist, G.S., Letowitz, B. and Hynam, S. (1999) 'Expanding the frontier of treatment research', *Prevention and Treatment*, 2: 1–10. (Available at <http://journals.apa.org/prevention/volume2/pre0020001ahtml>.)

O'Farrell, M.K., Hill, C.E. and Patton, S. (1986) 'Comparison of two cases of counseling with the same counselor', *Journal of Counseling and Development*, 65: 141–5.

Ogles, M.M., Lunnen, K.M. and Bonesteel, K. (2001) 'Clinical significance: history, application, and current practice', *Clinical Psychology Review*, 21: 421–46.

Orlinsky, D.E., Ronnestad, M.H. and Willutzki, U. (in press) 'Fifty years of psychotherapy process-outcome research: continuity and change' in M.J. Lambert (ed.) *Bergin and Garfield's Handbook of Psychotherapy and Behavior Change*, fifth edition. New York: Wiley.

Orlinsky, D.E. and Howard, K.I. (1986) 'Process and outcome in psychotherapy', in S.L. Garfield and A.E. Bergin (eds) *Handbook of Psychotherapy and Behavior Change*, third edition. New York: Wiley.

Orlinsky, D.E. and Russell, R.L. (1994) 'Tradition and change in psychotherapy research: notes on the fourth generation' in R.L. Russell (ed.) *Reassessing Psychotherapy Research*. New York: Guilford Press.

Orlinsky, D.E., Grawe, K. and Parks, B.K. (1994) 'Process and outcome in psychotherapy: *noch einmal*' in A.E. Bergin and S.L. Garfield (eds) *Handbook of Psychotherapy and Behavior Change*, fourth edition. New York: Wiley.

Parry, G. (2000) 'Evidence-based psychotherapy: an overview' in N. Rowland and S. Goss (eds) *Evidence-based Counselling and Psychological Therapies: Research and Applications*. London: Routledge.

Parry, G. and Watts, F.N. (1996) *Behavioural and Mental Health Research: a Handbook of Skills and Methods*, second edition. Hove: Erlbaum.

Paul, G. (1967) 'Strategy in outcome research in psychotherapy', *Journal of Consulting Psychology*, 31: 109–18.

Porter, E.H., Jr (1943a) 'The development and evaluation of a measure of counseling interview procedures' I, *Educational and Psychological Measurement*, 3: 105–25.

Porter, E.H., Jr. (1943b) 'The development and evaluation of a measure of counseling interview procedures' II, *Educational and Psychological Measurement*, 3: 215–38.

Quality Assurance Project (1984) 'Treatment outlines for the management of schizophrenia', *Australian and New Zealand Journal of Psychiatry*, 18: 19–38.

Rachman, S. (1971) *The Effects of Psychotherapy*. Oxford: University Press.

Rice, L.N. and Greenberg, L.S. (eds) (1984) *Patterns of Change*. New York: Guilford Press.

Robinson, L.A., Berman, J.S. and Neimeyer, R.A. (1990) 'Psychotherapy for the treatment of depression: a comprehensive review of controlled outcome research', *Psychological Bulletin*, 108: 30–49.

Rogers, C.R. (1942) *Counseling and Psychotherapy*. Boston MA: Houghton Mifflin.

Rogers, C.R. (1951) *Client-centered Therapy: its Current Practice, Implications, and Theory*. Boston MA: Houghton Mifflin.

Rogers, C.R. (1957) 'The necessary and sufficient conditions of therapeutic personality change', *Journal of Consulting Psychology*, 21: 95–103.

Rogers, C.R. and Dymond, R.F. (eds) (1954) *Psychotherapy and Personality Change*. Chicago: University of Chicago Press.

Rogers, C.R., Gendlin, E.T., Kiesler, D.J. and Truax, C.B. (1967) *The Therapeutic Relationship and its Impact: a Study of Psychotherapy with Schizophrenics*. Madison WI: University of Wisconsin Press.

Rosenthal, R. and Rosnow, R.L. (1991) *Essentials of Behavioral Research: Methods and Data Analysis*, second edition. New York: McGraw-Hill.

Roth, A. and Fonagy, P. (1996) *What Works for Whom? A Critical Review of Psychotherapy Research*. New York: Guilford Press.

Roth, A. and Fonagy, P. (in press). *What Works for Whom? A Critical Review of Psychotherapy Research*. second edition. New York: Guilford Press.

Rowland, N. and Goss, S. (eds) (2000) *Evidence-based Counselling and Psychological Therapies: Research and applications*. London: Routledge.

Rowland, N., Godfrey, C., Bower, P., Mellor-Clark, J., Heywood, P. and Hardy, R. (2000) 'Counselling in primary care: a systematic review of the research evidence', *British Journal of Guidance and Counselling*, 28: 215–31.

Ryle, A. (1990) *Cognitive-Analytic Therapy: Active Participation in Change*. Chichester: Wiley.

Seligman, M.E.P. (1995) 'The effectiveness of psychotherapy: the Consumer Reports study', *American Psychologist*, 50: 965–74.

Sexton, T.L. and Whiston, S.C. (1994) 'The status of the counseling relationship: an empirical review, theoretical implications, and research directions', *Counseling Psychologist*, 22: 6–78.

Shadish, W.R., Matt, G.E., Navarro, A.M. and Phillups, G. (2000) 'The effects of psychological therapies under clinically representative conditions: a meta-analysis', *Psychological Bulletin*, 126: 512–29.

Shadish, W.R., Matt, G.E., Navarro, A.M., Siegle, G., Crits-Christoph, P., Hazelrigg, M.D., Jorm. A.F., Lyons, L.C., Nietzel, M.T., Prout, H.T., Robinson, L., Smoth, M.L., Svartberg, M. and Weiss, B. (1997) 'Evidence that therapy works in clinically representative conditions', *Journal of Consulting and Clinical Psychology*, 65: 355–65.

Shapiro, D.A., Barkham, M., Reynolds, S., Hardy, G.E. and Stiles, W.B. (1992) 'Prescriptive and exploratory psychotherapies: toward an integration based on the assimilation model', *Journal of Psychotherapy Integration*, 2: 253–72.

Shapiro, D.A., Barkham, M., Rees, A., Hardy, G.E., Reynolds, S. and Startup, M. (1994) 'Effects of treatment duration and severity of depression on the effectiveness of cognitive-behavioral and psychodynamic-interpersonal psychotherapy', *Journal of Consulting and Clinical Psychology*, 62: 522–34.

Shapiro, D.A., Rees, A., Barkham, M., Hardy, G.E., Reynolds, S. and Startup, M. (1995) 'Effects of treatment duration and severity of depression on the maintenance of gains following cognitive-behavioral and psychodynamic-interpersonal psychotherapy', *Journal of Consulting and Clinical Psychology*, 63: 378–87.

Shapiro, D.A. (1996) 'Outcome research' in G. Parry and F.N. Watts (eds) *Behavioral and Mental Health Research: a Handbook of Skills and Methods, 2nd Edition*. Hillsdale, NJ: Lawrence Erlbaum Associates, Inc.

Silberschatz, G. and Curtis, J.T. (1986) 'Clinical implications of research on brief dynamic psychotherapy II. How the therapist helps or hinders therapeutic progress', *Psychoanalytic Psychology*, 3: 27–37.

Sloane, R.B., Staples, R.F., Cristol, A.H., Yorkston, N.J. and Whipple, K. (1975) *Psychotherapy versus Behavior Therapy*. Cambridge MA: Harvard University Press.

Smith, M.L. and Glass, G.V. (1977) 'Meta-analysis of psychotherapy outcome studies', *American Psychologist*, 32: 752–60.

Smith, M.L., Glass, G.V. and Miller, T.I. (1980) *The Benefits of Psychotherapy*. Baltimore MD: Johns Hopkins University Press.

Snyder, W.U. (1945) 'An investigation of the nature of nondirective psychotherapy', *Journal of General Psychology*, 33: 193–223.

Steinbrueck, S.M., Maxwell, S.E. and Howard, G.S. (1983) 'A meta-analysis of psychotherapy and drug therapy in the treatment of unipolar depression with adults', *Journal of Consulting and Clinical Psychology*, 51: 856–63.

Stiles, W.B., Shapiro, D.A. and Elliott, R. (1986) 'Are all psychotherapies equivalent?' *American Psychologist*, 41: 165–80.

Stiles, W.B., Elliott, R., Llewelyn, S.P., Firth-Cozens, J.A., Margison, F.R., Shapiro, D.A. and Hardy, G.E. (1990) 'Assimilation of problematic experiences by clients in psychotherapy', *Psychotherapy*, 27: 411–20.

Strupp, H.H. (1980a) 'Success and failure in time-limited psychotherapy. A systematic comparison of two cases: comparison 1', *Archives of General Psychiatry*, 37: 595–604.

Strupp, H.H. (1980b) 'Success and failure in time-limited psychotherapy. A systematic comparison of two cases: comparison 2', *Archives of General Psychiatry*, 37: 708–16.

Strupp, H.H. (1980c) 'Success and failure in time-limited psychotherapy, with special reference to the performance of a lay counselor', *Archives of General Psychiatry*, 37: 831–41.

Strupp, H.H. (1980d) 'Success and failure in time-limited psychotherapy: further evidence (comparison 4)', *Archives of General Psychiatry*, 37: 947–54.

Strupp, H.H., Horowitz, L.M. and Lambert, M.J. (eds) (1997) *Measuring Patient Changes in Mood, Anxiety, and Personality Disorders: Towards a Core Battery*. Washington DC: American Psychological Association.

Taube, C.A., Burns, B.J. and Kessler, L. (1984) 'Patients of psychiatrists and psychologists in office-based practice, 1980', *American Psychologist*, 39: 1435–7.

Thornicroft, G. and Slade, M. (2000) 'Are outcome measures feasible in mental health?' *Quality in Health Care*, 9: 84.

Truax, C.B. (1961) 'A scale for the measurement of accurate empathy', *Psychiatric Institute Bulletin* (Wisconsin Psychiatric Institute, University of Wisconsin) 1: 12.

Truax, C.B. and Carkhuff, R.R. (1967) *Toward Effective Counseling and Psychotherapy: Training and Practice*. Chicago: Aldine.

Truax, C.B. and Mitchell, K.M. (1971) 'Research on certain therapist interpersonal skills in relation to process and outcome' in A.E. Bergin and S.L. Garfield (eds) *Handbook of Psychotherapy and Behavior Change*. New York: Wiley.

Wampold, B.E. (2000) 'Outcomes of individual counseling and psychotherapy: empirical evidence addressing two fundamental questions' in S.D. Brown and R.W. Lent (eds) *Handbook of Counseling Psychology*, third edition. New York: Wiley.

Wampold, B.E. (2001) *The Great Psychotherapy Debate: Models, Methods, and Findings*, Mahwah NJ: Erlbaum.

Wampold, B.E. and Poulin, K.L. (1992) 'Counseling research methods: art and artifact' in S.D. Brown and R.W. Lent (eds) *Handbook of Counseling Psychology*, second edition. New York: Wiley.

Wampold, B.E., Mondin, G.W., Moody, M., Stich, F., Benson, K. and Ahn, H. (1997) 'A meta-analysis of outcome studies comparing *bona fide* psychotherapies: empirically, 'all must have prizes''', *Psychological Bulletin*, 122: 203–15.

Ward, E., King, M., Lloyd, M., Bower, P., Sibbauld, B., Farrelly, S., Gabbay, M., Tarrier, N. and Addington-Hall, J. (2000) 'Randomised controlled trial of non-directive counselling, cognitive-behaviour therapy, and usual general practitioner care for patients with depression' I. 'Clinical effectiveness', *British Medical Journal*, 321: 1383–88.

Waskow, I.E. (1975) 'Selection of a core battery' in I.E. Waskow and M.B. Parloff (eds) *Psychotherapy Change Measures*. DHEW Publication No. (ADM) 74–120. Washington DC: US Government Printing Office.

Waskow, I.E. and Parloff, M.B. (eds) (1975) *Psychotherapy Change Measures*. DHEW publication No. (ADM) 74–120. Washington DC: US Government Printing Office.

Watkins, C.E. Jr and Schneider, L.J. (1991) *Research in Counseling*. Hillsdale NJ: Erlbaum.

Whitehorn, J.C. and Betz, B. (1954) 'A study of psychotherapeutic relationships between physicians and schizophrenic patients', *American Journal of Psychiatry*, 3: 321–31.

Wing, J.K., Beevor, A., Curtis, R.H., Park, S.B.G., Hadden, S. and Burns, A. (1998) 'Health of the Nation Outcome Scales (HoNOS): research and development', *British Journal of Psychiatry*, 172: 11–18.

Wolfe, B. and Goldfried, M.R. (1988) 'Research on psychotherapy integration: recommendation and conclusions from an NIMH workshop', *Journal of Consulting and Clinical Psychology*, 56: 448–51.

3 Qualitative Research Methods in Counselling Psychology
JOHN McLEOD

As an academic discipline, psychology has shown a historical tendency to identify with the methods and values of the 'hard', natural sciences. Any graduate of a psychology degree course will be aware of the importance of measurement, experimentation and statistics in achieving valid knowledge. Nevertheless, many psychologists will also be aware that there exists an alternative to the traditional positivist approach. This alternative is often known as 'qualitative' research, and occupies a niche within the 'soft' end of psychology concerned with topics such as personality and social psychology. Some signs of the increasing significance of qualitative methodology in psychology include the popularity of discourse analysis in social psychology (Potter and Wetherell, 1987), the emergence of feminist approaches to psychological inquiry (Burman, 1989; Hollway, 1989), and the influential book by Smith et al. (1995). Before that, anti-positivism in the 1970s and 1980s was represented by the 'new paradigm' approach advocated by Reason and Rowan (1981) and supported by the philosophical critique developed by Harré and Secord (1972) and Shotter (1975).

However, it is important to recognize that qualitative research has in fact been a part of psychology from the very beginning. The founding figures of psychology, Wundt and Dilthey, both argued that a true 'human science' could be based only on the analysis and interpretation of meaning, and that the role of experimental methods should be confined to areas such as perception, neuropsychology and memory (Rennie, 1994e). Another of the early psychologists, William James, wrote a book, *Variety of Religious Experience* (1902), based on qualitative accounts of spiritual experience. Phenomenological psychology, which evolved from the work of nineteenth-century philosophers such as Brentano and Husserl, continues to generate research (Valle and Halling, 1989). Finally, psychoanalysis, the starting point of so much counselling and psychotherapy, is built on the study of qualitative single case studies (Kvale, 2000). A fascinating account of the historical development of methods in psychology, which emphasizes the role of qualitative and action research methods, can be found in Danziger (1990, 1997).

Over the past decade, there has been an increase in the interest in and acceptability of qualitative methods in the social sciences in general. The productivity of qualitative researchers in disciplines such as anthropology, sociology, criminology, education, social work, management, organizational studies, cultural studies and nursing is demonstrated in the *Handbook of Qualitative Research*, edited by Denzin and Lincoln (2000). The impact on counselling psychology of this trend can be observed in the increasing emphasis given to qualitative research in methods textbooks such as Heppner et al. (1992), McLeod

(1994) and Watkins and Schneider (1991). The most recent edition of the *Handbook of Psychotherapy and Behavior Change,* Bergin and Garfield, anticipating future trends in psychotherapy research, predicted that 'the growing endorsement of narrative, descriptive and qualitative approaches represents a rather significant shift in attitude that is likely to become more and more manifest in the conduct and reporting of inquiries' (1994: 828). The impact of qualitative methods in counselling psychology and psychotherapy has also been reflected in the publication of specialist texts on this approach (Frommer and Rennie, 2000; McLeod, 2001).

Qualitative research is generally defined as research built around the collection and analysis of the accounts or stories that people offer regarding their experience. The data of qualitative research are therefore 'words' rather than 'numbers'. However, to describe qualitative research merely in terms of the *absence* of quantification and statistics is to miss the point. At a more fundamental level, the aim of qualitative research is to illuminate and clarify the *meaning* of social actions and situations. The outcome of qualitative research is understanding rather than explanation. Qualitative research is therefore part of a broad interpretive or hermeneutic tradition in social science and the humanities (Messer et al., 1988; Taylor, 1979). Good qualitative studies rely on detailed descriptive accounts of the phenomena being researched, with theoretical formulations arising inductively from this material. Some branches of qualitative research also aim to be reflexive, with priority given to the role of the researcher in the creation of meaning, or may strive to be participative, with the goal of involving and empowering research informants as 'co-researchers'. Qualitative research is often 'discovery-oriented' or 'heuristic' in nature.

Qualitative research is based in a 'social constructionist' perspective on knowledge (Gergen, 1985), which assumes that, in the sphere of social and psychological inquiry, there is no fixed external reality to be 'objectively' known but a fluid 'social reality' which is co-constructed. The task of the researcher is therefore to construct (or deconstruct) versions of this social reality. One of the implications of this philosophical position is that qualitative researchers do not claim to generate 'universal' truths or scientific laws, but rather are striving to build meaningful 'local knowledges'.

This chapter introduces the main principles of qualitative research, and explores the ways in which the techniques can be used in research into counselling and psychotherapy. The chapter will primarily focus on the following topics: methods of gathering qualitative data, approaches to the analysis of qualitative data, the application of these ideas within counselling psychology and criteria for assessing the validity of qualitative studies.

Methods of gathering qualitative data

The process of doing qualitative research involves finding appropriate informants, the collection of detailed descriptive material, and then codification, categorization and interpretation of data. There are a range of different approaches to gathering qualitative data, and many researchers intentionally build into their research design the possibility of combining types of data, to enable 'method triangulation' by checking the extent to which different types of information generate the same themes or meanings. For example, face-to-face interviews are always to a greater or lesser extent *reactive*, with the attitudes and personality of the interviewer shaping what the informant will say. If interview data are combined with personal diaries kept by informants, the researcher can examine the degree to which informants say the same kinds of things in both media.

In designing qualitative studies, it is necessary to be aware that principles and assumptions about *sampling* are quite different from those relevant to quantitative research. Qualitative research is *intensive*, with a single case or a small number of cases being explored in depth. It is impossible to carry out effective qualitative research with very large samples of people, since, as *n* increases, so does the difficulty of doing justice to the mass of qualitative material that is produced. In qualitative research, informants or cases are selected on the basis of their theoretical significance rather than in accordance with rules of randomized or stratified sampling. (See Strauss and Corbin, 1998, and Yin, 1994, for more detailed discussion of sampling issues.)

Interviews

The most widely used method of gathering qualitative data is the research interview. Interviews can be constructed around schedules of questions (Lofland and Lofland, 1984) or can be more open-ended in nature (Kvale, 1996). The advantage of the face-to-face interview is that it represents a flexible technique for gathering accounts of experience. The researcher can readily monitor whether the informant is understanding the meaning or wording of questions, and can check out his or her own understanding of what the informant has disclosed by reflecting back at regular intervals. However, the time required for setting up and conducting an interview may be a problem for both researcher and participant. Also, the time involved in transcribing interview tapes is considerable. Variants on the standard one-to-one research interview are the telephone interview and the group interview. In market research, for example, *focus groups* (Greenbaum, 1998; Morgan and Krueger, 1997; Stewart and Shamdasani, 1998) are often used to generate rich qualitative data on consumer perceptions of products. The issues involved in using all kinds of qualitative research interviews are critically reviewed by Fontana and Frey (2000).

Open-ended questionnaires

Many qualitative researchers find that the use of the open-ended questionnaire represents a practicable alternative to the interview. Although questionnaires are less flexible and sensitive than interviews, the researcher can reach a much greater number of informants, and the time needed for data analysis is reduced by eliminating the necessity to transcribe tapes. In some situations, informants may find it easier to disclose confidential or sensitive material through an anonymous questionnaire than in a personal interview. Examples of open-ended questionnaires in research in counselling psychology have been studies where clients have been asked to describe the 'most helpful' or 'least helpful' aspects of a session.

Stimulated recall techniques

Interviews and questionnaires are generally used to explore events that happened some time in the past, and it is reasonable to suppose that informants may not remember significant aspects of what they actually experienced at the time of the event itself. Elliott (1986) and other psychotherapy researchers have developed the use of stimulated recall methods to overcome this problem. The main technique in this area, *interpersonal process recall* (IPR), was devised by Kagan (1984) as a training technique. An audio or video tape was made of a counselling session, and the trainee counsellor was invited to play the tape back, stopping whenever he or she recalled what they had been feeling or thinking during the original counselling session. In becoming more aware of his or her momentary reactions to the client, and range of behavioural intentions, the trainee counsellor was helped to evolve a wider repertoire of therapeutic responses. Elliott (1986), Rennie (1990) and others have adapted this approach to explore the in-session experiences of both clients and therapists for research purposes.

Projective techniques

Implicit in the use of stimulated recall is an assumption that informants may frequently 'know more than they can tell' (Nisbett and Wilson, 1977), and consequently require some assistance from researchers in retrieving experiential material that is transient or pre-verbal. The same assumption lies behind the use of projective techniques in qualitative research. Methods such as making up fantasy stories, finding images, creative drawing and finishing incomplete sentences are all ways in which informants can be helped to express themselves through metaphorical and figurative language. The data from projective techniques can be difficult to interpret at times, but can add a valuable dimension to interview or questionnaire-based studies (Branthwaite and Lunn, 1985).

Documentary sources

All the qualitative data-gathering methods described so far require active initiation on the part of the researcher, and as a result evoke some sort of reactivity on the part of the informant. Inevitably, informants will wonder why a particular question is being asked, or how much they can trust a researcher with a particular piece of information. The use of qualitative data gained from personal and official documents is therefore of special interest to researchers. Diaries, letters, memos and case notes may yield material that might never be disclosed in an interview.

Participant observation

Within disciplines such as sociology and anthropology, one of the principal modes of qualitative data gathering is through participant observation. Ethnographic studies that aim to capture the rituals or way of life of a group or culture rely on months or years of painstaking observation by researchers who participate in the day-to-day activities of the people being studied. Participant observation offers a uniquely detailed and intimate type of knowledge. Unfortunately, ethical and practical difficulties inhibit the use of participant observation in counselling and psychotherapy research. For example, who would tolerate the presence of a researcher sitting in on therapy sessions, or accompanying a client home to observe how his or her behaviour toward family members changed following that session? Further discussion of the use of ethnographic methods in counselling research can be found in McLeod (2001).

Inquiry groups

The final approach to generating qualitative research data is through the human inquiry group. This is a technique devised by those within the 'new paradigm' research tradition (Reason, 1988; Reason and Rowan, 1981) to reflect the distinctive values of their radically humanistic approach to human inquiry. The human inquiry group consists of a group of co-researchers who meet to examine their own experience of a phenomenon. The group itself decides on how data will be collected, and how the authenticity and validity of material will be evaluated. This is a research method that places a significant emphasis on the human capacity for reflexivity.

Approaches to the analysis of qualitative data

There are a number of approaches that can be taken to the analysis of qualitative research data. It is quite possible to gather qualitative material, such as transcripts of therapy sessions, and then apply quantitative techniques such as coding or content analysis at the analysis stage of the study. Usually, however, the term 'qualitative research' is reserved for studies that apply a more open-ended, interpretive style of data analysis. Although the field of qualitative research is fragmented, with a huge diversity of analytical techniques and procedures used by different researchers, it is nevertheless possible to identify four main schools of qualitative analysis: phenomenology, grounded theory, narratology and discourse analysis. In qualitative research, data collection and analysis tend not to form discrete stages of a piece of research, with all the data being gathered and then, once that stage is complete, being subjected to analysis. Instead, qualitative researchers will often move back and forward between data gathering and analysis in a cyclical process, deliberately using the analysis of early data to guide the choice of new cases, informants or research sites.

Phenomenological methods

The aim of phenomenological research is to achieve an authentic and comprehensive description of the way in which a phenomenon is experienced by a person or group of people. Phenomenological studies tend to use data based on informants' written or spoken accounts of their experience. The task of the researcher is to immerse himself or herself in this material until the 'essence' of what it means, its essential meaning, becomes clear. In this process of immersion, the researcher needs to 'bracket off' his or her assumptions about the phenomenon. The researcher is in effect suspending his or her 'natural' or 'taken for granted' attitude toward the phenomenon, in the search for new and underlying meanings. Each set of meanings that is 'bracketed' in this way becomes part of the final descriptive representation of the phenomenon. This ultimate representation can be seen as comprising ever widening 'horizons' of meaning. It is a mistake to imagine that this process can ever reveal any ultimate 'true' meaning. The methodology is, instead, intended to enable the researcher to open up an area of human experience, not to arrive at a once-and-for-all definition of it. The similarities between phenomenological inquiry and the work of the therapist, particularly therapists within the client-centred or person-centred tradition, should be obvious. The contrast between the inductive and open-ended nature of phenomenological research and the attempts by Rogers and his colleagues to develop 'operationalized' phenomenological measures such as the self–ideal self Q-sort will also be apparent.

In practice, phenomenological research is difficult to do, requiring sufficient self-belief to be willing to suspend normal 'ways of seeing', and also making great demands on the ability of the researcher to construct a readable account of what he or she has done. Further information about the use of phenomenological methods in psychological research is available in Becker (1992), Moustakas (1994) and Osborne (1990). Although relatively little 'pure' phenomenological research has been carried out in the field of counselling and psychotherapy, it is essential to recognize that all other approaches to qualitative research draw heavily on the phenomenological tradition.

Grounded theory analysis

Grounded theory was devised by two sociologists, Barney Glaser and Anselm Strauss, in the 1960s (Glaser and Strauss, 1967). Their aim was to develop a form of research that would allow theoretical statements to be clearly 'grounded' in experiential data. So, from their point of view, phenomenological research, in restricting itself to description rather than model building, did not go far enough. Conversely, traditional quantitative methods erred in the opposite direction by imposing pre-decided categories and variables on the data, and therefore sacrificing the potential to generate new ideas and concepts by listening closely to what informants actually have to say about their lives. Grounded theory studies typically use observational, documentary or transcribed interview data, to which the researcher applies a systematic step-by-step analysis. First, the material is segmented into 'meaning units', which may be as short as a word or phrase or as long as a paragraph or page. Then the researcher attempts to code the meaning of these units in as sensitive and open a manner as possible. Rather than just assigning one meaning to each segment, the researcher will strive to imagine all the different meanings that might be applied. A careful record is kept of each meaning or 'concept' that arises, along with its corresponding piece of text. The researcher goes on to explore similarities and differences between the concepts that have been produced in this way, and merges similar concepts into 'categories'. The accuracy and generality of these categories is checked by tracking through all the data, looking for counter-instances. Finally, the researcher finds a smaller set of 'main categories' that effectively capture the meaning of the material as a whole, and is then able to construct a model, or theoretical framework, for understanding the phenomenon being studied. This description of grounded theory analysis is, for reasons of space, somewhat over-simplified, and the reader is urged to consult Glaser and Strauss (1967), Glaser (1978), Strauss and Corbin (1998) or Rennie et al. (1988) for fuller accounts of what is involved in using this method.

The attraction of grounded theory is that it offers qualitative researchers an explicit, practicable set of steps to follow when dealing with qualitative data. However, some observers have argued that the practice of grounded theory analysis is an art that relies on intuition and creativity that must be learned through apprenticeship rather than acquired by following a book (Stern, 1994).

Narrative analysis

A third tradition in qualitative research involves close attention to stories and conversations. In phenomenological or grounded theory analysis, informant narratives tend to become transformed into more general themes or categories. There is therefore a tendency to lose sight of individual built-up sequences of meaning (stories, for example) in the search for the underlying content of what the stories are *about*. With the various forms of narrative analysis, by contrast, it is assumed that the structure of the actual story or conversation sequence serves as an important vehicle for meaning. Narrative analysis, or 'narratology', is an approach that:

> examines the informant's story and analyses how it is put together, the linguistic and cultural resources that it draws on, and how it persuades a listener of authenticity. Analysis in narrative studies opens up the forms of telling about experience, not simply the content to which language refers. We ask, why was the story told *that* way? (Riessman, 1993: 2)

Narrative approaches to qualitative research have been developed from a variety of different analytic perspectives. One widely used approach takes as its focus the ways in which self and personal identity are expressed in narrative and conversation (Josselson and Lieblich, 1993; Riessman, 1993; Rosenwald and Ochberg, 1992). Another quite different approach is taken by the proponents of *discourse analysis*, who place their main emphasis on the social functions of language. The aim of this type of study is to gain an understanding of the pre-existing linguistic resources or social discourses which speakers draw upon in making any statements (Wetherell and Potter, 1988). *Conversation analysis* (Madill et al., 2001), by contrast, focuses on sequences of interaction within segments of 'talk', such as transcripts of therapy sessions.

The common ground between different styles of narrative analysis is the close attention that it pays to the subtle and complex ways in which people construct meaning, and also to the influence of context on the kinds of stories that people tell. These intricacies can be captured only by looking in detail at samples of conversation, and it is usual in narrative research to include segments of transcript material in the text of the research article. Typically, narrative researchers may interview several informants to gain a general sense of the phenomenon in which they are interested, but then present their conclusions through the vehicle of an in-depth analysis of a single case. For example, in her research into marital violence, Riessman (1994) uses the words of one woman to represent the experience of deciding to leave a violent marriage. The informant is allowed to tell the reader directly how it was for her, while the commentary provided by the researcher points to some of the wider cultural meanings of her words.

The qualitative researcher as *bricoleur*

These three qualitative research approaches – phenomenology, grounded theory and narratology – have been selected as the forms of data analysis most applicable to topics in the field of counselling psychology. However, it is misleading to take the view that any of these methods represent analytical procedures that can be followed mechanistically in the hope of producing acceptable qualitative returns. The practice of qualitative research involves personal engagement with the phenomena being studied, and the employment of *any* tools likely to facilitate understanding. One of the features of qualitative research has been the creativity and innovation with which investigators have developed new analytical and data presentation techniques. The vast range of analytical strategies that have been invented are reviewed in Miles and Huberman (1994) and Bryman and Burgess (1994). Denzin and Lincoln (1994) have suggested that it is helpful to see qualitative research as a *bricolage* (a pieced-together solution to a specific problem in a concrete situation), and the qualitative researcher as *bricoleur* (a kind of professional do-it-yourself person). They write that:

> The *bricoleur* is adept at performing a large number of diverse tasks, ranging from interviewing to observing, to interpreting personal and historical documents, to

intensive self-reflection and introspection. The *bricoleur* reads widely and is knowledgeable about the many interpretive paradigms (feminism, Marxism, cultural studies, constructivism) that can be brought to any particular problem. ... The *bricoleur* understands that research is an interactive process shaped by his or her personal history, biography, gender, social class, race and ethnicity, and those of the people in the setting .... The product of the *bricoleur's* labour is a bricolage, a complex, dense, reflexive, collage-like creation that represents the researcher's images, understandings, and interpretations of the world or phenomenon under analysis. (Denzin and Lincoln, 1994: 2–3)

The metaphor and image of the *bricoleur* capture the complexity, difficulty and also the excitement of qualitative research. They also illuminate the attraction of qualitative research for many counselling psychologists, since the effective therapist is similarly required to integrate understandings of the personal, cultural and historical, and find meaning in complexity.

Applications of qualitative methods in counselling psychology research

It has been argued by Mishler (1990) that in practice most researchers tend not to construct studies according to abstract principles of research design and philosophy of science. Instead, researchers are influenced by 'exemplar' studies, investigations that have applied a particular technique and have produced credible new knowledge. In this section, some exemplar qualitative studies in the field of counselling psychology are introduced and discussed.

The client experience of the therapy hour

The work of Rennie (1990, 1992) embodies one of the most rigorous and sustained applications of qualitative methodology within psychotherapy research. Working within the person-centred tradition, the aim of this programme of research has been to construct a detailed and comprehensive understanding of the client's experience of a therapy session. These studies have involved the use of IPR interviews carried out with fourteen therapy clients. During the recall interview, a tape recording of the session is played to the client, who is invited to stop the tape whenever he or she has any comment to make about what he or she was experiencing at that moment of the therapy session. These IPR interviews are transcribed, and then analysed according to the procedures of grounded theory. A full account of the data-gathering and analysis process can be found in Rennie (1994d). This method enabled Rennie (1990, 1992) to construct a general representation of the client's experience of the therapy hour, built around three main categories: the client's *relationship with personal meaning*, the client's *perception of the relationship with the therapist*, and *awareness of outcomes*. In further, more fine-grained thematic explorations of the same material, Rennie has examined the client's experience of processes of resistance (Rennie, 1994c), storytelling (Rennie, 1994b) and deference (Rennie, 1994a). Angus and Rennie (1988, 1989) used a similar technique to explore client experiences of the use of metaphor in therapy sessions. This set of studies illustrates the systematic use of IPR and grounded theory in the service of developing a convincing and practically valuable model of therapeutic process.

Client evaluations of family therapy

Howe (1989) was invited by a family therapy team in a British social services department to carry out an evaluation of their therapeutic work with families. Members of thirty three families were interviewed. Twenty-two of the families had received therapy and ten had turned down the offer of this type of help. Open-ended interviews were carried out between four and seven weeks after the completion of treatment, and again after one year. Case notes and agency files were also examined. This mass of qualitative data was analysed in an 'interpretive' style loosely based on grounded theory. Howe presented his account of the clients' experience of family therapy in terms of three main categories: 'to be engaged', 'to understand' and 'to be understood'. These themes converged in a discussion of client 'verdicts' on their treatment. Howe found strikingly low levels of client satisfaction. He noted that 'the overwhelming verdict was captured in a phrase that cropped up in almost all interviews with those families that felt dissatisfied: "it was a waste of time"' (1989: 77). In fact, only three families felt that the therapy had helped them. The kind of analysis undertaken by Howe (1989) in this research allows the creation of a comprehensive and well rounded account of what the clients felt and thought about the therapeutic help they had received. It yields an estimate of overall success rates that stands comparison with the type of data produced by traditional quantitative outcome studies, but has the advantage of being able to place these evaluations in the context of a framework for understanding why and how the effects were generated.

Patterns of client change in short-term counselling

Cummings et al. (1994) demonstrate one of the ways in which open-ended questionnaires can be used along with narrative analysis in counselling research. Ten clients engaged in time-limited (eight to eleven sessions) counselling were asked after each session to write in response to five open-ended questions: 'What was the most important thing that happened in this session?' 'Why was it important and how was it helpful or not helpful?' 'What thoughts and feelings do you recall experiencing/having during the session?' 'What did you find yourself thinking about or doing during the time in between sessions that related in any way to the last session?' and 'Are you experiencing any change in yourself, and if so, what?' The researchers read through these written accounts, and constructed a narrative summary of what the client had reported. Other independent judges compared the original data with the narratives to check for bias or inaccuracy. The set of narratives produced by each client was analysed to identify the pattern of change that had occurred for that individual. Over the sample of ten cases, three different change patterns were found: consistent change, interrupted change and minimal change. Although clients categorized as showing 'consistent' and 'interrupted' change both appeared to gain from counselling, these contrasting patterns were associated with distinct sets of client experiences and needs. This small-scale study contributes to an understanding of change processes, by offering the reader vivid examples drawn from participants' written accounts, while at the same time raising important theoretical issues relevant to any assumption that the change process is the same for all clients.

The process of problem formulation in therapy

Davis (1986) represents an effective application of discourse analysis in the field of psychotherapy research. The aim of the study was to explore the way in which the stories that clients tell about their 'troubles' become transformed into 'problems' suitable for psychotherapeutic intervention. The background to the study is given by Davis (1986) as arising from feminist critiques of psychotherapy. From a feminist perspective, when women go to see a psychotherapist, their problems are taken out of their social context and individualized. The woman is therefore pathologized, with 'problems which many women have in common and which are related to the oppressive exigencies of their living and working conditions [being] shorn of all political significance' (Davis, 1986: 46). However, as Davis (1986) pointed out, there had been no research that examined just *how* this happened within therapy sessions. Davis selected a video of a first session with a woman client and an expert, 'highly respected' male therapist. The video had been employed for teaching purposes, and was used because it could be regarded as an example of good practice. The conversation between therapist and client was transcribed, and a detailed analysis of conversation sequences was carried out. Davis (1986) concluded that, during the course of the session, the therapist carried out a *reformulation* of the client's problems, offered the client *documentation* of the reformulation through examples drawn not only from her initial statements but also from her in-session behaviour, and finally achieved the client's *consent* to his views. In the particular session analysed by Davis the client began by describing a set of difficulties relating to her role as a full-time housewife and mother who was pregnant. The formulation offered by the therapist was that these difficulties arose from not being able to express her emotions openly, and striving to keeping up a facade of control. Davis observes: 'more than half of the therapy session is devoted to persuading the client that the facade-problem is what she needs to work on' (1986: 65). This piece of research is inevitably limited in its generalizability (for example, would other therapists act in a similar fashion?). However, a significant strength of this approach is that a fair amount of the session transcript is included in the paper, so the reader can independently assess the plausibility of the analyses made by the author.

Lesbian self-disclosure of sexual orientation to health professionals

Hitchcock and Wilson (1992) explore the processes and issues surrounding the decision of lesbian health care clients to disclose their sexual orientation to health professionals. This paper has broad terms of reference, in looking at disclosure to all kinds of health professionals, and not just psychotherapists. It is nevertheless relevant to counselling psychologists, in focusing on a significant issue and also in acting as an example of the use of grounded theory methods. Hitchcock and Wilson carried out interviews with thirty three self-identified lesbians. Each interview was tape-recorded and transcribed, and 'in keeping with conventions associated with the discovery of grounded theory method, data collection and analysis took place simultaneously and in a nonlinear fashion' (1992: 179). The material was coded, with a multiplicity of codes then condensed into more general categories, and finally a set of core concepts emerged. This process continued until no new meanings appeared in the data. The analysis Hitchcock and Wilson carried out revealed that lesbian health care users shared a *fear* of disclosure, and attempted to cope with this feeling through a process of *personal risking*. On first contact with a health professional, for example, many of the informants engaged in *scouting out*: 'collecting information about health care providers before deciding whether they are safe' (1992: 180). Following this initial information gathering, the lesbian client takes one of four possible stances on whether or not to let the health professional know about her sexual orientation: *passive disclosure, passive non-disclosure, active disclosure* and *active non-disclosure*. The decision to disclose is also affected by factors such as relationship status (that is, whether or not in a primary relationship), past experience with health professionals, and the relevance of sexual orientation to the health problem. This study offers a detailed appreciation of the experiences of lesbian clients. The message comes through strongly that lesbian clients feel it is risky to disclose any information about their sexuality, and take every precaution to do so as carefully as possible. It is of particular interest that this study was carried out in the San Francisco Bay area, a region with a tradition of tolerance of lesbian and gay people. The degree of fear and risk might well be assumed to be much higher in other places.

The experience of 'schizophrenia'

The research carried out in the late 1950s by the psychiatrist R.D. Laing and reported in *The Divided Self* (1960) and *Self and Others* (1961) remains a powerful example of the application of the phenomenological method. Laing's aim in this work was to understand the experience of being 'schizophrenic', to 'reconstruct the patient's way of being himself in his world' (1960: 25). In achieving this aim he needed to undertake a great deal of 'bracketing-off' of assumptions. His training as a doctor and psychiatrist, for example, had given him a language that acted as a barrier to an appreciation of what patients might be experiencing. Laing (1960: 18) wrote that 'as a psychiatrist, I run into a major difficulty at the outset: how can I go straight to the patients if the psychiatric words at my disposal keep the patient at a distance from me?' It was therefore necessary for him to 'deconstruct' the meaning of psychosis by developing a critique of the ways that 'psychiatric words' were used in practice. Having done this, he was able to explore the experiential world of 'schizophrenic' people from a fresh perspective. His phenomenological investigation of this way of 'being-in-the-world' resulted in two kinds of research output. First, there was a series of sensitive case studies of individual patients. Second, the recurring themes in these case studies were conceptualized in existential-phenomenological terms through ideas such as *ontological insecurity, engulfment, implosion, petrification, pretence* and *elusion*. Taken as a whole, this set of studies introduced the possibility of understanding the lives and experiences of people who are 'mad'. Unfortunately, the subsequent career of R.D. Laing progressed in directions that became increasingly difficult to reconcile with the world of research, even phenomenological research, and as a result these early studies have been neglected and discredited.

The history and organization of a counselling agency

In their book *Whom God hath Joined Together* Lewis et al. (1992) present a historical account of the development of the National Marriage Guidance Council, the leading British agency dealing in couples counselling. Lewis et al., draw together data from a variety of sources: interviews, personal and official documents, and observation. Their investigation provides a good example of *triangulation*: using agreement between data from different sources as a check on validity. They also attempted to establish the accuracy of their data and analysis by asking a member of the agency to comment on a draft of their report.

Exemplar studies of the use of qualitative methods in counselling psychology research: some conclusions

These examples illustrate what can be done with qualitative methods. The same set of general research approaches and techniques could in principle be applied to a large number of questions of interest to counselling psychologists. It is perhaps worth noting a number of features of the qualitative research paradigm. First, it requires intense personal involvement on the part of the researcher. In the studies by Rennie, for example, the task of coding and categorizing interview transcripts took years of careful work. In other exemplar studies, good-quality data could be obtained only through a capacity to form genuine relationships with informants, in which they felt safe enough to disclose sensitive personal information. Secondly, reflexive self-awareness on the part of the researcher is necessary. Davis (1986), for instance, was clear about the feminist values informing her approach. Laing has written in many places about his own understanding of schizophrenia and his personal experiences in relation to this topic. If a qualitative research report is a 'construction' of a segment of social reality, it is important to know the ways in which the personal beliefs and values of the researcher have played a part in the inquiry process. Thirdly, good qualitative research is challenging. A qualitative study that merely presents a version of what is 'obvious' is not very interesting. The studies reviewed earlier go beyond the obvious and reveal new aspects of phenomena, new horizons of meaning. Rennie describes the ways in which clients 'defer' to their therapists, keeping quiet when the therapist has misunderstood the client or said something unhelpful. Many health professionals who would see themselves as accepting of gay and lesbian clients might well feel uncomfortable on reading the study by Hitchcock and Wilson (1992). The three core values exhibited in these exemplar studies – authentic personal involvement, reflexivity and challenge – embody the core of the qualitative approach to research.

Criteria for evaluating the validity of qualitative studies

The criteria used in assessing the quality of a piece of qualitative research are quite different from those employed in traditional, experimental, positivist psychology. For example, concepts such as predictive or construct validity, inter-rater or test–retest reliability are defined through, and depend on, statistical operations. The assumption that underpins these traditional concepts of validity is that there does exist an objective reality, and that the methods of science can be used to gain ever more accurate models of that reality. Qualitative research, by contrast, is built on an assumption that the world of persons is a co-constructed social reality (Gergen, 1985). Different participants in a social world will, therefore, each possess a somewhat different version of what is 'real' or 'true'.

The fundamental criterion for evaluating the products of this type of human science was described by Weber and Dilthey as *Verstehen*, or a 'sense of understanding', close to the counselling notion of *empathy*. In practice, this concept has at least two sides to it. First, readers must recognize the 'world' or set of experiences that the researcher is describing as authentic and credible. Secondly, the analysis, interpretation or conceptualization carried out by the researcher should lead to new insights into the object of study. It is clear that these criteria are highly subjective. Readers may well differ in the degree to which they regard a research account as authentic or providing insight. As a result, a number of attempts have been made to elaborate a more specific set of quality control criteria for qualitative research (Henwood and Pidgeon, 1992; Kirk and Miller, 1986; Lincoln and Guba, 1989; Stiles, 1993). These efforts have been motivated in part by a desire on the part of qualitative researchers to see their work published in mainstream psychology journals. In the past, journal editors and reviewers unfamiliar with qualitative research have not known how to evaluate the merit of qualitative papers submitted to them, and have often refused to publish such work. Elliott et al. (1999) have produced a useful set of guidelines for evaluating qualitative research.

In relation to qualitative research in the field of counselling psychology, some of the central issues in assessing the validity of a study are: adequacy of information given about the context of the study and procedures employed, the extent to which conceptualization is explicitly grounded in data, the credibility of the researcher, the degree to which research participants have been empowered by their involvement in the study, and the success with which conclusions have been 'triangulated' against different sources of data. More detailed discussion of these issues can be found in McLeod (1994) and Stiles (1993). Many of the issues have been most clearly identified and addressed by feminist researchers (Finch, 1984; Mies, 1983; Oakley, 1981). A central theme in this area concerns the role of researcher *reflexivity* (Berg and Smith, 1988; Steier, 1991). In qualitative research the personal experience of the researcher is an important source of data. The researcher may often, for example, choose to include in a research report an account of his or her reflexive involvement in the research process (Wolcott, 1990).

Qualitative research in counselling psychology: future directions

It is necessary to be aware of some of the limitations of qualitative research in counselling psychology. For example, very little qualitative research has been carried out in the field of outcome research. Although Howe (1989) and Cummings et al. (1994) demonstrate that therapy can be evaluated using qualitative methods, it is not clear how or whether it would ever be possible to compare effectiveness rates across studies or carry out meta-analyses using *effect sizes* (see Chapter 2) from a qualitative perspective. One solution to this problem might be to develop 'mixed' or 'pluralist' studies in which qualitative and quantitative methods are combined. However, the different epistemological assumptions underlying the two approaches can make it difficult to integrate data from these two very different sources (Brannen, 1992: McLeod, 1994). A critical analysis of the role of qualitative methods in outcome research can be found in McLeod (2001).

Another limitation of qualitative research arises from the amount of time and effort required to accomplish a satisfactory qualitative study. Basic qualitative research tasks such as interviewing, transcribing tapes and coding data are very labour-intensive. Also, the art or craft of writing reports based on qualitative data can be highly demanding. The rapidly advancing availability of personal computer software for analysing qualitative data (Weitzman, 2000) may eventually attenuate these difficulties. The method of 'consensual qualitative research', developed by Clara Hill and her colleagues (1997) also represents a pragmatic approach to qualitative work. Hill et al. (1997) describe procedures through which teams of researchers can work together to share out the tasks of qualitative data collection and analysis.

A third limitation or dilemma arising from the use of qualitative methods is that these approaches have been generally used in a 'discovery-oriented' or 'heuristic' manner. In other words, qualitative researchers enter the field with relatively few presuppositions about what they may find, and are primarily interested in developing *new* insights or models. It is not clear whether qualitative methods are equally applicable during the verification or theory-testing phase of a research programme. On the whole, qualitative researchers take the view that concepts or categories should emerge inductively from the data that are gathered. If a researcher began a study with a well defined set of concepts (for example, derived from psychodynamic or person-centred theory) this inductive or naturalistic process could not occur in the same manner.

It is also important to recognize that qualitative research in counselling psychology is in its infancy. Up to now, relatively few qualitative studies have been carried out in this area. Nevertheless, it is apparent that this style of research has an important contribution to make. Some of the advantages of qualitative research are that it respects the complexity of the phenomenon being studied, invites the active participation of informants, and takes as its goal the enhancement of understanding. Qualitative research is, therefore, highly consistent with many of the values of counselling psychology, and is therefore more likely to be perceived as credible and relevant by practitioners. In addition, doing qualitative research is similar to doing therapy. The good qualitative researcher uses empathy, genuineness and acceptance in developing relationships with informants (Mearns and McLeod, 1984). As a result, it is possible that qualitative research may be a style of inquiry that many counselling psychologists are able to do well.

In a review of the evolution of psychotherapy research Orlinsky and Russell (1994) argue that this field of research has entered its fourth major phase. The first phase was characterized by the need to establish the legitimacy of scientific research into therapy. The second phase was marked by a search for greater rigour. The third phase represented the expansion and consolidation of the field. They regard the fourth, current, phase, which began in the mid-1980s, as encompassing a powerful sense of dissatisfaction with prevailing research methods and increasing openness to a radical reformulation of research practice. Qualitative research and human science are essential elements of this new movement.

References

Angus, L.E. and Rennie, D.L. (1988) 'Therapist participation in metaphor generation: collaborative and noncollaborative styles', *Psychotherapy*, 25: 552–60.

Angus, L.E. and Rennie, D.L. (1989) 'Envisioning the representational world: the client's experience of metaphoric expressiveness in psychotherapy', *Psychotherapy*, 26: 373–9.

Becker, C.S. (1992) *Living and Relating: an Introduction to Phenomenology*. London: Sage.

Berg, D.N. and Smith, K.K. (eds) (1988) *The Self in Social Inquiry: Researching Methods*. London: Sage.

Bergin, A.E. and Garfield, S.L. (1994) 'Overview, trends and future issues' in A.E. Bergin and S.L. Garfield (eds) *Handbook of Psychotherapy and Behavior Change*, fourth edition. New York: Wiley.

Brannen, J. (ed.) (1992) *Mixing Methods: Qualitative and Quantitative Research*. Aldershot: Avebury.

Branthwaite, A. and Lunn, T. (1985) 'Projective techniques in social and market research' in R. Walker (ed.) *Applied Qualitative Research*. Aldershot: Gower.

Bryman, A. and Burgess, R.G. (eds) (1994) *Analyzing Qualitative Data*. London: Routledge.

Burman, E. (ed.) (1989) *Feminists and Psychological Practice*. London: Sage.

Cummings, A.L., Hallberg, E.T. and Slemon, A.G. (1994) 'Templates of client change in short-term counseling', *Journal of Counseling Psychology*, 41 (4): 464–72.

Danziger, K. (1990) *Constructing the Subject: Historical Origins of Psychological Research*. Cambridge: Cambridge University Press.

Danziger, K. (1997) *Naming the Mind: How Psychology found its Language*. Thousand Oaks CA: Sage.

Davis, K. (1986) 'The process of problem (re)formulation in psychotherapy', *Sociology of Health and Illness*, 8 (1): 44–74.

Denzin, N.K. and Lincoln, Y.S. (1994) 'Introduction: entering the field of qualitative research' in N.K. Denzin and Y.S. Lincoln (eds) *Handbook of Qualitative Research*. London: Sage.

Denzin, N.K. and Lincoln, Y.S. (eds) (2000) *Handbook of Qualitative Research* second edition. Thousand Oaks CA: Sage.

Elliott, R. (1986) 'Interpersonal Process Recall (IPR) as a psychotherapy process research method' in L.S. Greenberg and W.M. Pinsof (eds) *The Psychotherapeutic Process: a Research Handbook*. New York: Guilford Press.

Elliott, R., Fischer, C.T. and Rennie, D.L. (1999) 'Evolving guidelines for the publication of qualitative research studies in psychology and related fields', *British Journal of Clinical Psychology*, 38: 215–29.

Finch, J. (1984) '"It's great to have someone to talk to": ethics and politics of interviewing women' in C. Bell and H. Roberts (eds) *Social Researching: Politics, Problems, Practice*. London: Routledge.

Fontana, A. and Frey, G. (2000) 'The interview: from structured questions to negotiated text' in N.K. Denzin and Y.S. Lincoln (eds) *Handbook of Qualitative Research*, second edition. Thousand Oaks CA: Sage.

Frommer, J. and Rennie, D.L. (eds) (2000) *Qualitative Psychotherapy Research: Methods and Methodology*. Berlin: Pabst.

Gergen, K. (1985) 'The social constructionist movement in modern psychology', *American Psychologist*, 40 (3): 266–75.

Glaser, B.G. (1978) *Theoretical Sensitivity: Advances in the Methodology of Grounded Theory*. Mill Valley CA: Sociology Press.

Glaser, B.G. and Strauss, A. (1967) *The Discovery of Grounded Theory*. Chicago: Aldine.

Greenbaum, T.L. (1998) *The Handbook for Focus Group Research*, second edition. Thousand Oaks CA: Sage.

Harré, R. and Secord, P.F. (1972) *The Explanation of Social Behaviour*. Oxford: Blackwell.

Henwood, K.L. and Pidgeon, N.F. (1992) 'Qualitative research and psychological theorising', *British Journal of Psychology*, 83: 97–111.

Heppner, P.P., Kivlighan, D.M., Jr and Wampold, B.E. (1992) *Research Design in Counseling*. Pacific Grove CA: Brooks Cole.

Hill, C.E., Thompson, B.J. and Nutt-Williams, E. (1997) 'A guide to conducting consensual qualitative research', *Counseling Psychologist*, 25: 517–72.

Hitchcock, J.M. and Wilson, H.S. (1992) 'Personal risking: lesbian self-disclosure of sexual orientation to professional health care providers', *Nursing Research*, 41 (3): 178–83.

Hollway, W. (1989) *Subjectivity and Method in Psychology: Gender, Meaning and Science*. London: Sage.

Howe, D. (1989) *The Consumers' View of Family Therapy*. Aldershot: Gower.

Josselson, R. and Lieblich, A. (eds) (1993) *The Narrative Study of Lives*. London: Sage.

Kagan, N. (1984) 'Interpersonal Process Recall: basic methods and recent research' in D. Larsen (ed.) *Teaching Psychological Skills*. Monterey CA: Brooks Cole.

Kirk, J. and Miller, M.L. (1986) *Reliability and Validity in Qualitative Research*. London: Sage.

Kvale, S. (1996) *InterViews: an Introduction to Qualitative Research Interviewing*. London: Sage.

Kvale, S. (2000) 'The psychoanalytic interview as qualitative research' in J. Frommer and D.L. Rennie (eds) *Qualitative Psychotherapy Research: Methods and Methodology*. Berlin: Pabst.

Laing, R.D. (1960) *The Divided Self: an Existential Study in Sanity and Madness*. London: Tavistock.

Laing, R.D. (1961) *Self and Others*. London: Tavistock.

Lewis, J., Clark, D. and Morgan, D. (1992) *Whom God hath Joined Together: the Work of Marriage Guidance*. London: Routledge.

Lincoln, Y.S. and Guba, E.G. (1989) 'Judging the quality of case study reports', *Qualitative Studies in Education*, 3: 53–9.

Lofland, J. and Lofland, L. (1984) *Analyzing Social Settings: a Guide to Qualitative Observation and Analysis*, second edition. Belmont CA: Wadsworth.

Madill, A., Widdicombe, S. and Barkham, M. (2001) 'The potential of conversation analysis for psychotherapy research', *Counseling Psychologist*, 29 (3): 413–34.

McLeod, J. (1994) *Doing Counselling Research*. London: Sage.

McLeod, J. (2001) *Qualitative Research in Counselling and Psychotherapy*. London: Sage.

Mearns, D. and McLeod, J. (1984) 'A person-centred approach to research' in R. Levant and J. Shlien (eds) *Client-centered Therapy and the Person-centered Approach: New Directions in Theory, Research and Practice*. New York: Praeger.

Messer, S.B., Sass, L.A. and Woolfolk, R.L. (eds) (1988) *Hermeneutics and Psychological Theory: Interpretive Perspectives on Personality, Psychotherapy and Psychopathology*. New Brunswick NJ: Rutgers University Press.

Mies, M. (1983) 'Towards a methodology for feminist research' in G. Bowles and R.D. Klein (eds) *Theories for Women's Studies*. London: Routledge.

Miles, M. and Huberman, A. (1994) *Qualitative Data Analysis: a Sourcebook of New Methods*, second edition. London: Sage.

Mishler, E.G. (1990) 'Validation in inquiry-guided research: the role of exemplars in narrative studies', *Harvard Educational Review*, 60 (4): 415–42.

Morgan, D.I. and Krueger, R.A. (1997) *Focus Group Kit I–VI*. Thousand Oaks CA: Sage.

Moustakas, C. (1994) *Phenomenological Research Methods*. London: Sage.

Nisbett, R.E. and Wilson, T.D. (1977) 'Telling more than we can know: verbal reports on mental processes', *Psychological Review*, 84: 231–59.

Oakley, A. (1981) 'Interviewing women: a contradiction in terms' in H. Roberts (ed.) *Doing Feminist Research*. London: Routledge.

Orlinsky, D.E. and Russell, R.L. (1994) 'Tradition and change in psychotherapy research: notes on the fourth generation' in R.L. Russell (ed.) *Reassessing Psychotherapy Research*. New York: Guilford Press.

Osborne, J.W. (1990) 'Some basic existential-phenomenological research methodology for counsellors', *Canadian Journal of Counselling*, 24 (2): 79–91.

Potter, J. and Wetherell, M. (1987) *Discourse and Social Psychology: Beyond Attitudes and Behaviour*. London: Sage.

Reason, P. (ed.) (1988) *Human Inquiry in Action: Developments in New Paradigm Research*. London: Sage.

Reason, P. and Rowan, J. (eds) (1981) *Human Inquiry: a Sourcebook of New Paradigm Methods*. Chichester: Wiley.

Rennie, D.L. (1990) 'Toward a representation of the client's experience of the psychotherapy hour' in G. Lietaer, J. Rombauts and R. Van Balen (eds) *Client-centered and Experiential Therapy in the Nineties*. Leuven: University of Leuven Press.

Rennie, D.L. (1992) 'Qualitative analysis of the client's experience of psychotherapy: the unfolding of reflexivity', in S.G. Toukmanian and D.L. Rennie (eds) *Psychotherapy Process Research: Paradigmatic and Narrative Approaches*. London: Sage.

Rennie, D.L. (1994a) 'Clients' deference in psychotherapy', *Journal of Counseling Psychology*, 41 (4): 427–37.

Rennie, D.L. (1994b) 'Storytelling in psychotherapy: the client's subjective experience', *Psychotherapy*, 31: 234–43.

Rennie, D.L. (1994c) 'Clients' accounts of resistance in counselling: a qualitative analysis', *Canadian Journal of Counselling*, 28: 43–57.

Rennie, D.L. (1994d) 'Strategic choices in a qualitative approach to psychotherapy process research: a personal account' in L. Hoshmand and J. Martin (eds) *Method Choice and Inquiry Process: Lessons from Programmatic Research in Therapeutic Practice*. New York: Teachers' College Press.

Rennie, D.L. (1994e) 'Human science and counselling psychology: closing the gap between research and practice', *Counselling Psychology Quarterly*, 7: 235–50.

Rennie, D.L., Phillips, J.R. and Quartaro, J.K. (1988) 'Grounded theory: a promising approach for conceptualization in psychology?' *Canadian Psychology* 29: 139–50.

Riessman, C.K. (1993) *Narrative Analysis*. London: Sage.

Riessman, C.K. (1994) 'Making sense of marital violence: one woman's narrative' in C.K. Riessman (ed.) *Qualitative Studies in Social Work Research*. London: Sage.

Rosenwald, G.C. and Ochberg, R.L. (eds) (1992) *Storied Lives: the Cultural Politics of Self-understanding*. New Haven CT: Yale University Press.

Shotter, J. (1975) *Images of Man in Psychological Research*. London: Methuen.

Smith, J.A., Harré, R. and van Langenhove, L. (eds) (1995) *Rethinking Methods in Psychology*. London: Sage.

Steier, F. (ed.) (1991) *Research and Reflexivity*. London: Sage.

Stern, P.N. (1994) 'Eroding grounded theory' in J.N. Morse (ed.) *Critical Issues in Qualitative Research Methodology*. London: Sage.

Stewart, D.W. and Shamdasani, P.N. (1998) 'Focus group research: exploration and discovery' in J.L. Bickman and D.J. Rog (eds) *Handbook of Social Research Methods*. Thousand Oaks CA: Sage.

Stiles, W.B. (1993) 'Quality control in qualitative research', *Clinical Psychology Review*, 13: 593–618.

Strauss, A. and Corbin, J. (1998) *Basics of Qualitative Research: Techniques and Procedures for Developing Grounded Theory*, second edition. Thousand Oaks CA: Sage.

Taylor, C. (1979) 'Interpretation and the science of man' in P. Rabinow and W. Sullivan (eds) *Interpretive Social Science: a Reader*. Berkeley CA: University of California Press.

Valle, R.S. and Halling, S. (eds) (1989) *Existential-Phenomenological Perspectives in Psychology: Exploring the Breadth of Human Experience*. New York: Plenum.

Watkins, C.E., Jr and Schneider, L.J. (eds) (1991) *Research in Counseling*. Hillsdale NJ: Erlbaum.

Weitzman, E. (2000) 'Software and qualitative research' in N.K. Denzin and Y.S. Lincoln (eds) *Handbook of Qualitative Research*, second edition. Thousand Oaks CA: Sage.

Wetherell, M. and Potter, J. (1988) 'Discourse analysis and the identification of interpretive repertoires' in C. Antaki (ed.) *Analysing Everyday Explanation: a Casebook of Methods*. London: Sage.

Wolcott, H.F. (1990) *Writing up Qualitative Research*. London: Sage.

Yin, R.K. (1994) *Case Study Research: Design and Methods*, second edition. London: Sage.

4 Establishing Practice-based Evidence for Counselling Psychology
MICHAEL BARKHAM AND CHRIS BARKER

This chapter sets out the central concepts of evaluation research and shows how these provide the basis for developing an evidence base for counselling psychology that is rooted in everyday routine practice (i.e. practice-based evidence). We wish to emphasize the continuity between evaluation and other forms of research, and accordingly have drawn upon the previous two chapters in their accounts of research methods and substantive findings. Knowledge of a broad range of research methods is fundamental to the task of evaluation, and the acquisition of such knowledge is an essential aspect of counselling psychology training. We regard well conducted evaluation and research to be fundamental to the development of the profession of counselling psychology and concur with Barker et al.'s (1994) view that 'evaluation should be a routine part of applied psychology: much clinical and counselling work is based on custom and practice rather than any formal knowledge base, and evaluating it is a way of seeing whether or not it lives up to its claimed benefits' (pp. 196–7).

This chapter has seven parts. The first summarizes the key concepts and definitions used in evaluation research, and the second presents some preliminary issues which counselling psychologists need to consider before setting up an evaluation. The third part looks at the central issues of measurement, the fourth looks at design, and the fifth gives examples of evaluation studies. The sixth examines how to assess the significance of the findings and how to communicate them to others. The seventh and final part places all the preceding components within a developing paradigm of investigation, namely 'practice-based evidence'.

General concepts and definitions in evaluation research

'Evaluations are concerned with whether or not programs or policies are achieving their goals and purposes' (Berk and Rossi, 1990: 15). In this context a program can refer to something large, like the service provided by a national institution such as Relate (a British organization that provides low-cost couples counselling), medium-sized, such as a student counselling service at a university, or small, such as the work of an individual counselling psychologist. We assume that many readers of this chapter may be working on their own and are looking for ways to monitor their own work. We argue that the central principles of evaluation apply to all types of service, including one-person operations.

Evaluation research addresses issues that are contained within the current 'policy space': that is, it aims to address issues that particular policy makers (or 'stakeholders') consider to be important. A major factor in determining the nature of the evaluation is whether the impetus for it derives from the counselling psychologist(s) or from external stakeholders such as funding agencies or users' groups. An evaluation driven by a counselling psychologist's own desire to look at his or her work imposes little restriction. By contrast, an evaluation driven by external demands needs to attend to the requirements of the stakeholders.

Research is sometimes divided into pure research (often referred to as basic or scientific research) and applied research (or evaluation). Pure research is that which addresses fundamental psychological processes (e.g. the role of cognitive biases in explaining one's own behaviour) whereas applied research or evaluation addresses a particular service at a particular time (e.g. the effectiveness of a student counselling service based on cognitive-behavioural principles). However, it is usually better to think of the pure–applied distinction as a continuum rather than a dichotomy, with most examples of research falling somewhere in the middle. Since counselling psychology is an applied discipline, counselling research always has an element of the applied in it (see Barker et al., 1994).

Because it is applied and policy-oriented, there is a tendency to view evaluation as less rigorous than traditional scientific research. Indeed, several characteristics of evaluation research appear to create tensions between it and the scientific basis of research (Cowen, 1978). Service settings are often organizationally messy, politicized, chaotic and pressured – an environment that may be hard to reconcile with one's noble ideals of dispassionately evaluating one's own work. However, our view is that the fundamental principles of scientific research apply equally well to evaluation research, but that evaluation researchers must also be adept at the art of compromise and knowing how to do the best they can under adverse circumstances.

In evaluating counselling practice, three particular descriptions of activities are most commonly used: service audit, quality assurance, and evaluation. We describe features of each of these.

Service audit refers to an examination of some aspect of a service delivery system. Writers, for example Firth-Cozens (1993), have focused on a comparison with an agreed standard. Hence, an audit of a counselling service in a primary care setting may be based on a standard of 90 per cent of clients being seen within a month of referral. However, preliminary research may need to be carried out to determine what is a reasonable standard initially, although this research may not strictly be considered an audit. The standard ought to be based upon several criteria. For example, it ought to be a balance between psychological knowledge (i.e., presumably the sooner clients are seen the better, but is a four-week delay twice as bad as a two-week delay?), and pragmatism (i.e., it is unrealistic to expect all clients to be seen within two weeks).

Quality assurance refers to instituting procedures that help maintain a high standard of service. Cape (1991) outlines four types of procedure. One is clinical audit (see above) and another is consumer surveys (discussed below). The third procedure comprises guidelines and standards which refer to quality targets (e.g., 'All counselling sessions will occur in a quiet, comfortable and private location', 'After the first or second interview, counsellors will discuss with the client their formulation of the client's presenting problems and their opinion about which intervention would be most helpful'). The fourth method, peer review, refers to members of the service meeting regularly to examine the service that is delivered, such as when psychotherapists use peer-group supervision to monitor the quality of therapy. Peer review may be formalized by having explicit criteria for case selection. Examples include cases involving long-term counselling (e.g., all cases seen for more than twenty sessions), clients from a particular ethnic group, or all clients at risk of suicide.

Evaluation has been classified into two categories: 'formative' and 'summative' (Scriven, 1972). Formative evaluations feed back continuously to inform and modify the service as it develops and are particularly appropriate for enhancing the design and implementation of new services. In contrast, summative evaluations provide a definitive evaluation of an already existing service: they provide a comprehensive summary of how the service was functioning at the particular time the evaluation was done. Both audit and evaluation are retrospective in that the information they provide can then be fed back into the system and changes made accordingly. This feedback system becomes a 'quality cycle' or 'audit loop' (Firth-Cozens, 1993; Shaw, 1986). In contrast, quality assurance attempts to be prospective in setting up standards and procedures to ensure that no problems arise in the future operation of the system.

Having looked at some of the background concepts, we will now turn to the issues involved in putting evaluation into practice. Fortunately, there is a large evaluation literature to draw on (e.g., Cook and Campbell, 1979; Rossi and Freeman, 1993; Shadish et al., 1991; Weiss, 1972). We look first at preparatory issues in building evaluation into counselling psychology services, and then at some of the choices that need to be made about which research methods to employ.

Preliminary issues in evaluating a service

Much groundwork needs to be done before evaluation can be successfully conducted. Some of the tasks are socio-political, having to do with the dynamics of the organization in which the evaluation is being carried out, others are conceptual, having to do with thinking clearly about what the service is trying to do and what is the rationale behind its operations.

Socio-political issues

One major issue is the impact of evaluation on the organization or system being evaluated. Let us take a simple example at the level of the individual counselling psychologist. An increasingly important component in ensuring the delivery of good therapy is peer-group supervision (Cape, 1991; Cape and Barkham, 2002). One way to ensure that the supervision is based on what actually was said rather than the therapist's recall of what was said is to ensure that tape recordings are made of therapy sessions. For counsellors who are not used to taping their sessions, this can be a threatening experience, and there is a small literature on the kinds of things which psychologists have done to avoid taping their sessions (such as saying, 'My clients would be too uncomfortable with a tape recorder,' or forgetting to turn the machine on). The point is that the threat felt by many people at this individual level can become considerable when the evaluation is being made of a system or organization.

When evaluating a larger organization, counselling psychologists need to employ their skills of empathizing with and accepting people's fears, and disclosing their own intentions and needs (Barker et al., 2002). An example of a project in which this issue has been addressed is in the recent evaluation of Relate counselling, in which Shapiro and Barkham (1993) addressed head-on the range of 'hopes' and 'fears' that would likely be encountered by members of the organization. This was achieved by running sessions facilitated by an external consultant (i.e., one of the researchers) in which members of the organization were able to list both their 'hopes' and their 'fears' relating to the evaluation which was planned. Such a task enables issues arising from an evaluation procedure to be addressed more productively by focusing on them rather than on specific individuals.

Conceptual issues

Before the evaluation proper can be conducted, it is important to be clear about what the service is intending to do and how it is intending to go about it. This task can usefully be broken down into a series of steps. Rossi and Freeman (1993), whose text is a key reference on evaluation research methods, set out six stages: (1) formulating the service's aims and objectives, (2) specifying the impact model, (3) specifying the target population, (4) estimating the extent of the target problem in the target population, (5) assessing the need for the service and (6) specifying the delivery system design. We will address each of these stages in turn.

Aims and objectives

Aims can be defined as overall statements of the desired outcomes of the service. These are often stated in a relatively idealized manner. For example, the aims of a counselling service in a health centre might be as follows: 'To provide an efficient service that reduces the psychological distress of patients who are referred to it,' 'To reduce the number of inappropriate consultations with GPs for psychological problems,' and 'To raise the level of psychological well-being in the local community'. In order to address such aims, objectives need to be set which specify how the aims are going to be achieved. For example, one objective related to the second and third aims above might be to provide a monthly anxiety management workshop that is open to everyone in the local community. The objectives also specify how to assess that the aims of the service have been met. Thus a measurable objective might be to reduce the number of prescriptions for anti-depressants by 5 per cent in the first year that the counselling service is operating.

The impact model

The impact model is a way of specifying the rationale behind what the service is trying to do to meet its objectives. 'An impact model takes the form of a statement about the expected relationships between a program and its goal, setting forth the strategy for closing the gap between the objectives set during the planning process and the existing behavior or condition' (Rossi and Freeman, 1993: 120). The impact model comprises three types of hypotheses: a causal hypothesis, an intervention hypothesis and an action hypothesis. The *causal* hypothesis describes what causes or maintains the target problem which the service is seeking to address (e.g., the hypothesis is that patients use doctors inappropriately because they have no one else to tell their troubles to). The *intervention* hypothesis specifies how the proposed intervention will affect the causal determinant (e.g., that the counselling service will provide an alternative, more appropriate place for patients to discuss their psychological problems). Finally, the *action* hypothesis specifies that the intervention will reduce the target problem (e.g., that the existence of the counselling service will reduce the number of inappropriate GP consultations). The model, together with the above examples, is depicted in Figure 4.1. The purpose in specifying the impact model is to make the rationale for the service's actions as explicit as possible and to subject them to empirical test, although it is not always feasible, or desirable, to test all three components.

The target population

The target population is those people at whom the service is aimed. There are two types of targets: direct and indirect. *Direct* targets are the people for whom the intervention is designed. In effect, this becomes the unit of analysis for any statistical work carried out later. Often the unit of analysis will be 'the individual' (e.g., people attending a clinic). However, for marital work the unit of analysis may more appropriately be the couple, where the aim of the counselling is to see if the relationship between the two people can be sustained. Similarly, work focused on families may adopt 'the family' as the unit of analysis in the same way that group work may adopt 'the group' as the appropriate unit of analysis. Of course, given the interactive way in which people live, there will usually be effects experienced by others as a result of one person experiencing change. Consequently the *indirect* targets consist of those other people

Figure 4.1   The impact model

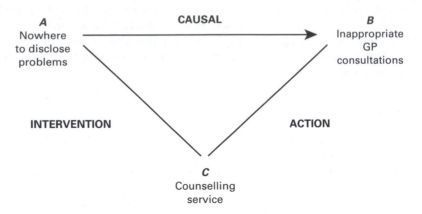

who will benefit from the service (e.g., the parents or siblings of adolescents who attend a counselling service).

The extent of the target problem

The next task is to estimate the extent of the problem in the target population. Three terms from epidemiology are useful. *Incidence* refers to the number of new cases occurring during a specified time period (e.g., one year). *Prevalence* is the number of existing cases either at a particular point in time (termed point prevalence) or during a specified time period, usually taken as twelve months or a lifetime. *Population at risk* refers to a subset of the general population who are at greater risk for the problem under evaluation (e.g., gay men are a population at risk of HIV infection). Rossi and Freeman (1993) identify some methods of estimating the extent of the target problem in the target population. First, surveys and censuses of the target population, which provide direct estimates of the size and severity of the problem. Second, rates under treatment in similar services elsewhere can be used to estimate the size of the problem, although often the number of people using a service is a small fraction of the people who are suffering from the problem that the service addresses. For example, the United Kingdom National Survey of Psychiatric Morbidity found that fewer than 14 per cent of people with a neurotic disorder were currently receiving any form of formal treatment (Bebbington et al., 2000). Finally, there is the method of key informants, in which influential members of the community are interviewed to gain their estimates of the size of the problems.

Assessing the need for the service

As suggested above, it is important not to assume that the extent of the target problem corresponds to the need for the service. Health planners (e.g., Stevens and Gabbay, 1991) make the useful distinction between need (as seen from a professional perspective), demand (what people ask for) and supply (what is available). For example, there is a need for reducing smoking among teenage girls (because of its adverse health risks), but there may not be a demand for counselling services designed to prevent girls smoking (because smoking may be perceived as glamorous or daring). So when designing a service, one must take account of demand and need, as well, of course, as supply, which depends on the available resources.

Delivery system design

Having gone through all these preliminary steps, you are in a good position both to design a service that is matched to the size, needs and demands of the target population and to evaluate the extent to which the service's aims and objectives are met. In the next section we look at the selection of research methods that can be used to carry out such an evaluation. Before we do, it is important to reiterate the point that in carrying out an evaluation of counselling practice the researcher is continually weighing up various options and trying to make decisions which are defensible but not necessarily ideal.

When planning any study, it is useful to distinguish between measurement and design (Barker et al., 2002). Measurement consists of specifying the concepts or variables that you will be studying (e.g., depression, well-being, safe sex) and how you will be measuring them (self-report or observation, qualitative or quantitative methods). Design consists of when you will be assessing them (e.g., at one moment in time or several, whether or not there is a control or comparison group, etc.). We will look first at measurement, then design.

Measurement

The measures used in an evaluation study should be derived from the aims and objectives of the programme. Well formulated aims and objectives will have direct implications about what to measure and in turn will determine the programme's success or failure. However, it is sometimes useful to have a classification scheme as a way to think about which aspects of a service to measure. One widely adopted taxonomy is Maxwell's (1984) list of six criteria for quality assessment: (1) access to services, (2) relevance to need, (3) effectiveness, (4) equity, (5) social acceptability and (6) efficiency/economy, which Parry (1992) uses in order to look at research evaluating psychotherapy services. Firth-Cozens (1993) expands these six quality areas and combines them with Donabedian's (1980) distinction between structure, process and outcome, which we will term *levels*. This combination creates a matrix (see Table 4.1) which identifies the differing tasks which need to be addressed within each quality area at each of the three levels. Although the language used in the table is medically oriented, it provides a useful basis for thinking about which variables to examine in evaluation.

Table 4.1   Matrix of levels and quality areas involved in developing an audit

	Structure	Process	Outcome
Equity and access	Availability of psychotherapy service. Day hospital relief for carers. Standards set for level of community staff. Condition in community homes	Minority languages catered for in terms of interpreters, bilingual professional. Waiting times for assessment, outpatients. Patient's Charter	Does 'Did not attend' (DNA) rate reduce when interpreters avilable?
Acceptability and responsiveness	Patient satisfaction with wards, community homes, access to senior staff. Are the services offered reflecting patient needs?	Patient and carer's satisfaction with communication, responsiveness to needs, frequency of appointments, etc.	Was outcome acceptable in terms of quality of life, satisfaction, family dynamics, etc?
Appropriateness	Do we still have appropriately trained staff for the patients we see? Survey of security arrangement of rooms used by psychiatrists to assess emergency referrals. Conditions of consulting rooms	Are our physical investigations appropriate? Are we giving CBT, psychotherapy, OT, play therapy, group therapy, etc., when appropriate? Are particular patient groups seeing appropriate levels and types of professional? Are patients receiving appropriate psychometric testing? OT and nursing assessment	Does drop-out reduce when appropriate assessments are conducted?
Communication	Are our notes maintained in an acceptable manner? Do we have easy access to information for patients? Are our confidentiality procedures adequate?	Do letters to GPs have sufficient information? Are our communications to each member of the team acceptable? Do we make it clear to patients' relatives the treatment options that are possible/available?	Is outcome communicated sufficiently well to patients/relatives, GPs and other community staff?

(Continued)

Table 4.1 *Continued*

	Structure	Process	Outcome
Continuity	Where continuity of care is not possible, are notes maintained to ensure similar care?	Do patients have continuity of care from one person where that is called for? Follow-up of patients referred from general hospital to addiction unit	Is there continuity in after-care? Respite care
Effectiveness	Are wards/hostels, etc. sufficiently clean?	Is alcohol/drug dependency 'absent' at each appointment? Are we maintaining patient compliance in drug therapy? Are community patients competent in necessary life skills? Is our proportion of bedsores meeting national standards?	Are our outcomes in short-term therapy as good as they should be? What are our long-term outcomes for substance abuse, truancy, carers' health, marital discord, sexual abuse, independence, etc? Is our relapse/readmission rate meeting our standards?
Efficiency	Procedure for reducing non-attendance is being followed	Are tests, procedures, seclusions, drugs, therapies given only when indicated? Time spent travelling	Is the length of therapy no longer than is necessary according to research?

Reprinted from J. Firth-Cozens, *Audit in Mental Health Services* (1993), by kind permission of Lawrence Erlbaum Associates Ltd., Hove.

In terms of Donabedian's (1980) three levels, structure is the measure of the physical resources available to the service: the physical environment and facilities, and the location of the service. Although less interesting psychologically, structural issues are important to clients, who often stress the importance of being seen in a pleasant and easily accessible setting. Their views about structural (and all other) aspects of a service can usefully be assessed via client satisfaction surveys. However, client satisfaction surveys tend to produce positive results: often around 80 per cent of clients say that they were satisfied with the service they received (Lebow, 1983). So it is usually better to also probe directly about client dissatisfaction and elicit suggestions for improvements in the service.

Measures of process concern how the service is being delivered. One set of measures assesses which clients come to the service: whether they are representative of the intended target population. The important issue here is the extent of potential bias (Rossi and Freeman, 1993), that is, the tendency of a service to address a small, unrepresentative and usually more privileged subsection of the population, such as Schofield's (1964) well known acronym of the YAVIS psychotherapy client: Young, Attractive, Verbal, Intelligent and Successful. Another important source of bias is along ethnic lines. Members of minority ethnic groups are often poorly served by established psychological services. It is obviously important to monitor service delivery to see that such biases do not occur and correct them if they do.

The other set of process measures concerns what service is being delivered. How many sessions do clients typically come for? If a structured service is being given, such as in HIV pre-test counselling, to what extent do counsellors adhere to the protocol for that service? Otherwise, what happens in counselling sessions? Post-session reports or tape recordings of sessions are useful ways to address this.

Measures of outcome

Donabedian's third level of evaluation – outcome – raises the crucial question: do clients benefit from the service? There is an enormous literature on psychotherapy outcome research to draw upon here (see Chapters 2 and 3) and a bewildering array of possible measures. We have compiled a list of seven criteria which provide a benchmark against which to evaluate any outcome measure.

- It should be easy to use (i.e., not require specialist professional skills).
- It should be relatively short. Many measures are developed in research settings where participants may be more tolerant of completing long questionnaires than in standard service settings. In addition, an evaluator may want to tap a wide range of variables, hence requiring more than one measure.
- The measure should be clinically sensitive in that it will detect change when it has occurred.
- It should be psychometrically sound in terms of standard parameters (e.g., test–retest reliability, internal consistency, construct validity, etc.).
- There should exist normative data on the measure. Ideally, there should be norms for differing populations (e.g., client and non-client populations) as well as for differing cultural groups if that is appropriate. These should be contained in manuals which provide standard guidance on the implementation of a measure. Without this, considerable discrepancy can be introduced unwittingly. An aspiration is that there should be appropriate versions of the measure for ethnic minorities.
- The measure should be atheoretical. At first, this may appear inconsistent with psychologists' constant search for theory. However, if the measure is based on a specific theory, it becomes a test of that one theory rather than being a more generic measure of change derived from an empirical base.
- The measure should be cheap or, more preferably, in the public domain.

One central issue relating to evaluation measures is that it is probably easier to show change arising from a reduction in symptomatology than a rise in personal well-being. This reflects the fact that reductions in symptomatology may be tapping effect sizes which are medium or large. In contrast, raising levels of personal well-being in people already functioning within a 'normal' range will be tapping a small effect size and will be appreciably harder to detect reliably.

A critical problem in evaluation is not only the diversity of measures but also the large number of one-off measures. For example, Froyd et al. (1996) reviewed 348 outcome studies in twenty selected journals from 1983 to 1988 and identified 1,430 outcome measures, of which 840 were used just once. This makes comparisons with other studies very difficult and fails to contribute to the overriding need for comparative (i.e., normative) data. It is usually better not to rely solely upon one outcome measure. Although adopting more than one outcome measure will increase the burden of evaluation on both the participants and the investigator, if only one measure is used, then outcome and the constraints of that single measure are inextricably bound together and partly reflect its over-specificity and unreliability. In addition, data from another measure can be viewed as concurrent replication.

A further issue arises from what has been referred to as the 'bandwidth-fidelity' dilemma. While researchers are keen to use measures with proven psychometric qualities (i.e., high fidelity) which often entails their focusing on narrowly defined constructs, practitioners wish to tap a broad range of issues (i.e., broad bandwidth): for example, general functioning, levels of subjective distress, quality of life, interpersonal issues, etc. Hence practitioners wish to tap 'bandwidth' and accordingly require 'good enough' measures rather than pure (fidelity) measures which researchers might adopt. This is a pervasive issue in evaluation research and in counselling psychology and psychotherapy research in general.

One measure that goes a considerable way towards meeting the criteria listed above is the Clinical Outcomes in Routine Evaluation – Outcome Measure (CORE-OM). The CORE-OM was designed for simple, face and construct-valid measurement of a core set of phenomena and followed a programme of development (Barkham et al., 1998; Evans et al., 2000), validation (Evans et al., 2002) and utility (Barkham et al., 2001). The CORE-OM comprises thirty four items chosen to cover four domains: problems, social functioning, well-being and risk. It is sensitive to change and has UK appropriate norms (both clinical and non-clinical). It is pan-theoretical and is free to users (but copyright). It has also been incorporated into part of the 2000 Psychiatric Morbidity Follow-up study which will provide more exacting UK norms. The CORE-OM provides meaningful baseline, outcome and change parameters for a broad span of counselling and the psychological therapies, for a broad spread of problems in a broad spread of settings, including primary and secondary care. The CORE-OM comprises one part of the larger CORE system which has been developed (Mellor-Clark et al., 1999). With a measure such as the CORE-OM available, this should lessen the barriers that impede counselling psychologists using an outcome measure as part of routine practice (see Figure 4.2).

Figure 4.2 CORE system: sample portions of therapy assessment and CORE-OM forms

CLINICAL OUTCOMES in ROUTINE EVALUATION
THERAPY ASSESSMENT FORM vi

Site ID ☐☐☐☐ Age ☐☐
Client ID (letters / numbers) Male ☐ Female ☐
Sub Codes (Therapist ID / OC2 numbers / SC2 numbers) Employment ☐ ☐
Referrer(s) Ethnic Origin ☐ ☐

Referral date D D / M M / Y Y Y Y — Total number of assessments ☐
First assessment date attended D D / M M / Y Y Y Y — Previously seen for therapy in this service? Yes ☐ No ☐ Episode ☐
Last assessment date D D / M M / Y Y Y Y — Months since last episode ☐☐☐ — Is this a follow up/review appointment Yes ☐ No ☐

Relationship/support please tick as many boxes as appropriate

Living alone (age including)	☐	Full time carer (of etc)	☐
Living with partner	☐	Living in shared accommodation (eg lodgings)	☐
caring for children under 5 years	☐	Living in temporary accommodation (eg hostel)	☐
caring for children over 5 years	☐	Living in institution/hospital	☐
Living with parents/guardian	☐	Other ☐	
Living with other relatives/friends	☐		

Current/previous use of services for psychological problems? please tick as many boxes as appropriate (current / < 1 year / > 1)

Primary	GP or other member of primary care team (eg practice nurse,counsellor)	☐	☐	☐
Secondary	In primary care setting	☐	☐	☐
	In community setting	☐	☐	☐
	In hospital setting on sessional basis	☐	☐	☐
	Day care services (eg day hospital)	☐	☐	☐
	Hospital admission < = 10 days	☐	☐	☐
	Hospital admission > = 11 days	☐	☐	☐
Specialist	Psychotherapy/psychological treatments from specialist team?	☐	☐	☐
	Attendance at day therapeutic programme	☐	☐	☐
	Inpatient treatment	☐	☐	☐
Other	Counsellor in eg voluntary, religious, work, educational setting	☐	☐	☐

Is the client currently prescribed medication to help with their psychological problem(s)? Yes ☐ No ☐
If yes, please indicate type of medication:
Anti-psychotics ☐ Anti-depressants ☐ Anidolytics Hypnotics ☐ Other ☐
Full time carer (section wrong)

CLINICAL OUTCOMES in ROUTINE EVALUATION
END OF THERAPY FORM v.2

Site ID ☐☐☐☐ — Number of sessions planned ☐☐☐
Client ID (letters / numbers)
Sub Codes (Therapist ID / SC4 numbers / SC5 numbers) — Number of sessions attended ☐☐☐
Date therapy commenced D D / M M / Y Y Y Y
Date therapy completed D D / M M / Y Y Y Y — Number of sessions unattended ☐☐☐

What type of therapy was undertaken with the client? *Please tick as many boxes as appropriate*

Psychodynamic	☐	Person-centred	☐
Psychoanalytic	☐	Integrative	☐
Cognitive	☐	Systemic	☐
Behavioural	☐	Supportive	☐
Cognitive/Behavioural	☐	Art	☐
Structured/Brief	☐	Other (*specify below*)	☐

What modality of therapy was undertaken with the client? *Please tick as many boxes as appropriate*

Individual	☐	Family	☐
Group	☐	Marital/Couple	☐

What was the frequency of therapy with the client?

More than once weekly	☐	Less than once weekly	☐
Weekly	☐	Not at a fixed frequency	☐

Which of the following best describes the ending of therapy?

Unplanned ☐		**Planned** ☐	
Due to crisis	☐	Planned from outset	☐
Due to loss of contact	☐	Agreed during therapy	☐
Client did not wish to continue	☐	Agreed at end of therapy	☐
Other unplanned ending (*specify below*)	☐	Other planned ending (*specify below*)	☐

CLINICAL OUTCOMES in ROUTINE EVALUATION
OUTCOME MEASURE

Site ID (letters only / numbers only) — Age — Male ☐ Female ☐
Client ID (Therapist ID numbers only (1) numbers only (2))
Sub Codes
Date form given D D / M M / Y Y Y Y
Stage Completed: S Screening, R Referral, A Assessment, F First Therapy Session, P Pre-therapy (unspecified), D During Therapy, L Last therapy session, X Follow up 1, Y Follow up 2 — Stage ☐ Episode ☐

IMPORTANT – PLEASE READ THIS FIRST
This form has 34 statements about how you have been OVER THE LAST WEEK.
Please read each statement and think how often you felt that way last week.
Then tick the box which is closest to this.
Please use a dark pen (not pencil) and tick clearly within the boxes.

Over the last week	Not at all	Only Occasionally	Sometimes	Often	Most or all the time	OFFICE USE ONLY
1 I have felt terribly alone and isolated	☐0	☐1	☐2	☐3	☐4	F
2 I have felt tense, anxious or nervous	☐0	☐1	☐2	☐3	☐4	P
3 I have felt I have someone to turn for support when needed	☐4	☐3	☐2	☐1	☐0	F
4 I have felt O.K. about myself	☐4	☐3	☐2	☐1	☐0	W
5 I have felt totally lacking in energy and enthusiasm	☐0	☐1	☐2	☐3	☐4	P
6 I have been physically violent to others	☐0	☐1	☐2	☐3	☐4	R
7 I have felt able to cope when things go wrong	☐4	☐3	☐2	☐1	☐0	F
8 I have been troubled by aches, pains or other physcial problems	☐0	☐1	☐2	☐3	☐4	P
9 I have thought of hurting myself	☐0	☐1	☐2	☐3	☐4	R
10 Talking to people has felt too much for me	☐0	☐1	☐2	☐3	☐4	F
11 Tension and anxiety have prevented me doing important things	☐0	☐1	☐2	☐3	☐4	P
12 I have been happy with the things I have done	☐4	☐3	☐2	☐1	☐0	F
13 I have been disturbed by unwanted thoughts and feelings	☐0	☐1	☐2	☐3	☐4	P
14 I have felt like crying	☐0	☐1	☐2	☐3	☐4	W

Please turn over

Source: Printed by kind permission of the CORE System Trustees

While practitioners need to take into account all the above considerations when deciding on the selection of measures, they also need a guiding strategy through the selection of measures. We identify three areas of measurement: outcome, process and change processes. In providing some initial guidance within each of these three areas, we acknowledge that the actual area which has priority for the practitioner will vary and depend very much on what question is being asked. At the level of outcome, practitioners may select a global standardized measure, for example the CORE-OM (Barkham et al., 2001; Evans et al., 2002) or a standardized measure targeting a specific presenting problem, for example the Beck Depression Inventory for depression (BDI; Beck et al., 1988). They might then add an individualized measure which is idiographic (i.e., has items identified by the client) rather than nomothetic (i.e., where the items are invariant across clients). Examples include variants of the Personal Questionnaire (Mulhall, 1976; Phillips, 1986). At the level of process, practitioners need to decide between asking clients to complete session-based measures of aspects of the process or obtaining audio tapings of the sessions and having these rated at some future date. Of course, both can be done but practitioners may not wish to overload themselves with material. Examples of session-based measures include those tapping the therapeutic alliance (e.g., the Working Alliance Inventory; Horvath and Greenberg, 1994) or impressions of the session itself (e.g. the Session Evaluation Questionnaire and Session Impacts Scale; Stiles et al., 1994). At the level of change processes, practitioners can utilize a combination of the other two levels in order to set the context and then employ a strategy of interviewing the client or carrying out detailed analysis on the audio recordings. In particular, there is considerable merit in focusing on significant events within sessions, as these are likely to be a cost-effective means of advancing practitioners' understandings about what specifically leads to change.

Effectiveness and efficiency

The final two quality areas in Table 4.1 denote effectiveness and efficiency. There has been a move towards assessing not just outcome, which looks at absolute change, but effectiveness, which looks at relative change. (Note, however, that the term 'effectiveness' has come into use in another sense: the phrase 'effectiveness research' is used to denote evaluations of actual working services, as opposed to 'efficacy research', which is conducted under controlled conditions in a research setting.) Berk and Rossi (1990) make the point that effectiveness must always address the issue 'Compared with what?' They identify three forms of effectiveness: (1) marginal effectiveness, where the issue is one of dosage, where the evaluator is making a judgement concerning more or less of some intervention; (2) relative effectiveness, where the comparison is between an active treatment versus no treatment, or between two or more active treatments; (3) cost-effectiveness, where comparisons are made in terms of units of outcome per unit of expenditure (e.g., pound or dollar).

A further task may be required, namely to evaluate efficiency. Efficiency can be construed as effectiveness but expressed in terms of financial or other resources. There is a potential tension here between practitioners devising models of intervention which are effective and managers addressing the question of efficiency. For example, a particular intervention may be shown to be clinically effective but at such a large financial cost that it raises questions about its efficiency. Clearly, it is a matter of balancing these two criteria.

Design

Design refers to when and how the measures are collected: design issues can usefully be thought of independently of measurement issues. (The term *design* is sometimes used in a broader sense to encompass measurement as well. However, we will adhere to the more precise usage.) Design is an enormous topic, that we can touch on only briefly here; more extended treatments are given in texts on research methods (e.g., Barker et al., 2002; Cook and Campbell, 1979; Kazdin, 1994; Parry and Watts, 1996; Rossi and Freeman, 1993). There is no one best design for all purposes; the type of design is determined by the aims of the evaluation. We will look at three key design issues here: (1) whether one or more groups are studied (e.g., whether a control or comparison group is used), (2) whether a single case or a larger sample size is used, and (3) whether several assessment points are used over time.

Control or comparison groups

Psychologists are often socialized into believing that they must have a control or comparison group in order to be doing good research. Of course, control and comparison groups are vital for addressing certain research questions, mainly those which address the explanation of change processes or questions of relative effectiveness. However, evaluations are frequently not concerned with explanations, but simply seek to establish that a service is beneficial: why it is beneficial, or whether it is more beneficial than other services, can be left to subsequent inquiry. Thus it is often sufficient to adopt a one-group design in which a single group of clients, perhaps receiving a specific form of counselling for a specific presenting problem, are studied. (Note that the word 'group' here is a technical design term: we are not implying that group rather than individual work is being evaluated.) For example, forty clients who come to a University Counselling Centre for help with relationship difficulties may be assessed before and after brief psychodynamically oriented counselling.

Single-case designs

The extreme example of a one-group design is an *n* of 1, or single-case design, which looks at the work of a single counselling psychologist with a single client. They are congenial designs for practitioners who wish to evaluate the effectiveness of their own counselling. One or more measures can be administered to clients at frequent intervals. For example, a client's anxiety may be assessed weekly, or a married couple may record the quality of their interactions every day. In this way the counsellor can look closely at improvement as it occurs over time. The type of improvement is usually obvious from a simple graphical inspection of the data, but statistical methods can also be used. A good example of a single case study is Parry et al.'s (1986) case of the 'anxious executive'. It used the Personal Questionnaire method (Mulhall, 1976; Phillips, 1986) in which the client selected items to capture his problems and rated them throughout the course of therapy. The ratings were supplemented by data on the therapist's views of themes and the client's views of helpful and unhelpful events within the sessions. The data set thus provided frequent measures across therapy on the processes of change for a range of issues salient to the client.

One advantage of this form of evaluation is that it can be readily extended to other clients, and thereby become what is known as a clinical replication series (Hayes et al., 1999). Such a procedure enables practitioners to become informed about possible important variables. For example, suppose a practitioner carries out a simple evaluation in which the first series of clients can be described as 'young' (e.g., under thirty five years old) and these cases are deemed successful. The practitioner then evaluates a series of clients who might be described as 'older' (e.g., over fifty) and these cases are not so successful. The practitioner then sees another series of younger clients for whom the outcome is successful. Such data may begin to inform the practitioner about the clients with whom she is more successful. Clearly, she must consider other variables which might covary with age (e.g., occupational status or social support network). However, it provides practitioners with a means of evaluating their practice by testing competing hypotheses. In this design it is the approach which is dominant. That is to say, the practitioner may employ any given instrument or instruments; the power of the design lies in the replication with a series of clients.

Number of assessment points

In group designs and single case designs alike the number of assessment points over time is determined by the aims and objectives of the evaluations. In some cases (e.g., evaluating clients' satisfaction with the service) a single time point may suffice. In others, usually concerned with evaluating outcome, several measurement points are valuable. While there is much interest in the interactive nature of process and outcome in psychotherapy and counselling psychology (e.g., Greenberg, 1986), it is hard to argue against the inclusion of a pre–post evaluation of a psychological intervention. Here the question being asked is 'At the end of an intervention, has something changed as compared with before the start of the intervention?' The change which is being monitored could be, for example, a fall in the client's level of distress or a rise in the client's sense of personal well-being or quality of life.

Assessing clients prior to an intervention is essential in order to describe the severity of their presenting problems. In evaluating the intervention, it then becomes essential to determine their well-being and psychological functioning after the intervention. This is the logic which leads to pre-post assessments, which are necessary but not sufficient for evaluating change. The critical point is the nature and psychological process of change. Data at two points in time may tell us that initially a client's score was high (i.e., reflecting poor psychological functioning) and then improved after the intervention. If we are interested only in end-point analyses, then this might be sufficient. However, there are a range of problems. First, many psychological experiences run in cycles, hence the post-assessment may well reflect improvement, but this ignores the naturally occurring increase a few months later. Second, two data points give only two shots at tapping any psychological process, and this is not particularly stable. More data points provide more stable data; post-counselling change needs to be followed up. And, third, only a straight line can be drawn between two data points, and it seems unlikely that a straight line reflects the only change process. Thus, in addition to collecting intake data, we suggest measurement points half-way through counselling (provided there is an estimate of the total course of the intervention), at the end of the counselling and at a three-month or six-month follow-up if possible.

A different or complementary strategy to collecting 'batched' data as above is to administer an instrument at every session – that is, collect data continually across the course of counselling. Although this may at first seem a huge task, several points are worth noting. First, batched data tend to be biased towards the clients who remain in counselling. Data are rarely available (other than at intake) on clients who terminate counselling unilaterally. This raises the issue of trying to determine the outcomes of clients who do not complete counselling. However, if data were available on *all* clients at *all* sessions, practitioners and managers would be able to assess the benefits gained from people terminating counselling prior to completing either a mid- or end-of-counselling assessment. Second, such data from all clients enable practitioners and researchers to have a far better understanding of the natural ebb and flow of change across the course of counselling. Third, the data can be used to 'track' clients' progress as a way of helping to identify interventions that may not be best matched to clients' needs. Although the administrative load of implementing continual measurement is high, in many respects it is easier to administer a measure at every session than trying to remember the exact point where a measure needs to be completed. In other words, it becomes the norm rather than the exception. The requirements for an evaluation system such as this have been well documented (e.g., Wiger and Solberg, 2001).

In the context of the above, it is now appropriate to consider some sample evaluation studies.

Evaluation studies

At the beginning of this chapter we stated that evaluation could be carried out on large and medium-size organizations as well as at the level of the individual counselling psychologist. This section summarizes examples of evaluation studies. The first is a study of part of a large national organization (i.e., Relate). The remaining studies are of medium-size organizations (e.g., a university counselling service, clinical psychology services) which include more direct examples of audit. Published examples of studies carried out at the individual level are rare.

National organization

Shapiro and Barkham (1993) present a report of an evaluation of one region within the Relate organization (which, as we said above, is a charitable organization operating throughout the United Kingdom to provide cheap and accessible counselling for individuals and couples about relationship problems). Clients completed the twelve-item version of the General Health Questionnaire (GHQ-12; Goldberg and Williams, 1988) and questionnaires about their relationship with their partner (as improving this is a natural aim of counselling). The pre-counselling data set was drawn from 352 clients and suggested that a very high percentage (83 per cent) met a definition of 'caseness' on the GHQ. Similarly, the measure of relationship difficulties indicated that 51 per cent of clients reported 'severe' or 'very severe' difficulties. A subsample of 101 clients who completed pre- and post-counselling questionnaires were analysed further. The GHQ-12 revealed a substantial pre–post effect size for a change of one standard deviation, which was probably an underestimate due to the large number of clients obtaining maximum scores pre-counselling and minimum scores post-counselling. However, given that the GHQ was designed as a health status measure, there are concerns about it being used to determine change (Firth-Cozens, 1993). Change on the relationship measure was less, with the pre–post effect size of 0.54 standard deviation units (compared with an expected change of 0.85 standard deviation units). Hence, clients showed substantial benefits in their general well-being, but this did not have an equivalent effect on their relationships. The study found high satisfaction rates, with over 80 per cent of clients having 'most' or 'almost all' of their needs met, and 97 per cent of clients were 'mostly' or 'very' satisfied.

Medium-sized organizations

Mathers et al. (1993) present an evaluation of short-term counselling in a university setting. The period of evaluation was fourteen months, during which ten counsellors saw a total of 401 clients. Of this total, 142 were attending for their initial appointment and were the focus of the study. The scores of 45 clients were compared pre- and post-counselling, using the GHQ-12 and showed a significant reduction from pre- to post-counselling (mean pre-, 23.1; mean post-, 13.8). Skaife and Spall (1995) report on an evaluation of a clinical psychotherapy service and place importance on the independence of the person carrying out the evaluation (in this case an audit). They sampled

44 discharged clients who were selected randomly and mailed a questionnaire. Responses were returned by 20 clients. Information was obtained in the areas of clients' introduction to the department, the process of therapy, outcome, and suggestions for improvements in the service. What is of note in this report is that the authors presented an 'action' plan based on the results and organized under Donabedian's (1980) three levels: 'structure', 'process' and 'outcome'. In terms of structure, consideration was given to moving the psychology department to the district hospital. At the level of process, a leaflet focusing on details of the service clients would receive was prepared and sent to clients. At the level of outcome, it was decided that the most sensible use would be as a baseline against which to compare subsequent data.

A study of therapist and client evaluations within the psychology department of a large Scottish psychiatric hospital was carried out by Neilson (1994). The sample comprised seven clinical psychologists and 36 clients. Interestingly, measures of process and outcome were used, being completed by therapists and clients. Results suggested that therapists were less positive in their evaluation of therapy than clients, a finding repeatedly observed in outcome studies. In general, therapists may have been more guarded than clients in their evaluations because they held a more long-term model of the impact of change. However, such a finding might also be influenced by how outcome was evaluated in this study. Rather than basing the evaluation on clients' and therapists' ratings of current 'state', questions were asked about the amount of improvement achieved and whether therapy had been successful or not. This procedure 'collapses' the evaluation of change into a single judgement rather than it being determined by calculating the difference between clients' degree of distress at pre-therapy and then at any point subsequently. Where no pre-therapy data are available, this is the only option. However, as stated earlier, it is less satisfactory than building-in evaluation from the beginning of a client's contact with the service and then administering subsequent measures in order to obtain data on whether clients have improved or not. The study also found that all clients were satisfied with the service provided. This finding, whilst initially gratifying to those in the service, supports our point made earlier that more information may be obtained by asking clients about their dissatisfactions with the service.

Individual-level studies

As noted above, there are fewer examples in the literature of studies conducted at the individual level, possibly because such studies may be carried out but not published. One recent example is Elliott's (2002) presentation of the 'hermeneutic single-case efficacy design'. This method provides a systematic way of looking at the process and outcome of change within an individual client, and evaluating competing causal explanations for any change that there might be.

Weighing up and communicating the findings

Having collected the data, how can you determine that meaningful change has occurred? Let us consider three broad approaches to how 'change' can be determined: criterion, statistical and clinical.

Determining change

Criterion change

A criterion approach makes comparisons with categorical levels of a particular behaviour. Hence, if a target is set, say of all clients being offered an initial appointment within three weeks of seeking help, when that target has been achieved the criterion can be said to have been met. At the level of the individual client, suppose a client presents with a social phobia. Then a criterion approach would be that the counselling is considered successful if the client's behaviour at the end of counselling meets certain criteria agreed upon at the beginning of counselling; for example, she is able to feel relaxed at social gatherings, is able to initiate social relationships, and so on.

Statistical change

Traditionally, researchers have tended to adopt the statistical change approach, which aims to establish whether the observed change could reasonably have been expected to occur by chance. The level of 0.05 has become established as the norm: if there is less than a one in 20 chance of the change happening by chance, it is deemed statistically significant. However, many issues are raised by this approach, the most important of which can be highlighted by the following example. Suppose 25 people who weigh between 125 kg and 165 kg take part in a programme to reduce weight because they are deemed to be at a heightened risk of a heart attack. Suppose they all lose 5 kg by the end of the programme. This pre–post change will be significant, but, with their weights now being 120 kg to 160 kg respectively, it is unlikely that they are at any appreciably less risk of a heart attack. The same principle applies to scores reflecting psychological well-being, in that a group of clients' scores on a measure may show a statistically significant reduction and yet their psychological state may still be very distressed.

Reliable and clinically significant change

Recent approaches have tended to look not just at statistical significance but also at reliable and clinical significance (Evans et al., 1998; Jacobson and Truax, 1991). Reliable and clinically significant change comprises two components, which can be phrased as separate questions. First, is the change which has occurred 'reliable'? This question can usually be operationalized as 'Is the client's movement from when they were previously tested greater than the measurement error of the instrument?' Consider the difference between measuring someone's weight and their psychological well-being. While there will be variability in a person's weight and psychological well-being at two points in time, it is likely that there will be considerably more measurement error in psychological well-being than weight. That is, the instruments for determining weight are relatively precise, compared with asking a client to complete a self-report measure on well-being. In order to take account of the fact that some change measures are more reliable than others, Jacobson and Truax (1991) propose the use of a reliable change index, which, broadly speaking, requires demonstrated change on a measure to be greater than the error arising from its unreliability of measurement.

The second component can be phrased in the form 'Where has the client moved to on the measure of interest?' This question focuses on the stage or level to which the client has moved rather than the actual amount of change. Questions of clinical significance ask about the meaning of a client's state at the end of counselling. Do their scores on various measures represent a return to functioning within the normal range, or at least a move out of the range of a dysfunctional group? The various criteria by which these notions might be encapsulated are summarized by Jacobson et al. (1999). Generally, they focus on whether a practitioner wishes to identify as 'improved' a client whose score moves out of the dysfunctional range (i.e., the client no longer belongs to the dysfunctional population but equally cannot necessarily be said to belong to the normal population) or whether a client's score has to enter the normal range (i.e., the client is likely to be a member of the normal population). A final criterion enables the practitioner to state whether a client is likely be a member of one population rather than another. Which of these criteria one adopts in any given application depends on the objectives of the intervention.

Presenting data to stakeholders

In presenting data to a stakeholder, it is important to consider its impact: data presented to one party may not be appropriate to present to another party. There is a considerable variety of ways of presenting data to stakeholders (e.g., see Barkham, 1992). Let us consider the issue of presenting data concerning client follow-up. A manager will be interested in the number of clients who can be identified as likely not to need further services. One method which might be seen as the most stringent would be to set a criterion on a primary outcome measure which was equivalent to clients being asymptomatic. Using a definition based either on a specific criterion or on reliable and clinically significant change, it is possible to determine the percentage of clients who meet such criteria. This approach carries with it the advantage of 'specificity': a specified percentage of clients are being stated as improved. However, serious consideration needs to be given to espousing a criterion which may be unrealistic. Identifying criteria which are met and which indicate a real improvement in the quality of clients' lives may be as, if not more, appropriate. For example, in evaluating people who have developed a fear of leaving the house, it might be reasonable to apply the criterion 'Is able to leave the house alone.' This presents a real improvement. However, we also know that such improvement can also carry with it other difficulties in terms of changes to family dynamics. Hence, utilizing more comprehensive criteria which incorporate the family dynamics may show a relatively mixed outcome: a deterioration in the familial context but significant gains for the individual client in respect of their social skills.

Towards a practice-based evidence paradigm

The components presented in this chapter comprise the basic procedures for designing and implementing effectiveness research in routine practice. However, as indicated earlier, the prevailing paradigm is that of evidence-based practice. The evidence-based practice places a premium on randomized controlled trials which are used by policy makers to guide and inform routine practice. Essentially this is a 'top down' model of the relationship between research and practice. Informative though it is, there are those who have been critical of it being the sole basis for guiding practice and who have offered a complementary paradigm – namely that of 'practice-based evidence' (Barkham and Mellor-Clark, 2000; Margison et al., 2001). The argument is that practice-based evidence is the natural complement to the current focus on evidence-based practice because it presumes a 'bottom up' model in which practitioners collect standardized data derived from routine practice. The combination of information obtained from both evidence-based practice and practice-based evidence paradigms then provides a much richer and more informed knowledge base for determining what interventions under what situations delivered by what professionals are most effective. The twin tracks of evidence-based practice and practice-based evidence are shown in Figure 4.3. As can be seen, they are not merely parallel processes but rather complementary activities that inform and feed into each other.

Practice-based evidence incorporates a broad range of activities. Hence, it utilizes the concept of practice research networks (PRNs) as integral to the *structure* (or rather infrastructure) required to deliver practice-based evidence. Practice research networks are, in effect, networks of practices collecting common data and supported by a research centre (see Audin et al., 2001). An immediate impact of the PRN is to reduce the isolation of the individual counsellor and also to provide the basis for multiple counsellors delivering sizeable data sets. The practice-based evidence paradigm also takes a rigorous position on quality evaluation as central to the *process* of delivering practice-based evidence. The point here is that, like any research enterprise, the activity can be designed and implemented along a quality continuum from 'good' to 'poor'. The majority of the components addressed in this chapter speak to the issue of 'quality evaluation' via issues of design and methodology. And, in terms of

Figure 4.3   The efficacy-effectiveness model

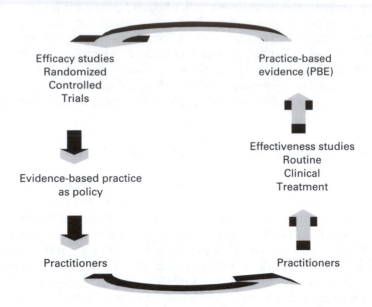

outcomes, practice-based evidence incorporates the principles and practice of clinically significant change methodology to complement other data utilization methods. Through this procedure, analyses emphasize both the individual and the sample as a whole. Overall, these are subtle changes that give rise to a more pluralistic and inclusive approach to the collection of evidence.

Conclusion

We conclude that evaluation is central to the process of quality control in any service delivery system. However, the scope of the evaluation very much depends on the resources available and the interested stakeholders. The former can be increased by bidding to appropriate funding agencies and stakeholders for support money. In this chapter we have provided a picture of the wide range of methods available to interested practitioners and how these can be honed into yielding a practice-based evidence for counselling psychology. Certainly it is our view that there is sufficient range of methods available to match the resources, interests and values of most counselling psychology practitioners.

References

Audin, K., Mellor-Clark, J., Barkham, M., Margison, F., McGrath, G., Lewis, S., Cann, L., Duffy, J. and Parry, G. (2001) 'Practice Research Networks for effective psychological therapies', *Journal of Mental Health*, 10: 241–51.

Barker, C., Pistrang, N. and Elliott, R. (1994) *Research Methods in Clinical and Counselling Psychology*. Chichester: Wiley.

Barker, C., Pistrang, N. and Elliott, R. (2002) *Research Methods in Clinical Psychology: An Introduction for Students and Practitioners, second edition*. Chichester: Wiley.

Barkham, M. (1992) 'Understanding, implementing and presenting counselling evaluation' in R. Bayne and P. Nicolson (eds) *Counselling and Psychology for Health Professionals*. London: Chapman & Hall.

Barkham, M. and Mellor-Clark, J. (2000) 'Rigour and relevance: practice-based evidence in the psychological therapies' in N. Rowland and S. Goss (eds) *Evidence-based Counselling and Psychological Therapies: Research and Applications*. London: Routledge.

Barkham, M., Evans, C., Margison, F., McGrath, G., Mellor-Clark, J., Milne, D. and Connell, J. (1998) 'The rationale for developing and implementing core batteries in service settings and psychotherapy outcome research', *Journal of Mental Health*, 7: 35–47.

Barkham, M., Margison, F., Leach, C., Lucock, M., Mellor-Clark, J., Evans, C., Benson, L., Connell, J., Audin, K. and McGrath, G. (2001) 'Service profiling and outcomes benchmarking using the CORE-OM: towards practice-based evidence in the psychological therapies', *Journal of Consulting and Clinical Psychology*, 69: 184–96.

Bebbington, P.E., Meltzer, H., Brugha, T., Farrell, M., Jenkins, R., Ceresa, C. and Lewis, G. (2000) 'Unequal access and unmet need: neurotic disorders and the use of primary care services', *Psychological Medicine*, 30: 1359–67.

Beck, A.T., Steer, R.A. and Garbin, M.G. (1988) 'Psychometric properties of the Beck Depression Inventory: twenty-five years of evaluation', *Clinical Psychology Review*, 8: 77–100.

Berk, R.A. and Rossi, P.H. (1990) *Thinking about Program Evaluation*. Newbury Park CA: Sage.

Cape, J. (1991) 'Quality assurance methods for clinical psychology services', *Psychologist*, 4: 499–503.

Cape, J. and Barkham, M. (2002) 'Practice improvement methods: conceptual base, evidence-based research, and practice-based recommendations', *British Journal of Clinical Psychology*, 41: 285–307.

Cook, T.D. and Campbell, D.T. (1979) *Quasi-experimentation: Design and Analysis for Field Settings*. Chicago: Rand McNally.

Cowen, E.L. (1978) 'Some problems in community program evaluation research', *Journal of Consulting and Clinical Psychology*, 46: 792–805.

Donabedian, A. (1980) *The Definition of Quality and Approaches to its Assessment*. Ann Arbor MI: Health Administration Press.

Elliott, R. (2002) 'Hermeneutic single-case efficacy design', *Psychotherapy Research*, 12: 1–21.

Evans, C., Margison, F. and Barkham, M. (1998) 'The contribution of reliable and clinically significant change methods to evidence-based mental health', *Evidence Based Mental Health*, 1: 70–2.

Evans, C., Connell, J., Barkham, M., Margison, F., Mellor-Clark, J., McGrath, G. and Audin, K. (2002) 'Towards a standardised brief outcome measure: psychometric properties and utility of the CORE-OM', *British Journal of Psychiatry*, 180: 51–60.

Evans, C., Mellor-Clark, J., Margison, F., Barkham, M., McGrath, G., Connell, J. and Audin, K. (2000) 'Clinical outcomes in routine evaluation: the CORE-OM', *Journal of Mental Health*, 9: 247–55.

Firth-Cozens, J. (1993) *Audit in Mental Health Services*. Hove: Erlbaum.

Froyd, J.E., Lambert, M.J. and Froyd, J.D. (1996) 'A review of practices of psychotherapy outcome measurement', *Journal of Mental Health*, 5: 11–15.

Goldberg, D. and Williams, P. (1988) *A User's Guide to the General Health Questionnaire*. Windsor: NFER-Nelson.

Greenberg, L.S. (1986) 'Change process', *Journal of Consulting and Clinical Psychology*, 54: 4–9.

Hayes, S.C., Barlow, D.H. and Nelson-Gray, R.O. (1999) *The Scientist Practitioner: Research and Accountability in the Age of Managed Care, second edition*. Needham Heights MA: Allyn & Bacon.

Horvath, A.O. and Greenberg, L.S. (eds) (1994) *The Working Alliance: Theory, Research, and Practice*. New York: Wiley.

Jacobson, N.S. and Truax, P. (1991) 'Clinical significance: a statistical approach to defining meaningful change in psychotherapy research', *Journal of Consulting and Clinical Psychology*, 59: 12–19.

Jacobson, N.S., Roberts, L.J., Berns, S.B. and McGlinchey, J.B. (1999) 'Methods for defining and determining the clinical significance of treatment effects: description, application, and alternatives', *Journal of Consulting and Clinical Psychology*, 67: 300–7.

Kazdin, A.E. (1994) 'Methodology, design, and evaluation in psychotherapy research' in A.E. Bergin and S.L. Garfield (eds) *Handbook of Psychotherapy and Behavior Change*, fourth edition. New York: Wiley.

Lebow, J.L. (1983) 'Research assessing consumer satisfaction with mental health treatment: a review of findings', *Evaluation and Program Planning*, 6: 211–36.

Margison, F., Barkham, M., Evans, C., McGrath, G., Mellor-Clark, J., Audin, K. and Connell, J. (2000) 'Measurement and psychotherapy: evidence-based practice and practice-based evidence', *British Journal of Psychiatry*, 177: 123–30.

Mathers, N., Shipton, G. and Shapiro, D.A. (1993) 'The impact of short-term counselling on General Health Questionnaire scores', *British Journal of Guidance and Counselling*, 21: 310–18.

Maxwell, R.J. (1984) 'Quality assessment in health', *British Medical Journal*, 288: 1470–2.

Mellor-Clark, J., Barkham, M., Connell, J. and Evans, C. (1999) 'Practice-based evidence and need for a standardised evaluation system: informing the design of the CORE System', *European Journal of Psychotherapy, Counselling and Health*, 3: 357–74.

Milne, D. (1987) *Evaluating Mental Health Practice: Methods and Applications*. Beckenham: Croom Helm.

Mulhall, D. (1976) 'Systematic self-assessment by PQRST', *Psychological Medicine*, 6: 591–7.

Neilson, J. (1994) 'Therapist–client concordance on therapy process and outcome and its implications for service evaluation', *Clinical Psychology Forum*, 73: 5–7.

Parry, G. (1992) 'Improving psychotherapy services: applications of research, audit and evaluation', *British Journal of Clinical Psychology*, 31: 3–19.

Parry, G. and Watts, F.N. (1996) *Behavioural and Mental Health Research: a Handbook of Skills and Methods*. second edition. Hove: Erlbaum.

Parry, G., Shapiro, D.A. and Firth, J. (1986) 'The case of the anxious executive: a study from the research clinic', *British Journal of Medical Psychology*, 59: 221–33.

Phillips, J.P.N. (1986) 'Shapiro Personal Questionnaire and generalized personal questionnaire techniques: a repeated measures individualized outcome measurement' in L.S. Greenberg and W.M. Pinsof (eds) *The Psychotherapeutic Process: a Research Handbook*. New York: Guilford Press.

Rossi, P.H. and Freeman, H.E. (1993) *Evaluation: a Systematic Approach*, fifth edition. Newbury Park CA: Sage.

Schofield, W. (1964) *Psychotherapy: the Purchase of Friendship*. Englewood Cliffs NJ: Prentice Hall.

Scriven, M. (1972) 'The methodology of evaluation' in C.H. Weiss (ed.) *Evaluating Action Programs*. Boston MA: Allyn & Bacon.

Shadish, W.R., Cook, T.D. and Leviton, L.C. (1991) *Foundations of Program Evaluation: Theories of Practice*. Thousand Oaks CA: Sage.

Shapiro, D.A. and Barkham, M. (1993) *Relate: Information Needs Research. Final report to Department of Social Security*. Rugby: Research and Policy Unit, Relate Marriage Guidance.

Shaw, C. (1986) *Introducing Quality Assurance*. London: King's Fund.

Skaife, K. and Spall, B. (1995) 'An independent approach to auditing psychology services for adult mental health clients', *Clinical Psychology Forum*, 77: 14–18.

Stevens, A. and Gabbay, J. (1991) 'Needs assessment needs assessment', *Health Trends*, 23: 20–23.

Stiles, W.B., Reynolds, S., Hardy, G.E., Rees, A., Barkham, M. and Shapiro, D.A. (1994) 'Evaluation and description of psychotherapy sessions by clients using the Session Evaluation Questionnaire and the Session Impacts Scale', *Journal of Counseling Psychology*, 41: 175–85.

Weiss, C.H. (1972) *Evaluation Research*. Englewood Cliffs NJ: Prentice Hall.

Wiger, D.E. and Solberg, K.B. (2001) *Tracking Mental Health Outcomes: a Therapist's Guide to measuring Client Progress, analyzing Data, and improving your Practice*. New York: Wiley.

Part III
Perspectives on Practice

5 The Psychodynamic Paradigm
MICHAEL BURTON AND TOM DAVEY

... the error bred in the bone of each woman and each man
Craves what it cannot have,
Not universal love
But to be loved alone. (W.H. Auden, 'September 1st, 1939',
Selected Poems)

the neurotic is one who refuses the loan of life in order not to pay
the debt of death. (Otto Rank)

Psychodynamic counselling is a broad church, and different versions derive inspiration from selective readings of Freud, Jung and a wide range of later theorists. There is still no obvious ascendant core text or belief system. There are some broad separations geographically in terms of the influence in America of self or ego psychology, in the United Kingdom of British object relations, including Klein, and European traditions, including Freud, Lacan and postmodern theorists. Many English trainings also place emphasis on narrativity and linguistics, sociology, cognitive sciences and phenomenology. Other influential areas of theory include psychology, feminism and humanism (Messer, 1998). What is emerging is an increasing trend toward eclecticism; see Mander (2000) and Jacobs (1999) for typical texts. The term *counselling*, or counselling psychology, rather than psychotherapy seems to be used in reference to the following dimensions:

- Cost and length of training.
- Relative weighting of experimental versus clinical evidence.
- University versus training body accreditation.
- Low dosage.
- Focus of aims.
- Degree of regression.
- Use of transference.
- Symptom relief versus insight.
- Conscious versus unconscious.
- Low intensity.
- Fantasy versus reality.

In comparing psychodynamic counselling with short-term psychodynamic psychotherapy it is difficult to sustain any of these differences as crucially discriminative, and issues of power, authority and money (training cost) appear to play as important a role in this debate as practice. In the years since the first edition this somewhat sterile debate about hegemony seems to have given way to more specific reports of particular practices with particular client groups using a range of validated process and outcome measures; see for instance Hemmings (2000) and Ross and Fonagy (1996).

There is an increasing trend toward using brief psychodynamically oriented treatments for borderline personality disorders, as well as for unresponsive and chronically ill psychiatric patients. These moves seem to have laid to rest debates about depth and length as prerequisites of a successful psychodynamic outcome (Guthrie, 1999; Cookson et al., 2001; White et al., 2001). The counselling psychologist as scientist/practitioner is no longer so clearly a third position in this debate with respect to the application of the techniques of social science to assess the truth claims of particular hypotheses. Increasingly psychotherapists and counsellors are including in their training the use of qualitative and quantitative methodologies. What remains far more problematic is that such social science positioning may assume particular philosophical and political premises, for instance the pathologizing that may occur from normative, behavioural and theoretical assumptions (Parker et al., 1995). As the field becomes more mature an increasing range of philosophical and sociological criticisms have been brought to bear (Frosh, 1997).

One contribution of psychology to counselling has been to develop and buttress the importance of critical debate, often at some cost to the certainties of conventional psychology. The very different philosophical and political premises from which particular brand loyalties of therapy derive now seem more a subject for discussion rather than polemical debate. The notion is that the analysis of particular positionings which derive from such beliefs can be examined in terms of which aspects of therapeutic outcome they might enhance or impair (Kobos and Bauer, 1995; Peake et al., 1988). The issue of what constitutes therapeutic outcome remains as thorny as ever but at least more sophisticated philosophical discussions are available to counsellors to replace the combative certitudes of yesterday (Le Bon, 2001). It is possible to begin to imagine that 'integrative' may mean more than arbitrary and eclectic.

In this chapter we will represent the contrasts between positionings by considering how proponents of particular theories respond to core concepts in the psychodynamic field. In the best traditions of British liberal egalitarianism, psychodynamic counselling in Britain has often sought to present aspects of many positions, sometimes resulting in inconsistency and incoherence, but also generating a richness and critical stance lacking in many psychodynamic psychotherapy trainings. If, as we will argue, part of the counselling process is an appreciation of the multiplicity of narratives by which our lives may be represented, an appreciation of the plurality of influences is an important part of counselling training (see McLeod, 1997). The more so when these influences can be traced to major historical movements. This seems especially important in considering post-colonial literature and the imperialism of Western thought. There is little doubt that with a multiplicity of journals and scholarly work psychodynamic counselling and psychotherapy continue to foster a wealth of clinical and theoretical work.

One issue of debate is whether psychodynamic counselling any longer has as much need to acknowledge its historical roots as solely in psychoanalysis, given the increasing diversity and influence of other sources (Frosh, 1987, 1989). Recent developments in cognitive analytic therapy (Ryle, 1995), conversational therapy (Hobson, 1985), communicative psychotherapy (Sullivan, 1999) and solution-focused therapy (Messer, 1998) have brought notions of working with defences through the therapeutic relationship to a wider Anglo-Saxon audience. These therapies all derive some of their sources from the work of Freud's daughter Anna, whose work highlighted the role of early interpersonal relationships via the mechanisms of ego growth and defence. It was left to Hartmann to attempt to describe the psychic structure of the ego and to argue that its development could result in a conflict-free adaptation to social reality. These ideas were taken up by the self psychologists Kohut and Kernberg, who argued that the child is symbiotically linked with adults and their experience and in effect initially borrows and subsequently internalizes notions of an object world from them in the form of self objects. This shifts the entire emphasis of psychodynamic thinking away from the fundamental impossibility of knowing represented by Freud's notion of the unconscious towards a vision of adaptation, social integration and normalcy (see Elliot, 1994). In this reading, the task of both development and cure is fundamentally an educative one related to the development of a conscious ego.

Other sources for psychodynamic counselling in Britain as represented by, for instance, the published texts of Noonan (1983) and Jacobs (1999), draw on Freud, the object relation theorists and attachment theory, in particular the work of Klein, Winnicot and Bowlby (see Elliot, 1994, for discussion). Emphasis is given to the vicissitudes of early development and the crucial role of early parenting in the formation of a sense of self and the other (often expressed in terms of attachment). In this vision human beings are relationship- or object-seeking, rather than, as in Freud's vision of development, largely self-organized in terms of the satisfaction of libidinal drives. This leads to considerable interest by the counsellor in the difficulties of early childhood relationships with significant others, particularly the mother, and more recently siblings. In some hands this can become a narrative of the patient in terms of being a victim of parental oppression and offers as a vision of cure the possibility of a reparative relationship with the therapist as the 'good enough' mother. The positioning of the counsellor can easily become deeply seductive (for both parties) and the problems of such an approach in practice centre on issues of separation and loss when the mutual fantasy comes to an end or is challenged by discussion of the end. Some brief therapists would argue that such an outcome, sometimes called a transference neurosis, can be avoided by structuring therapy in such a way as to minimize such regressive or symbiotic invitations. Clients are seen seated, not on the couch, the time limits are spelt out from the beginning, and therapy is conducted at low intensity. The logical extension of this has been to reduce therapy to a single or double encounter (see Barkham, 1989). Nonetheless, there are many who would argue that within such a relationship the mix of supportive and challenging elements provides a perfect setting in which to rework the dysfunctional interpersonal dramas of childhood, and that surviving ending and frustration are fundamental to leading a full life in a postmodern world (see Hobson, 1985, for a discussion).

The third influence derives from an existential/phenomenological tradition and a rereading of Freud which emphasizes the essential unknowability of the unconscious and the fragmented and incoherent conscious 'I' that seeks to deny this essential alienation by placing itself at the centre as speaking subject. In this the patient is encouraged to recognize that he or she is, in Heidegger's words, 'neurotic because they are in love with the truth', and that essential to existence in a postmodern world is toleration of difference, unknowability and the internal inconsistency of a self which is resultant from a multitude of influences. Although in the hands of Lacan the truth claims are meant to be universal, later exponents see it much more as description of particular socio-cultural angsts of the late twentieth century (see Grosz, 1990, for a review). In this view the parental drama is an important mythology of the late twentieth century which has extensive narrative power but which also easily entraps people into a victim position. Consistent with this view is the psychological evidence of the inconsistent predictive power of early traumas in later pathology, the importance of other family members, and feminist critiques of the positioning of women in the vision of the maternal (Izzard and Barden, 2001). A contemporary of Freud's, Karl Kraus, is reported as describing Freud's acolytes as 'lustful rationalists' creating 'psychoanalysis', which, with its truth claims, was 'the disease it sought to cure'.

A fourth influence comes from brief therapy, where economic and situational pressures (often military or related to emergencies) have led to the development on all continents of psychodynamic therapeutic systems based on a limited number of sessions (Peake et al., 1988; Koss and Shiang, 1994, who list twenty one different variants, for a full review). Early innovators, such as Ferenczi and indeed Freud himself, were concerned at the general inflationary spiral that has characterized psychoanalysis and sought via a more active role by the analyst to shorten the process. There has always been considerable tension between what many analytic therapists might deem appropriate and what many patients are able to afford, tolerate or indeed want.

However, some analytic therapists have seen in the constraints of short-term working a reality-based discipline that permits a profound exploration of the transient and yet important aspects of human relations, permitting 'experiential learning' or 'corrective emotional experiences' or 'core conflictual relationship themes' to be enacted and explored (Luborsky, 1993). Others have emphasized the motivational aspects of brief work and the anxiety-rousing quality of realizing that the offer is of strictly limited duration (Mann, 1982). Yet others have gone on to argue that anxiety constitutes an arena for change which should be generated both by situational factors and by therapists' confrontation of patients' patterns. Davanloo took this to its logical conclusion in arguing that it is possible in the dynamic interaction between patient and therapist to unlock unconscious patterns by relentlessly challenging patterns of defence, resistance and relating, although many have found the level of challenge and coercion hard to stomach (see Flegenheimer, 1982, for a review).

The work of Robert Hobson and his associates represents a new dynamic strand, with its emphasis on the relational dynamic and the use of language as narrative. This has led to a widespread interest in the nature of therapeutic narrative and a convergence between psychodynamic and systemic therapy (Papadopoulos and Byng-Hall, 1997).

This notion that there might be particular demands or skills involved in brief therapy has been explicitly taken up by many authors, particularly those who have emphasized the planned ending or contract as an important reality-based element in containing and interpreting the fantasized elements of understanding and support. This raises a central issue for dynamic therapy in the notion of death and mortality where every ending is seen to signify the larger ending that awaits us all, and close attention is therefore given to the termination of sessions and the therapy as a whole as revealing of the kinds of defensive structures that patients mobilize to protect themselves from awareness of transience and mortality. What is interesting is that in offering a system of therapy that specializes in being predictable and thought through, patients may be being inducted into cure characterized by the fantasy of the world as predictable and knowable. It may be that to be 'sane' in a postmodern world involves such a suspension, a triumph of hope over reality (see Parker, 1997).

The underlying theory of personality and motivation

Freudian theory attempted to resolve a considerable range of philosophical and psychological problems within a biological and positivistic framework, and as we have suggested above, component sub-theories have been taken up by the various theorists to the extent to which they meet their philosophical, political and emotional ends. Thus within the Freudian opus can be found theories of the structure and function of mind, the nature of child development, the development of gender differences, the nature of socialization. The exact relationship between these theories was a matter of concern to Freud and all those who followed him. As with any prolific writer, Freud was often more concerned with developing new ideas than integrating them with the old, but he might also have warned against assuming that any singular theory of personality could catch the multiply determined motives – conscious and unconscious – of the human subject.

Thus a radical critique of this section heading might question the assumption concerning the singularity and predictability of traits or types, and the unitary self of psychology, and the power that derives from the normative assumptions of psychology (Foucault, 1961). A more radical psychodynamic reading would wish to challenge the centrality of the unitary self or *subject* (Kennedy, 1998) and present such assumptions as a core and delusional construct of consciousness in which constructs of mastery and narrative coherence consistently attempt to present the world, self and others as predictable and known. Motivation in this view derives from a desire to reimpose a sense of primordial singularity that derives from the human infant's loss of early fusion with its mother (Benvenuto, 1989), and anything that appears to hold out such a prospect is seen to be salient and desirable. In this view, then, initial alienation leads to a lifelong search for unity, and motivation is seen as an implicit function of the knowledge-seeking organism casting its neural net over William James's sea of confusion. This contrasts with the alternative reading of drive theory where cognitive development is seen as a resultant of motivation. A fundamental challenge to most current therapeutic theories is to resolve the relative priorities to give to cognition and motivation. A more radical challenge might question the attempt to formulate such theories as a defence against the absurdity or uncertainty of human existence and thus as part of the construction of technological social myths of the late twentieth century. These views have been expressed most forcefully by the social constructionists and linguistically oriented psychologists (Parker, 1997). They can be placed in opposition to evolutionary and cognitive psychologists who argue for a variety of forms of biological determinism (see Lakoff and Johnson, 1999, for a discussion). The answer, as so often, probably lies somewhere in between, with the need to find expression in psychodynamic theory for both an embodied and social self.

If our categorization of the world is both learnt and hierarchical, the child (and its socialization) is seen by most psychodynamic theorists to be the author of the adult personality. In as far as this implies entry into a public domain and shared language, developmental tasks are fundamentally about the repression of difference and conflict. Notions of personality may serve to map out the trajectory and history of these losses. This is not to deny the importance of development but rather to emphasize that what is of interest to the therapist is the utility in the patient's current drama that their recollections and responses play. The stage on which such recollections and responses will be marshalled and played out may well depend on the particular cognitive style and developmental achievements, but whether these constitute stable types or more transient adaptive traits is unclear in psychodynamic theory, although it is worth noting that tests such as Myers-Briggs or Eysenck draw on concepts that at least share a common signifier with those in Jungian and Freudian theories (see Deary and Matthews, 1993, for a review). Although it is difficult to define any general theories of personality or motivation which are common to all those who might describe themselves as psychodynamic, some terms do seem to be used in common parlance.

The notion of *depth* which often appears to equate with the hypothesized age of developmental arrest or difficulty is fundamental to object relations, attachment and ego psychology. This raises a further shibboleth of much psychoanalytic thinking in the concept of *transference* in which early patterns of fantasy and behaviour (classically unconscious but latterly in some schools both conscious and unconscious) are re-enacted with the therapist and are dealt with by interpretation of the underlying conflicts which led to the arrest in development and which are being re-experienced in the current relationship. There is some consensus amongst object relations-influenced therapists that transference interpretations are not as helpful in short-term work and that sustaining a focus on present behaviour and minimizing regressive invitations and negative transference is preferable, although others would prefer to structure the session around the client rather than around the theory. Further, for research purposes so many complex aspects of interpersonal relatedness have become compressed into the single term 'transference' that it has lost much of its utility. It has therefore been replaced by more specific terms (see below).

The notions of depth and transference in the hands of many counsellors become comforting theoretical crutches in the formulation of the relationship and enable the counsellor to treat the client as an arrested infant, avoiding those elements of the interaction between two adults, such as sexuality, power, money and professional convenience, which appear to trouble most therapists (see Langs, 1986, for a discussion of the defensive potential of these terms in protecting the therapist's position and power). The complex interrelationship of unconscious intra-personal modes of relating and conscious, external, inter-personal, collaboration is an area which separates many analytic therapists, who emphasize the primacy of the former, from psychodynamically oriented counsellors, who tend to work with an amalgam of both.

This raises a second key concept, that of the *unconscious*, and with it notions of *repression* and psychodynamic theories of memory. There is fundamental agreement that people are often unable to recall aspects of their past or current behaviour. The particular claims of psychoanalysis are that this forgetting is motivated (it is not simply that painful things are forgotten but that even the forgetting is forgotten) and that repressed memories are subject within the unconscious to mechanisms of displacement and deferral characterized by metaphorical and metonymic (primary) processes different from the inductive and deductive logic of conscious awareness (secondary process), particularly in relation to traumatic or conflicted events (see Erdelyi, 1984). Many of these claims have been assessed experimentally and the picture that emerges appears rather more complex. Generally trauma *per se* does not cause amnesia, although adults and children will often actively attempt to avoid discussing it. These processes appear more akin to denial or disavowal than repression. What does seem clear from experiment is that memory is radically reconstructive in the light of current salient meanings, rather than veridical (Laplanche, 1992). This has raised particular anxieties with respect to *false memory syndrome*, where patients or their relatives have claimed that memories of abuse or childhood trauma are fabrications encouraged by the therapist. In many respects the controversy has echoes of the earlier one where Freud decided that the reports of infantile sexual abuse by his female patients generally represented not actual abuse but the operations of imagination and fantasy in the face of unresolved childhood internal conflicts. The experimental manipulation of memory via suggestion of one kind or another has spawned a considerable research industry often associated with roles as expert witnesses for and against the veracity of such recall (see Mollon, 1998, for a review). What is important to the psychodynamic vision is not that it has a dogmatic position but rather that it invites us to consider how our current narratives and recollections act to serve a particular, singular and ultimately entrapping vision of ourselves. It also throws into question the function of rationality; there seems increasing evidence that we construct a world of meaning based upon salience and convenience but then report its construction as representing the processes of logic (see Gilovich, 1991, for a review).

In psychodynamic terms, entrapping responses are termed *defences*.

> An overall definition of a defence is an individual's automatic psychological response to internal or external stressors or emotional conflict. Defences generally act auto-matically, that is, without conscious effort. ... Character traits are in part made up of specific defences which individuals use repetitively in diverse situations. Individuals tend to specialize using a prototypical set of defences across a variety of stressors ... defences affect adaptation ... there is a clear hierarchy of defences in relation to the overall adaptiveness of each one ... the least adaptive protect the individual from awareness of stressors and/or associated conflicts at the price of constricting aware-ness, freedom to choose and flexibility in maximizing positive outcomes. When defences are most adaptive, they maximize the expression and gratification of wishes and needs, minimize negative consequences, and provide a sense of freedom of choice. (Perry, 1993)

Symptoms in this account are compromises which serve to express some aspects of the original conflict whilst keeping others at bay. Freud's idea of defences was developed by a number of workers to include responses to exter-nal as well as internal stimuli, and to incorporate the idea that it was the fan-tasy induced by a stimulus, not the stimulus itself, that was crucial.

One important concept that emerges from the idea of defence is that of patient *compliance*. As we have hinted extensively, although psychodynamic theorists have not always been as aware of it as Freud was, the issue is crucial to an understanding of the possibilities of cure and the extent to which the task of therapy is compliance with the normalizing authority of the therapist. If what ails people is precisely how the demands of society impact upon their lives to define them in ways that deny their difference and diversity, it may well be that the body and symptoms become a method of both expressing dis-ease but at the same time of distancing the self from its implication by declaring one's problems medical. Psychodynamics is often torn between a desire to hitch-hike on the status and esteem of the medical model of mental illness and the more radical deconstructive challenge that suggests that we are trapped precisely by a vision of ourselves that splits off unacceptable parts or declares them alien from our being. Whilst the record of psychodynamic therapy is no better than that of any other therapeutic system in terms of cure, we might sug-gest that its ability consistently to reopen and challenge the premises of illness and symptom places it in a unique position: as one therapist when faced by a long reiteration of symptoms said, 'Talk about something else.' The problem is that considerable career investment by both patients and physicians in a medical system is profoundly challenged by such a suggestion. Not surprisingly, if the measures of success are to do with symptom reduction, social acceptance or compliance, psychodynamics can show no particular benefit and the benefits it might show may lie outside the arena of conventionally measured psychologi-cal and medical variables.

The assessment process

The process of analytic therapy presupposes the ability to engage in a certain kind of reflexive conversation, involving both the ability to recognize the 'as if' quality, as in 'It is as if you are my father,' etc., and to tolerate the imposition by the therapist of boundaries concerning time, attendance, payment and discussion of the ongoing relationship with the therapist. In addition it may require the ability to tolerate levels of antisocial behaviour on the part of the therapist in not answering or in failing to respond politely but rather in insisting that all the patient's comments, intended or otherwise, can be understood to be relational and positional. Not surprisingly, high drop-out rates have been widely reported and short-term interventions, in this view, are appropriate to only a limited group of relatively 'robust' clients (Malan, 1963). However see White et al. (2001), Guthrie (1999), and Cookson et al. (2001) for an entirely contrary view. Other schools have emphasized the notion of depth and claim a continuum with counselling and short-term therapy best addressing issues that derive from relatively late on in childhood development of an Oedipal nature. This notion of developmental arrest has led some workers to propose, after Klein, that particular periods of childhood are characterized by different cognitive coping processes and that these arrests are represented in adult life by particular defences. Some forty two possible mechanisms of defence have been described.

This has led to the formulation of hierarchies of defences based on developmental models and to the assessment and categorization of patients in terms of the defences manifested in presenting sessions. In as far as these categorizations turn upon particular theories they are subject to all the caveats described so far. They do represent a bridge between psychiatric and psychodynamic classificatory systems, and the terms 'psychotic', 'neurotic', 'borderline', 'mature' and 'immature' that derive from them have very much entered popular parlance, albeit in practice they seem less easy to apply.

The view that ego mechanisms are hierarchically organized, proposed originally by Semrad, has been tested in a number of studies that group defences into four (or five if we include image-distorting, which subsumes both borderline and narcissistic) categories along a dimension from least to most adaptive – psychotic, immature, neurotic and mature. These categories are characterized by specific defences (Table 5.1) and inversely correlated with measures of global health, from psychotic to mature (see Perry, 1993). The problem for such categorical schemes with their medical overtones is that they label the patient and offer the marginalized prospect of a career as a patient and position the counsellor or therapist as expert.

In our experience the issues of assessment turn not so much on any hypothesized madness in the patient as on the ability of the therapist and organization to tolerate certain kinds of behaviour or defence, specifically impulsive or violent behaviour, failure to attend or to attend in a fit state (focused around addictive behaviours of a variety of kinds) and the production of discourses

Table 5.1   Taxonomy of defences

Psychotic	Immature	Image distorting	Neurotic	Mature
Delusional projection	Avoidance	Splitting of others' images	Displacement	Sublimation
	Acting out		Dissociation	Altruism
Psychotic denial distinction	Neurotic denial	Splitting of self-images	Asceticism	Humour
	Fantasy	Devaluation	Reaction formation	Anticipation
	Projection	Omnipotence		Suppression
			Repression	
	Hypochondriasis	Manic denial		
			Rationalization	
	Passive aggression	Bland denial Projective identification	Undoing	
			Isolation	
		Primitive idealization	Intellectualization	

Source: Perry (1993), by permission.

that profoundly challenge or ignore the therapist. Such people have often been termed psychotic, borderline or narcissistic. Interestingly these are precisely the 'heartsink' patients who are often allocated to neophyte counsellors in public-sector settings, on the grounds that more experienced therapists and physicians prefer not to work with them!

What does change mean and how is it brought about?

As with all matters psychodynamic, there are considerable disagreements as to what might constitute change and as to how such change is to be achieved. There seems some consensus that early difficulties in parenting lead to developmental arrests that in turn lead to currently inappropriate modes of responding and thinking. Major differences arise as to whether these problems of thought, speech or response are best addressed directly as symptoms, or whether constitutive elements of early learning, or even early fantasies, need to be addressed first or as well. Many dynamic therapists would argue that correction or re-education alone is not enough for lasting change; what is required is a reparative experience with the therapist in terms of reparenting, or of enacting previously learnt behaviours under similar affective conditions but achieving a different cathartic outcome. This raises an important debate between the ideas of enactment and analysis. In the latter the task is to bring into consciousness by interpretation, repressed material and to thus allow new and more adult defensive structures to be mobilized and in turn analysed. In this vision the client's responses and use of the therapist, in the absence of knowledge or information concerning the therapist, allows both parties to hypothesize as to the structure of the client's inner world. This vision of the therapist as somewhat distant is, as already discussed, mostly a fiction and supportive comments seem part of all therapeutic practices. Nonetheless the notions of therapy as anxiety-inducing, different and fundamentally unknowable are common to many theories of short-term work as a motivating factor in uncovering buried conflicts and unconscious processes.

What these approaches take for granted is the nature of the subject of self that is to be the end project of the therapeutic enterprise; thus considerable bodies of research exist in short-term dynamic therapy concerning client and therapist variables that are prognostic of good outcome (see below).

The nature of the relationship between counselling psychologist and individual client

The pressures of training courses and developments in the registration of counsellors, counselling psychologists and psychotherapists have led to an intense interest in the defining and discriminating factors that separate and demarcate different schools of therapy. The academization of therapy has also led to increasing intellectual scrutiny of the counselling process, which has in turn led to attempts to formulate counselling psychology in terms of identifiable skills and practices. Much of this work in the arena of psychodynamic counselling psychology has been conducted in America, where the premises of ego psychology, and in particular the idea of a reality-based collaboration between counsellor and client, the so-called ego or working alliance, have been more acceptable. In Britain the idea of such a collaboration has more often been seen as an example of unresolved positive transference resulting from the unconscious projection of the client's idealizing fantasy and therefore to be interpreted rather than studied or encouraged.

Attempts to study the ego or working alliance have led to the development of a number of research instruments (see Horvath et al., 1993, for a review), and a good deal of work has been done attempting to map the changes in client and counsellor perceptions across a series of sessions. It is probably premature as yet to come to anything more than tentative conclusions but some of the results seem to fly in the face of popular beliefs. Studies by Bordin (1976) and by Luborsky et al. (1993) appeared to show that what was crucial was not the therapist's attitude but the client's perception of it. Subsequent studies by Safran et al. (1990) and others suggested that this conclusion needed to be modified to track the changes that occurred across sessions and that the working alliance and client–therapist attitudes might follow a cyclic form. Thus Horvath et al. (1993) suggest that there may be an initial honeymoon phase peaking at or around session three where the client develops attitudes toward the therapist based upon the client's perceptions of the relevance and potency of the interventions offered. This involves the therapist being able to communicate to the client the important link between therapy-specific tasks and the overall goals of treatment and to maintain awareness of the client's commitment to these activities, and to intervene effectively if resistance is present. A major difficulty here is the disparity between the client's desire for relief from pain and symptoms in the shortest possible order and the therapist's awareness of the longer-term plan of therapy and the necessity of delayed gratification.

In the second phase after alliance building the presence of dysfunctional interpersonal relationship schemas reactivated in therapy needs to be challenged by the therapist, which leads to an increase in the client's perception of having sympathy withdrawn and an increase in negative feelings about the therapy and therapist. If these issues are taken up, the argument is that the therapeutic alliance can be repaired ready for another cycle of challenge. There seems to be some evidence to support this contention in that skilled therapists appeared more attentive to the timing of interpretations and were better at retaining clients. Equally strength of commitment to the shared goals of therapy appears to be a good predictor of positive outcome. Interestingly there was little evidence that interpretation *per se* or reference to the relationship improved outcome; what seemed critical was close attention to the client's best interests, although relationships in which no challenge occurred would be simply collusive with the dysfunctional schema of the patient. The problem with all such generalizations is that they assume patients are in a common presenting state whereas the evidence on diagnosis suggests that for some patients a very extended period of alliance building may be necessary before any challenge can be tolerated. It is a fine calculation as to when collaboration shades into collusion.

Common to a number of recent formulations, then (Luborsky, 1993), is the idea that counsellor behaviour may have to change to meet certain client and situational demands. Thus Steenbarger attempts to integrate research findings on brief therapy, proposing a three-stage process and a changing pattern of counsellor behaviour as a result. To put the claim in simple commonsense terms, initially you have to listen carefully to understand what is being said, and this induces a sense of understanding and concern in the other. During this process certain discrepancies and inconsistencies or repetitions become clear which can be discussed and challenged. This makes demands on the client to be different, which they respond to more or less positively, posing problems as to how to integrate the changes into their own and others' visions of them, especially in the absence of the therapist's support. Not surprisingly many of the processes of change can be shown to go on after the cessation of therapy, which places the notion of short-term therapy in a different perspective. Despite claims to the contrary these changes can be shown to hold up for sustained periods after therapy has ceased but appear to do so most effectively where the ending has been planned and the problems of isolation have been discussed. Clients commonly discuss carrying an internalized model of the therapist within them.

An alternative view often described as phenomenological or existential is that counselling is fundamentally an ethical activity in which the therapist seeks to 'meet with' the other as profoundly as possible by entering into an ethical relationship (Gans, 1988). What is in question is the understanding and experience of what is relationally possible between two people. The therapist's offer is to monitor and report whenever they sense that this relating is checked by the therapist's inability or difficulty, and consistently to wonder as to the particular forms and practices being mutually employed. What this poses is a radical challenge to the expertise of the therapist which is profoundly uncomfortable to the patient because of the challenge to the projection of authority. It challenges both patient's and therapist's notions of expertise and questions the moral force of the particular value systems both may espouse and is therefore radically uncomfortable for anyone seeking the comfort of received authority or wisdom. It does acknowledge the extraordinary complexity of the human mind and our endless pursuit of a knowing which seeks to make the world predictable; this all too often leads to an ossification of meanings in which we become trapped within our own narrative closure.

Family, group and organizational applications

Although psychodynamic theories are fundamentally about the formation of singular selves, both Freud and Jung included the collective group unconscious in their formulations (de Mare, 1972). There is a large body of literature devoted to what happens when aggregations of selves collide in differing contexts. Broadly speaking, family, group and organizational applications of psychodynamic theory have become entities in their own right and have not been subsumed into counselling psychology, at least not until recently in Britain. Indeed, to some extent these applications remain opposed to individual ways of working, as they represent a different view: of society as a single entity as opposed to an aggregation of individual selves that is often assumed in individual work. If one believes in the multiplicity of narratives running through human discourse, family, group and organizational applications of psychodynamic theory offer arenas for airing these narratives and therefore the registration of difference (see Papadopoulos and Byng-Hall, 1997, for a discussion). Although the validity of extrapolating models of early development to generalized models of society is open to question, these applications challenge individual counselling's assumption of the primacy of singular selves with an alternative vision from sociology, of society as singular, which has echoes in the social deconstructionist movement. In emphasizing the homoeostatic and causal feedback loops between the internal and external, and between the individual and the group, family, group and organizational therapists have often emphasized the circularity of cause and effect and criticized the linear formulations of individual psychotherapists. However, in Freud's notion of the idea of primary and secondary gains the idea certainly exists that symptoms can not merely serve as the representation of repressed material, but are also socially functional. This leads to a new class of question concerning what may be obscured by virtue of an individual's or group's obsession with a particular issue. Such a view may offer a radical critique of the current obsession with 'symptom' support groups (anorexia, alcohol, etc.) in that whilst it may mobilize people's political power it may also serve to obscure in silence issues of difference. In the group analytic tradition of Foulkes (1964) where the group itself is seen to be its own psychotherapist such a selection would be seen as contra-indicated in creating a monologic and obsessed therapist. The counselling psychologist in espousing belief in the importance of the falsification of theories may be uniquely placed to recognize the heuristic utility of identification and group compliance in creating an identity, but also to see the loss that may result from the failure to address issues of difference. The effectiveness of these two modes of symptom reduction versus individuation is a subject for empirical testing, but is also a function of personality and developmental issues.

This raises an important contribution of counselling psychology, as it brings to the debate on individuation a raft of empirical research. It is perhaps one of the ironies of psychodynamic practice that it has in its family, group and organizational applications emphasized the importance of context and group fantasy which are often invaluable insights into understanding the ways that institutional influences are encoded in the work of the counselling psychologist. For reviews of these applications see Hoffman (1981) for family therapy applications, de Mare (1972) for group therapy applications and Hinshelwood (1979) for organizational applications.

Research evidence about effectiveness

Research on the outcome of psychodynamic therapy has been reviewed in two celebrated papers by Luborsky and his associates (Luborsky et al., 1975, 1993) which take their title from the caucus race in *Alice in Wonderland* of which the dodo says: 'Everyone has won and all have won prizes.' This refers to the number of celebrated meta-review studies which show that no particular method or theoretical stance is particularly advantaged with respect to any other (see Miller et al., 1993, for review). Luborsky summarizes his own study of research rigorously assessed to meet nineteen criteria as follows: 'group versus individual; time-limited versus time-unlimited; client-centred versus other psychotherapies; behaviour therapy versus other therapy; and dynamic therapy versus other therapies ... the main trend is the non-significant difference effect' (Luborsky et al., 1975). There was a tendency for psychotherapies with medication to be better than therapy alone, and an overwhelming superiority of psychotherapy versus no psychotherapy.

In its psychoanalytic incarnation psychodynamic therapy proposes therapy five or six times a week for several years as constituting a minimum commitment, with an investment of tens of thousands of pounds. The prospect that a few sessions of cognitive analytic therapy can achieve the same result invites at best a sharp intake of breath and at worst an action under the Trade

Table 5.2   Results of meta-analysis

	Measured at termination	Mesured at follow-up
Dynamic therapies better	1	1
Non-significant difference	14	5
Other psychotherapies better	2	2

Source: Adapted from Luborsky et al. (1993) by permission.

Descriptions Act! As we have argued, psychodynamic counselling makes no such time or frequency demands, but there is in the field a creeping tendency toward the belief that more is better and, as we have seen, deeper. There are a few studies that address this issue, although the vast majority of studies have been reported as short-term work, whether it be five or fifty sessions.

Table 5.2 summarizes Luborsky's results. It offers no satisfaction to any claim of the superiority of dynamic treatment versus any other kind and it would seem that the dodo was correct, at least in this race. Smith et al. (1980) summarized their finding by saying that 'A typical therapy client is better off than 75 per cent of untreated individuals.'

A variety of explanations are offered for these results. The most obvious argument proposed by protagonists of the psychodynamic view is that the results are relevant only to short-term therapy and that studies of longer-term therapy would be more impressive. Bacharach et al. (1991) summarized the results from six studies of psychoanalysis with a total *n* of over 500 and claimed improvements were in the 60–90 per cent range, which appears to be comparable to but not better than other treatments, although these were not comparison studies. There is some evidence to show that psychotherapy plus medical treatment does better than medicine alone in a variety of psychosomatic treatments and that this reduces calls on medical resources; panic attacks may be best dealt with by cognitive therapies and mild phobias by behaviour therapy, whilst schizophrenics benefit from family therapy and social skills training. The development of variants such as cognitive analytic therapy, solution and time-focused therapy has increasingly blurred the borders between what is cognitive, integrative, supportive, relational and psychodynamic. Thus whilst there are numerous caveats in a field plagued by methodological difficulties, it may well be that when psychodynamic therapy wishes to make claims for special status it has had to look to studies of specific therapy with specific populations to show positive effect (see Ross and Fonagy, 1996, for a review). What is clear to these authors is that treatment regimens which have been carefully considered, and which are provided by therapists who believe in what they are doing and are adequately supported to do it, tend to diminish rather than increase patients' perceptions of the world as mad.

Whilst valuable contributions have been made by research in removing some of the mystique of the counselling process – it has, for instance, been possible to produce training protocols that pay attention to research findings and that improve the therapeutic outcomes of counsellors who previously seemed to lose clients and to produce rather low working alliance ratings – a danger is that a skills-based approach may assist counsellors to improve client retention in the short term at the cost of development in later stages of expertise (see Skovholt and Ronnestad, 1992, for discussion). Thus computer instanciations of expert systems have gone some way to emphasize the importance of tacit or fuzzy logic calculations. It is our concern that to be human is to be able to tolerate enormous confusion and to make and correct huge inductive and deductive leaps. The question therefore is not a matter of learning to act the part but of being it. But what may it mean to be human? There have been countless attempts to specify the critical processes in operational terms but a brief examination of English literature might suggest that the complexity of an answer continues to provide a creative source for generation after generation.

Rather than further review research attempts to specify the crucial processes in therapy, we suggest that the therapeutic task is to be able to sustain without panic, and even with it, the unknown or painfully familiar feelings that are engendered by the presence of the *other*, to come to accept that we are always at the mercy of the other because we are created by others and not vice versa. This view is so subversive to the *subject* of much psychological investigation, and to the rationalist and positivistic positions prevalent in the West, that it tends to engender powerful opposition. To be other than is desired by the client, to frustrate their demands to make us into what they want, is so contrary to the notions of ethical committees and customers' charters that it is often far simpler for both parties to talk about symptoms, or lapse into reparative fantasies of reparenting or take up the authoritative stance of the healer. The phrases 'to give people the space to start experiencing themselves' and 'to slouch toward Bethlehem with them' are ways people have tried to articulate this in the literature. But what it means operationally is presumably to emphasize the uniqueness of the relationship, which can be unique only if counsellor and counsellee can both bear the feelings that acknowledging difference involves. What claims such an enterprise can expect to make upon the public purse is unclear; there is little room in our current visions of efficiency and cure for not knowing. It is relevant that the authors have racked up at least ten years of personal therapy between them and regard it as time and money well spent. But, in the celebrated words of Mandy Rice Davis, 'They would say that, wouldn't they?'

Psychology has always struggled with such ideographic data to say something of generality, failing often to recognize the essential paradox inherent in doing so. The situation often seems not dissimilar to the training of Buddhist monks who demand of the master that he tells them the secret of mastery. He tolerates but never answers until the monks cease finally to question and can accept there is no answer other than the process of living itself, albeit reflexively. In an age of technological fixes this is never likely to be an attractive proposition in the West but we believe it should find some room for articulation in the processes of counselling and training.

In the words of one researcher, Luborsky, after summarizing all the current studies and showing no conclusive difference in therapeutic outcome between different therapeutic interventions:

Question: Don't you feel, despite all the evidence for the non-significant difference effect, that dynamic therapies have some special virtues to offer that are still not well enough recognised?

Answer. ... Yes. The studies have not yet dealt with possible long-term benefits, nor ... with the distinction between changes in symptoms and changes in general adjustment. (Luborsky et al., 1993: 511)

Or, in the words of Alan Bennett, 'There is always a little bit in the corner that you can't get out.' It may well be that one can achieve the same behavioural outcome via a range of means: most parents of small children will have run the gamut from bribery, through seduction, to coercion, to diversion, many times in an average day and will report varied degrees of success with each of these methods. The choice of method will be seen to turn on the familial dynamics, social context and the personalities of the participants. One explanation of the widespread adherence to psychodynamic methods as at least part of an eclectic mix is that it fits well into the dominantly white middle-class presuppositions of its protagonists. We would argue that there is nothing inherently wrong with therapist comfort other than that it requires an awareness of the counsellor's positioning, power and needs in its exercise. Psychodynamic counselling in its dogmatic claims is as authoritarian and wrongheaded as any 100 year old piece of positivism is likely to be; in its radical and subversive deconstruction of the unitary subject it profoundly challenges many of the sacred cows of late twentieth-century Western mythology. As such it deserves to be part of the armoury of any therapist. We may in the face of the other's pain and need decide to accept the offer of authority and cure them, but at least we can seek to defend ourselves against the seductions of expertise and charisma inherent in the process, and hope to be braver tomorrow.

References

Bacharach, H., Galatzer-Levy, R., Slolnikoff, A. and Waldron, S. (1991) 'On the efficacy of psychoanalysis', *Journal of the American Psychoanalytic Association*, 39: 871–916.

Barkham, M. (1989) 'Exploratory therapy in two plus one sessions: rationale for a brief psychotherapy model', *British Journal of Psychotherapy*, 6 (1): 79–86.

Benvenuto, B. (1989) 'Once upon a time: the infant in Lacanian theory', *British Journal of Psychotherapy*, 5 (3): 409–22.

Bergin, A.E. and Garfield, S.L. (1994) *Handbook of Psychotherapy and Behavior Change*, fourth edition. New York: Wiley.

Book, H.E. (1997) *How to practice Brief Psychodynamic Psychotherapy: the Core Conflictual Relationship Theme Method*. Washington DC: American Psychological Association.

Bordin, E.S. (1976) 'The generalizability of the psychoanalytic concept of the working alliance', *Psychotherapy: Theory, Research and Practice*, 16: 252–60.

Cookson, A., Espie, J. and Yates, K. (2001) 'The Edinburgh Project: a pilot study for the psychotherapeutic treatment of borderline and other severe personality disorders', *British Journal of Psychotherapy*, 18 (1): 68–88.

Coren, A.(1997) *A Psychodynamic Approach to Education*. London: Sheldon.

Deary, I.J. and Matthews, G. (1993) 'Personality traits are alive and well', *Psychologist*, 6: 299–311.

Early, J. (2000) *Interactive Group Therapy: Integrating Interpersonal, Action Oriented and Psychodynamic Approaches*. New York: Brunner Mazel.

Elliot, A. (1994) *Psychoanalytic Theory*. Oxford: Blackwell.

Erdelyi, M.H. (1984) *Psychoanalysis: Freud's Cognitive Psychology*. San Francisco: Freeman.

Flegenheimer, W.V. (1982) *Techniques of Brief Psychotherapy*. London: Jason Aronson.

Foucault, M. (1961) *Madness and Civilization*. London: Tavistock.

Foulkes, S.H. (1964) *Therapeutic Group Analysis*. London: Allen & Unwin.

Frosh, S. (1987) *The Politics of Psychoanalysis*. London: Macmillan.

Frosh, S. (1989) *Psychoanalysis and Psychology*. London: Macmillan.

Frosh, S. (1997) *For and Against Psychoanalysis*. London: Routledge.

Gans, S. (1988) 'Levinas and Pontalis: meeting the other as in a dream' in R. Bernasconi and D. Wood (eds) *The Provocation of Levinas*. London: Routledge.

Gilovich, T. (1991) *How We know What Isn't So*. New York: Free Press.

Grosz, E. (1990) *Jacques Lacan: a Feminist Introduction*. London: Routledge.

Guthrie, E. (1999) 'Psychodynamic Interpersonal Therapy', *Advances in Psychiatric Treatment*, 5: 135–45.

Hemmings, A.H. (2000) *A Systemic Review of Brief Psychotherapies in Primary Health Care*. London: Trust for the Study of Counselling in Primary Care.

Henry, W.P., Strupp, H.H., Schacht, T.E. and Gaston, L. (1994) 'Psychodynamic approaches' in A.E. Bergin and S.L. Garfield (eds) *Handbook of Psychotherapy and Behavior Change*, fourth edition. New York: Wiley.

Hinshelwood, R. (1979) *Therapeutic Communities*. London: Routledge.

Hobson, R. (1985) *Forms of Feeling*. London: Routledge.

Hoffman, L. (1981) *Foundations of Family Therapy*. New York: Basic Books.

Horowitz, M.J. (1988) *Introduction to Psychodynamics*. New York: Basic Books.

Horvath, A., Gaston, L. and Luborsky, L. (1993) 'The therapeutic alliance and its measures' in N.E. Miller, L. Luborsky, J.P. Barber and J.P. Docherty (eds) *Psychodynamic Treatment Research*. New York: Basic Books.

Izzard, S. and Barden, N. (eds) (2001) *Rethinking Gender and Therapy: the Changing Identity of Women*. Oxford: Oxford University Press.

Jacobs, M. (1999) *Psychodynamic Counselling in Action*. London: Sage.

Kennedy, R. (1998) *The Elusive Human Subject*. London: Free Association Books.

Kobos, G. and Bauer, J. (1995) *Brief Therapy: Short-term Psychodynamic Intervention*. Northvale NJ: Aronson.

Koss, M.P. and Shiang, J. (1994) 'Research on brief psychotherapy' in A.E. Bergin and S.L. Garfield (eds) *Handbook of Psychotherapy and Behavior Change*, fourth edition. New York: Wiley.

Lakoff, G., and Johnson, M. (1999) *Philosophy in the Flesh*. New York: Basic Books.

Langs, R. (1986) *Madness and Cure*. New York: Aronson.

Laplanche, J. (1992) 'Interpretation between determinism and hermeneutics: a restatement of the problem', *International Journal of Psycho-Analysis*, 73: 429–45.

Le Bon, T. (2001) *Wise Therapy*. New York: Continuum.

Luborsky, L. (1993) 'How to maximize the curative factors in dynamic psychotherapy' in N.E. Miller, L. Luborsky, J.P. Barber and J.P. Docherty (eds) *Psychodynamic Treatment Research*. New York: Basic Books.

Luborsky, L., Diguer, L., Luborsky, E., Singer, B., Dickter, D. and Schmidt, K.A. (1993) 'The efficacy of dynamic psychotherapies: is it true that everybody has won and all must have prizes?' in N.E. Miller et al. (eds) *Psychodynamic Treatment Research*. New York: Basic Books.

Malan, D. (1963) *A Study in Brief Psychotherapy*. New York: Plenum.

Mander, G. (2000) *A Psychodynamic Approach to Brief Therapy*. Thousand Oaks CA: Sage.

Mann, J. (1982) *A Casebook in Time-limited Psychotherapy*. New York: McGraw-Hill.

de Mare, P.B. (1972) *Perspectives in Group Psychotherapy*. London: Allen & Unwin.

McLeod, J. (1997) *Narrative and Psychotherapy*. Thousand Oaks CA: Sage.

McLoughlin, B. (1995) *Developing Psychodynamic Counselling*. Thousand Oaks CA: Sage.

Messer, S.B. (1998) *Models of Brief Psychodynamic Therapy*. New York: Guilford Press.

Miller, N.E., Luborsky, L., Barber, J.P. and Docherty, J.P. (eds) (1993) *Psychodynamic Treatment Research*. New York: Basic Books.

Mollon, P. (1998) *Remembering Trauma: a Psychotherapist's Guide to Memory and Illusion*. New York: Wiley.

Noonan, E. (1983) *Counselling Young People*. London: Methuen.

Northcut, T.B. and Rovinelli, N. (eds) (1999) *Enhancing Psychodynamic Therapy with Cognitive Behavioural Techniques*. Northvale NJ: Aronson.

Papadopoulos, R.K. and Byng-Hall, J. (eds) (1997) *Multiple Voices: Narrative in Systemic Family Psychotherapy*. London: Tavistock.

Parker, I., Georgaca, E., Harper, D., McLaughlin, T. and Stowell-Smith, M. (1995) *Deconstructing Psychopathology*. London: Routledge.

Parker, I. (1997) *Psychoanalytic Culture: Psychoanalytic Discourse in Western Society*. London: Sage.

Patton, M.J. and O'Meara, N.M. (1992) *Psychoanalytic Counselling*. New York: Wiley.

Peake, T.H., Borduin, C.M. and Archer, R.R. (1988) *Brief Psychotherapies*. London: Sage.

Perry, J.C. (1993) 'Defences and their effects' in N.E. Miller, L. Luborsky, J.P. Barber and J.P. Docherty (eds) *Psychodynamic Treatment Research*. New York: Basic Books.

Rana, R. (2000) *Counselling Students: a Psychodynamic Perspective*. London: Macmillan.

Ross, A. and Fonagy, P. (1996) *What Works for Whom: a Critical Review of Psychotherapy Research*. New York: Guilford Press.

Ryle, A. (ed.) (1995) *Cognitive Analytic Therapy*. New York: Wiley.

Safran, J.D., Crocker, P., McMain, S. and Murray, P. (1990) 'The therapeutic alliance rupture as a therapy event for empirical investigation', *Psychotherapy*, 27: 154–65.

Skovholt, T.M. and Ronnestad, M.H. (1992) *The Evolving Professional Self: Stages and Themes in Therapist and Counsellor Development*. Chichester: Wiley.

Smith, M.L., Glass, G.V. and Miller, T.I. (1980) *The Benefits of Psychotherapy*. Baltimore MD: Johns Hopkins University Press.

Sullivan, M. (ed.) (1999) *Unconscious Communication in Practice*. Oxford: Oxford University Press.

White, J., Berry, D., Dalton, J., Napthine, G., Prenderville, B. and Roberts, J., (2001) 'Holding and treating severe disturbance in the NHS: the containment of borderline personality disorders in a therapeutic environment. *British Journal of Psychotherapy*, 18 (1): 89–105.

6 The Humanistic Paradigm
JOHN McLEOD

The use of the concept of 'paradigm' to describe different approaches in counselling psychology derives from the work of the philosopher of science Thomas Kuhn (1962), who argued that knowledge is created through the collective activity of communities of scientists. A 'scientific community' comprises not only theory and concepts, but also a wide range of shared experiences such as exposure to similar types of training, readership of a common set of books and journals, and participation at conferences. This notion of a community of like-minded inquirers matches very well the conditions surrounding the origins of humanistic psychology. In the early 1950s, particularly in North America, academic psychology was dominated by behaviourism, and psychotherapy was dominated by psychoanalysis. However, at the same time, a growing number of psychologists were becoming convinced that neither behaviourism nor psychoanalysis could adequately account for the key questions of human experience. Many of these psychologists had been influenced by the European philosophical traditions of phenomenology and existentialism (Misiak and Sexton, 1973). Gradually, members of this group began to develop a new professional and academic identity: humanistic psychology.

The standard-bearers of the humanistic psychology movement were the Association for Humanistic Psychology, founded in 1962, and the *Journal for Humanistic Psychology*, founded in 1961. The intellectual scope and aims of humanistic psychology were summarized in the first editorial of that journal in the following terms:

> The *Journal of Humanistic Psychology* is being founded by a group of psychologists and professional men and women from other fields who are interested in those human capacities and potentialities that have no systematic place either in positivistic or behavioristic theory or in classical psychoanalytic theory, e.g., creativity, love, growth, organism, basic need-gratification, self-actualization, higher values, ego-transcendence, objectivity, autonomy, identity, responsibility, psychological health, etc. This approach can also be characterized by the writings of Goldstein, Fromm, Horney, Rogers, Maslow, Allport, Angyal, Buhler, Moustakas, etc., as well as by certain aspects of the writings of Jung, Adler, and the psychoanalytic ego-psychologists. (Sutich, 1961: viii–ix)

This definition captures the central themes of the humanistic paradigm. First, it is an approach that is not based solely in psychology but also draws significantly from the 'other fields' of humanism such as literature, the arts and philosophy. Secondly, there is an emphasis on optimal functioning rather than on pathology. Thirdly, there is a conceptualization of the person as an individual 'self'. Fourthly, it does not employ a single clear theoretical focus, but instead relies on a loosely connected network of ideas. Finally, there is a sense of a set of ideas and practices that exist in opposition to the mainstream, that find their identity through *not* being psychoanalysis or behaviourism, rather than constituting a positive alternative that might seek to replace them.

The period since the inauguration of the 'third force' of humanistic psychology has seen major fluctuations in its popularity and influence. In the 1960s and 1970s, humanistic psychology was in tune with the spirit of economic expansion and personal freedom. The economic recession of the 1980s, accompanied by a demand for counselling and psychotherapy to be more accountable and problem-focused, resulted in a lessening of interest in humanistic approaches. Smith (1982) and Giorgi (1987) described this period as representing a crisis in humanistic psychology. More recently, however, there has been a resurgence in the humanistic orientation, with a steady growth in training opportunities, theoretical development and research activity.

The humanistic paradigm can be characterized as consisting of a number of discrete approaches to counselling psychology, each of which represents a distinct domain of theory, research and practice, but nevertheless draws on a core set of philosophical and psychological assumptions. The most important of these approaches are client-centred or person-centred counselling and psychotherapy, Gestalt therapy, and experiential psychotherapy. There are several other therapeutic approaches, such as existential therapy and the various transpersonal theories, that overlap significantly with humanistic psychology and therapy. Well known and widely used models such as transactional analysis and rational-emotive therapy have also been informed and influenced by humanistic theory and practice. However, for the purposes of this chapter, the humanistic paradigm will be discussed through examples drawn from the three approaches that most faithfully reflect the philosophy of humanism: person-centred, Gestalt and experiential.

The humanistic approach, as a relatively recent addition to the field of psychological therapies, has been dominated by the theories and teachings of two major figures: Carl Rogers, the founder of client-centred therapy, and Fritz Perls, founder of Gestalt therapy. The key ideas of these 'first generation' humanistic writers are well known and widely available (see Clarkson, 1989; Clarkson and Mackewn, 1993; Mearns and Thorne, 1998; Thorne, 1992). While acknowledging the enormous contribution made by Rogers and Perls, it is important to recognize that in recent years a 'second generation' of humanistic theorists has emerged, represented by Goff Barrett-Lennard, Art Bohart, Eugene Gendlin, Les Greenberg, Germain Lietaer, Dave Mearns, Erving Polster, David Rennie and Laura Rice.

In practice, humanistic therapy usually takes place either in one-to-one, hour-long sessions, or in groups led by a facilitator. Most humanistic practitioners rely on dialogue as a means of helping clients to explore the meaning of their troubles, although some will also employ enactments (such as Gestalt two-chair work), exercises (such as guided fantasy) or expressive media (clay, paint, voice, dance) to facilitate the therapeutic process. Humanistic counselling and psychotherapy have been used effectively in time-limited mode, and with couples and families.

The underlying theory of personality and motivation

Any counselling psychologist applying a humanistic approach in work with clients will draw upon a set of core theoretical assumptions and therapeutic principles. The basic theory of the humanistic approach, its theory of personality or concept of the person, constitutes what Maddi (1989) has called a *fulfilment* model. The 'root metaphor' of the paradigm is that of *growth*. The person is seen as striving to create, achieve or become. The need for fulfilment, actualization or transcendence is regarded as a fundamental human motive. This image of the person stands in contrast to the conflict model implicit in psychodynamic theory, and the problem management or coping model implicit in behaviourism. Fulfilment and growth, from a humanistic point of view, are achieved through the search for meaning in life. The centrality of meaning making and meaning creation in humanistic psychology places it in the constructivist movement in psychology and social science. The aims and scope of humanistic psychology are exemplified in Bugental (1967) and Schneider et al. (2001).

Within the broad framework supplied by the fulfilment model, humanistic theory makes sense of human experience through concepts of process, reflexivity, self, organism and experiencing. These concepts represent the fundamental assumptions underpinning any humanistic approach to counselling psychology, and can be viewed as a philosophical or value position adopted by humanistic counsellors and psychotherapists, an attitude towards the person.

One implication of the humanistic image of the person as actively seeking meaning and fulfilment is to give central emphasis to the concept of *process*. Actualization or fulfilment is not an end state to be attained, but a continual challenge or journey to be experienced. Humanistic counselling and psychotherapy view the client, and what happens during therapy, as a set of processes. From this perspective, any attempt to categorize or label the client – for example, by using a psychiatric diagnosis or personality test – can be seen as inappropriate and unhelpful, a misunderstanding of the true nature of persons. The humanistic conception of the person implies that change or becoming is inherent in the experience of being human. Humanistic therapists do not initiate or engineer change, but pay attention to the internal or external factors that prevent change from occurring. This is an essential aspect of the philosophical stance of humanistic counsellors and psychotherapists. Therapeutic change is not attributed to the actions, interventions or expertise of the therapist. It is not the interpretation of the therapist, or his or her use of behavioural techniques, that is responsible for change. People, and the systems in which they live, are systems that are inherently capable of evolving and renewing themselves, and the job of the therapist is to facilitate these processes.

The concept of *reflexivity* refers to the human capacity to monitor reactions to situations, actions and inner feelings. Humanistic theory, drawing on the older traditions of existentialism and phenomenology, stresses the importance of viewing persons as capable of reflecting on experience. The possibility of choice and agency arises from reflexivity, since the person does not respond automatically to events but acts intentionally, based on an awareness of alternatives. The existence of choice also brings with it the necessity to examine the values upon which choices are based. It is associated with an appreciation of the role of moral responsibility in intentional human action. Humanistic approaches consider value and responsibility issues to be central to therapy, for example through the Rogerian concept of 'internal' and 'external' locus of evaluation, or through the use of notions of authenticity and genuineness. The implications for therapy of notions of reflexivity and agency are explored by Bohart (2000; Bohart and Tallman, 1999) and Rennie (1998, 2000).

Another key concept in humanistic theory is that of *self*. One consequence of the human capacity for reflexivity is the possibility of gaining a sense of 'Who am I?' through reflecting on the totality of personal experience. The concept or definition of self possessed by a person is a product of both personal reflection and also of social interaction, as others attribute qualities and characteristics to self. The effort to reconcile the senses of self derived from the dialectic between an active, experiencing 'I' and a reactive, socially defined 'me' constitute much of the territory of humanistic therapy. The issue of how to understand the scope and domain of the self has been a recurring issue in humanistic psychology. For example, various writers have argued that any adequate definition of self must include its spiritual and political as well as interpersonal aspects.

Humanistic theory regards people as *organismic* beings, as embodied. This is not an attempt to reduce human experience to biology and genetics, but represents instead an awareness of the fact that the sense that people have of the world is usually experienced at a visceral, feeling level.

The final core concept of the humanistic paradigm in counselling psychology is that of *experiencing*. Indeed, some writers would describe all humanistic therapies as fundamentally experiential in nature. The concept of experiencing employed in humanistic psychology is fundamentally anti-reductionist in nature. Being a person is not reduced either to cognition or to emotion, nor are these two concepts conceived as polar opposites. Instead, life is apprehended through experiencing, which always involves an interplay of thought and feeling (Bohart, 1993). Similarly, current actions are not determined by past events or memories, since action is carried out with reference to experiencing, which always includes threads of meaning that relate to the sense the person has of their past, present and future. Moreover, experiencing is coloured by a sense of purposefulness or intentionality.

Limitations of space make it difficult to do justice to the philosophical basis of humanistic psychology. However, this brief overview should be sufficient to demonstrate that the paradigm represents a way of understanding persons that is coherent and distinctive.

The assessment process

Differences exist between the humanistic approach and other paradigms in counselling psychology in relation to the practice of assessing clients. In emphasizing the sense of person-in-process, and in seeking to understand the person from within his or her frame of reference, humanistic therapists and researchers find little value in conventional approaches to psychological assessment. For example, any attempt to fit a diagnostic label to the client is seen as likely to intrude into the relationship between client and therapist, and interfere with the task of understanding the client's experience from his or her own point of view. Identification of target problems or behavioural repertoires, as in behaviour therapy, would similarly represent a distraction from the aim of exploring the experiential dimensions of these behaviours. In either case, assessment procedures could well introduce into the therapeutic relationship an image of therapist as expert and authority figure, which would run counter to the intention of encouraging the growth of an internal locus of evaluation in the client. In humanistic work, therapist interventions are not initiated in response to global categorizations of the client (e.g. 'borderline') but are made in reaction to in-session events and are negotiated with the client.

The one area in which assessment occurs in humanistic counselling is in relation to the decisions made by both therapist and client to make a commitment to working together. Usually, a humanistic therapist will meet a prospective client before beginning therapy, to enable a process of mutual decision making to take place. From the point of view of the client, it is important to check out the credibility and humanity of the therapist. From the perspective of the counsellor or psychotherapist, there are two main objectives. First, the therapist is interested in the readiness and willingness of the client to engage in therapy (see Mearns and Thorne, 1998). Secondly, the therapist reflects on his or her own personal reactions to the client in order to discover whether there will be any personal barriers to being able to enter into an accepting and congruent relationship with them. To do this effectively, the therapist must have the capacity to trust his or her own feelings about the client. This kind of assessment therefore relies on interpersonal skills and awareness rather than on history taking or the use of questionnaires or other psychometric instruments. Where such standard measures are employed, the meaning of the data that are generated will be determined by the client.

Researchers working within the humanistic paradigm have also found it necessary to confront the issue of client assessment. Clearly, a great deal of published psychotherapy research relies on the administration of standardized assessment instruments. In the early years of research into the humanistic therapies, efforts were made to develop questionnaire measures of humanistic concepts such as self-actualization, self-esteem, self-disclosure and experiencing. Rogers and his colleagues (Rogers and Dymond, 1954) developed Q-technique as a tool for assessing self-acceptance in a way that was consistent with a phenomenological perspective. More recently, researchers have begun to explore the process of therapy using Interpersonal Process Recall (Elliott, 1986; Rennie, 1992), a method that calls on the active participation of the client and is highly sensitive to the nuances of the experiential world of the client.

Much of the impetus behind the construction of psychological tests, from the invention of the first intelligence tests, has arisen from the wish to screen or detect people with severe problems so that they can be directed towards special forms of help or control. However, the concept of psychopathology or 'abnormal' psychology does not sit easily with the philosophical and ideological assumptions of the humanistic paradigm. The few humanistic measures that have been constructed have emphasized aspects of mental 'health' (for example, self-actualization) rather than 'illness'. Nevertheless, the practical demands of dealing with clients, some of whom may indeed be highly disturbed, and the requirement to communicate with therapists and mental health professionals of other orientations, have led some humanistic psychologists to begin to evolve a set of classifications of disorders compatible with their approach (see Biermann-Ratjen, 1998; Mearns, 1994; Melnick and Nevis, 1998; Speierer, 1998).

In the past, the reluctance of many humanistic practitioners to participate in assessment of clients has denied them one of the most important means of professional influence and control. In the realm of service provision, counselling and psychotherapy are increasingly becoming assimilated into systems of managed patient care that require categorization of clients and demonstrable therapist competence in relation to specific presenting disorders. In research, there has been a trend toward the evaluation of specific interventions targeted on specific problems ('what works for whom'). In practice, this quest for specificity is made possible through the use of standardized assessment techniques. In their unwillingness to employ bureaucratized and depersonalized methods of assessment that result in the disempowering of persons, humanistic practitioners have taken a stance that has political implications as well as possessing theoretical consistency. Recently, however, researchers within the humanistic tradition have attempted to engage with the challenge of adapting humanistic therapies to the needs of clients with specific problems. Examples of the results of this work, in relation to client problems such as depression, PTSD, psychosomatic disorders and psychosis, can be found in Greenberg et al. (1998) and Thorne and Lambers (1998).

What does change mean and how is it brought about ... what psychological theory of learning is being employed?

Given the philosophy and concept of the person outlined above, how does a humanistically oriented counselling psychologist work with clients? What are the basic change processes occurring in humanistic therapy? Taking the humanistic therapy literature as a whole, it is possible to identify three core therapeutic principles: heightened awareness, carrying forward and 'meeting as healing'. Within the different schools of humanistic practice, different aspects of these themes are given greater or lesser emphasis. For example, the person-centred approach has tended to give greater prominence to the way that a productive therapeutic relationship (as a healing encounter) can be facilitated

Table 6.1   Strategies for working with awareness in humanistic therapy

The phenomenological stance of the therapist
Reflection of meanings and feelings
Therapist resonance
Therapist sensitivity to the client's 'edge of awareness'
Experiential focusing
Use of expressive media – art, movement, voice
Exploring the awareness continuum
Expressing aspects of experience through action and dialogue (e.g. Gestalt two-chair work)
Meditation

through the 'core conditions' of empathy, acceptance and congruence. The Gestalt tradition, on the other hand, has given priority to the here-and-now awareness of the client.

Awareness

Working with awareness in humanistic counselling or psychotherapy can take many forms. The assumption in humanistic therapy is that whatever is troubling the client is exhibited in the quality of their here-and-now awareness. The healthy or fully functioning person (Rogers, 1961) is open to experience, or in a state of 'flow', whereas the person who is troubled and seeking help is engaged in denying or distorting their awareness of self and others in order to avoid unacceptable or frightening areas of feeling or experiencing. From a Gestalt therapy perspective, awareness is an indicator of the quality of the contact between the person and his or her environment. Awareness that is reduced or constricted is associated with an impeded ability to interact with the environment, for example to perceive the wishes of others accurately.

There are significant similarities and differences between the humanistic understanding of the role of awareness in therapy and the psychodynamic understanding of the operation of unconscious fantasy and defence mechanisms. The similarity lies in an agreement that the current conscious awareness of the client may exclude essential data that he or she needs in order to resolve whatever life difficulties he or she may be experiencing. There are, however, two main differences between the humanistic and psychodynamic views on how to help the person in this situation. From a psychodynamic point of view, the client must gain insight into the buried or repressed unresolved childhood events that lie behind the present disturbance, so the primary task of the therapist is to offer interpretations of the links between present problems and past experience. From a humanistic perspective, by contrast, the primary task is to explore the ways in which the client is denying aspects of his or her *current* awareness, and to try out, or experiment with, strategies for becoming more aware. Some of the awareness strategies employed by humanistic therapists are listed in Table 6.1. Using these strategies may have the consequence, in some cases, of opening up areas of buried childhood experience, but uncovering this type of material is not considered necessary for effective therapy to occur. The second important difference between psychodynamic and humanistic conceptions of awareness arises from the question of the extent to which awareness or consciousness can be viewed as intentional. For a psychodynamic therapist, defences are *mechanisms* caused by childhood events, and the client has little control over whether and how these mechanisms operate. Humanistic therapists, on the other hand, assume that the person has a substantial degree of choice over his or her attention and awareness. The implication is that the person can choose to be more aware. An example of how this assumption might be applied in practice would be the Gestalt technique of inviting the client to use more direct language, such as 'I feel' rather than 'it feels'.

Exploration of client awareness is facilitated by a rigorous *phenomenological stance* taken by the therapist. The aim of the therapist is to become sensitive to as many of the client's horizons of meaning as possible, to gain as complete an understanding of the experiental world of the client as can be achieved. This process is similar to that of 'phenomenological reduction', in which any assumptions or interpretations about an experience are systematically 'bracketed off' in an endeavour to reach the core or essence of the phenomenon. The task for the humanistic therapist is to work with the client to open up the many facets of meaning implicit in an issue or problem, without imposing an externally derived or 'expert' interpretation of what the client is feeling. The rule of humanistic therapy is that the client is always the expert on his or her experience. The aim of the therapist is to accept and give value to the meaning or content of whatever the client is exploring, while actively facilitating the process of exploration. The slogan for therapists coined by Greenberg et al. (1993) is to 'direct process, not content'.

Perhaps the clearest articulation of the humanistic sense of awareness as an active process of experiential processing can be found in the notion of the *awareness cycle* that has been developed in Gestalt therapy. This model of awareness provides a way of making sense of how the on-going flow of living and relating can be blocked in a number of different ways. For example, a client working on a relationship problem could be open to the feelings he has about the situation, but may be stuck at the stages of mobilizing energy and taking action that would bring about change. The awareness cycle model can be useful for the therapist in helping him or her to focus on the tasks the client might need to complete in order to re-establish a healthy flow of experiencing.

Carrying forward

The second fundamental principle of humanistic therapy can be described as carrying forward. This principle is based on the philosophical assumption that some kind of search for fulfilment or 'growth' is inherent in being human, and that as a result there is always a sense of movement, emergence, direction or intentionality in attempts by clients to resolve difficult life dilemmas. The idea of carrying forward can be observed in the awareness cycle model, which is based in an assumption that the 'natural' state of affairs is continuous movement through these phases of experiencing. The writings of Gendlin (1984) on experiential focusing convey a similar perspective.

Bozarth has argued that the central task in client-centred or person-centred therapy is 'going with the client's direction, at the client's pace, and with the client's unique way of being' (1990: 63). Rennie (1990), in his research into the experiences of therapy clients, reports that they are frequently aware of a sense of direction, which he refers to as the client's 'track', in what they are working on:

> clients … increasingly have a sense of being on a path, or train of thought (client's track). There is a compellingness to the track: clients feel that they are on the edge of their experience; there is uncertainty whether words can be found to express what they are sensing. (1990: 160)

The therapeutic principle of experiential carrying forward is also evident in the use of process models of therapeutic change. The original global model of therapeutic process developed by Rogers (1961) described a series of seven stages through which successful client-centred therapy would proceed (Table 6.2). More recently, more specific micro-process change models have been constructed, identifying stages in effective empathic responding (Barrett-Lennard, 1981), focusing on a problem (Gendlin, 1981) and experiential processing of various kinds of emotional problems (Greenberg et al., 1993). The research carried out by the group led by Greenberg and Rice has been instrumental in developing a perspective on experiential processing that combines key elements of both person-centred and Gestalt practice. From Gestalt they have taken the idea that it is possible to identify discrete change events within each therapy session. These events are triggered by the client expressing a dilemma or emotion that acts as a 'marker' to initiate a distinctive set of experiential processing tasks. From the person-centred approach they have identified the therapeutic relationship as a whole, and therapist empathy in particular, as critical factors in enabling the client to carry out processing tasks effectively.

From a humanistic point of view, learning is always *experiential* in nature and is always a *process* that occurs in a *relational* context (Kolb, 1981; Rogers, 1969). Whereas other orientations would stress the cognitive (for example, insight or reframing), behavioural or emotional/cathartic elements in therapeutic learning, from a humanistic perspective all these elements are seen as facets of one experiential process. Working experientially involves taking account of the interplay between thoughts, action and feelings rather than attending rigidly to any one of these modes in isolation.

The nature of the relationship between counselling psychologist and individual client

The third element of the humanistic approach to enabling therapeutic change is based in an acceptance of the healing power of the relationship between therapist and client. In humanistic therapy the practitioner strives to meet the client as a person, in as genuine a manner as possible. Active, sensitive, empathic

Table 6.2   The process of change

Stage 1

Communication is about external events. Feelings and personal meanings are not 'owned'. Close relationships are construed as dangerous. Rigidity in thinking. Impersonal, detached. Does not use first-person pronouns

Stage 2

Expression begins to flow more freely in respect of non-self topics. Feelings may be described but not owned. Intellectualization. Describes behaviour rather than inner feelings. May show more interest and participation in therapy

Stage 3

Describes personal reactions to external events. Limited amount of self-description. Communication about past feelings. Beginning to recognize contradictions in experience

Stage 4

Descriptions of feelings and personal experiences. Beginning to experience current feelings, but fear and distrust of this when it happens. The 'inner life' is presented and listed or described, but not purposefully explored

Stage 5

Present feelings are expressed. Increasing ownership of feelings. More exactness in the differentiation of feelings and meanings. Intentional exploration of problems in a personal way, based in processing of feelings rather than reasoning

Stage 6

Sense of an 'inner referent', or flow of feeling which has a life of its own. 'Physiological loosening' such as moistness in the eyes, tears, sighs, muscular relaxation accompanies the open expression of feelings. Speaks in present tense or offers vivid representation of past

Stage 7

A series of felt sense connecting the different aspects of an issue. Basic trust in own inner processes. Feelings experienced with immediacy and richness of detail. Speaks fluently in present tense

Sources: Klein et al. (1986), Rogers (1961)

engagement in the world of the client is fundamental to humanistic therapy (Bohart and Greenberg, 1997). The therapist does not assume that the feelings that the client has towards him or her are necessarily due to some kind of repro-duction of what was felt in previous relationships (with parents, for example), but are a real relationship between two people who are each reacting to the other in the here-and-now. The discussion by Shlien (1984) of the Freudian con-cept of transference makes this clear. Shlien (1984) acknowledges that clients may love or hate their therapist, but he disputes the view that this phenomenon must be seen as a repetition of previous patterns of relating. For Shlien, such feelings are expressed by the client in response to whether they feel themselves to be accepted and understood by the therapist:

> the therapist is responsible for two fundamental behaviors – understanding and misunderstanding – which account for love, or for hate, and their associated affects.

These, as well as other behaviors and the situation and personality of the therapist, may account – should first be held accountable – for the whole of what passes for transference. (Shlien, 1984: 177)

In his analysis of the origins of the concept of transference in the early work of Freud and Breuer, Shlien argues that ' "transference" is a fiction, invented and maintained by the therapist to protect himself from the consequences of his own behaviour' (1984: 153).

The formulation by Rogers (1957) of the 'necessary and sufficient conditions' for therapeutic change, which has subsequently become known as the '*core conditions' model*, suggests that effective therapy can only occur within a relationship between therapist and client in which the latter perceives the former as being accepting, empathic and congruent. Within Gestalt therapy, notions of therapist–client *contact* and *merger* are used to refer to the same kind of relationship qualities. Although much of the published work of Fritz Perls appears to depict a version of Gestalt therapy in which an on-going relationship with the client is not given any great emphasis, recent developments in Gestalt therapy have tended to favour the relational approach (Hycner, 1993; Hycner and Jacobs, 1995).

The kinds of therapeutic processes described above, involving the deepening of awareness and the carrying forward of experiencing, are more likely to occur in the context of a relationship in which the client feels enough trust and safety to take risks and be open. However, the view in humanistic psychology is that participation in a close, authentic relationship with another person is healing in itself. The therapeutic alliance or relationship is not merely a means to a set of therapeutic ends but is empowering and valuable in its own right. People are seen as becoming anxious, depressed or confused because they lack relationships that are affirming and supportive. The humanistic therapist aims to achieve authenticity and *transparency* (Jourard, 1971) in relation to the client. In practice, this means that the therapist is more willing to be known, for example being more open about his or her personal values or feelings, than would practitioners from other orientations. Van Balen (1990), Friedman (1992) and Schmid (1998) represent an important strand of humanistic thinking, influenced by the work of the philosopher Martin Buber, with their proposal that therapists should aim to enter into a *dialogue* with their clients, and accept the implication that to do so will involve a degree of *mutuality* in the relationship: 'we come to awareness of ourselves not just through our individuality … but in our dialogue with other selves – in their response to us and in the way they call us into being' (Friedman, 1992: 5).

These relationship qualities are actively constructed by humanistic therapists. For example, therapist transparency and genuineness can be communicated to the client through the use of *meta-communication* (Kiesler, 1988; Rennie, 1998). Rather than merely responding directly to the client, the counsellor may make reference to the feelings, intentions and understandings that lie behind his or her response. The therapist response may be offered in a tentative manner, to allow the client every opportunity to disagree with or correct the therapist's understanding of the situation. This style of communicating with the client has a number of advantages. It conveys the message that the client is in control, it encourages the use of the internal locus of evaluation of the client, and minimizes the likelihood of the therapist intruding on the internal processing or 'track' (Rennie, 1990) being pursued by the client. It also models for the client a means of dealing with the pervasiveness of meta-perspectives in everyday interactions. A further use of meta-communication is suggested by Kiesler (1988), who views it as a way of providing the client with feedback on his or her style of relating to others.

A final dimension of the counsellor–client relationship from a humanistic perspective concerns professionalization. Humanistic practitioners have generally done their best to reduce the status and power differences existing between client and helper. For example, while other approaches to counselling and psychotherapy have fought hard to fashion strong professional identities, there has been some ambivalence within the humanistic paradigm over this issue. The elements of professionalization put in place by members of other therapeutic orientations have included: professional associations with licensing and disciplinary powers, exclusion from practice of non-professionals, a significant presence in university-based training, a strong emphasis on research, representation in national professional bodies and a wide range of publishing outlets. Although the humanistic paradigm includes, in some form, all these elements of professionalization, the commitment and energy with which these professional goals have been pursued has not matched that exhibited by other approaches to therapy. To some extent this ambivalence over professional status reflects the origins of the humanistic paradigm as a 'third force' protest movement. The social philosophy or politics implicit in the humanistic paradigm has influenced adherents of this approach to be cautious about the increasing trend toward viewing counselling and psychotherapy as professional specialisms.

Traditionally, humanistic psychology has been developed either by individuals or by non-hierarchical, non-bureaucratic collectives. Key figures in humanistic psychology such as Fritz Perls, Sidney Jourard or Sheldon Kopp worked largely alone or in temporary collaborations with small groups of colleagues. The most important organizational centre during the early years of humanistic psychology, the Counselling Center at the University of Chicago, was led by Rogers but was characterized by 'maximum participation by all staff members in matters which concern the total group' (Gordon, 1951: 322). It is significant that, despite the dominant position in psychotherapy training and research held by the Chicago group during the 1950s, they did not establish a specialist journal or professional association for client-centred therapy.

It would be easy to attribute this ambivalence over professionalization to an individualism inherent in the humanistic approach. Holland (1977) and Masson (1988), for example, have criticized humanistic psychology for constructing an image of the person detached from any social or political context. It is certainly true that there exist some strands of extreme masculine individualism within humanistic writing. Nevertheless, there has also been a strong communitarian movement within the humanistic approach, a deep appreciation of collective experience, expressed through the writings of Rogers (1969) on the 'healing capacity' of the group (see also Barrett-Lennard, 1994; Wood, 1984). This sense of collective life has been rooted in experience in temporary community groups (up to about 100 members) that meet face to face and share a commitment to authentic dialogue. It is probably reasonable to conclude that people who have been exposed to this type of community group experience have a distrust of the operation of larger, more formal organizational groupings and institutions.

Although humanistic psychology grew out of the European philosophical traditions of existentialism and phenomenology, it took root originally in the United States, and as a result has assimilated American values around self-help and mistrust of experts (Sollod, 1978). Humanistic approaches in counselling have therefore been in the vanguard of the psychology that has been 'given away' so that it can be used by ordinary people. The humanistic paradigm includes many applications within self-help groups and counselling agencies staffed by non-professional helpers (for details see Larson, 1984). In addition, a number of books written by humanistic psychologists have been aimed at the popular market rather than merely at a readership of mental health professionals.

Family, group and organizational applications

The humanistic approach to counselling psychology has been applied in most of the major areas of counselling psychology practice. The emphasis of the approach on personal growth and empowerment has resulted in wide use within student counselling and private practice. The reliance on personal qualities and the ability of the counsellor to form a healing relationship, rather than on his or her ability to master abstract theory or complex technique, has led to extensive adoption of the approach in voluntary agencies. The humanistic-experiential model has also been implemented in work with families, couples and children, and with highly disturbed clients (see Lietaer et al., 1990; Greenberg et al., 1998; Thorne and Lambers, 1998 for examples of recent developments in these areas). Many models of group work and organizational development have drawn heavily on humanistic theory. Finally, humanistic ideas have been applied to a range of social and political problems (e.g. Rogers, 1978).

Research evidence about effectiveness

Some of the earliest controlled outcome studies of counselling and psychotherapy were carried out by Rogers and his colleagues at Ohio and Chicago in the 1940s (Cartwright, 1957; Rogers and Dymond, 1954). These studies provided evidence for the effectiveness of client-centred therapy in bringing about positive changes in client self-acceptance, self-awareness, confidence, emotional maturity and adjustment. However, subsequent research into humanistic therapy has placed less emphasis on the issue of outcome. Partly, this can be attributed to a realization that, from a phenomenologically informed perspective, any definition of outcome is complex and ambiguous:

> 'We have come to the conclusion that 'success', no matter how it is phrased or described, is not a usable or useful criterion for research in psychotherapy ... in every meaningful way we have given up the concept of 'success' as the criterion against which our research measurements will be compared. (Rogers and Dymond, 1954: 29)

In the 1960s and 1970s, therefore, the attention of humanistic researchers was drawn more to the question of therapy process, in particular to testing Rogers's (1957) 'necessary and sufficient conditions' process model. Reviews of the findings obtained by this programme of research can be found in Watson (1984) and Cramer (1992). Other factors contributing to the decline of outcome studies of humanistic counselling and psychotherapy were the failure of the approach to maintain its presence in the academic world, and also a general sense that the methods of empiricist psychology were not consistent with the values and philosophy of humanism (Giorgi, 1987).

Despite these constraints, a number of outcome studies of humanistic counselling and psychotherapy have been carried out in recent years. In an authoritative review, Greenberg et al. (1994) found thirty seven studies published between 1978 and 1992, involving 1,272 clients. Fifteen of these studies included comparisons with no-treatment or waiting-list groups, and twenty six studies compared humanistic therapy with another therapeutic orientation. Taken as a whole, the results of these studies provide strong evidence for the general efficacy of humanistic therapy, with a mean effect size (ES) of 1.30, which means that the average client would move from the fiftieth to the ninetieth percentile in relation to the pre-therapy sample. When compared with other forms of active intervention, humanistic therapy proved to be no more or no less effective than any other approach. It is of some interest that many of these studies were carried out by researchers employing client-centred therapy as a kind of placebo control. This circumstance would tend to lower expectation of positive outcomes, and would be consistent with the view that the research does not overestimate the effectiveness of humanistic therapy.

The relatively small number of studies carried out makes it difficult to estimate the efficacy of humanistic-experiential counselling and psychotherapy with reference to particular client groups. Greenberg et al. (1994) observe that there is some evidence to suggest that clients who are interested in their inner experience, have good social skills and a high need for intimacy are best suited to humanistic-experiential work. More favourable outcomes were obtained with clients with relationship problems, anxiety or depression, with less impressive results for more chronic or severe problems such as schizophrenia. These trends are similar to those found with other forms of therapy. Greenberg et al. conclude that 'there is as yet no clear evidence for selecting or deselecting experiential therapy in treating any specific disorder' (1994: 518).

To sum up, it is perhaps reasonable to comment that much more research needs to be carried out to evaluate the effectiveness of humanistic therapy with different client groups. By contrast, humanistically oriented studies of psychotherapy process have been at the leading edge of psychotherapy research. The development by Elliott (1986) of Interpersonal Process Recall as a research tool, the studies by Rennie (1990, 1992) into the experience of the client, and the introduction by Greenberg (1984) of task analysis methods have been instrumental in advancing studies of the 'interior' of the therapy hour. It is perhaps worth noting that these developments in process research have been carried out in North America and have relied on various qualitative approaches to research that are broadly consistent with the philosophy and values of the originators of humanistic psychology, whereas many of the more recent outcome studies, which have used traditional research designs, have been carried out in Europe. There has been no British research of any significance into humanistic therapy.

Conclusion

In the conclusion to this chapter, the current status of the humanistic paradigm will be evaluated by considering the strengths and weaknesses of the approach, and identifying some of the directions in which it appears to be moving. For an alternative perspective on the same topics, the reader is recommended to consult Rice and Greenberg (1992), Greenberg et al. (1998) and Schneider et al. (2001).

The weaknesses of the humanistic approach to counselling and psychotherapy are obvious to most psychologists. Historically, psychology has worked hard to legitimize its status as a scientific discipline by using research to distance it from the domain of commonsense belief and folk psychology. In the field of humanistic psychology, however, there has been a marked lack of research, not merely into the processes and outcomes of humanistic therapy, but into the personality theory and concepts that underpin it. Despite the influence of Rogers, a leading figure in psychotherapy research, there has evolved what could be described as an anti-intellectual bias in much humanistic writing and training. The leading journals, *Journal of Humanistic Psychology* and *Self and Society*, contain very little research material. There is no humanistic developmental psychology, or humanistic cognitive psychology. This absence of research activity places humanistic counselling psychologists at a growing disadvantage in a market place that increasingly demands accountability and evidence of effectiveness in relation to tightly defined client groups or presenting problems.

From a sociological perspective, humanistic therapy can be viewed as very much a product of a particular era in which the prosperity of Western industrial societies allowed greater than usual expression of individual creativity and freedom. It can be argued that humanistic therapy embodies a 'monocultural' image of the person (Holdstock, 1993) which has little relevance outside this specific time and place. Even within the cultural milieu in which it has evolved, humanistic psychology is silent on many critically important issues. For example, there has been no systematic attempt within humanistic therapy to assimilate the lessons of feminism or to confront the experience of racism and colonialism. It would be difficult to characterize psychoanalysis as a politically radical movement, but these debates have not been opened up in humanistic psychology to the extent they have within psychoanalysis. It is certainly true that individual humanistic practitioners have addressed such issues at a local level, but there has been little attempt to integrate what they have learned into the paradigm as a whole. On the other hand, there are those within the humanistic approach who would argue that its strong emphasis on authenticity and acceptance in relationships militates against systematic discrimination in the form of racism, sexism or ageism, and that equality of value for persons lies at the core of a humanistic orientation.

The issues being discussed here can be seen as representing significant gaps in the humanistic paradigm, and their existence can be attributed to a number of factors. The emergence of humanistic psychology as a protest movement in psychology in the 1950s has had the effect of 'humanizing' much of mainstream psychology, so that writers such as Wertheimer (1978) and Smith (1982) can claim that much of psychology as a whole is humanistic in nature. The more radical humanistic theorists and practitioners, those who have continued to argue for a distinctive humanistic agenda, have found little welcome within the academy. Most have made their living as practitioners, with limited time for scholarship and research. Those who have worked in universities have found it difficult to secure funding for humanistic research programmes. There is, however, a more basic difficulty that underlies the lack of advance in humanistic thought: the lack of a credible humanistic research method. The pioneering research into client-centred therapy carried out by Rogers and his colleagues attempted to accommodate phenomenological ideas within a traditional empiricist approach, without acknowledging the epistemological tensions implicit in this endeavour. On the other hand, research based on a rigorous application of phenomenological methods (see Valle and Halling, 1989) has had limited impact. Mainstream psychologists have been able to apply experimental methods to a wide array of research problems. Likewise, psychoanalytic scholars have been able to rely on an interpretive approach to research topics. By contrast, humanistic psychologists have not possessed a methodology for doing research that is consistent with the broader aims and values of the paradigm.

Nevertheless, humanistic approaches to counselling psychology also possess a number of significant strengths. The humanistic paradigm is built on a distinctive concept of the person, viewed as an active, aware, contextualized and intentional agent who must be understood as a complex whole. This way of seeing self and others is experienced by many people as affirming and facilitative. There exists a set of basic principles concerning the application of this concept of the person within therapy, through the creation of a helping or healing relationship. It is a flexible approach, and one that can be readily learned. It is a way of working with people that can be used in many different settings.

The humanistic paradigm in psychology is emerging from a period in which it was dominated by a handful of major figures such as Rogers and Perls. It is also emerging from a period in which its aims and values have not been favoured by the prevailing political and economic conditions. There are four trends that can be detected within the paradigm that represent possibilities for significant future advances in this approach These trends are:

- Integration of ideas from cognitive psychology,
- Development of a distinct research methodology,
- Theoretical assimilation of concepts of spirituality,
- Re-establishing links with broader humanistic traditions in literature and the arts.

Given that humanistic psychology is centrally concerned with the process of meaning making, the relevance of cognitive psychology has always been clear. Indeed, Gestalt therapy, which in many ways draws upon existential and biological/organismic concepts, was named in recognition of its debt to early cognitive psychologists such as Koffka, Kohler and Wertheimer. The connection between client-centred therapy and cognitive psychology can be seen in Wexler and Rice (1974). However, as Greenberg et al. (1993) observe, there has been substantial progress in cognitive psychology in recent years. Their own work has had the objective of developing an experiential psychotherapy which explicitly draws on contemporary cognitive theory and research in areas such as attention, memory and parallel processing. Their model is based on the idea that problems in living are associated with the operation of dysfunctional emotional schemes. This kind of careful, well informed use of insights from cognitive psychology in the context of a humanistic model of therapy (Greenberg et al., 1993) provides a powerful model for future developments in the field. The work of Toukmanian (1992) has also made a significant contribution to this trend.

The second important area of new thinking within humanistic psychology is related to the question of finding an appropriate research methodology. The increasing acceptance of qualitative methods in the counselling and psychotherapy research community (see Chapter 3) has resulted in the refinement of research approaches that are consistent with the underlying philosophical assumptions of humanistic psychology. These methods involve collaboration with informants or co-participants, along with sensitive strategies for gaining access to experiential material. The researcher is expected to be aware of his or her own role in the inquiry process, and to adopt a reflexive stance toward the data. The research strategies most widely used to achieve these aims are *human inquiry* (Reason, 1988; Reason and Rowan, 1981), the analysis of narrative and discourse (Riessman, 1993), *grounded theory* analysis (Rennie, 1990) and the application of methods of intensive single-case analysis (Elliott, 2001; Schneider, 2001). This movement in the direction of participatory, experientially informed inquiry has been characterized by Rennie (1994) as representing a return to Dilthey's conception of a human science.

A third challenge for the future of humanistic psychology lies in the area of spiritual experience. Despite research findings showing that at least one-third of people have at some point undergone a significant spiritual experience in their lives, counselling and psychotherapy have evolved as mainly secular activities which have tended to deny or ignore this area of human experience. Humanistic psychology, with its emphasis on meaning and higher-order needs, and its openness to ideas from Eastern religions, has always allowed a place for spiritual experience (West, 2000). However, although in the past the real concern for spiritual issues has been shown mainly in transpersonal therapies, there is increasing interest in finding ways of assimilating this dimension into more widely used humanistic therapies such as the person-centred approach (Purton, 1998; Thorne, 1992).

Finally, there are signs of renewed willingness in humanistic psychology to draw upon the much wider and deeper tradition of humanism found in the arts and literature. Many of the founders of humanistic psychology, such as Jacob Moreno, Erich Fromm and Henry Murray, were highly active in exploring the relevance to psychology of fiction and drama. The appreciation of this enormous cultural resource became lost as humanistic psychology became identified as a model of therapy rather than as an approach to psychology. The rediscovery of fiction by writers such as Polster (1987), and the powerful statement by Bruner (1986) of the importance of narrative ways of knowing, signify a return to this fundamental tradition in the humanistic approach. Perhaps there is now an opportunity to look in a fresh way at the roots of the humanistic approach, at those areas of human experience that Sutich (1961) characterized as the 'human capacities and potentialities that have no systematic place either in positivistic or behavioristic theory or in classical psychoanalytic theory, e.g., creativity, love [and] growth'.

References

Barrett-Lennard, G.T. (1981) 'The empathy cycle: refinement of a nuclear concept', *Journal of Counseling Psychology*, 28: 91–100.

Barrett-Lennard, G.T. (1994) 'Toward a person-centered theory of community', *Journal of Humanistic Psychology*, 34 (3): 62–86.

Biermann-Ratjen, E.-M. (1998) 'Incongruence and psychopathology', in B. Thorne and E. Lambers (eds) *Person-centred Therapy: a European Perspective*. London: Sage.

Bohart, A.C. (1993) 'Experiencing: the basis of psychotherapy', *Journal of Psychotherapy Integration*, 3 (1): 51–67.

Bohart, A.C. (2000) '"The client is the most important common factor": clients' self-healing capacities and psychotherapy', *Journal of Psychotherapy Integration*, 10: 127–48.

Bohart, A.C. and Greenberg, L.S. (eds) (1997) *Empathy Reconsidered: New Directions in Psychotherapy*. Washington DC: American Psychological Association.

Bohart, A.C. and Tallman, K. (1999) *How Clients make Therapy Work: the Process of Active Self-healing*. Washington DC: American Psychological Association.

Bozarth, J.D. (1990) 'The essence of client-centered therapy' in G. Lietaer, J. Rombauts and R. Van Balen (eds) *Client-centered and Experiential Therapy in the Nineties*. Leuven: University of Leuven Press.

Bruner, J. (1986) *Actual Minds, Possible Worlds*. Cambridge MA: Harvard University Press.

Bugental, J. (ed.) (1967) *Challenges of Humanistic Psychology*. New York: McGraw-Hill.

Cartwright, D.S. (1957) 'Annotated bibliography of research and theory construction in client-centered therapy', *Journal of Counseling Psychology*, 4 (1): 82–100.

Clarkson, P. (1989) *Gestalt Counselling in Action*. London: Sage.

Clarkson, P. and Mackewn, J. (1993) *Fritz Perls*. London: Sage.

Cramer, D. (1992) *Personality and Psychotherapy: Theory, Practice and Research*. Buckingham: Open University Press.

Elliott, R. (1986) 'Interpersonal Process Recall (IPR) as a psychotherapy process research method' in L.S. Greenberg and W.M. Pinsof (eds) *The Psychotherapeutic Process: a Research Handbook*. New York: Guilford Press.

Elliott, R. (2001) 'Hermeneutic single-case efficacy design: an oveview' in K.J. Schneider, J.F.T. Bugental and J.F. Pierson (eds) *The Handbook of Humanistic Psychology: Leading Edges in Theory, Research and Practice*. Thousand Oaks CA: Sage.

Friedman, M. (1992) *Dialogue and the Human Image: Beyond Humanistic Psychology*. London: Sage.

Gendlin, E.T. (1981) *Focusing*. New York: Bantam Books.

Gendlin, E.T. (1984) 'The client's client: the edge of awareness' in R.F. Levant and J. Shlien (eds) *Client-centered Therapy and the Person-centered Approach: New Directions in Theory, Research and Practice*. New York: Praeger.

Giorgi, A. (1987) 'The crisis of humanistic psychology', *Humanistic Psychologist*, 15 (1): 5–20.

Gordon, T. (1951) 'Group-centered leadership and administration' in C.R. Rogers (ed.) *Client-centred Therapy*. London: Constable.

Greenberg, L.S. (1984) 'Task analysis: the general approach' in L.N. Rice and L.S. Greenberg (eds) *Patterns of Change: Intensive Analysis of Psychotherapy Process*. New York: Guilford Press.

Greenberg, L.S., Elliott, R.K. and Lietaer, G. (1994) 'Research on experiential psychotherapies' in A.E. Bergin and S.L. Garfield (eds) *Handbook of Psychotherapy and Behavior Change*, fourth edition. New York: Wiley.

Greenberg, L.S., Rice, L.N. and Elliott, R. (1993) *Facilitating Emotional Change: the Moment-by-moment Process*. New York: Guilford Press.

Greenberg, L.S., Watson, J.C. and Lietaer, G. (eds) (1998) *Handbook of Experiential Psychotherapy*. New York: Guilford Press.

Holdstock, L. (1993) 'Can we afford not to revision the person-centred concept of self?' in D. Brazier (ed.) *Beyond Carl Rogers*. London: Constable.

Holland, R. (1977) *Self and Social Context*. London: Macmillan.

Hycner, R. (1993) *Between Person and Person: Toward a Dialogical Psychotherapy*. New York: Gestalt Journal Press.

Hycner, R. and Jacobs, L. (1995) *The Healing Relationship in Gestalt Therapy: a Dialogical/Self Psychology Approach*. New York: Gestalt Journal Press.

Jourard, S.M. (1971) *The Transparent Self*, second edition. New York: Van Nostrand Reinhold.

Kiesler, D. (1988) *Therapeutic Metacommunication: Therapist Impact Disclosure as Feedback in Psychotherapy*. Palo Alto CA: Consulting Psychologists Press.

Klein, M.H., Mathieu-Coughlan, P. and Kiesler, D.J. (1986) 'The Experiencing Scales' in L.S. Greenberg and W.M. Pinsof (eds) *The Psychotherapeutic Process: a Research Handbook*. New York: Guilford Press.

Kolb, D. (1981) *Experiential Learning*. New York: Wiley.

Kuhn, T.S. (1962) *The Structure of Scientific Revolutions*. Chicago: University of Chicago Press.

Larson, D. (ed.) (1984) *Teaching Psychological Skills: Models for Giving Psychology Away*. Monterey CA: Brooks Cole.

Lietaer, G., Rombauts, J. and Van Balen, R. (eds) (1990) *Client-centered and Experiential Therapy in the Nineties*. Leuven: University of Leuven Press.

Maddi, S. (1989) *Personality Theories: a Comparative Analysis*, fifth edition. Pacific Grove CA: Wadsworth.

Masson, J. (1988) *Against Therapy*. Glasgow: Collins.

Mearns, D. (1994) *Developing Person-centred Counselling*. London: Sage.

Mearns, D. and Thorne, B. (1998) *Person-centred Counselling in Action*, second edition. London: Sage.

Mearns, D. and Thorne, B. (2000) *Person-centred Therapy Today: New Frontiers in Theory and Practice*. London: Sage.

Melnick, J. and Nevis, S.M. (1998) 'Diagnosing in the here-and-now: a Gestalt therapy approach' in L.S. Greenberg, J.C. Watson and G. Lietaer (eds) *Handbook of Experiential Psychotherapy*. New York: Guilford Press.

Misiak, H. and Sexton, V.S. (1973) *Phenomenological, Existential and Humanistic Psychologies: a Historical Survey*. New York: Grune & Stratton.

Perls, L. (1992) 'Concepts and misconceptions of Gestalt therapy', *Journal of Humanistic Psychology*, 32 (3): 50–6.

Polster, E. (1987) *Every Person's Life is Worth a Novel*. New York: Norton.

Purton, C. (1998) 'Unconditional positive regard and its spiritual implications' in B. Thorne and E. Lambers (eds) *Person-centred Therapy: a European Perspective*. London: Sage.

Reason, P. (ed.) (1988) *Human Inquiry in Action: Developments in New Paradigm Research*. London: Sage.

Reason, P. and Rowan, J. (eds) (1981) *Human Inquiry: a Sourcebook of New Paradigm Research*. Chichester: Wiley.

Rennie, D.L. (1990) 'Toward a representation of the client's experience of the psychotherapy hour' in G. Lietaer, J. Rombauts and R. Van Balen (eds) *Client-centered and Experiential Therapy in the Nineties*. Leuven: University of Leuven Press.

Rennie, D.L. (1992) 'Qualitative analysis of the client's experience of psychotherapy: the unfolding of reflexivity' in S.G. Toukmanian and D.L. Rennie (eds) *Psychotherapy Process Research: Paradigmatic and Narrative Approaches*. London: Sage.

Rennie, D.L. (1994) 'Human science and counselling psychology: closing the gap between research and practice', *Counselling Psychology Quarterly*, 7: 235–50.

Rennie, D.L. (1998) *Person-centred Counselling: an Experiential Approach*. London: Sage.

Rennie, D.L. (2000) 'Aspects of the client's conscious control of the psychotherapeutic process', *Journal of Psychotherapy Integration*, 10 (2): 151–67.

Rice, L.N. and Greenberg, L.S. (1992) 'Humanistic approaches to psychotherapy', in D.K. Freedheim (ed.) *History of Psychotherapy: a Century of Change*. Washington DC: American Psychological Association.

Riessman, C.K. (1993) *Narrative Analysis*. London: Sage.

Rogers, C.R. (1957) 'The necessary and sufficient conditions of therapeutic personality change', *Journal of Consulting Psychology*, 21: 95–103.

Rogers, C.R. (1961) *On Becoming a Person*. London: Constable.

Rogers, C.R. (1969) *Freedom to Learn*. Columbus OH: Merrill.

Rogers, C.R. (1978) *Carl Rogers on Personal Power: Inner Strength and its Revolutionary Impact*. London: Constable.

Rogers, C.R. and Dymond, R.F. (eds) (1954) *Psychotherapy and Personality Change: Co-ordinated Research Studies in the Client-centered Approach*. Chicago: University of Chicago Press.

Schmid, P.F. (1998) '"Face to face": the art of encounter', in B. Thorne and E. Lambers (eds) *Person-centred Therapy: a European Perspective*. London: Sage.

Schneider, K.J. (2001) 'Multiple-case depth research: bringing experience-near closer' in Schneider, K.J., Bugental, J.F.T. and Pierson, J.F. (eds) *The Handbook of Humanistic Psychology: Leading Edges in Theory, Research and Practice*. Thousand Oaks CA: Sage.

Schneider, K.J., Bugental, J.F.T. and Pierson, J.F. (eds) (2001) *The Handbook of Humanistic Psychology: Leading Edges in Theory, Research and Practice*. Thousand Oaks CA: Sage.

Shlien, J.M. (1984) 'A countertheory of transference' in R.F. Levant and J. Shlien (eds) *Client-centered Therapy and the Person-centered Approach: New Directions in Theory, Research and Practice*. New York: Praeger.

Smith, M.B. (1982) 'Psychology and humanism', *Journal of Humanistic Psychology*, 22 (2): 44–55.

Sollod, R.N. (1978) 'Carl Rogers and the origins of client-centered therapy', *Professional Psychology*, 9: 93–104.

Speierer, G.W. (1998) 'Psychopathology according to the differential incongruence model' in L.S. Greenberg, J.C. Watson and G. Lietaer (eds) *Handbook of Experiential Psychotherapy*. New York: Guilford Press.

Sutich, A. (1961) 'Introduction', *Journal of Humanistic Psychology*, 1 (1): vii–ix.

Thorne, B. (1992) *Carl Rogers*. London: Sage.

Thorne, B. and Lambers, E. (eds) (1998) *Person-Centred Therapy: A European Perspective*. London: Sage.

Toukmanian, S.G. (1992) 'Studying the client's perceptual processes and their outcomes in psychotherapy' in S.G. Toukmanian and D.L. Rennie (eds) *Psychotherapy Process Research: Paradigmatic and Narrative Approaches*. London: Sage.

Valle, R.S. and Halling, S. (eds) (1989) *Existential-Phenomenological Perspectives in Psychology: Exploring the Breadth of Human Experience*. New York: Plenum.

Van Balen, R. (1990) 'The therapeutic relationship according to Carl Rogers. Only a climate? A dialogue? Or both?' in G. Lietaer, J. Rombauts and R. Van Balen (eds) *Client-centered and Experiential Therapy in the Nineties*. Leuven: University of Leuven Press.

Watson, J.C., Greenberg, L.S. and Lietaer, G. (1998) 'The experiential paradigm unfolding: relationship and experiencing in therapy' in L.S. Greenberg, J.C. Watson and G. Lietaer (eds) *Handbook of Experiential Psychotherapy*. New York: Guilford Press.

Watson, N. (1984) 'The empirical status of Rogers's hypotheses of the necessary and sufficient conditions for effective psychotherapy' in R.F. Levant and J. Shlien (eds) *Client-centered Therapy and the Person-centered Approach: New Directions in Theory, Research and Practice*. New York: Praeger.

Wertheimer, M. (1978) 'Humanistic psychology and the humane but tough-minded psychologist', *American Psychologist*, 33: 739–45.

West, W. (2000) *Psychotherapy and Spirituality: Crossing the Line between Therapy and Religion*. London: Sage.

Wexler, D.A. and Rice, L.N. (eds) (1974) *Innovations in Client-centered Therapy*. New York: Wiley.

Wood, J.K. (1984) 'Communities for learning: a person-centered approach' in R.F. Levant and J. Shlien (eds) *Client-centered Therapy and the Person-centered Approach: New Directions in Theory, Research and Practice*. New York: Praeger.

Yontef, G. (1998) 'Dialogic Gestalt therapy' in L.S. Greenberg, J.C. Watson and G. Lietaer (eds) *Handbook of Experiential Psychotherapy*. New York: Guilford Press.

7 The Cognitive-Behavioural Paradigm
MICHAEL J. SCOTT AND WINDY DRYDEN

The theoretical origins of cognitive-behaviour therapy can be traced back to the Stoic philosopher Epictetus, who in the first century AD observed that 'People are disturbed not so much by events as by the view which they take of them'. The implication of this observation is that situations (like objects in the visual world) are better viewed from some angles than from others and that, at least in principle, people choose their orientation. However, a person's 'orientation' is itself influenced by his beliefs about himself in relation to the world. Thus if I believe myself to be a football referee I will watch the football match from a different 'angle' from that used if I believe myself to be a football spectator. The task of cognitive-behaviour therapy is to relieve emotional disturbance by helping people change their maladaptive beliefs and behaviours.

Underlying theory of personality and motivation

From a cognitive-behavioural perspective human experience is viewed as a product of four interacting elements – physiology, cognition, behaviour and emotion (Figure 7.1). Thus if I am tense (physiology) when I come to write an essay this may lead me to think 'I am not going to write a good essay' (cognition), which in turn might lead me to feel anxious (emotion) and that might lead me to put my pen down and go for a walk (behaviour). The effect of going for a walk might be to reduce my tension (back to physiology). I may then be more inclined to think, 'In reality I actually do quite well on essays' (cognition) and this may make me feel in turn more relaxed (emotion). In this instance a behaviour (going for a walk) has broken down the negative chain reaction. This behaviour itself may have been energized by my general knowledge (cognition) that going for a walk lifts my mood.

Within the cognitive-behavioural tradition, the primary emphasis is on breaking out of negative chains via the cognitive and behavioural ports of entry. It should be noted, however, that it is perfectly possible in principle to break negative cycles via the physiological port, for example a relaxation exercise involving tensing and relaxing each muscle group in turn, or via the emotional port, for example playing a favourite music CD. Whilst the cognitive-behavioural approach to anxiety and depression and other emotional disorders has concentrated on changing cognitions and behaviours there has been a shift to include emotions as a port of entry when it comes to the treatment of personality disorders.

To return to our example, if I thought that 'I am not going to write a good essay' but also that 'I am a stupid person and worthless', such a belief might

Figure 7.1   The cognitive-behavioural model

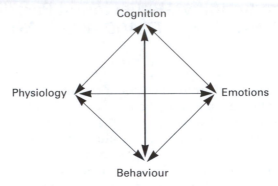

sabotage all my efforts. I might not even go for a walk in the first place. This distinction between thoughts and beliefs suggests that there is an architecture to cognitions with a foundation (beliefs) and a superstructure (thoughts), In keeping with this idea Persons (1989) suggested a two-level model. The first level is one of overt difficulties, with cognitions, emotions and behaviour reciprocally interacting (Figure 7.2). The second level is one of covert difficulties, and it is at this level that core beliefs operate, for example, 'I am stupid.' Core beliefs are the tacit beliefs people have about themselves and their relationship to the world. The core beliefs are rarely verbalized and usually operate at the edge of a person's awareness. They are beliefs inferred from a person's responses to a wide range of situations. The core beliefs are moulded in childhood.

There are reciprocal interactions between levels one and two. My belief that 'I am stupid' may make it more likely that I will automatically think 'I am going to make a mess of something' when confronted with a task. But if I can change such automatic thinking (what are called automatic thoughts) across a range of similar situations I may eventually change the core beliefs.

Beck (1995) has suggested two further refinements of the cognitive architecture, described above. (1) Clients may develop conditional beliefs or rules to avoid activating dysfunctional core beliefs/schemas. They are expressed in an 'if ... then' format, e.g. 'If I do everything perfectly then I do not have to think of myself as useless.' (2) Protective behaviours, designed to avoid activating the dysfunctional schema/core belief, e.g. working extremely long hours at work so that everything is done perfectly. The genesis of the core beliefs and rules can be explored in the counselling session and the client can experiment with challenging the protective behaviours, e.g. plan always to leave work by 5.30 p.m.

With disorders such as anxiety and depression, that is, the Axis 1 disorders in the *Diagnostic and Statistical Manual* fourth edition (*DSM* IV; APA, 1994), automatic thoughts tend to be the target, whereas with Axis 2 disorders in *DSM* IV the personality disorders, the core beliefs are the more direct focus. Individuals differ in their core beliefs and it is the omnipresence of an individual's core beliefs that makes his or her behaviour relatively predictable and confers on the individual a particular personality. Beck et al. (1983), for example, have drawn

Figure 7.2   Persons' (1989) model of client difficulties

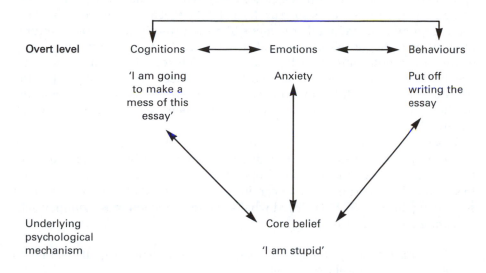

a distinction between autonomous and sociotropic personalities. The autonomous personality bases his sense of self-identity on his achievements and would have a core belief of the form 'If I am not the top then I am a flop.' The sociotropic personality on the other hand believes that he needs the approval of others. His core belief is of the form 'I am nothing if I do not always have other people's approval.'

Within a cognitive-behavioural paradigm the motivation of an individual is held to be a product of two sets of beliefs – self-efficacy and outcome expectancies (Bandura, 1982). Self-efficacy relates to the belief in one's ability to perform an action, whilst outcome expectancies relate to one's belief that the outcome is worthwhile.

The assessment process

A fundamental tenet of Beck's cognitive theory of emotional disorders is that emotional disorders are distinguished by their differing cognitive content (Alford and Beck, 1997). This suggests differing cognitive targets in different emotional states, e.g. Scott and Stradling (2001) have suggested that, among the post-traumatic states, post-traumatic stress disorder (PTSD) is characterized by 'what did happen', subsyndromal PTSD by 'what could have happened', depression by 'what I can't do now' and the associated features of PTSD by 'what I should/should not have done'. Cognitive-behavioural approaches have been developed differently for various disorders. It is therefore important to be able to identify and distinguish the different disorders. Though unstructured interviews are commonly used to assess clients' emotional difficulties in routine clinical practice, they have poor levels of agreement, 32–54 per cent (Beck et al., 1962), whereas the level of agreement using structured interviews such as the SCID (First et al., 1995) are over 90 per cent. Cognitive-behavioural treatment like the prescription of psychotropic medication is diagnosis-specific, and structured interviews ought to be a part of the armamentarium of CBT practitioners. Self-report measures are not a substitute for diagnoses but are useful as a measure of change. Having specific criteria for different conditions provides a basis for answering the fundamental research question 'Which treatment works best for which client?' (Paul, 1967).

Beck's cognitive theory of emotional disorders (Alford and Beck, 1997) states that it is cognitive distortions that give rise to maladaptive interpretations of the context in which the individual operates and of that context's relationship to self. But the distortions are not confined to content but also involve errors of processing. Burns (1980) has listed what seem to be the ten most common self-defeating thought processes.

- *All-or-nothing thinking,* seeing everything as black and white, e.g. 'If I am not in complete control, I will lose all control.'
- *Over-generalization*, where it is concluded from one negative event that other negative events are thereby likely, e.g. 'I wasn't successful at that and now everything is probably going to fall apart.'
- *Mental filter,* seizing on a negative fragment of a situation and dwelling on it, omitting consideration of any positive feature, e.g. 'Town was crowded, it was awful … Oh yes, I did get some great bargains and bump into some old friends … but it was so bad in town.'
- *Automatic discounting,* sensitivity to absorbing negative information and summarily discounting positive information, e.g. 'yes I was complimented, but he is nice to everyone'.
- *Jumping to conclusions,* where a conclusion is inferred from irrelevant evidence, e.g. 'Everyone stared at me because my stomach was bloated.' This often involves 'mind reading'.
- *Magnification and minimization,* magnifying imperfections and minimizing positive attributes.
- *Emotional reasoning,* using feeling as evidence of the truth of a situation, e.g. 'I feel guilty, therefore I must have done something bad'.
- *'Should' statements,* an overdose of moral imperatives, 'shoulds', 'musts', 'have to's' and 'oughts'.
- *Labelling and mislabelling,* Emotional reactions are in large measure a product of the label a person attaches to a phenomenon. An inappropriate label can produce a distressing reaction.
- *Personalization,* egocentric interpretation of interpersonal events relating to the self, e.g. 'Two people laughed and whispered something to each other when I walked by. They were probably saying I look odd.'

Alford and Beck (1997) propose that the information-processing biases are generic, i.e. not specific to any one emotional disorder, with the possible exception of all-or-nothing thinking, which appears to be a prominent feature of

Table 7.1   Core rubrics for personality disorders

Paranoid personality
   I am disliked by others
   Life is a competitive struggle against external enemies
   Therefore, I will excuse myself from blame and failure by attributing blame to others

Schizoid personality
   I am a misfit
   Life is a difficult place and human relationships are troublesome
   Therefore, it is better for me to keep my distance and maintain a low profile

Antisocial personality
   I am entitled to what I want
   Life is a jungle where dog eats dog
   Therefore, I will eat before I am eaten and defy their efforts to tame me

Obsessive-compulsive personality
   I am liable to be held responsible for what goes wrong
   Life is unpredictable
   Therefore, I have to be on guard against anything that might go wrong

borderline personality disorder. There is some overlap between the processes; it is not suggested that each self-defeating thought pattern is in a watertight compartment.

In recent years the attention of cognitive-behaviourists has shifted to a focus on personality disorders, partly because these disorders may coexist with an emotional disorder such as depression or anxiety and make it more difficult to treat the latter. Forgus and Shulman (1979) have provided a framework for examining the cognitive content of the personality disorders by asking clients to perform the sentence completion exercise below.

1   I am ...
2   Life is ...
3   So I ...

Whilst each individual's response will be unique to them, it is argued that there are families of responses that typify the personality disorders. Completion of the above sentences by a client would give a brief summary (rubric) of that client in relation to others and the strategies he or she uses. Certain rubrics are held to be prototypical of particular personality disorders; these are called core rubrics (Table 7.1).

To meet the diagnostic criteria for a personality disorder the client would not only have to manifest the criteria at the time of assessment but would also have to have exhibited such traits by early adulthood. It follows that the personality-disorderd client will have exhibited the same view of themselves (I am), view of the world (Life is) and strategies (Therefore), in early adulthood. Within the cognitive-behavioural framework the genesis of personality disorders is held to lie in the acquisition of maladaptive beliefs in childhood. These beliefs were probably functional in the context in which they originated but are maladaptive in the current adult situation. To trace the aetiology of personality disorder it is also useful to ask clients to complete the framework as if they were in childhood. Where the truthfulness of a client may be in question (for example, a client with a suspected antisocial personality disorder), evidence would need to be collected from significant others and 'slotted' into the framework. In moving from the treatment of emotional disorders to personality disorders there is a shift to a more historical focus, with a greater emphasis on childhood material. Beck et al. (1990) have developed a similar framework to Forgus and Shulman (1979) using the headings 'View of self' 'View of others' (a greater emphasis than in Forgus and Shulman on the interpersonal), 'Strategies' and 'Main beliefs' and have applied it to elaborate each of the personality disorders except for borderline personality disorder (BPD). Beck et al. were unable to explicate the specific thought content of BPDs and suggest that it is their thought processes such as all-or-nothing thinking that are the primary problem. In addition they suggest their compulsiveness and low frustration tolerance complicate matters. Beck et al. also suggest that their chronically low self-esteem has to be a prime therapeutic target.

Young (1990) contends that dysfunctional experiences with early socializing agents and peers can lead to the formation of Early Maladaptive Schemas (EMS). He defines EMS as 'extremely stable and enduring themes (regarding oneself and one's relationship with others) that develop during childhood and are elaborated throughout an individual's lifetime. These schemas serve as templates for the processing of later experiences' (1990: 9). They are most in evidence when the person shows high levels of affect and overreacts to situations. He identifies sixteen maladaptive schemas grouped under five headings.

- *Impaired autonomy*, expectations about oneself and the environment that interfere with one's perceived ability to separate, survive and function independently.
- *Disconnection*, expectation that one's need for nurturing, stable, trustworthy and empathetic relationships – social or intimate – will not be met in a predictable manner.
- *Undesirability*, the expectation that one will not be desirable to other people in terms of any of the following: physical attractiveness, social skills, inner worth, moral integrity, interesting personality, career accomplishment, etc.
- *Restricted self-expression*, inordinate restriction or suppression of one's emotions, impulses, natural inclinations or daily preferences in order to gain the respect of others or avoid guilt.
- *Insufficient limits*, excessive personal wants that lead to difficulty meeting others' expectations or one's personal goals.

Young educates clients on how they use schema maintenance strategies (for example, look for information that supports their schema and discount information that contradicts the maladaptive schema). He also introduces the notion of schema avoidance, where the client will not think about certain material because it is highly affect-laden; this seems consistent with defensive notions such as denial. The third process he highlights is schema compensation: engaging in behaviour to compensate for an activated maladaptive schema (for example, a person who proves to himself and others how strong he is to compensate for an activated 'weakness' schema). The focus of therapy is schema change. This is done by the counsellor identifying and labelling the client's schemas and challenging them. Extensive use is made of imagery to evoke memories and feelings.

What does change mean and how is it brought about?

Change within the cognitive-behavioural paradigm is often synonymous with symptom reduction and behaviour change. Thus success with an anxious client would be gauged by say a reduction in the number of and intensity of the symptoms. If the anxious client had also shown agoraphobic avoidance his/her improvement would also be assessed by his/her ability to venture forth alone. However, for some conditions, such as depression, lasting symptom reduction, that is to say, relapse prevention, is postulated to depend on the modification of core beliefs. Counselling psychologists are likely to consult not only clients who might merit a diagnostic label on *DSM* IV but also clients with problems in living; for both categories attention has been paid to the question of what constitutes clinical change. (This is an important question not only from the point of view of whether what the counselling psychologist does makes any 'real' difference to the client's life, but also from the point of view of the audits demanded of employers of counselling psychologists.) Jacobson and Truax (1991) have suggested three ways to operationalize clinically significant change:

- When the post-test mean score of a client falls beyond the mean of a comparative dysfunctional group by two or more standard deviations.
- When the post-test mean score of a client falls within two standard deviations of a normative group's mean.
- When the post-test mean score of a client is more likely to have been drawn from the normative than from the dysfunctional group's distribution.

For depression, norms for normal and dysfunctional groups are readily available (Nietzel et al., 1987), making the determination of clinically significant change easier than for other disorders where comparative data have yet to be assembled. Cognitive-behaviour therapy is not a single therapy and it may be that some cognitive-behaviour therapies turn out to be better than others at bringing about change with some disorders. They can be categorized under four main headings: coping skills, problem-solving, cognitive restructuring and structural cognitive therapy. First the similarities of the cognitive-behaviour therapies are described and then the differences. The family members share the following characteristics.

Therapy begins with an elaborate, well planned rationale. This provides clients with an explanation of their disturbance and of the steps that they will be guided through to help them overcome their difficulties. In practice this means explaining that it is the interpretation and evaluation of an event (B) that is the major influence on emotional response (C), rather than the event/stimulus (A) *per se*. Analogies are useful to convey this message. For example, 'The mind is like a camera, it depends on the settings and the lenses you choose as to what sort of photographs of events you take. It is possible to teach people to choose the settings and lenses so that you get a more realistic picture of the situation than the ones that you are typically disturbed about.' The rationale for the behavioural dimension of therapy is usually explained in terms of activity as a prerequisite for a sense of mastery or pleasure. It is therefore necessary to overcome the inertia that emotional distress can produce.

The cognitive and behavioural dimensions overlap considerably. For example, a client may refuse to go to the theatre, something he once used to enjoy; that is, he resists the behavioural task on the cognitive grounds that 'I know I am not going to enjoy it, so why bother?' This roadblock would be tackled cognitively by suggesting that the thought that he would not enjoy the play was a hypothesis; he does not have a crystal ball and as such he needs to conduct an experiment to assess the veracity of his prediction. At the start of therapy it is also important to outline the time scale of therapy, the likelihood of success and the importance of homework assignments.

Therapy provides training in skills that the client can utilize to increase his effectiveness in handling his daily life. Clients are asked to record events between sessions that they experience as upsetting. These may be external events, such as being criticized by a spouse, or internal events, for example a sudden change of mood looking out of the window watching the traffic go by. Having identified the triggering events and the emotional responses to them, clients are asked to record what they may have said to themselves to get so upset, that is, to find the Bs of the ABC model. Clients may have greater or lesser access to the B, depending on whether it is at the forefront of their mind or at the edge of awareness. Part of the counselling psychologist's therapeutic skills lies in making the Bs explicit and then helping the client challenge whether or not they are valid and useful and by whose authority they are held. For example, a client who experiences a downturn in mood watching the traffic go by may have been saying to himself, 'Life is just passing me by, I'm always getting myself into a bad mood, I'll always be this way, I'm a failure.' A more rational response might have been, 'I am only forty, life begins at forty, some things I have done well, some badly. Join the human race.'

Therapy emphasizes the client making independent use of cognitive-behavioural skills outside the therapy context. If in the therapy session the therapist had, for example, drawn a client's attention to a constant theme of failure in his Bs, the client would be alerted that such thoughts could well be triggers for a lowering of mood outside the therapy session. Consequently the client would be given a mood-monitoring exercise to conduct outside of therapy. First the client might be instructed to pause when she noticed the first signs of emotional distress. Then she would have to review her defeatist talk for themes of failure. Having identified which theme or themes were operative, she would apply the alternative rational response which had been selected and practised in therapy in order to behave in a way that could enhance her sense of mastery or pleasure.

Therapy encourages the client to attribute his improvement in mood more to his own increased skilfulness than to the therapist's endeavours. If the client sees the improvement in his mood as a product of his own change in thinking habits and behaviour, and can continue using these skills, the therapist will be able to terminate therapy. Clients can be prepared to make such attributions by the therapist's constant emphasis on the importance of homework assignments. Essentially clients are being taught a skill for their independent use, and the more they practise it the more skilful they will become.

The cognitive-behaviour therapies can be categorized under four main headings, although there is some overlap between them.

Coping skills. A coping skill has two components: a self-verbalization or instruction and a resultant behaviour. A client's difficulty in managing particular situations may be due to a deficiency in a coping skill. For example, a depressed client's inability to be assertive may be due to a belief that they should never express their own needs, and consequent 'mumbling' at a time when they should express their needs. The Stress Inoculation Training (SIT) of Meichenbaum (1985) addresses both the cognitive and the behavioural aspects of coping skills and is the most well known therapy in this category. SIT is aimed at the reduction and prevention of stress. Stress is viewed as an interaction between the individual and the environment. Both need to be targeted for change. At an individual level clients may be taught what to say to themselves and how to respond in situations that they find difficult. At an environmental level the client might be encouraged to organize with others, say, a change in their shift pattern that was more to the workers' convenience.

Problem solving. The problem-solving therapies suggest that it is clients' deficiencies in problem solving that lead to the development and maintenance of their disturbance. Problem-solving therapy (Nezu et al., 1989) has been the most widely applied therapy in this category. Problem solving is conceptualized as involving the following stages:

- Problem orientation, i.e. 'locking on' to a problem.
- Precise definition of the problem.
- The generation of as many alternative solutions as possible.
- Choosing the best solution.
- Planning implementation of the solution.
- Reviewing progress.

If the chosen solution has not remedied the problem, or only partially so, another 'solution' is chosen, implemented and subsequently reviewed. This approach can be applied to both impersonal and interpersonal problems.

Cognitive restructuring. The two main therapies under this category are rational emotive behaviour therapy (REBT; Dryden, 1990) and cognitive therapy (CT; Beck et al., 1979). REBT contends that irrationality is a major determinant of emotional disorder. Ellis (1962) has suggested that much of the neurotic person's thinking is dominated by 'musts', 'shoulds', 'oughts' and 'have to's'. From the inappropriate use of these moral imperatives, three beliefs may develop:

- *Awfulizing*, which is the tendency to make grossly exaggerated evaluations of negative events.
- *Low frustration tolerance*, which is the tendency to believe that uncomfortable situations are impossible to bear.
- *Damnation*, which is the tendency to evaluate as 'bad' the essence or human value of self and/or others as a result of the individual's behaviour.

In cognitive therapy it is maladaptive interpretations of situations that are viewed as exercising a pivotal role with regard to emotional distress rather than irrational beliefs. Beck et al. (1990) contend, for example, that an interpretation of a situation that was adaptive in childhood may have become maladaptive in adulthood. For example, an abused child may well conclude on the basis of his/her experience that adults should be approached with great caution, and this may lead to unnecessary timidity with other people when he or she becomes an adult.

In cognitive therapy clients are asked to collect data on their current maladaptive interpretations of situations. These interpretations are cross-examined and if possible tested out empirically. The counselling psychologist may, say, seek to lift a depressed client's mood by tackling the client's inactivity. However, the client may protest that there is little point in activity because there will be no enjoyment. Rather than get into an argument as to whether the client will or will not enjoy the activity, in a spirit of what Beck terms collaborative empiricism the counselling psychologist might suggest trying the activity as the only sure way of finding out how it influences mood.

Structural cognitive therapy. In structural cognitive therapy (Liotti, 1986) the concern is with 'deep' structures. Three levels of cognitive organization are posited:

- *Core level*, beliefs (schemata) of the individual that have been formed, usually during childhood and adolescence, and that are tacitly held as unquestionable assumptions about some important aspect of self and reality.
- *Intermediate level*, verbalizable, explicit descriptions of the self, other people and the world.
- *Peripheral level*, the plans of action and problem-solving strategies that each individual is able to develop in the day-to-day confrontation with the environment.

A primary concern in structural cognitive therapy is to make the core level explicit. The treatment, for example, of an agoraphobic client would begin with behavioural strategies helping the client to try going gradually greater distances alone, but therapy would not be terminated when the client had learnt to travel alone. Therapy would also explore deeper issues such as 'Who am I getting out and about for, anyway?' In addition, the developmental origins of the disorder would be explored; for example, an agoraphobic may as a child have had a chronically unwell mother and found that he regularly had to go and stay with a variety of relatives.

The time scale for the application of the first three categories of CBT is brief compared with traditional psychotherapy, typically involving weekly sessions over three to four months. However, the time scale for the fourth category, structural cognitive therapy, is considerably longer, typically eighteen months, because its goal is to achieve fundamental changes in the individual. In many ways structural cognitive therapy reflects the recently evolved cognitive-behavioural approach to personality disorders. It is well established that if clients have not only an Axis 1 disorder, such as depression, but also an Axis 2 personality disorder, they are less likely to respond to psychotherapy. As between one-third and two-thirds of clients presenting with anxiety and depression have a coexisting personality disorder it has been important to develop treatment strategies accordingly (Scott et al., 1995).

Pretzer and Fleming (1989) have suggested the following guidelines for treating clients with personality disorders. (It should be emphasized, however, that none of the CB approaches for treating personality disorders has yet been empirically evaluated.)

- Interventions are most effective when based on an individualized conceptualization of the client's problems.
- It is important for the therapist and client to work collaboratively towards clearly identified shared goals.
- It is important to focus more than usual attention on the therapist–client interaction.
- Consider interventions that do not require extensive client self-disclosure.
- Interventions which increase the client's sense of self-efficacy often reduce the intensity of the client's symptomatology and facilitate other interventions.
- The therapist should not rely primarily on verbal interventions.
- The therapist should try to identify and address the client's fears before implementing changes.
- The therapist should anticipate problems with compliance.
- The therapist should not assume that the client exists in a reasonable or functional environment.
- The therapist must attend to his or her emotional reactions during the course of therapy.
- The therapist should be realistic regarding the length of therapy, goals of therapy and standards for self-evaluation.

The cognitive behaviour approaches to personality disorders are an expression of four trends in cognitive behaviour therapy that make dialogue and perhaps integration with other psychotherapies more feasible than hitherto.

- *Inclusion of non-conscious processes.* There is acceptance that schemata and personal rules are inferred constructs and not observable behaviours which operate covertly and without awareness, though this does not go as far as acceptance of the notion of a Freudian unconscious.
- *Emphasis on interpersonal process.* The salient cognitions to tackle in the personality disorders are thought to be those concerned with the view of self in relation to others.
- *Concern for emotional processes.* Whilst cognitive-behaviour therapists have long accepted the interdependence of cognition and affect there is increasing attention being given to affect as conveying information, and as an action disposition. Affect is given the same status as cognition as a therapeutic means by which the client can become less disturbed.
- *The importance of the therapeutic relationship.* Whilst a good therapeutic relationship has always been held to be a necessary part of teaching clients the various cognitive-behavioural skills, it is only recently in the treatment of personality disorders that it is coming to be understood as a possible laboratory or microcosm of the client's difficulties.

The nature of the relationship between counselling psychologist and client

Within cognitive-behaviour therapy the therapeutic relationship has received much less attention than the technical aspects of counselling. This has not been because the therapeutic relationship was thought unimportant but rather that it was taken for granted that a good therapeutic relationship was a necessary but not sufficient condition for client change. The cognitive-behaviour therapist would insist that both technical and relationship skills are necessary for client change, whilst some other schools of counselling see only the necessity for the relationship to be considered. The Therapist Client Rating Scale (TCRS; Bennun et al., 1986) has been used to assess the client's view of therapy sessions and also the counsellor's view. The client form consists of three scales: (1) Positive regard/interest, (2) Competence/experience, (3) Activity/guidance. The counsellor's form also consists of three scales: (1) Positive regard, (2) Self-disclosure/engagement, (3) Co-operation/goal orientation. Both forms are made up of twenty nine items with each item scaled 1 to 6 (e.g. 1 = very talkative to 6 = very quiet). The instrument has been used with phobic and obsessive–compulsive clients and a significant positive correlation was found between the client factor 'positive regard' and outcome of therapy.

Counsellors providing cognitive therapy for depression are assessed in research trials using the Cognitive Therapy Scale. The scale has three parts. Part 1, General Therapeutic Skills, and Part 2, Conceptualization, Strategies and Techniques, are of equal depth, reflecting the equal weighting given to the personal and technical in cognitive therapy. Part 3 is a brief section in which the rater indicates any additional considerations, for example a particularly difficult client, to be taken into account when rating the quality of the interview. The headings from Part 1 of the Cognitive Therapy Scale are shown below and the extent to which the counsellor met the goal for each heading on a scale 0 to 6 is indicated: 0 = poor; 1 = barely adequate; 2 = mediocre; 3 = satisfactory; 4 = good; 5 = very good; 6 = excellent.

Cognitive Therapy Scale

Part 1 General Therapeutic Skills

1   *Agenda* (0–6). Therapist worked with client to set an appropriate agenda with target problems suitable for available time. Established priorities then followed agenda.
2   *Feedback* (0–6). Therapist was especially adept at eliciting and responding to verbal and non-verbal feedback throughout the session, e.g. elicited reaction to session, regularly checked for understanding and helped summarize main points at end of session.
3   *Understanding* (0–6). Therapist seemed to understand the client's internal reality thoroughly and was adept at communicating this understanding through appropriate verbal and non-verbal responses to the client, e.g. the tone of the therapist's response conveyed a sympathetic understanding of the client's 'message'. Excellent listening and empathic skills.
4   *Interpersonal effectiveness* (0–6). Therapist displayed optimal levels of warmth, concern, confidence, genuineness and professionalism appropriate for this particular client in this session.
5   *Collaboration* (0–6). Collaboration seemed excellent. Therapist encouraged client as much as possible to take an active role during the session, for example by offering choices, so they could function as a team.
6   *Pacing and efficient use of time* (0–6). Therapist used time very effectively by tactfully limiting peripheral and unproductive discussion and pacing the session as rapidly as was appropriate for the client.

Thus in the treatment of Axis 1 disorders the therapeutic relationship has been an important, albeit infrequently discussed, aspect of the counselling process. With regard to the counselling of Axis 2 personality disorders the role of the therapeutic relationship assumes even greater importance. For example, if a client has an avoidant personality disorder, the key feature of the disorder is that others are seen as critical and demeaning; the therapeutic implication of this is that the counsellor can very easily be cast as 'just like all the others' and special care has to be taken to elicit from the client whether anything has been said or done by the therapist that has upset them. By contrast, a less solicitous stance would be needed with a client with a dependent personality disorder, where the key feature is a belief that they cannot function independently. Thus the counsellor's approach to the relationship is not uniform across the personality disorders.

Family, group and organizational applications

The reciprocal interaction of cognitions, emotions, behaviours and physiology, shown in Figure 7.1 above, takes place in an environment which may to varying degrees be toxic. The individual may 'inhale' the fumes through any or a combination of the four ports of entry – cognitions, emotions, behaviours and physiology. The cognitions port is always implicated in emotional distress, though the cognition need not necessarily be conscious, as it is now well established in cognitive psychology that people do process information outside of conscious awareness.

The environments which have so far been given consideration in cognitive-behaviour therapy are current partner or family and the organizational environment at work. These are now considered in turn.

Current partner and family

In some instances it is recognized that it may be appropriate to target the faulty cognitions in the environment rather than the individual. For example, a depressed child may be better helped by the counsellor challenging maladaptive family constructs (i.e. family-held beliefs) with his/her parents and perhaps siblings. So that, though the target for change is the child's symptoms, the most efficient way forward might be to challenge the reasonableness of the parents' expectations of him/her and what they communicate to him/her about his/her worth. Cognitive family therapy may in such circumstances be the best way forward. Even in instances of adult depression, marital therapy may be the counselling modality of choice rather than individual therapy. It has been found that 50 per cent of women with depression have severe marital problems, and that the provision of cognitive-behavioural marital therapy, to couples willing to participate, not only improves marital satisfaction but also lifts depression. By contrast, providing individual cognitive therapy to depressed women whilst lifting the depression does not improve marital satisfaction (O'Leary and Beach, 1990).

Cognitive-behavioural marital therapy involves behaviour exchange contracts, practice in communication skills and the challenging of beliefs that disrupt relationships (see Scott, 1989). The beliefs targeted for change in cognitive-behavioural marital therapy tend to cluster under five headings.

- *Disagreement is destructive.* 'When my partner and I disagree, I feel like our relationship is falling apart.'
- *Mind reading is expected.* 'People who have a close relationship can sense each other's needs as if they could read each other's minds.'
- *Partners cannot change.* 'Damage done early in relationships probably cannot be reversed.'
- *The sexes are different.* 'Misunderstandings between partners generally are due to inborn differences in the psychological make-up of men and women.'

- *Sexual perfectionism.* 'I get upset if I think I have not completely satisfied my partner sexually.'

Organizations

The most popular model of stress is a transactional one, that is, stress resides neither in the individual nor in the environment, but arises when there is a poor fit between the individual and the environment. Within the work context, stress can arise at the individual (I)/organization (O) interface. By organization is meant the immediate line managers of the individual, who may act as conduits of the organization's belief system. Richman (1988) has contended that individuals may possess vocational irrational beliefs (VIBS) and that the nature of these will be different at various points of the career cycle. Similarly, organizations may be purveyors of VIBS. A list, by no means exhaustive, of I/O VIBS is shown below.

At entry:

- 'I have to show my boss I can do an excellent job or I will be a failure.'
- 'If I do not like the post right away I will never find a post that is for me.'
- 'I am bright and talented and therefore should not have to do the mundane jobs.'
- 'I cannot stand not using my potential.'

VIBS of a demoralizing boss:

- 'New recruits must learn the job slowly, going through every single step.'
- 'New recruits cannot have anything to contribute and therefore should not have their views considered.'
- 'Beginning recruits should do as we say and not ask questions or expect feedback unless we choose to give it.'
- 'New recruits should be given the easiest tasks.'
- 'New recruits should be tested out by being assigned to do the most difficult tasks right away.'

Mid-career:

- 'I should have achieved a higher position by this age in my life.'
- 'I cannot stand that I may never accomplish my career goals.'
- 'I am worthless as a person because others of my age have gone further.'
- 'I cannot stand looking after younger workers who may move up beyond my position.'
- 'I should not level off in my career or redefine my goals because that will mean I am weak and not ambitious enough.'

Organizational VIBS:

- 'He/she has done well enough in their specialism, they should not want to make any kind of change.'
- 'He/she has too many concerns about their family, they can no longer be trusted as a committed member of the company.'
- 'He/she should not suddenly try to make a name for themselves at this stage in their career.'
- 'I should not offer him/her any growth opportunities since their time here is limited.'
- 'Mid-career workers seem too conflicted and unmotivated to be given any challenging assignments.'

Resolving many of the so-called 'personality clashes' within industry is actually about identifying and modifying individual and organizational VIBS.

Group

The cognitive-behavioural approaches that have been described for Axis 1 disorders are essentially psycho-educational and lend themselves easily to group treatment. The intent in group cognitive-behaviour therapy, it should be noted, is different from other group psychotherapies where the focus is on group processes and dynamics. The group cognitive-behavioural approach is commended because it is seen as a cost-effective way of bringing about change. For example, Scott and Stradling (1990) have demonstrated that group cognitive therapy for depression produces as much change as individual cognitive therapy. Group cognitive-behavioural programmes have also been described for anxiety and bulimia. Given the scarcity of counsellor resources and long waiting lists in the United Kingdom, group cognitive-behavioural approaches are likely to become more common, with counsellors having difficulty finding time for the lengthier individual CBT treatments of personality disorders developed primarily in the United States.

Research evidence about efficacy

There is now no disorder to which cognitive-behaviour therapy has not been applied, including teaching psychotic clients to control their symptoms. But this is not to say that CBT has proved to be equally effective with each disorder. Further, there are too few studies on some disorders, so that the interventions must be regarded as promising but 'not proven'.

One way of assessing the efficacy of a therapy is to subtract the mean score of the treatment group at the end of treatment from the mean score of the comparison group e.g. waiting list. The difference is then divided by a measure of the spread of results in the control group i.e. the standard deviation, to give an effect size (ES). Thus an ES of 0.5 would indicate that the mean outcome score of the treatment group was half a standard deviation larger than the mean outcome of the control group. Effect sizes have been categorized along a continuum

Table 7.2   Comparisons of cognitive therapy with no treatment, waiting list and placebo controls

Disorder	Average effect size	% of CT patients superior to controls
Adult unipolar depression	0.82	79
Adolescent unipolar depression	1.11	87
General anxiety disorder	1.04	85
Panic disorder with or without agoraphobia	0.91	82
Social phobia	0.93	82
Childhood depression and anxiety disorders	0.90	82
Marital distress	0.71	76
Anger	0.70	76
Childhood somatic disorders	0.47	68
Chronic pain (not headache)	0.46	68

of no effect (ES < 0.2), low (0.2 = < ES < 0.5), medium (0.5 = < ES < 0.8) and high (ES > = 0.8) (Cohen, 1988). Butler and Beck (2000) have reviewed 325 studies covering fourteen disorders or populations. The comparisons of CBT to inert controls are shown in Table 7.2. Butler and Beck (2000) have also compared CBT with alternative treatments. A comparison of CBT with antidepressant medication in the treatment of depression showed CBT to be slightly superior (average effect size 0.38). However, one year after treatment discontinuation, depressed clients who had undergone CBT had half the relapse rate of patients who had been treated with antidepressant medication (30 per cent versus 60 per cent).

For disorders such as post-traumatic stress disorder and bulimia nervosa there have been so few comparison studies that it has not been possible to calculate an effect size in the way Butler and Beck (2000) have done, but in other meta-analyses a different effect size has been utilized involving subtraction of post-treatment mean from pre-treatment mean and dividing by the pooled standard deviation, making it possible to include uncontrolled studies. Whilst this methodology is not as reliable as that used in the Butler and Beck (2000) review, the meta-analses do yield large effect sizes for CBT, for example Van Etten and Taylor (1998) considered thirteen studies of some form of CBT in the treatment of PTSD and found an average effect size of 1.89. The next highest ES was for the class of drugs that include Prozac and Seroxat 1.43. Such findings suggest that CBT is promising for these disorders.

As more outcome studies become available it will become possible to include a wider range of disorders in the type of meta-analyses conducted by Butler and Beck (2000). This will help ensure that CBT is approached in an evidence-based framework and that realistic claims are made.

Controlled trials are used to establish the efficacy of an intervention, but though an intervention may be found efficacious at a research centre it cannot be assumed that the findings will translate to routine clinical practice, e.g. whilst a trial may have high internal validity it may not have high external validity.

Trials of psychological interventions in the settings in which they are to be administered are relatively rare. This has led practitioners to have some scepticism about the 'scientific' trials, and to a scientist–practitioner gap. Efficacy studies arguably mark just the beginning of the development of evidence-based interventions.

References

APA (American Psychiatric Association) (1994) *Diagnostic and Statistical Manual of Mental Disorders*, fourth edition. Washington DC: American Psychiatric Association.

Alford, B.A. and Beck, A.T. (1997) *The Integrative Power of Cognitive Therapy*. New York: Guilford Press.

Bandura, A. (1982) 'Self-efficacy mechanism in human agency', *American Psychologist*, 37: 122–47.

Beck, J. (1995) *Cognitive Therapy: Basics and Beyond*. New York: Guilford Press.

Beck, A.T., Epstein, N. and Harrison, R. (1983) 'Cognition, attitudes and personality dimensions in depression', *British Journal of Cognitive Psychotherapy*, 1: 1–16.

Beck, A.T., Freeman, A. and associates (1990) *Cognitive Therapy of Personality Disorders*. New York: Guilford Press.

Beck, A.T., Rush, A.J., Shaw, B.F. and Emery, G. (1979) *Cognitive Therapy of Depression*. New York: Wiley.

Beck, A.T., Ward, C.H., Mendelson, M., Mock, J.E. and Erbaugh, J.K. (1962) 'Reliability of psychiatric diagnoses: a Study of consistency of clinical judgements and ratings', *American Journal of Psychiatry*, 199: 351–7.

Bennun, I., Hahlweg, K., Schindler, L. and Langotz, M. (1986) 'Therapists' and clients' perceptions: the development and cross-cultural analysis of an assessment instrument', *British Journal of Clinical Psychology*, 25: 275–85.

Burns, D. (1980) *Feeling Good: the New Mood Therapy*. New York: New American Library.

Butler, A.C. and Beck, J.S. (2000) 'Cognitive therapy outcomes: a review of meta-analyses', *Journal of the Norwegian Psychological Association*, 37: 1–9.

Cohen, J (1988) *Statistical Power Analyses for the Behavioral Sciences*, second edition, Hillsdale NJ: Erlbaum.

Dryden, W. (1990) *Rational-Emotive Counselling in Action*. London: Sage.

Ellis, A. (1962) *Reason and Emotion in Psychotherapy*. New York: Lyle Stuart.

First, M.B., Spitzer, R.L., Gibbon, M. and Williams, J.B.W. (1995) *Structured Clinical Interview for DSM IV Axis 1 Disorders: Patient Edition* (SCID-I/P version 2.0). New York: Biometrics Research Department, New York State Psychiatric Institute.

Forgus, R. and Shulman, B. (1979) *Personality: a Cognitive View*. Englewood Cliffs NJ: Prentice Hall.

Jacobson, N.S. and Truax, P. (1991) 'Clinical significance: a statistical approach to defining meaningful change in psychotherapy research', *Journal of Consulting and Clinical Psychology*, 59: 12–19.

Liotti, G. (1986) 'Structural cognitive therapy' in W. Dryden and W. Golden (eds) *Cognitive-Behavioral Approaches to Psychotherapy*. London: Harper & Row.

Meichenbaum, D. (1985) *Stress Inoculation Training*. New York: Pergamon Press.

Nezu, A.M., Nezu, C.M. and Perri, M.G. (1989) *Problem Solving Therapy for Depression*. New York: Wiley.

Nietzel, M.T., Russell, R.L., Hemmings, K.D. and Gretter, M.L. (1987) 'Clinical significance of psychotherapy for unipolar depression: a meta-analytic approach to social comparison', *Journal of Consulting and Clinical Psychology*, 55: 156–61.

O'Leary, K.D. and Beach, S.R.H. (1990) 'Marital therapy: a viable treatment for depression and marital discord', *American Journal of Psychiatry*, 147: 183–6.

Paul, G.L. (1967) 'Strategy of outcome research in psychotherapy', *Journal of Consulting Psychology*, 31: 109–18.

Persons, J.B. (1989) *Cognitive Therapy in Practice: a Case Formulation Approach*. New York: Norton.

Pretzer, J. and Fleming, B. (1989) 'Cognitive-behavioral treatment of personality disorders', *Behavior Therapist*, 12: 105–9.

Richman, D.R. (1988) 'Cognitive psychotherapy through the career cycle' in W. Dryden and P. Trower (eds) *Developments in Cognitive Psychotherapy*. London: Sage.

Scott, M. (1989) *A Cognitive-Behavioral Approach to Clients' Problems*. London: Tavistock/Routledge.

Scott, M.J. and Stradling, S.G. (1990) 'Group cognitive therapy for depression produces clinically significant reliable change in community-based settings', *Behavioural Psychotherapy*, 18: 1–19.

Scott, M.J., Stradling, S.G. and Dryden, W. (1995) *Developing Cognitive-Behavioural Counselling*. London: Sage.

Scott, M.J. and Stradling, S.G (2001) 'Determining the cognitive ports of entry amongst the posttraumatic states: treatment implications', *Behavioural and Cognitive Psychotherapy*, 29: 245–50.

Telch, M.J., Lucas, J.A., Schmidt, N.B., Hanna, H.H., Jaimez, T. LaNae and Lucas, R.A. (1993) 'Group cognitive-behavioural treatment of panic disorder', *Behaviour Research and Therapy*, 31: 279–87.

Van Etten, M.L. and Taylor, S. (1998) 'Comparative efficacy of treatment for posttraumatic stress disorder: a meta-analysis', *Clinical Psychology and Psychotherapy*, 5: 126–44.

Young, J. (1990) *Cognitive Therapy for Personality Disorders: a Schema Focused Approach*. Sarasota FL: Professional Resource Exchange.

8 The Existential-Phenomenological Paradigm
ERNESTO SPINELLI

The existential-phenomenological approach presents a radical challenge to many of the fundamental assumptions brought to the theory and practice of counselling psychology. Equally, it forms the basis of numerous qualitatively focused models of research whose concerns lie with the analysis of the central features of the counselling process and their influences upon its outcomes. Much of this challenge derives from the explicitly philosophical origins of existential-phenomenological psychology, whose centrality continues to provide the approach with its primary critiques of the natural science framework that underlies currently dominant trends in psychological theory and research.

Phenomenology refers to the study of phenomena (or 'the appearance of things') in order to clarify how the object world is humanly experienced and presents itself to our consciousness. As such, phenomenology attempts to investigate more adequately the human condition as it manifests itself in lived experience. The *existential* focus of phenomenology takes the question of 'being' itself as its primary focus for investigation. In doing so, it specifies two inter-related avenues of inquiry: *ontological* inquiry, which focuses upon the intrinsic, universal features of existence, and *ontic* inquiry, which examines 'the specific individual ways in which each of us is in the world' (Cohn, 1997: 12). Taken within the context of psychology, 'existential-phenomenological psychology … has become that psychological discipline that seeks to explicate the *essence*, *structure*, or *form* of both human experience and human behavior as revealed through essential *descriptive* techniques including disciplined reflection' (Valle and King, 1978: 6, original emphasis). The discovery and elucidation of the ontological givens (or interpretative limits) of our experience form one major aspect of existential-phenomenological inquiry, just as the attempt to discern the impact of the personal, socio-cultural and psychologically derived ontic biases and assumptions forms the second, equally significant, concern.

Phenomenology, as a philosophical system, arose in the early years of the twentieth century. Its founder, Edmund Husserl (1859–1938), initially a student of mathematics and the natural sciences, sought to establish phenomenology as the fundamental philosophy of all scientific investigation (Husserl, 1977). In attempting such, both Husserl and his principal assistant, Martin Heidegger (1889–1976), confronted the bedevilling 'dualistic split' between subject and object upon which modern-day natural science is based.

Whereas dominant views of philosophy, psychology and therapy impose a separateness or distinction between subject and object (or between 'self' and 'other'), the existential-phenomenological approach denies this distinction and proposes, in its place, a co-constituted view of existence which argues that everything that we are, or can be, aware of, all that we reflect upon, define or distinguish is interrelationally derived. The very experience of 'being', for instance, is opened to conscious reflection only when it is placed in the contextual relationship of being-in-the-world (or 'Dasein').

The structural tendency, or 'given', through which relations emerge has been termed by existential-phenomenological theory as *intentionality*. Intentionality explicitly refers to the directional nature of consciousness. All consciousness is of something. So, to perceive is to perceive something; to love is to love something; to imagine is to imagine something; and so forth. In this sense, intentionality serves as a descriptive psychology of conscious processes (Ihde, 1998). However, at a more significant level, intentionality can be understood to be the foundational correlational rule of existential phenomenology. In this latter sense, intentionality points toward the interrelatedness and interdependence of what a natural science tradition refers to and separates as 'subject' and 'object'. From the standpoint of intentionality, however, neither term makes sense in and of itself, nor can one be dealt with, defined and understood in isolation from the other. Considered from the standpoint of existence, the experience, knowledge and understanding of either the subject or the object can emerge only via this correlational *a priori*. Intentionality reveals that through the process of constructing the meaning-possibilities of those 'things' with which we are in relation (i.e. the investigated 'object'), we also reconstruct the meaning-possibilities of the 'thing-constructing' being (i.e. the investigating 'subject'). As such, the notion of intentionality reveals that both 'self' and 'other' (or, more generally, 'the world') are made meaningful, or are opened to disclosing investigation through their interdependent, co-constitutional relations (Heidegger, 1962). One of the important consequences of this argument is that each of us is actively involved, or implicated in construing, or attempting to make meaningful, our experience of the world – which includes our experience of ourselves, of others, and of all those features, objects and mental processes that make up our lived reality.

This view stands in stark opposition to the natural science assertion that posits that we can speak with impersonal certainty about the true, or objective, nature of reality. Instead, the existential-phenomenological approach argues that we can never know the real world, only the interpreted world – the world that emerges through our reflections upon it. As such, all our statements about the world, or any aspect of the world – including, of course, ourselves – are, at best, approximations. We can never truly speak of 'facts' with any final certainty because all our statements reveal limitations and assumptions that impede our ability to describe or understand things as they are independent of our experience of them. Heidegger, in particular, insisted upon the impossibility of deriving 'truth' in any natural scientific sense. Instead, for Heidegger, the notion of truth reached back to the notion of *aletheia* – that which is disclosed, or revealed, and which emerges from the interrelatedness of a being with the world (Cooper, 1996). The therapeutic implications of this perspective were most clearly expressed by Leslie Farber, who argued that for the process of therapy, 'speaking truthfully is a more fitting ambition than speaking the truth' (Farber, 2000: 10).

The main means through which the existential-phenomenological approach explores and clarifies questions of essence and existence is via a particular method that enjoins investigators to seek (1) to suspend, or bracket, their biases and presuppositions in order to allow openness to one's experience; (2) to remain at a descriptive level of interpretation in order to focus upon the immediate, or primary, data of experience; and (3) to horizontalize the items of description by avoiding placing any immediate hierarchies of importance or significance upon them – particularly during the early stages of investigation (Ihde, 1986; Spinelli, 1989). While this method must always remain an attempt that can never be final or complete, it serves to make explicit with increasing adequacy those biases and assumptions – both (at least partially) 'bracketable' and 'given' (or invariable) – that we bring to any encounter with the world.

Underlying theory of personality

According to the existential-phenomenological approach, human existence reveals 'the total, indissoluble unity or interrelationship of the individual and his or her world ... In the truest sense, the person is viewed as having no existence apart from the world and the world as having no existence apart from persons ...' (Valle and King, 1978: 7).

When applied to life sciences such as psychology, existential phenomenology approaches the question of human nature from the assumption that it is open-ended, and capable of an enormous range of experience (Cohn, 1997; Deurzen-Smith, 1988). Such a view eschews the trend in modern personality theories which seeks to categorize or 'typologize' individuals or which attempts to divide and reduce people in terms of various 'parts' or components. Instead, it aims to remain at a descriptive and open-ended level of analysis of human experience that simultaneously acknowledges both the ontic uniqueness of each 'being-in-the-world' and the species-shared ontological 'givens' of being human that set the invariant boundaries for the possibilities of our experience.

Unlike other living organisms, whose sensory characteristics may be different, or attuned in differing ways, human beings are governed by certain fixed 'invariants' which exist at the species level. In addition, however, all manner of other biasing influences exist at a socio-cultural level that further affect both the way that we process our perceptions and the meanings we provide for the interpreted objects of our perceptions. Psychologists interested in perceptual processes have pointed out a substantial number of such invariants – both at the species and socio-cultural levels (Merleau-Ponty, 1962; Spinelli, 1989; Yalom, 1980). Furthermore, there also exist biasing influences that are individually derived – that is to say, that are formed from the unique experiences and interactions each of us has with the world. All such limitations lead to the conclusion that, as humans, we interpret the world within the 'givens' of our species possibilities, from biases and perspectives derived from socio-cultural influences, and from the consequences of our own unique development.

   This stance provokes a deeply unsettling perspective, since, in one stroke, it places human personality and experience in an uncertain, relativistic realm of being wherein whatever meaning we may 'find' for ourselves can no longer be seen to be certain in that it has no fully independent, or external, basis. In addition, because existence is co-constituted, each 'being-in-the-world' is characteristically open-ended, in constant flux, or plastic, rather than fixed or fully definable. If we consider this conclusion further, however, we can understand that, as well as being unique and plastic, existence is also never fully sharable, since the variables that make up each human being's experience of the world are not accessible, in any complete or final manner, to any other human being. At best, what attempts one may make to provide another with some sense of one's experience of the world can be seen to be increasingly adequate but never total or complete. Viewed from the standpoint of existential-phenomenological psychology, this perspective concludes that each of us is alone in our experience of reality. 'And yet, paradoxically, this "aloneness" emerges precisely because we are *in relation* to one another' (Spinelli, 1994: 294, original emphasis).

   The existential-phenomenological approach employs the term *angst* to refer to the inevitable existential anxiety of being. It is the anxiety that comes with the acceptance that there are no meanings in the world apart from the relative ones that we create, that we cannot rely upon the certainty of facts, or of purpose, that we cannot know what happens to us when we are thrown out of the world, when we cease to be as humans. This temporality, which expresses both our awareness of our inevitable movement toward nothingness and the unavoidable uncertainty as to how and when our humanly embodied existence will come to an end, is viewed to be our most fundamental source of angst (Cohn, 1997; Deurzen-Smith, 1988; Heidegger, 1962; Spinelli, 1997; Yalom, 1980).

   In our efforts to avoid the experience of angst we resort to a variety of truth-distorting stances toward our experience of being. For instance, we might seek out the security of fixed external truths, permanent meanings, statements from on high concerning the true point and purpose of our lives. Alternatively, we might attempt to deny our experience via various forms of denial and dissociation (Spinelli, 1997). Such strategies have been referred to as inauthentic (Heidegger, 1962) or as expressions of bad faith (Sartre, 1956), and their frequency and appeal lie precisely in that they serve to allay the unease and uncertainty of being-in-the-world (Cohn, 1997; Spinelli, 1997).

   This deception or denial of being can be seen as the central focus for the application of the existential-phenomenological approach to the practice of counselling psychology, since many of the issues that clients present reveal their attempts to avoid angst in any number of ways. For instance, clients may express a view of themselves, or their identity, as defined by certain fixed characteristics, attitudes, patterns of thought and so forth, and, when experientially confronted with evidence to the contrary, or with experiences that expand the 'meaning' they have given themselves, they reject, or disown, the evidence in order to maintain their fixed meaning rather than accept their own evidence and reshape or extend their meaning of themselves. In doing so, such individuals deny the possibilities of experiential freedom, or choice, that they have available to them.

'The existential-phenomenological idea of choice has often been misunderstood to suggest that we possess unlimited freedom to choose how and what "to be". This view, quite simply, is wrong' (Spinelli, 1994: 295). The choices that we are free to make arise within a *situated* freedom, which is to say, that freedom whose boundaries lie within the intentional relationship through which each of us, as a 'being-in-the-world' is co-constituted. Rather than being free to choose what we want, we are, rather, free to choose how to respond to the unavoidable and unpredictable 'stimuli' of the world. In fact, more accurately speaking, 'we are *condemned* to choose' (Sartre, 1956, emphasis added). As such, our choice is interpretative, not at the event – or stimulus – level.

'Equally, choice should not be understood to be solely at the level of "choosing between optional stimuli" or even between "optional meanings of stimuli"' (Spinelli, 1994: 296). Even if we may have fixed or sedimented particular meanings so that no optional alternative seems available, we remain free to choose to acknowledge or accept that one sedimented meaning. While this point may strike some readers as a trick of logic so that the view that we always choose can be maintained, on reflection it should prove to be not the case at all. For instance:

> Many of the problems and issues that clients bring to therapy originate through this self-same 'unwillingness to choose the one choice available'. In this stance … clients … place themselves in the position of 'passive victims of circumstance'. The one choice may remain the same regardless of the position I adopt toward it, but the experience of 'being' varies significantly depending on whether I choose to accept its presence in my relational world or whether I deceive myself by denying its presence (and, at times, further deceive myself by believing that another choice option is available). (Spinelli, 1994: 296–7)

Further, existential phenomenology emphasizes the *interrelational dimension* of choice in that it insists that our choices, and their possibilities and consequences, cannot be considered solely from a subjective perspective but must take into account their intersubjective impact upon those with whom we are in relation, and, as well, upon others' world relations (Goldenberg and Isaacson, 1996; Spinelli, 2001a).

Existential choice emerges through the acceptance of the uncertainties with which life presents us. Angst, then, is not, properly speaking, a disturbing aspect of life which counselling psychologists must assist clients in alleviating, removing or resolving. Rather, angst exposes us to the possibilities and responsibilities of being — be they joyous or despairing, life-enhancing or confrontative of our eventual human nothingness.

The assessment process

It is highly unusual for existential-phenomenological counselling psychologists to employ any formal assessment procedures or diagnostic tests. Their avoidance of such procedures rests upon their insistence that diagnosis is a medical, rather than psychological, dichotomy designed to distinguish health from illness. As has been argued by David Pilgrim, '[t]he psychiatric question "Is this person suffering from a mental disorder or not?" becomes transformed by a psychologist into "How do we account for this person's actions and experience in this particular context?"' (Pilgrim, 2000: 302). Further, as with many other psychologists, existential-phenomenological practitioners continue to express their concern regarding the persistent lack of conceptual and predictive validity of diagnostic classifications (Pilgrim, 2000). Pilgrim, among others, has provided a critical summary detailing diagnostic classifications' persistent inability to specify the aetiology of functional diagnoses and the lack of validity of symptom profiles with regard to the distinction between different states of abnormality and, indeed, between normality and abnormality (Pilgrim, 2000). More broadly, existential phenomenologists argue that diagnostic labels compare poorly with more everyday descriptions of lived disturbance. While the former are reductionist, impersonal and negatively judgemental in their language, the latter 'are more sensitive about the psychosocial context of behaviour and experience' (Pilgrim, 2000: 303).

Beginning with the descriptively oriented and pioneering work of the psychiatrist Karl Jaspers, existential-phenomenological approaches have emphasized the clarification and analysis of psychic experience (and disturbance) from the standpoint of how it is lived and what meaning is placed upon it by those individuals who seek out our expertise 'according to the perspectives of self-awareness, style of self-report and perceptual processes rather than by diagnostic grouping' (Fewtrell and O'Connor, 1995: 13). Such attempts (which Jaspers termed 'not-knowing' (Jaspers, 1963) and which, more recently, the present author has referred to as un-knowing (Spinelli, 1997)) make it the aim of the counselling psychologist to expose and explore the meanings being expressed through their clients' responses in order that they may attempt to discern that which is *understandable within what is initially experienced as being un-understandable.*

> Existential-phenomenological psychologists and psychotherapists suggest that the attempt to unfold both what the client is experiencing reflectively at any given moment, and how that currently lived experience is imbued with meaning relative to the whole of the client's reflected life-experience, is of inestimable value to client and psychologist/psychotherapist alike. This undertaking permits a clarification of the preoccupations and evaluations that are attributed by the client to his or her experience, as well as the wider meanings that these have upon the client's sense of his or her overall life-experience. In addition, through these clarifications, the psychologist/psychotherapist is in a position to assist the client by accurately reflecting back the experience and challenging it insofar as the challenge reflects the implicit beliefs, values, judgements, contradictions and assumptions that are embedded within the meanings given to, and the inter-relational stances derived from, these experiences. (Spinelli, 2001b: 63–4)

Emmy van Deurzen-Smith has suggested that existential-phenomenological counselling is particularly suitable for persons who experience themselves as alienated from the *mores* and demands of their society or who are at a point of crisis such as confronting death or experiencing meaninglessness and isolation, who have lost their sense of relatedness to themselves, to 'significant others' and/or to the world in general or who are attempting to cope with sudden and dramatic changes in a variety of personal circumstances. Similarly, she has indicated that the existential-phenomenological model is beneficially applicable to those who inhabit a foreign culture or who are members of a minority group within a dominant culture and society (Deurzen-Smith, 1988).

The question of assessment within the existential-phenomenological model must also address the qualities of counselling psychologists who wish to work effectively within this standpoint. As well as being expected to demonstrate sound and wide-ranging theoretical knowledge and professional training, existential-phenomenological counselling psychologists should demonstrate suitable maturity and life experience that infuse their ability to confront and deal with their own existential dilemmas. Critical self-reflection, wide-ranging engagement with various cultures, environments and work-related situations, the ability to express and acknowledge the humour, tragedy and absurdity of living, and an ongoing curiosity about, and tolerance of, the different ways people opt to 'be-in-the-world' are considered to be essential features of effective existential-phenomenological counselling psychologists.

The question of change

The existential-phenomenological approach views the person as constantly self-disclosing through his or her on-going relations with the world. Its primary concerns lie with the descriptive exploration and clarification of the various interrelational orientations that define and provide meaning for persons at all levels of their existence. Further, it seeks to facilitate a process whereby these relations may be clarified and confronted in ways that promote an attitude of openness to the possibilities and limitations of human existence.

The problems and issues that people bring to the counselling psychologist are seen as being, first and foremost, *problems in interrelational living* which reflect the attempt to avoid the uncertainty and angst provoked by *being-in-the-world-with-others*. As such, the challenge for the existential-phenomenological counselling psychologist lies principally in assisting people not to remove or evade anxiety but, rather, to confront and clarify their stance toward it and, through that, to reflect more honestly upon what the impact of this stance might be both with regard to their 'presenting problems' and to their wider ways of being or *world-view*.

While the question of change can be viewed as an inevitable and on-going feature of life, the task of the existential-phenomenological counselling psychologist lies in assisting persons to recognize their resistance to, and attempts to control, the changes in their lives rather than guide them in any direct manner towards novel ways of change. Paradoxically, it is via the very process of clarifying and challenging people's stance towards change that the benefits of 'therapeutic change' can be seen to occur.

Although it acknowledges the integrity and experiential freedom of human beings, this approach eschews any notions of 'self-actualization', 'inherent tendencies toward self-integration' and the 'innate positive nature' of human beings. Instead, it places equal emphasis upon the human quest for relation, meaning and truth as well as those underlying uncertainties, dilemmas and anxieties of living which challenge the person's attempts to establish and maintain a secure and fully integrated foundation. Similarly, while it addresses all possible dimensions of experience (such as the personal, social, physical and ideal/spiritual dimensions), it avoids any assumptions regarding the meaning, purpose or independent truth or reality of such dimensions.

In adopting this stance, the existential-phenomenological approach avoids bestowing upon the counselling psychologist the role of superior, objective instructor who distinguishes for the client those beliefs, attitudes and behaviours which are assumed to be 'irrational' and who attempts to replace them with 'rational' ones. Similarly, rather than present themselves as 'symptom removers', 'treatment providers', 'directive educators' or 'professional helpers', existential-phenomenological counselling psychologists seek to *attend* to their clients in that, through descriptively focused interpretations, they attempt to clarify their clients' meaning-world with them, thereby providing them with the experience of being heard – and hearing themselves – in a manner that is non-judgemental and accepting of the stance they maintain. This attempt 'to accept the being who is present' promotes the possibility of the clients' greater willingness and courage to confront the fixed, or sedimented, biases and assumptions they hold with regard to their relations with themselves, others and the world in general, and how these sedimented stances may themselves have provoked their current 'problems in living'.

As the existential-phenomenological approach urges counselling psychologists to maintain a flexible approach and attitude towards their therapeutic 'style', it is characteristically critical of any emphasis upon a specific technique or set of 'doing' skills. Instead, it emphasizes the personal or 'being' qualities of the counselling psychologist as essential components of the therapeutic relationship.

The nature of the relationship between counselling psychologist and client

It is the case that virtually all psychological research into the therapeutic process – whether it be process- or outcome-oriented – has concluded that the relationship within the therapeutic process is the primary recurring variable to be singled out by both counselling psychologists and clients as essential to the success of therapy – however 'success' may be defined or measured (Howe, 1993; Norcross and Goldfried, 1992; Spinelli, 1994). Nevertheless, what there might be about this particular relationship that is so significant – or, indeed, 'particular' – remains largely unclear.

Perhaps more explicitly than any other current model, the existential-phenomenological approach bestows undisputed centrality upon the relationship between counselling psychologist and client. Existential phenomenologists have argued that is through this relationship itself that the client's issues are manifested or 'brought forth' for examination. In other words, the therapeutic relationship is seen to be the 'microcosm' through which the 'macrocosm' of the client's lived reality is expressed and opened to inquiry.

But, equally, in order for this inquiry to reflect 'microcosmically' the 'macrocosmic' experience of the client in a suitably adequate, or 'good enough' fashion, existential-phenomenological counselling psychologists must be both willing and able to 'place' themselves into the relationship. This notion of *encounter* requires both the counselling psychologist and the client to be present in a manner that acknowledges their co-constitutionality.

Placed in this context, existential phenomenology argues that the very enterprise of therapy is principally dependent upon the establishment and maintenance of a relationship which both explores and expresses the possibilities and limitations of interrelational being. Via this stance, it once again reveals its implicit critique of the dominant natural science model of counselling psychology which concentrates upon what counselling psychologists do (partly because these factors can be measured, taught and assessed, at least to some extent). It should be clear that the situation is not necessarily an either/or one in that, ideally, one would hope to find in one's therapist both sufficient professional expertise and personal qualities that will allow suitable attendance.

Nevertheless, existential phenomenology expresses the view that, if alienated from the *being qualities* of the counselling psychologist, the doing of counselling psychology becomes 'technologized' to such an extent that it distorts the therapeutic relationship in serious ways (raising, among other issues, the question of unnecessary power imbalances weighted heavily in favour of the counselling psychologist) which may well be deeply antagonistic to its fundamental aims and possibilities (Cohn, 1997; Spinelli, 1989, 1994). As such, while by no means dismissing the value of learned skills or knowledge, what is being argued is that these should be placed within a perspective that emphasizes 'doing' as an extension of, and not a substitute for, the therapist's 'being' in the relation. In this way, what counselling psychologists 'do' should be always understandable within, and an expression of, their attempts to acknowledge and enter into the client's world-view rather than be the means of asserting their 'taking charge' of the therapeutic encounter.

One existentially informed theorist who stressed these points and pointed out that they may well contain within them the very key to the clarification of many of the issues that clients express as deeply problematic was R.D. Laing. Throughout his writings Laing argued that mental distress and disturbances, rather than being primarily a form of 'illness' best dealt with via medical models of treatment, could be more adequately understood as expressions of deeply felt and divisive unease, conflict and fragmentation of various facets of one's experience of one's own being as expressed through one's relations with oneself and with others. These various expressions of existential disturbance could be seen to be focused upon concerns surrounding one's *essence* ('that I am'), *existence* ('what I am') and *identity* ('who I am') (Laing, 1960). Further, Laing, together with his colleague Aaron Esterson, argued the case that ontological insecurity arises precisely when the distinction between who one is and what one does (or must/mustn't be or do) remains unclear or indistinguishable through one's relations (Burston, 2000; Laing and Esterson, 1964; Spinelli, 1989, 1994).

An important implication of a 'being' focus in counselling psychology is that it allows counselling psychologists to acknowledge themselves as changing beings whose current manner of existence is expressed through their interactive relationship with their clients. As such, it concedes to counselling psychologists a far greater range of possibilities of relating to clients in differing, if apposite, ways rather than requiring them to maintain a similar stance regardless of the situation or relationship encountered.

While this viewpoint might initially — if mistakenly — suggest a *laissez-faire* attitude to the therapeutic process, in fact it requires existential-phenomenological counselling psychologists to participate in a respectful encounter that is as likely as not to expose them to their own human frailties and limitations. Deeply influenced by Martin Buber's notion of the *interhuman* possibilities of dialogue, the existential analyst Leslie Farber has provided the most detailed, and moving, examinations surrounding the *moral* issues to be faced by therapists who attempt to engage with their clients as 'person to person'. Farber was among the first therapists to insist upon the need to 'bring the world back into the consulting room' by explicitly acknowledging the importance of the client's wider world relations, the impact of the therapeutic relationship upon these, and, in turn, their impact upon the therapeutic relationship (Farber, 2000; Spinelli, 2001a).

Existential phenomenology urges counselling psychologists to be *with* and be *for* their clients. While closely related, and mutually inclusive, these two stances point out emphases whose implications are worth more detailed consideration.

> In 'being with' the client, existential-phenomenological counselling psychologists stay with '*the experienced truths of the client as they are being related* in order that they, and whatever implications such truths may hold, may be exposed to further investigation and clarification by both the [counselling psychologist] and the client. (Spinelli, 1994: 315, original emphasis)

'Being for' the client seeks to remind existential-phenomenological counselling psychologists that, within the confines of each sessional encounter, they are there to attempt to 'enter' the experiential world of the client for the sole reason of allowing the client a specific form of encounter with *another who seeks to be the self*. This process can be seen once again to subvert the likelihood that the existential-phenomenological counselling psychologist will perceive his or her role as being that of '"truth-bringer", "healer" or "helper" in any purposive or direct manner' (Spinelli, 1994: 317) regardless of whether the client assumes it to be such.

The distinction between 'being with' and 'being for' can be seen to be both subtle and significant. While the notion of 'being with' the client focuses on the existential-phenomenological counselling psychologist's willingness to accept the experiential reality of the client, the notion of 'being for' the client urges the counselling psychologist to try to enter that lived reality in order that the counsellor may experience it, if only in part, in a manner that approaches the client's way of being.

The injunctions to 'be with and for' the client are by no means easy ones for counselling psychologists to adhere to (not least because the experience may be disturbing, destabilizing and even frightening), nor is it possible for them ever to be fully completed.

Equally, explanations regarding this attempt which employ terms such as 'transference and counter-transference' have been criticized by existential phenomenologists in that, rather than point out important areas of unconscious conflict in either the client or the therapist (as these latter terms would imply), the difficulties encountered may more accurately reflect unwillingness to engage in this kind of 'being' encounter. Indeed, such explanations may in themselves be seen as defensive and protective barriers or obstacles which serve to distance both the counselling psychologist and the client from the acknowledgement and exploration of the direct experience each has of themselves, the other, and of themselves-in-relation-to-the-other (Cohn, 1997; May, 1983; Spinelli, 2001a).

In a similar fashion, it would be erroneous to assume that the project of 'being with and for' the client equates with the person-centred model's notion of 'mirroring' or 'reflecting back'. Rather than seek to present themselves as 'reflective screens', existential-phenomenological counselling psychologists explicitly acknowledge their own input to the relationship via descriptively focused interpretations that seek to clarify and challenge both the overt and the tacit meanings and assumptions suggested within clients' statements so that their significance to and implications for the client's lived reality can be disclosed and considered. Secondly, the project of 'being with and for' the client makes it clear that existential-phenomenological counselling psychologists are not being asked to 'be themselves' (in the sense of the 'real self' as the person-centred model would suggest) but, rather, that the 'self' that the counselling psychologist is attempting to be is a self-in-relation, whose focus resides in 'the other' (that is, the client) .

Briefly, the existential-phenomenological model's focus upon the various issues of 'being' allows the counselling psychologist to approach the inter-relational world through challenges and clarifications that focus upon the 'what and how' of the client's experience, and hence remain at a descriptive level of the client's current orientation.

The present author has suggested that such explorations should examine four interrelated existential realms of the client's lived experience. The *I-focused* realm concerns itself with the client's experience of being him/herself in any given relationship. It asks, in effect, 'What do I tell myself about my current experience of being in this encounter?' The *you-focused* realm examines the client's experience of 'the other, or others' being in relation with him or her ('What do I tell myself about my experience of the other in any given encounter?'). The *we-focused* realm examines the client's currently lived experience of being with another (the counselling psychologist) at any point during the therapeutic relationship ('What do I tell myself about us in the immediacy of this encounter?). Finally, the *they-focused* realm concerns itself with 'the client's experience of how those who make up his or her wider world of 'others' (extending beyond the other who is the [counselling psychologist]) experience their own interrelational realms in response to the client's current way of being and, as well, to the novel ways of being that have presented themselves as possibilities to the client through psychotherapy' (Spinelli, 2001a: 33).

While all approaches to counselling psychology address the first two realms, existential phenomenology places critical emphasis upon the third realm as the principal means available to adopt a stance of being with and for the client. Finally, the fourth realm permits specific acknowledgement of the 'world dimensions' contained and implicated in any given individual's experience of being and, by so doing, permits a shift in the therapeutic enterprise from the subjective to the intersubjective. This shift, in turn, brings a 'world-conscious' moral dimension to the arena of psychotherapy, the lack of which has been justifiably criticized by 'insiders' and detractors of therapy alike (Masson, 1989; Smail, 1996).

Via the exploration of the above interrelational realms of encounter the existential-phenomenological counselling psychologist is better able to assist the client in making explicit a number of underlying themes, values, beliefs and sedimented assumptions that are contained within the client's stances but which are likely to have remained implicit or unexamined. The clarification of these is seen to be, in itself, a major means for the client to gain a more substantial, and often novel, awareness of the presenting problems (Binswanger, 1963; Deurzen-Smith, 1988; Spinelli, 1994).

In taking such stances, existential phenomenology focuses upon clients' conscious experience of themselves-in-relation. Again, while not denying that much of experience remains unreflected, in that it is not properly clarified and attended to, it need not be the case that this can be understood solely (or even primarily) in terms of unconsciously repressed material. Again, while some existential phenomenologists retain the notion of the unconscious in so far as it expresses the idea of potential awareness that persons cannot, or will not, allow themselves to reflect consciously upon (May, 1983), others have restated the question of the unconscious from the standpoints of dissociation and sedimentation of self-constructs (Spinelli, 1994, 2001a; Strasser and Strasser, 1997). In either case, while by no means denying the experiential features and variables associated with bringing to conscious reflection that which has been previously distorted, denied or unreflected upon, the existential-phenomenological approach demystifies the underlying ideas associated with psychoanalytic notions of the unconscious as the repository for 'repressed' material whose meaning requires interpretative 'decoding'.

It must be said that the adoption of this model asks a great deal of counselling psychologists. For not only does it remove from them much of their professional mystique, and a good deal of the power that comes with this, it also confronts them with the question of their willingness to attend to clients whose issues may provoke all too painful reminders of their own deceits and anxieties. At the same time, the willingness to encounter another in this fashion may also remind counselling psychologists of the immeasurable wonder and joy that are possible when beings encounter themselves through one another.

Family, group and organizational applications

In line with the above, the existential-phenomenological approach does not merely tolerate, but, more correctly, values and embraces the diversity of living as expressed in terms of culture, race, gender and sexual orientation. Concerned as much with the 'universals' of human experience as it is with individual uniqueness, existential phenomenology has been shown to be of particular value to the clarification of various psychological factors relevant to multicultural counselling (Deurzen-Smith, 1988; Eleftheriadou, 1993; Vontress and Epp, 2001) and its effectiveness as a model for psychotherapy provided by and for members of the black community in the United Kingdom has been espoused (Asmall, 1997). The existential-phenomenological has also been successfully applied in the fields of nursing and health care (Becker, 1992). With regard to the on-going debates concerning sexuality and sexual orientation, existential-phenomenological authors such as Maurice Merleau-Ponty (1962), Hans W. Cohn (1997), as well as the present author (Spinelli, 2001a), have provided highly innovative contributions emphasizing the interrelational dimensions of embodied sexual being, as opposed to medically derived concerns of 'normal' and 'abnormal' sexual practices and typologies.

While most existential-phenomenological counselling psychologists tend to work with clients on a one-to-one basis, couple therapy and, less commonly, family therapy is by no means unfeasible. Hans W. Cohn's pioneering contributions to existential-phenomenological group therapy have revealed this model's unique expertise in the analysis and exploration of the individual's experience of relational encounters within various group settings (Cohn, 1997). In like fashion, Strasser and Strasser have developed a widely applicable schedule for short-term, or time-limited, existential-phenomenological therapy (Strasser and Strasser, 1997). Existential phenomenology has begun to be successfully applied to the arena of legal and family mediation (Coleman et al., 2000).

Research

The existential-phenomenological approach has often been presented as being antagonistic to, or uninterested in, psychological research. This contention is far from the truth. Rather, it has played a major role in the development of qualitatively focused approaches to research (Churchill and Wertz, 2001; Giorgi,

1985; Karlsson, 1993). At the same time, the existential phenomenologists' view of suitable counselling psychology research stands in direct contrast to the natural science viewpoint and its underlying assumptions, principally because the questions they pose and the methods they employ are grounded in a carefully articulated, but undeniably different, set of philosophical assumptions.

First, unlike traditional natural science psychological research models, the existential-phenomenological approach denies the possibility of truly objective observation and analysis. Rather, it assumes an indissoluble relationship between observer and observed.

A second major divergence rests on the notion of consciousness. Although the study of consciousness has resurfaced within psychology (Davies and Humphries, 1993), and while, in many cases, the analyses employed rely upon a phenomenological paradigm (Hunt, 1995), nonetheless, in the more general psychological research model the nature of consciousness, *per se*, rarely surfaces as an issue. From the standpoint of existential-phenomenological psychological research, consciousness, or more accurately conscious experience, is central to all inquiry, since the primary aim of existential-phenomenological investigation is to describe as adequately as possible direct and immediate experience. As a clarification of what is being argued here, consider the following example, originally presented in Valle and King's *Existential-Phenomenological Perspectives in Psychology* (1978). Imagine that you are transcribing the musical notes that make up the melody from the first movement of Tchaikovsky's Fifth Symphony. If you then rewrite this melody as transposed by one octave, you will transcribe a quite different set of musical notes. Though the two notations reveal surface distinctions from one another, their underlying melody remains the same. While natural science psychological research typically focuses on the notes, existential-phenomenological psychological research seeks to disclose the melody – that is, more broadly speaking, the foundational structure of conscious experience.

Third, existential-phenomenological psychological research rejects the common notion of causality in its linear form as being valid for the subject matter it investigates. Therefore individuals are not studied or understood in a manner that would suggest that something that happened in their past is a direct cause of their later behaviour. While by no means denying the importance of the past as 'meaning giver' to one's experience, existential-phenomenological psychology sees the importance of past events principally in terms of how they are currently understood, weighted and interpreted by the individual. In this way it construes the past as being far more plastic and dependent upon the present (as well as future expectations) than do most other forms of psychological inquiry. This view expresses the existential-phenomenological stance of 'the-past-as-presently-lived-and-future-directed' since any statement of the past depends upon our current, or present biased perceptions, as well as, of course, our future-directed aims and expectations (Cohn, 1997; Spinelli, 1994). It should be evident, therefore, that this stance rejects standard research notions of control groups, dependent and independent variables, preliminary hypotheses, and so forth, since they all suggest and rely upon, to a greater or lesser degree, the notion of linear causality.

Fourth, as Romanyshyn and Whalen, among others, have pointed out, while existential-phenomenological psychology, too, initiates its investigations from a naive realism, or natural attitude, it takes as its principal task the elucidation and investigation of this self-same natural attitude and 'seeks to describe the advent of experience's meaning prior to any commitment to philosophical positions of realism or idealism' (Romanyshyn and Whalen, 1978: 27).

Fifth, existential-phenomenological research is principally *qualitative-interpretative*, focusing upon descriptive methodologies which focus on questions of 'what' and 'how' something is, rather than 'why' it is. In so doing, it seeks to remain as faithful as possible to the data of experience. In other words, it seeks to understand rather than to explain, and, by so doing, it searches for meaning rather than seeks to collect facts. As Gunmar Karlsson has clarified this distinction:

> Facts are conceived of as objective and independent of consciousness, while meaning is considered subjective and idiosyncratic. In line with logical empiricism, traditional psychology neglects to study meaningful experience in a 'direct' way. Instead, one *operationalizes* variables so as to turn them into observable facts. [Existential phenomenology] rejects the idea that there exist objective facts, *independent* of a subject or a subjective consciousness. The 'objectively' given fact is always present in relation to … a constituting and meaning-imbuing subject …. (Karlsson, 1993: 16, original emphasis)

In a similar fashion, David Rennie (1994) has discussed a model for human science research which closely parallels the principal characteristics of existential-phenomenological research in that it emphasizes the researcher's striving to remain as open as possible to the emergent data rather than testing the accuracy of a hypothesis. In doing so, Rennie has pointed out the necessity of clarifying the philosophical foundations for human science research and has concluded that the natural science model typical of psychological research methodology is unsuitable to its subject matter.

Colaizzi's *Reflection and Research in Psychology* (1973), Valle and King's *Existential-Phenomenological Perspectives in Psychology* (1978), Giorgi's *Phenomenology and Psychological Research* (1985), Karlsson's *Psychological Qualitative Research from a Phenomenological Perspective* (1993) and the present author's own text, *The Interpreted World* (Spinelli, 1989), all provide wide-ranging explorations, critiques and research studies focusing on many of the major areas of experimental and applied psychology as considered from an existential-phenomenological perspective. Equally, the *Review of Existential Psychology and Psychiatry*, the *Journal of Phenomenological Psychology* and the *Journal of the Society for Existential Analysis* regularly publish articles and papers relevant to counselling psychology research and practice. Recent developments in existential-phenomenological research methodologies relevant to counselling psychology research have focused upon hermeneutic single-case efficacy design (Elliott, 2001) and multiple-case depth research (Schneider, 2001).

Generally speaking, existential-phenomenological research begins with the investigator's clarification of his or her own involvement, biases and aims. He or she must first clarify how his or her personal inclinations and predispositions influence the 'how and what' elements that form the focus of investigation, thereby explicitly acknowledging the investigator's role in the research. In addition, however, this self-same process allows the investigator to refine the focus of inquiry so that he or she can construct a formal statement which will provide the preliminary basis with which to formulate research questions. The success of such questions will depend upon how well they are able to 'tap into' the co-researchers' (that is, the 'subjects'') experience so that they can describe and clarify it concretely.

Once the responses have been obtained (usually via face-to-face interviews or written questionnaires), the researcher's task becomes that of extracting significant statements relevant to the focus of inquiry so that their general, or foundational, meanings, clusters of themes and idiosyncratic statements can be integrated into an adequately reflective description of the investigated phenomenon in as unequivocal a statement of identification of its formal structure as possible. In most instances, this statement is discussed with each co-researcher in order to ascertain its adequacy in conveying the co-researcher's experience and, possibly, bringing to light previously unexplored, misunderstood or inadequately expressed experiential variables. In this way, the aim of existential-phenomenological research can be seen to be that of providing descriptive statements whose adequacy is measured on the basis of their ability to express and contain the richness and diversity, as well as the invariant elements, of a given focus experience. This approach stands in direct contrast to the more typical attempts on the part of psychological research to reduce, deny, denigrate or transform experience into a form of operationally defined behaviour.

While the notions of reliability and validity which remain central elements of a natural science research methodology are not directly employed by existential phenomenology, the approach relies upon the *verifiability* of the researcher's conclusions in so far as verifiability refers to 'whether another researcher can assume the perspective of the present investigator, review the original protocol data, and see that the proposed insights meaningfully illuminate the situations under study' (Churchill and Wertz, 2001: 259).

With regard to research evidence for the effectiveness of the existential-phenomenological model, it must be acknowledged that few studies are specific to this issue. Irvin Yalom has noted that the effectiveness of this model is 'as rational, as coherent, and as systematic as any other' (Yalom, 1980: 5). Some preliminary verification of this assertion has emerged from the successful outcome studies of the *Soteria* project focused upon the existentially derived treatment of severe mental disturbances (Mosher, 2001).

Nevertheless, it remains the case that researchers associated with the existential-phenomenological model remain highly critical of much of the research focused upon quantitative outcome studies that has been carried out, pointing out that the natural science approach typically adopted to analyse and measure the effectiveness of therapeutic interventions is at best limited and often unsuitable to the subject matter (Rennie, 1994; Kaye, 1995) and that models incorporating new paradigm research such as those advocated by Reason and Rowan (1981), human science research favoured by Giorgi (1985), Rennie (1994) and discovery-oriented research as advocated by Mahrer (2000) are far more likely to provide more suitable means of exploring the effectiveness of this, or any other, model relevant to counselling psychology. Likewise, the recent 'shift from randomized controlled trials to that which NIMH [National Institute of Mental Health] terms "effectiveness" research' (Schneider, 2001: 673) in the United States stands in significant contrast to the more narrowly focused quantitative 'evidence-based' bias that has become prevalent in the United Kingdom and may yet have its influence in future British research protocols.

Conclusion

While it is hoped that this brief overview of the existential-phenomenological approach has convinced readers of its specific and unique paradigm characteristics and contributions to counselling psychology, it would be misleading to suggest that existential phenomenology seeks to present itself solely as a separate and independent approach to counselling psychology research and practice. While it undoubtedly fulfils these requirements, an equally significant 'thrust' of the approach lies in its attempts to demonstrate its relevance to other counselling psychology models in that, via its principal method of investigation, it provides an original and important means of exposing and clarifying the underlying, often implicit, assumptions contained in all theoretical models and their applications. Via the critical stance that it advocates, its inclination towards the suspension of judgement, and in its questioning of assumed truths, facts and the soundness of inferences that all models adopt, the existential-phenomenological approach reveals a healthy scepticism that is much needed in the psychological investigation of counselling and psychotherapeutic theories and practices.

In this latter sense, the existential-phenomenological approach can be more accurately seen to be an attitude or stance taken towards thinking about and 'doing' counselling psychology. Such input will serve both to delineate the boundaries of counselling psychology and to clarify its unique place and contributions to psychological theory and research in general.

References

Asmall, I. (1997) 'Existentialism, existential psychotherapy and African philosophy', *Journal of the Society for Existential Analysis*, 8 (2): 138–52.

Becker, C.S. (1992) *Living and Relating: an Introduction to Phenomenology*. London: Sage.

Binswanger, L. (1963) *Being-in-the-World: Selected Papers of Ludwig Binswanger*, ed. S. Needleman. New York: Basic Books.

Burston, D. (2000) *The Crucible of Experience: R.D. Laing and the Crisis of Psychotherapy*. Cambridge MA: Harvard University Press.

Churchill, S.D. and Wertz, F.J. (2001) 'An introduction to phenomenological research in psychology: historical, conceptual, and methodological foundations' in K.J. Schneider, J.F.T. Bugental and J.F. Pierson (eds) *The Handbook of Humanistic Psychology*. London: Sage.

Cohn, H.W. (1997) *Existential Thought and Therapeutic Practice*. London: Sage.

Colaizzi, P.F. (1973) *Reflection and Research in Psychology*. Dubuque IA: Kendall Hunt.

Coleman, B., Coleman, S., Spinelli, E. and Strasser, F. (2000). 'Caught in the middle: training MP's in dispute resolution' in G. Power (ed.) *Under Pressure: Are we Getting the most from our MPs?* London: Hansard Society.

Cooper, D.E. (1996) *Thinkers of our Time: Heidegger*. London: Claridge Press.

Davies, M. and Humphries, G.W. (eds) (1993) *Consciousness*. Oxford: Blackwell.

Deurzen-Smith, E. van (1988) *Existential Counselling in Practice*. London: Sage.

Eleftheriadou, Z. (1993) 'Applications of a philosophical framework to transcultural therapy', *Journal of the Society for Existential Analysis*, 4: 116–23.

Elliott, R. (2001) 'Hermeneutic single-case efficacy design: an overview' in K.J. Schneider, J.F.T. Bugental and J.F. Pierson (eds) *The Handbook of Humanistic Psychology*. London: Sage.

Farber, L.H. (2000) *The Ways of the Will*. New York: Basic Books.

Fewtrell, D. and O'Connor, K. (1995) *Clinical Phenomenology and Cognitive Psychology*. London: Routledge.

Giorgi, A. (1985) *Phenomenology and Psychological Research*. Pittsburgh PA: Duquesne University Press.

Goldenberg, H. and Isaacson, Z. (1996) 'The narrow ridge where I and Thou meet', *Journal of the Society for Existential Analysis*, 7 (2): 118–30.

Heidegger, M. (1962) *Being and Time*, trans. J. Macquarrie and E. Robinson. Oxford: Blackwell.

Howe, D. (1993) *On Being a Client: Understanding the Process of Counselling and Psychotherapy*. London: Sage.

Hunt, H.T. (1995) *On the Nature of Consciousness*. London: Yale University Press.

Husserl, E. (1977) *Phenomenological Psychology*. The Hague: Nijhoff.

Ihde, D. (1986) *Experimental Phenomenology: an Introduction*. Albany NY: State University of New York Press.

Ihde, D. (1998) *Expanding Hermeneutics: Visualism in Science*. Evanston IL: Northwestern University Press.

Jaspers, K. (ed.) (1963) *General Psychopathology*, trans. J. Hoenig and W. Hamilton, Manchester: Manchester University Press.

Karlsson, G. (1993) *Psychological Qualitative Research from a Phenomenological Perspective*. Stockholm: Almqvist & Wiksell.

Kaye, J. (1995) 'Postfoundationalism and the language of psychotherapy research' in J. Siegfried (ed.) *Therapeutic and Everyday Discourse as Behavior Change*. Norwood NJ: Ablex.

Laing, R.D. (1960) *The Divided Self*. London: Tavistock Publications.

Laing, R.D. and Esterson, A. (1964) *Sanity, Madness and the Family*. Harmondsworth: Penguin.

Mahrer, A.R. (2000) 'Philosophy of science and the foundations of psychotherapy', *American Psychologist*, 55 (10): 117–25.

Masson, J. (1989) *Against Therapy*. London: Collins.

May, R. (1983) *The Discovery of Being: Writings in Existential Psychology*. New York: Norton.

Merleau-Ponty, M. (1962) *The Phenomenology of Perception*, trans. C. Smith. London: Routledge.

Mosher, L. (2001) 'Treating madness without hospitals: Soteria and its success', in K.J. Schneider, J.F.T. Bugental and J.F. Pierson (eds.) *The Handbook of Humanistic Psychology*. London: Sage.

Norcross, J.C. and Goldfried, M.R. (eds) (1992) *Handbook of Psychotherapy Integration*. New York: Basic Books.

Pilgrim, D. (2000) 'Psychiatric diagnosis: more questions than answers', *Psychologist*, 13 (6): 302–5.

Reason, P. and Rowan, J. (1981) *Human Enquiry: a Sourcebook of New Paradigm Research*. Chichester: Wiley.

Rennie, D. (1994) 'Human Science in Counselling Psychology: Closing the Gap between Research and Practice', paper delivered to the first annual conference of the BPS Division of Counselling Psychology, May.

Romanyshyn, R.D. and Whalen, B.J. (1978) 'Psychology and the attitude of science' in R.S. Valle and M. King (eds) *Existential-Phenomenological Perspectives in Psychology*. New York: Plenum Press.

Sartre, J.P. (1956) *Being and Nothingness: an Essay on Phenomenological Ontology*, trans. H. Barnes. London: Routledge (1991).

Schneider, K.J. (2001) 'Multiple-case depth research: bringing experience-near closer' in K.J. Schneider, J.F.T. Bugental and J.F. Pierson (eds) *The Handbook of Humanistic Psychology*. London: Sage.

Smail, D. (1996) *How to Survive without Psychotherapy*. London: Constable.

Spinelli, E. (1989) *The Interpreted World: an Introduction to Phenomenological Psychology*. London: Sage.

Spinelli, E. (1994) *Demystifying Therapy*. London: Constable.

Spinelli, E. (1997) *Tales of Un-knowing: Therapeutic Encounters from an Existential Perspective*. London: Duckworth.

Spinelli, E. (2001a) *The Mirror and the Hammer: Challenges to Therapeutic Orthodoxies*. London: Continuum.

Spinelli, E. (2001b) 'Psychosis: new existential, systemic and cognitive-behavioral developments', *Journal of Contemporary Psychotherapy*, 31 (1): 61–7.

Strasser, F. and Strasser, A. (1997) *Existential Time-limited Therapy: the Wheel of Existence*. Chichester: Wiley.

Valle, R.S. and King, M. (eds) (1978) *Existential-Phenomenological Perspectives in Psychology*. New York: Plenum Press.

Vontress, C.E. and Epp, L. R. (2001) 'Existential cross-cultural counselling: when hearts and cultures share' in K.J. Schneider, J.F.T. Bugental and J.F. Pierson (Eds.) *The Handbook of Humanistic Psychology*. London: Sage.

Yalom, I. (1980) *Existential Psychotherapy*. New York: Basic Books.

9 Feminist Approaches to Counselling Psychology
CAROLYN KAGAN AND CAROL TINDALL

What is the feminist approach to counselling psychology?

> At the heart of feminist counselling and therapy is the belief that the external world and internal world of women, the objective and subjective are fundamentally inter-connected. There is disagreement as to the specific dynamics between these, but what is clear is that both feminist theorists and therapists concur that changing our internal worlds and gaining currency and agency in the world will not make it less hostile or oppressive. (Day, 1992: 382)

It is a mistake to think of *the feminist approach* in counselling psychology as a unitary, homogeneous entity, and most feminist thinkers agree there are a number of different feminisms. Humm (1992) suggests that these differences in feminist thought arise from a complex process of ideas that emerge from and are intertwined with historical, social and political events. Thus feminisms develop differently in different places and at different times, for different reasons. Day (1992) argues for a different way of conceptualizing the differences in femi-nism – one that reflects different philosophical positions. She suggests a useful distinction is to be made between radical, socialist and black feminists (see Table 9.1). To these differentiations Enns (1993) adds liberal, cultural, existential, Marxist, lesbian, postmodern and psychoanalytic feminisms. Having said that, we can probably identify some common threads running through feminist thought and feminist therapeutic practice.

Russell (1996: 248) suggests that feminism is a perspective, based on a set of values, which are used to inform all aspects of practice. As she says:

> [feminism is] a way of construing the world, our experiences and the possibilities which we see for the future. It is a perspective which defies rigidity, while genuinely affording value to women's experience as of central importance and worth. ... Feminism is a way of seeing the world which works towards helping women take an equal place in society ...

Humm (1992: 1) sums up the core of feminism slightly differently, stressing the political dimensions.

> Feminism is a social force [which] depends on the understanding that, in all societies which divide the sexes in differing cultural, economic or political spheres, women are less valued than men. Feminism also depends on the premise that women can con-sciously and collectively change their social place. ... [it is] a belief in sexual equality combined with a commitment to eradicate sexist domination and to transform society.

Table 9.1 Analyses of women's oppression

Feminism	Analysis of women's oppression
Radical	Position of women flowed fundamentally from the exercise of male power in a patriarchal society
Socialist	Patriarchy takes particular forms and is shaped by the economic and social organization of a society
Black	Black women's experiences have to be understood through the prism of racism

Source: After Day (1992: 374)

Different theoretical and practice traditions emphasize various parts of a feminist approach differently, and outline different therapeutic goals and analyses (see, for example, Day, 1992; Enns, 1992; Russell, 1996; Worrell and Remer, 1993). Despite this, it is possible to identify some general principles and values which characterize and underpin feminist counselling psychology.

Principles of feminist approaches to counselling psychology

Socio-political analysis

'The personal is political' has been the cornerstone of feminist approaches to counselling psychology (Morrow and Hawxhurst, 1998) since the early 1960s.[1] Whatever the theoretical or counselling psychology position adopted, what feminist counselling psychologists share 'is a belief that women's experiences are a product of the interactions between their internal psyche and external material worlds, and thus are political' (Day, 1992: 375; see also Chaplin, 1988; Walker, 1990).

As we have seen, whilst there are different theoretical schools of feminism, all start with the recognition of the inferior status of women and the fact of their oppression. Women's position in society and their experiences of relationships are shaped by external factors, by social structures, and by cultural and ideological influences (Smail, 1991). These external structures are patriarchal, and feminisms, in their different forms, all offer critiques of patriarchy. In summary, women's social value and feelings of self-worth are anchored in patriarchal societal values and prescriptions about what it means to be female, and these must be understood, and eventually changed.

Emphasis on gender and sex role stereotyping

As part of a critique of patriarchy, a useful distinction is to be made between sex (the biological embodiment of differences between men and women) and gender (the social expectations of the masculine and feminine). Some experiences women have may be linked with their sex – such as processes of reproduction and fertility: however, the meaning of these experiences is *socially* constructed, and thus linked with their gender. Thus, for example, both men and women can become parents: however, in nearly all societies, the expectations of fathers and mothers are different. These are differences to do with gender, not sex. In most counselling psychology situations, it is the meaning of experience that is important, and thus it is with gender roles that we are concerned. Feminist counselling psychology aims to facilitate equality in personal power between men and women, and help clients to challenge culturally prescribed sex roles.

Nevertheless, 'It recognises that whilst men have also been victims of a sexist culture and its rigid patterns of socialisation, it is still men who hold the balance of power and receive a disproportionate share of social rewards and privileges' (Taylor, 1994: 320).

Woman-centred focus

Women's lives and experiences are at the core of feminist work. Not only do feminist approaches seek to unmask and understand sex role stereotypes and their contribution to women's problems, they also undertake socio-political analyses of women's position and, importantly, highlight women's strengths and potential. Gender roles are acquired through the process of socialization, and different expectations and pressures are brought to bear on women at different stages in their life cycle. Socialization, coupled with women's relatively weak structural position, gives rise to some of the unique problems women face, and that feminist counselling psychology seeks to address. Working mothers, for example, experience their lives very differently from working fathers, largely as a result of differing expectations and social value placed on their different activities. Elderly widowers will often receive more support and assistance from services than will elderly widows: not because their bereavement experiences are greater, but because of stereotyped expectations about their needs and capabilities.

In feminist work, the understanding and experience of gender roles and social expectations is just as relevant to practitioners as it is to clients. Women counselling psychologists have experienced, at first hand, some of the same sources of oppression as their clients, and we will see, below, how this influences the therapeutic process.

Power and powerlessness

The exploration of power, powerlessness and gaining power[2] are common in one way or another to all feminist approaches. Power is a multi-layered concept, and is of interest, not only in analyses of women's unequal access to social power in general, but also in considerations of the therapeutic relationship and processes. Power can be explored at the personal, interpersonal, and societal levels, and it is important to understand that all analyses of power are tied in to particular historical and cultural contexts. In a counselling psychology situation, as Taylor (1994: 320) points out:

> not all clients have a social history that includes ineffective and inappropriate uses of power, and a general lack of real power … however … it is likely that at the point when anyone seeks counselling s/he is feeling out of control, powerless and demoralised.

Feminist approaches seek to identify different forms and sources of power and powerlessness and help clients to a recognition of their potential for gaining access to both personal and social power. Acknowledgement is made of the power (often wielded by counselling psychologists, feminist ones included) within the therapeutic process.

However, where perhaps feminist approaches might differ from other approaches is in using power dynamics themselves as a conscious part of the therapeutic process itself (Morrow and Hawxhurst, 1998). Certainly a feminist approach would require that the role and nature of power is part of on-going reflection about practice.

Positive vision of the future

Feminist approaches share a commitment to work with women on their strengths, with a view to helping them develop their potential. As we have seen, this may be outside the restrictions of conventional sex role expectations. Central to this principle is to help women gain a sense of worth, and be recognized as valuable persons in their own right. Day (1992) considers the view that such a 'recognition of a person in her own right' might be consistent with humanistic counselling. Is, then, humanistic counselling also feminist? Day argues, and we would agree, that it is not necessarily feminist, in so far as 'an orthodox humanistic approach has been too inward, with scant regard paid to the *external structural constraints* which shape women's oppression and their internalisation of it' (Day, 1992: 381, our emphasis).

In addition to focusing on women's strengths and potential, feminist approaches offer positive visions of the future for women. These visions are of a more equitable society, in which being female is valued and in which social resources are allocated equitably. In an unequal society, it is argued, women's self-image, ability to be self-directed and ability to be happy are constrained by their lack of access to external power. Thus feminist approaches help women dream of – and achieve – a future in which they can be who they want to be, not just who they are expected to be (Brown and Liss-Levinson, 1981).

Commitment to social action and social transformation

Key to feminism is a commitment to social transformation, in order to achieve the liberation of women. This usually goes hand in hand with a commitment to some form of collective action in order to actively contribute to and create social change. Yet, without action, we have to recognize the limited contribution that counselling psychology might make to the position of women generally. Worell and Remer (1992: 24) put it thus: 'it is unsufficient to fix women for functioning in a dysfunctional society'.

We have seen, then, that a number of principles underpin feminist approaches. These include:

- Socio-political analysis of women's position (including an emphasis on sex role stereotypes).
- Adopting a woman-centred focus.
- The centrality of power and powerlessness.
- Retaining a positive vision of the future.
- A commitment to social action.

Within each of these principles, feminist approaches reflect a number of values.

Values of feminist approaches

Egalitarianism

The value of egalitarianism is revealed via the goals of feminist therapy, which seek to achieve a more equitable place for women in society, as well as via counselling psychology practice, which seeks to demystify the therapeutic process and render it transparent and open. To value egalitarianism is not to adopt a simplistic view of equality between counsellor and client, or to ignore actual power differentials. Rather it leads to a position where knowledge and understanding are shared and jointly negotiated between client and counselling psychologist.

This is not to deny that differences in knowledge and technique exist, but to make such differences transparent and open, accepting difference, not judging difference as less in some way. The egalitarian principles enshrined in feminist practice can be a model of relationships in general.

Care and commitment

The value of care and commitment directly informs the ethical base of feminist counselling psychology practice. Commitment to, and care towards, clients do not begin and end with the consultation session. Care for clients prior to their entering therapy requires us to be clear about what we can and cannot offer; what our skill and experiences are, and what our underlying values and principles are. Commitment to clients does not necessarily end once formal sessions have ended. For many women, whose psychological distress is closely linked with fractured relationships and sense of identity, as well as lives full of practical difficulties, it will sometimes be necessary to make contact outside therapy sessions.[3]

Diversity

To value diversity is to accept, welcome and celebrate difference, not to pathologize it. Many critiques of the prevailing mental health system have shown how assessment, diagnosis and treatment are all constructed along a construct of male-is-normal, female-is-abnormal dimension. Further, white able-bodied male is taken as the 'normal' alongside which black and/or disabled women are seen to be deviant. Enns (1993: 17–22) reports a telling account of a proposal to change *DSM*[4] categories in a way that would pathologize normally socialized men, rather than normally socialized women, as does the current diagnostic system (see also Brown, 1992).

A commitment to diversity would enable us to identify within our practice the harm done to people by the workings of a competitive, individualistic society, where perfection is expected and, by implication, those who are not perfect are seen as lesser and excluded. Feminist therapists must, according to Enns (1993) recognize, understand and work with the diversity brought by clients, including that which is 'conveyed by their various problems, racial/ethnic identifications, economic statuses, personality styles, and exposure to "isms" such as racism, sexism, ageism, and heterosexism'.

Reflexivity

Feminist practice values reflexivity – a process of continual reflection, analysis, evaluation and decision making. We are able to practise as feminists, in accordance with the principles and values outlined above, only if we have a high degree of self-awareness and a willingness to learn from others and from our own practices.

The value of egalitarianism requires us to have a degree of humility in terms of our own expertise and continual learning, and we can achieve this only through reflective self-awareness. Reflexivity is as important in terms of the micro-interactions we conduct with clients as it is as a mechanism for enabling us to scrutinize our ethical practice and prevent problems occurring. Both uses of reflexivity require us to become self-aware.

Self-awareness is a process, not a state. Kagan and Evans (1995: 230) suggest that:

> We will never achieve total self-awareness (how would we know we had it anyway?), but can work at making constructive use of our experiences throughout life, in order to enhance our personal relationships and make more effective use of our professional interpersonal skills.

We have seen, then, that, in addition to feminist principles, feminist values underpin feminist approaches to counselling psychology. These include the values of

- Egalitarianism.
- Care and commitment.

- Diversity.
- Reflexivity.

What might it look like in practice?

Interestingly, there is very little on *process* in the literature on feminist approaches to counselling psychology. This is surprising, as Seu (2000), among others, claims that therapists would describe their feminist stance more in terms of process than goals or outcome. We have seen, however, that feminism is a perspective, defined by a set of principles and values, which always involves the political as well as the individual. It is about being woman-centred, this is the heart of it. In terms of process, our feminist belief systems guide us as women as well as inform our professional practice. Consequently, feminist practice is always feminist, whatever the issue, from the obviously feminist such as rape or breast cancer to the less obviously feminist such as depression or stress at work, and whoever the client.

Let us now move on to explore how these feminist values and principles might operate in practice, how feminist values might shine through the process; how ideally we might work if feminist guidelines and principles are followed. As power is the underlying issue, it will not be addressed separately but rather will be considered within each exploration of how principles and values might appear in practice.

Socio-political analysis

The emphasis on political and social influences makes the practice of feminist counselling psychology different. As Taylor (1996: 209) states, 'The political and social influences on the personal and interpersonal lives of people coming into counselling is a proper area of exploration in counselling.' So feminist counselling psychology is about explicitly exploring the issues of power in people's lives, exploring the client's position within various social structures, from wider societal structures to more personal work, family and partnership issues. It is about consciousness raising and involves assisting clients to discriminate between external and internal contributions to their distress, as well as enabling clients to analyse the power issues at work in their everyday lives.

More specifically, gender position and stereotypical gender styles need to be addressed. Mainstream therapy often involves the adjustment model of encouraging women to change, to adjust to fit into their socially constructed roles within our patriarchal society, to conform to their socialization processes, to meet the needs of others before addressing their own needs. Within feminist counselling psychology how these social processes operate is highlighted, and adjustment to an existing oppressive environment is *not* a valued outcome. It is about enabling women to see that they have choices, they can be free of the shackles of stereotypes, they do not have to live up to others' norms and expectations. In fact Waterhouse (1993) claims that living up to these stereotypes, being what she calls an 'angel child', leads women into self-harm of one sort or another as well as depression. She urges women to turn their anger on society instead of on themselves, to get really wild with a social system that fails to take their experiences seriously and suggests that 'wild women don't get the blues'.

Offering, within counselling psychology practice, a political analysis of contemporary society and how societal values and norms influence their personal and interpersonal lives, gives clients new insights, new ways of understanding their experiencing other than as a personal pathology. Morrow and Hawxhurst highlight the significance of political analysis:

> The individual experiences of dis-ease experienced by women have their roots in the powerlessness and oppression of women as a class. ... Depression and other forms of psychological distress are created primarily by societal, cultural, and political forces. (1998: 40)

Russell acknowledges the dangers posed to women by 'adjustment' perspectives:

> the *status quo* surrounding individuals may be oppressive and destructive to their well-being. Locating responsibility for all the problems encountered by women within themselves is dangerous, as it leads to the adaptive model of mental health where women are seen to be neurotic in some way if they do not accept the social structures around them. (1996: 249)

Feminist counselling psychologists acknowledge that we do not exist in a vacuum, that we are all embedded within our socio-cultural context, that we need to work at both the individual and the political level to bring about change. Ussher (1991) reminds us that, within the process, we must look at the societal discourses that regulate and control women, but that we must not forget the reality of the pain and desperation for the individual client we are working with; both levels need to be operating. The intention according to Morrow and Hawxhurst is to 'combine personal healing with political transformation' (1998: 40).

Egalitarianism

Egalitarianism within feminist therapy works on two levels and reflects the attention paid to both the individual client within the counselling relationship and their everyday life within the current socio-political context. Within the therapeutic relationship, feminists do all that they can to establish 'a mutual, reciprocal, respectful and non-authoritarian relationship' (Taylor, 1996: 208). Essentially this involves the therapist and client openly exploring the power dynamics within the process and negotiating, not imposing, the contract right from the outset. This immediately focuses the process on analysis of power and begins to make the dynamics explicit. Clients are not passively in receipt of the therapist's analysis but rather together, collaboratively, therapist and client explore the possible power dynamics and their potential impact. Such a collaborative relationship involving both as active participants can also be a powerful illustration of how relationships might operate beyond the therapeutic session, in clients' personal and social worlds. It is acknowledged that clients are people who are currently vulnerable, seeking help, whereas the therapist is in a position of power, having the skills and knowledge to provide the help needed. Differences between client and therapist are not denied but made transparent. Difference is not judged as less in any way but is acknowledged and accepted. Power differentials within the therapeutic relationship are minimized as far as possible. The therapist needs to be open and receptive, reflexively aware, throughout, to ensure that a collaborative, non-abusive working relationship is established and maintained.

Simultaneously, egalitarianism beyond the therapeutic context is explored; clients' critical reflections are encouraged, with the aim of undermining the power of socially constructed gender roles and oppressive patriarchal values. To this end there is a thorough exploration of the role of different kinds of power in clients' lives. The intention is to encourage clients to value themselves and significant others equally and enable them to negotiate egalitarian personal relationships.

For example, women who have experienced abuse of one sort or another at the hands of violent men very often blame themselves for the abuse and look to themselves for a solution. They are aided and abetted in this focus by some traditional psychology theories that tend to 'victim-blame', hold the woman responsible for what are men's actions. Theories of co-dependence, for example, which pathologize women for their perceived neediness in relationships, rather than questioning why men are so violent. Even the terms commonly used focus on the women – 'battered wives', 'women who have experienced abuse', labelling the women rather than using the label 'violent men'. Numerous pop psychology books such as *Women who Love too Much* also encourage women to accept the burden of responsibility. Such a client in a feminist counselling psychology relationship might gain insights from a socio-political analysis of gender stereotypes and the power and powerlessness inherent in the roles being played out. Insights into how sexist society requires women to undertake the affective work of society, both within the family and beyond, in the workplace, may also be valuable. The aim is to enable clients to shrug off socially constructed roles and play the roles they choose in the ways they choose. The process of change is one of liberation from oppressive societal constraints to explorations of new possibilities. Instead of attempting to fit themselves into socially predetermined roles they have the insight and power to make their elected roles their own, to fit their roles around themselves. In this way clients are able to construct psychologically healthier and more comfortable lives for themselves and those around them.

Openness and transparency

A further practice difference that clients are likely to notice is the openness of the feminist counselling psychologist and the fact that she makes aspects of the process transparent. This is clearly also part of setting up an egalitarian, collaborative working relationship. Openness consists of the feminist therapist being prepared to answer questions, to self-disclose about her own experiences, including those of oppression and patriarchy. Disclosure is not always in the interests of the client, and only information which the counselling psychologist believes will facilitate the therapeutic process is disclosed. The quality of contact is different, less distant than other approaches. The sharing is two-way. Feminist counselling psychologists, unlike many other counsellors, will be clear from the outset about their feminist perspective, and the principles and values that underpin their work as well as their on-going commitment to explain the therapeutic process. The client is then in a position to make an informed choice of whether to take up the therapy on offer. Therapists too make a decision based on these initial discussions as to whether the client is likely to benefit from feminist therapy. Not everyone is open to feminist ways of working.

Suitability is assessed in terms of whether the client seems willing to explore the problem, herself and wider issues. Is she able to introspect and see patterns in her experiencing? Does she seem socially and politically aware? Essentially, does the client seem comfortable and able to engage with this way of working? If client and therapist decide not to work together, the feminist therapist will explain why she believes the client will benefit from a different type of therapy and will always endeavour to refer the client to an appropriate alternative. However, after the decision not to work together has been negotiated it may be some time before an alternative therapist is found. In that case the feminist will offer appropriate support and therapeutic help until a suitable therapist is found. If the decision is to work together, both client and counsellor negotiate the contract, including what issues they will work on and how they will work, within ethical and professional boundaries, which are discussed openly.

Care and commitment

As is already clear, the relationship between client and feminist therapist is different in kind from many other therapeutic relationships. A mutual, empathic caring relationship is worked for. Gilligan (1982) draws attention to a particular difference between male and female styles of relating, suggesting that men 'protect separateness' while women 'sustain connections'. It is this quality of mutuality and strength of connection which underlies the ethic of care apparent in feminist therapy. Counsellors demonstrate their care and commitment to their clients by expressing 'an emotional investment in the other person's well-being' (Stiver, 1991: 265).

Mutuality is evident in the process as counsellor and client move forward together on points of consensus and work together in ways that are mutually agreed. This involves constant interplay between issues to be worked with and ways of working. As women we have the potential for understanding other women, but it is only potential, not automatic. Being a woman is not the same as being woman-centred. Woman-centredness is about validating women's experiences, putting them at the heart of our work.

It is crucially important, given the therapist's investment of self and the client's vulnerability, that boundaries are clear and explicit. The ethos of care and commitment involves keeping both client and therapist safe, with clear and explicit boundaries, negotiated and not imposed upon clients. Boundaries within feminist approaches are often different not just because they are mutually agreed. For example, if a client is perceived to be vulnerable between sessions the feminist counselling psychologist may make contact in order to encourage her and ensure the client does not feel abandoned by the artificially imposed appointment system of therapy work. Such contact reminds clients that they have not been forgotten and in our experience is much appreciated.

A further feature of care and commitment within the feminist therapy process is the emphasis on the positive, at both the individual and the community level. Focusing only on clients' problems and negative aspects is a very easy trap to fall into. Feminist process would also emphasize positives, times when problems were dealt with, client strategies that work, current positive aspects of themselves (clients) and their lives. The feminist therapist is careful not to collude with the immersion in negative emotion and perception of inadequacy that clients often experience initially and aims to present a more realistic, balanced perspective.

A positive vision of the future is about doing what we can in our own communities and work lives to strive for a more equitable society, one which truly values the feminine as well as the masculine. We are committed to challenging paternalist structures that disadvantage women. This is done in academia at a theoretical level but action is also required to make a real difference in people's lives. Action is inherent in feminist principles and women who take part in feminist therapy often go on to community work of various kinds. Interestingly, although social action is still held as a principle of feminist therapy, as we will see, 'activism is difficult to combine, both financially and psychologically, with counselling practice' (Chester and Bretherton, 2001: 542).

Reflexivity

The important role played by self-awareness and reflexive practice was identified by feminist researchers in the early 1970s and thereafter (see, for example, Oakley, 1981; Finch, 1984) who recognized that a clear separation between researchers and those participating in the research was not possible, particularly if both were women, exploring life experiences which they had all shared. At this time it was recognized that the 'traditional' ways of conducting research, based as they were on pursuing the male values of objectivity, were inadequate for the task. Reflexivity is a core value of feminist counselling psychology, although it is paid scant attention in the literature. Wilkinson defines reflexivity as 'disciplined self-reflection' (1988: 493). It involves embracing rather than discounting our subjective involvement with the client and the process. We cannot stand separate from our practice or our clients and hold them at a distance, we are actively engaged with our clients and the process of change. Taylor makes the point well when she acknowledges, 'I reached the point in my work as a psychotherapist where I could no longer stand apart from my women clients and play dumb: the opaque mirror stance can be punitive' (1995: 109).

This high level of engagement with client and process is done from a position of humility: we make every attempt to work collaboratively, democratically, acknowledging that we too are active learners in the process. Just as we encourage clients to attend to their processing and highlight socio-political messages and values present in their lives, so we as practitioners must attend to our own processing, our own stories, which reflect the socio-political values we have adopted. We need to reflect constantly on our practice, particularly from the point of view of sexism and heterosexism. King (1996), although talking about research, acknowledges how attending to our own processing, particularly what is stirred up for us, is an additional source of insight.

To offer sound ethical practice, we need an ability to distinguish between clients' issues and our own, based in reflexive awareness and self-appraisal. An appreciation of how our gender, personality, style and levels of self-awareness impact on our therapeutic process is crucial in gaining the confidence to work as a critical reflective practitioner.

The emphasis is on change for both our clients and ourselves and the ability to learn from this change. To learn we need to reflect on our practice, including the power dynamics within and beyond the therapeutic relationship. It is crucial that we engage in our own critical reflection as well as encouraging clients to do so. Such critical self-awareness, reflection and learning facilitate the adoption of a flexible approach to practice.

The counselling psychologist, the client and the process are embedded in and saturated with culturally produced meanings and values. If we do not actively attend to such issues in ourselves, the client and the context, we run the risk of reproducing oppression in the therapeutic encounter. We must constantly engage in critical exploration to ensure that the therapeutic space we offer 'can be truly creative not persecutory or providing false comfort' (Seu, 2000: 252).

One of the places where we can attend to raising and maintaining critical self-awareness is in supervision. The tasks of supervision are many. Here we focus briefly on the reflexive aspects of supervision. Feminist supervision reflects feminist principles and values, gender and power issues are addressed, and a mutual, reciprocal and non-authoritarian relationship is worked for between supervisor and supervisee. There is an agreement that therapy and supervision reflect social values and that gender and power issues can contaminate the therapy and supervision process. As Taylor points out, 'therapy is always shaped to some extent by the value system of the therapist, which largely will be unconscious' (1994: 322).

Supervision is about identifying and addressing the effect of the therapist's value system on the therapy being scrutinized. This is partially achieved by incorporating a social analysis into supervision which clarifies the political nature of some of the therapeutic issues and results in addressing gender stereotypes which otherwise might remain as part of the therapist – client encounter. Supervision enables supervisees to clarify their own sex role identity and its impact on their practice and facilitates them working towards where they need to be, in order to be helpful to clients.

This is achieved within an egalitarian supervisory relationship that echoes the feminist therapeutic relationship in terms of negotiation, self-disclosure, working with strengths and mutuality. Such an egalitarian relationship, according to Maroda, 'maximises individual freedom and encourages a working partnership' (1991: 6). It is within this working partnership that both personal and therapeutic issues and how these are intertwined and impact on practice can be critically explored.

Dilemmas and tensions

In this section we shall assess the extent to which feminist counselling psychology really does reflect its underlying values and principles. In doing so, we will draw heavily on two recent studies which have sought information about what it is that feminist practitioners say they do.

Marecek and Kravetz (1998: 15) undertook a small-scale interview study, in the United States, of twenty-five practitioners who 'identified themselves either as feminist therapists or said they brought a feminist perspective to their work' (sixteen of them were psychologists). Chester and Bretherton (2001) report a questionnaire study of 140 (138 women and two men) Australian counsellors who identified themselves as feminist, accessed largely through feminist and psychology networks.

Both studies sought to explore the extent to which feminist principles and values were reflected in practice. Whilst there were some differences in the findings of the studies, largely due to differing methodology, there were also some similarities. Feminist practitioners by and large agreed on the values underpinning feminist practice, in particular its emphasis on woman-centredness, commitment to social action, a critique of patriarchy, egalitarianism and a commitment to a positive vision of the future and social action. However, in practice some of these values had little impact on the therapy itself.

Are the values reflected in feminist counselling psychology?

Nearly all the therapists in both studies reported that they adhered to feminist values in their lives, and that feminism constituted a strong belief system for them. However, a tension was revealed by Marecek and Kravetz's therapists. They reported that, in practice, they adopted a value-neutral stance – validating and acknowledging their women clients' own values and choices. However, they also claimed their work was underpinned by feminist values, which, as we have seen, are not neutral. These therapists, too, along with many in Chester and Bretherton's study, said that they did not reveal their feminist stance to clients, thus breaching the value of egalitarianism. The reluctance to declare one's feminism is probably a response to what is known as the backlash to feminism, which is, in itself, a complex phenomenon. On the one hand, feminism has been incorporated into the mainstream, and thereby, as Enns (1993) and Hollway (1991) argue, depoliticized. On the other hand, feminism has been promoted as something negative and to be feared as undermining social stability by reactionary media, and, as a result, this cultural backlash means that 'to speak about feminism necessarily means speaking to and from the narratives about feminism in the culture at large' (Marecek and Kravetz, 1998: 24).

Yet feminism values openness and transparency. In order for clients to exercise choices about the type of therapy and therapist they work with, clarifying one's value position from the outset is essential (Hare-Mustin et al., 1979). Marecek and Kravetz (1998: 25) share our own concern with the tendency to remain silent on one's feminism as a therapist.

> Although we sympathize with the difficult position of being a feminist in a time of backlash, we find the justificatory practices troubling. They [the therapists] run the risk of dishonesty, of patronizing women, and of disrespecting clients' ability to think for themselves.

There is, then, agreement on values underlying feminist counselling psychology but not necessarily congruence between belief in the values and practice. To what extent, then, are the principles of feminist practice borne out in practice?

Are the principles reflected in feminist practice?

Feminist principles do seem to underpin, to some extent, feminist counselling psychologists' practice.

Woman-centredness and diversity

The principle of *woman-centredness*, incorporating gender role analysis, featured in all the self-declared feminists' work. However, there was a tendency to assume that being about women was being feminist. As Marecek and Kravetz (1998) suggest, there has been a conflation of 'woman' with feminism. They remind us that not all counselling (and, by implication, not all counselling psychology) with women is feminist, and that the general incorporation of 'feminist' into practice with women, which fails to adhere to the different feminist principles outlined here, has led to the dominance of therapeutic goals over feminist goals. Therapists' professional identities overlay their feminist identities. As Enns (1993: 63) puts it, 'Psychologists cannot assume the label of feminist therapist by merely adding feminism and stirring [and] defining oneself as a feminist does not automatically mean that one is a feminist therapist.'

Figure 9.1   Different approaches to counselling psychology in terms of values and flexibility

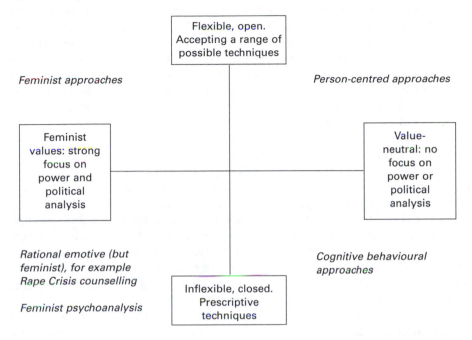

It is interesting to consider, though, the extent to which different professional models of counselling psychology can be mapped on to dimensions of feminist practice. Some perspectives fit feminist values and principles better than others. (See Worrell and Remer, 1992: 122, for a framework that can be used to examine the feminist possibilities of different psychological theories.) In Figure 9.1 we have mapped different counselling psychology perspectives on to key dimensions of feminist practices, namely clarity of values and political analysis, and flexibility of approach, as reflected in a commitment to egalitarianism, diversity and power sharing. Whilst feminist theory and practice within some theoretical traditions are well developed, the principles and values of feminist counselling psychology, as outlined in this chapter, do not always follow. For example, Orbach (2001) outlines developments in feminist psychoanalytic theory but only partially reflects the feminist value of egalitarianism within the therapeutic process.

All approaches to counselling psychology can be mapped on to these two dimensions. Where would you put the different approaches?

Practising therapists also highlighted a central dilemma of both feminism and feminist counselling psychology, namely the issue of 'gender essentialism', the view that there is an inevitable and universal female nature, and that an understanding of the connectedness of all women is pivotal to feminist work. The goal of feminist therapy, then, is to celebrate the uniqueness of women's contributions and to encourage women to seek fulfilment in their female gender roles. Such a view directly challenges the value of diversity and the recognition of the differences within and between women's lives (Burman et al., 1998). A critique of patriarchal society and women's oppression does not inevitably lead to the assumption of commonality between all women in either the nature of the oppression or their experience of it. It seems that the US, more than the Australian, feminist practitioners held simplistic views of feminism and woman-centredness that were not underpinned by an understanding of theoretical feminism, and thus the conflation of women and feminist.

Two further dilemmas arise from the principle of woman-centredness in counselling psychology, both to do with the role of men. First is the issue of whether feminist counselling psychologists can work with men, and second whether men can be feminist counselling psychologists. We see no reason, in principle, why feminist counselling psychologists cannot and should not work with men, still with a principle of being woman-centred. Marecek and Kravetz's therapists, however, did not all agree. Some said their feminist values prohibited them from working with violent men, for instance. The opposite view was taken by most of the participants in Chester and Bretherton's study. They argued that working with men on, for example, domestic violence, sexual abuse or issues connected with adapting to changing gender roles was being woman centred.

The second dilemma, whether men can be feminist counselling psychologists, is more problemmatic. We would prefer to suggest, with others (for example, Adu-Poku, 2001) that men, adhering to feminist principles and values, can work in pro-feminist ways, whilst not working as feminists.[5] Enns summarizes this position well when she says, 'principles of profeminist practice call for men to confront sexist behaviour, redefine masculinity according to values other than power, prestige and privilege, and actively support women's efforts to seek justice' (1993: 38–40)

Adu-Poku (2001: 166) argues for the need to incorporate different ethnic and gender interests – diversity – into debates and practices that are feminist. He asks: 'How can women's situations be reformed if [black] men continue to be silent accomplices to sexism, by shying away from the opportunity to join the women's struggle? How can one become an effective advocate of anti-racism if sexism is unchecked?' This view is supported by Burman et al. (1998: 293), who call for broad awareness, knowledge and sensitivity.

> The task for us therapists and practitioners is … to grapple with the complexities of the lived experiences of our clients, without presuming any particular mapping between social category and lived experience. Here the current vogue for 'not knowing' is often put forward … we would caution against overstating the extent of 'not knowing', for we must know how to 'not know' and be vigilant about those (cultural and gender, for example) assumptions that we want not to know.

Without supporting a gender essentialism position, though, feminist approaches might also seek, as we have seen, similarities between women, united as they may be by their position in an oppressive social system. We have seen that there is no one system of feminist counselling and counselling psychology practice, and that socio-historical contexts directly influence client and counsellor experience. We have seen, too, that the nature and role of power are central to feminist counselling psychology. These observations make it even more important for feminist practitioners to engage in a continual process of reflection, reconsideration and action.

Social action and the role of power

This feature of feminism is, perhaps, the most difficult to reconcile with counselling psychology, and certainly seems to be the principle least often put into practice (Chester and Bretherton, 2001; Marecek and Kravetz, 1998).

Some feminist counselling psychologists (for example, in Chester and Bretherton, 2001) argue that therapy is a form of action in itself. A similar case, for writing as a political strategy, has been made by academic feminists (for example, Burman et al., 1996: 179). Resolution of this issue may well depend on the extent to which action and social change are considered to be a legitimate goal of feminist counselling psychology. The current view of practitioners appears to be that distress is individual, and it is possible for women to participate in social action only if they have resolved any personal issues first. Day (1992: 382), who recognizes the political nature of social action, suggests that 'changes in the external fabric of women's lives have to be fought for on the political terrain, but may be also by women who not only are able to cope with the external and oppressive world, but who want to change it'.

She seems to suggest that women who undertake therapy are not such women. From this perspective, power and empowerment (legitimate feminist goals) are inner power. Feminist counselling psychology would, then, serve to help women identify and strengthen their inner power, and would be best achieved by one-to-one therapeutic work. Chester and Bretherton's participants, however, did acknowledge more the role of social action, although they did not see it as a priority for intervention. For both groups of feminist counsellors, social action was seen as practice they engaged in as separate from their therapeutic work. Social action is possible only when women act collectively, sometimes in alliance with men, on issues of joint concern and that lead to change for women. Groups offer one means by which women's collective interests can develop and be validated (as is recognized in the Australian study), although there appears to be relatively little attention paid to group work in contemporary feminist therapy.

Enns (1992, 1993) offers a historical explanation for this. She outlines different patterns of feminist counselling over time, and suggests that the emphasis on collective action characterized earlier stages of feminist therapy, and features in radical and socialist feminist traditions. Certainly the decreased emphasis on social and collective action would be consistent with the depoliticization of feminism, discussed above.

The picture that emerges, then, is somewhat cloudy, confused and the inevitable gaps between theory and practice are evident. Marecek and Kravetz (1998: 13) highlight this point: 'Feminists who are therapists operate in a space of contradiction, ambiguity, and perhaps even incommensurability.' The difficulty of reconciling action with therapy has led some to argue that therapeutic work, by definition, cannot be feminist (Kitzinger and Perkins, 1993). However, as we will see, there are some models of practice that can incorporate action within counselling psychology endeavours.

Holland (1988, 1992) presents a model of emancipatory psychotherapeutic practice (see also O'Hara, 1997) in which she challenges the split between inner strength and social action. She suggests that (in this case) depressed women may begin with individual therapy to explore and strengthen their self-concepts, move on to group work with a view to helping them locate their difficulties within a social context, and experience commonalities with other women, and then, collectively, engage in social action, highlighting mental health difficulties locally and developing facilities that may change some of the environmental conditions giving rise to depression in the first place. She describes this as helping women 'through psychic space into social space and so into political space' (1988: 134). Her work makes explicit the legitimate role that therapeutic practitioners can play in supporting women in moves towards social action, reflecting the goals and principles of feminist practice. There would be an argument that group work might help women overcome a sense of isolation and increase their sense of connectedness with others before entering individual therapy. However, for this to then contribute to social action, opportunities for interconnected and collective activity would need to follow.

In our experience, it is not so much a matter of first finding personal strength and then proceeding to collective action: women may, for example, engage in collective action first and therein find inner strength.

Research

There is scant research on how feminist principles and values inform the change process, although gender bias is evident in research too. We need to challenge what Day (1992) refers to as the gender-blind assumptions of therapy, that is, that the emotional worlds of women and men are the same. Gender issues are for the most part marginalized or invisible in both psychology and counselling texts. If we take the main psychology theories underpinning popular counselling psychology approaches we see that it is men who are the focus of much of the research, who are doing the research, who are interpreting the research and who are consequently contributing to psychological knowledge. The maleness involved at every level of theory development is not acknowledged, but assumed to apply to all. It is therefore not surprising that the therapeutic world can be seen to collude with the patriarchal *status quo*, with the adjustment model of mental health and the consequent reinforcement of women's unequal position in society.

It was not until 1981, when men, in this case Reason and Rowan, published their new paradigm research, which incorporated feminist values, that research based on feminist principles was adopted by mainstream researchers. As we have seen, feminists had been researching and writing about their collaborative, ethical and reflexive ways of doing research since the early 1970s, but their work was marginalized, never given centre stage. We are concerned that feminism is not more central, given the prevalence of women in the therapeutic world. Russell (1996) reflects that therapy is in danger of replicating traditional roles in the production of knowledge, with women doing the hands-on, caring aspects of the work and men producing the discourses of counselling (and counselling psychology). We need to do what we can to ensure that research and practice based on feminist values are brought into mainstream counselling psychology.

So what we need is research that informs gender-conscious practice (Orbach, 1990), that works towards enabling women to take an equal place in society. Effective research based on feminist values, which concerns itself with practice issues, with developing understanding and not simply data gathering, will help us get away from the notion of psychotherapeutic work as a tool of conformity, 'a coercive framework for constructing and interpreting experience' (Burman, 1995: 47). We need, in Russell's words, 'to recognise the importance of feminist theory as part of mainstream counselling and to initiate practices and codes which enable us to develop an integrated and anti-sexist approach' (1996: 259).

Conclusion

We have outlined the principles and goals of feminist counselling psychology and shown how these can be implemented in practice, but also some of the tensions and dilemmas that are revealed through practice. Although we have touched on historical changes in feminist therapeutic work, it seems clear that contemporary feminist approaches seem to be drifting away from the radical routes of feminist alternatives to mental health work. In our view it is time these radical routes were revived and that the role of social action became incorporated, once again, into legitimate feminist counselling psychology practice. Perhaps it is in the work of prevention and participation, two popular contemporary political and professional concepts, that the future of feminist counselling psychology practice and research lies. By encouraging the participation of clients in, for example, decisions about the priorities, practices and resource allocation of counselling psychology, we might be able to fulfil feminist values and feminist principles in new and innovative ways, but it will be possible only if we fully commit ourselves to the feminist values of egalitarianism, diversity, care and commitment and reflexivity.

Notes

1 Feminist approaches emerged earlier than the 1960s (Russell, 1996), but other commentators locate contemporary feminist counselling psychology as a product of the 'second wave' feminism of the 1960s and 1970s (see, for example, Enns, 1993).

2 We are deliberately avoiding suggesting that 'empowerment' is the feminist principle. Whilst it may be a feminist goal, we take the view that the process of empowerment, by which one person enables another to have power, is in and of itself a disempowering stance. People cannot be given power, they must acquire it.

3 In the United States, recognition that feminist counselling and therapy raised particular ethical issues led to the development of a code of ethical practice for feminist practitioners (Enns, 1993: 49).

4 *DSM* refers to *Diagnostic and Statistical Manual of Mental Disorders*, published by the American Psychiatric Association and used widely in the West for assessment and diagnostic purposes. The accounts given by Enns (1993) refer to the 1987 version, *DSM*-III-R.

5 We are grateful to Ian Parker for this distinction (see also Adams, 1988; Ganley, 1988).

References

Adams, D. (1988) 'Treatment models of men who batter: a profeminist analysis' in K. Ylö and M. Bograd (eds) *Feminist Perspectives on Wife Abuse*. Newbury Park CA: Sage.

Adu-Poku, S. (2001) 'Envisioning (black) male feminism: a cross-cultural perspective', *Journal Gender Studies*, 10 (2): 157–67.

Brown, L. (1992) 'A feminist critique of the personality disorders' in L.S. Brown and M. Ballou (eds) *Personality and Psychopathology: Feminist Reappraisals*. New York: Guilford Press.

Brown, L. and Liss-Levinson, N. (1981) 'Feminist therapy' in R. Corsini (ed.) *Handbook of Innovative Therapies*. New York: Wiley.

Burman, E. (1995) 'Identification, subjectivity and power in feminist psychotherapy' in J. Siegfried (ed.) *Therapeutic and Everyday Discourses as Behavior Change*. Norwood NJ: Ablex.

Burman, E., Gowrisunkur, J. and Sangha, K. (1998) 'Conceptualizing cultural and gendered identities in psychological therapies', *European Journal of Psychotherapy, Counselling and Health*, 1 (2): 231–56.

Burman, E., Alldred, P., Bewley, C., Goldberg, B., Heenan, C., Marks, D., Marshall, J., Taylor, K., Ullah, R. and Warner, S. (eds) (1996) *Challenging Women: Psychology's Exclusions, Feminist Possibilities*. Buckingham: Open University Press.

Chaplin, J. (1988) *Feminist Counselling in Action*. London: Sage.

Chester, A. and Bretherton, D. (2001) 'What makes feminist counselling feminist?' *Feminism and Psychology*, 11 (4): 527–45.

Day, L.G. (1992) 'Counselling for women: the contribution of feminist theory and practice', *Counselling Psychology Quarterly*, 5 (4): 373–84.

Enns, C.Z. (1992) 'Toward integrating feminist psychotherapy and feminist philosophy', *Professional Psychology: Research and Practice*, 23 (6): 453–66.

Enns, C.Z. (1993) 'Twenty years of feminist counseling and therapy: from naming biases to implementing multifaceted practice', *Counseling Psychologist*, 21 (1): 3–87.

Finch, J. (1984) '"It's great to have someone to talk to": the ethics and politics of interviewing women' in C. Bell and H. Roberts (eds) *Social Researching: Politics, Problems, Practice*. London: Routledge.

Ganley, A.L. (1988) 'Feminist therapy with male clients' in M.A. Dutton-Douglas and L.E. Walker (eds) *Feminist Psychotherapies: Integration of Therapeutic and Feminist Systems*. Norwood NJ: Ablex.

Gilligan, C. (1982) *In a Different Voice: Psychological Theory and Women's Development*. Cambridge MA: Harvard University Press.

Hare-Mustin, R.T., Marecek, J., Liss-Levinson, N. and Kaplan, A.G. (1979) 'Rights of clients, responsibilities of therapists', *American Psychologist*, 36: 1494–505.

Holland, S. (1988) 'Defining and experimenting with prevention' in S. Ramon and M. Giannichedda (eds) *Psychiatry in Transition: the British and Italian Experiences*. London: Pluto Press.

Holland, S. (1992) 'From social abuse to social action: a neighbourhood psychotherapy and social action project for women' in J. Ussher and P. Nicolson (eds) *Gender Issues in Clinical Psychology*. London: Routledge.

Hollway, W. (1991) 'The psychologization of feminism or the feminization of psychology?' *Feminism and Psychology*, 1: 29–37.

Humm, M. (1992) *Feminisms: a Reader*. London: Harvester Wheatsheaf.

Kagan, C. and Evans, J. (1995) *Professional Interpersonal Skills for Nurses*. London: Chapman & Hall.

King, E. (1996) 'The use of self in qualitative research' in J.T.E. Richardson (ed.) *Handbook of Qualitative Research for Psychology and the Social Sciences*. Leicester: BPS Books.

Kitzinger, S. and Perkins, R. (1993) *Changing our Minds: Lesbian Feminism and Psychology*. New York: New York University Press.

Marecek, J. and Kravetz, D. (1998) 'Power and agency in feminist therapy' in B. Seu and C. Heenan (eds) *Feminism and Psychotherapy*. London: Sage.

Maroda, K. (1991) *The Power of Countertransference: Innovations in Analytic Technique*. Chichester: Wiley.

Morrow, S.L. and Hawxhurst, D.M. (1998) 'Feminist therapy: integrating political analysis in counseling and psychotherapy', *Women and Therapy*, 21 (2): 37–50.

Oakley, A. (1981) 'Interviewing women: a contradiction in terms' in H. Roberts (ed.) *Doing Feminist Research*. London: Routledge.

O'Hara, M. (1997) 'Emancipatory therapeutic practice in a turbulent transmodern era: a work of retrieval', *Journal of Humanistic Psychology*, 37 (3): 7–33.

Orbach, S. (1990) 'Gender and dependency in psychotherapy', *Journal of Social Work Practice*, 4 (3–4): 1–15.

Orbach, S. (2000) *The Impossibility of Sex: Intimacies between the Therapist and Patient*. Harmondsworth: Penguin.

Orbach, S. (2001) *Towards Emotional Literacy*. London: Virago.

Parker, I. (ed.) (1999) *Deconstructing Psychology*. London: Sage.

Reason, P. and Rowan, J. (eds) (1981) *Human Inquiry: a Source Book of New Paradigm Research*. Chichester: Wiley.

Russell, J. (1996) 'Feminism and counselling' in R. Bayne, I. Horton and J. Bimrose (eds) *New Directions in Counselling*. London: Taylor & Francis.

Seu, I.B. (2000) 'Feminist psychoanalytic psychotherapy: reflections on a complex undertaking', *Changes*, 18 (4): 244–53.

Smail, D. (1991) 'Towards a Radical Environmentalist Psychology of Help', *The Psychologist*, 4 (2): 61–4.

Stiver, I.P. (1991) 'The meaning of care: reframing treatment models' in J.V. Jordan (ed.) *Connection: Writings from the Stonecenter*. New York: Guilford Press.

Taylor, M. (1994) 'Gender and power in counselling and supervision', *British Journal of Guidance and Counselling*, 22 (3): 319–26.

Taylor, M. (1995) 'The feminist approach' in M. Walker (ed.) *In Search of a Therapist: Peta – a feminist's problem with men*. Milton Keynes: Open University Press.

Taylor, M. (1996) 'Feminist paradigm' in W. Dryden and R. Woolfe (eds) *Handbook of Counselling Psychology*. London: Sage.

Ussher, J. (1991) *Women's Madness: Mysogyny or Mental Illness?* New York: Harvester Wheatsheaf.

Walker, M. (1990) *Women in Therapy and Counselling*. Milton Keynes: Open University Press.

Waterhouse, R. (1993) 'Wild women don't have the blues: a feminist critique of person-centred counselling and therapy', *Feminism and Psychology*, 3 (1): 55–71.

Wilkinson, S. (1988) 'The role of reflexivity in feminist psychology', *Women's Studies International Forum*, 11 (5): 493–502.

Worrell, J. and Remer, P. (1992) *Feminist Perspectives in Therapy*. Chichester: Wiley.

Worrell, J. and Remer, P. (1993) *Feminist Perspectives in Therapy*, second edition. Chichester: Wiley.

Acknowledgement

We dedicate this chapter to our colleague and friend, Maye Taylor, whose work as a feminist counselling psychologist has been both challenging and inspirational.

10 Counselling Psychology Practice: A Transpersonal Perspective
JOHN ROWAN

Transpersonal counselling is for me not a school of counselling with a separate identity – although some people may see it that way – but rather a dimension of all counselling which can be given a chance or ignored. Petrūska Clarkson (1995) has shown that the transpersonal relationship has its place alongside the working alliance, the transference–countertransference relationship, the authentic relationship and the developmentally needed relationship. It needs just as much attention, just as much respect, as any of these other and more widely accepted relationships. Her work is brilliant and very useful here. But Clarkson herself has rather an eccentric version of how the transpersonal should be seen: she does not quote any of the main accepted writers in the field, but tries to hack out her own version of it, based on the notion of *physis*.

Transpersonal psychology is now a well defined field, with two international journals and a multitude of excellent texts. We shall be referring to this literature many times. But at the same time it is important to say that the transpersonal is a human dimension available to all, which most of us have come across in one way or another. It is not something strange or marginal, but a readily available resource. Most of the people who are reading this, for example, will probably have had what Maslow (1973) calls a peak experience. One's reactions while watching a beautiful sunset or listening to an especially moving piece of music, for example, can lead to peak experiences. According to the classic psychological account from the work of Abraham Maslow, peak experiences tend to be triggered by intense, inspiring occurrences. 'It looks as if any experience of real excellence, or real perfection … tends to produce a peak experience'. (Maslow, 1973: 175). The lives of most people are filled with long periods of relative inattentiveness, lack of involvement or even boredom. In contrast, in their broadest sense, peak experiences are those moments when we become deeply involved in, excited by and absorbed in the world.

This can happen through very natural experiences, if we will let it happen. Tanzer (1967) found that childbirth could be a potent source of peak experiences, if the mother (in suitable circumstances) allowed it to be, and ways were found of teaching mothers how to have such experiences. Instead of having a painful and distressing time, these mothers often had 'a great and mystical experience, a religious experience, if you wish – an illumination, a revelation, an insight' (Maslow, 1973: 183).

The most powerful peak experiences are relatively rare. They have been portrayed by poets as moments of ecstasy, by the religious as mystical experiences. For Maslow the highest peaks include 'feelings of limitless horizons opening to the vision, the feeling of being simultaneously more powerful and also more helpless than one ever was before, the feeling of great ecstasy and wonder and awe, the loss of placing in time and space …' (1970: 164). This now ties in with our understanding of the transpersonal. We can say that a peak experience of this latter kind may give us a glimpse at least of the transpersonal realm. And such glimpses can be genuinely helpful, as Anthony and Ecker (1987) make clear.

For those who have not come across the term very much before, it is perhaps as well to point out the fact, first noted by Ken Wilber (1983), that in the process of our psychospiritual development there are three broad phases: the prepersonal, where we have not yet achieved full rationality; the personal, where we have been fully initiated into language, and mathematics, and science; and the transpersonal, where we go beyond the conventional bounds of time and space and do not find ordinary notions of rationality enough to encompass our experience. To put it another way, there is the personal unconscious as described by Freud and others; there is the conscious and the preconscious, which are much more accessible and familiar; and there is the superconscious, as described in psychosynthesis (Assagioli, 1991), as well as the collective unconscious, as described by Jung (1968). The transpersonal is the realm of the superconscious.

It is as well, perhaps, to say that the transpersonal is not the same as spirituality. There are many definitions of spirituality, and in the most general of them it makes perfect sense to say that there can be prepersonal spirituality (very often based on fear), personal spirituality (often based on integrity and authenticity) and transpersonal spirituality, which has to do with the divine, the numinous, the sacred, the holy.

The clearest guide to the transpersonal realm is still Ken Wilber (1997) and it will be convenient to use his categories. He has said that there are four great divisions within this realm, and we shall find this a useful way of dividing up the field. He calls them the Centaur (the first level of the transpersonal, still partly in the personal, but characterized by a mystical experience called the discovery of the real self); the Psychic/Subtle, which I shall label as the Subtle (the great realm of symbols and images and archetypes and big dreams and deity figures); the Causal (the deep water of spirituality, where all the symbols disappear, and we are alone with the infinite divine); and the Nondual, where all categories disappear, and the self too – the ultimate mystical experience.

If we accept this broad schema, it becomes clear that humanistic psychology has taken possession of the Centaur stage, because all of the therapies described as humanistic believe in the real self, and in the kind of ecstasy which can be described as a peak experience. This is perhaps only the foothills of mysticism, but it does have a place for the kind of experience which James Horne (1978) describes as 'casual extraverted mysticism'. Gestalt therapy talks about the 'mini-satori', psychodrama talks about the 'cathartic breakthrough', primal integration talks about 'personal transformation', person-centred therapy talks about 'becoming real', humanistic-existential therapy talks about 'being authentic', and so forth. But this is all on the edges of the transpersonal proper, because it still retains the 'skin-encapsulated ego' described by Alan Watts and referred to by Joanna Macy (1991).

If we want to go to the heartland of the transpersonal as it reveals itself in therapy, we have to move on to the Subtle level. It is here that we find the phenomena which truly go beyond the personal. It is here we find what Henri Corbin (1969) has called the 'imaginal world', what Schwartz-Salant (1986) has called 'the subtle body', what Whitmont (1987) has called 'the guidance self', what Assagioli (1975) has called 'the higher self', what Hillman (1997) has called 'the soul', what Jung (1968) has called 'the high archetypes', what Buddhists (Govinda, 1973) have called 'the sambhogakaya', and so forth. We all have access to this level, the level of the Subtle self, if only we will engage in the practices which can make it real for us. Brant Cortright has laid out this field with a masterly and comprehensive conspectus. He says: 'A transpersonal orientation implies an openness to transpersonal content when it arises in the course of psychotherapy' (1997: 237). He also says, quite unequivocally, that 'Transpersonal psychotherapy is heart-centred' (p. 239). Compassion is very important at this level, and it is a kind of juicy compassion, not like the earnest compassion of the Centaur or the calm, unwavering compassion of the Causal.

In Table 10.1 we can see how this works out in practice. Column 1 is the most common level of therapy, where we try to put right whatever has gone wrong, and both therapist and client work at the level of what Wilber calls the Mental Ego – the most common and everyday form of consciousness. Column 2 is the realm of the Centaur, and both therapist and client are involved in the process of contacting the real self, which is an experience of freedom and authenticity. Column 3 is what we are mainly talking about in this chapter – the realm of the Subtle, the realm of soul, the realm of heart. Column 4 is put in just to emphasize that the Subtle is not the end of the road, and also to give a hint of the disciplines which the therapist may wish to follow in order to be able to see the Subtle more clearly. It is easier to appreciate a given level when one has passed through it and in a sense left it behind (though in reality nothing is left behind). Coming back to the Subtle, or column 3, let us look at it more closely, and hear what it has to say, and come into deeper contact with it.

If we want to start working on this level, we have to go through the process of entering it, which usually involves some kind of ritual or initiation.[1] As with the real self, this is often at first only a glimpse, which we cannot retain. We had it, and it is gone again. But if we persevere with our psychospiritual development, it can become a plateau experience which lasts longer – perhaps for the length of a therapy session or a workshop. And if we persevere further, we tend to get very interested in and insightful about mythology, altered states of consciousness, dreams, auras, devas, heart compassion, symbol systems and all the other aspects of the Subtle. It can then become a permanent acquisition, so that we have access to it at all times.

Because this is an unfamiliar realm for most people, many confusions and errors are possible as we start to get into it. The most common one, according to Wilber (1983), is to confuse the Subtle realm with the Magic/Mythic realm of the prepersonal. This is the realm of superstition and all kinds of practices based on fear. If we approach the transpersonal through the realm of the Centaur we are much less likely to make these mistakes, because it is at the Centaur stage

Table 10.1   A comparison of four positions in personal development

Wilber level	1 Mental Ego	2 Centaur	3 Subtle	4 Causal
Rowan Position	Instrumental Self	Authentic Self	Transpersonal Self (1)	Transpersonal Self (2)
Buddhism	Nirmanakaya	Nirmanakaya	Sambhogakaya	Dharmakaya
Great Exemplar	Milton Erickson	James Bugental	Roberto Assagioli	Shankara
Ego	dominant	transformed	light	open
Story Example	Erickson	May or Wheelis	Naropa	George Fox
Process	healing – ego-building	development – ego-extending	opening – ego-reduction	enlightenment
Traditional role of Helper	physician analyst	growth facilitator	advanced guide	priest(ess) sage
Representative approaches	hospital treatment chemotherapy some psy-ana directive behaviour mod cognitive-behavioural some TA crisis work REBT brief therapy solution based	primal integration Gestalt therapy some psy-ana psychodrama open encounter bodywork therapies some TA person-centred co-counselling regression experiential	psychosynthesis some Jungians some pagans transpersonal voice dialogue Some Wicca or magic Kabbalah some astrology some Tantra Shamanism core process	mystical Buddhism Raja Yoga Taoism monasticism Adi Da Christian mysticism Sufi goddess mystics some Judaism Advaita impersonal
Representative names	Freud Ellis Meichenbaum Beck Eysenck	Maslow Rogers Mahrer Perls Searles	Jung Hillman Starhawk Assagioli Gordon-Brown	Eckhart Shankara Dante Tauler Suso

(Continued)

Table 10.1 *(Continued)*

Wilber level	1 Mental Ego	2 Centaur	3 Subtle	4 Causal
Rowan Position	Instrumental Self	Authentic Self	Transpersonal Self (1)	Transpersonal Self (2)
	Skinner	Laing	Mary Watkins	Ruysbroeck
	Lazarus	Moreno	Jean Houston	Nagarjuna
	Watzlawick	Winnicott	Bolen	Lao Tzu
	Bandler	Lomas	Grof	George Fox
	Haley	Bugental	Boorstein	Julian of Norwich
	Erickson	Hycner	Epstein	Sheng-Yen
	Linehan	Bohart	Field	Suzuki
	Dryden	Clarkson	West	Osho
	Ivey	Satir	Fukuyama	al-Ghazali
	Egan	Bozarth	Maguire	Maharshi
Questions	what is the best method?	what is the best relationship?	how far can we go together?	dare you face the loss of all your words?
Key issues	efficiency respect	autonomy authenticity	openness vision	essence commitment

that we have faced and dealt with our own Shadow. I argue that, unless we deal with our Shadow material in the Centaur stage, there are great dangers in entering the Subtle stage of consciousness, because we shall probably project our own Shadow material into it, and perhaps open ourselves up to really unpleasant and frightening experiences. This often happened in the days when LSD was a popular drug, because it has the power to propel us into the Subtle region with no preparation (Huston Smith, 2000).

In my own work (Rowan, 1993) I have also pointed to the danger of confusing the transpersonal with the extrapersonal. The extrapersonal is the realm of those 'wild talents' which enable some people to see ghosts, bend spoons, stop clocks, stick needles through themselves without drawing blood – all those things which are so characteristic of fakirism and the paranormal generally.

If we assume that we have avoided all these pitfalls and entered the Subtle, I think the best mnemonic to hang on to is to say that we are working at the level of soul (Hillman, 1997). At this level we are at last out of the skin-encapsulated ego and our defensiveness has gone down by another notch. We can genuinely let go of our boundaries and be with another person's soul (as some people would say, heart to heart). This goes well beyond the usual definitions of empathy, and is more like what Rosemary Budgell has called *linking* (Rowan, 1998b). It is a new kind of being, which allows therapy to go much deeper, and to touch the soul. In view of what follows, it seems important to say at this point that working in therapy at a transpersonal level is more about being than about doing. As Bill Wahl has said:

> The transpersonal can also, especially in the Zen tradition, be experienced as 'nothing special', as ordinary, as just doing the dishes or feeling that baby in your arms. You offer a number of definitions of the transpersonal. Sometimes I think it's simply experiencing with no recourse to self or ego. Sometimes this is fantastic, sometimes it's just the feel of the soapy water. (Wahl, 2001)

But if this is the story about being, what about doing? It is all very well to outline what kind of experience it is to work at the level of soul, but what does one actually do? How does this help with therapy? What I am interested in here is the question – OK, so there is such a thing as the transpersonal; but what does a therapist actually do that is any different from what any therapist does? The general answer is that the therapist who is able to access Subtle consciousness becomes more creative in all respects. But, to be more specific, there are, I believe, eleven main ways in which the transpersonal can become relevant in the therapeutic relationship.

Spiritual emergencies

A very important issue which has come to prominence in recent years is the appreciation of the difficulties which can arise when people move into the Subtle area. This is particularly difficult when people are suddenly exposed to spiritual experiences which they are not ready for. Christina and Stanislav Grof (1990) have outlined ten specific problems which can come out of such events.

- *Peak experiences.* These can be so overwhelming for someone who has never been ecstatic before that there can be fears of going crazy. To be out of touch with ordinary reality, even for a short period of time, is for some people an impossibly worrying event.
- *Kundalini energy awakening.* Sometimes through yoga, body work, or even quite spontaneously, the energy of the chakras can combine to give an overwhelming experience. Probably this is worst for people who have no conception of such a thing, and who live in a social context which is unsympathetic to it. But it is essentially a healing experience if it can be contained and lived through.
- *Near-death experiences.* These are the experiences when people are declared physically dead, and are then revived. Even an approximation to this, through an accident, for example, can result in a full-blown near-death experience. This may often give a glimpse of the Subtle level. The difficulty may come from the people around at the time, who may be very worried by what the person says, and perhaps later for the person involved, in owning it and in talking about it.
- *Past-life memories.* If a person has, for any reason, a vivid memory which appears to refer to a previous life, this may be very disturbing for the person, particularly if they do not believe in reincarnation. Often such memories have a life-or-death quality which may make them hard to take, at the same time as it makes them very meaningful. People may be quite unafraid of death after such an experience.
- *Opening to life myth.* Here the person seems to go on a journey to the centre, to the central meaning of life. But because it takes place on a Subtle level, the whole process can be dramatic and overwhelming. The person may feel that they are at the centre of global or even cosmic events. Death and rebirth, masculine and feminine energies – these can be central concerns on a grand scale. There are here great dangers of ego inflation, and this state needs to be handled very carefully and with real understanding, so as not to fall into the error of assuming that it is a manic episode. It can be healing and very positive, if handled correctly. Emma Bragdon (1990) makes the point that these experiences usually last no more than forty days. Interestingly enough, they often last exactly forty days.
- *Shamanic crisis.* This is an initiatory crisis often involving a visit to the underworld, where annihilation takes place, followed by rebirth and perhaps ascent to heaven. Power animals are often involved, sometimes in quite horrifying ways. But if the person can be encouraged to stay with the experience and work through it, it can be genuinely initiatory, taking the person to a Subtle level of consciousness, at least temporarily.
- *Psychic opening.* This is the arrival of psychic powers of one kind or another, perhaps quite suddenly and surprisingly. All sorts of paranormal phenomena may be involved, including poltergeist phenomena. Out-of-body experiences are quite common – apparent journeyings through space, leaving one's solid body behind. Loss of identity may be experienced, and this can be frightening, too. There may be experiences of synchronicity, which may be confused with delusions of reference. This again can give glimpses of the Subtle.
- *Channelling.* The arrival of spirit guides or discarnate entities offering to use one as a channel for communication can be very disconcerting. It can be a healing and transforming experience for the recipient, and other people may also feel benefited. The dangers of ego inflation are large here, too, and so it is very important to discriminate

what is prepersonal from what is transpersonal. Jon Klimo (1988) has written well about this.

- *UFO encounters*. Contact with UFOs can be frightening and challenging, and such an experience often carries with it, as do many of these other experiences, the feeling that one cannot talk about it. One may be regarded as crazy, or at least as self-deluding. Yet such experiences can be genuinely illuminating for the person involved. They can partake of the nature of initiations. Again ego inflation may result, and has to be watched out for.

- *Possession*. Here there is a sense that one has been taken over completely by an entity which may be good or evil. If it is voluntary, as in some rituals where the participant is supposed to be taken over by a god or goddess, there is usually no problem. But if it is involuntary, and particularly if the entity seems to be evil or alien, it can be very frightening, both to the person and to those around. But 'when the person is given an opportunity to confront and express the disturbing energy in a supportive and understanding setting, a profound spiritual experience often results, one that has an extraordinary healing and transformative potential' (Grof and Grof, 1990: 99).

There is now a world-wide network of therapists who are willing and able to handle such states, and this is something which all those involved in the transpersonal may be able to help with.

Other cultures

It has been pointed out that there is a particular role for the transpersonal therapist in the field of cross-cultural or transcultural work, because of the increased respect for all religious experiences which comes with transpersonal development. Cinnirella and Loewenthal (1999), for example, show that members of communities such as white Christian, Pakistani Muslim, Indian Hindu, Orthodox Jewish and Afro-Caribbean Christian have many different attitudes to counselling and psychotherapy. Some of these make them particularly suspicious of Western types of therapy. It is the transpersonal understanding of the Subtle (not mentioned in Cinnirella and Loewenthal) which would be the most likely bridge for such people to use, in order to get the benefit of adequate therapy.

Not quite in the same category, but offering the same kind of disconcerting experiences, is the cross-cultural work involving discarnate entities of one kind and another, ranging from gods and goddesses to demons and devils, and from loas, orishas and zar to ghosts and witches. A great deal of fear may be aroused by such material for the client, and may be picked up by a therapist who is not well versed in this area. The transpersonal therapist is of course much better able to handle such material than other therapists, because their experience of the Subtle realms, and the transformations of consciousness, will stand them in good stead. (See Wilber et al., 1986.) Also the whole idea of the pre/trans fallacy may be important, in placing the phenomenon into the right place.

Here is an example, taken from an interview with a patient in a mental hospital detailed by Eugenie Georgaca, which goes like this:

Interviewer: So did, did something specific happen yesterday that made you feel so bad?

Patient: Yeah.

Interviewer: What was it?

Patient: Those spirits. Spirits have been following me, spirits that, you know, they are coming up, they are coming out.

Interviewer: Yeah. So what type, I mean, what type of spirit is it?

Patient: I would say a mind spirit.

Interviewer: Yeah, yeah, I mean, obviously that's, I mean, you haven't seen it or heard it or anything, you just ...

Patient: I feel it.

Interviewer: Yeah, you're just feeling it. So how do you know it's a spirit then?

Patient: The world made up of, the world made up of body I just think it's spirit.

Interviewer: Hmmmm, but it doesn't do anything else to you, does it?

Patient: That it makes me sick, it makes me sick.

(Georgaca, 2000: 233)

The interviewer goes on to avoid all the issues raised by this conversation, and to retreat to a rational form of dismissal of the experience as delusional. The first questions a transpersonal therapist might ask could be: 'Does this spirit have a name?' 'Does it have a personality?' 'What does it want?' Because the interviewer had no understanding of the mind-set of the patient, such a question could not be asked. But it is a well known fact among people who believe in spirits that once you know the name of a spirit it gives you much more control of them. It makes it much easier to talk to the spirit and have a dialogue with it. This means that the transpersonal approach can be particularly valuable in cross-cultural work where the culture of origin of the client is very different from the host culture.

Until recently this was an uncharted area, but now the excellent book by Fukuyama and Sevig (1999) is available to help us with a multitude of research studies and a great deal of insight.

Big dreams

This is a colloquial term, meaning dreams which have an archetypal meaning or significance. Such dreams, according to Jung (1968), have peculiar numinosity, a sacred quality. Unless they are treated with a proper transpersonal respect, they may well be undervalued and not given due attention. Crittenden Brookes (1996) has a good discussion of how to work with big dreams of this kind, and so does Dina Glouberman (1995). Kelly Bulkeley (1999) shows that people have been interested in big dreams all through history and in many different countries. Barbara Somers (2000) has a good deal to say about various aspects of dreams, including their transpersonal aspects at different stages in the life cycle. It is clear that there is a huge area here which only a transpersonal approach can do justice to.

A mythological vision

If we know our mythology, we can be more helpful to people who have mythological dreams or visions. Stephen Larsen (1990) has some useful things to say about this, and shows how masks can help in working with such issues. David Feinstein and Stanley Krippner (1997) have a great deal to say about ways in which we can work with the Subtle realm, using a mythological approach. There is a kind of awareness here of the depths which storytelling can reach. It is curious that the narrative approach to psychotherapy, which lays so much stress on the story, has had virtually nothing to say about this mythological aspect of the matter. John McLeod (1997) has an interesting discussion as to why this might be so, and at the same time points out how important fairy stories can be. Fairy stories are often mythological in character, and contain archetypal material, as Dieckmann (1986) points out at length and Stein and Corbett (1991, 1992) have collected many examples. Of course the queen of them all in this respect is Marie-Louise von Franz (1970, 1974, 1977).

Intuition

As I have explained elsewhere (Rowan, 1993) there are at least six different things we could look at under the heading of 'intuition', but here it suffices to say that therapists of all kinds actually rely a great deal on intuition, though it is not popular to say so on training courses. But there are good books, such as the one by Philip Goldberg (1983), which are encouraging and helpful when developing one's intuition. The essential thing about the type of intuition which belongs to the Subtle stage of development (which I have called the 'surrendered self' type of intuition) is that it feels as if the thought, speech or intervention comes from somewhere else. As someone said: 'I can find myself making a suggestion about something or saying something to a client which I don't feel comes entirely from me' (West, 2000: 107).

Another useful book here is the one by Will Parfitt (1990), which has some good remarks on intuition and also some exercises useful for therapists who want to get on terms with the transpersonal area of work.

Symbol systems

If we have a good grasp of any one symbol system, whether it be astrology, the tarot, the I Ching (Walker, 1986), the runes, a polytheistic pantheon of deities (Hillman, 1981) – all these can be very useful in helping a client to deal with things that are just on the borders of consciousness. They can give useful clues as to where the client might be, and where he or she needs to go next. For example, a person's astrological chart may show an opposition between two traits, two tendencies, and these can be put out on to separate chairs so that a dialogue may be conducted between them. Similarly with tarot cards, particularly significant cards for the client can be put out on chairs and again dialogues can take place between them. Sallie Nichols (1980) shows how the tarot can relate to the work of Jung, while Barbara Walker (1984) has a more feminist consciousness.

Symbol systems are also useful for reminding us that there is more than one kind of person in the world. Astrology, for example, gives us twelve sun signs, but then doubles that number by bringing in the moon sign, and then multiplies it again by looking for oppositions, angles, the mid-heaven and so forth. The Jungian approach of Liz Greene (Greene and Sasportas 1987, 1989), for example, gives us something very rich. The wonderful book by A.T. Mann (1979) is also inspiring.

For some people, such ideas may be offputting, because they regard all this as New Age, or superstition, or both. And certainly the ideas are so ambiguous as to lend themselves to all sorts of uses at all sorts of different levels. That is the beauty, and the danger, of symbols. All I am saying is that they can serve the soul, they can open up the channels of intuition, and be a good way of communicating with some clients at their own level.

Shamanic journeying

Shamanic experiences, in the hands of a good leader, such as Leo Rutherford or Caitlin Matthews, can be an excellent initiation into experiences of other worlds. Even Leslie Kenton (1998) can suggest useful exercises and fantasies to use in training oneself to work in this realm (e.g. pp. 77–8). Similarly, books like the one by William Bloom (1998) can open our eyes to the world of the Subtle, which is present at all times but ignored by most of us most of the time. (See note 1 again.)

Meditation or prayer

Prayers of openness are in general more useful than other kinds of prayers, and they are very similar to meditation in the Eastern traditions, and contemplation in the Western. They can be compatible with the work of psychotherapy, because they have no ego-laden content.

Meditation is of course quite popular in the West at the present time, but it seems to me that people are often put off by its dryness and its seeming impossibility. An instruction such as 'Count your breaths up to ten without having any distractions' is almost certainly bound to produce an experience of failure, in my experience. I have developed a pattern of meditation which overcomes some of these problems by starting with something very simple, and gradually working onwards from there through experiences of success rather than failure.

Figure 10.1   John Rowan's instructions for meditation

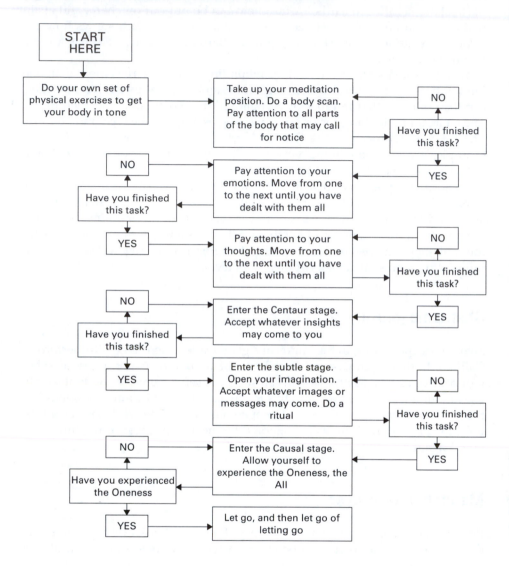

Osho (1992) contains many useful suggestions for particular types of meditation practice, as for example a meditation for smokers. Lawrence LeShan (1974) is more conventional but can be helpful.

Spirit releasement

Sometimes a transpersonal practitioner may need to know about the work of people like William Baldwin. If a person becomes possessed, this needs to be distinguished from something more mild like a subpersonality on the one hand, and something more severe like dissociated identity disorder on the other. According to Baldwin, the most common kind of involuntary possession is by the remnants of a dead person.

> Earthbound spirits, the surviving consciousness of deceased humans, are the most prevalent possessing, obsessing or attaching entities to be found. The disembodied consciousness seems to attach itself and merge fully or partially with the sub-conscious mind of a living person, exerting some degree of influence on thought process, emotions, behaviour and the physical body. (Baldwin, 1992: 13)

Baldwin says that an attachment of this kind can be 'benevolent in nature, totally self serving, malevolent in intention, or completely neutral. Attachment to any person may be completely random, even accidental' (p. 14). There can be more than one, since it takes up no physical space.

Treatment of this problem, according to Baldwin, is quite different from dealing with subpersonalities, which are mostly in the normal range, or attempting to treat dissociated identity disorder, which is a psychiatric condition. But the general rules of therapy still apply:

> The therapist must work with whatever material emerges, whatever memories and images are presented by the client. The map is not the territory, the description is not the experience. The words describing the event, memory or experience are but inadequate symbols of the feelings and perceptions of a real or imagined experience which had impact on the client. It is the impact which is being uncovered. The residues of that impact are the focus of healing. (p. 53)

There are six steps in spirit releasement therapy, but this is not the place to describe them, since like all forms of therapy it needs to be experienced by the therapist before being used with clients.

Imagery

Imagery is one of the most useful entries into the world of the transpersonal, because it is so flexible. People like Dina Glouberman (1995) have shown that imagery covers a wide range of possibilities. One of the earliest books to appear is still one of the best (Stevens, 1971), and it seems to have been kept in print. Jean Houston is a mistress of the art of dealing with imagery, and her books (1982, 1987) give all the details of how she uses it to address the transpersonal. The book by her follower Jay Earley (1990) is also excellent.

Obviously imagery is not necessarily transpersonal. It can be prepersonal, personal or transpersonal, but it does offer, just as do dreams, an opening which sometimes leads to the transpersonal. The well known book by Paolo Ferrucci (1982) gives a good deal of information as to how this may be so. The thing to remember is that Subtle consciousness is immensely and continuously creative, because of offering no barriers to inspiration and intuition, and hence new techniques may be invented in every session – often involving imagery in some form. For example, in working with resistance, it is often useful to personify the resistance, dialogue respectfully with it, and then ask the client to visualize it transforming in some way.

The Shadow

One of the most important areas of transpersonal work is what Jung calls the Shadow. I use this term to include all the negative, hateful and frightening aspects of the psyche. One of the characteristics of the transpersonal, which distinguishes it from the prepersonal, is that it believes that evil can always be transformed and never needs to be destroyed or banished. And this results in some very practical ways of working. For example, if we come across a shadow figure – perhaps from a dream or vision, perhaps from childhood, perhaps from a present-day partner or boss – we can put it on an empty chair and work with it in that way. Sometimes, when we do that, the person is too scared to talk to the shadow figure, and sometimes, in such cases, it is appropriate for the therapist to sit beside the client and give support. I call this 'siding with the client', and have written up a full case example of working in this way (Rowan, 1987, abridged version 1992).

Another useful technique, which I believe comes from psychosynthesis, although I have never seen it written down, is to draw the shadow figure on a piece of paper – preferably a large piece (I usually have an A3 pad for this) – using felt pens or other bright colours. Then I ask the client to stand on the paper, right in the middle of the figure that has been drawn. The instructions then go like this:

> Imagine that all the energy of that figure is contained in that paper you are standing on. All the energy, all the meaning, all the essence of that figure is down there underneath your feet. [*Pause.*] And now that energy is rising up into your feet and ankles. [*Pause.*] And now it is rising up into your calves and knees. [*Pause.*] And now it is rising up into your thighs, hips and genitals. [*Pause.*] And now it is rising up into your stomach, abdomen, and your back, and your chest. [*Pause.*] And now it is flowing into your hands and arms. [*Pause.*] And now it is rising up into your shoulders and neck. [*Pause.*] And now it is rising up all the way to the top of your head. [*Pause.*] And now let your body take up the posture, the position, that goes with that energy that is now filling you up. [*Pause.*] Let your whole body express the sense of that energy. [*Pause.*] And now you are that energy, you embody it fully, and I am going to ask you three questions. [*Pause.*] What do you want? [*Wait for answer.*] Thank you for that answer. Now – what do you need? [*Wait for answer.*] Thank you for that answer. And – what do you have to offer? [*Wait for answer.*] Thank you for that answer. Now you can let go of all that energy, and go back to your seat [*or couch*].

Then of course it is the time for processing whatever came out. This is often a big learning experience, and quite a lot of emotion can be expressed. As always, it is better to experience this exercise yourself before using it on anyone else. As always, appropriateness is all. The time to use it is when the client has got tired of avoiding the shadow material and is ready to deal with it properly.

Never forget that the therapist may not have dealt with all his or her shadow material: the shadow of the therapist needs to be taken into account too. At this level the old phrase 'the therapist's use of self' becomes translated into 'the therapist's use of soul'.

Conclusion

What we have been saying, then, is that most therapists, most of the time, just operate on the usual levels which are most familiar. But if they have done sufficient work on themselves to feel confident to be able to handle the Subtle level, with all its strange phenomena, they may well wish to use other techniques.

All the specific techniques mentioned have to be used with sensitivity and discretion, as always in counselling. It is a question of tuning in to what the client is ready for. At the moment when the client wants to do something, and does not know how to do it, the techniques of the counsellor can be acceptable and useful. But the main thing is the awareness of the spiritual realm.

For further details and references on spirituality generally see Ken Wilber (1987, 2000). There is also a good discussion of these issues in Rothberg and Kelly (1998).

To sum up, what I have been trying to say in this chapter is: (1) the transpersonal is a dimension of experience, not a school of psychotherapy; (2) the basic thing necessary is some degree of Subtle consciousness, the basic state of *being* which makes work at the level of soul possible; and (3) that once these things are given, there is an extraordinarily rich field here, with a wonderful range of possibilities. In fact, I think the transpersonal approach is the most creative of all. There are of course some specific risks. It is possible to get so enthusiastic about the myriad possibilities that one forgets that it is the relationship with the client that is the most important thing. As Richard Hycner so wisely says: 'So-called techniques need to arise out of the *between*.' (Hycner, 1993, p. 58)

Research

When we come to consider the research aspects of the transpersonal, we find that not only is there a great deal of research available, there is also a whole transpersonal approach to research itself.

The grandfather of research in the field of transpersonal therapy is of course Stanislav Grof. His first book in English (1979/1975) reported on research using LSD in therapy (in the days when it was legal) from 1956 to 1966 in Czechoslovakia (as it was then) and from 1967 to 1973 as chief of psychiatric research at the Maryland Psychiatric Research Center and research fellow at Johns Hopkins University. In a later book (1980) he summed up more again of this work, and presented a large amount of original artwork by patients to illustrate his findings. In later years he pursued his research using breathing and music to produce altered states of consciousness, and has published several more books (1988, 1992) about this work. Briefly, what he has found is that when the deepest layers of the unconscious are reached three realms are opened up: the biographical unconscious, as described in psychoanalysis, and particularly in Object Relations; the pre- and perinatal unconscious, as found also by Frank Lake (1980) in England; and the superconscious (Assagioli) or the realms of the transpersonal. In his 1988 book he has collected the fullest list of transpersonal states I have seen anywhere. This is a remarkable body of work.

Not only has a great deal of research been carried out, but there is now a flourishing literature on a transpersonal approach to research itself. A good example is Braud and Anderson (1998), which details five 'expanded methods of disciplined inquiry', and gives many examples of them in use. For example, the paper by Dorothy Ettling on 'Levels of Listening' ends up with the remark that 'this research project literally changed my life'.

Another important book came out in the same year (Bentz and Shapiro, 1998), which takes a specifically Buddhist angle on the matter. Instead of talking about the scientist practitioner, Bentz and Shapiro speak of the scholarly practitioner. Obviously the scholarly can include the scientific, but is not restricted to that. And they raise important philosophical questions, such as 'What makes something count as knowledge?' When they give advice to the researcher, of course, they cover the usual things, like taking care and checking up, but also introduce new things, such as 'Cultivate a boundless heart toward all beings'.

My own chapter on transformational research (Rowan, 1998a) makes some other points, such as the importance of intuition as a fourth form of knowledge, along with propositional, practical and experiential knowledge. And my paper on linking (Rowan, 1998b) brings together a mass of information about the transpersonal relationship in therapy.

As well as being and doing, which we have seen are important for practice, there is also of course thinking, which is important for theory. Bits of theory have been scattered through this chapter, but as a help to the reader I have put an asterisk against those names in the bibliography which are particularly important theoretically.

The Causal

Finally, just a word about the Causal stage of consciousness, which is the next level, according to Wilber, after the Subtle (see Figure 10.1). This is less used in therapy, because it is the deep water of spirituality, where there are really no problems. There are no symbols or images here. It is further along the psychospiritual path, and really only attained by meditation that is sustained and regular.

I used to say that it was virtually impossible to conduct therapy at this level, because here there are no problems, and clients usually want their problems taken seriously. But I now believe that there are people who do work at this level, partly because I have had experience now of doing it myself.

Someone who has written insightfully about this particular matter is Mark Epstein (1996), who gives a better sense than most of what working at the Causal level would be like. David Brazier (1995) also has some interesting things to say about this level. Amy Mindell (1995) makes explicit links with working at the Buddhist level of no-mind (*mu-shin*), and quotes a roshi who says it can also be translated as 'creative mind'. A.H. Almaas (1988) speaks of working at the level of Essence, which appears to mean the same thing.

What I also believe is useful is that practitioners have their own spiritual practice, which may well lead them personally into the realm of the Causal. As usual with all these transitions, this is usually in the form of glimpses at first, followed by plateau experiences if the practice is continued and sustained, followed by access on a permanent basis with further and deeper practice. From a position in the Causal, it is much easier to work at the Subtle level, because it can be seen in the round, so to speak.

Note

1 Suitable rituals of initiation may be found on the following web sites, all of which also feature books which can be used for further study. They often have links to other sites with similar orientations.

www.hallowquest.org.uk John and Caitlin Matthews, two of the most prominent and experienced people in the field of shamanism and Western mysteries, put on a number of different workshops.

www.shamanism.co.uk Leo Rutherford is one of the main British leaders of shamanism, and his Eagle's Wing organization puts on many workshops.

www.martinj.dircon.co.uk/index.html Martin Jelfs is a leading exponent of Tantra in Britain, and his centre Transcendence puts on a number of workshops each year.

www.qed-productions/lkjrney.htm Leslie Kenton has an interesting approach called Journey to Freedom, embodying many different ideas from the soul realm, and offers workshops on it.

References

Almaas, A.H. (1988) *The Pearl Beyond Price*. Berkeley CA: Diamond Books.
*Anthony, Dick and Ecker, Bruce (1987) 'The Anthony typology' in D. Anthony, B. Ecker and K. Wilber (eds) *Spiritual Choices*. New York: Paragon House.
Assagioli, Roberto (1975) *Psychosynthesis*. Wellingborough: Turnstone Press.
Assagioli, Roberto (1991) *Transpersonal Development: the Dimension Beyond Psychosynthesis*. London: Crucible.
Baldwin, William (1992) *Spirit Releasement Therapy: a Technique Manual*, second edition. Falls Church VA: Human Potential Foundation Press.

*Bentz, Valerie Malhotra and Shapiro, Jeremy J. (1998) *Mindful Inquiry in Social Research.* Thousand Oaks CA: Sage.

Bloom, William (1998) *Working with Angels, Fairies and Nature Spirits.* London: Piatkus.

Bragdon, Emma (1988) *A Sourcebook for Helping People in Spiritual Emergency.* Los Altos CA: Lightening Up Press.

*Braud, William and Anderson, Rosemarie (1998) *Transpersonal Research Methods for the Social Sciences: Honoring Human Experience* Thousand Oaks CA: Sage.

Brazier, David (1995) *Zen Therapy.* London: Constable.

Brookes, Crittenden E. (1996) 'A Jungian view of transpersonal events in psychotherapy' in S. Boorstein (ed.) *Transpersonal Psychotherapy*, second edition. Albany NY: SUNY Press.

Bulkeley, Kelly (1999) 'The interpretation of spiritual dreams throughout history' in S. Krippner and M.R. Waldman (eds) *Dreamscaping*. Chicago: Lowell House.

Cinnirella, Marco and Loewenthal, Kate Miriam (1999) 'Religious and ethnic group influences on beliefs about mental illness: a qualitative interview study', *British Journal of Medical Psychology*, 72 (4): 505–24.

Clarkson, Petruska (1995) *The Therapeutic Relationship.* London: Whurr.

Corbin, Henri (1969) *Creative Imagination in the Sufism of Ibn 'Arabi.* Princeton NJ: Princeton University Press.

*Cortright, Brant (1997) *Psychotherapy and Spirit: Theory and Practice in Transpersonal Psychotherapy.* Albany NY: SUNY Press.

Dieckmann, Hans (1986) *Twice-told Tales: the Psychological Use of Fairy Tales.* Wilmette IL: Chiron.

Earley, Jay (1990) *Inner Journeys: a Guide to Personal and Social Transformation.* York Beach ME: Samuel Weiser.

Epstein, Mark (1996) *Thoughts without a Thinker.* London: Duckworth.

Feinstein, David and Krippner, Stanley (1997) *The Mythic Path.* New York: Tarcher/Putnam.

Ferrucci, Paolo (1982) *What we may be.* Wellingborough: Turnstone Press.

Franz, Marie-Louise von (1970) *Interpretation of Fairy Tales.* New York: Spring.

Franz, Marie-Louise von (1974) *The Feminine in Fairy Tales.* New York: Spring.

Franz, Marie-Louise von (1977) *Individuation in Fairy Tales.* Zurich: Spring.

Frank, Marie-Louise von (1983) *Shadow and Evil in Fairy Tales.* Dallas TX: Spring.

Fukuyama, Mary A. and Sevig, Todd D. (1999) *Integrating Spirituality into Multicultural Counselling.* Thousand Oaks CA.: Sage.

Glouberman, Dina (1995) *Life Choices, Life Changes.* London: Thorson.

Goldberg, Philip (1983) *The Intuitive Edge: Understanding Intuition and Applying it in Everyday Life.* Los Angeles: Jeremy Tarcher.

Govinda, L. (1973) *Foundations of Tibetan Mysticism.* New York: Weiser.

Greene, Liz and Sasportas, Howard (1987) *The Development of the Personality: Seminars in Psychological Astrology* I. London: Routledge.

Greene, Liz and Sasportas, Howard (1989) *Dynamics of the Unconscious: Seminars in Psychological Astrology* II. London: Arkana.

Grof, Christina and Grof, Stanislav (1990) *The Stormy Search for the Self.* Los Angeles: Tarcher.

Grof, Stanislav (1979, original publication 1975) *Realms of the Human Unconscious: Observations from LSD research.* London: Souvenir Press.

Grof, Stanislav (1980) *LSD Psychotherapy.* Pomona CA: Hunter House.

Grof, Stanislav (1988) *The Adventure of Self-discovery.* Albany NY: SUNY Press.

*Grof, Stanislav (1992) *The Holotropic Mind.* San Francisco: Harper

Hillman, James (1981) 'Appendix – Psychology: Monotheistic or Polytheistic', in D.L. Miller (ed.) *The New Polytheism.* Dallas: Spring Publications.

*Hillman, James (1997) *The Soul's Code*. New York: Bantam Books.

*Horne, James (1978) *Beyond Mysticism*. Waterloo, Ont.: Wilfred Laurier University.

Houston, Jean (1982) *The Possible Human*. Los Angeles: Tarcher.

Houston, Jean (1987) *The Search for the Beloved: Journeys in Sacred Psychology*. Los Angeles: Tarcher.

Hycner, Richard (1993) *Between Person and Person: Toward a Dialogical Psychotherapy*. Highland NY: Gestalt Journal Press.

*Jung, Carl Gustav (1968) *The Archetypes and the Collective Unconscious*, second edition. London: Routledge.

Kenton, Leslie (1998) *Journey to Freedom*. London: Harper Collins.

Klimo, Jon (1988) *Channelling*. Wellingborough: Aquarius.

Lake, Frank (1980) *Constricted Confusion*. Oxford: Clinical Theology Association.

Larsen, Stephen (1990) *Mythic Imagination.* New York: Bantam.

LeShan, Lawrence (1974) *How to Meditate*. London: Crucible.

Macy, Joanna (1991) *World as Lover, World as Self*. Berkeley CA: Parallax Press.

Mann, A.T. (1979) *The Round Art: the Astrology of Time and Space*. Cheltenham: Paper Tiger.

*Maslow, Abraham H. (1970) *Religions, Values and Peak Experiences*. New York: Viking Press.

Maslow, Abraham H. (1973) *The Farther Reaches of Human Nature*. London: Penguin.

McLeod, John (1997) *Narrative and Psychotherapy*. London: Sage.

Mindell, Amy (1995) *Metaskills: The Spiritual Art of Therapy*. Tempe, AZ: New Falcon Publications.

Nichols, Sallie (1980) *Jung and the Tarot: an Archetypal Journey*. York Beach ME: Samuel Weiser.

Osho (1992) *Meditation: The First and Last Freedom*. Cologne: Rebel Publishing House.

Parfitt, Will (1990) *Walking through Walls: Practical Esoteric Psychology.* Shaftesbury: Element.

Rothberg, Donald and Kelly, Sean (eds) (1998) *Ken Wilber in Dialogue*. Wheaton IL: Quest.

Rowan, John (1987) 'Siding with the client' in W. Dryden (ed.) *Key Cases in Psychotherapy.* Beckenham: Croom Helm (abridged version in J. Rowan (ed.), *Breakthroughs and Integration in Psychotherapy*, London: Whurr, 1992).

*Rowan, John (1993) *The Transpersonal: Psychotherapy and Counselling* London: Routledge.

Rowan, John (1998a) 'Transformational research' in P. Clarkson (ed.) *Counselling Psychology: Integrating Theory, Research and Supervised Practice*. London: Routledge.

Rowan, John (1998b) 'Linking: its place in therapy', *International Journal of Psychotherapy*, 3 (3): 245–54.

Schwartz-Salant, Nathan (1986) 'On the subtle-body concept in clinical practice' in N. Schwartz-Salant and M. Stein (eds) *The Body in Analysis*. Wilmette IL: Chiron.

Smith, Huston (2000) *Cleansing the Doors of Perception: the Religious Significance of Entheogenic Plants and Chemicals*. New York: Putnam Tarcher.

Somers, Barbara (2000) 'Dreaming in depth' in N. Wellings and E.W. McCormick (eds) *Transpersonal Psychotherapy*. London: Continuum.

Stein, Murray and Corbett, Lionel (1991, 1992) *Psyche's Stories* I–II. Wilmette IL: Chiron.

Stevens, Jon (1971) *Awareness: Exploring, Experimenting, Experiencing*. Moab UT: Real People Press.

Tanzer, D.W. (1967) 'The Psychology of Pregnancy and Childbirth'. Unpublished doctoral dissertation, Waltham MA: Brandeis University.

Wahl, Bill (2001) Personal communication.

Walker, Barbara G. (1984) *The Secrets of the Tarot: Origins, History and Symbolism*. San Francisco: Harper & Row.

Walker, Barbara G. (1986) *The I Ching of the Goddess*. San Francisco: Harper & Row.

*West, William (2000) *Psychotherapy and Spirituality*. London: Sage.

Whitmont, Edward (1987) 'Archetypal and personal interaction in the clinical process' in N. Schwartz-Salant and M. Stein (eds) *Archetypal Processes in Psychotherapy*. Wilmette IL: Chiron.

*Wilber, Ken (1983) *Eye to Eye*. Garden City NY: Anchor.

Wilber, Ken (1987) *A Sociable God*. New York: McGraw-Hill.

*Wilber, Ken (1997) *The Eye of Spirit*. Boston MA: Shambhala.

*Wilber, Ken (2000) *Integral Psychology*. Boston MA: Shambhala.

*Wilber, Ken, Engler, Jack and Brown, Daniel P. (1986) *Transformations of Consciousness*. Boston MA: Shambhala.

11 The Constructivist Paradigm
DAVID A. WINTER

Constructivism, which has its roots in the writings of such philosophers as Vico and Kant, is a term which is now applied to certain postmodern approaches in numerous fields of knowledge. This chapter will outline the increasing influence of constructivism, in its various forms (Neimeyer and Mahoney, 1995; Neimeyer and Rood, 1997; Neimeyer and Raskin, 2000), in the areas of counselling psychology and psychotherapy. However, before considering how it is applied in this sphere, the essential features of the constructivist approach and of the theories which it encompasses will be described.

The underlying theory of personality and motivation

In psychology, constructivism 'refers to a family of theories that share the assertion that human knowledge and experience entail the (pro)active participation of the individual' (Mahoney, 1988: 2). In other words, the psychological constructivist believes that people actively construct their worlds.

Two other features which Mahoney considers to be shared by constructivist psychological theories are emphases on 'morphogenic nuclear structure' and 'self-organizing development'. The former refers to the view that people are structured in such a way that core processes constrain more peripheral aspects of the person's functioning. The latter essentially means that each of us organizes our development so that our identity and equilibrium are maintained: to quote Guidano (1987: 3), 'the maintenance of one's perceived identity becomes as important as life itself'. As we shall see, both of these characteristics of constructivism are central to its approach to psychological counselling.

Personal construct theory

The basic features of constructivist meta-theory are fleshed out in somewhat different ways in the various constructivist theories. As it is probably the most elaborate of these, and that which has been used most extensively in the field of counselling psychology and psychotherapy, and has generated the most research, George Kelly's (1955) personal construct theory will now be described as an example of the constructivist approach.

Personal construct theory is based upon the philosophical assumption of 'constructive alternativism', which states that 'all of our present interpretations of the universe are subject to revision or replacement' (Kelly, 1955: 15). Therefore, not only do we construct our worlds but, as the client may discover during counselling, we can reconstruct them. Optimally, each of us functions like a scientist, formulating hypotheses, testing them out, and if necessary revising them. This essentially anticipatory nature of human functioning is expressed in the 'fundamental postulate' of personal construct theory: 'A person's processes are psychologically channelized by the ways in which he anticipates events' (Kelly, 1955: 4).

Kelly elaborated his fundamental postulate in eleven corollaries, which detail the process of construing. Central to this is the development by each individual of a system of bipolar personal constructs. Their bipolarity means that each of our constructs presents us with a 'pathway of movement' (Kelly, 1955: 128). For example, Tom, who employed a construct contrasting being assertive with being reasonable, was resistant to moving down the path of becoming more assertive because of its implication of also becoming more unreasonable. In choosing which pole of a construct to apply to an event, the person will select that option which is most likely to increase his or her capacity to anticipate the world. This notion may make even the most apparently self-destructive behaviour comprehensible, as in Fransella's (1972) finding that stutterers would not trade stuttering for fluency until the latter carried as many implications for them, and therefore possibilities of anticipating their world, as did stuttering. As is evident from these examples, people differ from each other in their personal construct systems. Construing another person's construction processes is the essence of intimate relationships, or, to use Kelly's term, role relationships.

In Kelly's view, we each organize our constructs in a hierarchical system, such that some constructs are superordinate to others. The particular relationships between constructs in our system determine the predictions which we make about our world. For example, the relationship within Tom's construct system between the constructs 'dislike meeting people – like people's company' and 'unselfish – demanding' implied predictions not only about other people but also about how he might change were he to see himself as more interested in meeting people.

Our predictions may be validated or invalidated by our experience of subsequent events. Experience of invalidation may lead to reconstruing, which may take various forms. For example, if Tom were to meet a person whom he construed as liking meeting people and unselfish, he could respond to the invalidation of his prediction by reconstruing the person as selfish. Alternatively, after several such invalidations, he might reverse the relationship between the two constructs, or 'loosen' this relationship, concluding that people who like meeting others may or may not be selfish. More fundamentally, he might decide that the 'dislike meeting people – like people's company' construct is not particularly useful, perhaps developing a new construct to replace it. Finally, he might avoid reconstruing by attempting to force the world to comply with his construction, for example by making such demands on a person who likes meeting others that the person rejects the demands, and as a result is construed as selfish. This latter strategy was equated by Kelly with hostility. The particular response which a person makes to invalidation will depend, among other things, on the type of construct which has been invalidated. For example, research indicates that a person's superordinate constructs are particularly resistant to invalidation, perhaps because the number of implications which they carry means that the effects of their invalidation are likely to reverberate through the system much more than the effects of invalidation of a more subordinate construct.

Those superordinate constructs which are central to an individual's identity were termed *core constructs* by Kelly. They are particularly resistant to change, since threat is 'the awareness of imminent comprehensive change in one's core structures' (Kelly, 1955: 489). A subset of core constructs, termed *core role constructs*, concern one's construing of one's characteristic mode of interaction with others. For Kelly, guilt was the experience of an 'apparent dislodgement from his core role structure' (1955: 502). It is important to note that this does not necessarily involve an individual engaging in behaviour which is bad in a conventional moral sense: for example, in the case of Tom, whose core role involved unassertive behaviour, occasions on which he found himself acting assertively evoked guilt. A further emotion considered by Kelly was anxiety, which he equated with the awareness that one's constructs do not equip one to predict the events with which one is confronted.

Individuals may adopt various strategies in an attempt to avoid anxiety. They may constrict their worlds to those events which they can predict, or alternatively dilate their perceptual fields in the hope that from their new experiences may develop a system of constructs which may be applied to these. As we have seen above, they may loosen their construing to avoid invalidation and the anxiety associated with it, or tighten construct relationships in an attempt to build a system 'designed to be anxiety-tight' (Kelly, 1955: 849). Optimal functioning involves the cyclical interplay of such contrasting strategies as these, whereas in psychological disorder the individual tends to employ a particular strategy exclusively. For example, to use psychiatric nosological categories, there is evidence that people diagnosed as thought-disordered schizophrenics tend to be characterized by loose construing, and those diagnosed as neurotic by tight construing (Winter, 1992). However, the essential characteristic of psychological disorder is that the individual fails to reconstrue despite persistent invalidation of some construction.

As with other constructivists, Kelly took a holistic view of the person, and did not make the traditional distinctions between cognition, affect and conation. As the examples above demonstrate, he equated emotion with the awareness of a transition in one's construing, the nature of the emotion depending upon the particular transition involved. He saw no need for a concept of motivation, since he viewed the person as a 'form of motion', not requiring any motivational force to set him or her moving. Nevertheless, Kelly's view of choice, discussed above, does provide an explanation of the individual's direction of movement, and may also be reframed in terms of the individual moving away from the anxiety associated with inability to anticipate events. Finally, although Kelly did not employ a concept of the unconscious, he did acknowledge that an individual's constructions are at different levels of cognitive awareness, and that therefore people may not always be aware of the bases for their choices. Some of the constructs at a low level of awareness are preverbal, their lack of verbal labels often being because they were developed before the person had the use of words.

Guidano and Liotti's approach

Although Kelly did not consider in depth the development of construing, greater attention has been paid to this area by other constructivists, in particular by drawing upon attachment theory. Guidano and Liotti (1983), for example, consider that attachment processes, particularly in the relationship between child and parent, are central to the development of an individual's knowledge of self and the world, or 'personal meaning organization'. Guidano (1987) also considers the developmental process to involve an interplay of cognitive growth and emotional differentiation, the latter including the development of 'emotional schemata' which are employed in assimilating the individual's experiences. Clusters of schemata form 'scenes' portraying aspects of the person's experience, and similar repeated experiences lead to the development of prototypical 'nuclear scenes', each involving cyclical interplay between two clusters of emotional schemata. Rules for the connection of nuclear scenes are developed in the form of 'scripts' which provide a stable and coherent sense of self in the world, and which may be further organized into 'meta-scripts', which, in effect, provide a programme for the individual's life. The emotional schemata and scripts are at a more tacit level of knowledge than the person's explicit models of self and the world.

Guidano equates normal functioning with a personal meaning organization which is able to develop flexibly and resiliently towards increasing levels of complexity by a dialectical process of assimilating its contradictions. In such a system, there is an 'essential tension between opponent processes', including that between processes of maintenance and change. The dynamic balance that is achieved requires abstract processing which involves a 'decentring' from the world of immediate experience and a 'recentring' on, and commitment to, the self. The individual will tend to attend selectively to data which are consistent with his or her personal identity, but when it is necessary to process experiences inconsistent with the individual's self- or world-view this will be achieved by a reconstruction of personal identity. However, in 'cognitive dysfunctions' the view of the self is too rigid to permit reconstruction and the individual therefore distorts information which is inconsistent with it, and attributes to external causes, such as illness, the emotional distress which accompanies this information, which often involves change in the view of a significant figure.

In both neurotic and psychotic disorders, there is a too concrete processing of experiences, and the latter disorders are in addition associated with interference in the individual's 'self-synthesizing ability'. Guidano considers that particular patterns of 'closure' of personal meaning organization, resulting from specific developmental pathways, correspond to certain clinical patterns, of which he has identified four major types: the depressive, agoraphobic, eating disorders, and obsessive-compulsive patterns.

Neuro-linguistic programming

Another essentially constructivist approach is neuro-linguistic programming, which was devised by Bandler and Grinder on the basis of their study of the patterns employed by outstanding therapists. They consider that people construct maps of their worlds by applying various filters, including language, to their perceptions (O'Connor and Seymour, 1990). Experiences are represented internally primarily through the visual, auditory and kinesthetic systems, and each person has a preferred system for constructing such representations as well as a 'lead system' for bringing memories into conscious awareness. There are submodalities within each of these systems (for example, colour and brightness within the visual system), changing which will change the emotional impact of a particular memory.

The assessment process

George Kelly's 'first principle' was that 'if you do not know what is wrong with a person, ask him; he may tell you' (1955: 322–3). Constructivists have devised various ways of asking their clients what is wrong with them, and several of these have been described by G.J. Neimeyer (1993).

The principal concern of constructivist assessment procedures is, of course, the elicitation of the client's view of the world. Moreover, the initial focus will be on the exploration of this view in the client's own terms rather than in terms of a framework imposed by the counselling psychologist. To use one of Kelly's (1955) terms, the counselling psychologist will begin by adopting a 'credulous approach' in the assessment, taking what the client says at face value. This does not preclude the subsequent use by the counsellor of a set of diagnostic constructs in attempting to understand the client's situation. The personal construct counselling psychologist may, for example, apply Kelly's emotional constructs or his notions of tight and loose construing or constriction and dilation to material elicited by the assessment process. A counsellor following Guidano and Liotti's approach might frame diagnostic hypotheses in terms of the feelings, patterns of self-deception and developmental courses typically associated with particular personal meaning organizations. While Guidano and Liotti draw to some extent upon the ideas of Piaget, the influence of these ideas is particularly evident in the assessment process in another constructivist approach, Ivey's (1986) 'developmental therapy'. This involves employing Piaget's concepts of developmental stages metaphorically to identify the client's developmental level so that appropriate interventions may be selected.

The constructivist assessment process will be less concerned with identifying the frequency or intensity of beliefs held by the client than with revealing the relationships between the client's constructs, including their hierarchical organization. A major concern will be with assessing the avenues of movement open to the client rather than, as in a traditional psychiatric diagnosis, providing a static description of the client's predicament. Furthermore, the constructivist counselling psychologist will take the view that assessment and therapeutic intervention are closely interwoven. Rather than striving for an assessment process which does not influence the subject of the assessment, the constructivist will accept that assessment always generates change, and may select assessment procedures to facilitate particular types of reconstruing.

Constructivist assessment techniques tend to be idiographic and interactive, involving either some variant of a structured interview approach or interaction between the subject and him/herself. As R.A. Neimeyer (1993) has described, they may be usefully categorized in terms of whether they focus primarily on the structure or on the process of the client's construing.

Structure-oriented assessment techniques

The most well known structure-oriented constructivist assessment approach is Kelly's repertory grid technique. The counselling psychologist employing this technique will first elicit from the client a set of 'elements', or aspects of his or her experience. Most commonly these will be names of people supplied by the client to fit certain role titles (e.g. 'a man you dislike'; 'your partner'), together with aspects of the self (e.g. 'yourself now'; 'your ideal self'; 'how you will be following counselling'). In the typical procedure, the client will then be presented with successive groups of three of these elements, and asked, for each group, how two of the elements are similar and thereby different from the third. In answering this question the client will reveal one of his or her constructs. The final stage in the procedure is for the client to sort all the elements in terms of all the constructs thus elicited, usually by rating or ranking them.

While some aspects of the client's construing will be evident from visual inspection of a repertory grid, detailed analysis generally requires the use of one of the computer packages devised for the purpose. A variety of measures may be derived from such a package, including those which indicate similarities and differences between the client's construing of different elements (for example, whether the client's partner is construed as similar to some other significant figure in his or her life), those which reveal similarities in meaning between constructs (for example, indicating how the client's problem is construed) and measures of the degree of tightness of the construct system.

Although a repertory grid may provide some indication of the hierarchical relationships between constructs in a client's system, such information may be obtained more directly by two further techniques. In *laddering* the client is presented with one of his or her constructs and asked to which pole they would prefer to be assigned, and why. The reason for the client's preference will be a construct more superordinate than the first, and the procedure may be repeated to trace further levels of superordinacy. In the bipolar version of the implications grid (Fransella, 1972), the client is asked, for each of his or her construct poles, which other construct poles would apply to a person so described. Figure 11.1 shows the negative implications of construct poles concerning sexual responsiveness which this procedure revealed in a man who was unable

Figure 11.1   Negative implications of sexual responsiveness in a client's pre-treatment implications grid

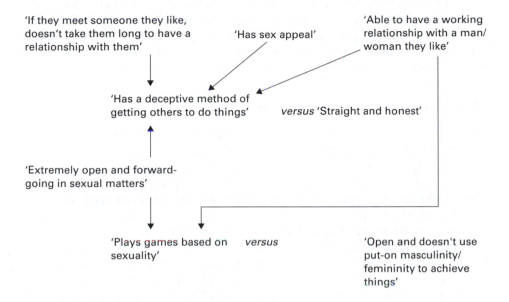

to ejaculate. These implications suggested that were he to be able to be more sexually responsive he would have to see himself in a less favourable light.

Process-oriented assessment techniques

Process-oriented assessment techniques tend to focus upon narrative material, since it may reveal something of the flow of a person's construing. One such technique which was developed by Kelly is the self-characterization, in which the client is asked to write a character sketch of himself or herself as if it were written by a sympathetic friend. Variations on this procedure include sketches of the self at different points in time (for example, as a child; if I lost this particular problem). A more extensive written narrative procedure which can provide access to the client's construction and reconstruction processes is for him or her to keep a personal journal. Open-ended interviews may also be employed, as in a procedure developed by Viney and Westbrook (1981: 48) in which the client is asked to 'talk to me for a few minutes about your life at the moment – the good things and the bad – what it is like for you'. Various content analysis scales may be applied to the interview transcript in order, for example, to assess emotions, including anxiety in Kelly's sense of the term. These scales may also be applied to transcripts of counselling sessions to monitor changes in the client.

A further technique which can provide access for both counsellor and client to the client's construing processes is Mahoney's 'stream of consciousness' procedure, in which 'the client is invited to attend to and, as best one can, report ongoing thoughts, sensations, images, memories, and feelings' (1991: 295). The client is not required to share with the counselling psychologist all this material, and the counsellor will generally be less concerned to provide interpretations of what is reported than to elicit its meaning for the client.

Neuro-linguistic Programming assessment

Assessment in neuro-linguistic programming explores both the structure and the process of the client's view of the world. A particular concern is to identify the client's preferred representational system by noting 'accessing cues', such as eye movements, gestures, or speed and tone of speech. For example, if the client's eyes move upwards at some point, or become defocused and look straight ahead, the counselling psychologist will suspect that he or she is visualizing something. The counsellor's interventions may then be matched to the client's preferred system. The psychologist employing this approach will also be concerned to 'calibrate' the client's emotional states by noting the non-verbal expressions of these states. Turning to the client's use of language, the counsellor will employ the 'meta-model', which involves asking questions to elicit information which, because of omissions, distortions or generalizations, is not transferred from the client's 'deep structure' to the 'surface structure' of his or her speech. For example, if the client says, 'I was hurt,' the counselling psychologist might ask, 'How and by whom?' Among the particular issues which the counsellor will wish to clarify are the client's desired outcomes, and their ecological context, which may be appreciated by asking the client to consider in what way other aspects of his or her life would be affected if each outcome were achieved.

What does change mean and how is it brought about?

Constructivists view therapeutic change as a process of reconstruction. This process may take many forms, as Kelly (1969: 231) described in listing the approaches to their task which a therapist and client might adopt.

- The two of them can decide that the client should reverse his position with respect to one of the more obvious reference axes.
- Or they can select another construct from the client's ready repertory and apply it to matters at hand.
- They can make more explicit those preverbal constructs by which all of us order our lives in considerable degree.
- They can elaborate the construct system to test it for internal consistency.

- They can test constructs for their predictive validity.
- They can increase the range of convenience of certain constructs, that is, apply them more generally. They can also decrease the range of convenience and thus reduce a construct to a kind of obsolescence.
- They can alter the meaning of certain constructs; rotate the reference axes.
- They can erect new reference axes.

The earlier items in this list, involving changes in the use of the client's existing constructs, clearly involve more superficial reconstruction than do the later items, involving modification of these constructs or their replacement by new constructs. The level of reconstruction which is attempted may also be viewed in terms of the type of constructs which it involves. For example, counselling may be contrasted with psychotherapy in that it will generally not attempt to produce changes in a client's core constructs.

The variety of possible types of reconstruction is matched by the range of techniques which the counsellor may employ to facilitate the changes. The counselling psychologist will base the selection of the particular type of reconstruing on which to focus, and therefore of the technique to be employed, on his or her assessment of the client's construct system. Of particular concern will be the selection of interventions which are 'ecologically sound', in that they foster the evolution of the client's construct system without disrupting its integrity (Neimeyer and Harter, 1988). For example, there will be concern not to dismantle some aspect of this system until a viable alternative is available, and not to present a fundamental challenge to a client's core constructs. If the counsellor fails to take such matters into account, the result is likely to be a highly anxious and/or threatened client, who will resist the psychologist's efforts in order to preserve his or her construct system. It is also important to note that, whatever type of reconstruction is aimed for, the constructivist counselling psychologist will not be attempting to persuade the client to adopt some particular view of events, but simply to help the client to discover that it is possible to view events in alternative ways. The client's construing should thereby be set in motion again.

Personal construct psychotherapy

In the personal construct approach, one of the counsellor's first concerns may well be a continuation of the process of elaboration of the client's construct system which is likely to have commenced during the assessment process. This will involve exploring the implications of the client's constructions, initially particularly those relating to the presenting complaint, and identifying, and perhaps resolving, any inconsistencies in his or her construing. This process may be facilitated by the use of the assessment procedures described in the last section, by asking the client to imagine the outcome of alternative courses of action, or by 'casual enactment'. This last approach involves short spells of role playing by the client and counselling psychologist of situations involving the client and/or significant or hypothetical figures in his or her life. One of the benefits of enactment is that it may allow the client to experiment with some new behaviour while disengaging core constructs from the experimentation and thereby avoiding the threat which it might otherwise involve.

While enactment is usually employed in a relatively informal way during therapy, Kelly also devised a more formal enactment procedure, known as fixed-role therapy. The counselling psychologist who employs this approach will initially write a sketch of a hypothetical character for the client to enact. In writing this sketch, the counsellor will generally draw upon the client's self-characterization and other assessment material, and will be attempting to describe a person who is orthogonal to, rather than the opposite of, the client. The sketch will also attempt to elaborate some theme which it might be valuable for the client to explore. If the role portrayed in the sketch appears plausible to the client, he or she will be asked to 'become' this character for two weeks, during which there will be frequent rehearsals of the role with the counsellor, focusing on progressively more threatening or anxiety-provoking situations. The aim of the exercise is not to transform the client permanently into the new character, but to provide 'one good, rousing, construct-shaking experience' (Kelly, 1955: 412), which will demonstrate to the client that he or she need not be trapped in one particular role and corresponding set of reactions from other people. The procedure is a good example of the 'invitational mood' in which personal construct counselling is conducted, the client being encouraged to experiment by approaching events as if some new construction of them were correct. It is, however, only one of many possible ways of facilitating experimentation during this form of counselling.

The personal construct counselling psychologist will at times be concerned either to loosen or to tighten a client's construing. Loosening may serve several functions, such as allowing certain aspects of the client's experience to be encompassed by their constructs; setting the stage for realignment of constructs; and facilitating the attachment of a verbal label to a preverbal construct. It may be achieved in various ways, including relaxation, free association of the type employed in psychoanalysis, encouragement of reporting of dreams, and uncritical acceptance of the client's construing. While loosening may be a necessary component of reconstruction, the client's new constructions will need to be tightened if testable predictions are to be derived from them. Many of the techniques used in elaborating a client's construing will have a tightening effect, as will such behavioural procedures as self-monitoring of behaviours or thoughts. A particular set of tightening techniques suggested by Kelly involves 'binding' a construct to the time or person it was initially developed to anticipate. This and other personal construct techniques are illustrated in the following case example.

In exploring the unfavourable constructions of sexual responsiveness which had been revealed by the client's implications grid (see Figure 11.1 above), it became apparent that these had their basis in his child-hood experience of a mother who manipulated others with her sexuality. He was therefore encouraged to view these constructions as an anachronism, which had served a useful purpose when first developed but were now inappropriately applied in his adult relationships. Since he had dealt with the inconsistencies in his view of sexuality by constricting his world to exclude sexual experiences, he was encouraged to elaborate his construing in this area to reduce the anxiety which it occasioned. The procedures used included asking him to keep a daily record of his sexual urges, to complete a repertory grid in which the elements were sexual situations and to experiment with homework tasks designed to enhance his awareness of pleasurable bodily sensations. He eventually reported that he had been able to have his first orgasm, and further grid assessments revealed that this was accompanied by the development of a more favourable construction of sexual responsiveness.

Process-oriented cognitive therapy

The basic features of Guidano's non-rationalistic, process-oriented cognitive therapy are the facilitation of the client's self-awareness and of a flexible response to incongruities so that these may be assimilated into a more abstract self-image. The experience of affect during therapy, particularly in the context of the therapeutic relationship, is considered crucial in prompting reorganization. Therapy, in effect, involves training in self-observation by a 'moviola' technique in which the client is encouraged to 'zoom in' on and out of particular scenes from their life, and to view events from both a 'subjective' and an 'objective' viewpoint. Homework assignments involve focusing self-observation on particular items between sessions, and techniques borrowed from other therapeutic approaches may be employed to foster experimentation.

The self-observational process in itself, with its emphasis on clients disengaging themselves from their beliefs and viewing them as hypotheses, is likely to modify the client's view of the self and of the events which are being considered. Reorganization of the client's view of the self will also be promoted by explanations offered by the therapist which are discrepant from the client's own explanations, provided that the client is sufficiently emotionally involved in the therapeutic relationship. One such therapeutic explanation will be the therapist's initial reformulation of the client's problem in terms of the personal meaning organization which underlies it. The 'internal' focus of this reformulation will be likely to be inconsistent with the client's view of his or her problem, which may tend to focus on external attributions such as symptoms of illness.

The strategy adopted in therapy is a stepwise one in which the client is encouraged to move on to a new level of self-observation only when stability has been achieved at the level previous to this. During the initial focus on the client's immediate experiences, the client comes to appreciate that emotional states are constructions associated with perceived imbalances in an affective relationship. The next stage is generally a reconstruction of the client's 'affective style' involving analysis of the client's history of affective relationships. Guidano considers that most clients obtain relief from their presenting problems without the necessity for a final stage of analysis of how their developmental pathways led them to arrive at their personal meaning organizations. However, with those who are interested in exploring this area a self-observational process may again be employed, but with the client being asked to compare their subjective viewpoint of an event not only with their present objective viewpoint but also with the perspective of the self at the age when the event occurred.

Guidano's (1991) treatment of Sandra, who presented with phobic anxieties concerning both going out and staying at home alone, began with a reformulation of her difficulties as a fear of loss of control which she experienced in situations which she perceived either as constrictive or as not affording her sufficient protection. Focusing self-observation on this experience, she came to view her fears as 'tests of strength' which she constructed to demonstrate to herself that, since she was liable to lose control, she required her husband to 'keep an eye on her'. Shifting the focus to her marital relationship, it became apparent that, to preserve her sense of self, she had excluded from awareness feelings connected with her husband's affair with another woman and her own subsequent affair with his best friend. These feelings could then only be viewed by her as an uncontrollable fear of being alone or losing control which, paradoxically, kept her closer to a husband whom she might otherwise have considered leaving. Exploration of the affective history of her relationships, by focusing on critical scenes from those relationships, allowed the identification of a pattern of oscillation between need for protection and need for freedom and independence. Then, focusing on her early developmental history, it became increasingly apparent that her phobic meaning organization largely derived from inhibition of her exploratory behaviour and autonomy by the ostensibly loving attentions of her mother, the indirectness of this inhibition preventing her from recognizing it at the time. Her reconstrual of her mother was associated with Sandra apparently viewing the world as less threatening and exposing herself to previously avoided situations, such as making a journey by aeroplane.

Developmental therapy

Ivey's developmental therapy aims to help the client progress through a series of stages equivalent to those which Piaget used to characterize child development. If therapy is successful, the client develops into a formal operational thinker, who is able to identify consistently repeating patterns in his or her experiences, or a 'post-formal thinker', who can appreciate that reality is constructed dialectically. For this process to occur, there needs to be an appropriate equilibration between assimilation and accommodation. Ivey (1986: 40) describes the counselling psychologist's task as 'to provide a new environment that provides more useful and accurate environmental feedback and thus returns the client to the process of growth and development'.

Depth-oriented brief therapy

Ecker and Hulley's (1996) depth-oriented brief therapy makes use of the concept of 'position', which they define as 'a constructed version of reality plus a strategy for responding to that reality' (p. 13). Of particular relevance to therapy are the client's conscious anti-symptom position and their unconscious pro-symptom position, which is assumed always to accompany it. The counselling psychologist's main tasks are 'radical inquiry', in which the pro-symptom position is elucidated by such means as asking the client to view the world from a symptom-free perspective, and 'experiential shift', in which there is experience of transformation of the constructs comprising this position. Two possible types of therapeutic resolution may occur: either a 'direct resolution', in which the pro-symptom position changes so that the symptom no longer seems necessary, or a 'reverse resolution', in which the anti-symptom position changes so that the symptom no longer appears to be a problem.

Neuro-linguistic programming

Neuro-linguistic programming tends to be rather more directive than other constructivist approaches in its employment of techniques, sometimes facilitated by the use of trance, to modify clients' ways of viewing their worlds. One such technique is the association of certain stimuli, or 'anchors', from different representational systems with some resourceful state which the client wishes to bring to bear in particular problematic situations. By using the anchors (for example, saying a word internally, visualizing an image, and/or making a certain movement) in the situations concerned, the client will be able to summon up the required resources. Another technique which may be employed to reconstruct some past traumatic event is to ask the client to imagine watching himself or herself watching the event on a screen; and then to ask the client to alter the picture's submodalities (such as brightness or size) to change the negative feelings which it brings forth. Next, the client may be asked to join his or her younger self on the screen, bringing resources from the present to cope with the traumatic incident. Finally, the client may be invited, in imagination, to practise coping with similar events in the future. 'Reframing' may also be used in neuro-linguistic programming, the counsellor offering alternative meanings of the client's statements. For example, a behaviour which is presented as a problem by a client may be reframed as a strength in certain circumstances, and the client then helped to employ it in only those contexts, and to develop alternative ways of acting in other contexts.

Therapy as narrative reconstruction

A variant of the constructivist approach which is growing in prominence is to view people as storytellers (Mair, 1988), whose narratives may be rewritten in therapy. For example, White and Epston (1990) have developed various 'narrative means to therapeutic ends' which allow clients to externalize their problems and then 'reauthor' their lives, perhaps freeing them from 'subjugating' stories; while Neimeyer (1994) has described the use of client-generated written narratives in therapy. Viney (1993) considers that an approach which involves the telling and retelling of stories may be particularly useful with older clients.

Technical eclecticism

It should now be apparent that constructivist approaches to therapy and counselling psychology are technically eclectic in that they may borrow the techniques of other approaches, but will conceptualize their action in terms of the particular constructivist model concerned rather than the model from which they are derived. For example, both personal construct psychotherapy and the approach of Guidano and Liotti may employ behavioural techniques as aids to experimentation. The latter authors consider that, by changing superficial structures, such techniques may facilitate the identification of the rules which underlie these structures.

The relationship with the individual client

Kelly viewed the relationship between therapist or counselling psychologist and client as analogous to that between a research supervisor and student. Guidano and Liotti also use the metaphor of scientific research in describing this relationship, the therapist serving as a model of the scientific attitude for the client. They, like Kelly, emphasize the importance of creating a co-operative, collaborative therapeutic relationship, stressing that this is one which the client can perceive as a 'secure base' from which to explore his or her emotional life and identity. In their view, this requires the therapist to recognize and respect the client's identity, while not confirming its 'basic pathogenetic assumptions'. They also consider that the process of exploration may usefully focus upon the therapeutic relationship itself, and that the client's construing of the therapist, for example, may provide a basis for assessment and change of such aspects of the client's cognitive structures as his or her models of attachment figures. The therapist's own self-awareness is enhanced as he or she attends to the emotions accompanying his or her perceptions of the client, and this increases the therapist's involvement in the therapeutic relationship. Guidano (1991) considers the final stages of therapy as involving a transformation of the therapeutic relationship into one of supervision. He considers that emotions associated with the separation from the therapist should be employed to clarify further the client's bonding style and to renegotiate the 'rules' of the client–therapist relationship.

The constructivist approach which perhaps most emphasizes the importance of the intimate personal relationship between counselling psychologist and client is Leitner's (1995) experiential variant of personal construct psychotherapy. He stresses that since such intimate relationships always pose the danger of invalidation of core constructs, counselling may be a terrifying experience. Such invalidation may be less likely if an optimal therapeutic distance, involving a balance between connection and separatedness, is maintained between counselling psychologist and client.

Taking a credulous, respectful attitude towards the client's view of the world (or 'pacing' the client, to use a term from neuro-linguistic programming), the constructivist counselling psychologist will not try to impose his or her own constructions on the client. As Guidano puts it:

> The therapist should try to work only on those areas of experience which have shown themselves to be critical on the basis of a previous reconstruction of the same basic themes of the client's personal meaning, refraining from an exaggerated intervention in other domains despite the fact that one's own conception of life might seem better and more suitable than those exhibited by the client. (1991: 209)

Since the constructivist counsellor in effect 'suspends' his or her own constructions during counselling, the impact on the psychologist's approach of differences between counsellor and client in terms of such areas as gender, race, class or sexual orientation should be minimal. However, counselling is likely to be more effective if the counselling psychologist is sufficiently familiar with the client's milieu and cultural background to have some awareness of the sources of validation which are available to the client.

Family, group and organizational implications

While the constructivist approaches described above initially focused primarily on the individual's construing of the world, later developments of some of these approaches have demonstrated their applicability to couples, families and broader social groups. For example, Procter (1981) and other post-Kellyan personal construct theorists have developed a family construct psychology, based on the notion that a family (or indeed any social group) may be considered to have a construct system, the properties of which are essentially similar to those of an individual's construct system. Such personal construct assessment techniques as the self-characterization and repertory grid have been adapted for use with couples, families and groups, allowing not only the identification of features of construing shared by the individuals concerned but also indications of the extent to which each individual's construing deviates from this consensus and is understood by other members of the family or group. Similarly, adaptations of methods used in individual personal construct counselling have been employed in marital and family counselling. Their applications in organizational settings have, for example, facilitated conflict resolution and greater awareness by managers and staff of each other's constructions. Neuro-linguistic programming has also been fruitfully employed for such purposes, particularly in the business context.

Constructivist counselling may usefully be conducted in a group setting, since the group provides an interpersonal laboratory which offers a rich source of validational evidence for clients' constructions. Kelly's (1955) approach to group psychotherapy was based on the view that groups pass through a series of developmental stages, at each of which certain therapeutic techniques are appropriate. One technique of which he and later personal construct therapists have made particular use in groups is enactment. A further personal construct group approach, the *interpersonal transaction group*, has been devised by Landfield and Rivers (1975) to foster the development of role relationships. Such a group involves brief, non-critical dyadic interactions between group members, who rotate at the end of each interaction until each member has been paired with every other. There is then a plenary discussion of members' experience of the interactions, topics for which are selected for their relevance to the clients' problems.

In addition to applications to couples, families and other groups of constructivist approaches to individuals, several systems theory approaches may themselves be considered essentially constructivist (Feixas, 1992). The methods which they employ are directed towards the elicitation of a family's construing, or their interacting stories (Dallos, 1997), and the promotion of reconstruction. For example, in the Milan group's 'circular questioning' technique (Selvini-Palazzoli et al., 1980), each family member, in front of the others, states his or her construction of some issue, such as the relationship between two other members and the comparison of these with a third. The interactions thus generated may lead constructions to be revised. More precisely, many modern family therapy approaches may be classified as social constructionist (McNamee and Gergen, 1992). Although being similar to the constructivist position in assuming that we construct our worlds, they differ in emphasizing that this construction arises through social interaction and is mediated by language. Family counselling from this perspective may be considered to involve the 'co-construction of realities' by means of conversation between a family and its therapists. This may be facilitated by such devices as allowing a family to observe the family counselling team discussing them, and then to discuss their observations with the team (Andersen, 1987).

Research evidence about effectiveness

There are numerous single-case reports and uncontrolled group studies demonstrating the effectiveness of constructivist counselling or psychotherapy with a wide range of clients, of all ages, including not only those presenting with psychological disorders but also physically ill people and those with disabilities. (See Winter, 1992, for a review of the literature on personal construct psychotherapy and counselling.) There are also a few controlled studies of the effectiveness of constructivist techniques, such as fixed-role therapy, employed in the context of another approach or in a modified form which departs significantly from the original. However, controlled outcome studies of relatively 'pure' constructivist approaches are rare. One of the first of these, by Bannister et al. (1975), found only slightly more improvement in thought-disordered schizophrenics treated by personal construct psychotherapy than in a control group. The authors argue that more favourable results might have been achieved had they been able to have more control over the validational fortunes of their clients' construing. Evesham and Fransella (1985) carried out a controlled study of a personal construct psychotherapy treatment method for stutterers which Fransella (1972) had found to produce a significant reduction in disfluencies. Comparing an approach that incorporated this method with one that solely involved training in speech techniques, they found somewhat less change post-treatment in the former group but that its clients had a significantly lower relapse rate over the following eighteen months.

Viney (1990) has investigated personal construct crisis intervention counselling for people hospitalized for medical problems and personal construct psychotherapy for elderly people presenting with psychological problems. In both these client groups, those treated by the personal construct approach not only showed such psychological changes as reductions in anxiety, depression and indirectly expressed anger, and increases in expressed competence, but also greater improvements in physical health than did controls. In another study with older people, Botella and Feixas (1992–93) found evidence of reconstruction during a personal construct-oriented autobiographical group. At the other end of the age spectrum, personal construct groups for adolescents have been found to lead to gains in self-esteem, compared with a control group, and increased ease of understanding other group members (Jackson, 1990); similar gains in social maturity as do psychodynamic groups (Viney et al., 1995); and to help members attain their therapeutic goals (Truneckova and Viney, 1997). Interpersonal transaction groups have also been found to be comparable in effectiveness to process groups in reducing depression and alleviating distress, although not in enhancing social adjustment, in women who had been sexually abused as children (Alexander et al., 1989).

In a study which revealed significant differences in the process of personal construct and cognitive therapies (Winter and Watson, 1999), these therapies were found to be comparable in their effectiveness with clients with neurotic disorders (Watson and Winter, 1997). Limited evidence has also been provided that personal construct group psychotherapy may enhance the effectiveness of exposure therapy for agoraphobia (Winter et al., 1999), while a more positive outcome on measures of depression, hopelessness and construing has been found in clients presenting with deliberate self-harm who received a personal construct psychotherapy intervention than in those in a 'normal practice' condition (Winter et al., 2000).

Although the results of most of these investigations are encouraging, and indicate effect sizes in personal construct psychotherapy which are similar to those in cognitive-behavioural and psychodynamic therapies (Viney, 1998; Winter, 2003), there is clearly a need for further controlled outcome research on constructivist approaches to counselling and psychotherapy.

Conclusion

Constructivist counselling psychology, although sometimes sharing techniques with other approaches, offers a distinct, alternative construction of the problems which may lead an individual to seek counselling, and of how these problems might best be addressed. Like a behavioural approach, it is likely to encourage the client to experiment, but unlike such an approach it is primarily concerned with the constructions underlying the client's behaviour. In contrast to rationalist cognitive approaches, it does not consider that there is a correct, rational way of viewing events, and is less concerned with the client's beliefs than with the structures and processes involved in those beliefs. Unlike the psychodynamic approach, it will not necessarily focus upon the client's past, does not generally consider that people should pass through a fixed sequence of developmental stages, and will view interpretation less as providing the client with insight than as demonstrating that an alternative construction of the client's situation is possible. It has greater commonality with those approaches, such as the humanistic and systems paradigms, which reject the deterministic, reductionist assumptions underlying the behavioural, rationalist cognitive and psychodynamic approaches. However, it differs from the humanistic approach in its view of emotions, and in making greater use of diagnostic constructs in assessing the client's predicament. It differs from some systemic approaches in its less adversarial view of the counsellor–client relationship.

Despite the contrasts between constructivism and traditional versions of many of the other counselling paradigms, there are constructivist trends in several of these paradigms, as in most other areas of human knowledge. Whatever its theoretical base, a counsellor's practice is likely to benefit if he or she takes the view that there are numerous alternative viable constructions of the client's predicament and of a successful outcome of counselling.

References

Alexander, P.C., Neimeyer, R.A., Follette, V.M., Moore, M.K. and Harter, S. (1989) 'A comparison of group treatments of women sexually abused as children', *Journal of Consulting and Clinical Psychology*, 57: 479–83.

Andersen, T. (1987) 'The reflecting team: dialogue and metadialogue in clinical work', *Family Process*, 26: 415–28.

Bannister, D., Adams-Webber, J.R., Penn, W.I. and Radley, A.R. (1975) 'Reversing the process of thought disorder: a serial validation experiment', *British Journal of Social and Clinical Psychology*, 14: 169–80.

Botella, L. and Feixas, G. (1992–93) 'The autobiographical group: a tool for the reconstruction of past life experience with the aged', *International Journal of Aging and Human Development*, 36: 303–19.

Dallos, R. (1997) *Interacting Stories: Narratives, family beliefs, and therapy*. London: Karnac Books.

Ecker, B. and Hulley, L. (1996) *Depth Oriented Brief Therapy*. San Francisco: Jossey Bass.

Evesham, M. and Fransella, F. (1985) 'Stuttering relapse: the effects of a combined speech and psychological reconstruction programme', *British Journal of Disorders of Communication*, 20: 237–48.

Feixas, G. (1992) 'Personal construct approaches to family therapy' in R.A. Neimeyer and G.J. Neimeyer (eds) *Advances in Personal Construct Psychology* II. Greenwich CT: JAI Press.

Fransella, F. (1972) *Personal Change and Reconstruction: Research on a Treatment of Stuttering*. London: Academic Press.

Guidano, V.F. (1987) *Complexity of the Self: a Developmental Approach to Psychopathology and Therapy*. New York: Guilford Press.

Guidano, V.F. (1991) *The Self in Process: Towards a Post-rationalist Cognitive Therapy*. New York: Guilford Press.

Guidano, V.F. and Liotti, G.A. (1983) *Cognitive Processes and Emotional Disorders*. New York: Guilford Press.

Ivey, A.E. (1986) *Developmental Therapy*. San Francisco: Jossey Bass.

Jackson, S. (1990) 'A PCT therapy group for adolescents' in P. Maitland (ed.) *Personal Construct Theory Deviancy and Social Work*. London: Inner London Probation Service/Centre for Personal Construct Psychology.

Kelly, G.A. (1955) *The Psychology of Personal Constructs*. New York: Norton.

Kelly, G.A. (1969) 'Personal construct theory and the psychotherapeutic interview' in B. Maher (ed.) *Clinical Psychology and Personality: the Selected Papers of George Kelly*. New York: Wiley.

Landfield, A.W. and Rivers, P.C. (1975) 'An introduction to interpersonal transaction and rotating dyads', *Psychotherapy: Theory, Research, and Practice*, 12: 366–74.

Leitner, L.M. (1995) 'Optimal therapeutic distance: a therapist's experience of personal construct psychotherapy', in R.A. Neimeyer and M.J. Mahoney (eds) *Constructivism in Psychotherapy*. Washington D.C.: American Psychological Association.

Mahoney, M.J. (1988) 'Constructive metatheory I. Basic features and historical foundations', *International Journal of Personal Construct Psychology*, 1: 135.

Mahoney, M.J. (1991) *Human Change Processes: the Scientific Foundations of Psychotherapy*. New York: Basic Books.

Mair, M. (1988) 'Psychology as storytelling', *International Journal of Personal Construct Psychology*, 1: 125–37.

McNamee, S. and Gergen, K.J. (1992) *Therapy as Social Construction*. London: Sage.

Neimeyer, G.J. (ed.) (1993) *Constructivist Assessment: a Casebook*. Newbury Park CA: Sage.

Neimeyer, G.J. and Rood, L. (1997) 'Contemporary expressions of constructivist psychotherapy' in G.J. Neimeyer and R.A. Neimeyer (eds) *Advances in Personal Construct Psychology* IV. Greenwich CT: JAI Press.

Neimeyer, R.A. (1993) 'Constructivist approaches to the measurement of meaning' in G.J. Neimeyer (ed.) *Constructivist Assessment: a Casebook*. Newbury Park CA: Sage.

Neimeyer, R. and Harter, S. (1988) 'Facilitating individual change in personal construct therapy' in G. Dunnett (ed.) *Working with People: Clinical Uses of Personal Construct Psychology*. London: Routledge.

Neimeyer, R.A. (1994) 'The role of client-generated narratives in psychotherapy', *Journal of Constructivist Psychology*, 7: 229–42.

Neimeyer, R.A. and Mahoney, M.J. (1995) *Constructivism in Psychotherapy*. Washington DC: American Psychological Association.

Neimeyer, R.A. and Raskin, J.D. (2000) *Constructions of Disorder: Meaning-making Frameworks for Psychotherapy*. Washington DC: American Psychological Association.

O'Connor, J. and Seymour, J. (1990) *Introducing Neuro-linguistic Programming*. London: Aquarian.

Procter, H.G. (1981) 'Family construct psychology: an approach to understanding and treating families' in S. Walrond-Skinner (ed.) *Developments in Family Therapy*. London: Routledge.

Selvini-Palazzoli, M., Boscolo, L., Cecchin, G. and Prata, G. (1980) 'Hypothesizing–circularity–neutrality: three guidelines for the conductor of the session', *Family Process*, 19: 3–12.

Truneckova, D. and Viney, L.L. (1997) 'Assessing the Effectiveness of Personal Construct Group Work with Problematic Adolescents', paper presented at the twelfth International Congress of Personal Construct Psychology, Seattle.

Viney, L.L. (1990) 'A constructivist model of psychological reactions to physical illness and injury' in G. Neimeyer and R. Neimeyer (eds) *Advances in Personal Construct Psychology*. I. New York: JAI Press.

Viney, L.L. (1993) *Life Stories*. Chichester: Wiley.

Viney, L.L. (1998) 'Should we use personal construct therapy? A paradigm for outcomes evaluation', *Psychotherapy*, 35: 366–80.

Viney, L.L. and Westbrook, M.T. (1981) 'Measuring patients' experienced quality of life: the application of content analysis scales in health care', *Community Health Studies*, 5: 45–52.

Viney, L.L., Henry, R.M. and Campbell, J. (1995) 'An Evaluation of Personal Construct and Psychodynamic Group Work with Centre-based Juvenile Offenders and School-based Adolescents', paper presented at the eleventh International Congress of Personal Construct Psychology, Barcelona.

Watson, S. and Winter, D. (1997) 'A Comparative Process and Outcome Study of Personal Construct, Cognitive and Psychodynamic Therapies in a British National Health Service Setting', paper presented at the twelfth International Congress of Personal Construct Psychology, Seattle.

White, M. and Epston, D. (1990) *Narrative Means to Therapeutic Ends*. New York: Norton.

Winter, D.A. (1992) *Personal Construct Psychology in Clinical Practice: Theory, Research and Applications*. London: Routledge.

Winter, D.A. and Watson, S. (1999) 'Personal construct psychotherapy and the cognitive therapies: different in theory but can they be differentiated in practice?' *Journal of Constructivist Psychology*, 12: 1–22.

Winter, D.A., Gournay, K. and Metcalfe, C. (1999) 'A personal construct psychotherapy intervention for agoraphobia: theoretical and empirical basis, treatment process and outcome' in J.M. Fisher and D.J. Savage (eds) *Beyond Experimentation into Meaning*. Lostock Hall: EPCA Publications.

Winter, D., Bhandari, S., Metcalfe, C., Riley, T., Sireling, L., Watson, S. and Lutwyche, G. (2000). 'Deliberate and undeliberated self-harm: theoretical basis and evaluation of a personal construct psychotherapy intervention' in J.W. Scheer (ed.) *The Person in Society: Challenges to a Constructivist Theory*. Giessen: Psychosozial-Verlag.

Winter, D.A. (2003) 'Personal Construct Psychotherapy: the evidence base', in F. Fransella (ed.) *Personal Construct Psychotherapy Handbook*. London: Wiley.

12 The Systems Paradigm
ROBERT BOR AND CHARLES LEGG

The systems approach in therapy is relatively new when compared with the psychoanalytic, humanistic or existential-phenomenological paradigms. In terms of therapeutic 'technology', perhaps only Freudian psychoanalysis compares in terms of the approach being as paradigm driven (Jones, 1993). The origins of the systems approach in therapy in the late 1950s can be traced back to three trends: (1) the emergence of systems theory in organizational psychology; (2) the theoretical works of Bateson (1972); and (3) the involvement of families in the understanding and treatment of major psychological problems (Bateson et al., 1956). In common with most paradigms, theory, research and practice have evolved almost beyond recognition, giving rise to important refinements and the emergence of subschools. It is interesting to note, however, that the systems paradigm appears to be more deeply embedded within clinical psychology and social work practice in the United Kingdom than within counselling psychology. In a recent survey of British counselling psychologists, only 8 per cent of respondents listed 'systems' as their preferred theoretical approach, which was considerably less than an integrative (38 per cent), cognitive behavioural (21 per cent) or psychodynamic (18 per cent) approach (Bor and Achilleoudes, 1999).

Systems is both a school of therapy in counselling psychology and a metatheory. It can be used to understand and explain a wide range of phenomena in therapy while being compatible with a range of therapeutic approaches. It differs from most of the other theoretical paradigms described in this book in a number of respects. First, there is no underlying theory of personality or motivation. Secondly, the assessment process is an integral part of the therapeutic process and cannot meaningfully be considered separately from it. Thirdly, change is viewed as a change in the functional properties of the system rather than the individual characteristics of any member of the system. Hence concepts such as the 'theory of learning' are seen as inappropriate. Fourthly, because it is a systems approach, family, group and organizational issues are inherent in the approach and cannot be meaningfully abstracted from this context. Although these issues will be addressed in this chapter, we have chosen to subdivide the material in a different manner from other chapters in this part of the book. The chapter reviews the application of a systems approach in counselling psychology. Drawing on published research, we describe the underlying theory, the assessment process, change through therapy and developments in contemporary practice. Systems theory is principally about understanding ideas in the wider social context, and it is appropriate therefore to begin this review with a brief description of the context and historical roots of the paradigm. We use the terms 'counselling' and 'therapy' throughout to refer to activities conducted within, and legitimized by, the discourse of counselling psychology.

Background to the systems paradigm

The systems paradigm shifts the focus from the individuals to the social context in which they are embedded. Instead of asking 'What is wrong with this person and how can it be corrected?' the systemic therapist asks 'How does the social system containing the individual operate to create "symptoms" in the identified "patient" and how might I create change in the system so that it no longer generates the symptoms?' The underlying concepts were derived from cybernetic theory and applied to human thought and action by Bateson (1972). Initial systems thinking focused on the family as the primary symptom-generating social system but more recent approaches have taken more account of the wider social context.

Initially, systemic theory and specific therapeutic practices went hand in hand, but there is no logical connection between the two. All therapeutic interventions take place in a social context that extends beyond the consulting room and all therapists should consider the impact of this social context on the long-term outcome of their interventions. It is possible to have a systemic view of the origins of problems while using therapeutic techniques that operate at the individual rather than the system level. This is particularly true of approaches like solution-focused or narrative therapies that identify the origins of problems in the attempts of individuals to negotiate their way through the maze of power relationships in which they are enmeshed but seek to help clients by encouraging them, as individuals, to develop new narratives or positions that redefine their relationships with a socio-political framework that is, itself, unchanged by therapy.

The basic tenets of the systems approach can be summarized as follows (see Bor et al., 1998, for a more detailed explanation of these points).

- Psychological problems need to be understood within a social and political context. Systemic counselling is always contextual.
- Interaction (reciprocity) is at the heart of all psychological inquiry and counselling practice.
- Relationships between people (whether they are family members or colleagues) are punctuated by beliefs and behaviours.
- Problems may occur at particular developmental stages of individuals or families. They may also arise when people deny 'reality'.
- Problems that present to therapists are generally expressed in language and in the course of conversation. Systems theory has contributed significantly to insights into the language of therapy.
- As with most counselling psychology approaches, the systemic therapist strives to be empathic. Counselling is a collaborative activity with the client.

The underlying theory of the systems paradigm is described below.

'Personality' and systemic theory

Personality is not a thing, it is a theoretical construct advanced to account for recurrent patterns of human behaviour. Personality-based theories of human action take an essentially ballistic view of the human mind, according to which we are hewn by early experience from the material created by our genetic endowment and then launched into adult life to continue in the trajectory established by these early experiences. Personality-based theories in counselling focus on identifying failures in this process as the source of problems in adulthood and seek to promote change by reversing the harm done in earlier life. Our view is that, when counselling psychologists talk about 'personality', they are really talking about the issue of how psychological and interpersonal problems develop. This section is written in that spirit.

Systemic theorists offer an alternative account of recurrent patterns of behaviour, one that focuses on their maintenance in the present by feedback within the system. It does so by considering the social context of the behaviour rather than the characteristics of the individual displaying that behaviour. The family offers an example of a problem-generating social system and, as already pointed out, much of the early systemic work concentrated on the clients' families as the primary source of difficulties (Jones, 1993). The principles of systemic thinking can be illustrated by descriptions of the evolution and resolution of problems in the family system, as described below. The underlying problem-generating processes may be the same in the wider social system but the interventions necessary to resolve these problems are clearly going to be different when it is impossible to bring the whole system into therapy.

Families, by definition, satisfy the minimum criteria for being a system. There is a series of elements, the family members, and they are interconnected, in that what one member of a family does affects the other members of the family. The elements and the connections between them are also enduring. The family is both a biological and a social construct and the two do not need to match. An individual may be defined socially as part of one's family but not biologically, as in the case of adoption. Although the family serves a biological function, the *experience* of an individual as a family member cannot be determined biologically.

How do family processes lead to psychological problems?

What most psychologists view as 'symptoms' systems theorists view as the product of attempted *solutions* to the problems in the family. Those problems can come about for a number of reasons. Many theorists focus on problems in communication (Bateson et al., 1956) while others focus on problems stemming from transitions within the family (Andolfi et al., 1983).

Change in the family

As family members age, so the dispositions of the individuals and the appropriateness of particular patterns of care will change. This process of change may result in psychological problems for individuals in the family (Andolfi et al., 1983; Carter and McGoldrick, 1989). According to Andolfi et al. (1983) psychological problems develop either when families *create* inappropriate solutions or when families attempt to resist change, while Carter and McGoldrick (1989) argue that problems arise when families attempt to *apply* inappropriate solutions to the problems created by change.

Andolfi et al. (1983) identify two types of family in which a developmental event is translated into individual pathology. One is the 'at risk' family, in which the tensions involved in passing through a major developmental stage are resolved by one member of the family developing symptoms in such a way as to allow the rest of the family to complete its restructuring. The other is the 'rigid' family, in which restructuring is resisted by means of an individual developing symptoms. They give as an example of an 'at risk' family one in which the maternal grandfather has died and the maternal grandmother has come to live with the family. This is a family coping with two developmental events simultaneously, the death of a member and the acquisition of a new member of a household. One solution to this problem may be for a child to regress developmentally, as a consequence of which the grandmother may acquire someone to care for, the child, and the parents can focus their anxiety on the child rather than the tensions created by having the grandmother living with them. Rigidity, they suggest, may underlie disorders like depression, where the development of depressive symptoms in the child may remove the need to restructure the family following the child's leaving home.

Andolfi et al. (1983) pointed out that 'rigidity' is not necessarily an inherent property of a family system but something that develops out of the family's attempt to deal with developmental transitions. Thus the distinction between an 'at risk' and a 'rigid' family is that the former changes its organization and the latter does not. Although the necessary modelling has not yet been carried out, there are enough formal similarities between family systems and the simple networks that have been simulated in recent years to suggest that each family may have the potential to apply different solutions to the same developmental event. That is to say, whether or not the family progresses through at the expense of the well-being of one member or gets stuck may be more a function of accidents and incidents occurring during the transition than of the properties of the family prior to the transition. Having said that, there are likely to be pre-existing family structures that make some families more prone to maladaptive outcomes than others.

While Andolfi et al. (1983) view the family as being creative, Carter and McGoldrick (1989) view the family as essentially conservative. Following from Bowen, they put forward a dual stressor model in which liability to psychological problems is the result of interactions that have persisted across a number of generations. According to this approach, life-cycle transitions create psychological problems when the family attempts to apply, inappropriately, the solutions developed by previous generations of the family. For example, if one's parents reacted to the birth of children by panicking, one would be inclined to do the same thing. Carter and McGoldrick's approach is best viewed as an extension of Andolfi et al.'s, since it reminds us that, when faced with problems, most people attempt to solve them heuristically, by applying solutions that were used in the past for similar problems. It is incomplete as a model for the development of psychological problems because it lacks an explanation of how family attitudes, taboos and expectations develop.

Psychological assessment in systemic counselling

Systemic counselling differs from other approaches in two ways. The first is in the methods used in the assessment process and the second is in the nature of the hypotheses entertained about the processes underlying the problem. The methods involve asking clients questions about relationships, the choice of operation at any point being guided by the counselling psychologist's current hypothesis about the origins of the client's problems. Typically, the hypotheses revolve around the relationships between the client and their social context, rather than intrapsychic processes (Liddle, 1983; Selvini-Palazzoli et al., 1980b; Tomm, 1984).

One of the strengths of the systems approach is that it encourages the counselling psychologist to consider the possibility that the 'problem' is located outside the identified patient. People come to counselling when there is a 'problem' but it would be naive to believe that the individuals who have been referred are always the ones with the problem. Clients may also be referred because of problems with the referring agency or with the relationship between the client and the referring agency (Selvini-Palazzoli et al., 1980a). In these circumstances the aim of the counselling psychologist would not be to deal with the referred problem but to deal with the relationship between the client and the referring agency.

The referring agency may have a very clear idea of the 'problem', as seen from their point of view, but since the aim of counselling is to work within the framework of the client it is essential to find out what they view as the problem. One of the advantages of working in the family setting is that it will remind the counselling psychologist that there may not be a single problem but there may be as many as there are members of the family, as each family member has a different perspective on the situation. At this stage the aim is to build up a picture of what the family members think the problem is as a prelude to forming a hypothesis about the underlying family dysfunction. In addition to feeding into the hypothesis-forming stage, this stage is vital for engaging the client, as it is a means of showing the client that they are being listened to.

The fundamental process in assessment is creating a hypothesis about the presenting problem in the terms of the conceptual framework with which the counselling psychologist operates. A hypothesis directs the counselling psychologist to think about the problem in a particular way and to seek particular types of information from the client. The process of counselling is therefore concerned with the refinement of a hypothesis rather than their generation of one *de novo*.

There are a number of schools of systemic therapy and, according to Liddle (1983), they differ in their approaches to the hypothesis-formation stage. We can divide them into two broad categories; those that attempt to place families along universal dimensions of family function, such as Bowen's approach (see Liddle, 1983), and those that attempt to view the family from within its own frame of reference, such as the Milan team's systemic approach (Selvini-Palazzoli et al., 1980b).

Bowen's approach is to view the family from the outside, collecting data from the parents on a number of aspects of family functioning, including the history of symptom(s) and the interaction between the nuclear family. This information is often organized using a genogram (Liddle, 1983; McGoldrick and Gerson, 1989). The aim of this information gathering is to determine, among other things, the family's level of anxiety, the degree of 'differentiation of self' of each family member, the flexibility–rigidity of the family and the family's responsiveness to stress.

Approaches like Bowen's recognize that families act as complex systems but they deal with them by trying to measure high-level system variables that are emergent properties of the system. Such an approach is possible only from a fixed reference point. The variants of the systemic approach (Liddle, 1983; Selvini-Palazzoli et al., 1980b; Tomm, 1984) explicitly deny the possibility of dealing with universal system variables. Instead of viewing the family from the outside inwards, the systemic therapist attempts to view the world from within the frame of reference of the family and thus look outwards from within.

The task of the systems therapist is to construct a model of the family's model of itself. Expressing the problem in this way highlights the point that the therapist can never come to experience the world in exactly the same way as a member of the family, although they may be able to get an idea of what it might be like to be one. The problem is that therapists always view the world through their own sets of constructs, which will not be the same as those of the family members. Most systemic therapists adopt Bateson's approach to information, which holds that:

- Information is a difference,
- Difference is a relationship (or a change in a relationship).

Thus information is a relationship, which means that the systemic therapist can concentrate on collecting the details of the relationships (or, more properly, relationships between relationships, since the concern is the relationship between the position someone holds in the family and the way that they behave towards other family members) between family members, using techniques like circular questioning and future-oriented questions (Selvini-Palazzoli et al., 1980b; Tomm, 1984). For many therapists the use of questions constitutes an assessment tool and a therapeutic intervention.

Circular questions (Penn, 1982) are difficult to define individually, as their circularity depends upon the context. The essence of the approach is for the counselling psychologist to ask questions that generate feedback that provides the basis for subsequent questions. There are a number of ways that the feedback can be obtained. For example, the counselling psychologist may attend to the non-verbal and paralinguistic cues provided by the client. Used in a family setting, circular questioning links the family members together, as one person's answer to a question can be used to generate a question to another member of the family. Circular questioning may prove a useful tool for elaborating the nature of the problem and getting the family to develop a representation of its own dynamics.

Penn (1985) suggests the technique of challenging the family with future-oriented questions. Instead of asking the family about how they feel and act now and how they felt and acted in the past, Penn proposes asking them about how they will deal with events in the future. This approach has two benefits. The first is that it may enable the client to explore alternative ways of acting that may be more adaptive for the client. By allowing the client to explore them in an environment of 'positive connotation', the counselling psychologist may facilitate the client's adopting these other modes of action in the future. The other advantage is that it allows the counselling psychologist and client to investigate the implicit assumptions, the 'premises', underlying the client's way of adapting to change, and thus to work on those premises. Having identified a premise, the counselling psychologist can ask the client to consider what might happen if they violated the assumption in some way.

In all counselling approaches, it is necessary to determine the point at which the relationship should be terminated. This is problematic because it is assumed that the 'problem' extends beyond the symptoms of the identified patient. Furthermore, the identified patient may have a problem, such as a terminal illness or brain damage, which is not susceptible to counselling. Faced with these problems, the counselling psychologist has to negotiate the end point rather than impose it. As a consequence, this process is intimately related to the process of establishing each person's expectations of therapy. It will be difficult, if not impossible, to negotiate an acceptable end point with a family that expects therapy to remove the symptoms of the identified patient without there being a change in themselves or their relationships. Following on from this point, the process must also be viewed as a therapeutic intervention as well as part of the assessment phase since it will involve getting families to think about how their lives might be different following therapy.

Assessment in systemic counselling might be expected to be much more complex than assessment in individual counselling but, in many ways, the systemic counselling context is a liberating one. Not only may systemic counselling allow one to approach problems that are inaccessible to individual methods but it also makes explicit what is implicit in most individual counselling methods, which is that most problems of individual adjustment are influenced, if not determined, by the individual's relationship with their family, and this allows the counselling psychologist to collect information about this relationship from a number of sources, rather than just from the individual client.

The systems approach to the therapeutic relationship

It is impossible to make generalizations about the therapeutic relationship within the systems framework because there are so many different approaches adopted. Clients will experience the different forms of systems-based therapy in different ways. For example, the approach of Selvini-Palazzoli et al. (1980b) recommends maintaining strict neutrality to all family members, a neutrality reinforced by the stylized assessment tools (like circular questioning) advocated by this group. At the other extreme, Andolfi et al. (1983) recommend taking an active part in the family group, even to the extent of appearing to form alliances with particular family members. The narrative approach, which has grown out of the systems approach, favours a collaborative approach that involves neutrality towards individuals but a distinctly partisan approach to the narrative themes they present. It is not always clear how therapists can be experienced as neutral by clients who are espousing either preferred or non-preferred narrative themes.

Contemporary systemic ideas: the narrative metaphor

Most psychological therapies themselves undergo change as new ideas influence practice and vice versa, and the systems approach is no exception to this. The systems approach was established with the idea that problems emerge from, and are maintained by, the immediate dynamics of social relationships. Change communication within the family and you dissolve the problem. However, disruption is a haphazard therapeutic strategy, and Bateson and his followers never satisfactorily dealt with the issue of how therapists could ensure that new, non-problematic modes of family interaction could be guaranteed to emerge from temporary changes in communication pattern. Follow-up research has indicated that, in many instances, the changes wrought in therapy are only temporary and that relying on the family to provide information about itself may lead to conspiracies of silence designed to stabilize problems in the face of therapeutic interventions (Palazzoli et al., 1989). Moreover, if 'symptoms' are the result of an entire family's attempt to resolve a problem generated by its interaction with the wider social system, disruption of communication within the family may lead only to the replacement of one problematic solution with another. How to stabilize change and how to enable change when 'problems' are solutions to the demands of the wider social context are issues addressed by the narrative approach.

The narrative approach has widened the scope of context to include social and political forces (such as gender and sexuality) and how these shape context and experience. It takes into consideration both the here-and-now experience of the client as well as history in the aetiology of problems, including the political issues referred to above, by considering how one's experience of being in a family, embedded in the power relations of a broader socio-political context, may lead one to create a story about oneself, which is carried over into other contexts. The emphasis in therapy is on language and the construction of reality (ideas).

From a narrative metaphor perspective, there is an emphasis on meaning and the importance of language as a mechanism of change (White and Epston, 1990). Therapy involves freeing the client from a particular kind of account or 'story' and opening the way to alternatives of greater possibility and promise. This approach looks to the effects of literary traditions, social conditions, cultural values and, most important, social processes. This evolution in therapy has been very greatly influenced by ideas of power and knowledge loosely based on the work of Foucault (Foucault, 1980; Rabinow, 1984), from social constructionism (Gergen, 1991) and deconstructionism (Hepburn, 1999). Finally, these ideas are situated in a narrative metaphor and much of the current thinking on narrative has been influenced by Jerome Bruner (Bruner, 1986).

Foucault's influence has made systemic therapy more responsive to issues associated with gender, power, sexual orientation and social structure. Until recently these have not featured prominently in systemic theory and practice. At best the strategic position of the therapist's neutrality towards family process and structures may have inadvertently preserved the *status quo* in the same systems. At worst, discrimination and injustice within family systems may have gone unquestioned. The narrative approach introduces the idea that it is neither ethical nor therapeutic to omit discussion about these issues in sessions.

Narrative metaphor

In a narrative metaphor people are seen as organizing their experience in the form of stories. According to Lynn Hoffman, 'It is as if reality consists of the tales people tell themselves to make sense of the world and to navigate within it' (Hoffman, 1993: 71). Narrative produces experience, and vice versa, and the relationship between narratives and experience is a circular one. A narrative metaphor proposes that people 'story' their lives and it is through storying that people structure and give meaning to their lives. This is different from saying that people describe their lives by stories, the difference being that stories lend structure to life and provide meaning. The stories by which people conduct their lives also shape them and have real effects on them. The function of narratives may be expressed as follows: 'we tell ourselves stories in order to live' (Didion, 1979: 11). People usually have several stories about their lives, with one story invariably being more dominant and influential. No single story can capture the range of richness of people's experience: 'Life experience is richer than discourse. Narrative structures organize and give meaning to experience, but there are always feelings and lived experience not fully encompassed by the dominant story' (Bruner, 1986: 143).

When individuals and families seek the help of a counselling psychologist, they usually present this dominant story which contains the so-called problem (White, 1989). It may be helpful for the counselling psychologist to think of problems as stories that people have agreed to tell themselves to justify their behaviour, and to understand exceptions as deviations from the customary or ordinary. Within this framework it is assumed that people seek counselling 'when the narratives in which they are "storying" their experience, or in which they are having their experience "storied" by others, do not sufficiently represent their lived experience. In these circumstances, there will be significant aspects of their experience that contradict these dominant narratives' (White and Epston, 1990).

It is important to note that within the narrative metaphor experience is regarded as a primary variable. This shift is part of the evolution in thinking in systemic counselling. Another major shift is the move away from thinking about positive explanations and associated ideas of circular causality. Positive explanation proposes that events take their course because they are driven in that direction, which raises ideas about causes, forces and impacts (Bateson, 1972). Narrative approaches attend more to the Batesonian emphasis on negative explanation and restraints. Negative explanation proposes that events occur in certain ways 'instead of' in other ways: 'We consider what alternative possibilities could conceivably have occurred and then ask why many of these alternatives were not followed, so that a particular event was one of those few that would, in fact, occur' (Bateson, 1972: 399).

Any event, behaviour, belief or discourse may be thought of as 'restraint' in that, when they are selected and attended to, others may not be noticed. The emphasis in thinking is no longer on 'because of' ideas (even though the 'cause' was 'circular') but rather 'instead of' ideas. One of the client's narratives may become the one that acts as a restraint, especially when there is a problem-saturated story. This narrative informs the client's thinking, and its informing ideas restrain him from noticing alternatives. The perspective of 'restraints' rather than 'causes' is fundamental to an understanding of recent developments in the theoretical underpinnings of counselling.

Implications for practice

The objective of counselling is shifted when problems are seen as 'restraints'. Previously, the client or the client's family may have been viewed as the problem, or the problem may even have been seen as serving a function. From the narrative perspective neither the person nor their relationships are viewed as the problem. 'Rather the problem becomes the problem, and the person's relationship with the problem becomes the problem' (White and Epston, 1990: 40). The objective of counselling becomes revealing stories about their relationships. The history of the problem is viewed as a story of restraint rather than of cause and effect. The counselling interview is conducted with a curiosity that seeks to investigate what has restrained the person from participating in alternative possibilities. The narrative of influence must be considered to be the overarching constraint or to contain the ideas that restrain. Problems are viewed as separate from the person, that is, existing in their ideas, beliefs (discourses) or the behaviours, but not the person. Thinking 'instead of' rather than 'because of' appears to have the effect of empowering people. The client is never given the impression that the problem is a consequence of personal inadequaces, incompetences or imperfections. It is no longer sufficient simply to try to change their behaviour without first hearing the narratives clients use to make sense of their life. The counselling psychologist will address these restraints and provide a context that will enable each client to see a world of alternative possibilities and expanding options rather than limitations and constraints. The counselling process can be conceived of as a journey of liberation from oppressive constraints to new possibilities.

The narrative metaphor introduces processes such as deconstructing, reconstructing and restorying. The counselling psychologist puts these into practice by helping the client to generate an alternative story. There is no one or 'right' way of doing this. Pioneering work in the thinking and practice of the narrative metaphor has been carried out by Michael White (1989) and David Epston (1989), and readers should consult these references to gain further insight into the practice of the narrative metaphor. Michael White, who is significantly influenced by Foucault's ideas of power and the subjugation of persons by systems of political thought, addressed the restraints by 'externalizing' the problem (White, 1989). This approach is one that encourages clients to objectify and at times to personify the problem that they experience as oppressive. The problem then becomes a separate entity and therefore external to the person or the relationship that has ascribed the problem. The process of 'externalizing' the problem can be understood as a way of loosening the restraints by separating people from them.

There is a significant difference between internalizing and externalizing discourses about the problem. Internalizing discourses locate the problem or the 'cause' of the problem in the persons' families. Externalizing discourses locate the problem in meaning systems that influence persons or families. This creates a completely different context for change.

Collaboration

Collaboration is presented as a hallmark of the current approaches within a narrative metaphor to counselling. Counselling psychologists no longer present themselves as 'experts'; counselling psychologists' experience and knowledge (called theory and expertise) are no longer privileged over the validity of the client's experience and knowledge, especially of the problem. The power of therapists resides in their ability to control the therapeutic conversation to privilege accounts of the clients' lives that the therapists deem more appropriate (Gale, 1991; Gale and Newfield, 1992; Kogan, 1998; Kogan and Gale, 1997), rather than in their knowledge of individual psychology. Therapists constrain therapeutic discourse rather than direct it. Counselling psychologists and clients are said to 'co-construct' an alternative story to the 'problem-full' one initially told by the client or family. The 'new' story is a possibility-filled one generated and co-authored in equal partnership by the two parties.

Strongly associated with the presentation of a collaborative partnership between counselling psychologist and client is the idea of openness. Counselling psychologists are encouraged to situate their ideas and questions in their own experience and to be available to answer any questions their clients may have about their thinking (White and Epston, 1990). In current practice, counselling psychologists are trying to let clients hear what they are saying about them, as when reflecting teams discuss their ideas in front of the family or client. This is in contrast to the earlier practice of a team discussion behind the one-way mirror with team 'messages' then 'sent' to the clients via the therapist.

With the significant change in the nature of the power exercised by counselling psychologist and client, there is a transformation in the counselling process, which has become less rigidly structured and managed. Thus an anthropological, research-type approach has infiltrated and influenced the format of the traditional counselling interview. According to Mischler (1986: 8), 'in the mainstream tradition [of interviewing] the idea of discourse is suppressed. Questions and answers for example are regarded as analogues of stimuli and responses rather than as forms of speech.' While he is referring to a research interview, Mischler's ideas may equally well be applied to the counsellor–client interview. Clients (interviewees) may be regarded as informants or competent observers while counselling psychologists (interviewers) are regarded as reporters or investigators who also build up 'archives' of knowledge about the nature of the problem, from the information given by the interviewees. Recent developments are characterized by counselling psychologists yielding control to clients of the flow and content of the interview, entering into a collaborative relationship and attending to what and how clients may learn from their efforts to respond meaningfully to questions within the context of their own worlds of experience.

Research evidence about effectiveness

After more than three decades, it is incorrect to suggest that research into systemic therapy is in its infancy. The results are broadly supportive of this approach across a wide range of psychological problems (Shadish et al., 1995).There are also several well established international journals in this field, including *Family Process, Journal of Family Therapy, Journal of Marital and Family Therapy, Family Systems and Health* and *Journal of Systemic Therapy*. Qualitative research methods and theoretical discussions dominate the literature in this field. Nevertheless, both outcome and process studies have been carried out.

Long-term follow-up of 'Milan' systemic therapy yielded disappointing results. Problematic patterns of interaction re-emerged and detailed debriefing of families indicated that they had often collaborated to hide significant family secrets from the therapeutic team (Palazzoli et al., 1989). On the other hand, White (White and Epston, 1990) has carried out follow-up studies on the efficacy of narrative therapy and reports clear improvements in a large proportion of cases. Process studies of conventional systemic therapy are rare, but there have been a number of such studies of narrative approaches (Gale, 1991; Gale and Newfield, 1992; Kogan, 1998; Kogan and Gale, 1997). According to these studies, therapeutic efficacy depends on tight control of the therapeutic agenda. Therapists use a variety of conversational strategies to ensure that exceptions and solutions to problems remain in play, while reiterations of problems are discouraged. There are methodological difficulties associated with these studies (Wynne, 1988), but these limitations are not confined to the assessment of the effectiveness of the systems approach (Roth and Fonagy, 1998; Rowland and Goss, 2000).

Critique and conclusion

The systems approach in counselling psychology is relatively new in comparison with some other approaches. Recent developments in the field will be most clearly viewed and assessed at a distance and by the next generation of practitioners. The future of the systems approach belongs to practitioners who work towards the integration of different approaches within the systems paradigm, rather than to those who seek to develop 'brand name' approaches (Broderick and Schrader, 1991). Nonetheless, there are some strikingly creative and interesting approaches being developed for a range of topical issues, such as working with gays, lesbians and their families (Bepko and Johnson, 2000), different cultural groups (Park, 2000) and with families coping with the chronic illness of one of their members (Cohen, 1999).

The systems approach can be criticized at the level of the adequacy of the metaphor and the lack of a clear statement of mechanisms of cognitive and behavioural change. The problem of the metaphor is simply stated. At the level of generality at which the concept is applied to counselling, the systems metaphor lacks predictive or prescriptive power. When systems theory is articulated into coherent models that possess predictive and prescriptive power, however, such as negative feedback systems, they do not map on to counselling because cybernetic systems tend to be inherently conservative while therapy is about creativity and change. Systemic counselling models, including those based on the narrative metaphor, contain no explicit account of how emotional, cognitive or behavioural events arise and change. The Batesonian model provides an incomplete description of systems, because it does not describe the properties of the individual elements that make up family systems. In their more extreme forms (Paré, 1995) narrative models expressly deny the value of proposing that people have properties over and above the stories they tell about themselves. The models, therefore, give us an account of how change might take place but not *why* problems are problems because there is no account of how either family dynamics or the development of specific narratives might cause the distress that motivates pursuit of therapy, nor of how distress might motivate the development of problematic solutions.

There has been a large-scale swing away from using the cybernetic/biological machine-type metaphor for conceptualizing about counselling to the more narrative-type metaphors where ideas of interest are those of narrative, semantics and linguistics. Essentially informing ideas of these metaphors are that they are psychologically non-objectivist but reify social and political constructs (Madigan, 1992; Paré, 1995; Pilgrim, 2000). That is to say, they use a political framework to make psychological constructs problematic. The strength of systemic, including narrative, approaches is that they stand in direct opposition to deficit models, focusing on the creativity and resourcefulness of clients in the face of problems, rather than their limitations.

References

Andolfi, M., Angelo, C., Menghi, P. and Nicolo-Corgliano, A.M. (1983) *Behind the Family Mask: Therapeutic Change in Rigid Family Systems*. New York: Brunner Mazel.

Bateson, G. (1972) *Steps to an Ecology of Mind*. New York: Ballantine.

Bateson, G., Jackson, D.D., Hayley, J. and Weakland, J. (1956) 'Toward a theory of schizophrenia', *Behavioral Science*, 1: 251.

Bepko, C. and Johnson, T. (2000) 'Gay and lesbian couples in therapy: perspectives for the contemporary therapist', *Journal of Marital and Family Therapy*, 26 (4): 409–20.

Bor, R. and Achilleoudes, H. (1999) 'Survey of BPS Division of Counselling Psychology Members, 1999', *Counselling Psychology Review*, 14 (4): 35–44.

Bor, R., Miller, R., Latz, M. and Salt, H. (1998) *Counselling in Health Care Settings*. London: Cassell.

Broderick, C.B. and Schrader, S.S. (1991) 'The history of professional marriage and family therapy' in A.S. Gurman and D.P. Kniskern (eds) *Handbook of Family Therapy* II. New York: Brunner Mazel.

Bruner, J. (1986) *Actual Minds, Possible Worlds*. Cambridge MA: Harvard University Press.

Carter, B. and McGoldrick, M. (1989) 'Overview: the changing family life cycle – a framework for family therapy' in B. Carter and M. McGoldrick (eds) *The Changing Family Life Cycle: a Framework for Family Therapy*, second edition. Boston MA: Allyn & Bacon.

Cohen, M. (1999) 'Families coping with childhood chronic illness: a research review', *Families, Systems and Health*, 17 (2): 149–64.

Didion, J. (1979) *The White Album*. New York: Simon & Schuster.

Epston, D. (1989) *Collected Papers*. Adelaide SA: Dulwich Centre.

Foucault, M. (1980) *Power/Knowledge: Selected Interviews and Other Writings 1972–1977*. New York: Pantheon Books.

Gale, J.E. (1991) *Conversation Analysis of Therapeutic Discourse: the Pursuit of a Therapeutic Agenda*. Advances in Discourse Processes XLI. Norwood NJ: Ablex.

Gale, J. and Newfield, N. (1992) 'A conversation analysis of a solution-focused marital therapy session', *Journal of Marital and Family Therapy*, 18: 153–65.

Gergen, K.J. (1991) *The Saturated Self*. New York: Basic Books.

Hepburn, A. (1999) 'Derrida and psychology: deconstruction and its ab/uses in critical and discursive psychologies', *Theory and Psychology*, 9: 639–65.

Hoffman, L. (1993) *Exchanging Voices: a Collaborative Approach to Family Therapy*. London: Karnac.

Jones, E. (1993) *Family Systems Therapy*. Chichester: Wiley.

Keeney, B. (1983) *Aesthetics of Change*. New York: Guilford Press.

Kogan, M. (1998) 'The politics of making meaning: discourse analysis of a "postmodern" interview', *Journal of Family Therapy*, 20: 229–51.

Kogan, S.M. and Gale, J.E. (1997) 'Decentering therapy: textual analysis of a narrative therapy session', *Family Process*, 36: 101–26.

Levine, D.S. (1991) *An Introduction to Neural and Cognitive Modelling*. Hillsdale NJ: Erlbaum.

Liddle, H.A. (1983) 'Diagnosis and assessment in family therapy: a comparative analysis of six schools of thought' in J.C. Hansen and B.P. Keeney (eds) *Diagnosis and Assessment in Family Therapy*. Rockville MD: Aspen.

McGoldrick, M. and Gerson, R. (1989) 'Genograms and the family life cycle' in B. Carter and M. McGoldrick (eds) *The Changing Family Life Cycle: a Framework for Family Therapy*, second edition. Boston MA: Allyn & Bacon.

Madigan, S.P. (1992) 'The application of Michel Foucault's philosophy in the problem externalizing discourse of Michael White', *Journal of Family Therapy*, 14: 265–79.

Mischler, E.G. (1986) *Research Interviewing*. Cambridge MA: Harvard University Press.

Paré, D.A. (1995) 'Of families and other cultures: the shifting paradigm of family therapy', *Family Process*, 34: 1–19.

Park, R. (2000) 'Beyond white and middle class: cultural variations in families – assessments, processes and policies', *Journal of Family Psychology*, 14 (3), 331–3.

Penn, P. (1982) 'Circular questioning', *Family Process*, 21: 267–80.

Penn, P. (1985) 'Feed-forward: future questions, future maps', *Family Process*, 24: 299–310.

Pilgrim, D. (2000) 'The real problem for postmodernism', *Journal of Family Therapy*, 22: 6–23.

Rabinow, P. (1984) *The Foucault Reader*. New York: Pantheon.

Raimy, V. (ed.) (1950) *Training in Clinical Psychology*. New York: Prentice Hall.

Roth, A. and Fonagy, P. (1998) *What Works for Whom?* London: Routledge.

Rowland, N. and Goss, S. (2000) *Evidence-based Counselling and Psychological Therapies*. London: Routledge.

Selvini-Palazzoli, M., Boscolo, L., Cecchin, G. and Prata, G. (1980a) 'The problem of the referring person', *Journal of Marital and Family Therapy*, 6: 3–9.

Selvini-Palazzoli, M., Boscolo, L., Cecchin, G. and Prata, G. (1980b) 'Hypothesizing–circularity–neutrality: three guidelines for the conductor of the session', *Family Process*, 19: 3–12.

Selvini-Palazzoli, M., Cirillo S., Selvini, M. and Sorrentino, A.M. (1989) *Family Games: General Models of Psychotic Processes in the Family*. London: Karnac.

Shadish, W., Ragsdale, J., Glaser, R. and Montgomery, L. (1995) 'The efficacy and effectiveness of marital and family therapy: a perspective from meta-analysis', *Journal of Marital and Family Therapy*, 21 (4): 345–60.

Tomm, K. (1984) 'One perspective on the Milan systemic approach' II, 'Description of session format, interviewing style and interventions', *Journal of Marital and Family Therapy*, 10: 253–71.

White, M. (1989) *Selected Papers*. Adelaide SA: Dulwich Centre.

White, M. and Epston, D. (1990) *Narrative Means to Therapeutic Ends*. New York: Norton.
Wynne, L. (ed.) (1988) *The State of the Art in Family Therapy Research*. New York: Family
   Process Press.

Acknowledgement

We are very grateful to Isobel Scher, who contributed to some of the ideas in this chapter.

13 The Eclectic and Integrative Approach
HENRY HOLLANDERS

The title of this chapter may be somewhat misleading. The use of the definite article suggests that there may be such a thing as *the* eclectic and/or *the* integrative approach to counselling, in much the same way as there is, broadly speaking, *the* Psychodynamic approach, *the* Person-centred approach, or *the* Cognitive-behavioural approach. This is not the case. In practice eclecticism and integration take many different forms. What unites eclectic or integrative practitoners is a desire to move beyond the boundaries of a single approach in order to make use of the rich diversity that characterizes the field of counselling. Basically, it is an attempt to leave behind the narrow confines of 'schoolism', so often associated with exclusivism and dogmatism, and to enter into the unending challenge of finding out what contributes to an effective and truly therapeutic encounter between *this* therapist and *this* client, in *this* situation

Practitioner 'stances'

When faced with the challenge of practising counselling with a particular client, any counselling psychologist is bound to take up one of a number of different stances. Possible stances, relevant to the subject of this chapter, include: Purist, Eclectic, Integrative, Pluralistic, Holistic and Syncretistic. A stance may be taken up either explicitly (intentionally) or implicitly (by default). Moreover, the stance that is taken up may be maintained throughout the counselling, or it may be shifted from session to session and, perhaps, even from time to time within the session. The position taken up in this chapter is that it is in the best interests of both the client and the practitioner for the stance to be both explicit and maintained throughout the counselling. To take up a stance implicitly, and to move frequently from one implicit stance to another, is likely to be subjecting the client to the worst, rather than the best, of all worlds.

The purist stance

The purist identifies herself with only one particular therapeutic approach. She will profess to be true to this approach and will refuse to be seduced by techniques and procedures from elsewhere. Purism may take at least two forms, superficially similar to each other, but basically very different. The first is associated with schoolism. Schoolism is characterized by binary thinking (i.e. 'This', over against 'That'), and those immersed in schoolistic attitudes are likely to defend passionately the 'truth' of their own school and attack with vigour the 'errors' of rival schools. The second form purism may take, however, is less pugnaciously evangelistic and more akin to pluralism. A counselling psychologist may adopt a purist approach to her work because she sees the value and wisdom of adhering to a single orientation, and of belonging to the community of practitioners associated with that orientation. It need not follow from this that she will brand all other ways of working as 'erroneous' and 'dangerous' (see, for example, Klein, 1999). She may recognize her own approach simply to be one among many, but, importantly, it is the one she has chosen (presumably because, at some level, she considers it to be the best), and she will follow it consistently throughout her practice. Nevertheless, she will be prepared to acknowledge its weaknesses as well as delight in its strengths.

The eclectic stance

Those who take up an eclectic stance towards practice will be prepared to adopt a range of techniques and procedures from different approaches. If, however, they are to avoid what has been dubbed as 'haphazard' eclecticism (Dryden, 1984; Lazarus, 1990) they must find some way of making systematic and coherent treatment choices that will enable them to practise consistently over time. This has been attempted in a number of different ways. Some practitioners have adopted a 'mainstream' orientation, to which they add whatever seems to be useful from other approaches for particular clients. Others have opted for a more recognizable eclectic framework that enables them to make systematic use of a variety of skills and techniques by matching them with different stages in the counselling process. Examples of such frameworks are Egan's Skilled Helper model (Egan, 1998; Jenkins, 2000) and Lazarus's Multi-modal therapy (Lazarus, 1981; Palmer, 2000). Eclecticism, in this sense, is sometimes referred to as Systematic Eclecticism (Dryden, 1991) or Technical Eclecticism (Norcross and Newman, 1992; Lazarus, 1992).

The integrative stance

'Integration' covers a wide range of attitudes and perspectives. In the literature the terms 'Integrative' and 'Eclectic' are often used interchangeably (Hollanders, 1996, 2000b). When a distinction is drawn, however, it is usually along the lines of making out that eclecticism is primarily concerned with techniques, whereas integration is primarily concerned with theories. Thus, on the one hand, the systematic eclectic will seek to bring a number of techniques together into some coherent whole without necessarily having regard to the theory of origin. The integrationist, on the other hand, will seek to combine different theories into a new theory that is more comprehensive than any of the individual theories it has brought together. An example of this kind of integration is Cognitive Analytic Therapy (CAT) (Ryle, 1991; Crossley and Stowell-Smith, 2000), which combines theoretical elements from Object Relations theory, Systems theory,

Cognitive theory and Personal Construct theory. The result is an approach with a unique theoretical foundation that translates well into a form of practice.

It is likely, however, that this kind of distinction between eclecticism and integration (i.e. techniques versus theories) is too clear-cut and narrow to be meaningful to grass-roots practitioners. There is some evidence that many who tentatively describe themselves as 'integrative' are working with a much broader concept of what integration means in practice (Norcross and Prochaska, 1988; Hollanders and McLeod, 1999). In his 'Introductory Statement' for the first issue of the *Journal of Psychotherapy Integration* (*JPI*), Arkowitz (1991) writes:

> In psychotherapy integration, representatives of different therapy approaches have shown a willingness to look beyond the confines of their own orientations in order to discover what can be learned from other ways of thinking about psychotherapy and change. In its most general sense, psychotherapy integration encourages an attitude of openness and exploration to help understand why people change, how they change, and how to better help them change, unrestrained by the limitations imposed by adherence to one particular approach or theory. (p. 1)

It is this broader definition that is favoured by Goldfried (1999), who speaks of integration as 'an umbrella term that encourages flexibility in how we think about the change process and how we can work clinically' (p. 237).

In this broad sense, then, an integrative stance is one in which a practitioner seeks to remain open in her thinking and flexible in her way of working. She will have a clear theoretical base but will consider it to be an open rather than a closed theory, and will be prepared to make any changes that may be called for as a result of her own, and others', reflective practice and research. She will be ready to explore widely and be creative in ways that will take her beyond a single theory. At grass-roots level this may be almost indistinguishable from an eclectic stance (Hollanders 2000b), and for this reason, for the most part, the term 'integration' will be used in the remaining sections of this chapter to cover both the integrative and the eclectic stances.

The pluralist stance

From a philosophical perspective Ayer (1982) describes pluralism as 'denying that there is a single world, which is waiting there to be captured, with a greater or lesser degree of truth, by our narratives, our scientific theories or even our artistic representations'. According to this perspective 'there are as many worlds as we are able to construct by the use of different systems of concepts, different standards of measurement, different forms of expression and exemplification' (p. 13). Writing from a more psychotherapeutic perspective, Samuels (1989) considers pluralism to demonstrate 'an attitude to conflict that tries to reconcile differences without imposing a false resolution on them or losing sight of the unique value of each position' (p. 1). According to this view pluralism is also concerned with 'oneness', not so much by trying to bring everything together into an integrated whole as by recognizing that diversity has its place within 'a unified version of the field, a cohesive vision of psycho-therapy' (Samuels, 1993: 320). Thus pluralism is an attempt to hold unity and diversity in balance.

In practice it is likely that a practitioner who takes up a pluralist stance will work within a single approach because she considers that to be the most con-sistent way of working. However, she will not hold to that approach as though it is *the* truth. Indeed, she will recognize that other approaches also have gen-uine, and even equal, value. If she feels confident and competent enough to work with a number of different approaches she will be happy to do so, *but not with the same client*. Ideally, a pluralist practitioner will work closely with col-leagues from a number of different orientations, to whom she can refer when she considers that particular clients will gain more benefit from an approach other than her own. In this sense the pluralist stance is similar to the more liberal purist stance described above. The main difference between the two is probably in the realm of epistemology, in that the liberal purist is more likely to consider her particular approach to be closer to *the* truth than any other, whereas the pluralist will not think of *the* truth at all!

The holistic stance

While Holism has been mainly associated with the Humanistic schools of ther-apy (Graham, 1986; West, 2000), it is a concept that has been taken up by some integrationists (Clarkson, 1993; Goldberg, 1996; O'Brien and Houston, 2000). Broadly, a holistic stance will involve seeing the individual as a whole person within her/his total context. The holistic practitioner will be concerned with the body as well as with the mind, with the socio-economic context as well as the internal world, with culture and culturally embedded beliefs as well as emotional and cognitive states, with the meaning and influence of 'universal' symbols as well as with individually created metaphors, with community values and norms as well as with the process of self-actualization. Precisely how this will be done will depend on the philosophical and theoretical base of each therapist, but clearly it is an immensely demanding task. Inevitably, the responsible holistic practitioner will be broadly integrative in the sense that in such a wide-ranging undertaking she will need to draw from many different disciplines. She must also find some way of doing so within a coherent and ethical form of practice.

The syncretistic stance

'Syncretism' is the term used by Norcross and Newman (1992) to denote 'uncritical and unsystematic combinations' of theories and techniques. They further explain, 'This haphazard "eclecticism" is primarily an outgrowth of pet techniques and inadequate training, an arbitrary, if not capricious, blend of methods "by default"' (p. 20). In this sense, the Syncretistic stance is not a stance at all but a kind of shifting around the field without a map, or with a number of disconnected map fragments. Consequently there is no clear direction or purpose.

A question of commitment

A superficial observation on the above stances may be that only the purist practitioner seems to have anything like a genuine and clear commitment to a position. The others, to varying degrees, appear to be uncommitted and are, therefore, more likely to lack conviction and direction when it comes to practice. Indeed, this is the main thrust of the criticism levelled by Szasz (1974) against eclecticism:

> The eclectic psychotherapist is, more often than not, a role player; he wears a variety of psychotherapeutic mantles, but owns none and is usually comfortable in none. Instead of being skilled in a multiplicity of therapeutic techniques, he suffers from what we may consider, after Erikson, 'a diffusion of professional identity'. In sum, the therapist who tries to be all things to all people may be nothing to himself; he is not at one with any particular method of psychotherapy. If he engages in intensive psychotherapy, his patient is likely to discover this. (p. 41).

Whilst this criticism may be true of *some* eclectic practitioners, it is more relevant to those who take up a syncretistic stance. Interestingly, Prochaska (1984) has applied Perry's (1970) model of intellectual and ethical development to the development of the psychotherapist. (It can, of course, be applied equally to the counselling psychologist.) In this view, the process of development runs through four primary stages – 'Dualistic' (*this* is *the* truth, *that* is error); 'Multiplistic' (*the* truth, which I have in its fullest form, can be found in a partial form in other systems); 'Relativistic' (truth is relative rather than absolute and will be constructed in different ways in different situations by different people – however, I have a lingering sense that my construction will be better than yours!); and finally 'Committed' (a recognition that none of us has *the* truth – the best we can do is to go on with humility, trying to find/construct meaning together). Following this developmental line, it can be seen that 'commitment', in this sense, is quite different from rigid adherence to a single therapeutic orientation. Instead, the commitment that characterizes the mature practitioner is to the whole project of therapy – a project in which she is jointly engaged with a great variety of equally committed partners from diverse backgrounds.

A brief outline of the development of integration in counselling and psychotherapy

The concept of integration in psychotherapy is by no means new or novel. It is true that the early history of counselling and psychotherapy is dominated by the development of different schools, each eager to assert its superiority over the others. Nevertheless, even within that early adversarial climate, another strand of development can be traced. As early as 1932, French, in an address delivered to the American Psychiatric Association, sought to draw attention to the commonalities he considered to exist between Freudian psychoanalysis and Pavlovian conditioning (French, 1933). His presentation received a mixed, but largely unenthusiastic, reception. In the ensuing years eclecticism/integration did not flourish, though there is some evidence for the existence of a 'therapeutic underground' (Goldfried and Davison, 1976; Wachtel, 1977) made up of those practitioners who publicly identified themselves with a single orientation but who, in the privacy of their own studies and consulting rooms, were prepared to open themselves to influences from other approaches. Some lone voices were raised intermittently in favour of a more eclectic/integrative therapeutic stance in the 1930s, 1940s and 1950s (e.g. Rosenzweig, 1936; Watson, 1940; Dollard and Miller, 1950), but it was only in the 1960s that a discernible movement towards eclecticism/integration began to emerge and gather momentum (e.g. Alexander, 1963; Marmor, 1964; Marks and Gelder, 1966; Paul, 1966; Weitzman, 1967; Bergin, 1968; Kraft, 1969). It was in this decade that Jerome Frank published his important work *Persuasion and Healing* (1961), in which he sought to distil the prime factors that produce change in the lives of individuals. This volume has been described by Arkowitz (1992) as 'one of the most influential early writings on common factors' (p. 277). In 1967 Arnold Lazarus, working along different lines from those of Frank, introduced the concept of 'technical eclecticism' (Lazarus, 1967).

By the 1970s practitioners were beginning to openly identify themselves as eclectic in growing numbers. Surveys of American practitioners conducted by Garfield and Kurtz (1974, $n = 855$) and Jayaratne (1978, $n = 489$) both indicated that 55 per cent of those surveyed adopted the label 'eclectic' to describe their therapeutic orientation.

In 1975 Gerard Egan published the first edition of *The Skilled Helper*, setting out an eclectic framework for a 'problem management approach' to the counselling process. Egan began from an essentially humanist position but in subsequent revisions of his work (2001 being the latest) he shifted progressively towards a more action-oriented form of helping. The counselling process is presented as going through three main stages: Exploration, Understanding and Action (later to be retitled Present Scenario, Preferred Scenario and Getting There), with each stage having an appropriate set of skills associated with it. Egan's approach has had a major influence on training programmes for counsellors in the United Kingdom.

An important contribution to the debate on integration in the 1970s was made by Paul Wachtel with the publication of *Psychoanalysis and Behavior Therapy* (1977). Wachtel retained the psychoanalytic concepts of the unconscious, dynamic conflict, and the influence of the 'inner world' on interactions with the 'outer world'. At the same time, however, he paid attention to a number of behavioural principles, including the importance of the present environmental context in which problematic behaviour takes place; the real influence of present as well as past interpersonal relationships, and the need for active interventions by the therapist in working with clients/patients towards identified goals. In the 1980s Wachtel developed his approach more fully, using the term 'cyclical dynamics' to describe it (Wachtel, 1987).

During the 1980s and 1990s a number of surveys of practitioners indicated that the broad trend among counsellors, psychologists and psychotherapists towards eclecticism/integration was continuing (Hollanders, 2000a). However, many of these surveys were conducted in America among clinical psychologists. From the few surveys that were conducted in the United Kingdom there were some indications that clinical psychologists were less likely to identify themselves as eclectic than their American counterparts (O'Sullivan and Dryden, 1990; Norcross et al., 1992).

The formation of the Society for the Exploration of Psychotherapy Integration (SEPI) was a hugely significant event in the development of a professional identity for integrative practitioners. The society's first newsletter appeared in 1983, and by 1991 there was sufficient growth in the membership to warrant the publication of the first issue of its official journal, the *Journal of Psychotherapy Integration*.

Publications on eclecticism and integration increased dramatically in the 1980s and 1990s. Some significant publications that appeared during these years included:

- *The Integration of the Psychotherapies* (Mahrer, 1989).
- *Handbook of Eclectic Psychotherapy* (Norcross, 1986), later substantially revised and produced as *Handbook of Psychotherapy Integration* (Norcross and Goldfried, 1992).
- *Comprehensive Handbook of Psychotherapy Integration* (Striker and Gold, 1993).
- *Key Concepts in Psychotherapy Integration* (Gold, 1996).

Important British contributions to the debate included:

- 'Questions of training: a contribution from a peripatetic cousin' (Dyne, 1985).
- *Eclecticism and Integration in Counselling and Psychotherapy* (Dryden and Norcross, 1990): mainly American contributors, but with a British editor and put together and published in Britain.
- *Cognitive Analytical Therapy* (Ryle, 1990).
- 'A multiplicity of psychotherapeutic relationships' (Clarkson, 1990), later expanded into *The Therapeutic Relationship* (Clarkson, 1995).
- *Integrative and Eclectic Therapy* (Dryden, 1992), mainly American contributors, but with a British editor and publisher.
- 'Searching for integration in counselling practice' (Fear and Woolfe, 1996).

Publications on eclecticism and integration have continued to appear regularly in the first two years of this century, the most recent being:

- *Integrative and Eclectic Counselling and Psychotherapy* (Palmer and Woolfe, 2000).
- *Integrative Therapy: A Practitioner's Guide* (O'Brien and Houston, 2000).
- *Integration in Counselling and Psychotherapy* (Lapworth et al., 2001).

These represent just a few of the many publications now available to those who are concerned to go further into the subject. Those who want a more detailed history of the eclectic/integrative movement are referred to Hollanders (1996, 2000a).

Current trends influencing the movement towards integration

A number of trends can be identified that have had some influence on the development of integration within the field of counselling. Constraints on space prevent an analysis of all of them, but in the following sections we will highlight those trends related to the maturation of the field of counselling, and those related to philosophical developments associated with postmodernism.

The maturing field

The movement towards integration could be seen as an almost inevitable part of the process of maturation of the whole field of counselling. This process has a number of strands.

A movement away from chaos towards order

The history of counselling has been marked by a great proliferation of approaches. By the mid-1980s in excess of 400 different varieties of coun-selling/psychotherapy had been identified (Karasu, 1986). Though some may consider this to be indicative of richness, it has become increasingly difficult to avoid the criticism that the field is in a state of chaos, with no sense of unified identity. One factor that gave impetus to the movement towards integration was a growing sense of the need to take stock, to consolidate, rather than to continue to multiply. In the light of this it is somewhat unfortunate that, to date, integration has succeeded only in adding yet more (integrative) approaches to the already crowded pool. Nevertheless, the task of creating a more visibly unified field is important if counselling is to gain credibility as a profession.

A movement away from charismatic leaders towards a more critical analysis of systems, irrespective of personality factors

In earlier days, the mainstream counselling approaches were closely associated with the charismatic personalities of the founders. The status of 'guru' was actively sought by some, while others had it conferred on them by their follow-ers irrespective of their own contrary inclinations. The teaching associated with the different schools was of a dogmatic kind that required faith from the adher-ents. The danger was that counselling would become a kind of quasi-religious movement. However, there were those of a more philosophical or scientific frame of mind, who were concerned to apply a more critical analysis to the 'belief' systems, irrespective of the kudos of the founders. This kind of analysis was bound to raise important questions, such as 'What actually works?' 'If it works, what is it that makes it work?' 'Who does it work for?' 'Do some things work better for some clients, while other things work better for other clients?' As long ago as 1967 Paul was urging practitioners to move beyond the narrow boundaries of the different approaches by asking more closely,' *What* treatment, by *whom*, is most effective for *this* individual with *this* specific problem, and under *which* set of circumstances?' (Paul, 1967: 111).

Answers to such questions cannot be found convincingly in dogma. They can be truly explored only through the processes of research. While the questions must concern all practitioners, it is only the practitioner with an integrative spirit who can address them from outside the constraints of a single orientation. This is not to suggest that integrationists have been any more successful than any one else at research, but simply to point out that they have placed themselves in a position in which there is greater potential for addressing the questions more comprehensively than those who confine themselves to a single approach. If this is so, then it is also the case that eclectic/integrative practitioners have a greater responsibility to engage more comprehensively in the processes of research.

Away from individual pursuits towards collective professional responsibility

The gradual development of counselling into a regulated profession raises many questions that cannot be addressed here. The process of professionalization, however, implies that at some level there is a recognized need for individuals to form themselves into a more coherent body of practitioners, with a unified professional identity under the title of 'Counselling'. For this to happen in any meaningful way, two basic conditions must be fulfilled. First, the emphasis on the freedom of the individual to do 'her own thing' must give way to a greater sense of collective professional responsibility. Secondly, there must be a readiness by practitioners to listen to each other, to be prepared to move closer to each other wherever possible, and to become more 'ecumenical' in spirit if they are to live in one house, under one roof. In the end, it may be neither possible nor desirable to develop a single, shared paradigm, but if counsellors are to form a credible profession occupying a place alongside other related professions, the different parts of our diverse field must be prepared to actively engage with each other. It is within this ethos that the project of integration, in its broadest sense, has found its place.

The philosophical climate

Another major influence on the movement towards integration has been the change in the philosophical climate during the last century. Counselling, like every other movement, is influenced by the philosophical trends of the day. This can be seen most overtly in the humanistic and existential approaches, but it is no less true of the other approaches. As a philosophical movement, postmodernism, though difficult to define in a precise way, had a profound effect on life in the second half of the twentieth century. Some postmodern themes relevant to counselling in general, and to integration in particular, can be summarized as follows.

The demise of the meta-narratives/discourses

A meta-narrative is a way of seeing and understanding the world. It is a kind of 'big story', which shapes our thinking, structures our experience and influences all the ways in which thought and experience are expressed. It is the ground out of which our concepts of self emerge, the boundaried territory within which we gain some way of evaluating our life. The meta-narratives pervade all our texts as forms of 'truth' that are so basic to the coherence of the whole that it does not occur to us to question them – or even to notice them! However, with the rapid advances in the realms of science and technology it has become increasingly difficult for the old meta-narratives (e.g. those related to the established structures of power and authority) to continue to hold sway. The technological revolution has produced a way of life that is moving at a breathtaking pace. New positions, ideas, movements and concepts are bombarding us from every direction, and with a rapidity that means that as soon as an idea has been formulated it is broadcast, and a moment later (or so it seems) it has become redundant in the face of a new one (Gergen, 1996). Under this onslaught, the old established certainties are crumbling. What were once considered to be enduring universal truths have begun to look like nothing more than constructions produced under social, political, cultural and economic influences.

The importance of the process of deconstruction

If we are to uncover the ways in which the meta-narratives have infiltrated our stories about ourselves and our world (including the world of counselling) we must engage in the process of deconstruction (Karasu, 1996; Parker, 1999). It is important, however, to distinguish between deconstruction and destruction. Deconstruction is not a blatant act of destruction that sweeps everything away. Rather, it is a careful taking apart, piece by piece, in order to make clear the way our apparently 'enduring truths' are actually no more, and no less, than socially and culturally embedded constructs. This is no merely academic exercise. It is a radical process, and requires great courage (some might say foolhardiness!), since what is being deconstructed is the very foundation on which we are standing. In the face of such a daunting challenge, which carries with it the risk of disintegration, some may take refuge in a deeper entrenchment in the meta-narratives (e.g. the resurgence of fundamentalism in all its forms, and its purist counterpart in counselling). For those who take up the challenge, however, there is the prospect of new kinds of constructions emerging out of very different perspectives on what constitutes 'knowledge' and how it is formed. These new constructions will themselves be subjected to the process of deconstruction and reconstruction, over and over again, thus opening up the possibility of endlessly creating and recreating our 'selves' and the world around us. At the end of the day, total deconstruction may be impossible, since we may never be able to situate ourselves fully outside the meta-narratives. Nevertheless, all who are concerned that the constructs with which they are working should not become fixed in forms that fail to relate to the rapidly changing contexts in which they are situated must take the challenge it presents very seriously.

The role of language in the creation of 'realities'.

To the postmodernist, 'truth' (or, better, 'knowledge') is neither absolute nor fully objective. It is not something that exists 'out there', waiting to be delivered through a process of revelation (religion). Nor is it 'in here', within the closed system of the universe, waiting to be found through a process of discovery (science). Rather, knowledge is created through a process of construction, and always under personal, social, political, cultural and economic influences. In this process of construction language plays a central role. Language is considered to be actively engaged in the creation of concepts rather than simply the means by which concepts are expressed. Much postmodern philosophy is concerned with the way language functions in the creation of an illusion of 'realities', while at the same time conveying the impression that it is describing only 'realities' that actually exist. In other words, philosophy (at least in its postmodern form) is finally giving up the quest for 'the truth' beneath the surface, and, instead, is focusing its attention on the 'surface' (language) itself, since the surface is all there is – and all that is needed!

The philosophical themes summarized above face counsellors with a challenge. Like everything else, counselling came into being in a cultural and social context produced by the meta-narratives, and it continues to function within that context. The theoretical orientations are not enduring truths to be preserved at all costs. Rather, they must be seen as constructs that are socially, politically, culturally and economically 'embedded'. As such they must be subjected to a continual process of deconstruction. Karasu (1996) sees this process as an 'integral part of the search for new shapes and structures without necessarily negating those of the past, paving the way for unprecedented possibilities that better befit contemporary needs' (Karasu, 1996: viii). In the end, of course, we may choose to reject this whole analysis of our current situation, but we may be in danger of becoming stuck in a backwater if we ignore the great flow of influence postmodernism has already had on society, and the consequential implications for our practice. Whilst in no way implying that all integrationists are postmodernists or social constructionists, it is in the climate created by this kind of radical pluralist philosophy that integration, in the broadest sense, has emerged as a deeply significant movement in the counselling world.

Issues confronting the 'would-be' integrative practitioner

Becoming a responsible integrative practitioner demands considerable rigour, and there are a number of issues that those who are seeking to develop a more integrative approach to their practice must begin to get to grips with. Some of these are summarized briefly in this section.

Integration: an approach or a process?

How are you to conceptualize integration? Is it an approach you are seeking to find, or a process, without an end point, to be engaged in? For some, integration means to embark on the quest for an approach that will incorporate what is useful from other approaches to such a degree that it will gain widespread, possibly even universal, acceptance. When arrived at, this will become *the* approach that will give definition to the whole field. It is clear, however, that we are nowhere near such a position, and it is highly unlikely that it will be achieved in the foreseeable future, if ever. For others, less ambitiously, integration involves the adoption of an existing integrative (or eclectic) approach, within which they can practise in a coherent way (e.g. cognitive analytic therapy (Ryle, 1990), or multi-modal therapy (Lazarus, 1981). There are others, however, for whom integration is not about the creation or adoption of specific approaches at all. For these practitioners integration is an on-going process. They retain their existing theoretical orientation, but from this base they engage in an integrative process that constantly presents them with the challenge of making responsible use of the riches to be found in the therapeutic world and beyond.

Where is the 'locus of integration': external or internal?

Following on from the first issue, the 'would-be' integrative practitioner needs to consider her own primary 'locus of integration'. Where does integration take place? For some it takes place primarily in an approach that brings things together in a coherent way (external). For others it takes place primarily in the therapist as she engages in each new therapeutic relationship (internal) (Clarkson, 1995; Gold, 1996; Wosket, 1999). Of course, these two perspectives are not diametrically opposed to each other, and most integrative practitioners will, no doubt, consider that they have both an external and an internal 'locus'. Any approach needs to be internalized before it can be used effectively, and any internal integration needs to gain some form of expression in practice that can at least be described and given a rationale. Nevertheless, it is clear that a specific integrative approach is essential to those for whom the primary locus of integration is external. For those to whom it is internal, however, the emphasis is not so much on the application of an approach as on the moment-by-moment use of self-in-relationship in the counselling session.

How can 'incommensurable paradigms' be held together at the same time?

Kuhn (1970) used the term 'the incommensurability of paradigms' to express the idea that an individual cannot view the world in two fundamentally different ways at the same time. This is an important issue for the would-be integrative practitioner, since it strikes at the heart of the integration movement, raising the question of whether it is a viable project at all. It is, perhaps, a particularly disturbing issue for those who hold on to the hope that one day, through the process of integration, some kind of 'grand theory of everything' will emerge to replace all existing partial theories. It is less troubling, however, for those who view integration from a constructionist perspective. For these, since there is no accessible absolute reality, all paradigms are only constructions of 'what is' (Gergen, 1996, 1997). Each paradigm may have its own validity as a construction, but none has validity as 'absolute truth'. Viewed in this way, it is entirely possible to see things first from this perspective, and then from that. The therapeutic task can then be understood to be one in which the client's 'story' (or narrative) is explored from as many constructed perspectives as possible, in order for her to make use of them in a creative reconstruction of her own. The question for the constructionist now becomes quite different from that posed at the beginning of this section. Rather than asking whether it is possible to hold conflicting paradigms together, the constructionist, as an integrative practitioner, must ask what is the most responsible way to move around, and between, the different constructions whilst retaining a sense of coherence, in the best interests of the client?

Issues related to language and community

Most counsellors would be likely to agree that it is not good to practise in a kind of splendid isolation. Identification with a community which gives a sense of belonging is important. The question for the 'would-be' integrationist is 'Where will you go to find friends with whom you can communicate in such a way as to feel understood rather than regarded with suspicion?' The Counselling Psychology Division of BPS provides some form of community identification, but only in a general way. Cognitive-behavioural practitioners have a broad community with which they identify, and within which they speak the same language. The same is true of both Humanistic and Psychodynamic practitioners. Those within these communities can engage in debates with a reasonable expectation of being understood. But with which community is the integrationist to identify herself and which language is she to speak? If she has a theoretical home base along mainstream lines she may be inclined to identify herself with that particular community, but since she doesn't totally commit to that way of theorizing and practising this may be problematic for both the practitioner and the community. This issue has been partially addressed through the formation of the Society for the Exploration of Psychotherapy Integration (SEPI), which has begun to provide integrationists with a broad communal identity of their own.

What constitutes good practice, supervision and training?

This three-part question requires a book of its own. All that can be done here is to highlight the issues that the 'would-be' integrationist must find some way of addressing. The question of good practice is, in some ways, closely related to the issue raised immediately above, in as much as, at some level, the community is likely to be the arbiter of what constitutes good practice. For example, the cognitive behavioural community will determine good cognitive behavioural practice. However, in the absence of a clearly defined community, who is to determine good practice for the integrationist? In extreme form, in the context of a court of law, where will an expert witness be found if the practitioner in question is integrative? For those integrationists who practise within a recognized integrative approach the issue is less acute, since there is some identifiable form of practice that the practice of the individual can be set against. For those integrationists who rely on the use of self-in-relationship as the integrative factor, however, the issue is more problematic. In that case, is the individual practitioner alone to be the judge of good practice? This leads into the related issues of training and supervision. The communities in which integrative practitioners are trained carry considerable responsibility for setting out sound and rigorous principles that can be used by the individual in determining good practice. This, of course, is the responsibility of all training providers, integrative or not, but it is heavier and more urgent for those who offer an integrative programme which is not contained within a wider theoretically orientated community. Likewise, the supervisor must play her part in determining with the counsellor what is good or bad practice. Although a number of integrative approaches to supervision are being developed (Carroll and Tholstrup, 2001), it may not be necessary for the integrative practitioner to have an integrative supervisor. Indeed, a good case can be made out for having a succession of supervisors from different mainstream orientations. What *is* necessary, however, is for the supervisor to be sympathetic to integration, so that there can be a collaborative and creative process of matching, in a careful and responsible way, what the supervisor has to offer with the integrative practice of the supervisee.

There is, however, another, and quite different, way of approaching the issue of what constitutes good practice. From this perspective, good practice is determined by the outcomes achieved rather than by the consensus of the community. We will return to this later under the heading of 'Client-led integration' (below).

Integration in practice

From issues confronting the 'would-be' integrationist we turn to considering ways in which some have already begun to put integration into practice. Reference has been made earlier to technical eclecticism, pluralism and theoretical integration as ways of conceptualizing and working towards integration in practice (see Practitioner 'stances', above). The limitation of space prevents further discussion of these here. In this section we will focus briefly on: 'common factors'; 'the place of the relationship in integration'; 'using a "home base" in the integrative process' and 'client-led integration'.

The common factors approach to integration

This is based on the idea that there seems to be a broad equivalence of outcomes among the main-line therapies (Luborsky et al., 1975; Smith et al., 1980; Stiles et al., 1986). If so, the truly therapeutic factors in each are likely to have more to do with similarities than with differences. Further, it is also likely that these similarities are more to do with non-specific factors than with any overlaps of theory between the different approaches. Karasu (1986) identified three common factors that he considered were shared by all the therapeutic approaches: affective experiencing, cognitive mastery and behavioural reformulation. Norcross and Grencavage (1989) examined the writings of fifty different 'common factors practitioners', grouping the common factors identified by each under the headings: client characteristics, therapist qualities, processes of change, treatment structures and relationship elements. The client characteristics reported most frequently as being favourable to positive outcomes were 'hope' and 'faith'. As might be expected, in the light of this, the most frequently reported therapist qualities were the ability to generate hope and expectation of change. Under 'relationship elements', there was general endorsement of the importance of the alliance.

The common factors pathway to integration may be seen as a kind of preliminary research project that has potential for leading to the development of a specific approach that makes more overt and effective use of the commonalities. One attempt at building such an approach is the somewhat loosely structured Eclectic Therapy of Sol Garfield (1992). More recently Lapworth et al. (2001) have built their integrative approach around what they consider to be the generic elements of counselling and psychotherapy. Their list of sixteen elements, which they claim has been compiled on the basis of research studies, reading the literature and practice experience, includes: the therapeutic alliance; being listened to so as to be able to listen to oneself; being acknowledged; empathy; normalizing experience; challenging and confronting; structuring time for reflection, and consistency and continuity. However, it is not necessary for the common factors concept of integration to lead to the formation of a new approach. It has a less formal application, in that studies along this line of inquiry may simply provide counsellors with some insights to be put to good use in their existing practice.

The place of the relationship in integration

One factor that all the therapies have in common is the therapeutic relationship, and this has become a focus of considerable interest across the therapies in recent years (Feltham, 1999). It has, of course, always been of paramount importance to the psychodynamic and humanistic therapies, though in quite different ways. For many integrationists, the relationship is the central integrating factor (Kahn, 1997; Gold, 1996), and a number of integrative approaches have been based on the idea that different uses are made of the relationship, and different things are required from it, at different times in the therapy (Clarkson, 1990, 1995; Murphy and Gilbert, 2000). 'Reading' the relationship, using oneself in the process of developing and understanding the relationship, and being able to 'translate' diverse therapeutic interventions into the relationship, whilst experiencing and observing their effect on the relationship, are all important aspects of the integrative process.

Using a 'home base' in the integrative process

It is likely that most integrative practitioners in the United Kingdom retain a home base in one of the main-line therapies (Hollanders, 1996). For these practitioners, however, having a home base doesn't mean being confined to home! They are prepared to go out and about and to embark on a process of exploration and discovery that will enable them to bring back home whatever may be useful. In reality (as distinct from the metaphor!) this is not a simple process. '*What* is to be brought back?' and '*How* is it to be incorporated into the home base?' are questions of crucial importance. To take something from one context and place it into another is bound to produce some change in the item itself (the intervention), or in the context into which is it brought (the base theoretical orientation), or in both. In more formal terms, the question here is whether the process of integration is to be primarily assimilative or accommodative.

Assimilative integration places the emphasis on the imported intervention and the need for it to be moulded to fit the shape of the place given to it in the home base. For example, two-chair work originated in Gestalt as a way of enabling different polarities within the self to be explored, and to facilitate dialogue between them. This technique has occasionally been imported into behaviour therapy as part of the process of rehearsal, in which a client rehearses in the therapy an interaction between herself and another individual, in preparation for putting it into practice outside the session. It is clear that in the process of assimilating the technique into the behavioural home base it has become quite a different kind of intervention.

Accommodative integration, on the other hand, focuses more on the way the home base may need to be adjusted to make a space for the imported intervention. Inevitably every bit of accommodation changes, to some degree, the nature of the accommodating orientation. Thus, returning to the example used above, rather than simply taking the two-chair technique and using it in a thoroughly behavioural way, the accommodative integrative/behaviour therapist will allow herself to be challenged by the original purpose of the intervention, and will be prepared to explore the ways in which her current theory base and practice may be appropriately adjusted to accommodate it. In reality, those who approach integration from a mainstream 'home base' are very likely to be both assimilative and accommodative to some degree. Which perspective predominates will probably depend on how tightly/loosely the integrationist is attached to the home base. What is generally agreed, however, is that whatever is assimilated or accommodated should come out of/be subjected to the processes of empirical research. Those who wish to explore this more fully than can be done here are referred to a special edition of the *Journal of Psychotherapy Integration* (Messer, 2001) where these issues are debated in some depth.

Client-led integration

Jacobson (1999), though making no claims to be an integrationist, and even professing to be ignorant of what integration is about, made an interesting and challenging contribution to the debate from the perspective of a radical behaviourist. He suggested that if therapists are shaped by the naturally reinforcing contingencies in their environment it is likely that they will move closer to each other in the way they practise, and, in consequence, a kind of integration will take place:

> I am wondering whether or not, over time, therapists working with similar types of clients look more and more alike, regardless of theoretical orientation, as their clients shape them by reinforcing certain behaviours and punishing others. If so, we may find in the natural environment, a kind of integration of techniques that explains the common refrain you hear from clinicians all the time, 'I do whatever works.' (p. 227)

This all depends, however, on whether a therapist is open to such reinforcing contingencies or is bound defensively to a paradigm. This, in turn, is related to whether a therapist is reinforced in her behaviour by processes validated and valued by the paradigm or by positive outcomes for the client. In practice, to be paradigm-bound, and reinforced by processes, means that if the paradigm values emotional catharsis (for example), and the therapist manages to produce emotional catharsis in the client during a session, then the therapist will be reinforced in her beliefs and behaviours, irrespective of whether or not this has any positive effect on the client's actual problem outside the session. Similarly, if the paradigm places the relationship between client and therapist in a central position, and a warm and mutually accepting relationship is produced, then, again, the therapist will be reinforced in her practice, even if this bears no relation whatsoever to improvement in the client's actual condition outside the therapy session. Jacobson comments:

> clients can think their therapists are wonderful, refer other people to them, even though it is obvious to everyone that the client has not changed at all. I am astounded by how often this happens. I have known dozens of people in therapy ... where literally nothing has changed except that they now have a therapist they think is wonderful. (p. 232)

On the other hand, if a therapist is reinforced by outcomes, and allows what she does in her practice to be moulded by how much a client actually improves in her life (e.g. the depression lifts, or the panic attacks are fewer), then it is likely that she will find that she is practising in ways that are similar to other therapists who are also moulded and reinforced by outcomes. It is in this sense that clients' actual 'in life' behaviour will shape and reinforce practitioners' therapeutic behaviour, and, at the same time, unwittingly assist in the process of integration. All of this, of course, is open to discussion – particularly Jacobson's somewhat narrow and, perhaps, naive understanding of what is involved in the use of the therapeutic relationship. Nevertheless, the call to all therapists to examine what it is that reinforces their practice is timely and challenging, and entirely relevant to the integration debate.

Integration in research

Careful research into counselling at all levels is being increasingly recognized as a necessity if this emerging profession is to take its place alongside other related and more established professions. Steps have been taken in this direction and, though still in its early stages, a research base is being gradually built up by most main-line approaches (e.g. Bergin and Garfield, 1994; Roth and Fonagy, 1996; Chambless and Gillis, 1993; Department of Health, 2001). Since a major emphasis of the integration movement is on the need to go on discovering and using what works best, what has been empirically validated, rather than being bound by theoretical dogma, it might be expected that research would be high on the integrationist's list of priorities. To some extent this is the case. Nevertheless, it is generally agreed that insufficient outcome research into eclectic/integrative approaches has been undertaken (Barkham, 1992; Lambert, 1992; Glass et al., 1993; Glass et al., 1998). Glass et al. (1998) have highlighted five main areas in which research has already been undertaken, but more is needed. These are:

- Combining techniques from existing approaches.
- Prescriptive matching of client characteristics with an eclectic selection of interventions.
- Research on common and specific change factors across different pure-form therapies.

- Psychotherapy derived from integrative theories of psychological disorders (i.e. integrative treatment packages for specific disorders).
- Psychotherapy derived from integrative models of therapeutic change.

Although a number of research studies are cited by the authors in each of these areas, more are called for. In particular, Glass et al. (1998) point out that since 'integrative and eclectic theorists and clinicians have often claimed that their more flexible and broader-based therapies are *more* effective than pure-form therapies', it is crucial to the whole project of integration that these approaches should be subjected to rigorous research. While this is an area in which research is sparse, there are some integrative approaches that have made good progress in this direction. These include the Transtheoretical Approach of Prochaska and DiClemente (1992), and Ryle's Cognitive Analytic Therapy (1990). Those who wish to pursue particular research studies are referred to Roth and Fonagy (1996), Chambless and Gillis (1993), Glass et al. (1998) and Mackay and Barkham (1998).

The way ahead

It is likely that integration in counselling will continue to develop in the twenty first century, and that it will be pursued along four main lines:

- *The on-going quest for an all-embracing theory* that will provide a universally agreed definition of what counselling is all about. In spite of the seemingly insuperable theoretical and philosophical problems connected with this project, it is likely that some will continue to pursue it.
- *The development of specific eclectic/integrative approaches.* During the second half of the twentieth century a number of integrative approaches emerged and disappeared. Some, however, have been more durable, and these continue to draw a considerable amount of interest. Most notable among them, for British readers, are Cognitive Analytic Therapy and Interpersonal Dynamic Therapy, which developed out of Hobson's Conversational Therapy (Hobson, 1985). We can expect more eclectic/ integrative approaches to be developed in the twenty first century.
- *The continued development of assimilative and accommodative integration.* It is likely that most grass-roots integrative practitioners will continue to retain their base theoretical orientations and go on finding creative ways of building a wide range of diverse (and preferably empirically validated) interventions into them. It is possible that, in time, some predominantly accommodative integrationists will find that accommodation has been pursued to such a degree that a new approach has emerged. This, however, is not the prime purpose, and if it does turn out to be the case the newly emerged approach must itself be subjected to on-going accommodative processes in order to remain truly integrative.
- *The development of the integrative 'statesperson'.* It is hoped that in the coming years we may see the emergence of integrationists who will function as 'statespersons' within the profession. Rather than pursuing a purely personal interest in integration, they will have the experience and expertise to take on the role of developing 'connected-ness' between the different parts of the whole field. Their task will be to stand

between the various schools, encouraging dialogue, debate and, even, creative conflict. They will not be against the existence of the distinctive individual schools of therapy, but will work with what already exists, and will do what they can to encourage each school to push its boundaries to the limit. There are some therapeutic pathways that can be traced only from the position of the psychodynamicist, others that only the cognitive behaviourist will be able to find, and the same will be true of each of the mainstream orientations. The integrationists will strive to act as interpreters of the ensuing developments and of their relevance to the field as a whole. They will do what they can to facilitate a growing sense of unity within continuing diversity, to bring the 'many' into a sense of connectedness with the 'one'. Though not directly related, we might make a link between this and an interesting suggestion from Josephine Klein (1999), that a new tier should be developed within the profession. It would consist of specially trained and experienced 'assessment consultants' or 'referral consultants', who would have the specialist task of assessing clients for therapy. She considers that it would be important for those in such a role to be broad in their vision and to be in touch in a thoroughly informed way with a whole range of therapies, in order to be able to make appropriate referrals.

Of course, it is not possible to tell precisely how integration will develop in the coming years, but all the evidence points to its continuation and growth as a major movement in the therapeutic world.

References

Alexander, F. (1963) 'The dynamics of psychotherapy in the light of learning theory', *American Journal of Psychiatry*, 120: 440–8.

Arkowitz, H. (1991) 'Introductory statement: psychotherapy integration come of age', *Journal of Psychotherapy Integration*, 1 (1): 1–3

Arkowitz, H. (1992) 'Integrative theories of therapy' in D.K. Freedheim (ed.), *History of Psychotherapy: a Century of Change*. Washington DC: American Psychological Association.

Ayer, A.J. (1982) *Philosophy in the Twentieth Century*. London: Unwin.

Barkham, M. (1992) 'Research on integrative and eclectic therapy' in W. Dryden (ed.) *Integrative and Eclectic Therapy: a Handbook*. Buckingham: Open University Press.

Bergin, A.E. (1968) 'Technique for improving desensitisation via warmth, empathy and emotional re-experiencing of hierarchy events' in R. Rubin and C.M. Franks (eds) *Advances in Behavior Therapy*. New York: Academic Press.

Bergin, A.E. and Garfield, S.L. (eds) (1994) *Handbook of Psychotherapy and Behavior Change*, fourth edition. New York: Wiley.

Carroll, M. and Tholstrup, M. (eds) (2001) *Integrative Approaches to Supervision*. London: Jessica Kingsley.

Chambless, D.L. and Gillis, M.M. (1993) 'Cognitive therapy of anxiety disorders', *Journal of Consulting and Clinical Psychology*, 61: 248–60.

Clarkson, P. (1990) 'A multiplicity of psychotherapeutic relationships', *British Journal of Psychotherapy*, 7 (2): 148–63.

Clarkson, P. (1993) *On Psychotherapy*. London: Whurr.

Clarkson, P. (1995) *The Therapeutic Relationship*. London: Whurr.

Crossley, D. and Stowell-Smith, M. (2000) 'Cognitive analytic therapy', in S. Palmer and R. Woolfe (eds) *Integrative and Eclectic Counselling and Psychotherapy*. London: Sage.

Department of Health (2001) *Treatment Choice in Psychological Therapies and Counselling: Evidence Based Clinical Practice Guideline*. London: Department of Health Publiciations.

Dollard, J. and Miller, N.E. (1950) *Personality and Psychotherapy: an Analysis in Terms of Learning, Thinking and Culture*. New York: McGraw-Hill.

Dryden, W. (1984) 'Issues in the eclectic practice of individual therapy' in W. Dryden (ed.) *Individual Therapy in Britain*, London: Harper & Row.

Dryden, W. (1991) *A Dialogue with John Norcross: Towards Integration*. Milton Keynes: Open University Prss.

Dryden, W. (ed.) (1992) *Integrative and Eclectic Therapy: a Handbook*. Buckingham: Open University Press.

Dryden, W. and Norcross, J. (eds) (1990) *Eclecticism and Integration in Counselling and Psychotherapy*. Loughton: Gale Centre.

Dyne, D. (1985) 'Questions of 'training': a contribution from a peripatetic cousin', *Free Associations* 3: 92–145.

Egan, G. (1975) *The Skilled Helper*. Pacific Grove CA: Brooks Cole.

Egan, G. (1998) *The Skilled Helper*, sixth edition. Pacific Grove CA: Brooks Cole.

Fear, R. and Woolfe, R. (1996) 'Searching for integration in counselling practice', *British Journal of Guidance and Counselling*, 24: 399–411.

Feltham, C. (ed.) (1999) *Understanding the Counselling Relationship*. London: Sage.

Frank, J.D. (1961) *Persuasion and Healing*. Baltimore MD: Johns Hopkins University Press.

French, T.M. (1933) 'Interrelations between psychoanalysis and the experimental work of Pavlov', *American Journal of Psychiatry*, 89: 1165–203.

Garfield, S.L. (1992) 'Eclectic psychotherapy: a common factors approach', in John C. Norcross and Marvin R. Goldfried (eds) *Handbook of Psychotherapy Integration*. New York: Basic Books.

Garfield, S.L. and Kurtz, R. (1974) 'A survey of clinical psychologists: characteristics, activities and orientations', *Clinical Psychologist*, 28: 7–10.

Gergen, K.J. (1996) Keynote address delivered at the World Congress on Psychotherapy, Vienna, July.

Gergen, K.J. (1997) *Realities and Relationships*. Cambridge MA: Harvard University Press.

Glass, C.R., Victor, B.J. and Arnkoff, D.B. (1993) 'Empirical research on integrative and eclectic psychotherapies' in G. Striker and J.R. Gold (eds) *Comprehensive Handbook of Psychotherapy Integration*, New York: Plenum Press.

Glass, C.R., Arnkoff, D.B. and Rodriguez, B.F. (1998) 'An overview of directions in psychotherapy integration research', *Journal of Psychotherapy Integration*, 8 (4): 187–209.

Gold, J.R. (1996) *Key Concepts in Psychotherapy Integration*. New York: Plenum Press.

Goldberg, C. (1996) 'Critical issues confronting the profession of psychotherapy: now and into the new millenium', *International Journal of Psychotherapy*, 1 (1): 23–33.

Goldfried, M.R. (1999) 'A participant-observer's perspective on psychotherapy integration', *Journal of Psychotherapy Integration*, 9 (3): 235–42.

Goldfried, M.R. and Davison, G.C. (1976) *Clinical Behavior Therapy*. New York: Rinehart & Winston.

Graham, H. (1986) *The Human Face of Psychology*. Milton Keynes: Open University Press.

Hobson, R.F. (1985) *Forms of Feeling: the Heart of Psychotherapy*. London: Tavistock Publications.

Hollanders, H.E. (1996) 'Eclecticism/Integration among Counsellors in Britain in Relation to Kuhn's Concept of Paradigm Formation'. Ph.D. thesis, Keele: University of Keele.

Hollanders, H.E. (2000a) 'Eclecticism/integration: historical developments' in S. Palmer and R. Woolfe (eds) *Integrative and Eclectic Counselling and Psychotherapy*. London: Sage.

Hollanders, H.E. (2000b) 'Eclecticism/integration: some key issues and research' in S. Palmer and R. Woolfe (eds) *Integrative and Eclectic Counselling and Psychotherapy*. London: Sage.

Hollanders, H.E. and McLeod, J. (1999) 'Theoretical orientation and reported practice: a survey of eclecticism among counsellors in Britain', *British Journal of Guidance and Counselling*, 27 (3): 405–14.

Jacobson, N.S. (1999) 'An outsider's perspective on psychotherapy integration', *Journal of Psychotherapy Integration*, 9 (3): 219–33.

Jayaratne, S. (1978) 'Characteristics and theoretical orientations of clinical social workers: a national survey', *Journal of Social Service Research*, 4 (2): 17–30.

Jenkins, P. (2000) 'Gerard Egan's skilled helper model' in S. Palmer and R. Woolfe (eds) *Integrative and Eclectic Counselling and Psychotherapy*. London: Sage.

Kahn, M. (1997) *Between Therapist and Client: the New Relationship*. New York: Freeman.

Karasu, T.B. (1986) 'The specificity versus non-specificity dilemma: toward identifying therapeutic change agents', *American Journal of Psychiatry*, 143: 687–95.

Karasu, T.B. (1996) *The Deconstruction of Psychotherapy*, Northvale NJ: Aronson.

Klein, J. (1999) 'Assessment – what for? Who for?' *British Journal of Psychotherapy*, 15 (3). 333–45.

Kraft, T. (1969) 'Psychoanalysis and behaviorism: a false antithesis', *American Journal of Psychotherapy*, 23: 482–7.

Kuhn, T.S. (1970) *The Structure of Scientific Revolutions*, second edition. Chicago: University of Chicago Press.

Lambert, M.J. (1992) 'Psychotherapy outcome research: implications for integrative and eclectic therapists' in J.C. Norcross and M.R.Goldfried (eds) *Handbook of Psychotherapy Integration*. New York: Basic Books.

Lapworth, P., Sills, C. and Fish, S. (2001) *Integration in Counselling and Psychotherapy: Developing a Personal Approach*. London: Sage.

Lazarus, A.A. (1967) 'In support of technical eclecticism', *Psychological Reports*, 21: 415–16.

Lazarus, A.A. (1981) *The Practice of Multimodal Therapy*. New York: McGraw-Hill.

Lazarus, A.A. (1990) 'Why I am an eclectic (not an integrationist)' in W. Dryden and J.C. Norcross (eds) *Eclecticism and Integration in Counselling and Psychotherapy*. Loughton: Gale Centre.

Lazarus, A.A. (1992) 'Multimodal therapy: technical eclecticism with minimal integration' in J.C. Norcross and M.R. Goldfried (eds) *Handbook of Psychotherapy Integration*. New York: Basic Books.

Luborsky, L., Singer, B. and Luborsky, L. (1975) 'Comparative studies of psychotherapies: is it true that "Everybody has won and all must have prizes"?' *Archives of General Psychiatry*, 32: 995–1008.

Mackay, H. and Barkham, M. (1998) 'Report to the national and psychological therapies clinical guidelines group: evidence from Cochrane Reviews, published reviews and meta-analyses 1990–1998'. University of Leeds, Psychological Therapies Research Centre, Memo 369. Leeds: University of Leeds.

Mahrer, A. (1989) *The Integration of Psychotherapies: a Guide for Practising Therapists*. New York: Human Sciences Press.

Marks, I.M. and Gelder, M.G. (1966) 'Common ground between behaviour therapy and psychodynamic methods', *British Journal of Medical Psychology*, 39: 11–23.

Marmor, J. (1964) 'Psychoanalytic therapy and theories of learning' in J. Masserman (ed.) *Science and Psychoanalysis* VII. New York: Grune & Stratton.

Messer, S.B. (ed.) (2001) Special issue: Assimilative Integration, *Journal of Psychotherapy Integration*, 11 (1).

Murphy, K. and Gilbert, M. (2000) 'A systematic integrative relational model for counselling and psychotherapy' in S. Palmer and R. Woolfe (eds) *Integrative and Eclectic Counselling and Psychotherapy*, London: Sage.

Norcross, J.C. (1986) 'Eclectic psychotherapy: an introduction and overview' in J.C. Norcross, *Handbook of Eclectic Psychotherapy*. New York: Brunner Mazel.

Norcross, J.C., Dryden, W. and Brust, A.M. (1992) 'British clinical psychologist: a national survey of the BPS Clinical Division', *Clinical Psychology Forum*, 40: 19–24.

Norcross, J.C. and Goldfried, M.R. (eds) (1992) *Handbook of Psychotherapy Integration*. New York: Basic Books.

Norcross, J.C. and Grencavage, L.M. (1989) 'Eclecticism and integration in counselling and psychotherapy: major themes and obstacles', *British Journal of Guidance and Counselling*, 17 (3): 227–47.

Norcross, J.C. and Newman, C.F. (1992) 'Psychotherapy integration: setting the context' in J.C. Norcross and M.R. Goldfried (eds) *Handbook of Psychotherapy Integration*, New York: Basic Books.

Norcross, J.C. and Prochaska, J.O. (1988) 'A study of eclectic (and integrative) views revisited', *Professional Psychology: Research and Practice*, 19 (2): 170–4.

O'Brien, M. and Houston, G. (2000) *Integrative Therapy: a Practitioner's Guide*. London: Sage.

O'Sullivan, K.R. and Dryden, W. (1990) 'A survey of clinical psychologists in the South East Thames Health Region: activities, role and theoretical orientation', *Clinical Psychology Forum*, October: 21–6.

Palmer, S. (2000) 'Multimodal therapy' in S. Palmer and R. Woolfe (eds) *Integrative and Eclectic Counselling and Psychotherapy*. London: Sage.

Palmer, S. and Woolfe, R. (eds) (2000) *Integrative and Eclectic Counselling and Psychotherapy*. London: Sage.

Parker, I. (ed.) (1999) *Deconstructing Psychotherapy*. London: Sage.

Paul, G.L. (1966) *Insight versus Desensitization in Psychotherapy*. Stanford CA: Stanford University Press.

Paul, G.L. (1967) 'Strategy in outcome research psychotherapy', *Journal of Consulting Psychology*, 31: 109–18.

Perry, W. (1970) *Forms of Intellectual and Ethical Development in the College Years: a Scheme*. New York: Holt Rinehart & Winston.

Prochaska, J.O. (1984) *Systems of Psychotherapy: a Transtheoretical Analysis*, second edition. Homewood IL: Dorsey Press.

Prochaska, J.O. and DiClemente, C.C. (1992) 'The transtheoretical approach' in J.C. Norcross and M.R. Goldfried (eds) *Handbook of Psychotherapy Integration*. New York: Basic Books.

Rosenzweig, S. (1936) 'Some implicit common factors in diverse methods in psychotherapy', *American Journal of Orthopsychiatry*, 6: 412–15.

Roth, A. and Fonagy, P. (1996) *What Works for Whom? A Critical Review of Psychotherapy Research*. New York and London: Guilford Press.

Ryle, A. (1990) *Cognitive Analytical Therapy: Active Participation in Change – New Integration in Brief Psychotherapy*. Chichester: Wiley.

Ryle, A. (1991) Reformulation (revised 1991), CAT course notes. London: UMDS, Guy's Hospital.

Samuels, A. (1989) *The Plural Psyche: Personality, Morality and the Father*. London and New York: Routledge.

Samuels, A. (1993) 'What is a good training?' *British Journal of Psychotherapy*, 9 (3): 317–323.

Smith, M.L., Glass, G.V. and Miller, T.J. (1980) *The Benefits of Psychotherapy*. Baltimore MD: Johns Hopkins University Press.

Stiles, W.B., Shapiro, D.A. and Elliot, R. (1986) 'Are all psychologists equal?' *American Psychologist*, 41: 165–80.

Striker, G. and Gold, J.R. (eds) (1993) *Comprehensive Handbook of Psychotherapy Integration*. New York: Plenum Press.

Szasz, T.S. (1974) *The Ethics of Psycho-analysis: the Theory and Method of Autonomous Psychotherapy*. London: Routledge.

Wachtel, P.L. (1977) *Psychoanalysis and Behavior Therapy: Toward an Integration*. New York: Basic Books.

Wachtel, P.L. (1987) *Action and Insight*. New York: Guilford Press.

Watson, G. (1940) 'Areas of agreement in psychotherapy', *American Journal of Orthopsychiatry,* 10: 698–709.

Weitzman, B. (1967) 'Behavior therapy and psychotherapy', *Psychological Review,* 74: 300–17.

West, W. (2000) *Psychotherapy and Spirituality: Crossing the Line between Therapy and Religion.* London: Sage.

Wosket, V. (1999) *The Therapeutic Use of Self.* London: Routledge.

Part IV
Psychological Interventions: Developmental Themes

14

The Life Course as a Meta-model for Counselling Psychologists
LÉONIE SUGARMAN

The notion of life-span development was gathered fairly late under the umbrella of psychology. It was not until 1980 that it received the accolade of a paper devoted to it in the *Annual Review of Psychology*. Here life-span developmental psychology was defined as being 'concerned with the description, explanation, and modification (optimization) of developmental processes in the human life course from conception to death' (Baltes et al., 1980: 66). Whilst this definition still holds true today, its manifestation in research and practice has not remained static. Thus 'descriptions' have tended to shift from the search for the universal to the understanding of the particular, 'explanations' have become increasingly contextualized and 'modifications' increasingly client-centred.

As in a figure–ground relationship, life-span developmental psychology provides counselling psychologists with a framework in which to locate their practice. It provides what Egan calls a working knowledge – that is, a theoretical and research knowledge translated into 'the kind of applied understandings that enable helpers to work with clients' (1990: 17). Clients are seen as 'existing at the centre of a matrix where life events combine and conspire with the ageing process to present each person, at any one time, with a unique set of challenges' (Woolfe, 2001: 347). Development remains, however, a contested concept. It is not the same thing at all points in the life course, if only because in adulthood development is less dependent than during childhood on biological and maturational processes (Baltes, 1987). Instead, social, cultural and cohort influences are paramount. Rather than focusing on life-span development, therefore, it is sometimes better to concentrate on the life course as a site for theorizing concepts – that is, as a framework for exploring flexible biographical patterns within a continually changing social system (Featherstone and Hepworth, 1989). The life course also provides a framework within which the relevance and limitations of concepts developed in relation to one life stage can be refined by exploring their application to other life stages.

Methodologically, research in life-span developmental psychology frequently repudiates theoretically derived hypothesis testing in favour of:

> more basic descriptive work, including a more systematic use of autobiography, storytelling and conversation, diaries, literature, clinical case histories, historical fiction, and the like, with a new emphasis upon the person's construction and reconstruction of the 'life story,' rather than what might be considered a more objective account of what happened. (Datan et al., 1987: 154).

It shares this position with much research in the field of counselling psychology (see, for example, Lynch, 1997; McLeod, 1997, 2000) and both disciplines have played a significant role in the narrative turn that engulfed the social sciences in the latter years of the twentieth century.

Order in the life course

Life-span developmental psychology has consistently addressed the question of the extent to which the shape and content of the human life course are ordered and predictable. Such order as is found has traditionally been conceptualized as a series of stages that predominantly reflect either the maturational unfolding of an individual's potential or the age-based norms, expectations and pressures prevailing within the person's social and cultural environment. Erikson's (1980) theory of eight developmental crises stretching from infancy to old age underpins many stage-based accounts of the life course. Whilst acknowledging the importance of the environment, particularly the social environment, Erikson's theory nonetheless veers towards an internal rather than external locus of the developmental imperative. It borrows from embryology the epigenetic principle that 'anything that grows has a ground plan, and out of this ground plan the parts arise, each part having its time of special ascendency, until all forms have arisen to form a functioning whole' (Erikson, 1980: 53). Jung, likewise, depicts each phase of the life course as having its own characteristics, potentialities and limitations: 'we cannot live the afternoon of life according to the program of life's morning, for what in the morning was true will at evening be a lie. Whoever carries into the afternoon the law of the morning ... must pay with damage to his soul' (1972: 396).

Building on the work of Erikson, Jung and others, Levinson's (1990, 1996; Levinson et al., 1978) description of the 'seasons' of adult life has become one of the most widely cited stage-based accounts of the adult life course. Levinson's model is non-hierarchical in that whilst each phase of life is seen as having its defining characteristics, later stages (or 'seasons') are not necessarily seen as better. Whilst not all researchers have replicated Levinson's findings (Clausen, 1993), and the supposed universality of Levinson's stages has been questioned, the overall shape, or rhythm, of the life course that Levinson suggests has much to offer the counselling psychologist. The primary concept in Levinson's theory is that of the life structure – an amalgam of the person and their immediate socio-cultural world (people, things, places, institutions and culture) – that evolves through alternating structure-changing and structure-building phases, each lasting several years. Structure-changing phases comprise periods of reappraisal during which earlier decisions, current life-style and future plans are questioned and often reformulated. Structure-building phases are primarily periods of consolidation, during which we build a new structure around the key choices we have made, and pursue our goals and values within it. Clients' needs will vary according to their position in this sequence – with, perhaps, an emphasis on exploration and decision making during transitional periods, and a focus on implementation of plans, maintenance of effort, and evaluation of outcome during the structure-building periods. This sequence mirrors to a considerable extent the sequence of stages in the transtheoretical model of change (Prochaska et al., 1992): pre-contemplation, contemplation, preparation, implementation and maintenance.

Levinson's not inconsiderable emphasis on chronological age has been a main point of criticism of his theory. Other stage-based accounts of the life course place greater emphasis on stages as a consequence, not of chronological age *per se*, but of society's age-related roles and expectations (Kohli and Meyer, 1986). This approach, exemplified by the work of Neugarten (1977), whilst recognizing that some regularities of the life cycle do arise from within, focuses attention on how the life course is defined, constituted and changed by external occurrences. It examines how we use common life events as markers to anticipate what form our life course will and, as we may believe, 'should' take. Many of these events correlate with age, and together they comprise an age-grade system – 'a prescriptive timetable for the ordering of life events' (Neugarten, 1977: 45). Aspects of this timetable may be institutionalized, as when upper and/or lower age limits are set for such activities as school attendance, marriage, voting or retirement. However, most aspects of a society's age-grade system are consensual rather than formal, comprising a general although perhaps unarticulated assumption that there are 'right' and 'wrong' ages for such activities as getting married, finishing our education or throwing a tantrum in public. Such social norms can be and are challenged – many elements of the United Kingdom's age-grade system are less rigid than in the past. However, most people feel some degree of pressure to conform to prevailing age-graded conventions and may be worried about deviating from the norm. We operate in relation to a 'social clock' (Schlossberg et al., 1979) which enables us to state whether we are 'early', 'on time' or 'late' for a wide range of significant life events. Deviations from age norms tend to attract both negative self-assessments and criticism from others. Understanding the nature, source and mutability of these norms provides an important research role for counselling psychologists. Similarly, exploring the taken-for-granted nature of these norms and their validity for a particular client – often centring around what a person feels he or she 'ought' or 'ought not' to be doing at their age or life stage – can be an important element of practice from a life-span perspective.

The waning of the stage concept

Life-span developmental psychology most completely embraced the concept of life stages during the 1970s and 1980s. Phrases such as the 'mid-life crisis' and the 'male menopause' became common, and books with titles such as *Passages* (Sheehy, 1974) and *The Seasons of a Man's Life* (Levinson et al., 1978) became best-sellers. It indicated a recognition that adulthood was not a featureless, unchanging plateau. The idea of there being 'predictable crises of adult life' – to borrow the subtitle of Sheehy's (1974) book – brought some order to this awareness, transferring to adult life a framework of understanding that had long been applied to the years of infancy and childhood.

Levinson's (1996) study of women's adult development did not achieve the same level of attention as his earlier study of men. This is perhaps not surprising. Although Levinson (1996) does discuss gender differences, the theory proposed in *The Seasons of a Woman's Life* is not very different from that in the earlier book (Levinson et al., 1978), and during the eighteen years between their publication the stage concept of adulthood had, at least in academic circles, fallen somewhat out of favour. Inevitably there are exceptions to this generalization – Loevinger's (1976) theory of ego development, for example, was revised during the 1990s (Hy and Loevinger, 1998). Furthermore, interest in stages remains high in more focused developmental domains – for example, with regard to cognitive development beyond the stage of formal operations (Commons et al., 1989).

Since the 1980s the increasing lack of predictability of the life course has become more widely expected and accepted. Few, for example, would now anticipate a 'job for life', and notions of boundaryless (Arthur and Rousseau, 1996) or portfolio (Handy, 1989) careers have replaced the assumptions of Super's (1957, 1980) sequence of growth, exploration, establishment, maintenance and decline. Similarly outdated is the idea of a single normative description of the family life cycle (for example, Haley, 1973; Carter and McGoldrick, 1980) – with clear-cut stages involving a couple having, raising and launching two or three children in the context of a lasting marriage. It is not that such a sequence does not exist, but rather that it is merely one of many possibilities.

Stage-based descriptions of the life course have regularly pleaded their flexibility. But whilst Levinson (1996), for example, protests that his model 'is not a blueprint for the concrete course of an individual's life' (p. 414), such claims have frequently been unheard or sceptically dismissed. Stage theories, however broadly construed, will often strain to accommodate diversity. There is also resistance to their seemingly prescriptive quality of indicating not only what life 'is' but also what it 'ought' to be at a particular point in the life course.

A shift towards themes

Some theorists, perhaps tired of adding caveats and qualifications to stage-based accounts of life-span development, have abandoned stages for themes. Thus Jacobs (1998) reworked his earlier (Jacobs, 1985) account of the life course around the concept of continuing themes rather than overlapping and interconnecting stages. He shows the issues of trust and dependence, authority and autonomy, and co-operation and competition as emerging sequentially in the way depicted by Erikson, thereby indicating a degree of retention of the stage concept. However, having emerged, each issue then stays centre stage and finds its place among the other themes, rather than fading from view whilst different issues take over.

Although it has sometimes been marginalized, a thematic approach to life-span development is not new. Nor is it necessarily an alternative to a stage approach – thus there are what Schlossberg et al. (1995) term 'single domain' stage theories for many aspects of physical, personal, social and mental development. Piaget's theory of cognitive development and Kohlberg's theory of moral development are but two of many possible examples. The themes selected for attention by counselling psychologists may reflect their theoretical predilections, or be determined primarily by the nature of the client group and the espoused purpose of a particular therapeutic service.

The transitional phases in Levinson's model, with their focus on discontinuities and major reorganizations of the life structure, have sparked greater interest and comment than the structure-building phases, which emphasize consolidation and more gradual, incremental changes. Similarly, the aspect of Levinson's work that talks about tasks running through several developmental periods has also been largely sidelined. His task of forming a Dream and giving it a place in the life structure might receive mention, but his analysis of the tasks of forming a mentoring relationship, an occupation, and a love relationship, marriage and family often go unremarked, save for a critique of his stereotypical view of gender roles. This is a reflection of the emphasis at the time when his model was first promulgated on the differences rather than the similarities (or continuities) between different life stages. A 'thematic' approach to the life course draws attention to continuities of development. It provides a counterbalance to the emphasis on discontinuous change that characterizes the 'stage' approach, and also emphasizes that continuity is not synonymous with stagnation or stasis. The restitution of the theme of continuity also characterizes contemporary work on psychosocial transitions or turning points, another mainstay of both life-span development and counselling psychology.

Continuity in transition

In addition to being landmarks in a person's life course, age-graded, cohort-specific and non-normative life events can also be viewed as psychosocial processes or transitions. In the mid-1970s Hopson and Adams (1976) developed from research on a range of transitions a general framework describing the cycle of reactions and feelings that accompany such events. They proposed a seven-phase sequence of experiencing a disruption (Immobilization, Minimization), gradually acknowledging its reality (Depression, Acceptance of reality and letting go), testing oneself (Testing), understanding oneself (Search for meaning) and incorporating changes in one's behaviour (Internalization). Variants of this model have, knowingly or unknowingly, been used to describe a wide range of transitions – expected and unexpected, sudden and gradual, chosen and imposed, desired and unwanted. Over the years the nature, and indeed the existence or extent, of virtually every aspect of this model has been debated, but the issue that most reflects current debate concerns the extent, nature and desirability of 'letting go' (see, for example, Klass et al., 1996; Neimeyer, 2001b).

The stage of 'letting go' is a pivotal point in the transition cycle – often it occurs at an emotional low point, involves relaxng one's hold on the past and marks the point at which a person begins more to look forward than to look back. The point at issue is what is meant by 'letting go'. Does it necessarily imply the severance of links – 'putting the past behind us' – or can these links be renegotiated rather than broken, with a place for our past being found in our current life structure?

Studies of bereavement and other forms of grief have perhaps provided the richest source of material about this issue. Traditionally, at least in twentieth-century Western societies, a main goal of grief has been disengagement, with continued attachment to the deceased being interpreted as symptomatic of psychological problems. During the 1990s, however, and accompanying the narrative turn that reflected that decade's postmodern *Zeitgeist*, attention turned from an emphasis on detachment during transitions (specifically bereavement) towards a consideration of continuity (see, for example, Attig, 2001; Hagman, 2001; Neimeyer, 2001b). Attention turned to the ways in which a dead person 'is lost and then refound, rather than clung on to before being ultimately relinquished' (Walter, 1996: 9). Ties with the past are not relinquished, but are reformulated as we reconstruct our personal biography. Physical separation from another person, place or role, even if permanent, does not, as tradition dictates, mean that we must 'move on without them' (Walter, 1996: 20), but rather that we work to 'find a secure place' (Walter, 1996: 20) for them in our present life. This framework applies not only to bereavement and mourning. Gearing (1999), for example, in a study of former professional footballers found that the memories of their career, irrespective of how successful or unsuccessful they had been, often 'made it easier to get on with life in the present' (p. 56).

From this perspective, grief and other transitions can be seen as on-going processes of redefining over time the meaning and impact of loss (Silverman and Klass, 1996; Attig, 2001). This draws attention to the search for meaning phase in Hopson and Adams's model, making it a theme throughout the transition. Whilst the boundaries between transition stages have always been seen as blurred and fluid (although this has sometimes been ignored by critics), there has been a distinct trend over the last decade or so to emphasize different aspects of the response to transition as coexisting, unique and on-going rather than separate, universal and time-bounded. As with the ascendency of themes over stages as a model of the life course, so the ascendency of continuing rather than breaking bonds during transition reflects compatibility with the concept of narrative coherence.

The ascendance of the narrative framework

In the life-span literature there is a sense in which most, if not all, roads lead towards envisaging the life course as a process of narrative construction. This is not a new idea. Salmon (1985) described narrative – or 'life as story' – as a key metaphor for encapsulating our sense of our lives, and Cohler (1982) proposed the construction of a personal narrative as a way of imposing order on an inherently chaotic life course. Since the 1980s, however, this perspective has increasingly been incorporated into mainstream psychology.

Narrative and the life course

McAdams (1985: 57) epitomizes the narrative view of the life course when he defines identity as 'a life story which individuals begin construing, consciously or unconsciously, in late adolescence'. Drawing, like many contemporary theorists of the life span, on the work of Erikson, McAdams (1993) suggests how, through infancy, childhood and adolescence the key features of a unique life story develop so that by the time we reach early adulthood we have available to us the tools we need to fashion our life experiences into a coherent, purposeful and meaningful story. He records how, during infancy and childhood, we develop a pervasive *narrative tone* (a general sense of optimism or pessimism), a library of *personal images* (the feelings, knowledge and inner sensations associated with particular events), and characteristic *motivational themes* (organized around our needs for agency and communion) that reflect what we want and how these goals might be achieved. During adolescence these elements are placed within an *ideological setting* that both defines and is defined by our beliefs about morality and truth. Now, at the brink of adulthood, the scene is set for the development and enactment of our personal narrative. During early adulthood, characters or *imagoes* that reflect internalized complexes of actual or imagined people are incorporated into the narrative. During middle adulthood, McAdams suggests, we tend to turn our attention to a *generative denouement* to our life story – that is, to an envisioned ending that allows some aspect of our self to live on after us. Finally, in late adulthood, McAdams identifies a period of *narrative evaluation* through which a person strives to review, judge, reconcile and accept his or her life story. In this scheme stages and themes combine as the embryonic narrative elements developed in the early years thread their way through the personal narrative constructed from late adolescence onwards. It is a more flexible framework than those dictated by either a maturational or a social-role view of stages.

Forms of life story

McAdams's distinction between a positive or optimistic and negative or pessimistic narrative tone suggests two different forms that a personal narrative can take across the life course. In distinguishing between progressive and regressive narratives Gergen (1988) uses a similar evaluative distinction to describe how events in a personal narrative move a person towards or away from valued end points: 'as one succeeds in approaching the valued goal over time, the story becomes more positive; as one goes through a series of negatively valued steps towards a negative endpoint, the story moves in a negative direction'

(p. 99). As these evaluations change over time a person's characteristic story line develops into something that can be represented in the lifeline or life graph exercise that forms part of many career and life planning programmes. If everything in a person's life is perceived as going right, or, alternatively, if everything is perceived as going wrong, their narrative can be described as unchanging with regard to its evaluative endpoint. This would be reflected as a straight horizontal line on a life graph – what Gergen (1988) calls a *stability* narrative. If, however, things are getting better, this comprises a *progressive* narrative – represented as a rising slope on the lifeline. When things are getting worse, this *regressive* lifeline (regressive in the sense of moving away from a valued end point) is represented as a downward slope on the lifeline. To these directional concepts of stability, progression and regression Gergen adds the notion of dramatic tension. A steep rather than gentle upward or downward incline in the lifeline indicates high levels of dramatic tension resulting from rapid movement towards or away from a desired goal. Further dramatic tension is provided by points at which the lifeline changes – either the degree of incline may suddenly alter or, more particularly, a line may change direction. These points represent turning points, transitions or key events in a person's life (Wethington et al., 1997).

Whilst the particulars of every individual's lifeline and life story will be unique, it has long been suggested by literary scholars that there are only a limited number of story forms: comedy, romance, tragedy and irony (or satire) (Frye, 1957, 1965). It has also been proposed (Fear and Woolfe, 1999) that these forms underpin different therapeutic orientations, and that congruence between personal philosophy and theoretical orientation is a necessary condition for practitioners' continuing professional development. To see life as a comedy is to believe that it is basically safe and secure, and that all will be well in the end. The romantic view is one of idealism, with love, commitment and integrity having the power to transform adversity. Both convey an optimistic narrative tone. In contrast, the tragic and ironic views of life acknowledge disappointments, personal flaws and insurmountable obstacles. Salmon (1985) suggests we present comic views of the life course to children (for example, in stories where people 'live happily ever after'), are indulgent of adolescent romantic visions, but will often see the realism of tragedy and irony as a hallmark of adult maturity. Murray (1986) identified in the work of three life course researchers (Gould, 1978; Levinson et al., 1978; Sheehy, 1974) the narrative structures of, respectively, satire, tragedy and romance. Frye (1957) links his four narrative structures, albeit not without criticism (Gergen, 1988), to the seasons of the year. There are echoes here of Jung's description of the life course.

Story content

McAdams (1993) identifies the person's need for agency and communion – for power and love – as key themes around which the substance of a person's personal narrative coalesces. With regard to more specific story lines, he identified (McAdams, 1985) in the life stories of a sample of American adults evidence of one or more of the story lines found in Elsbree's (1982) taxonomy of generic plots: establishing or consecrating a home; engaging in a contest; taking a journey; enduring suffering; and pursuing consummation.

The theme of *establishing or consecrating a home* reflects a concern with sustaining human community and creating order out of chaos. Reflected not only in the literal task of home building, it is evidenced, for example, in the tasks of creating a stable life structure, putting down roots, making commitments and establishing a more organized life that are recurrent themes in Levinson's (1986) model of adult development. Similarly, whilst Erikson's (1980) task of generativity – establishing and guiding the next generation – is usually expressed through parenthood, it may also be expressed through other forms of creativity and altruistic concern.

Elsbree's second generic plot – *engaging in a contest* – is illustrated in Sheehy's (1974) description of the task mid-life being to achieve through battle victory over our 'inner custodian' – a 'nasty tyrant' within the self which commands us to meet the demands made on us by others, notably our parents. Erikson's (1980) depiction of life-span development as a sequence of 'battles' or crises is illustrative of this theme on a grander scale, and, in similar vein, Levinson et al. (1978) see all stages of development being characterized by conflicting tasks. For example, in the phase now termed the Entry Life Structure for Early Adulthood phase (Levinson, 1990), young adults need both to keep their options open in order to explore possibilities and to make choices and commitments in order to create a stable life structure. Whilst work on one of these two tasks may predominate, the other is never totally absent.

The image of *taking a journey* permeates Levinson et al.'s account of adult development. The Early Adult Transition, for example, is described as 'a preliminary *step* into the adult world' (1978: 56, emphasis added) and all major transitional phases as *bridges*, or *boundary zones*, between two *states* of greater stability. Unresolved problems are described as '*baggage* from the past' (p. 322). This image of a journey imbues our day-to-day thinking and language. Do we 'know where we are going'? It is 'better to travel hopefully than to arrive'? It is one of the most pervasive images of the life course.

The *enduring of suffering* is inevitable as the fidelity of our life choices is tested and we face mounting pressure to change. Again it is a theme that permeates accounts of the life course. The severance during transitions of ties or bonds with our past, even if they are subsequently reformulated, involves the experience of loss (Parkes, 1971). Similarly, the structure-changing periods in Levinson et al.'s model are periods of upheaval, both exciting and frightening, during which individuals must, among other things, confront the painful task of coming to terms with their own limitations, flaws and mistakes.

Elsbree's final generic plot, that of *pursuing consummation*, is enshrined in many definitions of development proffered by life-span researchers. Thus Bühler (Bühler and Massarik, 1968), describes an 'effective' person as one who leads a goal-directed life, striving for self-fulfilment and self-actualization. Through this striving, basic needs can be transformed into life goals and, ideally, 'ultimate purposes'. Likewise, Levinson et al. identify as key developmental tasks of early adulthood the establishment of a Dream and the discovery of ways of living it out. This Dream 'has the quality of a vision, an imagined possibility that generates excitement and vitality' (1978: 91). That many life stories fall short of full consummation is indicated in the emphasis within both life-span and counselling psychology on the process rather than end state of development – one is a developing, not a developed person. Thus Kaplan describes the concept of development as 'pertaining to a rarely, if ever, attained ideal' (1983: 188).

Several of Elsbree's generic plots may coexist within the same story. When Rogers writes that the good life is 'a *process*, not a state of being' and 'a direction, not a destination' (1967: 186) he invokes the themes of taking a journey and pursuing consummation. A brief quote from Gould (1980) illustrates, in varying degrees, all the above five plots. Personal growth is described as a search for security (illustrating the plot of maintaining a home), as a conflict (engaging in a contest), and as a journey (to arrive somewhere new) in which we must endure suffering (through the disturbance of safety patterns) in order to pursue consummation (the licence to be):

> As we expand our potential, we disturb the patterns within ourselves (our defensive system) and our relationship to those close to us. ... That is why growth is a conflict – the disturbance of safety patterns; and that is why growth is more than learning and practicing new activities or changing by will power. It is a transformation of self in which we enlarge the license to be, only after going through mythical dangers in order to arrive at a new secure place that in turn will be left when the feelings of stagnation and claustrophobia initiate another cycle. (1980: 58)

For Gould the thrust of adult development is towards the realization and acceptance of ourselves as creators of our own lives, and away from the assumption that the rules and standards of childhood determine our destiny. Thus, whilst Levinson et al. talk of the evolving life structure, Gould talks of 'the evolution of adult consciousness as we release ourself from the constraints and ties of childhood consciousness' (1978: 15). He envisages this occurring as we sequentially correct the false assumptions we have lived by until then, and which have restricted and restrained us unnecessarily.

Story styles

How a story is told and its relationship to other stories in a person's personal narrative may be as important as *what* it contains. Roberts (1994) uses the categories *intertwined, isolated, frozen, incomplete, unspoken* and *evolving* to describe different aspects of storytelling styles.

When stories *intertwine*, the similarities and differences between stories of different times and places resonate with each other. This can be used as a resource to enlighten current concerns, but if stories become enmeshed rather than merely intertwined, it may inhibit creativity. Present stories can become mired in past interpretations and meanings, making re-authoring all the more difficult. The tangled web may need to be unravelled so that each story can stand on its own, with its uniqueness and integrity respected. As often, this separation is a double-edged sword. Just as stories can become overly intertwined, so too may they be overly *isolated*, thereby precluding us from learning from experience. Here, then, the task may be to look for links, continuities and themes rather than for differences.

Like overly intertwined stories, *frozen* stories are rigid and unbending. They are told repeatedly in the same way, becoming so familiar and unquestioned that the teller is oblivious to alternative perspectives. Such stories, whilst they may feel safe, can also be stultifying. They are the antithesis of a narrative view of the life course, which emphasizes development as the regular reinterpretation of the past in the light of new experiences and insight.

Incomplete stories contain possibly irretrievable gaps. Through a range of disruption and loss – bereavement, geographical relocation, family break-ups – people lose contact with the places, people, things and symbols that may inhabit their stories. A concern with life course issues leads to efforts to weave into a personal narrative that material which is available, to imagine what other stories there might have been, and what these would have meant. *Unspoken*, or silenced, stories are those that are too risky or difficult to express. Meanings may be unclear, there may be gaps that cannot be openly acknowledged. The therapeutic setting may be a place where the narrative can be put together in a safe and protected way, and where clients can address the questions of whether, when and how unspoken stories might be declared and shared. In the final resort perhaps therapy can be conceived of as a process of assisting clients to create a different story to account for their lives.

A life-span perspective promotes the nurturance and encouragement of *evolving stories*. Personal, family and other cultural stories need to be told (and heard) repeatedly across the life course so that new experiences and information can be incorporated into the interpretation of events:

> If we do not know the old stories, it is sometimes hard to move on to the new ones, because we are unsure of what it is we want to keep from our heritage and what it is we want to change. Understanding what has been given to us through the stories in our lives, while having an ongoing dialogue about the new stories that are being created, lets us both hold the past and move on with the present and future. (Roberts, 1994: 21)

The life-span perspective

By now it should be clear that life-span developmental psychology does not comprise a single theory. It is best thought of as a family of theoretical propositions (Baltes, 1987) that provide a framework for encompassing a range of more narrowly focused descriptions, explanations and modifications, and act as a set of orienting principles for practitioners. The following interrelated theoretical principles (Baltes, 1987; Rutter, 1996) draw together and sum up the threads of a life-span, or life course, perspective.

Development is a lifelong process

It is assumed that throughout the life course there is the potential for both continuous growth, which is gradual, incremental, cumulative and quantitative, and discontinuous development, which is rapid, innovative, substantial and qualitative. This contrasts with earlier privileging within developmental psychology of childhood as the main period of growth and development, a period of 'becoming', with adulthood assumed to be a stable plateau, a period of 'being' rather than becoming, and old age again a period of change, but this time characterized by decline and loss – almost a period of 'ceasing to be'.

Development is multidimensional and multidirectional

Clients will often be struggling with conflicts between different developmental trajectories – for example, between the roles of worker and home maker, of spouse and parent, or of child and parent. Whilst therapeutic services are frequently organized around particular life stages or themes, adopting a life-span perspective encourages a more holistic view of the person. Life-span developmental psychology adopts a total life space (Super, 1980), as well as a total life-span perspective. It is recognized that different elements of the person – intellectual, social, career, family, for example – may follow developmental trajectories that are at least partially independent. Gardner's (1993) concept of multiple intelligences is informative here. It is further assumed that, even within one domain, the concept of development need not be bound by a single criterion of growth or progress.

Development involves loss as well as gain

Development is seen as a joint expression of growth (gain) and decline (loss). Thus decision making inevitably involves the closing off of some options, and moving forward inevitably involves leaving aspects of the past behind, even if links with the past are reformulated rather than totally severed. By the same token, losses can result in developmental gains – for example, in the form of new opportunities or the development of new coping skills. The underlying assumption is that any developmental progression displays both new adaptive capacity and loss of previously existing capacity. Gould speaks of the danger inherent in pursuing personal growth through transformation: 'As we push the boundary to gain internal freedom, we automatically destroy pieces of the illusion of absolute safety' (1980: 64).

Development shows plasticity

Plasticity denotes the potential for a particular developmental path within a particular individual to be modified by life conditions and experiences. It refers to the potential for within-individual rather than between-individual variability.

The developmental preoccupations of childhood are likely to show greater correlation with age and less plasticity than those of adulthood. Perceptual, motor and cognitive development during the first months or years of life does follow a relatively fixed order and timetable. This is reinforced, at least within any one society, by regularities in child-rearing practices and education. Whilst still affected by social conventions and practices, adulthood is less bound by such ordered and timed processes. It is to be expected, therefore, that there will be a wider range of developmental possibilities for adults. The limiting of options for many older people through perceptual, motor and cognitive decline and through social exclusion may reduce the plasticity of the developmental possibilities of this life stage.

Development is historically and culturally embedded

Social and cultural environments change over time, both in terms of specific events such as wars or economic recession, which will be experienced by some generations but not by others, and in terms of developments such as techno-logical advances and changing social trends. Similarly, the particular life-styles that are condoned and sanctioned vary across time and culture.

Changing trends may involve qualitative as well as quantitative changes. Datan charts the progression: 'the exceptional becomes the scarce, the scarce becomes the infrequent, the infrequent becomes the acceptable, and finally, the acceptable becomes the norm' (1983: 41). A changed definition of 'normal' development is thus achieved. Married women's participation in the work force passed through this sequence of stages during the twentieth century. Whereas cultural differences serve to highlight the inappropriateness of trans-ferring concepts of development from one social group to another, historical differences serve to make the past an uncertain and unreliable guide to the future.

Development as the outcome of individual–environment transactions

Whilst there is less tendency than in the past for psychologists to assume that the locus of development lies exclusively, or even predominantly, within either the person or the environment, the life-span perspective continues to be instru-mental in promoting an interactive, contextual or systems view of the person: an active organism within an active environment (Dowd, 1990). Thus identity development is seen as an iterative process of person–context transactions

(Bosma and Kunnen, 2001) and psychological turning points as triggered by major life events, personally or socially significant role transitions, or symbolic indicators of ageing and mortality (Wethington et al., 1997). This draws attention to the need to look to the outer as well as the inner worlds inhabited by both client and therapist.

Development is a multidisciplinary concept

As adult development emerged as a field of study during the 1980s it drew largely on the disciplines of psychology and sociology – reflected in the distinction between life stages as evidence of unfolding psychological maturation, on the one hand, and as indicators of a society's socially defined sequence of age-graded roles on the other. Gerontology, with its long tradition of challenging stereotypes and myths of ageing, and debating what might be meant by successful ageing, has also made a special contribution to a life-span perspective on development.

The broad and encompassing perspective adopted by life-span developmental psychologists encourages the consideration of a range of different systems that influence development, each with associated disciplines of study. The environment can be thought of as a hierarchical nest of systems in which the individual is embedded (Bronfenbrenner, 1977), and which can each influence individual development to a varying degree, and with varying degrees of directness (Kohli and Meyer, 1986). Anthropology, for example, is informative with regard to cultural influences (such as language, social *mores*, folk tales), and sociology with regard to the impact of societal institutions (government, health services, education, etc.). Psychology makes its major contribution in relation to processes within the individual, interactions between individuals and the different personal settings in which they live, and interactions between different settings. At the sub-individual level we can look at the development of various biological or chemical processes, for example. Baltes (1987) issued a plea for efforts at integrating the knowledge derived from different disciplinary perspectives. Together these different influence systems provide the biological, personal, social and cultural milieu in which the individual develops.

Implications for practice

As life-span researchers seek to document, explain and enhance development over the life course they become involved in finding, co-constructing and interpreting the stories people create and use to describe and understand their lives. It has by now almost become a truism to say this is also the role taken by therapists. We live in a storied world, and there exist many strands of narrative-informed counselling and psychotherapy (McLeod, 2000). Spence's (1982) description of the central mission of therapist and client as the construction of the client's life story holds for practitioners from a range of theoretical backgrounds – although the type of story they construct will be influenced by their theoretical orientation and their personal philosophy (Fear and Woolfe, 1999). If the life story the client tells is problematic in some fundamental way then serious story repair, or rebiographing, may be indicated (Howard, 1991). A major goal of intervention from a life-span perspective is, therefore, to work with the client to construct *self-empowering rather than self-limiting life stories* (Viney, 1993).

Despite the waning of the stage concept, a life-span perspective can still *suggest developmental problems or issues* that may occur during the life course (Rodgers, 1984). Jacobs (1998), whilst rejecting stages in favour of themes as an organizing framework for considering life-span development, also acknowledges the usefulness of stage theories in suggesting 'tasks and attitudes – whether physical or intellectual, or stages of emotional development – which a therapist might expect to find at different ages, and which generally can be said to constitute adult maturity' (p. 11).

If a current way of life is rewarding and satisfying or, at the very least, providing the security of a familiar routine, the temptation to resist internal and external pressures to change can be considerable. It is exacerbated when combined with the, probably implicit, assumption that it should not be necessary to change once adulthood is reached. Appreciation of the rhythms and patterns of life-span development enables practitioners to be involved in helping clients to *become aware of age-graded expectations* within their society, and to create individual goals in relation to this normative timetable (Rodgers, 1984). This does not imply conforming to all social expectations and age-norms, but rather that adherence to and deviation from them should be undertaken consciously, with consideration being given to the likely impact of so doing. The life events and developmental tasks that comprise a society's age-grade system operate as 'a kind of culturally specific guidance system' (Reinert, 1980: 17), and clients can be helped to choose whether to challenge or comply with its dictates.

To the extent it is accepted that development is cumulative, present problems may result, at least in part, from *inadequate or incomplete resolution of earlier developmental issues*. Cumulative or hierarchical models such as Erikson's 'can also be used as a template to locate possible sources of personal difficulty' (Jacobs, 1998: 11). Erikson (1980) suggests, for example, that the abandonment of self that is necessary to resolve successfully the crisis of Intimacy versus Isolation is not possible until the crisis of Identity versus Role confusion has been addressed to the extent that the individual has a secure sense of who he or she is. It may therefore be necessary to address issues beyond those impinging on clients' current life stage – both issues from earlier stages which may have been ignored or need reworking and issues likely to arise in the future and which clients may wish to prepare for.

If it is accepted that the life course is characterized by a regular need to initiate and/or respond to change, but that this is not necessarily recognized or accepted by clients, then it seems likely that many individuals will *lack effective change-management skills*. Transition management, goal setting, action planning and implementation – with all their associated techniques of brainstorming, force-field analysis, prioritizing, etc. – become potentially relevant issues for clients to address.

The life-span perspective sees both positive and negative life events as an inevitable part of life and as potential growth points. This comprises a *developmental rather than a disease perspective on life events*, whereby 'crises are perceived as normative human experiences that pose a challenge and an opportunity for developmental adaptation and growth' (Woolfe, 2001: 347). Overall, there is an emphasis on well-being rather than sickness.

Conclusion

The metaphor of the story provides not only an informative image of the life course, but also a link between the disciplines of life-span development and counselling psychology – with life construed as the stories we create and live by; psychological disturbance as stories awry and incoherent; and therapy as exercises in story repair and reconstruction (Howard, 1991). Within this framework, whilst the concept of stages may be subordinated to that of themes, it has by no means disappeared. In both the academic literature (Arnett, 2000) and the media (Rice, 2000) new life stages are being proposed. Arnett (2000) advocates a stage of 'emerging adulthood' and Rice (2000) a 'new' pre-teen generation of 'tweenies' or 'tweenagers' – children (primarily girls) between eight and twelve years of age who are 'sassy, sophisticated and self-possessed' (p. 18).

The redirection of gaze away from stage and towards theme helps to counter-balance any over-emphasis on change by, like narrative, embracing the concept of continuity and overarching coherence. It is, however, a dynamic under-standing of continuity – not to be equated with stasis or stagnation. In practice this implies recognition that clients' needs change over time.

Taking a life course perspective is not a simple option. It demands casting aside the blinkers of disciplinary specialism, tolerating ambiguity and living with the concept of 'both–and' rather than 'either–or'. However, by retaining an emphasis on the particular and the contextual it can supplement rather than replace depth with breadth. It requires the ability to think dialectically – to resolve, albeit temporarily, contradictory factors in a particular situation; something that denotes cognitive (for example, Commons et al., 1989) or personal (for example, Kolb, 1984) maturity, and is seen as the foundation for integration in therapeutic practice (Fear and Woolfe, 1996).

References

Arnett, J.J. (2000) 'Emerging adulthood: a theory of development from the late teens through the twenties', *American Psychologist*, 55: 469–80.

Arthur, M.B. and Rousseau, D.M. (eds) (1996) *The Boundaryless Career: New Employment Principle for a New Organizational Era*. New York: Oxford University Press.

Attig, T. (2001) 'Relearning the world: making and finding meanings' in R.A. Neimeyer (ed.) *Meaning Reconstruction and the Experience of Loss*. Washington DC: American Psychological Association.

Baltes, P.B. (1987) 'Theoretical propositions of life-span developmental psychology', *Developmental Psychology*, 23: 611–26.

Baltes, P.B., Reese, H.W. and Lipsitt, L.P. (1980) 'Life-span developmental psychology', *Annual Review of Psychology*, 31: 65–110.

Bosma, H.A. and Kunnen, E.S. (2001) 'Determinants and mechanisms in ego identity development', *Developmental Review*, 21: 39–66.

Bronfenbrenner, U. (1977) 'Toward an experimental ecology of human development', *American Psychologist*, 32: 513–31.

Bühler, C. and Massarik, F. (eds) (1968) *The Course of Human Life: a Study of Goals in the Humanistic Perspective*. New York: Springer.

Carter, E. and McGoldrick, M. (1980) *The Family-life Cycle: a Framework for Family Therapy*. New York: Gardner.

Clausen, J.A. (1993) *American Lives: Looking Back at the Children of the Great Depression*. New York: Free Press.

Cohler, B.J. (1982) 'Personal narrative and the life course' in P.B. Baltes and O.G. Brim (eds) *Life-span Development and Behavior* IV. New York: Academic Press.

Commons, M.L., Sinnott, J.D., Richards, F.A. and Armon, C. (eds) (1989) *Adult Development, Volume 1: Comparison and Applications of Developmental Models*. New York: Praeger.

Datan, N. (1983) 'Normative or not? Confessions of a fallen epistemologist' in E.J. Callahan and K.A. McKluskey (eds) *Life-span Developmental Psychology: Non-normative Life Crises*. New York: Academic Press.

Datan, N., Rodeaver, D. and Hughes, F. (1987) 'Adult development and aging', *Annual Review of Psychology*, 38: 153–80.

Dowd, J.J. (1990) 'Ever since Durkheim: the socialization of human development', *Human Development*, 31: 138–59.

Egan, G.E. (1990) *The Skilled Helper: a Systematic Approach to Effective Helping*. Monterey CA.: Brooks Cole.

Elsbree, L. (1982) *The Rituals of Life: Patterns in Narrative*. New York: Kennikat.

Erikson, E.H. (1980) *Identity and the Life Cycle: a Reissue*. New York: Norton.

Fear, R. and Woolfe, R. (1996) 'Searching for integration in counselling practice', *British Journal of Guidance and Counselling*, 24 (3): 399–411.

Fear, R. and Woolfe, R. (1999) 'The personal and professional development of the counsellor: the relationship between personal philosophy and theoretical orientation', *Counselling Psychology Quarterly*, 12: 253–62.

Featherstone, M. and Hepworth. M. (1989) 'Ageing and old age: reflections on the postmodern life course' in B. Bytheway, T. Keil, P. Allatt and A. Bryman (eds) *Becoming and Being Old: Sociological Approaches to later Life*. London: Sage.

Frye, N. (1957) *Anatomy of Criticism*. Princeton NJ: Princeton University Press.

Frye, N. (1965) *A Natural Perspective: the Development of Shakespearean Comedy and Romance*. New York: Columbia University Press.

Gardner, H. (1993) *Frames of Mind: the Theory of Multiple Intelligences*, second edition. London: Fontana.

Gearing, B. (1999) 'Narratives of identity among former professional footballers in the United Kingdom', *Journal of Aging Studies*, 13: 45–58.

Gergen, M.M. (1988) 'Narrative structures in social explanation' in C. Antaki (ed.) *Analysing Everyday Explanation: a Casebook of Methods*. London: Sage.

Gould, R.L. (1978) *Transformations: Growth and Change in Adult Life*. New York: Simon & Schuster.

Gould, R.L. (1980) 'Transformational tasks in adulthood' in S.I. Greenspan and G.H. Pollock (eds) *The Course of Life: Psychoanalytic Contributions toward Understanding*

Personality Development III, *Adulthood and the Aging Process*. Washington DC: National Institute of Mental Health.

Hagman, G. (2001) 'Beyond decathexis: toward a new psychoanalytic understanding and treatment of mourning' in R.A. Neimeyer (ed.) *Meaning Reconstruction and the Experience of Loss*. Washington DC: American Psychological Association.

Haley, J. (1973) *Uncommon Therapy*. New York: Norton.

Handy, C. (1989) *The Age of Unreason*. London: Arrow.

Hopson, B. and Adams, J. (1976) 'Towards an understanding of transition: defining some boundaries of transition dynamics', in J. Adams, J. Hayes and B. Hopson (eds) *Transition: Understanding and Managing Personal Change*. London: Martin Robertson.

Howard, G.S. (1991) 'Culture tales: a narrative approach to thinking, cross-cultural psychology and psychotherapy', *American Psychologist*, 46: 187–97.

Hy, L.X. and Loevinger, J. (1998) *Measuring Ego Development*, second edition. Hillsdale NJ: Erlbaum.

Jacobs, M. (1985) *The Presenting Past: an Introduction to Practical Psychodynamic Counselling*. Milton Keynes: Open University Press.

Jacobs, M. (1998) *The Presenting Past: the Core of Psychodynamic Counselling and Therapy*. Buckingham: Open University Press.

Jung, C.G. (1972) 'The transcendent function' in H. Read, M. Fordham, G. Adler and W. McGuire (eds) *The Collected Works of C.G. Jung* VIII, *The Structure and Dynamics of the Psyche*. London: Routledge.

Kaplan, B. (1983) 'A bio of trials', in R.M. Lerner (ed.) *Developmental Psychology: Historical and Philosopical Perspectives*. Hillsdale NJ: Lawrence Erlbaum.

Klass, D., Silverman, P.R. and Nickman, S.L. (eds) (1996) *Continuing Bonds: New Understandings of Grief* London: Taylor & Francis.

Kohli, M. and Meyer, J.W. (1986) 'Social Structure and social construction of life stages', *Human Development*, 29: 145–9.

Kolb, D. (1984) *Experimental Learning: Experience as the Source of Learning and Development*. Englewood Cliffs NJ: Prentice-Hall.

Levinson, D.J. (1990) 'A theory of life structure development in adulthood' in C.N. Alexander and E.J. Langer (eds) *Higher Stages of Human Development*. New York: Oxford University Press.

Levinson, D.J. (1996) *The Seasons of a Woman's Life*. New York: Random House.

Levinson, D.J., Darrow, D.N., Klein, E.B., Levinson, M.H. and McKee, B. (1978) *The Seasons of a Man's Life*. New York: Knopf.

Loevinger, J. (1976) *Ego Development*. San Francisco: Jossey Bass.

Lynch, G. (1997) 'The role of community and narrative in the work of the therapist: a postmodern theory of the therapist's engagement in the therapeutic process', *Counselling Psychology Quarterly*, 10: 353–63.

McAdams, D.P. (1985) *Power, Intimacy, and the Life Story: Personological Inquiries into Identity*. Homewood IL: Dow Jones-Irwin.

McAdams, D.P. (1993) *Stories we Live by: Personal Myths and the Making of the Self*. New York: Morrow.

McLeod, J. (1997) *Narrative and Psychotherapy*. London: Sage.

McLeod, J. (2000) 'The development of narrative-informed theory, research and practice in counselling and psychotherapy: European perspectives', *European Journal of Psychotherapy, Counselling and Health*, 3: 331–3.

Murray, K. (1986) 'Literary pathfinding: the work of popular life constructors' in T.R. Sarbin (ed.) *Narrative Psychology: The Storied Nature of Human Conduct*. New York: Praeger.

Neimeyer, R.A. (2001a) 'Meaning reconstruction and loss' in R.A. Neimeyer (ed.) *Meaning Reconstruction and the Experience of Loss*. Washington DC: American Psychological Association.

Neimeyer, R.A. (ed.) (2001b) *Meaning Reconstruction and the Experience of Loss*. Washington DC: American Psychological Association.

Neugarten, B.L. (1977) 'Adaptation and the life cycle' in N.K. Schlossberg and A.D. Entine (eds) *Counseling Adults*. Monterey CA: Brooks Cole.

Parkes, C.M. (1971) 'Psycho-social transitions: a field for study', *Social Science and Medicine*, 5: 101–5.

Prochaska, J.O., DiClemente, C.C. and Norcross, J.C. (1992) 'In search of how people change: application to addictive behaviors', *American Psychologist*, 47: 1102–14.

Reinert, G. (1980) 'Educational psychology in the context of the human lifespan', in P.B. Baltes and O.G. Brim (eds) *Life-Span Development and Behavior* III. New York: Academic Press.

Rice, M. (2000) 'What little girls are made of', *Observer Magazine*, 3 December: 18–27.

Roberts, J. (1994) *Tales and Transformations: Stories in Families and Family Therapy*. New York: Norton.

Rodgers, R.F. (1984) 'Theories of adult development: research status and counseling implications' in S.D. Brown and R.W. Lent (eds) *Handbook of Counseling Psychology*. New York: Wiley.

Rogers, C.R. (1967) *On Becoming a Person: a Therapist's View of Psychotherapy*. London: Constable.

Rutter, M. (1996) 'Transitions and turning points in developmental psychopathology, as applied to the age span between childhood and mid-adulthood', *International Journal of Behavioral Development*, 19: 603–26.

Salmon, P. (1985) *Living in Time: a New Look at Personal Development*. London: Dent.

Schlossberg, N.K., Troll, L.E. and Leibowitz, Z. (1979) *Perspectives on Counselling Adults: Issues and Skills*. Monterey CA: Brooks Cole.

Schlossberg, N.K., Waters, E.B. and Goodman, J. (1995) *Counselling Adults in Transition: Linking Practice with Theory*. New York: Springer.

Sheehy, G. (1974) *Passages: Predictable Crises of Adult Life*. New York: Dutton.

Sheehy, G. (1996) *New Passages: Mapping your Life across Time*. London: Harper Collins.

Silverman, P.R. and Klass, D. (1996) 'Introduction: what's the problem?' in D. Klass, P.R. Silverman and S.L. Nickman, *Continuing Bonds: New Understandings of Grief*. Washington DC: Taylor & Francis.

Spence, D.P. (1982) *Narrative Truth and Historical Truth: Meaning and Interpretation in Psychoanalysis*. New York: Norton.

Super, D.E. (1957) *The Psychology of Careers*. New York: Harper.

Super, D.E. (1980) 'A life-span, life-space approach to career development', *Journal of Vocational Behavior*, 16: 282–98.

Viney, L. (1993) *Life Stories: Personal Construct Therapy with the Elderly*. Chichester: Wiley.

Walter, T. (1996) 'A new model of grief: bereavement and biography', *Mortality*, 1: 7–25.

Wethington, E., Cooper, H. and Holmes, C.S. (1997) 'Turning points in midlife' in I.H. Gotlib and B. Wheaton (eds), *Stress and Adversity over the Life Course: Trajectories and Turning Points*. Cambridge: Cambridge University Press.

Woolfe, R. (2001) 'The helping process', *Psychologist*, 14: 347.

15 Psychological Counselling of Children and Young People
JIM DOWNEY

A typical referral to the counselling psychologist working with children can be used to illustrate some of the central issues in this field of work.

> A mother has sought referral of her three children for psychological counselling. In the first session she explains each child's behaviour has changed, becoming challenging or worrying since she and their father separated some months ago. From her description, each child is behaving quite differently and independently of each other. None of the children has asked to be referred and one of them has actually said she does not wish to see anyone. The mother's request, however, is that you will help the children to talk through their upset and help them accept the separation and imminent divorce of their parents.

In psychological terms the family has suffered a 'loss event', probably traumatic and unexpected for the children, if not the mother. We could safely predict all family members will also be struggling with the increased stress of sudden change, the loss of familiar patterns and routines and possibly continuing conflict between the parents.

Depending on each child's developmental status and position in the family, it is possible each will have a different experience and understanding of the separation of their parents, the present circumstances etc. The mother's request raises the following issues.

- *What is the most effective focus for intervention?* Do you immediately take the children on as clients and pursue the therapeutic goals outlined by the parent or do you investigate the possibility of increasing the mother's understanding of her children's adjustment reactions and needs and offer some practical advice on 'good' post-divorce parental arrangements?
- *Is there evidence to support the selection of particular therapeutic approaches?* If you do see the children and assess them to be in need of specialist help, what treatment approaches are likely to be most effective in facilitating positive change? This decision requires knowledge of the research into treatment efficacy.
- *What are the implications for therapy of developmental status differences between children?* The three children are of different ages and psychological capacities. How could this affect the choice of approach?

Other issues arise, too, such as being clear about who is the client; about children having the right to refuse therapy; and about the need to establish with everyone the limits to confidentiality in child work. These three questions are repeatedly posed by child work, and before any individual therapy can begin the counselling psychologist must make decisions in relation to each. They will be examined and developed across the chapter through reference to the scientific and developmental literature.

Plan of the chapter. The chapter falls into three broad sections. The first considers the most effective focus for intervention, the second looks at the scientific support for particular forms of therapy and the final section reviews developmental changes of childhood and the implication of such changes for the choice of therapy.

Before proceeding to the first section, however, there are a number of introductory points to be made followed by a brief consideration of the differences between children and adults in therapy.

Children's mental health

Children and young people, up to the age of eighteen years, represent 20–25 per cent of the total UK population. There are many difficulties in estimating the exact prevalence of mental health difficulties within the child population. There are significant variations in the classification of different types of childhood difficulty. Prevalence estimates are further complicated by factors such as age, gender and geographical location. Nevertheless authoritative surveys now produce estimates which indicate 5–40 per cent of children will experience mental health problems sufficient to significantly disturb their everyday lives and relationships. It is further estimated that between 5 per cent and 25 per cent of children and young people will experience more severe difficulties, known as mental health disorders, in the course of their childhood (Wallace et al., 1997). It is also reliably estimated that the incidence of children's mental health difficulties increases as they mature, with the adolescent population showing the highest rates of prevalence. Lastly, there is a much smaller group of children who might be identified as suffering from a diagnosable mental illness.

The counselling psychologist working with children will typically be asked to meet with children who may be described as suffering from mental health problems or disorders. This broad and ill defined group of children may present a wide range of difficulties, from isolated fears to persisting aggressive outbursts. However, the vast majority of children's problems can be described in terms of two broad categories: difficulties which take the form of an externalizing pattern, e.g. aggressive behaviour, and those which take an internalizing pattern, e.g. anxious rumination, etc.

The range of psychological approaches available to the counselling psychologist working in this field is highly diverse. Indeed, Kazdin (2000) identified over 500 differently named therapeutic types of approach described in a clinical literature relating to children. However, if the approaches are categorized according to their principal treatment method and focus they may be summarized as falling into four main categories: *community* approaches (e.g. school, neighbourhood), *family* approaches, *group* approaches and *individual* approaches. This chapter concentrates on therapeutic approaches offered to *individual* children, which have also received support and validation from scientific studies. Unfortunately this still does not leave room for any detailed account of therapeutic approaches, nor can any attempt be made to describe the treatment of particular childhood presentations. Rather the chapter will aim to offer guiding ideas and frameworks for the counselling psychologist working with this massively varied child population.

The central supra-theoretical theme which will be addressed is that of developmental change, its relevance to the understanding of childhood difficulties and the selection of therapeutic approaches and methods. The developmental perspective is paramount for effective and sensitive work with children and their families. It not only incorporates a body of knowledge concerning changes in the cognitive and social capacity of children but also offers a way of conceptualizing the responses of children to their experiences. This provides a framework for assessment and intervention activities irrespective of age, gender, experience or difficulty. In addition it should assist in the making of clinical decisions in respect of the level and focus of therapeutic effort.

Finally, it is important to say that this chapter is primarily written for and about children who are receiving a 'good enough' caring experience but whose developmental progress is at some level of risk, for example poor negotiation of a developmental task or life experience. More severely damaged children, whose care experience has been seriously inadequate or abusive, may require a more specialized account than can be given here.

The child in therapy

A consideration of some of the essential differences between child and adult work will be beneficial to the counselling psychologist faced with the questions raised above.

The counselling psychologist new to child work needs to be aware of two common errors which occur when adult therapists meet child clients. First there is a tendency to assume childhood distress and dysfunction are the same in their origin and experience as they are for adults (adultomorphic tendency). Secondly, there is a temptation to assume all children are psychologically alike and can therefore be treated in the same way (developmental uniformity myth). Once they have been identified, it is tempting to believe the possibility of committing these errors has been removed. However, the ability to avoid these misperceptions is not based on good intent but on good developmental understanding.

Therapeutic work with adults is based on a range of assumptions, differently described and emphasized, depending on clinical model and approach, but at or near their centre is a proposition which holds that personal autonomy and choice are possible at the level of individual action.

The validity of this proposition, notwithstanding the challenges and caveats from moral, political and philosophical schools, depends upon the presence of an easily overlooked cognitive capacity: the capacity to render one's own behaviour, thoughts and feelings the subject of personal examination. A related but even more sophisticated cognitive capacity is further assumed in adult work, the capacity to 'step outside' one's own intimate social context in order that relationships, shared beliefs and meanings can also be examined. Much of adult therapy is directed towards a point where the client can exercise these 'capacities' to their personal psychological benefit, for example through making new personal choices based on increased insight, awareness or understanding of their position.

For the counselling psychologist working with children it is vital to recognize that the capacity for self-reflection is a developmental acquisition born of biological maturation, social experience and cognitive ability. Nor is the capacity suddenly present; like all developmental capacities it emerges over extended time, becoming more robust, reliable and universally available to the child as use and experience establish it.

Attention to a particular child's developmental capacity for self-reflection must therefore be an early consideration in any direct work undertaken. Clearly the robust presence, early emergence or absence of a self-reflective capacity has serious and practical implications for the way therapy is conducted and for the therapeutic interventions considered appropriate and accessible for a given child.

A second and related issue of crucial relevance to direct child work is the need to recognize, and where possible work with, the child's primary social context, usually the family. Unlike adults, children are usually in no position, socially or psychologically, to 'leave' their family. The family is the social system which guides, controls and informs the child's development. It is from within the family that the child develops an idea of their own personal value, abilities and aspirations. Even as the child matures, personally and socially, and encounters extra-familial 'ideas', they are processed through the family's ideological 'filter'. In a very real sense the ideas and suggestions of the counselling psychologist may have only as much 'influence' as the child's family can tolerate or allow. It is vital therefore that the counselling psychologist develops an awareness of and stays respectful to the family's values, beliefs and practices.

Lastly, a number of more general points can be made about the child in therapy which may render its practice different from typical adult therapy. It is relatively rare for children of any age to refer themselves for therapy. They are invariably referred by others. This difference in referral raises questions about the child's motivation for therapeutic work and their acceptance or understanding of therapeutic goals. The child must therefore find therapy intrinsically interesting if he or she is to be engaged. The use of play activities is one means of engaging the child's interest. They also provide an often essential non-verbal means of communication for the child, whose verbal facility and comfort with extensive conversational exchange will be more restricted than an adult client's.

It should, however, be mentioned that the view about children's ability to contribute their own thoughts and opinions to therapeutic work is changing. Within the postmodern tradition new ways of engaging with children are being proposed. These changes come out of an awareness that children will make their contribution within a cultural context which often presumes and subtly enforces the dismissal of children's perspective when placed alongside that of an adult. Specifically within the family the process of discussion or debate is often didactic rather than dialectical, and this alternative form of engaging with children is placed at the centre of postmodern therapy. Hence within this tradition some therapists are proposing that children's 'thinking' rather than simply expressions of their feeling can be elicited in a way which extends our understanding of their experience and the meaning they give to it. Whilst the view probably has its origins within the postmodern narrative therapeutic tradition it is also evident in some areas of cognitive behavioural work, where again children as young as three are being approached in ways which allow them to articulate thoughts and beliefs which heretofore it had been thought would be too ill formed or beyond their capacity to articulate.

In summary, then, the child may be an unwilling, unsuspecting or unmotivated client whose commitment and interest in therapeutic work may be very low. In therapy sessions they will require verbal and non-verbal communication options. The goals and methods of therapy must be commensurate with the child's developmental competence and ability. Finally, the child is so dependent on and psychologically captive to his or her family and wider context that it is only in exceptionally rare circumstances that the child can be 'treated' in isolation.

The contextualized intervention

Individual psychotherapeutic work with children has a long history, and, whatever the actual therapeutic approach, the shared basic assumption is that through direct contact with the child the therapist can provide a corrective experience (catharsis, insight, reconditioning behaviour, restructuring cognitions, etc.) which will lessen or remove the child's difficulties. However, questions about the effectiveness or wisdom of seeing children in isolation were increasingly raised from the 1960s onwards. Shirk (1999) summarized current thinking in saying therapy 'cannot be restricted to the individual child but must encompass the social contexts, particularly the family context, in which the child develops'. There is evidence now that the vast majority of child therapists, practising in the United States or United Kingdom, routinely see a need to involve the child's parents at some level in the treatment process (Kazdin et al., 1990).

An applied appreciation of child development is critical to the understanding of child problems, the choice of therapeutic method and the evaluation of change. Children's needs and sensitivities vary with age, gender and experience, as does their vulnerability to different types of difficulty. The clinical and social significance of specific behaviours also changes with development and age. As stated earlier, it is imperative that the context in which development and behaviour are occurring is taken into account. Although the course of both normal and dysfunctional development is still poorly understood, it is clear that child behaviour and development are directly and indirectly influenced according to complex contextual relationships. Reliably identified risk factors for mental health difficulties in childhood include family and environmental characteristics (Pearce, 1993). A plausible hypothesis is that most contextual variables ultimately have their impact on children through some disturbance in family process, and more specifically in disrupted parenting practices (Fauber et al., 1990).

The 'Goodness of Fit' model proposed by Chess and Thomas (1984) makes connections between child and context and provides the therapist with a practical framework for conceptualizing a child's presented difficulty. The central proposition of the model holds that high levels of consonance between the child and his or her environment potentiates optimal positive development. Where the demands and expectations of the environment consistently exceed the child's capacities, motivations and behavioural style, the potential for maladaptive patterns of functioning and distortions in development is present. The primary objectives of human behaviour are conceived by the model as relating to social competence and task mastery goals where, in interactive fashion, progress towards one type of goal influences the child's progress towards the other. Changes in environmental demand on the child which are marginally ahead of current functioning will produce stress in the child–environment relationship which can be resolved through an extension of personal skills. Such mastery experiences are perceived as positive in nature and contribute to a positive sense of self. Repeated failure experiences can lead to chronic stress which the child will seek relief from but through strategies of impulse and avoidance rather than mastery. The result is likely to be reduced social competence and a weakening of self-esteem.

It has been mentioned earlier that this chapter is referring to those children who have received a good enough care experience. Clearly if it were to also incorporate children who had suffered poor attachment experiences in the early stages of life then this could become a predominant developmental framework for understanding many of their subsequent patterns of expression. Attachment theory and the Goodness of Fit model are not in contradiction with each other, rather it is a matter of which is most helpful in reaching an understanding of the child's areas of difficulty and the most appropriate focus of intervention.

The Goodness of Fit formulation helps structure a strategy of intervention that includes an assessment of the child's motivations, abilities and temperament, their behaviour patterns and their consequences, plus the expectations, demands and limitations of the environment. In all cultures children encounter points of transition which have been set by custom, belief and native awareness of when children are ready to meet a new demand. For instance, in

Great Britain school entry is determined by many factors unrelated to child development, but at three years plus it is also timed to coincide with the child's increasing ability to tolerate extended separation from primary and intimate carers. The success with which individual children meet the challenge varies enormously, dependent as it is on the child's temperament, early preparatory experiences, school and family response to the child's adjustment behaviour, and so on. The outcome is that most children master the challenge and become more competent, independent and confident about themselves. Unfortunately some considerable few experience enormous difficulties in making the adjustment and their future social development can be placed in jeopardy.

Not all challenges arise out of societal or familial traditions. For instance, although divorce is an increasingly common experience for children, it is a non-normative event and as such is not timed to coincide with the child's ability to cope with the impact. It is clear from the research (e.g. Hetherington, 1989) that children in different developmental phases are likely to respond in ways which can be understood in terms of their developmental capacities, individual temperamental style and personal experiences. The research further indicates that the child's adjustment to the divorce event can be greatly influenced, for good or bad, by their parents' actions, availability and sensitivity to the child's needs before and after the parental separation. Similar patterns of interactional change have been noted at other transition points in family life, for example bereavement, and found to be predictive of child adjustment.

The Family Life Cycle model (Carter and McGoldrick, 1989) attempts to describe the normative and non-normative transitions of family life. As with any developmental model, it suggests different families will negotiate different transitions more or less adaptively in terms of present and future functioning. The model requires the clinician to consider the child's presenting difficulty against the family's own developmental stage and current tasks. In a family where marital breakdown has occurred, for instance, the developmental tasks of individual children may be compromised or completely undermined by the changes in marital and parental functioning. The effects may be relatively short-lived or become persisting maladaptive patterns, for example a child assuming the role of parental confidante may have difficulties pursuing social independence goals. It can be seen that the utility of the Goodness of Fit framework and Family Life Cycle model is restricted only by the counselling psychologist's ability to move from a knowledge of the general to an ideographic appraisal of the particular child and his or her context.

The point to be emphasized is that in all child work cases the psychologist must pay serious heed to contextual variables. Any adequate formulation of childhood difficulties must acknowledge and include the dynamic and reciprocal relationships between children and their environment. Assessing family or parent–child 'interactions' is an important step in assessing the child's presented problem. Where patterns are found to be obstructing healthy developmental progress a fundamental goal of any therapy will be how to promote change in restricting patterns. However, the counselling psychologist must still decide whether it is best achieved via work with an individual child, the parent(s), the parent and child or the family. The final decision will depend on more than simply where the formulation indicates change is required. Another critical factor which must be taken into account is the expectation of therapy held by various family members. For instance, Houts et al. (1985) suggest that in some cases individual child therapy may be the only therapeutic option available if the parents are unwilling or unable to define the difficulty as a family, or even a parent–child, problem. (See Street et al., 1991, for another way of responding to this dilemma.)

Whether individual child work is decided by formulatory design or familial expectation, the therapeutic approach selected should ideally have a proven efficacy and be compatible with the child's developmental abilities and individual temperamental style.

The effectiveness of child therapies

A vast array of psychological therapies are reported in the child therapy literature but many are poorly described and most have not been seriously or scientifically evaluated. Notwithstanding the problems of definition (what constitutes psychotherapy) and measurement (what constitutes effectiveness) advances toward the identification of effective treatments have been particularly slow because of the complexity of child work. Issues of developmental change, individual variation, problem co-morbidity, the diversity of parent and family arrangements as well as the wide contextual variation in which child behaviour and development are located all contribute to the field's complexity. Furthermore, current research methodology is unable fully to identify and encompass the multi-level and multi-componented nature of interventions. This reduces the clinical validity of most studies, making it impossible to assert with any confidence that changes in the child's functioning are attributable to the individual work done with him or her. Moreover, research into treatment effectiveness has to date been predominantly concerned with the question of treatment.

Even so, the research is typically found to evidence one or more of the following methodological flaws:

- Use of small, unspecified samples.
- Absence of control groups.
- Use of global outcome measures only.
- Failure to monitor the integrity of treatment.
- The absence of meaningful follow-up.

Most major reviews of the evidence of child psychotherapy effectiveness (e.g. Kazdin, 1994; Target and Fonagy, 1996) conclude that the principal issues are still to be resolved, i.e. what works for whom under which conditions? Nevertheless meta-analytic reviews of the effectiveness research literature support two general conclusions. Firstly, they confirm the effectiveness of 'therapeutic intervention' over 'no intervention' (Casey and Berman, 1985; Shirk and Russell, 1992). Secondly they seem to provide increasingly persuasive evidence that cognitive/behavioural therapies are more effective than the non-behavioural therapies (Weisz et al., 1995). In the latter studies by Weisz the suggestion that the more empirically shaped cognitive behavioural therapies were unduly favoured within such meta-analyses was examined and found not to be supported.

As with all areas of psychotherapeutic input the child and adolescent therapy arena is coming under closer external scrutiny. Questions relating to the effectiveness and purpose of therapeutic services are being raised by society and taken up by the scientist practitioner community. Nevertheless it is a sense of change rather than change itself which is apparent in the clinical field.

At a service policy level the actual models of treatment delivery are being questioned. The conventional model of one-to-one individual therapy in an out-patient clinic is being seriously examined. Within the child field, studies such as Weiss et al. (2000) are likely to support this shift in emphasis. Weiss and his colleagues completed a two year follow-up assessment of typical child psychotherapy in US out-patient settings. The study was methologically robust and whilst it found some evidence of improvement in children receiving treatment it was not of an order which lent support to a claim for effectiveness of traditional psychotherapy nor did it identify the presence of a psychotherapy 'sleeper effect'. Even so, research evidence continues to have little apparent impact upon the practice of clinicians in general (Wilson, 1997).

A sign perhaps of the way things are moving is found in an approach to treatment around resistant conduct-disordered young boys known as multi-systemic therapy (MST) which focuses on the systems in which troublesome behaviour is embedded and attempts to alter those systems in direct and concrete ways (Henggeler et al., 1998). Although the broad approach is multi-systemic and fundamentally rewrites the notion of how services should support and intervene, it nevertheless represents a bringing together of several different therapeutic approaches and techniques, including that of individual child work, towards some convergent and collaborative plan with the child and family.

It should be mentioned that various clinical groups have voiced concern about the narrowness of empirical tests of evidence. For instance, advocates of post-structural perspectives would argue that empiricism is merely one possible way of describing (social) phenomena. Furthermore some psychotherapeutic orientations, e.g. psychoanalytical, phenomenological, consider empirical methods as inappropriate for the examination of therapeutic process and outcome.

Behavioural and cognitive approaches

There is more empirical research evaluating the effectiveness of behavioural methods in child work than any other clinical approach. (As an approach, it lends itself more readily to empirical evaluation.) However, the majority of studies are not of direct individual work with children but of triadic work. That is to say, the therapist works essentially with the parent, who receives advice on how changes in their own behaviour will lead to desired changes in the child's behaviour. Thus the parent–child dyad is the unit of analysis, the parental input is changed through education and coaching and the child may never be directly engaged by the therapist (e.g. Patterson et al., 1992). Nevertheless there are also many well controlled single-case studies in the behavioural literature which demonstrate the effectiveness of this clinical approach in direct work with individual children.

The clearest examples of effectiveness are usually found in clinical cases where anxieties and fears are the symptom to be addressed. Behavioural methods of *in vivo* exposure, modelling and various self-control strategies are all shown to be helpful (Ollendick and King, 1998). Other commonly treated problems with which behavioural methods are shown to be effective are anger management, social and interpersonal skills training. In spite of the generally supportive evidence it is important to note that the clinical literature plainly acknowledges the unpredictability of the effectiveness of behavioural interventions at an individual level.

Cognitive-behavioural therapy (CBT) emphasizes learning processes and the centrality of the individual's cognitive style in the remediation of psychological distress. Interventions are designed to change detrimental, maladaptive cognitions and cognitive styles that children may be developing. The approach offers the child active strategies and alternative cognitions which introduce more adaptive and individually beneficial styles.

Single-case and group comparison studies indicate CBT is effective in the treatment of a number of common childhood problems. For instance, impulsivity is addressed through the teaching of self-instructional talk and problem-solving skills. Anxious children are assisted through a combination of treatment strategies including systematic desensitization and relaxation training, modelling and the development of more helpful cognitions, e.g. cognitive restructuring where misperceptions and negative evaluative biases are challenged and replaced by more positive cognitions and images. As in adult therapy, however, it is with depressed children (usually adolescents) that CBT has been most frequently examined and found to be effective. A typical treatment might incorporate cognitive restructuring of maladaptive cognitions, the development of a coping template through the teaching of various self-control skills (self-monitoring, self-consequation, self-evaluation) and social skills training. Kendall (1993) provides a thorough review of the approach and its proven utility.

Of all the therapeutic approaches used directly with children it would appear the cognitive-behavioural is now the best supported by studies of treatment effectiveness. However, even here doubts have been raised over whether CBT's effectiveness does actually rest upon changes in faulty cognitions. While earlier studies failed to directly tap into cognitive change, more recently reported studies have done so and findings support the view that beneficial changes in thinking have occurred as a result of CBT (Wood et al., 1996).

Psychotherapeutic approaches

Many therapeutic activities attract the title 'child psychotherapy' by which is usually implied, at minimum, that the child–therapist relationship is the primary 'instrument' for promoting change in the thoughts, feelings and behaviour of the child. However, variation in practice or emphasis appears then to revolve around at least three dimensions: the degree to which treatment is directive or non-directive, interpretative or supportive, and conducted principally through verbal discourse or indirect communication.

Whatever its form, clinical evidence for the usefulness of child psychotherapy is most abundant at the level of descriptive clinical case report. Very few rigorous empirical studies of psychotherapeutic approaches have actually been conducted, and their scientific legitimacy has, surprisingly, yet to be established. A major retrospective study at the Tavistock Clinic (Target and Fonagy 1994) identified 299 children as presenting with anxiety and depressive disorders. A review of their clinical records indicated 85 per cent were described as considerably improved after an average of two years' treatment. However, the authors recognize the study's limitations: without a control group, without objective measures and where client improvement was estimated by the therapist involved. The findings are therefore no more than correlational, but nonetheless the study marks a serious attempt to subject psychodynamic therapy to empirical evaluation.

A point worth making, despite the paucity of convincing research, is that a very large proportion of child therapists will openly acknowledge that psychotherapeutic methods and concepts influence their formulation of a case and their broad therapeutic approach (such as the establishment of a good relationship with the child, the awareness of unconscious motivation, an interest in the process of therapy) if not their specific interventive inputs (Kazdin et al., 1990).

Therapy effectiveness: summary

The meagre conclusions which can be drawn from various meta-analyses of child therapy effectiveness (e.g. Weisz et al., 1995) are that:

- Psychotherapy in any form is better than no treatment for a large number of childhood problems, including anxiety, aggression, social withdrawal, etc.
- Differences in treatment effectiveness tend to favour behavioural over non-behavioural approaches.

In addition, it would seem that with short-term therapy contacts (the vast majority of child therapeutic work) superior gains are likelier to be achieved where:

- Specific techniques for change are used.
- Treatment goals are explicit and defined.
- Intervention focus is on overt behaviour.

- Therapeutic focus is on the present rather than on the past.
- The child is older (pre-adolescent upwards).
- The child is seen individually.

Although at first sight these conclusions appear to offer firm guidance on the selection of therapy it must be pointed out that the latter more specific claims are based on more tenuous evidence. In addition it should be remembered that many practitioners dispute the validity of empirical methodologies as the measure of psychotherapeutic practice. As Shapiro (1996) stated: 'the complexity of psychotherapy and the wide range of perspectives on its processes require a pluralistic approach to methodology'.

Therapist characteristics

Even less can be said about the therapist characteristics associated with good therapy. Kolvin et al. (1981), in one of the few studies to examine this area in any detail, reported therapists rated as extrovert, assertive and open were more likely to be associated with positive treatment outcome. More traditional therapist characteristics such as empathy, warmth and genuineness were not. It would seem unwise therefore to assume that what holds for adult therapy, in terms of therapist characteristics and non-specific core conditions, will also hold for child therapy. However, many agree that effective therapy is more likely where:

- The therapist has received formal training in therapy and the psychological formulation of contextual and developmental factors.
- The therapist has flexible interpersonal relationship skills: capable of being active, directive and controlling when required and of being non-directive, supportive and passive when appropriate.
- The therapist engenders a positive expectation of therapy in the child.

Child characteristics

What every clinical research study reveals and every clinician knows is that no single therapeutic approach is effective for every child; individual differences in responsiveness are always found. Clearly many factors may contribute to this phenomenon, including the nature and characteristics of the problem, contextual variables, and individual characteristics of the child, such as gender, age and ability.

At present relatively little solid research evidence exists, though meta-analytic evaluation of therapeutic effectiveness studies suggests the child's developmental ability and the nature of the child's difficulty are likely to be related to treatment efficacy. For instance, Blagg (1992), in a review of psychodynamic and behavioural approaches to school refusal, reports that the treatment outcome is consistently good for children between seven and ten years irrespective of the treatment approach. However, for older children (eleven to sixteen years) the outcome is far less predictable, tending to be less successful and more dependent upon the type of treatment used.

However, the term 'child characteristics' runs the risk of casting the child as separate from their environment. An evaluation of a CBT intervention for anxiety difficulties (Cobham et al., 1998) found that individual children's response to treatment was related to their own parents' anxiety features. Children with more anxious parents responded less well to the therapy even when age, gender and severity of anxiety were controlled for.

Summary point

The counselling psychologist is left with a mass of research evidence which does not provide clear evidence of treatment superiority (only of the broad effectiveness of most approaches) or of the therapist characteristics which are necessary for psychological change. Nevertheless, the responsible counselling psychologist must in his or her therapeutic practice attempt to maximize the value of what is known. In the field of child work this means combining knowledge about child development, knowledge of research findings in specific areas, e.g. divorce, bereavement, etc., and knowledge about effective treatments.

Differences in developmental capacity

A review of changing developmental capacity could occupy another chapter if not a whole book in its own right. What follows is a very abbreviated account of important developmental characteristics across broad phases of childhood.

Developmental psychology has greatly extended our understanding of the cognitive and social changes of childhood but the counselling psychologist must remain aware that each child's developmental profile is unique and that normative data can be used only as a point of comparison for any given child. In particular it must be appreciated that a child's environment and experience may accelerate, distort or delay a particular child's ability or behaviour in any given area. For example, if the three children in our earlier divorce scenario had already experienced a previous parental divorce, their understanding of its significance and their vocabulary for describing the event would probably be more 'sophisticated' than a sibship of similar ages who were experiencing divorce for the first time. Furthermore, a vital point for the clinician to keep in mind is that, although the developmental changes to be outlined are usually associated with particular phases and age periods of childhood, it would be a serious error to believe this must be so. Individual children may reveal erratic levels of developmental functioning, sometimes ahead and sometimes behind what might be expected from other aspects of their behaviour. Most reliable of all is that under conditions of high personal stress there will be a tendency for the child to function at social and cognitive levels lower than would otherwise be the case.

It was proposed earlier that two central requirements of adult therapies are the capacity to self-reflect and the capacity to 'step out' of one's immediate context so as to contemplate alternative possible arrangements. These socio-cognitive developmental capacities cannot be assumed to be available to children in therapy or, where they are in evidence, that they are as robust or as complete as they are for mature adults. It is primarily with these capacities in mind that the broad phases of childhood development will be reviewed.

Infancy and early childhood

- Toddlers know more than they can articulate and cannot yet examine what it is they know.
- For instance they know 'the routine and familiar order of life' and they know how 'to be' in various social situations.

Early school years (four to seven years)

- Thinking is dominated by the immediate and concrete rather than the psychological.
- An uninspected view of self, what 'they know' are the labels and expressed values of their immediate environment.
- Self-concept at this point fairly limited and based around two key domains: general competence (skills) and social acceptability. They also view others in fairly concrete and absolute terms, e.g. good, bad, strong, etc.
- Social comparison with others is possible but the child will tend to be more concerned with how *they did*, etc., i.e. egocentric bias.
- Understand feelings as being caused by external events and things but they may be given an internal physical location. In distress the child seeks adult reassurance.
- Ability to make cause and effect links between feelings and events is limited unless contiguous in space and time.

Late middle childhood (eight to twelve years)

- Capable of unprompted self-reflection using logic and reason, but in a fairly concrete and literal manner.
- Social comparisons and the concept of 'fairness' often dominate interpersonal analysis.
- Egocentric bias persists but more consistently the child is conscious of the needs and interests of others.
- Self-concept more elaborated, combining positive and negative aspects of self.
- Capable of recognizing thoughts, feelings and behaviour as related and with help that changing one can alter the others.
- In situations of distress the child will often have completed a level of self-evaluation and identified what they believe should happen to improve matters.

Adolescence

- Have begun to define self in unique identity terms.
- Capable now of locating self as 'object' in an abstracted personal history and interpersonal context.

- Emergence of global self-awareness is associated with increased preoccupation with self and sensitivity to the perceptions of others.
- Capable of maintaining mood state through active rumination but also capable of concealing affective state, even when in distress, whilst maintaining general functioning.
- An ambivalent view of adults as a helpful social resource.

Developmental status, developmental abilities and choice of therapeutic approach

In reviewing the changing socio-cognitive capacities of children it becomes clearer that therapeutic methods and approaches make different levels of demand on these developmental abilities. At this point therefore it is possible to reconsider the major therapeutic approaches and the degree of consonance they achieve with particular developmental phases of childhood.

The very young child does not have the capacity to enter any therapeutic approach which depends upon self-reflection and evaluation. Even more important, young children do not yet have the developmental capacities to learn about the 'world' or 'themselves' via verbal and cognitive processes. The child at this age learns primarily through repeated, active, experiential processes occurring in the context of secure, constantly available and guiding attachment relationships.

Only the psychoanalytic model of child therapy routinely structures therapy in such an intensive, extended and relationship-based manner. In most cases, however, it will be clear that any therapeutic assistance which may be offered will be most effective at the level of the child's carers. The commonest forms of intervention at this age are therefore indirect and likely to include elements of developmental counselling (explaining the behaviour) and (behavioural) advice on parental response in the area of concern, in a therapeutic relationship which supports and affirms parental competence.

Behavioural methods

The relationship created in typical therapeutic activity may be characterized as highly structured, problem-focused and prescriptive. The approach does not require insight into motives, awareness of feelings or thoughts nor even an understanding of the intervention rationale. However, in direct individual work it does depend on the child being motivated to trust/obey/please the therapist, being behaviourally self-aware and having developed a basic level of self-control. Under these conditions and via processes of modelling, skill rehearsal, active systematic desensitization and training in relaxation skills, children as young as four years of age may be engaged. Children of any age thereafter may also be assisted through entirely behavioural techniques, though their increasing cognitive sophistication and increasing need for reasons for action mean they may be more open to and assisted by cognitive-behavioural methods.

Cognitive-behavioural methods

The cognitive-behavioural approach makes gradually increasing demands upon the child client as the sophistication of the technique is raised. At the simpler level techniques belonging to self-control strategies such as self-instructional talking, self-reinforcement, cognitive management of anxiety, still require that the child is developmentally capable of cognitive and behavioural self-monitoring: of reporting on thoughts and feelings, of linking the two (intuitively or via rational processes) and assigning them an internal origin. An indication of a child who may be capable of these levels of developmental operation would be found where social comparisons are being routinely made and psychological processes are cited prominently in accounts of experience. As described earlier, these features of development begin to appear in late middle childhood.

Higher-level techniques of CBT – such as interpersonal problem-solving approaches – may also be within the developmental reach of the eight to twelve-year-old child, since such children can usually offer a simple account of the 'other's' perspective. However, in interpersonal situations of high arousal the ability to maintain this wider perspective is very quickly reduced. Realistic, action-based approaches in which role-play and rehearsal are prominent would be necessary for children at the lower end of the eight-to-twelve age range to benefit from such techniques. With the introduction of cognitive restructuring techniques, based on the evaluation and testing of cognitions, the identification of underlying assumptions, etc., the level of developmental functioning required is raised yet further. The child now needs to be capable of taking a third-person perspective in respect of themselves, their circumstances and their psychological experiences. In addition this last strategy would appear to involve the capacity to deal cognitively with multiple possibilities, multiple emotions and indirect causal links. These capacities are unlikely to be evident before pre-adolescence and are more likely to be reliably available to the young person of late adolescent years. With all age groups the cognitive behavioural therapist needs to be aware that in the area of interpersonal difficulties the problems may be rooted in emotional obstacles to the application of social-cognitive skills and not necessarily to a deficit or distortion in cognitions.

Psychotherapeutic methods

Although there are many variations, common elements of the child psychotherapies are the ideas of change occurring through experience of the therapeutic relationship itself, through the use of corrective, emotional experiences, through interpretation and the development of increased personal insight and awareness.

At ages younger than seven years – and even older where the development of an 'internal model' of relationship has been seriously impaired – the child is unlikely to gain significantly from infrequent, brief contacts with a therapist. Relationship-based therapies with this age group therefore need to consider arranging – at least initially – a number of sessions per week if the child is to develop an enduring and transportable sense of the relationship. For children beyond this age, who are capable of actively sustaining ideas of relationship and experience through thought, the frequency of contact can probably be reduced. Obviously developmental capacity is not the only factor here. The level of disturbance and the nature of the child's on-going experience are critical factors in deciding on the intensity of contact.

A primary concern with psychotherapeutic methods based on interpretation, insight and self-reflection is that they may frequently exceed a young child's cognitive-developmental capacity. In particular methods which relate present behaviour or emotional experiences to distant causes, internal, personal origin and unconscious motives are likely to be beyond the cognitive developmental capacities of most children younger than late middle childhood. High demands for self-reflection and interpretive comment may outstrip the child's emergent capabilities and actually increase the likelihood of an external and concrete ego-centric perspective being elicited. For instance, Shirk (1998) conducted an analysis of 'interpretations' offered to children in insight-oriented child therapy. He found that the causal structure implicit in many interpretations was far more complex than the causal reasoning capacities of most children up to pre-adolescence. Furthermore, in the consideration of intimate relations children of middle childhood through to adolescence and beyond may persistently demonstrate areas of egocentric distortion characteristic of less sophisticated levels. Psychodynamic phenomena, such as denial, dissociation, etc., therefore could equally be interpreted as signs that cognitive capacities have been exceeded by the therapeutic methods employed.

An important caveat to the foregoing is that many psychotherapeutic approaches and techniques offer the child experiences which may have their primary impact via emotional, right-hemispherical or unconscious processes. Experiences evoked via play therapy, metaphor and analogy could therefore be seen as bypassing the restrictions of conscious, logical cognitive developmental capacities. The research and developmental literature on the processes by which such approaches may have their therapeutic effect is entirely undeveloped. Nevertheless, even these indirect therapeutic activities must remain mindful of the child's tendency to resist and reinterpret experiences in a developmentally consistent fashion.

Finally the manner in which children's self-esteem is directly or indirectly addressed in therapy is of perhaps greater importance than the 'techniques' associated with different approaches. On this point it would seem that adult approval and positive regard may be of greater importance and therapeutic value for younger children. As the child becomes psycho-socially more mature, therapeutic activities which promote personally valued competences or increase belief in one's own self-efficiency become more effective methods for promoting self-esteem.

Evidence-based practice: pulling it together

Having reviewed the clinical and developmental literature the counselling psychologist is still left with a very wide goal in terms of how to shape therapy. However, a few simple ideas may further anchor and orient the counselling psychologist in the direction of evidentially supported therapy with individual children.

The available evidence suggests that working from within a cognitive behavioural model with children is reasonably well supported and yet the suggested model of working can often seem inappropriate to the child presenting. For example, in respect of the three children presented at the beginning of this chapter it may be difficult to enter a therapeutic contract with them which suggests or indicates their ways of thinking are in some way in error. Children are confused, perhaps in denial, and perhaps most assuredly unsure how this major change in their life arrangement has affected them. A useful starting place for work with almost all children emerges from the personal construct – self concept theoretical literature (Byrne, 1996). Within this broad class of theory there is an idea that life experiences have an effect upon the way we conceive of ourselves. This is often abundantly clear in children brought for therapy usually in the context of events or circumstances which are leading if not themselves then their caring environment to struggle in their understanding of them. In the example which began the chapter it is plausible to assume that the children's experience of their parents' divorce has had some effect upon the way they understand the world and ultimately themselves.

It will be recalled that developmental research suggests children have a 'sense of themselves' which they are capable of articulating to some degree from as young as four years of age. Although various theoretical models of the self-concept construct exist, they all suggest that thoughts, feelings and behaviours are important to its definition. At the clinical practice level the self-concept provides an easily shared idea which children can understand and find interesting to explore. It is referred to and developed in individual therapy by such simple phrases as 'Are you the sort of boy/girl who makes friends easily?' There are many well validated measures of self-concept and these can further extend the range and breadth of inquiry. What exploring a child's self-concept will allow is the development of a line of inquiry of interest to the child but also an entry route into the thoughts, feelings and behaviours of the child as understood and described by themselves. As this account of themselves becomes more elaborated and perhaps more focused around certain ideas and experiences, e.g. divorce of parents, and ideas, e.g. self before and after experience, the introduction of cognitive and behavioural methods becomes but a short step to take.

The suggestion here therefore is to take a well supported theoretical construct self-concept and to use it as an entry point for opening discussion/conversation with the child which quite readily elicits ideas and beliefs to which cognitive behavioural methods can be applied. It also provides parent and child with an easily shared explanatory framework for the therapy to be undertaken. Furthermore it is supported by a range of standardized, research-validated measures which can be routinely incorporated as an important element of the therapeutic process as well as a source of objective measurement in respect of individual change.

Self-concept provides a platform from which it makes sense to look at behaviour and ways in which behaviour might be changed, at thinking and ways in which thinking might be changed, at feelings and the ways in which feelings might be identified. It is not suggested here that self-concept equates with self-esteem, although certainly the two are recognized as being very closely linked. It is also the case that individual therapy with children does not necessarily have the objective of 'making a child feel good about him/herself' but rather has an aim of increasing the accuracy and usefulness of self-perceptions and supporting a sense of personal agency within the child. Finally any changes within the child can endure only if they are supported by significant others in their environment.

Conclusion

The processes of child therapy are embedded in and constrained by the child's developmental ability to participate. Whatever the clinical approach adopted certain elements will remain common across therapeutic encounters. For instance, all child therapies require and depend upon the transmission and reception of meaning between participants. Similarly all therapies require and depend upon the establishment of a *relationship* with the child which will support and sustain therapeutic activity. All major therapeutic approaches (behavioural, cognitive, psychotherapeutic) in child work rely to some degree upon the child's ability to engage in *self-reflection* – to reflect upon their own actions, feelings and thoughts when distant from the actual experiences being discussed. Yet others (cognitive and psychotherapeutic) may go further and expect the child to develop, through therapy, increased *insight* into their own motivational structures. Without labouring the point it is clear all of these therapeutic objectives and their associated methods are crucially influenced by the child's cognitive-developmental capacities. This is not to ignore or underestimate the influence each child's unique personal history has upon their experience and understanding of the 'world'. Rather it is an appeal for both facets to be considered in arriving at an understanding of any individual child's behaviour and communication.

In broad terms it seems wise to anticipate that, in comparison with adults, children will be:

- More likely to be restricted to *the present*, in their view of themselves and their situation. The representation of the past may not be possible and is less likely to be seen as relevant to present conditions.
- As likely to exhibit their difficulties behaviourally as symbolically.
- Less able or inclined to be self-reflective (until adolescence) and more oriented to action-based, experiential learning.

Furthermore, it must be borne in mind that child difficulties with the process or tasks of therapy need not always be attributed to the absence or fragility of cognitive sophistication. Therapy may, as an activity, be of such length, interpersonal intensity and novelty that an excessive load is placed upon specific cognitive functions, such as memory, attention, concentration, leading to distractibility, withdrawal or emotional abreaction.

As yet the empirical evidence does not exist which can allow a therapist to confidently select specific treatments for specific children. This chapter has attempted to underline the importance of context and developmental ability in making therapeutic choices. Of all client groups children are possibly the least defended against the well intentioned decisions and actions of therapists. The responsible counselling psychologist undertaking direct work with children must therefore show respect for the lack of secure evidence and act with appropriate caution and sensitivity. The steps to be taken, it has been suggested in this chapter, are that the counselling psychologist should first evaluate the most advantageous focus for intervention, secondly examine the scientific support for the approach to be used (and, if available, the research data relating to the difficulty in question) and thirdly consider the child's developmental presentation and its meaning for the therapeutic methods to be used. Finally, however, the course of therapy must be determined more by the actual responses of the child in therapy than by theoretical frameworks or nomothetic research findings.

References

Barnett, R., Docherty, J. and Frommelt, G. (1991) 'A review of child psychotherapy research since 1963', *Journal of the American Academy of Child and Adolescent Psychiatry*, 30: 1–14.

Blagg, N. (1992) 'School phobia' in D. Lane and A. Miller (eds) *Child and Adolescent Therapy: a Handbook*. Milton Keynes: Open University Press.

Byrne, B.M. (1996) *Measuring Self-concept across the Lifespan*. Washington DC: American Psychological Association.

Carter, B. and McGoldrick, M. (1989) *The Changing Family Life Cycle: a Framework for Family Therapy*, second edition. Boston MA: Allyn & Bacon.

Casey, R.J. and Berman, J.S. (1985) 'The outcome of psychotherapy with children', *Psychological Bulletin*, 98: 388–400.

Chess, S. and Thomas, A. (1984) *Origins and Evolution of Behavior Disorders: from Infancy to Adult Life*. New York: Brunner Mazel.

Cobham, V., Dodds, M. and Spence, S. (1998) 'The role of parental anxiety in the treatment of childhood anxiety', *Journal of Consulting and Clinical Psychology*, 66: 893–905.

Fauber, R., Forehand, R., Thomas, A.M. and Wierson, M. (1990) 'A mediational model of the impact of marital conflict on adolescent adjustment in intact and divorced families: the role of disrupted parenting', *Child Development*, 61: 1112–23.

Flavell, J. (1985) *Cognitive Development*, second edition. Englewood Cliffs NJ: Prentice Hall.

Herbert, M. and Iwaniec, D. (1981) 'Behavioural psychotherapy in natural home settings: an empirical *study applied* to conduct disorders and incontinent children', *Behavioural Psychotherapy*, 9: 55–76.

Hetherington, E. (1989) 'Coping with family transitions: winners, losers and survivors', *Child Development*, 60: 1–14.

Houts, A.C., Shutty, M.S. and Emery, R.E. (1985) 'The impact of children on adults' in B. Lahey and A. Kazdin (eds) *Advances in Clinical Child Psychology* VIII. New York: Plenum Press.

Kazdin, A.E. (2000) *Psychotherapy for Children and Adolescents: Directions for Research and Practice*. New York: Oxford University Press.

Kazdin, A.E., Siegel, T.C. and Bass, D. (1990) 'Drawing upon clinical practice to inform research on child and adolescent psychotherapy: a survey of practitioners', *Professional Psychology and Practice*, 21: 189–98.

Kazdin, A.E. (1994) 'Psychotherapy for children and adolescents', in A.E. Bergin and S.L. Garfield (eds) *Handbook of Play Therapy and Behavioral Change*, fourth edition. New York: Wiley.

Kendall, P. (1993) 'Cognitive behavioural therapies with youth: guiding theory, current status and emerging developments', *Journal of Consulting and Clinical Psychology*, 61 (2): 235–47.

Kolvin, I., Garside, R., Nichol, A., Macmillan, A., Wolstenholme, F. and Leitch, I. (1981) *Help Starts Here: the Maladjusted Child in Ordinary School*. London: Tavistock.

Ollendick, T. and King, N. (1998) 'Empirically supported treatments for children with phobic and anxiety disorders', *Journal of Clinical Child Psychology*, 27: 156–67.

Patterson, G.R., Reid, J.B. and Dishion, T.J. (1992) *Antisocial Boys*. Eugene, OR: Castazia.

Pearce, J. (1993) 'Child health surveillance for psychiatric disorder: practical guidelines', *Archives of Disease in Childhood* 69: 394–8.

Shapiro D. (1996) Models of change in psychotherapy', *Current Opinion in Psychiatry*, 9: 177–81.

Shirk, S. (1998) 'Interpersonal schemata in child psychotherapy: a cognitive interpersonal perspective', *Journal of Clinical Child Psychology*, 27: 4–16.

Shirk, S. (1999) 'Developmental therapy' in W.K. Silverman and T.H. Ollendick (eds) *Developmental Issues in the Clinial Treatment of Children*. Boston MA: Allyn & Bacon.

Shirk, S. and Russell, R. (1992) 'A re-evaluation of estimates of child therapy effectiveness', *Journal of the American Academy of Child and Adolescent Psychiatry*, 31: 703–9.

Street, E.C., Downey, J. and Brazier, A. (1991) 'The development of therapeutic consultations in child-focused family work', *Journal of Family Therapy*, 13 (3): 311–33.

Target, M. and Fonagy, P. (1994) 'The efficacy of psychoanalysis for children with emotional disorders', *American Academy of Child and Adolescent Psychiatry*, 33: 361–71.

Target, M. and Fonagy, P. (1996) 'The psychological treatment of children and adolescents' psychiatric disorders', in A. Roth and P. Fonagy (eds) *What works for Whom? A Critical Review of Play Therapy Research*. New York: Guilford Press.

Wallace, S.A., Crown, J.M., Cox, A.D. and Berger, M. (1997) *Child and Adolescent Mental Health: Health Care Needs Assessment*. Abingdon: Radcliffe Medical Press.

Weiss, B., Catron, T., and Harris, V. (2000) 'A two year follow-up of the effectiveness of traditional psychotherapy', *Journal of Consulting and Clinical Psychology*, 68 (6): 1094–101.

Weisz, J.R., Weiss, B., Hans, S.S., Granger, D.A. and Martin, T. (1995). 'Effects of psychotherapy and adolescents revisited: meta-analysis of treatment outcome studies', *Psychological Bulletin*, 117: 450–18.

Wilson, G.T. (1997) 'Treatment manuals in clinical practice', *Behaviour Response Therapy*, 35: 205–210.

Wood, A., Harrington, R. and Moore, A. (1996) 'Controlled trial of a brief cognitive behavioural intervention in adolescent patients with depressive disorders', *Journal of Child Psychology and Psychiatry*, 37: 737–46.

16 Psychological Counselling with Young Adults
CASSIE COOPER

Students of human development have always recognized the deep significance of the physical, psychological and social transformation of the period of life we label young adulthood. It has become conventional for writers on the subject to indicate that irresponsibility, unbridled sexuality, naive enthusiasms and anti-social behaviour patterns characterize this phase of life.

For many years these so-called 'behaviour problems' were seen as easily contained and considered to be a matter of concern for parents, teachers, neigh-bours and sometimes the police, but hardly a primary concern in society. The challenge and irrational potential of the young adult population could be dealt with by suppression, or the assumption that they were exhibiting an immatu-rity and frustration which would be 'cured' by time. In the latter part of the twentieth century the situation altered radically. The young adult now weighs heavily on the consciousness of society. Disaffection, disillusionment and depression mirror the social changes, the moral dilemmas and the ambiguities which characterize our twenty-first-century world. Contributors to journals of psychology and counselling make it clear that we continue to be markedly sub-ject to such stereotyped thinking. The traditional stereotype of the young adult with attributes of rebellious aggressiveness was dominant in the past but still has powerful currency today. Stereotypes held strongly enough tend in the end to justify themselves. It is easy to present behaviour which reflects that which is expected.

In contrast, there is literature which projects a differing image of the young adult, who can be hailed as the guardian of uncorrupted wisdom, a victim of adult exploitation and negligence or as a trend-setter for new fashions and trends, whose opinions are eagerly sought by advertising agencies and the media.

In working with clients in this age group, psychologists and counsellors can be susceptible to polarization – perceiving the client either as a threatening delinquent or the victim of an unscrupulous and materialistic society.

This is a period of passionate self-absorption, when consideration for the feelings of others has a low priority in the struggle to develop an identity. Striving towards adulthood highlights a number of uncomfortable truths about our society. This client group brings into sharp focus the fact that their parents are growing older, that the society their parents espoused is being supplanted and overtaken by new generations and that these sexually developed young men and women are about to overtake their parents in forming external relation-ships that will eventually supplant and replace their families.

They are 'difficult' clients finally relinquishing all those years of parenting and schooling. The counselling psychologist endeavours to provide reality-determined issues and concepts whilst considering how best he or she can make use of disciplined methods to understand the developmental tasks of this age group.

In a certain sense we can think of every young man and woman as a budding psychologist. The normal processes of maturation enable each and every one of us to develop a particular view of life and to operate strategies for predicting and responding to life events however traumatic they may be. We learn as we go which major physical and intellectual developments are taking place.

Psychological problems for the young adult (defined for the purpose of this chapter as the period from age eighteen to twenty five years) are generally concerned with personal difficulties occurring in relation to family and friends, the perception of the world, and around attitudes to their sexual development and identity. These problems, when they occur, can be characterized by feelings of anxiety or tension, dissatisfaction with their own behaviour, excessive worries about minor problems and body image and a sense of failure to meet desired goals and ambitions in life.

There are times when clients themselves appear to be unaware that they have a 'problem', until significant others, who may be adversely affected by their behaviour, have cause to complain about the situation, after watching their loved ones lose hope, become self-destructive, unhappy, often resorting to delinquent behaviour.

Young men and women in this age group may well be unemployed, divorced, in debt, facing discrimination by race, economic stringency, sexual, moral or religious demands, medical disability, bereavement and loss. We question if these problems stem from the life script formed in early childhood. We acknowledge that changes cannot evolve in a smooth untroubled process of transition and that painful and destructive dysfunctions and shifts are inevitable. We question if so-called changes in our clients really reflect growth and understanding – or are they an attempt by troubled young men and women to gain approval from parents, teachers, friends and counsellors?

For many years the field of psychology treated the topic of personality development in early adulthood and its ensuing problems with benign neglect. Psychologists concluded that, once the storms of adolescence had abated, the young adult would proceed to the calm of adulthood. He or she having completed their schooling could go on to higher education, become a member of the work force, leave home, get married and 'settle down'. Nothing more would be heard from them until they approached the periods highlighted by media spin – 'thirty-something', 'mid-life crisis', 'forty-year itch' and the generation gap which widens until the inevitability of old age and death. Things are not so straightforward; the young adult of the twenty first century does not enter or accept a period of tranquillity, sameness and predictability. Psychological theories have influenced, reflected and reinforced these beliefs.

Popular theories about independence are psychoanalytic in origin. They postulate that a successful transition from adolescence to young adulthood is achieved in individuation – a rejection of parental definitions of identity. Rejection means that at this time the young man or woman is torn between the longing to be regressive and loyal to past childhood association and facilitations and the alluring prospect of adult autonomy. Acceptance of this view acknowledges that you are now what you were once, only more so. Whatever occurs later in life is merely an elaboration or distillation of your early childhood experiences.

With this view, the outer trappings of leaving home matter less than a person's inner psychological state. It is assumed to be an act of independence to leave home, sometimes banging the door in fury and frustration, but this in no way guarantees psychological autonomy. To leave home and telephone one's parents twice a week, depending on the family for advice and for money, can be far less autonomous than those who choose to remain at home whilst living with parents but financially able to support themselves and feeling able to come and go as they please.

This chapter will examine the theoretical perspectives which provide highly contrasting solutions to the problems listed below.

- The stormy and peaceful transitions in the *individuation* processes.
- Problems of *separation* – the development of independence/ego-strength.
- Failure to establish a work pattern either in education or employment.
- Ideas of *success and failure*.
- Inability to develop the *capacity to involve and develop intimate relationships* with members of the opposite sex and/or members of the same sex.

The individuation process

It is a paradoxical proposition that, if you have been happily and securely attached to your family and to your parents, it is easier to establish your own identity and to leave home without things going wrong than if you are anxious about them or at war with them. (Bowlby, 1979)

Young adulthood is not necessarily a stormy period for everyone. Most young people manage the transition from home to the wider world without difficulty. The Central Policy Review Research Team in its 1999 survey (CSO 1999) estimated that 70 per cent of twenty four-year-olds had left home, most of them having married, or were living with 'partners', indicating that approximately four-fifths of the young adult population had left home. This figure may well have further declined, owing, in part, to the high cost of maintaining a student at university and the increase in house prices, which precludes purchasing a home of one's own until attaining a high standard of living. One-third of marriages contracted under the age of twenty result in divorce within the next ten years, and one-fifth of the marriages contracted between twenty and twenty four end in divorce. Marriage and/or partnership, when used as a means by which to leave home, appears to be successful only as a temporary stepping stone.

There is considerable evidence, however, that in both a physical and a psychological sense leaving home is becoming more difficult for the young. Since 1995 the proportion of young people between the ages of twenty and twenty nine living at home has increased by 35 per cent. This is clearly due to economic factors. Young men and women who may want to establish their own home and family are finding it much harder to do so. For this reason marriage has to be postponed. Marriage was seen to be the ceremonial point of no return in the individuation process which resulted in leaving the parental home, but the average age of marriage has risen from 22.8 for men and 20.3 for women (in 1950) to 34.8 for men and 31.4 for women (in 2000). Personality formation theories which echo the psychoanalytic theme of the need to 'break away' from childhood identities (the idea of leaving home, whether it be by one means or another) pose problems to this new generation by their assumption of what was meant by dependence and the omnipotence of parents. It is harder than ever to push oneself to a form of liberation from parents through study, work or marriage, and finally to assume the parental role oneself.

Dependence is a prime characteristic of human nature, but as we reach adulthood the need to prove ourselves as independent becomes a priority. Independence is widely accepted as part of Western culture and philosophy, and is highly valued in current society. It is associated with powerful words and images such as strength, individualism and leadership.

The notion of dependence is, in contrast, devalued and often associated with helplessness, indecision, weakness and childish behaviour. Dependence and independence are seen as opposite poles, delicately poised, which can tip in either direction, but the desirable weighting is seen to lie in the area of independence, the golden goal of achievement and growth. Although psychoanalytic theories stress the necessity for the child of an early period of dependence on his or her parents, it has never been seen as a positive goal. Dependence is viewed as a 'means to', a process which can lead to emotional security or ultimately to the achievement of independence.

Counselling psychologists would see part of their role as facilitating their clients to become more independent, but are any of us ever truly independent and is independence necessarily such a good thing? George Kelly (1955) argued that adults, like children, are dependent too but that they extend their dependence discriminatingly to more people, more things and more institutions. He went on to suggest that the attitude taken by 'helping professionals' should not be one of labelling their clients as dependent or independent but one where 'emphasis is placed upon variations in their dispersion', a salient aspect of personal growth.

According to Eric Erikson's (1981) still influential theories of psychological development, the young adult is struggling to attain, and perhaps more important to retain, a sense of ego identity, a sense of self that is free and distinct from the experiences of childhood and adolescence. This task, says Erikson, is accomplished during a 'psychosocial moratorium' when the young person is free to experiment with new possibilities – for example, in careers or ideologies – without having to make a firm commitment to any as yet.

Case study 1

My first client exemplifies a family's response to the experience of separation and loss related to the young adult's individuation process and the necessity for the counsellor to be ready and willing to meet this response in a flexible manner. There was, in this case, a failure of therapy where the client was already away from home and where her parents opposed the treatment because they found it threatening in the same manner that they found her emerging autonomy threatening. There was no alliance with the family which could have helped my client had it existed.

Mindu, an intelligent university student, was referred for counselling because she had unsatisfactory relationships with men and performed poorly in one field of study after another. She had changed courses from Psychology to Business Studies, each time feeling inadequate and intellectually inferior. Her immigrant father, a wealthy and domineering businessman, had never allowed her to associate with young men of a different religion from his (Muslim) and could not understand why she was bothering to study at all. Her mother was also unsympathetic and called Mindu frequently to say that she was hurting her father who felt that, whilst Mindu was able to take his money, she did not really love him. If she loved him she would give up messing about in university and just come home.

The father was part of a very large family business which had been built from scratch by the paternal grandfather. Each of the father's three brothers had brought a son into the business to carry on after the elders retired. Mindu's younger sister had rebelled against the system and was now living with an aunt in Kenya. The elder sister was married, living near the parents' home, and her husband had been taken into the business.

Even so, her father was unhappy. He was highly suspicious of 'outsiders' (her sister's husband) and felt that the only trustworthy person as a successor to himself would have to be a 'blood relation'. Having no sons, only daughters, he had focused on Mindu to follow him into the family business. He could not understand her needs and independent career aspirations, which seemed 'ridiculous' to him, and he devalued her fields of study as potentially leading to financial ruin.

I understood Mindu's failure in her studies as an expression of guilt over separation. Her parents fuelled her conflict, portraying her as a betrayer of family loyalties, attempting to thwart her moves towards independence and autonomy and wishing to ensure her safe return to the bosom of the family. Mindu verbalized this quite clearly. 'If I am not cut out for academic work and I do not have what it takes to get a reasonable degree, then perhaps I really belong back in the family business. Perhaps my father is right.' It was clear that Mindu was avoiding ambivalence and was daunted by the prospect of ever separating from the family.

Her father was angry and constantly urged her to stop counselling. She was wasting time and money and she had no right to seek 'outside' help when she should in fact be confiding in him. After three months of counselling she returned home for the Easter holidays. On her return to university the father began to phone her on a daily basis. He was feeling unwell, he really missed her, she was in his dreams at night. At the same time he began to quibble about the money and threatened to cut down on her 'need' for counselling.

Four weeks later her father telephoned and asked to speak to me about Mindu. When I pointed out that my relationship with her was completely confidential, he launched into a tirade. Mindu had become estranged from her family as a result of her studies at university. There were other members of the family 'infected' in this way, and a male friend of Mindu had 'meddled and analysed' her. When this statement was received in silence he went on to query my religious beliefs and practices. Was I a parent who encouraged and advised my own children to leave home? How long did I envisage carrying on my counselling relationship with his daughter? Two weeks after this phone call Mindu terminated her therapy. She sent me a bright shiny card with a large sunflower on the front that just said, 'Thank you.'

Mindu's confused mixture of loyalty and guilt forced her to seek a form of reparation for the difficulties between her father and his family. Splits in the family reinforced her own fear of becoming a success. Success meant that she became different from other members of the family, and this could be seen to be an abandonment of her relationship with them. Her fight for individuation and autonomy was regarded with suspicion and fear by her father and incompatible with his so-called ideas of 'femininity'. She was betraying her cultural and religious background by aiming to be like her non-Asian peer group.

Lawrence Wrightsman (1994) has cited the term 'cultural camouflage' to describe the universal tendency of Asian family members to avoid responsibility for their feelings, actions and destiny by attributing their differences either to their cultural and religious background or to the influence of Western ideas.

In the traditional Asian context women are identified more transactionally than individually, as daughters to their parents, wives to their husbands, daughter-in-law to their parents-in-law and in their most valued role as mother of sons. Traditionally a daughter is less valued than a son, as she has no significant ritual role to fulfil within her natal family – post partum depression is almost exclusively associated with the birth of female children in India (Guzder and Krishna, 1993). According to published figures the suicide rate for young Asian women is two to three times the national average.

Finding an identity is a critical preliminary step to success in the stages of development which follow – especially those which are concerned with forming intimate friendships and sexual relationships. Obviously leaving home can support the successful resolution of creating a separate identity, since it removes a young person from the direct control of parents, but the young person has to distinguish here between physically leaving home and doing so symbolically. If home is symbolic of primary childhood identification and influences and leaving is identified with questioning parental values and influences, then a symbolic leaving can be essential to attaining an adult identity – but if such a symbolic leaving becomes difficult, then it matters little whether the young person is able to leave in actuality.

Individuation is a bottleneck through which each person has to squeeze individually, but which, in most families, presents a potential crisis for all. It is a process that cannot be hurried – not simply an event, but a process which continues in a rather indefinite way and which everyone has to face sooner or later.

Young people are clearly perplexed by the separation process and there are few guidelines. Is there a right time for this or that? A right age to leave, or are there only specific individual cases? Do our current cultural perspectives offer any means of assuring a smooth transition into adulthood – with no clear social norms? Who is to tell a parent that they are clinging too long to their sons and daughters or, erring in the opposite direction, pushing them out of the door too soon?

It is not often appreciated just how important this transition is when young people break down at the very point when they should be taking off. Breakdown means not only mental breakdown, although that is included (75 per cent of newly diagnosed schizophrenics are aged between seventeen and twenty five) (Curran et al., 1980). It also means academic failure, drug abuse, overdoses, criminal activities, unwanted pregnancies and all the other problems that are so frequently associated with this age group (Kraemer, 1982)

Separation

The defiant way to leave home is, of course, to run away, but while an abrupt exit is perplexing for all concerned, the inner dynamics of a gradual separation can be equally paradoxical. At the time of separation, when the young man or woman is striving for autonomy, there are conflicting thoughts about abandoning the home base. It is comforting to believe that there is a home base to return to in time of need. Here is the difficulty. In order to separate, it is necessary to acquire a psychological detachment from parents; the simultaneous wish for distinctness and approval. If you are 'different' from your parents then you may feel separate from them but if parents feel different from their sons and daughters it could represent the loss of their love and support.

There is also the symptom of what could be termed 'paralysing apathy'. Jay Haley (1990) traces many of these problems to the need to preserve the family by sacrificing one's own growth. The young student's failure, for example, often serves to keep parents from confronting issues in their marriage that might otherwise have led to a divorce. If children are unable to separate and thus able to keep their parents intensely involved with their own problems, then parents may neglect their own difficulties. Young men and women are prepared to pay a high price – their own emotional growth – for the sake of so-called stability in their family life.

We understand these realignments of needs and wants as readjustments made necessary by increased anxieties and called forth by these acute life crises within the family. To label such reactions as 'pathological' or bad helps neither to understand the problems. To help chart a purposeful course of action towards them, their inner psycho-logic, their rationale must be understood.

This unfinished business of childhood provides the basis for adult development. As children we are fundamentally helpless in the face of both danger and inner passions of lust, rage and greed. We depend wholly on our parents to control both these threats and we analyse a series of false assumptions, illusions, that allow us to believe that we are perfectly safe. Maintaining these beliefs has the benefit of preserving our sense of security but it also has a cost. We are confined by the rules that bound us as children. We cannot get free of these confining inhibitions without facing the illusory nature of some of our most fundamental beliefs and without giving up the security they provide. But when we do get free we come to see reality more clearly and thus stop the unexpected shocks that must repeatedly occur when our illusions collide with life. And … we also gain from this process real freedom to be our own person, in touch with our inner needs and passions, living a vital and meaningful life (McCrae and Costa, 1990)

Thus, for the counselling psychologist, the work must be at this developmental level to shed major false assumptions in order to achieve further levels of adult maturity. According to Gould, for ages sixteen to twenty-two the developmental task is 'leaving our parents' world' and the major false assumption to be renounced is 'I'll always belong to my parents and believe in their world' (Gould, 1978). Young people want to be separate, they want their autonomy, but they are afraid that if they express their true feelings they will no longer be loved. They are not yet able to take hold of the idea that being 'different' need not make you unlovable. Disagreements with friends and parents are experienced as a kind of betrayal. The pressure in this age group is to be like everyone else.

Those young people who are unable to break away from the myth that 'I'll always be with my parents, they will always be there for me, I believe they know what is best for me' are sentenced to play out in their lives their parents' restricted attitudes and life-styles. Religious observance, sexual attitudes, political allegiances: when these unconscious controls reach a crescendo, how often do we hear the heartfelt cry 'I wish they were dead'? The stronger the fear of not being able to sever the umbilical cord, the greater the intensity of anger before leaving.

The critical developmental task of separation – individuation is negotiated always in the family setting. Successful maturation requires the helpful participation of the parents in providing a facilitating environment, a setting in which the young adult is emotionally supported whilst attempting to develop an integrated identity as a psychologically differentiated person.

When parents themselves suffer unresolved narcissistic fixations rooted in frustrating relationships in their own early development, the threat of their own offspring's separation can induce regression in themselves. When this occurs, parents are less able to relate to their child as a separate and independent centre of their own, but tend to relate to him or her as an extension of themselves, a self-object whom they feel they have the unquestionable right to possess and control. The resulting counter-separation attitudes and behaviour of parents present a profound interference to the nascent adult's developmental task.

A frequent scenario of this painful period is the abrupt and bitter exit from the family. Some of those who have to stay at home do so in a state of constant warfare, usually with the mother. Those who do leave home – for whatever reason – keep up a running battle, a hostile dependent entanglement between offspring and mother. In many cases they fail in the key tasks of young adulthood. Even when living alone they neither form meaningful relationships outside the family nor embark on a career other than that of 'a problem'.

Success and failure

Donald Super (1990) offers some of the most respected theories of life-stage development, particularly in the areas of work and higher education. In focusing on changes in the concept of self and how they affect inevitably the choice of education and career Super delivers a theory of occupational development, and in relation to the age group fifteen to twenty-five identifies this as the first stage, one of 'exploration and trial'.

But the world is changing faster than Alvin Tofler predicted, and the changes bring with them dismaying consequences. The relative stability of the get-rich 1980s has been replaced with real unease. Nothing seems to be safe or predictable, and the employment scene is one of the most dramatic demonstrations of this. Most young men and women of today feel less in control of their destinies – optimism is low and depression is high. Society responds by avoidance: we are not able to confront the realities of the dissonance between how we educate young men and women in preparation for the world of work that they will enter.

School leavers and graduates still worry about finding work. There are always too many young people between the ages of eighteen and twenty five who remain unemployed whatever government initiatives attempt to change. This age group appears to be the hardest hit of all. To be unemployed at the beginning of an adult work life is to head towards the term 'unemployable' – the vicious process of no experience/no work and so on. Society has been conditioned to believe that work is fundamental to our well-being. Most people want and need to work. Given the situation where we know that work is not obtainable, with signs that it may become scarcer still, by definition we have a large-scale mental health problem to face.

Those in this age group who may have elected for further and higher education question the usefulness of an education system founded on the assumption that work will follow learning. Seductive recruiting by educational institutions often results in students making unrealistic or passive choices of courses and careers with all the predictable sequels. 'Drop-outs' are the disenchanted or pessimistic students, rather than inadequate ones – their mood is often related to their ultimate chances of getting the kind of career structure they have been led (by parents, teachers and the media) to believe they desire and deserve.

Sobering studies of unemployment in this and other age groups highlight particular psychological problems. The appalling suicide rate of 'redundant' senior executives, family disturbances when the breadwinner is out of work, these are the problems with which the counselling psychologist is engaged. The case history of a young chronically unemployed person can read like a description of clinical depression. The initial failure to find work and so-called 'success' leads to renewed efforts which result in frustration and a sense of futility. Turned inwards, such thoughts become a sense of personal failure, leading to apathy, immobilization and depression – feelings which are not addressed by Social Security hand-outs and Jobcentre schemes. Families are distraught. Parents often blame their son or daughter for not getting a job – some blame themselves. Successful parents can be cynical and judgemental, others feel anxious and helpless. Some parents feel it keenly as a family disgrace. Young people resort to drugs and delinquency as a panacea for their enforced inactivity.

Suicide and para-suicide

Suicide is a highly sensitive, controversial and stigmatizing issue, whether carried out, attempted or merely considered. The problem of suicide is enigmatic in many ways. Contrary to a still common belief, it is not dependent on a specific illness or mental state and it cuts across all diagnostic categories.

The problem is complicated for the young adult because suicidal behaviour at this stage cannot be separated from the unique and challenging developmental processes of early adulthood and their tight connections with family dynamics and social context. Furthermore, research data on suicide attempts may vary widely depending on how the information was obtained – from hospital out-patient departments, psychiatric hospitals and clinics or the Samaritans.

Suicide rates have increased dramatically. In 1992 there were 4,362 male suicides – a 27 per cent increase over the previous twelve years. The male increase was most marked in the fifteen to forty-four age group (CSO, 1994). The report offered no explanation for the increase but the Samaritans suggested that men are reluctant to discuss their feelings with those who might help them. Young people contemplating suicide do not always go to their GP or a counsellor. Of those under thirty five, only one-fifth sought help in that time. One in ten will actually own their feelings of depression and 20 per cent will have used self-mutilation, covert or overt, as a means of expressing feelings of frustration and anger. For some, self-harm can become a way of life.

It is perhaps a sign of the times that when they feel troubled or alarmed by feelings precipitated by stress young people put off consulting a doctor because they do not see themselves as ill or for fear of being diagnosed as a 'basket case'. Mental illness still carries a stigma and they assume it could impair their career prospects. When they do seek help it is often after an 'attempt' at suicide.

On the whole counselling psychologists have not been well prepared for the subject. Many, even psychiatrists, share with laymen simple misconceptions about the scale of suicide. In fact we may feel so uneasy with the subject that we tend to deny, ignore and avoid confrontation. The violence and apparent irrationality of suicidal behaviours contribute to many of these observed individual or institutional defensive attitudes. In addition, the lack of specificity and poor predictive value of risk factors may be discouraging in clinical practice in spite of over 150,000 hospital attendances in Great Britain which relate to suicidal thoughts and behaviour (Winter, 2001).

The same is true of the so-called warning clues – e.g. failure in academic performance or obtaining a job and very often falling in or out of love. But suicide attempts are highly meaningful and are often dedicated symptoms of intense suffering. The acts appear to be a critical response to a usually long-standing series of unresolved overt or covert difficulties. One can only identify the pre-suicidal syndrome as a narrowing of personal capabilities and dynamic activities, the inhibition of aggression towards others and a turning of those feelings inwards, resulting in fantasies of death.

The young adult recklessly driving a stolen car or experimenting with drugs is aware of death and destruction, often owning to 'bad/evil' feelings, including the power to hurt and destroy others and themselves:

> becoming more aware of the many ways in which other persons, even loved ones, have acted destructively towards them. What is worse, the realization comes that they may have done irrevocably hurtful things to parents, lovers, friends, rivals ... but there is a positive aspect to this recognition of the capacity to be destructive. By recognizing one's power to tear down things, you can begin to realize how truly powerful one can be in creating new and useful forms of life ... powerful forces of destructiveness and of creativity coexist in the human soul and can be integrated in many ways though never entirely. (Levinson, 1980)

Young women get pregnant to have something productive to do. Ninety-six conceptions in every 1,000 are in this age group, with the subsequent number of abortions increasing dramatically from 68.5 per cent in 1993 to 73 per cent in 2000.

Finding a focus or not finding a focus can stir the family tremendously. The so-called success of one's children is the weakest link in the chain of family life and is therefore most likely to be broken if there is a problem. Perhaps the difficulties hinge on the fact that parents themselves have not emotionally been able to separate and, when confronted by their children, who in turn have chosen to become parents themselves, find that they are in two stages of life at the same time. There are other potential sources of tension at this time for the young adult. This is particularly so if they become professionally and financially more successful than their parents were or are. This is not only measured in terms of academic success, a happier marriage or a financially more rewarding career. Parents may very well seem to be both proud and supportive, but often young men and women, feeling in some way disloyal, are unable to grasp the opportunities before them. Betraying their parents if they go ahead and take hold of their good fortune. Faced with this situation, parents become stressed and cannot understand why it is that their son or daughter is 'determined to spoil his or her chances in life with bad and sometimes mad behaviour' (Kraemer, 1982).

David Levi, Helm Sterlin and Robert Sagard at the National Institute for Mental Health, New York (1980), reported on the rather grim clinical profiles of thirty families who came for counselling because of a troubled young adult. In nearly all cases their problems were linked with a crisis in the lives of their middle-aged fathers where the father was exhibiting deep doubts and uncertainties about the meaning of his own life. Options in both love and work which seemed open to offspring led these fathers to regret the choices they had made in their own lives. Fathers who do not have a strong sense of self-worth tend to feel threatened by moves in the family towards independence. They respond either with criticism or total disengagement.

Case study 2

Susan is the eldest of three children, a middle sister and younger brother. Her parents live in another city. Susan is married and has three young children, a girl and two boys. Her sister and brother remain unmarried but in long-term relationships.

Following her mother's difficult pregnancy and a prolonged and painful labour Susan entered the world by forceps delivery. In the process she was badly mauled and arrived bruised and weakened, with a misshapen skull. Susan's mother, shocked and exhausted, initially refused to look at, hold, nurse or name her daughter. Nurses cared for the baby, who quickly recovered from the ordeal. Her large, dark brown, beautiful eyes prompted the nurses to name her Susan. ('Brown-eyed Susie' was a popular ballad.)

Ten days later Susan and mother returned home. The baby was lightly marred by a small bump on the forehead which was soon covered by the growth of her curly brown hair. However, her mother remained aloof and awkward with the baby.

Susan's memories of childhood are of a non-tactile mother. All her babies were cared for adequately (with the help of au pairs). The lack of warmth was experienced evenhandedly. Susan remembered her sister often left to cry alone in the garden.

Susan feels personally responsible for the 'trouble' she caused with her difficult birth. She feels that she was a 'disappointment', imperfect and repulsive. In contrast, her brother and sister's birth had been without complication and they were born unblemished.

Susan compensated for her 'defects' by fulfilling the role of a perfect child, obedient, religious, studious, sociable and affable. However, shortly after her sixteenth birthday she disobeyed her father and went to a party which entailed her coming home at a late hour and at a time when her father (who was away on business) was unable to collect her. Susan accepted a lift home from a girlfriend who had only recently passed her driving test. On the way home there was a serious crash, Susan was catapulted through the windscreen; her friend escaped unhurt.

Shards of glass had entered Susan's eyes, requiring complex surgery to remove them. The parents were informed about the accident and subsequent surgery but it was twelve hours before her father arrived at the bedside. Her mother did not come. Susan's right eye recovered without ill effect but the left eye was injured and the sight permanently impaired.

The residual effect of this trauma has often been re-experienced and re-examined during the course of therapy, particularly the long hours left alone fearing the worst, both before and after surgery, feelings of guilt and anxiety about the reaction of her parents, which her father's presence did little to assuage. When Susan's mother visited the hospital a day later Susan did not reproach her for her absence.

During the process of recovery Susan's left eye was kept bandaged. Her fantasy grew that when the dressing was removed she would have to confront an empty void. She felt unable to discuss these fears with her parents. Again she was letting them down, they would have to put up with a disfigured child, and again she apologized, accepting responsibility for another 'catastrophe'.

Susan's presenting problem was 'depression'. It was a way of describing 'an inability to enjoy life'. The accident did not prevent her from successfully completing her education. She went on to travel abroad, returned to university and obtained a degree. At university she met and married Adam, her husband, and since gave birth to three healthy children. She continues to hold a responsible job in the social services.

Her life story exhibits a process of success in one way or another but it is success itself that forms the basis of her depression and inhibitions. Success is a 'worry'. Each time the family achieved success, each time she received praise at work, each decision that had to be taken, filled Susan with anxiety and foreboding. If success or happiness was 'taken for granted' it could place herself and her family at risk of disaster and retribution. The experience of enjoyment did not bode well for the family. Lowering her defences would invite punishment, 'making her pay'. Susan had to be ever vigilant and protective of herself and her loved ones.

There are obvious connections in these anxieties between Susan's birth trauma and later accident. Repression and avoidance had taken their toll. Her lack of confidence in discussing her feelings with her parents, made her frustratingly unable to express her anger or to confront them with their lack of sensitivity to the developmental needs of their children or the discomfort she now acknowledged in recognizing her own collusion with their dissociation and denial.

The sense of foreboding which has cast its shadow throughout Susan's life is recognized theoretically and therapeutically by the term 'nameless dread'. This concept is explained by Mario Maronne (2000). 'The term "nameless dread" was used by Bion (1967) to describe a state of anxiety without meaning which results from the mother being unable to provide a state of calm responsiveness and containment of her child's anxieties.' Maronne enlarges on this:

> A nameless dread is intense anxiety or anxiety-ridden feelings which a person experiences at a subjective level but to which they cannot give a name. In other words this is anxiety or pain which has no meaning. In terms of attachment theory, the main source of anxiety is insecurity of attachment. Furthermore, the anxiety is less likely to be processed when it is not possible to make sense of it, to reflect upon its sources.
>
> In some families it is difficult or impossible for children and parents to discuss attachment-relevant events in a reflective way. When these explorations do not take place, the child is left alone with unprocessed anxieties. Therefore, the impact of the anxiety is greater than it would have been if shared reflective communications had taken place.

I know, with Susan, that I am working with a very damaged person. My maternal counter-transference feelings are powerful and at times over-protective. When the mother's adaptation is not good enough, the infant may be expected to die physically from neglect and the failure of the maternal 'reverie'. If the child survives it creates a false identity for itself, traditionally assigning itself to the task of tending to the needs of others, being compliant rather than creative.

But, together, Susan and I are working on these 'nameless anxieties'. The emphasis in her therapy is to move toward a meta-construction of Susan's intended future. Trying and testing the various ways in which a more constructive bridging can be found. Ways in which Susan's past experiences of trauma can be acknowledged and affirmed but can also be transformed. Susan can challenge the memory of her tragic experiences, juxtaposing a different interpretation of her trauma, rewriting her story in ways which reflect a positive attitude to life and the future, with the ability to preserve hope alongside her despair.

The capacity to involve and develop intimate relationships

Although the emphasis in this chapter has been on the context in which I work – the application of psychodynamic theory to counselling psychology – it should be noted that there are well in excess of 250 theories of counselling and therapy. Small wonder, then, that there is no consensus on which theory in the context of working with the young adult stands out as more appropriate or more significant than any other.

There are those who argue for the all-persuasive importance of *social structures* to counselling and psychotherapy, whilst others, particularly in the field of family therapy, maintain that the *systems* approach is of equal importance. There are also those counselling psychologists who place the emphasis on consideration of *single variables* that may particularly affect this group – namely consideration of race and gender.

The influence of these perspectives for counselling practice is well defined by Jenny Bimrose, writing on counselling and social context (1993). She urges counsellors to become more familiar with the different dimensions of this debate so that they can identify the perspective from which they are operating or perhaps what their intended focus could be for the future. She illustrates this point by correlating the concept of social context in counselling with the actual practical skills required in each of three perspectives.

- *Individualist:* using the traditional theoretical perspectives of psychology plus core skills of empathy, acceptance and understanding, etc.
- *Integrationist:* counsellors offering their clients skills which can be used to change systems, e.g. working with special groups. This method is effective when used in conjunction with individual counselling.
- *Structuralist:* concerning oneself with single contextual variables such as race or gender which pose a particular challenge to the therapist.

A complex array of therapies, techniques, methodologies and arguments face the individual practitioner. If there is little agreement on any of these the one thing of which we can be certain is that there are increasing numbers of young people in this age group who experience symptoms that cause distress to themselves, their families and their friends.

The most important stage encountered in the developmental tasks of the young adult is that of establishing a workable and acceptable system of values and relationships, and this is by no means the prerogative of the most articulate and highly educated young people in our society. Young men and women who seek help from counselling show a genuine – if confused – concern with moral issues, with questions of social justice, violence and discrimination. Many of them have few illusions about the discrepancies between their own pretensions and performance. They are often acutely conscious of not living up to their own ideals and of the extent to which they fall short of what they might expect from themselves. Many of the moral principles they supported as schoolchildren, or were struggling at one time to realize, were very close to those adumbrated by traditional social or religious codes which, as they grew older, demanded new reasons for adhering to them and new sanctions to validate them. What is quite clear, however, is that the main touchstone for their assessment of their own and other people's moral standards lies in the quality of personal relationships and that this means more to each one than some of the traditional sanctions of morality. It could be that the bewilderment, uncertainty and experimentation on moral issues that they present are signs that with time and luck may provide a future morality characterized less by constraint, punishment and inhibition and more by autonomy, sympathy, altruism and love.

During the past forty years young people have indicated considerable concern, often at unconscious levels, with the threat of eventual annihilation. 'Why bother?' they ask. However, there is a real distinction between today's generation and that which preceded it. The focus of this concern in the new century has shifted to the possible pollution and degradation of 'space-ship Earth'. The awful predicament is the same but the means to eliminate life are in the hands of man and womankind.

All periods involve change, but it is unquestionable that the 1990s witnessed a culture of exceptionally rapid and complicated social change where society has manifested deep conflicts in its values and uncertainties in its attitudes to even the most fundamental aspects of human relationships. We still are too much in the midst of agonized debates on such issues as euthanasia, the teaching of contraception, the effect of HIV and AIDS on world populations, the problems of the Third World, etc. to recognize the symptoms. The basis of family life is itself subjected to reappraisal and criticism, and increased knowledge of the physical bases of bisexuality and androgyny is blurring what seemed to be clear-cut sexual distinctions.

Young adulthood has its own special characteristics, and its special contribution to psychological life and development rests on the premise that this is a period during which the young adult's mental picture of him- or herself, begun in adolescence, will have firmed up, and when a specific and fixed sexual identity will be established.

This is the time during which the person will seek to find answers through relationships, through various social and sexual experiences and responses. These hinge on previous conditionings as to what is acceptable to his or her conscience and ideals and what must, at all costs to their future psychological well-being be rejected or denied. Every process of development and maturation demands great bravery.

The entry into young adulthood is marked by compromise. Compromise between what we think we might want and what our conscience allows us to live with. Earlier ways of feeling male or female are put under a new kind of stress. Previous experiences in childhood and adolescence of finding pleasure and feeling cared for are put under pressure because of the presence of a sexually mature and developed body.

It appears that society has tried to avoid a basic clarification. We are all seemingly aware of the differences between a male and female, and generally we can agree about the concepts of masculinity and femininity, but we have made the mistake of assuming that maleness signifies masculinity whilst womanliness is construed as femininity. However, if people appear to conform to these expectations, they may well have been trained to do so. Gender schema theory attempts to explain how these misconceptions can occur.

Gender schema processing suggests that there is a readiness on the part of children to encode and organize information according to how culture defines sex roles. For example, a child may observe that boys are usually described as 'strong' or 'brave' whereas girls are more usually described as 'nice' or 'sweet'. Cultural stereotypes, therefore, become adopted because the child learns not only that the sexes differ but more importantly that certain attributes are associated more with one sex than the other. 'The extreme degree in which our society classified behaviour and objects into masculine versus feminine only intensified the development of a gender scheme'. (Bascow, 1992).

The emphasis placed on only one side of our sexual make-up costs us dear. The young adult has to face up to this deficiency. In regarding himself as 'masculine' the young man has to conceptualize himself as being tough, an achiever, powerful and potent as opposed to the feminine 'touchy-feely' orientation.

The notion of androgyny still remains controversial since it was introduced into psychological literature in the 1960s. Basically the word 'androgynous' is just a convenient way of defining those who are able to show a *combination* of high scores on both masculinity and femininity scales. Men who score high on the masculinity scale may well be classified as having higher self-esteem, higher achievement needs, to be dominant and aggressive. Femininity scales are related to differing behaviour – the ability to show empathy, social skills, sensitivity to other people's feelings. The androgynous person (by definition) has both sets of skills. This combination has shown itself to be most advantageous in the forming of long-standing relationships. In one set of studies male and female subjects with various combinations of masculinity and femininity scores met each other in a waiting room. The results may contradict some common assumptions. The lowest level of interaction and enjoyment was found among the pairs sex-typed as high in masculinity and femininity. In contrast, when *both* persons were androgynous, levels of interaction and mutual enjoyment were high (Ickes and Barnes, 1987–88).

Men and women have been socialized to behave in sexist ways and they have difficulty in developing and integrating new roles that are compatible with non-sexist behaviour. Sex role strain (a major presenting problem) is the result of the rigid gender roles which restrict people's ability to actualize their human potential.

Women are more likely to experience role conflict. They have limitations placed on them because of the pervasive ideas linked with the feminine sex role in our society – polarized between the page three 'Bimbo', the mother of children or the high-powered executive complete with briefcase. Young men face differing sexual conflicts. Being a 'man' creates oppressive effects. Masculine mystique still implies that femininity is inferior to masculinity as a gender orientation.

Rigid gender roles can lead – in some young men – to what has been labelled as 'fear of femininity' (O'Neill, 1981). This is defined as a strong concern if they are seen to possess feminine values, attitudes and behaviours that this will produce a negative effect. They will be seen as weak, submissive and dependent. This is obviously a restriction to expressing one's own feelings. The right to be seen to be tender and vulnerable. It can be seen in the continuation of homophobia – fear of being homosexual and prejudicial belief in stereotypes about what it means to be gay.

This is illustrated in the obsession with achievement and success, with the preoccupation with work and status in establishing either accomplishment or delinquent behaviour as a means of substantiating and exhibiting one's value (O'Neill, 1981).

Conclusion

The intention in this chapter has been to state my belief that the outcome of early childhood development and of its distortions becomes pronounced by the end of the period designated as young adulthood. In the past there will have been many occasions when psychological distress was allowed to accumulate without too much notice or concern, leaving the young man or woman to inherit severe distortions of their lives at best, with mental illness at worst.

In working with the young adult before the results are distorted about a sexual identity and a sense of self or meaning, there is always a possibility at this time of reversibility. We are made aware of the fact that many of them need not have reached the point of despair or illness that brings them to the therapist. Difference in their lives could well have been made earlier if they had been taken seriously and if their feelings had not been dismissed as a 'passing phase'.

The term 'pathologization of everyday life' is used by Vivien Burr and Trevor Butt, two personal construct psychologists. They offer ways of resisting such categorizations in their joint chapter 'Psychological distress and modern thought' (2000).

(a) Avoiding traps for oppression of clients as victims by posturing the therapist's role of possessing expert knowledge with some revision.
(b) Recognition that human experience is diverse.
(c) Offer liberating ways of helping people construe their experience in illness, such as networks, which do not label in a counselling way.
(d) Seeing the role of language as more constructive than just a communication tool.
(e) Consider that the counselling ways of depicting causation when it comes to matters such as illness are limited because we participate in wider constructions of who we are.
(f) We should attempt to be experimental in how we depict histories.

They add that psychologists need to know how to be enabling in helping patients 'to produce self narratives which allow them to live at peace with themselves'.

Depression and mental suffering are a problem not only for individuals but also for groups and societies. It is not disputed that suffering sometimes involves biology or that there are individual variations and thresholds for becoming depressed, or that some depressions can be genetically loaded. What this chapter has tried to articulate is that the problems of the young adult are associated with roles and relationships, with self-organization and self-value. The counselling psychologist is trained to recognize these human needs and to work on the problem of creating environments that are not psychologically toxic.

Erikson's (1981) three adult identity phases – finding intimate relationships in early adulthood, establishing social links with different generations in middle adulthood and engaging in a retrospective life review process in late adulthood – were reflected in a study by Kamptner (1989) which concerned the material possessions most valued and treasured in these age groups. The young adults referred to the social significance that their cars, jewellery, music equipment, photographs and general memorabilia symbolized and the pleasures they provided. The study highlighted changes that occur with age in the relevance of treasured possessions, from those connected with 'mother' in early life to self in middle childhood and later to others in adulthood. He noted that the younger person's concern with functional items – status-orientated and reinforced by peer group fads and fashions – was gradually substituted for more personal items until in the twenty-five to thirty age group it was replaced by items which indicated increasing concern with social networks and social history.

Young people are bombarded with pictures of people who are success stories, brighter, more wealthy, more beautiful. They are fed myths of the happy family (despite divorce rates of 40 per cent). Senior citizens get beaten up in their homes, the young drop out of work, roam the streets and are socially marginalized. Young adults are the casualties of our society, treated as subordinates and not regarded as agents of value, since there are so many media millionaires, pop stars and footballers competing for that role.

The consumer society gives them things too easily. Fifty years ago material objects were attractive and valuable only if earned by effort. 'When they hop in and out of bed young people begin to despise sex as such' (Winnicott, 1969). Obsession with style, with brand awareness, does mean something. It is the defence mechanism of young people who feel powerless. They have incredible choices in how to dress, what objects to have – choices which advertisers and manufacturers offer in abundance. Consumer choice has become a priority, offering a way of escape and a means of self-expression.

We have a social fabric that is orientated to social success. If we have failed this generation it is because we no longer act as humans and have forgotten our human need for love, respect and compassion (Lorenz, 1952). This is a consequence of early life histories of affectionless parenting, economic stress, past and present abuse and the rendering of young people into objects of glorification. Dysfunctional communication can also occur in intact families where there is no history of abuse, neglect, violence or separation. Many books and articles have been written on the subject. It is not unusual to see young men and women who come into therapy in a state of being unable to conceptualize their affective state. Only later, in the course of therapy, do they recognize that in their family it was not possible to talk about feelings and interpersonal events and to understand them in a meaningful way. The modern antidote is all that is available – just keep on taking the tablets.

References

Bascow, S.A. (1992) *Gender Stereotypes and Roles*. Pacific Grove CA: Brooks Cole.

Bimrose, J. (1993) 'Counselling and social context', *Counselling and Psychology for Health Professionals*, 35: 149–65.

Bowlby, J. (1979) 'Self-reliance and conditions that promote it', in *The Making and Breaking of Affectional Bonds*. London: Tavistock.

Burr, V. and Butt, T. (2000) 'Psychological distress and modern thought' in Dwight Fee (ed.) *Pathology and the Postmodern: Mental Illness as Discourse and Experience*. London: Sage.

Central Policy Review Staff and Central Statistical Office (1992) *People and their Families*. London: HMSO.

Central Statistical Office (1994) *Social Trends*. London: HMSO.

Erikson, E.H. (1980) *Identity and the Life Cycle: a Reissue*. New York: Norton.

Gould, R.L. (1978) *Transformations, Growth and Change in Adult Life*. New York: Simon & Schuster.

Guzder, J. and Krishna, M. (1993) 'Sita Shakti' in *Cultural Paradigms for Indian Women*. British Psychological Society, *Psychotherapy Newsletter* 13: 30–67.

Haley, J. (1990) *Leaving Home*. New York: McGraw-Hill.

Ickes, W. and Barnes, R.D. (1987–88) 'The role of sex and self-monitoring in unstructured dyadic interactions', *Journal of Personality and Social Psychology*, 35: 315–30.

Kamptner, N.L. (1989) 'Personal possessions and their meanings in childhood, adolescence and old age' in S. Spacapan and S. Oskamp (eds) *The Social Psychology of Aging*. London: Sage.

Kelly, G.A. (1955) *The Psychology of Personal Constructs*. New York: Norton.

Kraemer, S. (1982) 'Leaving home', *Journal of Adolescence*, 5: 51–62.

Levi, D., Sterlin, H. and Sagard, R. (1980) *Report of the National Institute for Mental Health*. New York: NIMH.

Levinson, D.J. (1980) 'Towards a conception of the adult life course' in N.J. Smelser and E.H. Erikson (eds) *Themes of Work and Love in Adulthood*. Cambridge MA: Harvard University Press.

Lorenz, K. (1952) *King Solomon's Ring*. London: Methuen.

Marrone, Mario (1998) *Attachment and Interaction*. London: Jessica Kingsley.

McCrae, R.R. and Costa, P.T., Jr (1990) *Personality in Adulthood*. New York: Guilford.

O'Neill, J.M. (1981) 'Patterns of gender role, conflict and strain: sexism and fear of femininity in men's lives', *Personnel and Guidance Journal*, 60: 203–10.

Peel, J. (1994) 'A family album', *Radio Times*, 20–6, August.

Super, D.E. (1990) 'A life-span, life-space approach to career development' in D. Brown, I. Brookes and associates (eds) *Career Choice and Development*. San Francisco: Jossey Bass.

Winnicott, D.W. (1969) *The Maturational Processes and the Facilitating Environment*. London: Hogarth Press.

Winter, David (2001) 'Self-harm and Reconstruction', paper presented at the BPS centennial conference, Glasgow.

Wrightsman, L.S. (1994) *Adult Personality Development*. London: Sage.

17

Counselling Psychology and Mid-life Issues
SIMON BIGGS

There are a number of issues that are striking about the study of mid-life which have implications for counselling psychology.

- First, mid-life has only recently been recognized as a part of the life course with its own particular contradictions and issues. This is particularly true in health and welfare contexts. There is therefore significantly less knowledge on which to base therapeutic intervention compared to other parts of the life course. Mid-life is poorly defined and often described as the stage of life where people are concerned with the needs of others, rather than those of their own development (Staudinger and Bluck, 2001).
- Second, the very idea of mid-life, or middle age, appears to be highly dependent upon social construction. At different historical periods, and in different cultural contexts, it has been identified or ignored, valued or denigrated as fashion dictates (Biggs, 1999). This has been the case, even when mid-life change, such as the menopause, appears to be rooted in a defined biological process (Lock, 1998).
- Third, mid-life issues are nevertheless real to the extent that social rules and values influence behaviour and individual expectations. Any biological or maturational influences will be interpreted and explained by that context.

The way that mid-life is constructed will have profound implications for that person's future development and the existential questions they ask about their lives. As Shweder (1998), a social anthropologist who has studied mid-life, points out, our 'cultural fictions are real things' which depend upon a shared point of view to make them a 'fact of experience'.

Defining mid-life

Given this background, it is perhaps unsurprising that definitions of mid-life are often indistinct and depend upon the particular interest of the researcher or practitioner involved. However, by looking at some attempts to define mid-life and the issues surrounding it, we may be able to identify some of the key issues that can arise in therapeutic contexts.

It is very rare for a specific age to be placed on mid-life. Some authors, such as Colarusso and Nemiroff (1985), have attempted to specify stages of mid-life and fix them to chronological age. They have identified a period of mid-life transition between forty and forty-five years, of entering middle adulthood (forty-five to fifty), an age fifty transition (fifty to fifty-five), a culmination of middle adulthood between fifty-five and sixty years and finally a late adult transition between sixty and sixty-five years. The therapeutic implication would be that clients' experience is judged accoring to its degree of fit with these stages. However, such attempts may be overdetermined. The majority of studies indicate that mid-life is an uncharted period which, whilst there is a tacit everyday understanding that it exists, depends largely on the subjectivity and social context of the individual (Staudinger and Bluck, 2001). Mid-life can be identified through certain processes and qualities rather than through chronological age, and will depend upon a combination of cultural factors and personal circumstances.

Bernice Neugarten (1968) examined the responses of 2,000 Americans between the ages of forty and sixty and describes mid-life as an 'awareness' issue. She found that:

> Middle-aged men and women, while they by no means regard themselves as being in command of all they survey, nevertheless recognise that they constitute the powerful age group *vis-à-vis* other age groups; that they are the norm-bearers and the decision-makers; and they live in a society which, while it may be oriented towards youth, is controlled by the middle-aged. (1968: 93)

Neugarten was particularly interested in how adults 'clocked' themselves in relation to what their society, their friends and media images conveyed as being 'age-appropriate' behaviour. If you were 'on time' in terms of the cultural expectations of your part of the life course, you were likely to be less stressed than someone who was 'off time'. Mid-life emerges as period of heightened sensitivity to one's position within a complex social environment, where the reassessment of the self is a prevailing theme, depending upon feelings of timeliness and of intergenerational relationships. She concluded that 'Middle-aged people look to their positions within different life contexts – body, career, family – rather than to chronological age for their primary cues in clocking themselves' (p. 94).

Manheimer (1999) continues the temporal theme, stating that a key task of mid-life is 'making peace with time'. In mid-life we become 'historical to ourselves' as we come to see our personal experiences in the context of public events, changed historical circumstances, situations and conflicts.

These views would suggest that the therapeutic task concerns accommodating mulitiple role expectations and socially constructed definitions of the point of the life course that the client is at. It also suggests a different perception of self that arises at this time.

Other writers have emphasized multiple challenges emerging in the family sphere. Ryff and Seltzer (1996) refer to mid-life as those years when children grow up into adulthood but parents are not yet themselves elderly, which, they maintain, is the longest period of the parental experience. For Weisner and Bernheimer (1998) 'Mid-life is not a sharply marked lifestage; it has very wide malleability in timing and salience in cultures around the world. We suggest that mid-life is marked by its being yoked with the adolescent developmental transition' (p. 212).

With changing demography, mid-life is increasingly being defined in relation to an ageing senior generation. This 'sandwiched' position has been interpreted as a defining source of tension, and also as a means of continuing relationships between generations (Davis, 1981). In mid-life 'Individuals are expected to have established a family, found a clear career direction in which they will peak ... and have taken on responsibility with respect to their children, their own aging parents and sometimes their community' (Staudinger and Bluck, 2001).

Mid-life emerges from these attempts at definition as being multiply determined and as being multi-faceted. It can be a period of considerable power and fulfilment, a period of intergenerational readjustment and a period of reassessment of personal goals. Issues can become manifest in the public and the private spheres, in work or family relations, and both can be expected to arise in therapeutic situations. Indeed, one of the key issues for the mid-lifer would appear to be the resources she or he has for dealing with that complexity.

The history of mid-life and the talking therapies

The historical development of counselling psychology and psychotherapy has itself been subject to different interpretations of mid-life, which has influenced the 'seriousness' with which particular approaches have addressed the problem. It is possible to see at least three phases in the conception of mid-life as an indicator of adult identity.

First, we can look at how classic theories of human growth and development, such as Freudian psychoanalysis, positioned mid-life. Generally speaking, psychoanalysis ignored distinctions in adulthood. However a few chance remarks by Freud himself created a climate in which change was increasingly seen as unlikely with age. Second, mid-life has been seen as a crisis. This view became prominent in the 1950s and 1960s and was seen as a way of 'solving' the problem of transfer of power between generations, linking identity with processes of economic production. In a third phase, mid-life has become a period of consumer activity, which, it is assumed, can continue indefinitely until deep old age and death.

Therapists would need to be aware of these different historical interpretations for a number of reasons. Views about mid-life and what is achievable with mid-life clients may be embedded in particular approaches. Also, whilst these differing perspectives were dominant at different times, they still exist as cultural categories that may influence clients' and therapists' expectations about mid-life itself. They are still kicking around.

Phase 1: rigidity and accomplishment

Freud very rarely commented on a specifically 'adult' life phase. He simply assumed that it was covered by his general mechanisms of how the mind worked. The few remarks on mature adulthood that he made were very early on in the genesis of psychoanalysis and can most famously be found in his paper 'On Psychotherapy' (1905).

> Psychotherapy is not possible near or above the age of fifty, the elasticity of mental processes, on which treatment depends, is as a rule lacking – old people are not educable – and the mass of material to be dealt with would prolong the duration of treatment indefinitely.

Curiously, Freud was himself forty-eight years old when he made these remarks, before he revised his own views and theory of mind. And adult age is hardly mentioned in his subsequent writings. Indeed, adult age is not required by psychoanalytic theory, which maintains that the uncounscious knows no time, is essentially chaotic and timeless, and that problems in adulthood are caused by the repetition of faulty 'solutions' adopted in childhood. As Abraham (1919) pointed out, it is the age at which a problem appears, rather than the age of the patient, that is of key significance.

However, if ever a message was grasped by the spirit of an age, this one was. By 1952 Hollander, a leading US analyst, had pronounced that people in their fifties had too little hope in the future to be motivated to change. And by the end of the 1950s psychoanalytic training was forbidden to people aged over forty. One analyst who disagreed with this position, Pearl King (1974), reports that during this period colleagues would secretly 'confess' their guilty secret of working with mid-life patients. She, failing to get her views accepted in neo-Freudian circles, had to present her work to the rival Jungian Society of Analytic Psychology. Analytic psychology has always been more open to notions of therapeutic change across the life course. Indeed, one of the reasons why Jung and Freud parted company was that Jung viewed psychoanalysis as simply clearing away the problems of childhood but saying very little about how to deal with the problems of adulthood itself. This period reflected the dominant turn-of-the-century view that adulthood consisted of (predominantly masculine) accomplishment: mature adults were fully formed and unlikely to benefit from therapeutic intervention.

Phase 2: crisis and fit

It comes as little surprise, then, that it was a therapist, Elliot Jaques, and social scientists, Bernice Neugarten and David Guttman, influenced by the Jungian tradition, who developed the notion of mid-life crisis. By the 1960s mid-life had become a key contradiction that had to be resolved by adult identity.

Jaques (1965) placed the crisis as occurring between thirty-five and sixty-five years. He was at first interested in the changes in creative and most notably artistic production with age, observing the way in which the immediacy of paintings, plays and novels produced by writers early in their career 'hot from the fire' became more reflective and melancholy with age. 'The paradox is,' he claimed, one 'of entering the prime of life, the stage of fulfillment, but at the same time the prime and fulfillment are dated – death lies beyond' (p. 512). The mid-lifer, then, looks both ways, back to early adulthood, but also forward, becoming aware of finitude and that there is limited time left to achieve what they desire.

Neugarten's (1968) research pointed to mid-life crisis as a relatively novel social phenomenon. It will be recalled that Neugarten's work concerned the way that people 'clocked' themselves in relation to accepted and largely unquestioned life stages. The 'timeliness' of a life event depended on whether it occurred at the point in the life course that majority behaviour, or social conformity, would predict. Being on time or out of time became a criterion of personal satisfaction and socially valued behaviour. However, with mid-life two social norms come into conflict: on the one hand adults are encouraged to excel at their chosen activities, be they at work or within their families and personal relationships. On the other, they are expected to hand over to a potentially more productive rising generation. Mid-life crisis is seen as a time marked at first by protest and then by accceptance of a new, but less valued, social role. So, at first, mid-lifers react against the social pressures and insecurities brought on by competition from younger workers. Then they come to adopt the new conformities that society demands. A gradual withdrawal from productive and reproductive labour takes place, in preparation for a social and eventually a bodily death.

Both Jaques's and Neugarten's observations can be seen as reflections and metaphors of a trend toward disengagement from society. Within the social atmosphere of the 1950s and 1960s mid-life became characterized as a period of transition that was both expected and in some way anti-normative. Social structuration of work and family made mid-life a turning point, which developed into a crisis because it also required the shedding of dominant sources of self-worth.

Phase 3: life-style and recycling

In the late 1980s and 1990s increasing awareness of diversity and the influence of consumerism on identity has produced a more fluid notion of mid-life. The question has been asked: Do people simply 'play' at having mid-life identities and crises? Is mid-life simply a script, a narrative that one can enter into as the fancy takes? Under such circumstances how far is it possible to simply choose not to grow old?

Featherstone and Hepworth (1983, 1989) note that contemporary mid-life-styles allow 'Individuals who look after their bodies and adopt a positive attitude toward life … to avoid the decline and negative effects of the ageing process and thereby prolong their capacity to enjoy the full benefits of consumer culture' (1989: 87). In Featherstone and Hepworth's view, mid-life is no longer a period of transition from productivity to disengagement. Rather, it has become 'ageless', a life course plateau, buoyed up by consumer life-styles and a sort of continual reinvention. This reinvention of mid-life as a life-style fits well with Giddens's (1991) observation that adult identity now depends on the 'capacity to keep a particular narrative going … a coherent, yet constantly revised biographical narrative … in the context of multiple choice'. He argues that talking therapies do not simply treat people when they cannot cope but are now used to maintain the narrative, to keep it going. Therapies of various sorts, self-help manuals on mid-life and life-style magazines, are all available to monitor and adapt one's own 'performance' (Biggs, 1999). The turn to life-style and narrative reinforce the view, most forcefully expressed by Featherstone and Hepworth (1989), that we are experiencing a 'blurring of what appeared previously to be relatively clearly marked stages and the experiences and characteristic behaviour which were associated with those stages' (p. 144). This focus on agelessness can produce considerable pressure to deny the effects of adult ageing 'when older citizens are encouraged not just to dress "young" and look youthful, but to exercise, have sex, take holidays, socialise in ways indistinguishable from those of their children's generation. There are no rules now, only choices' (Blaikie, 1999: 104).

Such obsevations fit well with McAdams's (1993) view that the therapeutic task is now to 'story' the life course from our own resources. In life course terms, 'Defining the self through myth may be seen as an ongoing act of psychological and social responsibility. Because our world can no longer tell us who we are and how we should live, we must figure it out on our own' (McAdams, 1993). Narrative therapies arguably provide techniques whereby a multiplicity of possibilities for identity can be negotiated in the absence of binding cultural guidelines.

The experience of mid-life can, however, be historically and culturally uneven. It may be absent among poor African-Americans living in inner cities (Newman, 1998) and disguised amongst Blaikie's affluent, retired and predominantly white mid-life-stylers. For some there is too little choice and for others too much. It is a fiction, in Shweder's (1998) sense, reinforced by the ritual marking of birthdays as decade transitions, yet is at the same time an early warning of physical and social decline which may, given the right social and economic resources, be effectively postponed.

During the twentieth century our understanding of the middle adult years changed markedly, from a period in which mid-life was not recognized as at all distinctive, and adulthood was a marker of excessive stability, to a period in which it was seen as a transition and a precursor to the relinquishing of productive power, and finally to the view that mid-life-style in some way insulates people from the predations of age and marks the maintainance of a consumer-driven agelessness. Each of these perspectives may occur in therapeutic conversations at times and at different levels of personal engagement. They have their own afterlife which lives on in modes of practice and the assumptive realities of both therapists and clients.

Each phase leaves us with different tensions which may manifest themselves in the therapeutic process. In the first case, therapists may unconsciously avoid issues of ageing, and even ageing clients (Woolfe and Biggs, 1997), associating mid-life issues as depressing and without solution. Further, a classical approach may focus disproportionately on 'causative' factors in the client's childhood, rather than those of looking forward, in life course terms, as well as back (Biggs, 1998). In the second, there may be a tendency to inflate everyday issues and problems, or ignore them, both reactions drawing on the expectation that issues should reach crisis proportions if they are 'mid-life' in nature. Finally, a focus on maintaining an ageless life-style may create false expectations of what is possible and fail to take into account the need for resilience to losses and adaptation to forms of decline (Heckhausen, 2001). Each is arguably dismissive of the role of ageism (Butler, 1975) as a factor in the environment of which therapy is a part. Issues, such as the menopause (Granville, 2002) and other physical changes, intergenerationally based transference between client and counsellor (Woolfe, 1998) and reflections of here-and-now issues with the counsellor's own ageing (Biggs, 1989) may be avoided. As with all therapeutic process, however, the first step is to recognize the presenting issues. Those issues is addressed in the next section.

Mid-life issues in therapy

Kleinberg (1995) suggests that clients 'Do not necessarily enter treatment to cope with a mid-life crisis. Instead they are interested in the relief of symptoms, in resolving family conflict, or in feeling more creative' (p. 207). In other words, issues which may be interpreted as mid-life problems may not be presented in life course terms, and it is only through the therapeutic process itself that an awareness of the adult life course dimension becomes more sharply defined. Kleinberg has observed that in mid-life presenting problems often belie a personal feeling of senselessness and aimlessness, and that much of the therapeutic task consists of 'working through stagnation'.

A number of investigators have identified problems that they specifically relate to mid-life, which are summarized below.

Work, family and timing

Neugarten (1968) identified a number of issues from her survey of 2,000 participants which include the following:

- Dealing with the different rhythms of life arising from different contexts such as the demands of work, family and relationships, which may, unsurprisingly, fail to achieve harmony.
- Being a bridge between generations and containing conflicts of interest, both at home and at work. This is often accompanied by an increased awareness of mentoring and modelling roles.
- An increased awareness of distance, emotionally, socially and culturally, between the mid-life self and younger adults, that marks one out as part of an ageing generation. This may also result in feeling closer to one's own parental generation and identifying with them.
- Increased awareness of bodily health and the death of contemporaries, which according to Neugarten, can lead to an increased sense of physical vulnerability in men and preparations for widowhood in women.

For both sexes, life is restructured in terms of 'time left to live' rather than 'time since birth', intimating increasing awareness of personal finitude and a spur to personal integration in what time one has left. Mid-life is also percei- ved as a time of maximum capacity in which one's ability to handle a com- plex environment and self is at its peak. The contradictions that this and other factors can bring, is encapsulated in the difference between wanting to be young and wanting to feel young. The mid-lifer has a substantial repertoire of strategies to draw on and is 'no longer learning from a book'.

King (1980) has identified the following sources of anxiety and concern that she found to be indications of mid-life disturbance. Fear of the diminution or loss of sexual potency and the impact this would have on relationships may be linked with anxieties arising from marital relationships after the children have left home, and parents can no longer use their children to mask problems aris- ing in their relationship with each other. At work, the threat of redundancy or displacement by younger people adds to an awareness of the possible failure of professional skills, and a feared loss of identity looming in retirement. King also points to increased awareness of personal ageing, possible illness and conse- quent dependence on others, and the anxiety it arouses. This may be accompa- nied by the realization that they may not now be able to achieve the goals clients set for themselves, with consequent feelings of depression or deprivation.

Kleinberg (1995) himself identifies eight areas for initial assessment, which may indicate whether the client has begun to consider the process of mid-life review. These include increased awareness of:

- The physical changes of ageing and their impact on work and other efforts.
- Increased awareness of mortality and finitude.
- The extent to which a career is fulfilling and can continue to fulfil personal values.
- Current and future satisfaction and conflicts in intimate relationships.
- The need for peer and mentoring relationships and means of fulfilling them in the future.
- The impact of family changes on role satisfactions.
- The need to plan for the retirement years.

Turning to process, Sherman (1994) suggests that adults make judgements about the ageing self on four dimensions. A *comparative* self draws conclusions about personal ageing by comparing oneself with others. These would include age peers and the ageing of younger generations, of siblings and the observa- tion of older kin. Peers, for example, might be used to compare how well one is ageing relative to people in the same cohort. Family comparisons may be used to assess where one is on an intergenerational scale, which generation one belongs to. A *reflected* self would be sensitized to the views others are believed to hold about oneself. Here others are perceived to be judging the self accord- ing to age-appropriate criteria which may include particular others or the general community. A *retrospective* self depends upon comparisons with former identi- ties. Here the past self acts as a sort of retrospective yardstick whereby bodily reminders such as changes in appearance, health and strength are logged.

Often this increases awareness of any contradictions between how one feels inside and outward appearances. Finally, Sherman identifies a *mature* self that is becoming freer, so that a client can construct his or her own identity. This final self allows movement beyond comparisons based on the other three.

Parental experiences

Looking at the parental experience of mid-life, surprisingly little attention has been paid to how having and raising children affects parents themselves, as opposed to the effects of parenting on child development. Ryff and Seltzer (1996) consider that mid-life covers 'the most interesting time in the parental experience'. It includes the period in which children grow from adolescence to adulthood and show how their strengths and weaknesses are played out in life choices, and thus when parents and children begin to develop adult–adult relationships. It is also the stage when parenting (as compared with parenthood) ends, marked by a series of gradual transitions rather than an 'empty nest'. Leaving is a process and not an event, and this view gives a criterion for successful transition in terms of relationship rather than an experience of loss. Gradually attention changes to how children have 'turned out'. From this perspective, the achievements and adjustment of adult children constitute an important lens through which mid-life parents evaluate themselves and their own achievements. The therapeutic task would inevitably privilege intergenerational factors in attaining adjustment and future well-being. Adolescent and mid-life transitions often coincide, giving rise to system tensions between emerging and declining sexuality, fertility and more global expressions of potency which require negotiation.

Silverberg (1996) notes that parents' self-appraised mental health is strongly influenced by the development of adolescent children. The pubertal processes, peer influences and relationships, independence and autonomy that emerge as issues during adolescence influence parental well-being. Factors would include the concurrence of daughters' and mothers' reproductive transitions and fathers' discovery of nurturant qualities hitherto suppressed.

These changes take place at a time when a mid-lifer's own parents may be dealing with developmental processes involving life reappraisal and personal re-evaluation. Nydegger and Miteness (1996) suggest that parental transitions from mid-life through into later life and personal ones into middle age are pressures on the sandwiched mid-lifers. This may not however, be exclusively a source of stress, and can provoke a reasssessment of parental relationships, now appearing on a more egalitarian footing. A mid-lifer's relationship with their own parents may develop from authority to friendship. It is not until the mid to late thirties that individuals can establish true mutual autonomy with other adult generations, with successful renegotiation of generational relationships depending upon an established personal life-style.

In summary, these observations indicate that the developmental trajectories of both parent and child must be incorporated to understand the mid-life parental experience. Weisner and Bernheimer (1998) conclude that for adults with children, mid-life needs to be understood as a relational stage of life experienced through one's children as well as a cultural life stage and personal transition. A key question for counselling becomes whether the family can tolerate the anxiety of renegotiating powers and limits during this period which raise powerful feelings around autonomy and encroaching dependence.

Gender issues

A series of observations have also been made about changing gender and relationship identities in mid-life. Guttman (1987) has observed that gender roles begin to 'cross over' in mid-life, as individuals reclaim powers that fixed gender roles denied them in their younger adult years. According to this view, women become more outwardly assertive, taking up roles in the public sphere, whilst men discover their nurturant inner selves. This occurs in mid-life (Huyuk and Guttman, 1999) because the forced role specialization and stereotyping during the 'female window of fertility' and 'parental emergency' of the child-rearing years begin to recede. Sheehey (1995) refers to life course changes in gender identity as the 'sexual diamond'. Here, it is claimed, from puberty until the mid-thirties, gender roles increasingly diverge, and then come together again in the late fifties. Around this period, women and men become more like each other, with a tendency for men to take on traditionally female attributes and women to take on male ones. Rosowsky (1999) has reviewed problems as experienced by hetero-sexual couples in mid-life. He observes that problems often arise around family members' capacity to care. Joint goals and common focus or purposes may no longer appear to be viable as priorities change which may produce a vacuum in marital relations. In such circumstances a couple's relationship may easily become a repository of blame for unfulfilled goals and achievements. There is a strong link here with both a need to respond to changing personal gender identities and compensatory development for parts of the self that may have been suppressed in earlier phases of the relationship during child rearing or career development.

According to Rosowsky, tasks for couples in mid-life include redefining important roles, for example those of spouse, sibling, parent and adult-child, each of which may impinge upon relationship issues. Frequent events precipitating a re-evaluation of relationships include retirement, the children being launched as independent adults, loss of one's parents, or the development of serious illnesses. Each may lead to redefined goals for the individual and for their primary relationship, mutual disclosure and sense of trust. Failure to address these and related transitional issues may result in a form of narcissism noted by Kernberg (1989). It may present as inability to enjoy sexuality, but also corresponds to inability to relate in depth to other human beings, lack of awareness of ambivalence and lack of capacity for mourning and regret over previous acts of aggression toward those who are loved. Aggression may be denied and replaced by a display of naivety at the consequences of one's behaviour.

This overview suggests that mid-life provokes reappraisal in the areas of personal identity, relationships and social roles. This is often concerned with life course transitions and requires the renegotiation of established roles and relationships. The concurrence of multiple transitions within and between different spheres of life would require considerable personal resources.

The dynamics of mid-life

So what may be driving the issues outlined above in terms of psychological processes? Three explanations will be summarized below, the first arising from King's psychoanalytic approach, the second, arising from Jungian analytical psychology, adapted to take social ageism into account, and a third examining a *rapprochement* between Eriksonian ego psychology and McAdams's narrative approach.

King and the psychoanalytic approach

Pearl King was one of the first psychoanalysts to revise thinking about mid-life and adult ageing, at considerable risk to her standing within the psychoanalytic community. Her great innovation was to extend the use of psychoanalytic techniques to this group of clients. Whilst Pearl King's writing tends to lump 'the middle-aged and elderly' together, she maintains that each developmental phase influences one's capacity to cope with the challenges of the next. 'The way we meet the tasks and crises posed by middle age will influence how we are able to meet old age' (1980: 153).

King made a number of points about the process of therapy with mature adults which are helpful to any therapist considering such an undertaking. She tends to assume that the therapist will be younger than her client, a reverse of the traditionally assumed situation, and thus the resulting transference will not follow the more familiar route of parental therapist and client-child. First, she notes that what might appear particularly daunting for the younger therapist is that mid-life and older patients are unwilling to trust someone younger and less experienced than themselves, and that this itself may require relationship 'work' within the session.

Second, therapists need to take into account what she calls the psychological time scale within which a client may be functioning. Because of the longer life course of the mature adult, imaginative work may take place on a number of different time scales with multiple possibilities for tranference. Tranference may reflect child–parent, parent–child, peer–lover relationships or those reflecting other experiences. This can be doubly surprising to the therapist used to working with clients younger than themself. In one instance they may find themselves in the child role in relation to their client, yet they may also find themselves receiving parental projections that reflect the power relations of the therapeutic situation.

Knight (1986) also confirms that, with both mid-life and older adult clients, the therapist may be encountered as representing a variety of figures, including their parents, children and even grandchildren.

However, whilst King is radical in her reappraisal of process, she is less so in her explanation of the therapeutic task. Here she follows mainstream psychoanalytic thinking in seeing mid-life issues as essentially a recapitulation of oedipal problems, passed, admittedly, through the lens of adolescence. King states that 'The developmental phases that most often need to be worked through in the transference of middle-aged patients are those of puberty and adolescence, the analyst being experienced (whatever his actual age) as significant adults from those phases of the patient's life cycle' (1980: 155). Moreover:

> the traumas and psychopathology of puberty and adolescence must be re-experienced and worked through in the transference whatever early infantile material is also dealt with ... the middle aged individual is having to face many of the same problems as he did in his adolescence, but this time in reverse. (1980:156)

These reversals are reflected in sexual and biological changes, role changes and their socio-economic consequences and conflicts about dependence and independence. One result of these challenges to the self is that established defences may break down, precipitating an identity crisis, in terms of self-perception and perception of the self by others. This would require changes in self-image and the marshalling of inner resources to ride out any accompanying narcissistic trauma and wounds to self-esteem.

Reactions to these assaults and reversals include acting out and 'behaviour more reminiscent of adolescence than middle age', including sexual promiscuity and rapid changes in employment. In the session itself inability to commit to an enduring course of therapeutic action may reflect a fantasy that by avoiding change or therapeutic improvement clients will be 'out of time and therefore avoid ageing and death'. The fantasy belief that therapy is 'keeping them alive' may also mean that mid-lifers can be both inconsistent and difficult to finish working with as clients.

King's explanation of the dynamic underlying mid-life draws heavily on the psychoanalytic understanding of adolescence, itself understood as a reworking of the oedipal conflict. Whereas the transition to adolescence marks a growth of personal potency, reflected in the emergence of genital sexuality, mid-life provokes anxiety because it represents a reversal of such potential and an intimation of death itself. According to this perspective, clients draw consciously and unconsciously upon previous experience of life course transitions in order to make sense of mid-life. The recommended approach does not vary greatly from psychotherapy at other points in the life course, except that transferential relationships may require some recalibration to accommodate the multiple identifications that a mature identity has collected over the life course to date.

Jung, individuation and masquerade

Carl Jung (1967) was one of the first psychotherapists to attempt a psychology of the adult mind that moved beyond the psychoanalytic preoccupation with childhood events. In adulthood, it is argued, new challenges and possibilities emerge that require a different conceptual framework. Key to Jung's view of the psychology of adulthood was the notion that the adult life course could be divided in two broadly different orientations, which he called the first and second halves of life. Mid-life occurs as a transitional period, spanning the move from young adulthood to later adulthood, a process which might begin as early as age thirty-five. In the first half of life a person's identity is said to consolidate around the personal will, and as part of this process the constraints of childhood are cast aside. It is in this sense that one can say that the first phase of adult identity looks backwards for its points of reference, even though it is experienced as a time of looking to the future. It is 'enough to clear away all the obstacles that hinder expansion and ascent' (Jung, 1967: IX, 114) , the object is to 'win oneself a place in society and to transform one's nature so that it is more or less fitted in to that kind of existence' (1967: IX, 771).

However, with the approach of mid-life the social conformity implied by the first half of life begins to pall. 'Passion now changes her face and is called duty; I want becomes the inexorable I must, and the turnings of the pathway that once brought surprise and discovery become dulled by custom' (1967: IV, 331). It is increasingly experienced as having provoked a 'diminution of the personality' as personal potential has become suppressed in the service of social achievements.

At first, however, the mid-life adult may become psychologically entrenched, clinging on to the familiar, if increasingly untenable, positions of the first half. A particular problem at this stage may be that mid-lifers mistake their true identity with that of the persona, the social mask which has been so usefully and carefully constructed to achieve their current social status, whatever it may be. Jung comments that, rather than a sign of psychological well-being, attempts to maintain the priorities of the first half of life into the second are an indication of poor life-course adjustment, which he describes as a delusion. 'As formerly the neurotic could not escape from childhood, so now he cannot part with his youth' (1967: VIII, 777) and that 'the very frequent neurotic disturbances of adult years all have one thing in common, they want to carry the psychology of the youthful phase over the threshold of the so-called years of discretion' (1967: IX, 139). This is perhaps unsurprising, given the fears of ageing that are so common among younger adults, and the projection of undesirable 'shadow' parts of the self on to older adults (Biggs, 1989).

However, it is argued, it is not so much serious physical decline which marks mid-life resistance as a required change in life course priorities. As a part of the mid-life transition the ageing adult begins to develop different existential priorities, which in Jungian thought is referred to as the process of individuation. This is provoked by a number of mid-life processes:

- First, as Stevens (2000) points out, mid-lifers have climbed to the top of life's hill, and can see both forwards and backwards. They can take in the complexity of diverse life course positions.
- Second, before them is a gentle decline, which invites an assesment of self in terms of 'time left to me' rather than 'time from childhood'. Thus life's projects are

no longer open-ended, and the youthful fantasy of eternal life, and thus the possibility of eternal procrastination, have to be shed.

- Third, those shadow elements of the self that were previously projected on to older others begin to return and require acceptance.
- Fourth, there are those aspects of personal potential that had to be suppressed during the first half of life, which now have the possibility of expression.

Individuation is the core task of the second half of life. For Jung this constitutes a turning away from the external exigencies of early adult identity, and toward reflection on the inner world of the self. As mid-lifers turn to the second half of life they should 'devote serious attention to themselves' and a divestment of the 'false wrappings of the persona'. The person becomes, or has the potential to become, conscious in what respects she or he is both unique and at the same time holds in common with other human beings. A key tool in the encouragement of individuation is the use of 'active imagination' (Chodorow, 1997). Here the individual is encouraged to engage with fantasy and dreamwork in order to help distinguish oneself from the unconscious contents of the imagination. Jung developed this method in order to overcome his own sense of being a 'middle-aged man in crisis'.

Thus Jungian psychology proposes a radical break between the priorities of the first half and second half of life, and sees mid-life as a period of transition between the two. Problems associated with the middle years are therefore seen to be rooted in tensions, resistances and adjustments to this life course transition.

Whilst Jung saw mid-life as a period in which the social mask is dissolved, allowing a more authentic expression of a more complete self, more recent writing has attempted to reconcile the individuation process with the continued existence of ageism. As, psychologically, the individual allows more of the self into consciousness and personal experession, this takes place in a social environment which is also increasingly hostile towards adult ageing. This has given rise to the observation that older adults often deploy a masquerade in order to protect the emerging self from this ageist environment (Woodward, 1991; Biggs, 1999). The protective function of the persona is something which has been traditonally underplayed within this approach. Individuation, then, takes place, but has to be disguised if its public expression is anti-normative.

In terms of therapeutic process, the deployment of a masquerade in the mature years means that:

- First, the therapist may need to pay special attention to their own anti-ageist practice in creating a facilitative environment for self-expression. This would require psychological work on attitudes to social and personal ageing.
- Second, the masquerade may be positively protective of emerging individuation, rather than being exclusively an impediment to that process. The uses to which the persona is put may need to be explored as part of the therapeutic process.
- Third, in addition to the enhancement of individuation itself, therapists would need to take into account the context within which individuated parts of the self will seek expression.

The key contribution that analytic psychology makes to our understanding of the dynamics of mid-life is that it locates it as a natural part of the human life course. It is a predominantly optimistic perspective, which views resistance to adult maturity as a consequence of irrational clinging on to existential goals which are no longer appropriate. More recently, awareness of the protective value of social masking has led to a reconsideration of the value of this phenomenon in situations in which ageism impinges on personal identity.

McAdams and narrative approaches to mid-life

Dan McAdams (1993; 2001) has taken a particular interest in the construction of mid-life identity, which he sees as a time of 'putting it together'. The hall-mark of a successful mid-life transition is perceived as 'integrating and making peace among conflicting imagoes in one's personal myth'. These imagoes are the alternative identities that McAdams believes have been collected by people in their thirties and early forties. Mid-life, which is seen as stretching from the forties to the late sixties, consists of a sorting out of these accumulated aspects of self, motivated by fascination with one's own life story's dénouement. By the time clients reach approximately forty years of age, they are likely to have developed a much more articulated and realistic understanding of who they are and in what ways they have acquired a mature identity. Mid-lifers realize, in terms of love and work, that life is not simple and not fully under their con-trol. The 'putting it together' in mid-life must accommodate a 'curious blend of resurgence and decline', requiring a personal myth that changes in narrative tone from earlier versions of the self, incorporates more tragic and ironic elements, and marks a rejection of absolutes and a focus on situation specific truths. The new narrative is provoked as part of a recognition and acceptance of contradictory or ambivalent positions, 'fundamental conflicts in the myth' that had previously been kept separate.

According to this approach, individuals in mid-life experience a 'growing real-ization that good lives, like good stories, require good endings' (1993: 202). The reorganization of life's material which McAdams recognizes as a core process of mid-life takes place in the service of the present: 'When the present changes, the good historian may rewrite the past – not to distort or conceal the truth, but to find one that better reflects the past in the light of what is known in the present and what can reasonably anticipated about the future' (p. 102). The task is to become one's own mythmaker and is seen to consist of a move towards what McAdams refers to as situationally specific solutions and logical infer-ences that are linked with particular contexts.

The mid-life narrative that McAdams describes is not a simple process. It includes elements of immediacy, of the here and now, which lead to identities that are pragmatically created to meet current needs. An emphasis on episodes and situations has largely replaced a focus on continuities with the past, with a premium being placed on one's ability to reconstruct the self based on immediate personal concerns. However, there is a simultaneous awareness of processes and changes in self-perception that relate to the life course as a whole. Narrative therapy describes a process which fits mid-life well. It simultaneously recognizes and attempts to rewrite the life course script. As McAdams has elaborated his views on mid-life counselling he has increasingly drawn on Erikson's life-stage model (McAdams, 1993; 2001). This is itself a strange combination in so far as the rigid formulation of tasks and stages does not gel easily with the open-endedness of narrative reinvention (Biggs, 1999). The Eriksonian stage that is most often identified as addressing mid-life is that of 'generativity' (Erikson, 1982), or, more accurately, the tensions created by 'Care' which may result in generativity at its positive pole and stagnation at the negative. In order to bridge these contradictions, the narrative approach interprets generativity as a process of fashioning endings and new beginnings in the making of personal myths. The 'generativity script' states McAdams, 'is an adult's plan for what he or she hopes to do in the future to leave a heroic gift for the next generation. We recast and revise our own life stories so that the past is seen as giving birth to the present and the future, so that beginning, middle and end make sense in terms of each other' (1993: 227). It facilitates:

> An inner narration of the adult's own awareness of where efforts to be generative fit into his or her own personal story, into contemporary society and the social world he or she inhabits. The generativity script functions to address the narrative need for a sense of an ending, a satisfying vision or plan concerning how, even though one's life will eventually end, some aspect of the self will live on. (p. 240)

McAdams's interest in generativity may reside in it as a concept binding the multiplicity of mid-life narratives into a unitary self. 'Human experience tends toward a fundamental sense of unity in that human beings apprehend experience through an integrative selfing process' (McAdams, 1997: 57). Selfing, here, refers to the making of something, some narrative one's own, a task which contemporary society and the multiple convergences of mid-life-styles make increasingly difficult to achieve. Generativity appears to offer a purposive centre: 'it is in the long middle when men and women make their most significant contributions to future generations and to society'(McAdams, 2001: 395). As such, generativity acquires more than a family resemblance to Erikson's next life stage: wisdom, characterized by tension between personal integrity and despair. The age at which these stages occur appears to vary in Eriksonian writing, and perhaps here reflects mid-life itself as a transitional phenomenon.

The popularity of narrative therapy is, perhaps, because it opens a critical distance between who we are and what we do. It allows a stance to be taken toward established roles and identity statements through the recognition that they are stories that clients tell therapists about themselves rather than an underlying state of reality. The therapeutic task is to create a workable narrative that draws on personal experience but refashions it to fit current well-being. Eventually one inhabits a narrative, rather as one inhabits a house which might become a home. It is both pre-existent and an occasion for self-creation. The use of narrative approaches to help understand mid-life suggests a process that is triggered by the need to make sense of the multiple stories created during earlier phases of adulthood, and increasing awareness of the contradictions between them. A new narrative emerges which better fits the social indeterminacy of contemporary ageing, yet grounds it in a sustainable narrative form.

Conclusion

Evidence on the use of counselling psychology with mid-life clients is limited. However, it is possible to identify a number of issues that may be specific to mid-life as a distinct phase of the life course. These issues include the management of multiple demands on identity in the spheres of work, family and personal relationships. They also indicate a series of existential priorities that emerge from an intensified subjective awareness of life as a finite progression, provoking an accompanying change in personal priorities. Mid-life is therefore socially, personally and biologically defined. Therapy with mid-life clients may be subject to social and historical interpretation that lives both in the minds of clients and in the techniques of therapy itself.

References

Abraham, K. (1919) *Selected Papers in Psychoanalysis*. London: Hogarth.

Biggs, S. (1989) 'Professional helpers and resistances to working with older people', *Ageing and Society*, 9: 43–60.

Biggs, S. (1998) 'The end of the beginning: a brief history of psychoanalysis and adult ageing,' *Journal of Social Work Practice*, 12: 135–41.

Biggs, S. (1999) *The Mature Imagination: the Dynamics of Identity in Mid-life and beyond*. Buckingham: Open University Press.

Blaikie., A. (1999) *Ageing and Popular Culture*. Cambridge: Cambridge University Press.

Butler, R. (1975) *Why Survive?* San Francisco: Harper & Row.

Chodorow, J. (1997) *Jung on Active Imagination*. London: Routledge.

Colarusso, C. and Nemiroff, R. (1985) *The Race against Time: Psychotherapy and Psychoanalysis in the Second Half of Life*. New York: Plenum.

Davis, R. (1981) *Aging: Prospects and Issues*. Los Angeles: Andrus.

Erikson, E. (1982) *The Life-cycle Completed*. New York: Norton.

Featherstone, M. and Hepworth, M. (1983) 'The mid-lifestyle of George and Lynne', *Theory, Culture and Society*, 1: 85–92.

Featherstone, M. and Hepworth, M. (1989) 'Ageing and old age: reflections on the postmodern lifecourse', in B. Byetheway (ed.) *Becoming and being Old*. London: Sage.

Freud, S. *On Psychotherapy in Collected Works* VII. London: Hogarth.

Giddens, A. (1991) *Modernity and Self-identity*. Cambridge: Polity Press.

Granville, G. (2002) 'Menopause: a time of private change to a mature identity', in M. Bernard, J. Phillips, L. Machin and V. Harding-Davies, (eds) *Women Ageing*. London: Routledge.

Guttman, D. (1987) *Reclaimed Powers*. London: Hutchinson.

Heckhausen, J. (2001) 'Adaptation and resilience in mid-life' in M. Lachman (ed.) *Handbook of Mid-life Development*. New York: Wiley.

Hollander, M. (1952) 'Individualising the aged', *Social Casework*, 33: 337–42.

Huyuk, M. and Guttman, D. (1999) 'Developmental issues in psychotherapy with older men' in M. Duffy (ed.) *Handbook of Counselling and Psychotherapy with older Adults.* New York: Wiley.

Jaques, E. (1965) 'Death and the mid-life crisis', *International Journal of Psychoanalysis,* 46: 507–14.

Jung, C.G. (1967) *Collected Works.* London: Routledge and Kegan Paul.

King, P. (1980) 'The life cycle as indicated by the nature of the transference of the middle-aged and elderly', *International Journal of Psychoanalysis,* 61: 153–60.

Kernberg, O. (1989) *Borderline Conditions and Pathological Narcissism.* New York: Aronson.

Kleinberg, J. (1995) 'Group treatment of adults in mid-life', *International Journal of Group Psychotherapy,* 45: 207–22.

Knight, B. (1986) *Psychotherapy with Older Adults.* Beverley Hills CA: Sage.

Lock, M. (1998) 'Deconstructing the change' in R. Shweder (ed.) *Welcome to Middle Age!* Chicago: University of Chicago Press.

Manheimer, R. (1999) *A Map to the End of Time.* New York: Norton.

McAdams, D. (1993) *The Stories we Live by.* New York: Morrow.

McAdams, D. (1997) 'The case for unity in the postmodern self', in R. Ashmore and L. Jussim (eds) *Self and Identity.* New York: Oxford University Press.

McAdams, D. (2001) 'Generativity in mid-life' in M. Lachman (ed.) *Handbook of Mid-life Development.* New York: Wiley.

Neugarten, B. (1968) *Middle Age and Aging.* Chicago: University of Chicago Press.

Newman, K. (1998) 'Place and race: mid-life experience in Harlem', in R. Shweder (ed.) *Welcome to Middle Age!* Chicago: University of Chicago Press.

Rosowsky, E. (1999) 'Couple therapy with long married older adults' in M. Duffy (ed.) *Handbook of Counselling and Psychotherapy with older Adults.* New York: Wiley.

Ryff, C. and Seltzer, M. (1996) *The Parental Experience in Mid-life.* Chicago: University of Chicago Press.

Samuels, A., Shorter, B. and Plaut, F. (1986) *A Critical Dictionary of Jungian Analysis.* London: Routledge.

Sheehey, G. (1995) *New Passages.* New York: Harper Collins.

Sherman, S. (1994) 'Changes in age identity' *Journal of Aging Studies,* 8: 397–412.

Silverberg, S. (1996) 'Parents' well-being and their children's transition to adolescence' in C. Ryff and M. Seltzer (eds) *The Parental Experience in Mid-life.* Chicago:University of Chicago Press.

Staudinger, U. and Bluck, S. (2001) 'A view of mid-life develoment from lifespan theory', in M. Lachman (ed.) *Handbook of Mid-life Development.* New York: Wiley.

Stevens, A. (2000) *On Jung.* London: Penguin Books.

Shweder, R. (ed.) (1998) *Welcome to Middle Age!* Chicago: University of Chicago Press.

Weisner, T. and Bernheimer, L. (1998) 'Children of the 1960s at mid-life', in R. Shweder (ed.) *Welcome to Middle Age!* Chicago: University of Chicago Press.

Woodward, K. (1991) *Aging and its Discontents.* Bloomington IN: Indiana.

Woolfe, R. (1998) 'Therapists' attitudes towards working with older people', *Journal of Social Work Practice,* 12: 141–9.

Woolfe, R. and Biggs, S. (1997) 'Counselling older adults: issues and awareness', *Counselling Psychology Quarterly,* 10: 189–95.

18 Psychological Therapy with Older Adults
FIONA GOUDIE

The 1990s saw the emergence of a substantial body of literature on psychological therapy and counselling with older people (see, for example, O'Leary, 1996; Terry, 1997; Knight, 1992, 1996). In print at least, there has been much to challenge the assumption made by Freud (1905) that after the age of fifty personality structures were too rigid to change.

In practice, however, older people continue to be under-represented on the case load of most psychologists and counsellors. Possible reasons for this range from ageism on the part of the referrer (Ford and Sbordone, 1980) to fear of dependence in the therapist (Martindale, 1989) or lack of knowledge about the availability of psychological therapy among older people themselves. Woolfe (1998) in a study of counsellors' attitudes to working with older people, suggests that fear of dependence may affect both therapists and older people. It seems that fears about their own mortality raised as a result of working on grief and loss issues as well as being confronted with issues relating to their own parents and grandparents may pose a threat to younger therapists. Whatever the reason, without sufficient experience of working with older clients individual therapists will be understandably nervous about addressing any complex issues that may arise in therapy. Counselling psychology services in general may be unsure about how to develop ways of working to meet the needs of more vulnerable older people. This will include those identified as priority groups by the National Service Framework for Older People (Department of Health, 2001) such as those in hospital, people with stroke, mental health problems, including dementia and frequent fallers.

This chapter aims to provide a theoretical and practical framework, using illustrative case examples to emphasize general models of psychological therapy which are valuable when working with older people while also referring to specific therapies or modifications which might need to be adopted with particular clients.

Models of psychological therapy

Cognitive behaviour therapy

This has one of the strongest evidence bases with older populations. Cognitive behaviour therapy has been demonstrated to be effective in treating older people with depression (Thompson et al., 1987; Teri et al., 1994; Scogin and McElreath, 1994), anxiety (Scogin et al., 1992) and chronic ill health (Rybarczyk et al., 1992). Applications have been developed for groups as well as individuals (Yost et al., 1986; Beutler et al., 1987) and for special populations such as people with dementia (Teri et al., 1997).

A useful summary for using cognitive behavioural psychotherapy (CBT) with older people is provided by Gallagher-Thompson and Thompson (1996). They have adapted the model developed by Beck and colleagues (Beck, 1976; Beck et al., 1979) for depression which used techniques to help clients evaluate and challenge negative thinking patterns and develop more adaptive points of view. Written records of negative thoughts and modifications, and the use of homework tasks such as behavioural assignments to check out negative beliefs are key elements of the Beck model.

Gallagher-Thompson and Thompson have developed a sixteen to twenty-session process at the Older Adult and Family Center, Department of Veterans' Affairs Health Care System in Palo Alto, California. They emphasize that CBT is not a 'bag of tricks' but, like other forms of therapy, relies on strong thera-peutic rapport between the therapist and client. The first three or four sessions are spent on this as well as on 'socializing' the client into treatment. This includes explaining what therapy is and is not (i.e. not a social visit, opportu-nity for medical review, or consultation about practical or financial support) as well as introducing certain techniques (recording forms, assessment question-naires, behavioural tasks like activity scheduling). There will also be some dis-cussion about how to stay on task with agreed goals of therapy and 'rules of engagement' such as the therapist not being rude if they interrupt a long dia-logue in order to stay on task and keep to time.

The treatment interventions in the early phase of therapy (possibly up to sessions 6–8) may be fairly behavioural and focus on concrete goals in the here and now. Monitoring links between activities and mood in order to plan ways of increasing pleasant activities or relaxation techniques to help cope with anxiety about socializing might be used. The middle phase will focus on links between events, thoughts and feelings, using various written and behavioural strategies to monitor, challenge and modify these. The client will be helped to practise and develop more adaptive ways in which to think and act when faced with a stressful situation.

The final phase involves helping the client to continue to use their new skills independently, with a written 'maintenance guide' for use when stressful situ-ations occur. Cognitive Behaviour Therapists also spend considerable time, as in other therapeutic approaches, exploring feelings and thoughts associated with the termination of therapy. This is seen as one of the most important aspects of the work, as many older people will have found therapy fills a signi-ficant gap in their lives.

Yost et al. (1986) describe similar strategies for use in group work with older people. They adopt a psychoeducational approach, with 'lecturettes' and the setting of homework as key elements of group sessions. Therapy is divided into four phases (preparation, collaboration and problem identification, cogni-tive change and consolidation/termination) over approximately fifteen to twenty sessions. The advantages which can be derived from group therapy in general – socialization, altruism and universality of problems – are seen by Yost et al. as giving group approaches the edge over individual therapy with older clients.

Psychodynamic approaches

There has been growing interest in the application of psychodynamic approaches to work with older people (Hildebrand, 1986; Knight, 1996; Semel, 1996). The Freudian position was that defences become more rigid and there is reduced motivation for change in later life (and therefore psychodynamic therapy may not be helpful). However, in his psychodynamic casework with older people Hildebrand (1986) found that older people often took the long view in relation to their problems, had greater self-reliance and were more able to deal with therapeutic tasks on their own. Knight (1996) while acknowledging some of the challenges of ageing which may affect therapy, such as memory changes and increased exposure to physical illness, argues that there is continual growth towards maturity throughout the life span. Maturity in this sense means increasing cognitive complexity (the capacity to understand argument, social change and an appreciation that people hold differing points of view) and emotional complexity (better comprehension and control of emotional reactions). From this perspective, rather than the younger therapist making allowances for the slowness and rigidity of the older client, it could be argued that older clients at times have to make allowance for the lack of diversity and mature reasoning in younger therapists.

Those writing about psychodynamic work with older people have tended to adopt a case study format (Hildebrand, 1986). This may foster the impression that psychodynamic therapy is suitable only for verbal, articulate clients. However, Terry (1997) has written movingly about its use with older people with dementia and their carers. He sees the aim of this work as helping the client resolve unconscious internal conflict underlying suffering and distress. He has undertaken psychodynamic work (through paying attention to his own responses and feelings) with a man who has severe dysphasia and 'behaviour problems'. He also describes support groups for staff to think about their own and their patients' feelings about being in an institutional setting and to help them understand that some of their own feelings may be unconscious communications from their patients.

Family therapy

The lives of older people are often deeply within their families – the family they came from, those they have married into and the ones they have initiated through having children. Increased life expectancy makes three, four and five-generation families more common and we can expect to have relationships with our parents and siblings as adults which last longer than the years of parent–dependent child or child–child relationships. Divorce and remarriage also serve to make relationships more complex across the generations. How do grandparents fit in when a son and daughter-in-law divorce, she remarries and moves with the children to live near her new husband's parents three hundred miles away?

While there has been limited research described within the family therapy literature on working with older people (see Qualls, 1996), practitioners from different 'schools' of family therapy *have* described and used clinical applications for ageing issues. The earliest dedicated text applied problem-focused brief therapy to older families (Herr and Weakland, 1979). Carter and McGoldrick (1980) acknowledged and described older age relationships as an important part of family culture and the life cycle. The work of Boszormenyi-Nagy and Krasner (1986) explores the balance of family obligations that are transmitted across generations (for example, obligations about caring for elders).

Whatever model or school is adopted it is likely that modifications of the approach will be needed. It may be necessary to take account of complex relationships and their geographical spread (requiring telephone contact with important members of the network), physical limitations of key family members and the involvement of important people and organizations outside the family such as paid carers and nursing home staff.

Models developed specifically for use with older people

Reality orientation

Reality orientation (RO) is not, strictly speaking, a model of psychotherapy. However, it is of historical importance as one of the earliest and most widely evaluated psychological interventions developed for use with older people. It originated in Veterans'Administration hospitals in the United States in the 1960s and was used with people with both long-standing psychiatric problems and those with dementia. However, research and practice have resulted in the approach being applied almost exclusively in dementia care settings.

The aim of the approach is to encourage people to remember and retain existing skills, abilities and sense of identity. Informal or twenty-four-hour RO is the cornerstone of the approach. The emphasis is on staff interaction with clients to increase awareness and interest in what is going on around them. Attention is paid to reducing barriers to awareness (sensory deficits, poor lighting, background noise), enhancing staff communication skills (tone of voice, non-verbal communication, sentence structure) and modifying the environment (using memory boards, signposts, colour coding). Informal RO is supplemented by formal or group RO. These are structured sessions, which involve repetition and rehearsal of information relevant to group members (for example, names and addresses, life circumstances, current affairs). The mode of repetition and rehearsal means this approach has lent itself to evaluation. Woods (1992) summarizes the research on RO.

While there is evidence for the effectiveness of group RO it has been criticized as rigid and encouraging clients to fail. However, this criticism is perhaps more appropriately aimed at those who have unthinkingly implemented the formal approach (focusing on endless repetition of day, date and weather, for instance) and paid insufficient attention to the informal approach (installing memory boards but not keeping them up to date, painting every door on a long corridor a uniform white instead of personalizing room doors or colour-coding toilet doors).

Reminiscence and life review

Until the 1960s reminiscence was seen as a negative activity, likely to over-emphasize past events and potentially cause distress to older people. Butler (1963) saw life review and related reminiscence activities as normative and undertaken by most people.

Reminiscence methods are used for a wide range of purposes, including oral history, enhancing social contact, maintaining old skills, improving cross-generational and cultural understanding, life review, therapy and for fun (see Bender et al., 1999, for a summary of purposes). Reminiscence activities are usually carried out in groups but can happen on an individual basis. They are increasingly used with people who have dementia. The rationale for this has been that remote memories of childhood and early adulthood are relatively well preserved until later in the course of dementia. Drawing on these memories can help the person maintain a sense of themselves as a person and enable them to feel confidence in some areas of memory even if day-to-day events are difficult to recall. Open-ended discussion around particular themes (childhood, first job and family life) may be a useful approach with people who have little cognitive impairment. However, it is more common to use a range of triggers to stimulate recall. These commonly include music, video tapes, photographic material and everyday objects of historical interest. Drama, art and literary projects may also have reminiscence as the focus. Some approaches involve individuals writing, using tapes or diaries.

Bender et al. (1999) emphasize the importance of staff 'doing their homework' in advance by getting an individual life history of the clients they will involve in reminiscence. Goudie and Stokes (1990), in the same vein, discuss the importance of *individual reminiscence profiles*. This information is needed to ensure that the subject matter is something people will be familiar with. Those who conduct reminiscence need to be confident about using a variety of stimulus material and have good non-verbal as well as verbal communication skills. In addition those running groups need good group-work skills and to be able to involve people with a range of cognitive abilities. At least two facilitators will be needed for a group of six. Certain people may not benefit from a group approach. Compulsive reminiscers (who may have unresolved feelings about an earlier life event) can dominate a group unhelpfully and some people have no real interest in reminiscing. For others, certain topics if introduced without thought or awareness of the individual's life history can trigger distress (for example, playing the sound of an air raid siren for someone who experienced bombing during a war). Overall, however, such groups appear to be stimulating and enjoyable to those who participate and increase staff awareness of the lives of the people they care for. Research into group reminiscence for specific problems like depression is in its infancy and a more structured approach which incorporates specific psychotherapeutic principles may be required (Fry, 1983).

Life-story work involves looking back over the past – usually on a one-to-one basis. It does not set out to resolve past or present problems but can be used to help families and carers gain greater understanding of the person they are caring for, to have something for families to pass on to carers if someone moves into a residential setting, to orientate the person to the reality of their life. Some work can take the form of a life-story book, with sections decade by decade through the person's life, but could also be a visual record of photos and memorabilia. Murphy (1994) describes good practice with people who have dementia.

Life review is a more focused and structured approach. The therapist and older person are usually working one-to-one on 'conflict resolution ... self acceptance and coming to terms with life' (Garland, 1994). The technique of recalling specific events and re-evaluating them may involve painful experiences. It is a psychotherapeutic approach requiring a trained therapist with access to supervision. Generally life review has been used with people who are not dementing, whereas reminiscence has a wider application.

Validation and resolution therapy

Validation therapy (Feil, 1990) was developed as a client-centred approach for listening to and understanding the apparently confused speech of people with dementia. Interpretation is linked with Feil's model of disorientation and the possibility of unresolved earlier life crises.

Resolution therapy (Goudie and Stokes, 1989; Stokes and Goudie, 1990) also emphasizes the use of counselling skills (reflective listening, exploration, warmth and acceptance) to try to understand and respond to what the person with dementia may be feeling. The focus is on what is going on in the here-and-now. So, for example, if someone was insisting they must go home to cook their husband's tea (even though he has been dead for years), the worker would *accept* that the person had been thinking about her husband and *reflect* this ('So you've been thinking about your husband and the meals you used to cook this afternoon?') while trying to *explore* what the current feelings behind it are ('It's very quiet here today. Are you feeling bored?') and *resolve* them ('Would you like to give me a hand with the tea trolley?').

These approaches emphasize the importance of the emotional life of people with dementia. By using them routinely, those working in dementia care can help promote psychological well-being as well as establishing a basis for positive relationships on which to offer more focused help if it is needed.

Key clinical areas

The National Service Framework for Older People (Department of Health, 2001) has identified a number of clinical areas as priorities for the National Health Service. These cover stroke, falls and mental health, including depression and dementia. The aim of this section is to demonstrate (using a case study approach) how elements of the models described earlier can be used therapeutically for clients or carers who have experienced these health problems.

Stroke

Case study 1   The Stroke Adjustment Group

The psychologist attached to a rehabilitation centre noticed that there was an increase in levels of depression among clients who had been attending for stroke rehabilitation and were due to be discharged in the next four to six weeks. The physiotherapists and occupational therapist had noticed that some clients relapsed during this period while others became hopeless about the future ('I thought I'd walk out of here, now I won't – I'm such a failure, I'll never cope alone') or angry with the team ('You've not done anything for me in a year. How can you discharge me?').

Because of the number of people who seemed to be experiencing similar feelings, the team felt a group approach might be useful (Barton et al., 2002). They set up an eight-week stroke adjustment group run by two team members. The group aimed to enable members to draw support from each other at a time when many felt vulnerable about the future, share feelings about losses associated with stroke as well as considering previously established coping strategies outside their life as a 'stroke patient' and how these might help them move beyond the 'stroke patient' role.

Elements of the framework described by Yost et al. (1986) were used, such as socialization of the group to therapy, preparation, consolidation, termination as well as some of the techniques they suggest (the idea of turn taking in 'rounds', mini-lectures about cognitions and coping strategies).

After the two or three sessions most group members were keen to speak during the rounds, both on their own behalf and in supporting and challenging each other, so the mini-lectures were shortened. The facilitators still started each session with homework/reflections on last week and introduced the agenda or theme for the session, with hand-outs for some of them.

For many members the group was the first time since their stroke they had been able to acknowledge that they would not regain their previous physical abilities or life-style. 'I was holding onto the idea that if I kept coming here I'd go back to normal eventually, even though I've been in a wheelchair for fourteen months.' The forthcoming discharge from the centre challenged such denial for group members and facilitators.

'I think we've kind of ignored his wife's remarks about his poor concentration, because we were like him – desperately hoping he could start driving and being the treasurer of his social club again.'

Over half the group's work was concerned with expressions of loss and regret. Members were often reluctant to consider the future, so a combined approach was used which allowed for reflection of feelings as well as more structured use of life review to consider previous ways of coping. This seemed to provide participants with a contained way of accepting the reality of their changed lives while maintaining continuity of strengths and resources (personal, social, material) to face their new life circumstances.

Certain themes emerged across a series of groups and were brought to peer supervision by the facilitators. These included dependence/ autonomy and rank ordering (hierarchies) of group members by one another according to the severity of their stroke or its consequences. Many group members believed the philosophy of stroke rehabilitation was to encourage independence and saw themselves as failing to achieve this and not then being helped to accept that they needed to depend on others (people, aids, alterations to the environment). The group facilitators tried to encourage discussions about the balance between dependence and autonomy, but some members felt it was too little too late and had strong feelings of shame and betrayal. The wider rehabilitation team felt they needed to revise the messages they gave when people started attending. Information leaflets were rewritten to include messages about appropriate support and sharing of care to modify the focus on maximizing independence.

There were some cross-cultural differences about dependence in a group with two male Asian members. Both men felt appropriately supported by their families and that at times the therapists had been urging them to become unnecessarily independent. One of them would continue to have a number of physical needs but could anticipate a future where he would continue to head his family and have an influence over the lives of his children and grandchildren. This contrasted with the often expressed and sometimes unrealistic desire among women members of the group to be 'totally independent' and 'not a burden on my family'.

The rank ordering or competitive hierarchy emerged with remarks like 'At least I'm not in a wheelchair' or 'Poor you, having to go into a home.' The facilitators struggled at times with how to address the underlying feelings of fear. Early modelling by facilitators of supportively challenging remarks ('How did you feel when Elsie made the remarks about the wheelchair?') and generalizing comments ('Sometimes it's easier to put other people down than admit to what we're most scared of') seemed helpful, and many group members began to respond to such remarks spontaneously ('I used to feel like that too, Elsie. I fought the idea for a long time').

The difference between those facing residential or nursing home admission and those remaining in their own home seemed to be a gulf that was too difficult to bridge in a group of this sort, and the facilitators felt that in future those going into care probably needed more space to reflect on the unique impact of this.

Falls

The consequences of falling, including the risk of hospitalization, increased risk of further falls and medical complications, have been identified as a key NHS target within the National Service Framework. A national programme of falls clinics and falls rehabilitation programmes is being developed. These focus on medical risk reduction and physiotherapy-based rehabilitation. Psychological aspects of falling are infrequently considered, despite the fact that fear of falling attributions about the reasons for a fall may be important risk factors for future falls (McKee et al., 1999).

Case study 2   A cognitive-behavioural intervention for frequent falling

Mrs Jones was eighty four and a widow living alone, with two daughters living near by with their families. She had received a hip replacement eighteen months previously and had never really regained the mobility she and the therapy team felt she would be able to. She spent most of the time sitting in her armchair next to a commode with important items (newspaper, glasses, flask, and television remote control) on a table in front of her. Her muscles were weak and when she did rise from the chair she lurched dangerously from one item of furniture to the next. She had had three further falls – usually when a family member was present. Her GP had suggested that she attend the new falls clinic at the nearby hospital but she said she was too afraid of moving to attend. The practice counselling psychologist agreed to see her at home in connection with the anxiety.

Mrs Jones had a range of negative thoughts about herself and her mobility. She felt that because she was old and scared the hip replacement operation had been a waste of NHS time and money. The panic and fearfulness (which were at their worst when she tried to stand and move to the commode or the bedroom) were not reducing. She put them down to old age and thought they would get worse in time. She believed her mobility problems were ruling every aspect of her life and that she was a nuisance to everyone.

The psychologist initially offered Mrs Jones a few one-to-one sessions to work on strategies for dealing with the panic and alternative ways of thinking about herself and her mobility. Mrs Jones thought this might be a waste of the therapist's time (and the counselling psychologist felt some of these feelings herself) but was very interested in any alternatives to medication for the panic attacks.

During the second session one of the daughters called. It was clear that she shared many of the same cognitions as her mother about old age and falling. She remarked to the psychologist: 'It's nice of you to come and give Mum a bit of company, but it would be better if you could sort a wheelchair for her – she'll need one soon enough.'

In supervision, the psychologist expressed her frustration about trying to carry out therapy in a home setting and wondered if it would be better to pass Mrs Jones on to the district nurse or physiotherapist. Her supervisor reflected that perhaps the psychologist was reacting to Mrs Jones's and her daughter's projections about ageing and hopelessness and might also be feeling some irritation at having to see someone away from the contained office environment where interruptions could be controlled.

At the subsequent session the psychologist suggested that a family meeting might be helpful. 'Why don't we invite everyone in the family who might be able to help us understand your fear of falling?' To her surprise, in addition to her two daughters, Mrs Jones suggested her twenty-one-year-old grandson.

The meeting was arranged with Mrs Jones, her two daughters, her grandson and the psychologist. A problem-solving focus was agreed for the session, in line with that proposed by Herr and Weakland (1979). For one daughter (Joyce) the ideal solution to Mrs Jones's difficulties was to get her a wheelchair and prevent her from putting herself at risk. She was frightened of the possibility of further falls, which could lead to hospitalization. The second daughter (Mary) was actually quite cross with her mother and sister and felt that her mother could do better and was 'putting on' the panic attacks for attention. The psychologist noted how they argued with each other and ignored their mother during the early part of the session. The grandson remained quiet through much of this. When asked to comment he said, 'This is just what it was like after Grandad died [five years previously] with Mum and Aunt Mary arguing. But then Aunt Mary was blaming Mum for not calling the ambulance quick enough and Mum couldn't believe he might have had a stroke. Gran was wringing her hands and didn't know what to say.'

There was a lengthy silence at this point. Slowly both daughters acknowledged this had been the case. Joyce said, 'I felt so guilty about

Dad that I want to wrap Mum up in cotton wool.' Mary acknowledged that she couldn't bear to think of losing her mother and was therefore possibly playing down the implications of any genuine aspects of frailty. Jeremy the grandson had always been close to his grandmother and had been party to many disclosures from her about how concerned she was to keep the peace between them.

The therapist felt this family session was invaluable to help them all understand the family's attitude to ageing as well as the aspects of Mrs Jones's helplessness which were to do with feeling 'stuck' between her daughters. It was possible to set some practical goals and teach the family anxiety management strategies, which they could help Mrs Jones with. At three-month follow-up she was going out for regular trips in the car and visiting her daughters' homes. She had accepted a walking frame and had been able to clear the clutter of furniture from her lounge so that she could slowly but more confidently move between lounge, kitchen and bedroom. She continued to feel panicky in certain situations (for example, if someone unexpectedly knocked at the door) but felt this was a realistic fear she could cope with.

The psychologist felt that she had been able to offer something useful to the family and believed that supervision and awareness of her own feelings had been crucial in avoiding premature discharge and collusion with the spirit of hopelessness.

Mental health

The feelings associated with receiving a diagnosis of dementia or stroke are similar to those associated with a diagnosis of cancer or other terminal illness and with bereavement and loss. Giving a diagnosis and discussing the implications can be stressful for health professionals and may generate feelings of panic, a desire to avoid the subject or pass the task on to someone they believe to be better qualified at dealing with bad news.

In services with a specific early diagnosis and treatment role, such as a memory clinic, the team may have developed their skills in pre- and post-diagnostic counselling. Grief counselling and therapy models such as Worden's (1991) can be valuable in relation to the post-diagnostic counselling work.

Many people with dementia never receive a diagnosis in the early stages of their disease. As their condition progresses they attend hospitals or day centres with other people who are obviously forgetful and have communication difficulties. Yet it is unusual for the treatment programmes in these settings to address directly the diagnosis and associated feelings for their service users themselves even though support groups for carers may discuss the issues directly.

Case study 3   Dealing with diagnosis in early dementia

This case study describes the work between Mary (forty three) a nurse-therapist, and Ernest (eighty) an attender at a newly opened day hospital for people with dementia. The therapeutic programme was group-based and included reminiscence, general knowledge and word quizzes, social activities and skill building (gardening, cooking).

Ernest was one of a small number of patients attending because they had been prescribed a new drug (cognitive enhancers for people with Alzheimer's disease). Some of the comments he made in groups during his first week included 'I don't know why I'm here – I think my wife wants rid of me,' 'I've been told I've got Alzheimer's and it would help coming here, but no one's told me what will help.' 'Everyone is confused here. Will I get like that?'

Ernest expressed interest in weekly one-to-one sessions with Mary on the theme of 'Coping with forgetting' instead of one of the group activities. Mary was concerned that the service was ignoring and avoiding the fears clients had about dementia. She thought that new attenders in particular were confused by the purpose of some of the group activities. She had previously worked as a counsellor in a breast cancer unit and used a psychodynamic approach.

Early sessions were information-orientated, at Ernest's request. 'I want to know why I'm taking these drugs.' He wanted the information written down to take home after the second session. The next morning his wife, Violet, phoned Mary to say that when Ernest had come home the previous evening with the information he had wanted to discuss it together. 'At first I was cross that he'd got hold of it himself, but then I realized we'd both been pretending to each other that everything was OK, ignoring the future but not really talking about now. We've always been so close. We cried together but it was such a relief.'

The sessions became more unstructured as Ernest gained the confidence to talk about his feelings of sadness at being denied information on his illness, anger at the early collusion between his wife and the health professionals and his fears and hopes for the future.

Ernest saw Mary weekly for eight weeks, then fortnightly for a further four sessions. The fortnightly sessions involved his wife. Mary was struck by the degree of support they were able to offer each other about marital tensions, the loss of their sexual relationship and certain friendships and the fact that Ernest had to stop driving. At times the couple joked about role reversal. Ernest had been the driver, the organized planner of trips and holidays, and more confident socially. Now Violet was having to take on these roles. However, they were also able to express their frustration and resentment as well as their sadness. Violet had never liked driving, and after a near miss got irritated with Ernest. 'If it wasn't for Ernest and his poor memory I wouldn't be driving.' Ernest was sad because he felt Violet was avoiding booking holidays. 'We'll never go abroad again. Violet feels embarrassed about me.'

Mary was able to reflect on these comments and suggest that at times they were projecting their own feelings on to the other. For example, Violet might feel irritated with herself about her neglected driving skills, and Ernest was perhaps embarrassed about his own memory lapses and lack of initiative in conversation.

They both felt positive about the sessions. Ernest felt they were no longer hiding things from each other and Violet commented that they often carried on talking about issues that had come up in a particular session long into the evening. At six-month follow-up they were using more home support, but both felt that their relationship was still good and they could face the future together with the support of their family.

There were some issues arising from this work for Mary in supervision. She admitted that she feared once she began the one-to-one work with Ernest she would never be able to stop it and would have him on her case load until he was admitted to long-term care (see Martindale, 1989, for more on this theme). However, she was able to reflect on the possibility of these feelings for Ernest and use them in therapy directly. This enabled both Ernest and Violet to share their fears of dependence in the future as well as the reality now and not catastrophize in advance. Instead of becoming dependent on Mary, Ernest was able to return to his confidante of a lifetime – Violet.

Mary had also been concerned about confidentiality and involving his wife in what had started out as individual work. However, it was important to acknowledge the reality of Ernest's memory problems and involve Violet in bearing witness to experiences he wanted to remember as well as helping with practical problem solving related to the consequences of Alzheimer's disease.

As someone with a psychodynamic background she had thought Ernest would see her as a parent figure but instead had the sense that Ernest and Mary saw her more as a well informed adult child who had to be let go. Biggs (1998) makes reference to the fact that therapy with older adults does not necessarily follow the psychodynamic tradition of transference, with the client projecting on to a 'parental' therapist. Indeed, Knight (1992) suggests that transference with older adults can take a number of forms (parent, child, grandchild, sexual partner) and the therapist needs to be alert to this.

Post-Traumatic Stress Disorder has become increasingly recognized as a psychological consequence of war service for veterans and for many civilians living through war. Specific symptoms include flashbacks, intrusive thoughts, auditory and visual re-experiencing of traumatic events, nightmares and the tendency to be easily aroused or startled.

For many older people who have experienced trauma in earlier life, avoidance of memories has been made possible for many years by engaging in physically demanding activities, working long hours and using tobacco and alcohol. However, late life losses associated with bereavement, reduction in physical ability and early dementia can lead to the reactivation of traumatic memories which have been successfully repressed for many years.

Case study 4   Depression and reactivation of war trauma following admission to residential care

Mr Zimbrowski was an eighty-four-year old Polish man who had been resident in 'The Elms' for six months since the death of his wife. A combination of severe arthritis and Parkinson's Disease had made it difficult to look after himself in his own home. Staff at 'The Elms' were concerned about his behaviour. He was hostile to staff and would remove food from other residents' plates at mealtimes and hoard it in his room. He was reluctant to eat in public. He appeared frightened of going to sleep and, when he did go to bed, he wanted to use the furniture to barricade himself into his room.

The head of the home and a visiting psychologist were able to develop enough of a relationship with Mr Zimbrowski and one of his daughters to find out that he had been a prisoner of war. He described how he had survived starvation and death in the camp. He had stayed awake at night to ensure his possessions were not stolen, and had sought out and then hidden any rations uneaten by the ill or dying. He had not talked about these experiences for decades, but the communal eating situation in the home and the noise of other residents and staff at night reactivated some of the old fears and behaviours. In the past he had been able to distract himself from certain memories by reading and watching television late at night. His concentration now affected his enjoyment of these activities. He also found the group reminiscence sessions organized by the home's activity co-ordinator intrusive. Even though he avoided the groups themselves, he felt nervous when other residents and staff joked together about how the city had changed and mentioned the war years. He was not sleeping, his appetite was poor and he was feeling depressed by his new surroundings.

A number of strategies helped Mr Zimbrowski and those caring for him to cope better with his traumatic memories and reactions. He and the psychologist established together that it was important for him to try to stay in the 'here and now' rather than being drawn back into the past. However, it was also important for staff to understand enough of his background to be able to empathize with him, without Mr Zimbrowski having to explain his past to each new staff member. With his daughter's help a life-story notice board was made with some of his mementoes and photographs. The board included recent photos of his children and grandchildren and information about work and hobbies as well as pre-war mementoes. It had two functions. It reminded staff of Mr Zimbrowski's Polish background and prisoner-of-war experiences and enabled them to empathize with him more readily. It also helped them to ground him in the here and now by drawing his attention to photos of his grandchildren, his long-service award from the local steelworks and his membership card for the Polish Club he still attended occasionally with his son. His hoarding of food was reduced by giving him his meals in his bedroom. He began to stay up late in the lounge with one or two other residents who enjoyed late-night television. As far as possible, the same two key workers on nights would help him get into bed. They would regularly repeat a conversation about the here and now which included a reminder of the date, current news, any recent or planned visitors, who they were and that they would be looking after him and his belongings overnight.

Some difficulties remained, particularly when staff changed, but Mr Zimbrowski felt much more settled and the home felt more able to cope on a day-to-day basis. The psychologist continued to offer the head of home some supervision sessions over a period of a few months, to enable her to reflect on and resolve any further difficulties.

Conclusion

This chapter has described the application of a range of approaches to psychological therapy and counselling with older people. The case studies illustrate some of the problems which older people and their carers may face and the different settings in which they can occur. While therapy with many older people will be little different from working with younger people, it has been the author's aim to demonstrate that psychological therapy and counselling can be of benefit to older people far beyond the confines of the one-to-one out-patient clinic. This demands an openness to change and an alertness to ageist assumptions in potential therapists.

Generational and cultural factors may mean that some older people have had little exposure to talking treatment and may not initially see its relevance. On the other hand there will be those who have children or grandchildren with experience of counselling and therapy. It is important to explain treatment approaches and their relevance as well as the structure that will be followed in a session (that it will be time-limited, that particular topics will be agreed as the focus of the work and that the therapist will bring them back to the point if they get sidetracked). If sessions end up as sociable chats it may be because the enthusiastic practitioner, keen to get on with 'the work', has not taken sufficient time to explain the purpose of the work and how it will be done.

Supervision has been emphasized in the case studies. While it is important with all client groups, it seems to be given less emphasis in work with older adults among some professional groups. This is a great mistake – particularly *early on* in the career of therapist and *early on* in the process of engaging in therapy with a particular client or group of clients. Early on in the career of the therapist it is important to become attuned to how the negative impact of ageism, relationships with parents and grandparents and fears about dependence and one's own ageing may affect the therapist's capacity to accept and work with older adults. Supervision is particularly important early on in the work, with individuals or groups, because it is at this point that most attention needs to be paid to clarifying what the relationship and therapeutic work are going to be about. Mutual avoidance of process issues (the feelings evoked in the client by the therapist and in the therapist by the client) at this stage can lead to premature discharge (as could have occurred with Mrs Jones in case study 2) or, conversely, a feeling in the therapist that they need to carry on supporting a frail client for ever as if they were a parent or grandparent.

Psychological therapy with older adults seems at times to engender apprehension in younger therapists. However, it can enrich our understanding of what life is like for older people now and what it may be like for us in the future. The richness and diversity of relationships and experiences increase with age and can appear to pose a greater challenge when things go wrong. Nonetheless, there is an encyclopaedia of learning to draw on and use – if we will listen.

References

Barton, J., Miller, A. and Chanter, J. (2002) 'Emotional adjustment to stroke: a group therapeutic approach', *Nursing Times*, June 4, 98 (23): 33–35.

Beck, A.T. (1976) *Cognitive Therapy and the Emotional Disorders*. New York: International Universities Press.

Beck, A.T., Rush, J., Shaw, B. and Emery, G. (1979) *Cognitive Therapy of Depression*. New York: Guilford Press.

Bender, M., Bauckham, P. and Norris, N. (1999) *The Therapeutic Purposes of Reminiscence*. London: Sage.

Beutler, L.E., Scogin, F., Kirkish, P., Schretler, D., Corbishley A. et al. (1987) 'Group cognitive therapy and alprazolam in the treatment of depression in older adults', *Journal of Consulting and Clinical Psychology*, 55: 550–6.

Biggs, S. (1998) 'The end of the beginning: a brief history of the psychoanalysis of adult ageing', *Journal of Social Work Practice*, 12 (2): 135–40.

Boszormenyi-Nagy, I. and Krasner, B. (1986) *Between Give and Take: a Clinical Guide to Contextual Therapy*. New York: Brunner Mazel.

Butler, R.N. (1963) 'The life review: an interpretation of reminiscence in the aged', *Psychiatry*, 26: 65–76.

Carter, E. and McGoldrick, M. (1980) *The Family Life Cycle: a Framework for Family Therapy*, second edition. New York: Gardner Press.

Department of Health (2001) *The National Service Framework for Older People*. London: Department of Health.

Feil, N. (1990) *Validation: The Feil Method,* second edition. Cleveland OH: Edward Feil.

Ford, C.V. and Sbordone, R.J. (1980) 'Attitudes of psychiatrists toward elderly patients', *American Journal of Psychiatry,* 137: 571–75.

Freud, S. (1905) *On Psychotherapy* in *Collected Works* VII. London: Hogarth.

Fry, P.A. (1983) 'Structured and unstructured reminiscence training and depression among the elderly', *Clinical Gerontologist,* 1 (3): 15–37.

Gallagher-Thompson, D. and Thompson, L. (1996) 'Applying cognitive-behavioural therapy to the psychological problems of later life', in S.H. Zarit and B.G. Knight, *A Guide to Psychotherapy and Aging.* Washington: American Psychological Association.

Garland, J. (1994) 'What splendour it all coheres: life review therapy with older people' in J. Bornat (ed.) *Reminiscence Reviewed: Perspectives, Evaluations, Achievements.* Buckingham: Open University Press.

Goudie, F. and Stokes, G. (1989) 'Dealing with confusion', *Nursing Times,* September 20, pp. 38–40.

Goudie, F. and Stokes, G. (1990) 'Reminiscence with dementia sufferers' in G. Stokes and F. Goudie (eds) *Working with Dementia.* Bicester: Winslow Press.

Herr, J.J. and Weakland, J.H. (1979) *Counselling Elders and their Families.* New York: Springer.

Hildebrand, P. (1986) 'Dynamic psychotherapy with the elderly' in I. Hanley and M. Gilhooly (eds) *Psychological Therapies for the Elderly.* London: Croom Helm.

Knight, B.G. (1992) *Older Adults in Psychotherapy: Case Histories.* Newbury Park CA: Sage.

Knight, B.G. (1996) *Psychotherapy with older Adults,* Newbury Park CA: Sage.

Magai, C. and Passman, V. (1997) 'The interpersonal basis of emotional behaviour and emotional regulation', in M.P. Lawton and K.W. Schaie (eds) *Annual Review of Gerontology and Geriatrics* XVII. Springer: New York.

Martindale, B. (1989) 'Becoming dependent again', *Psychoanalytic Psychotherapy,* 4: 67–75.

McKee, K., Orbell, S. and Radley, K.A. (1999) 'Predicting perceived recovered activity in older people after a fall', *Disability and Rehabilitation,* 21 (12): 555–62.

Murphy, C. (1994) *It Started with a Seashell: Life Story Work and People with Dementia.* Stirling: University of Stirling.

Murphy, C. and Moyes, M. (1997) 'Life story work', In M. Marshall (ed.) *State of the Art in Dementia Care.* London: Centre for Policy on Ageing.

O'Leary, E. (1996) *Counselling Older Adults.* London: Chapman & Hall.

Qualls, S.H. (1996) 'Family therapy with aging families', in S.H. Zarit and B.G. Knight (eds) *A Guide to Psychotherapy and Aging.* Washington DC: American Psychological Association.

Rybarczyk, B., Gallagher-Thompson, D. and Rodman, J. (1992) 'Applying CBT to the chronically ill elderly: treatment issues and case illustration', *International Psychogeriatrics,* 4: 127–40.

Scogin, F. and McElreath, L. (1994) 'Efficacy of psychosocial treatments for geriatric depression: a quantitive review', *Journal of Counselling and Clinical Psychology,* 62: 69–74.

Scogin, F., Rickard, H.C., Keith, S., Wilson, J. and McElreath, L. (1992) 'Progressive and imaginal relaxation training for elderly persons with subjective anxiety', *Psychology and Aging,* 7: 419–24.

Semel, V.G. (1996) 'Modern psychoanalytic treatment of the older patient' in S.H. Zarit and B.G. Knight (eds) *A Guide to Psychotherapy and Aging.* Washington DC: American Psychological Association.

Stokes, G. and Goudie, F. (1990) 'Counselling confused elderly people' in G. Stokes, and F. Goudie (eds) *Working with Dementia.* Bicester. Winslow Press.

Teri, L., Curtis, J., Gallagher-Thompson, D. and Thompson, L. (1994) Cognitive – behavioural therapy with depressed older adults' in L.S. Schneider, C.F. Reynolds, B.D. Lebowitz and A.J. Friedhoff (eds). *Diagnosis and Treatment of Depression in late Life: Results of the NIH consensus development conference.* Washington DC: American Psychiatric Press.

Teri, L., Logsdon, R.G., Uomoto, J. and McCurry, S.M. (1997) 'Behavioural treatment of depression in dementia patients: a controlled clinical trial', *Journal of Gerontology: Psychological Sciences*, 52: 159–66.

Terry, P. (1997) *Counselling the Elderly and their Carers*, Basingstoke: Macmillan.

Thompson, L.W., Gallagher, D. and Breckenridge, J.S. (1987) 'Comparative effectiveness of psychotherapies for depressed elders', *Journal of Consulting and Clinical Psychology*, 55: 385–90.

Woods, R.T. (1992) 'What can be learned from studies on reality orientation?' in G. Jones and B. Miesen (eds) *Care-giving in Dementia: Research and Applications*. London: Routledge.

Woolfe, R. (1998) 'Therapists' attitudes towards working with older people', *Journal of Social Work Practice*, 12 (2): 141–8.

Worden, W. (1991) *Grief Counselling and Grief Therapy*, second edition. London: Routledge.

Yost, E.G., Beutler, L.E., Corbishley, A.M. and Allendar, J.R. (1986) *Group Cognitive Therapy: a Treatment Approach for Depressed older Adults*. Elmsford NY: Pergamon Press.

Part V
Issues and Contexts

19 Counselling Psychology in Primary Care Settings
ROSLYN CORNEY

The main focus of this chapter is on the role of counselling psychologists in the primary care setting. This setting has seen a large expansion of the employment of counsellors and therapists and it has been proposed that, together with the workplace, it will become the largest sector of employment of counsellors and therapists in the future (Eatock, 2000). The chapter will end with a consideration of what additional expertise counselling psychologists can offer as well as future possible developments in other areas of health.

Changes in primary care over the 1990s

In the past, most patients who consulted their GP with a psychological problem were managed solely by their GP and only 10 per cent were referred to secondary mental health services based mainly in hospital (Goldberg and Huxley, 1992). Those referred were generally patients with overt mental health problems, including severe and chronic mental illness. Patients going through life crises or who were distressed were very dependent on the skills and interests of their GP. As NHS services became more primary care led, a number of mental health professionals started to spend time within the practice, mostly seeing patients directly but also advising members of the primary care team on assessment and management. These mental health professionals included psychiatrists, community psychiatric nurses and clinical psychologists. Offering a service within primary care was seen as having many advantages, particularly increased access and reduced stigma for the patient, plus a much higher uptake of first appointments (Corney et al., 1996).

Although originally the type of referral to these mental health professionals was wide-ranging, the first priority of these mental health professionals was the assessment and treatment of patients with more severe mental health problems (Corney et al., 1996). The bulk of problems seen within general practice are the more common mental health problems of anxiety and depression, often brought about by life crises and by personal and social problems. Psychological therapies and counselling were seen as a more relevant treatment option for this group of patients rather than the more traditional mental health services. General practitioners were also motivated to employ their own therapists in order to have more control over the service and to avoid the long waiting lists for secondary care services (Corney and Jenkins, 1992).

The first papers describing the work of counsellors and therapists in primary care were published in the 1970s but it was not until the 1990s that such professionals became well established in general practice settings. During the 1990s there was not only an increase in the number of attachments but also a gradual tightening of standards. Reports of schemes from the early 1990s suggested that the employment of counsellors and therapists was a haphazard affair, with many not having sufficient training or suitable supervision (Sibbald et al., 1993, 1996). A later national survey of primary care counsellors found that considerable changes had taken place; three-quarters of respondents had a diploma-level qualification, with 31 per cent also having a first or Master's degree (Mellor-Clark et al., 2001). Only six counsellors (out of 1,031) had no relevant qualification. Counsellors in the survey had an average of over six years' work experience in medical settings and 99 per cent had regular supervision. This study showed the extent of counselling provision, with 51 per cent of general practices having an arrangement with a practice counsellor, although group practices were still more likely to have a counsellor (56 per cent) compared with single-handed practices (37 per cent) (Mellor-Clark et al., 2001). This study found that only a small proportion of respondents were counselling psychologists. However, this is likely to change in the future as more counselling psychologists are being trained.

Changes in funding and arrangements for GP reimbursement were probably the main reasons why the provision of therapy increased so markedly (Corney and Jenkins, 1992). Under the new GP contract in 1990, GPs received extra payment for health promotion clinics. Many set up stress clinics staffed by psychologists and counsellors. Although this money was subsequently discontinued, it meant that many GPs had learnt to appreciate the value of having such a service on site and wanted to continue (Corney et al., 1996). The advent of GP fundholding meant that fundholding GPs could pay for the employment of therapists from their allocated budget. Although more recent changes have meant that fundholding has been abolished, the employment of therapists can now be commissioned by the new structure of primary care groups instituted in England (1999), local health groups in Wales, and local health care co-operatives in Scotland (Foster, 2000).

All these changes in general practice over such a short space of time have meant that the funding of therapists and counsellors in the setting has been precarious. Some therapists had their contracts terminated when the funding for stress clinics was withdrawn, or when the fundholding budgets were discontinued, or when primary care groups failed to continue with existing services. In addition to these job insecurities, the conditions of service in this setting have varied enormously. Counsellors and therapists were self-employed, employed, in student placements, or volunteers. There were no national pay scales, and no agreed conditions of employment or standards of training (Eatock, 2000; Foster, 2000). Many therapists were working in isolation, with little contact either with primary care team members or with other therapists for support.

The lack of agreed conditions of service led to the development of Guidelines for the Employment of Counsellors in General Practice (BAC, 1993) which was circulated to all English and Welsh practices in 1993. The national medical advisory committee of the Scottish Office Department of Health (1998) also developed a set of guidelines for good practice in primary care in 1998, as did the Counselling in Primary Care Trust (CPCT, 1995). The formation of the Association of Counsellors and Psychotherapists in Primary Care (CPC) in 1998 was another important step towards self-regulation and the adoption of agreed standards (Foster, 2000). The CPC represents all those providing counselling in primary care, including counsellors, psychotherapists, counselling psychologists, behaviour therapists and clinical psychologists. The CPC is working on the setting of a number of standards, including appropriate levels of training and accreditation for working in primary care and the need for adequate supervision of students in training. To become a registered member of the CPC, it is necessary to have a similar level of training and experience as that needed for BACP accreditation; this would mean that a qualified counselling psychologist would need 450 client hours' experience in primary care (Mellor-Clark et al., 2001). It is also recommended that therapists would need regular supervision from a supervisor with primary care experience, a supervision qualification as well as considerable experience of supervised practice (Burton et al., 1998).

The current and future situation

In general, it is likely that these changes will be positive for most therapists working in primary care. Certainly, conditions of service will be better regulated. The involvement of primary care groups where services are commissioned for all general practices within the group has meant that general practices are now operating on more equal provision of therapy and counselling, although this may mean that in the short term the existing provision may be spread more thinly (Foster, 2000). In addition, the new primary care groups (and more recently trusts) are more likely to purchase services from agencies or from trusts rather than employ individual independent therapists. These moves will encourage therapists to co-ordinate and integrate their services. It will be necessary for them to bring in a more uniform system of management and set agreed standards and principles. Although therapists may lose some of their earlier independence, the changes carry a number of advantages. Instead of working in isolation, they are more likely to work with a team of other therapists or other mental health professionals. Their terms and conditions of employment will be more likely to be regulated; they are more likely to receive administrative support and supervision within the service. Moreover, their contracts may include being paid for non-contact hours, giving them time to take notes, make contacts and attend meetings (Foster, 2000).

   In many areas, therapists have become employees of a NHS trust and a number have become an integral part of the trust's psychology service. The extent to which counsellors, therapists and clinical psychologists are now working together in the NHS is reflected in the number of departments of clinical psychology now calling themselves Clinical Psychology and Counselling Services. There is some evidence that they can work well together (Hall, 1997) and some services have been described that include a direct access psychology service in which clinical psychologists, psychotherapists, counsellors and assistant psychologists work together to provide a range of treatment in GP surgeries, out-patient settings and home visits (Burton, 1998). One of the main advantages of this arrangement is the closer integration of primary and secondary care services. A serious clinical problem seen by a therapist in primary care may need urgent referral to secondary care. Therapists working closely with secondary care services will have increased access plus greater knowledge and understanding of the resources available. It is also likely that, under these arrangements, counselling psychologists will find that their additional skills and background training in psychology will be particularly welcomed and appreciated, and their qualifications considered most suitable for employment in these posts.

These changes do mean that the days of the independent self-employed therapist working closely with the GP may be over. Therapists will increasingly be employed by other agencies and may find their loyalties divided between the demands and needs of the practices in which they work and those of the agencies which employ them. Improved employment conditions and reduced isolation may be obtained only by a reduction in independence.

Client base, ways of working and difficulties encountered

A number of studies in the past have suggested that some of the referrals from GPs are unsuitable for therapy or counselling. It is difficult to ascertain whether this is still the case and it seems likely that the problems occur less in well established schemes, particularly when some degree of collaboration has been developed. A GP with a new therapist in post may offload patients with long-standing and intransient problems but may gradually realize that this is not a productive use of their time (although shared care of this group may be helpful).

Most studies have found that high proportions of referrals are appropriate, including patients with depression, anxiety, stress, life crises and relationship problems. In the national survey, the great majority of counsellors reported treating depression, bereavement, anxiety, stress or stress-related illness, relationship problems and problems relating to physical health/adjustment to illness. Just over 70 per cent treated sexual problems and just over half reported treating social problems such as difficulties with housing or finances. Smaller proportions also reported treating certain problems that have been recommended by guidelines as more appropriate for the secondary care sector, such as self-harm or suicidal ideation (73 per cent), eating problems (73 per cent), aggressive or disruptive behaviour (66 per cent), substance abuse (47 per cent), hallucinations and delusions (21 per cent). While these latter conditions may be seen as inappropriate for referral to counselling (as proposed by the CPCT guidelines, 1995) it does depend on the severity of the difficulties and the associated problems experienced by these clients. For example, someone with a substance abuse problem may be referred because of a relationship problem or because they have become recently bereaved.

These findings suggest that although most referrals to counsellors and therapists are appropriate for their skills, GPs do not always adhere to the recommended guidelines. The survey asked whether counsellors had drawn up referral guidelines to assist their GPs in making an appropriate referral (Mellor-Clark et al., 2001). Only a quarter had done so; however, it is likely a higher proportion of counsellors had verbally discussed referral issues with GPs in order to obtain appropriate referrals.

One major feature of primary care therapy has been the short-term nature of the work. Because of the sheer volume of patients requiring help, most primary care practices have a predetermined limit of six, ten or twelve sessions, usually spread over a period of months (Hudson-Allez, 2000). This means that therapists may need to adapt their styles, becoming more focused; they may also need to be more pragmatic regarding the extent of help offered. They may find a need to include more cognitively based interventions or those involving problem solving (Hudson-Allez, 1997). How best to deal with a long waiting list may need to be an early consideration of therapists working in this setting; a variety of measures may need to be instigated, including the use of initial assessments prior to waiting for later treatment.

Because of some of these differences in ways of working, the Counselling in Primary Care Trust funded the development of a number of postgraduate Master's level qualifications in counselling in primary care. This included training and discussion on a number of issues relevant to primary care work, including the use of time-limited approaches; knowledge of the primary care system; knowledge of mental health and pharmacology; understanding of loss, grief and illness behaviour; working in a medical context, including interpersonal relationships, confidentiality, ethics, note taking; and being able to liaise with secondary care. Although most of the courses have been discontinued, it is important that other counselling courses address these issues and offer suitable training in these methods.

There have also been issues regarding the number of contact hours per week. There are a number of recommendations that most therapists should not work more than sixteen to twenty contact hours each week (Mearns, 1998). This may lead to difficulties if a therapist is employed full-time by one practice, although it is less problematic when therapists operate as part of a service involved in other activities and roles within primary care. These could include group work, providing advice and consultation to other primary care team members, and the supervision of students in training (Corney and Jenkins, 1992).

Another difficulty commonly encountered is the lack of close collaborative working with GPs. Working part-time (or working in several different practices) can make it very difficult for the therapist to meet other members of the primary care team and become more fully integrated. The different views on confidentiality of medical staff and therapists may also hinder integration. Most primary care team members consider that the boundaries of confidentiality regarding information about patients extend to include other practice members (or to other members within their profession when referred) while therapists may not wish to divulge counselling session information to anyone other than their supervisor. This can lead to problems, as the GP has prime responsibility for the patient and what is happening in the counselling sessions may impinge on the patient's health. Therapists who refuse to divulge any information about a client may seriously influence their integration into the primary care team and one of the main advantages of working in this setting may be lost.

These matters have been taken up by the Association for Counsellors and Psychotherapists in Primary Care, which has considered whether there should be a code of ethics and practice that is specific for therapists working in primary care (Hudson-Allez, 2000). In the meantime, it is important that confidentiality issues are discussed fully between therapist and GP, so that GPs, therapists and patients are aware of the issues and are in agreement with the procedures adopted.

There are also issues regarding the confidentiality of client notes. Therapists working in private practice own their notes, while ownership is not so clear when therapists are employed. If a therapist is employed by a trust, the trust can claim ownership and the right of access. Some therapists have suggested that therapists should have two sets of notes, one of which can be made available for public consumption, while the other is for the therapists' private use (Hudson-Allez, 2000). However, the courts can ask for all notes and the police have the power to search for private notes made by employed therapists or those working in private practice (Hudson-Allez, 2000).

In the national survey conducted by Mellor-Clark and colleagues, there was considerable evidence of a lack of close collaborative working (Mellor-Clark et al., 2001). Treatment outcomes and case progress were routinely discussed with GPs by only one-third of the sample; 20 per cent discussed more management issues such as treatment durations, waiting lists and case load. Smaller percentages discussed their case mix routinely (16 per cent) or their referral systems (17 per cent).

The survey also produced evidence suggesting that the supervision of therapists in primary care may not be fully adequate. Less than half the therapists had supervisors with the required supervision qualification and experience of primary care (although only 5 per cent had neither). Thus not all the therapists were considered to have a supervisor sufficiently qualified and experienced to provide insight and guidance to improve their practice (Burton et al., 1998).

Another difficulty encountered is the relatively high rate of clients who do not attend (DNA) their allotted appointment. This is a common problem for all professionals working in the primary care setting (including GPs) and most probably relates to the fact that the client is not paying directly for the service. Sometimes, practical measures can reduce the DNA rate, for example the client being asked to make an appointment with the receptionist rather than being sent an appointment letter through the post. Another alternative is to distribute a leaflet about the service to all new clients explaining why they need to cancel appointments in advance rather than by not turning up.

A number of these problems are due to counselling and therapy in primary care being a relatively new development. These services have grown because individual GPs perceived the need for them. This resulted in the *ad hoc* and haphazard way in which the services have been set up (often to the advantage of the GP and not the therapist). The introduction of guidelines and the adoption of a number of regulations and standards will hopefully mean that there will be less variation in conditions of service between practices in the future. It also means that issues such as confidentiality, supervision, work load and types of referral will be more thoroughly considered prior to setting up a service and suitable agreements made.

Efficacy and effectiveness

Under clinical governance, it is now mandatory for all NHS professionals to be both responsible and accountable for their own practice; to set standards of professional practice, conduct and discipline; and to monitor and evaluate their work in order to improve the quality of their service and safeguard high standards of care (Department of Health, 1998).

However, in addition to the need for clinical governance, counselling and therapy can become firmly and securely established within primary care only by showing that therapists are either effective in improving client outcomes or are cost-effective. Investigating effectiveness (let alone cost effectiveness) is a complex issue. How do we measure outcome? Lyons and colleagues (1997) suggested that there were three kinds of outcome in psychotherapy: clinical outcomes (a reduction in symptoms or an increase in quality of life); medical utilization outcomes (for example, a reduction in visits to the doctor, referrals elsewhere or a decrease in prescribing); and finally patient satisfaction.

Patient and GP satisfaction

If patient or GP satisfaction were considered the most important factors in assessing effectiveness, psychological therapy would have no difficulty in being accepted. The fact that many GPs have been willing to pay for a therapist out of their practice funds is proof enough of their satisfaction with the service (Corney et al., 1996). All studies that have investigated patient satisfaction have shown that clients appreciate and value the therapy. Patient satisfaction was shown to be high in the early studies of counselling (cited in Corney, 1992) as well as the more recent clinical trials which have also measured patient satisfaction (Boot et al., 1994; Friedli et al., 1997; Hemmings, 1997; Simpson et al., 2000).

The comprehensive review conducted by Hemmings also gives many examples of services with high patient satisfaction scores. Hemmings surveyed the grey literature as well as published work between 1992 and 1998. He obtained a range of material, including reports to the local health authorities and NHS trusts. His review summarised twenty-six reports which covered over 7,000 clients. Seventeen studies collected data on patient satisfaction; all were positive, with the number of participants who rated counselling as helpful to very helpful ranging from 66 per cent to 93 per cent. Ten studies investigated GP satisfaction; most GPs were similarly satisfied, believing that counselling was beneficial to their patients. In one area, 100 per cent of the GPs stated that the counselling was either important or essential to their service.

However, most studies of other treatments offered in primary care have also found high patient satisfaction rates (Corney, 1999). Subjective accounts are valuable, but need to be treated with caution. It may be very difficult to criticize a service, especially when arranged by the general practice upon which one relies. It is also possible that similar levels of patient satisfaction would have been obtained if clients were given the same amount of time by an untrained, warm and caring befriender or by a self-help group which could offer practical assistance on a longer-term basis.

Utilization of medical services

Other studies have considered whether counselling and therapy have had any effect on the utilization of medical services (Corney, 1992). The results have been used as a measure of outcome (for example, if the client visits the doctor less or stops taking psychotropic drugs he is assumed to be well or better) and also as a measure of costs. Many studies have shown a reduction in visits made to the doctor after the cessation of therapy in contrast with a period before. A similar number of studies have found a reduction in the number of psychotropic and other drugs prescribed. Other studies have indicated that there was a reduction in referrals to the mental health team after a therapy attachment had been instigated.

However, studies have reported a range of different findings and in the clinical trials reviewed by Rowland and colleagues (2000) there were no clear trends. For example, Boot and colleagues (1994) found a reduction in prescription of antidepressants for counselled patients but Friedli and colleagues did not (1997). Friedli, on the other hand, found a reduction in consultation rates (but only in the first three months) while Boot's study did not.

It could be argued that reduced consultation rates and prescription rates are not necessarily reliable indicators of outcome. Maintenance levels of antidepressants taken over a number of months may be important to prevent a relapse in depression and a therapist may feel that it is advantageous if patients are encouraged to visit their GP when appropriate occasions arise.

Clinical outcome

Studies investigating clinical outcome have to weigh up the need for either internal or external validity. The *internal* validity of a study refers to the extent to which the researcher has controlled for the existence of alternative or competing hypotheses that could account for the data. A study high in internal validity would be one that was conducted under laboratory conditions with all variables closely monitored and controlled for. The *external* validity of a study, on the other hand, refers to the degree to which its findings can be reliably and meaningfully generalized to other situations. Thus a study high in external validity would take place in circumstances as close as possible to natural conditions. Unfortunately studies high in internal validity (such as clinical trials) are often low on external validity and vice versa. Some compromise is usually necessary.

Studies high in internal validity are those that are most appropriate to measure the efficacy of the service. Efficacy research needs to be undertaken in a very controlled environment, with the type of patients and interventions strictly regulated. Effectiveness research, on the other hand, is the testing of the treatment in the real world of everyday clinical practice. In this type of research, the patients and therapy should be as similar as possible to what happens in real settings. Roth and Parry (1997) suggest three clear phases in any treatment research: theory, efficacy research and effectiveness research. These phases need different methodologies to validate them: randomized controlled trials for efficacy, naturalistic field trials for effectiveness.

Clinical trial methodology

In medicine, the efficacy of a treatment is determined by the use of clinical trials. In these studies, patients with a single tightly defined disorder are randomly assigned to treatment and control conditions (normally GP treatment as usual). Assessments occur prior to treatment and at set periods post allocation. The therapists are trained in a specifically defined therapy set down in a manual. They have to keep to this model of therapy in treatment and are monitored regularly to see that they do. The aim of this methodology is to keep as strict controls as possible so that the only difference between the two groups is the specified treatment.

It can be readily seen that such trials operate under very different conditions from everyday clinical practice. The trials that have been conducted have been generally very difficult to undertake and most are flawed, some more than others. In 1995 Seligman considered the efficacy study inappropriate for psychotherapy research, because 'it omits too many crucial elements of what is done in the field'. He argued that, in normal practice, the therapy is not always of fixed duration; the therapist does not keep to a set number of techniques but will vary the therapy according to the needs of the patients; patients often have multiple problems or co-morbidity rather than one tightly defined single disorder; and that the outcome measures (usually measuring symptoms) may be inappropriate, as they do not always relate to the objectives and goals of the therapist and client (Seligman, 1995).

There are a number of other reasons why the clinical trials conducted in this area have been flawed. First, randomizing patients as to treatment takes no account of patient motivation, an important factor affecting therapy which needs a high degree of patient participation. Secondly, the treatment received by the control group (and in the experimental group) is likely to be highly varied. It is usually considered unethical to restrict the GPs' treatment options, so patients in both groups will differ according to the medication received and which other agencies are involved. If the control group patients are seen by a skilled and conscientious GP, it may be more difficult to show an additional improvement due to therapy. Thirdly, there are difficulties in recruitment (often because GPs find it difficult to refer patients to a clinical trial), with many clinical trials having insufficient numbers to show a clinical effect even when one might be present. This is often exacerbated by attrition, participants dropping out of the trial at all stages of the process.

Some of these difficulties have been partially overcome by using the patient preference trial. These are trials in which patients with a strong preference for a particular treatment are not randomized but are allocated to the treatment of their choice. Their outcome is compared with the randomized groups. The increased acceptability of the trial to patients and referral agents may increase recruitment rates as well as improve whether participants represent the broader patient population. However, there are difficulties with analysing data from patient preference trials, as selection biases may operate in variables other than their preferences. For example, those wishing to be referred to a therapist may be more able to discuss their problems and be more psychologically minded, which in turn could affect the outcome.

All these methodological difficulties led Roth and Fonagy (1996), in a broad review of the efficacy and effectiveness of the psychotherapies in the United Kingdom, to suggest that the efficacy of counselling was particularly difficult to assess because of the lack of specificity and control in studies, the diversity of patient groups studied, the range and variation in the treatments administered, and the heterogeneity of contrast treatments.

Four systematic reviews have attempted to assess the efficacy of counselling in primary care as tested by clinical trial (Friedli and King, 1996; Godber, 1996; Roth and Fonagy, 1996; Rowland et al., 2000). Although the three earlier reviews indicated that there was no research evidence to suggest that counselling was either clinically or cost-effective, they included studies that evaluated other mental health professionals as well as counsellors. Rowland and colleagues were more careful in their criteria for inclusion and only included counsellors who were either accredited or eligible for BACP accreditation.

Rowland and colleagues conducted their review, working to established guidelines set out in the Cochrane Collaboration Handbook and by the NHS Centre for Reviews and Dissemination. These 'systematic reviews differ from other types of review in that they are explicit in their methodology and adhere to a strict scientific design in order to make them more comprehensive, to minimize the chance of bias, and so ensure their reliability' (Rowland et al., 2000). One major advantage of a systematic review is that it is often possible to produce a pooled summary statistic of the effectiveness of the intervention from the studies, including using a meta-analysis (Rowland et al., 2000).

Rowland and colleagues' review assessed randomized controlled trials and controlled patient preference trials of counselling in primary care. In order to assess counselling rather than some other form of psychological therapy conducted by other professional groups (for example, CBT), a decision was also made to only include trials of non-directive counselling by BACP accredited counsellors. They were also specific regarding the patient group to be included; they excluded specialist counselling interventions for patients with specific problems such as drug or abortion counselling.

Because of these strict inclusion criteria, they found only four appropriate trials (Boot et al., 1994; Friedli et al., 1997; Harvey et al., 1998; Hemmings, 1997), which resulted in a small sample size overall (487) for the meta-analysis. In this analysis, patients receiving counselling had significantly better psychological symptom levels post-intervention than patients receiving usual GP care. When the results were reanalysed excluding the studies with more methodological problems (Boot et al., 1994; Hemmings, 1997) counselling still compared favourably with usual GP care.

When clinical recovery was investigated (i.e. whether clients were assessed as recovered or not at follow-up) counselled patients were significantly more likely to have recovered than non-counselled patients. However, this analysis included only those who undertook follow-up assessments. A further intention to treat analysis, where all drop-outs were considered as 'non-recovered' (which is unlikely), found a small treatment effect in favour of those receiving counselling but it was not significant at the 5 per cent level.

The findings suggest that counselled patients tend to show modest but statistically significant improvement in symptom levels over those treated by GPs. The authors of this review conclude that 'there is very tentative evidence that counselled patients are more likely to recover than usual care patients, but this result needs further investigation' (Rowland et al., 2000).

There have been three more clinical trials that have reported since Rowland and colleagues' systematic review. The first was a complex patient preference trial which compared usual GP care, non-directive counselling and cognitive behaviour therapy (Ward et al., 2000). Patients who were depressed could choose their treatment or be randomized to one of the three treatments. While Ward et al. found significant differences in clinical outcome at four months between those receiving a therapy and usual GP care, no differences were found at twelve months. They found no differences according to type of therapy and no differences in outcome between those who were randomized to each psychological therapy and those who chose it.

The second study was also a randomized controlled trial with patient preference arms (Chilvers et al., 2001). However, in this study, depressed patients were either prescribed antidepressant drugs or generic counselling. No difference in outcome was found between groups, although there was some evidence that those receiving antidepressants recovered more quickly. The authors concluded that 'both counselling and antidepressants are effective' and 'that general practitioners should allow patients to have their choice of treatment'. However, the findings in this study differ from those of Ward and colleagues

(2000) in that patients who chose counselling did better than those who were randomly assigned to it.

In the third study, patients were included who had been depressed for six months or more (Simpson et al., 2000). This group was chosen as it has been shown that they are less likely to recover without outside help (Goldberg and Huxley, 1992). Depressed patients who were screened using GP attenders were referred either to counselling or to usual GP care. The study found no difference in outcome between groups at either six or twelve months; however, there was some evidence to suggest that more of the group receiving counselling were judged clinically improved than individuals in the control group.

Overall, these studies plus those reviewed by Rowland and colleagues (2000) suggest that counselling has a modest effect on clinical outcome but this may be only in the short term. When patients are followed up over a longer period, the differences between groups are reduced.

Other studies

The difficulties found in conducting clinical trials and their lack of external validity suggest that clinical effectiveness may be more appropriately measured using other methods. There has been increasing recognition of the need to supplement evidence from clinical trials with data from routine clinical practice (Mellor-Clark, Connell et al., 2001).

The review conducted by Hemmings included six studies in which clients were asked to rate symptoms pre- and post-therapy (2000). Each of these studies (with a total patient sample of 654) demonstrated a significant reduction in measured symptoms. One service measured symptom change in 385 participants and found consistent significant reductions in anxiety, depression and rumination plus an improvement in self-esteem (Baker, 1998, cited in Hemmings, 2000). While 'none of these studies used a randomised control design, all were consistent in showing a positive outcome with patients who had a moderate to severe level of morbidity' (Hemmings, 2000).

In a more recent evaluation Mellor-Clark, Connell and colleagues (2001) obtained agreement from nine services to take part. They included two services managed by clinical psychology departments, two managed by local health authorities, two managed by local NHS trusts, two consortiums of self-employed counsellors and a voluntary sector service. These services employed nearly 150 counsellors serving 200 practices. The evaluation used a specially designed and piloted audit and evaluation measure, with the counsellors being trained in its use. They used the CORE-OM, a thirty four-item client self-report questionnaire, which assesses the psychosocial domains of subjective well-being, symptoms, life/social functioning, risk to self and risk to others. In the study the measure was administered immediately prior to first contact and again at the last counselling session.

The counsellors also filled in a CORE therapy assessment form (TAF) at the end of the first counselling session that obtains a brief profile of the client. At discharge, the counsellor filled in the CORE end-of-therapy form (ETF) which collected data on the therapy and the counsellor's views on the effect of therapy on the client.

Mellor-Clark, Connell and colleagues calculated the amount of change necessary for clients to be regarded as significantly clinically improved. This was defined as the degree to which their profile was now more similar to a patient in a non-clinical population than in a clinical population. They also determined the amount of change necessary to be considered reliable rather than change due to measurement error.

They collected enough data to measure clinical change in 1,087 clients. The clients were either anxious or stressed, depressed or had relationship difficulties. The mean number of counselling sessions received was four. The results suggest that 59 per cent made a clinically significant change (changed from a clinical to a non-clinical population), 17 per cent made a reliable but not clinically significant change, 23 per cent made no reliable change and less than 2 per cent deteriorated reliably.

This study shows that it is possible to collect data systematically from a number of counselling schemes. All these studies are very positive and yield a range of very useful data, leading to the possibility of finding out the types of client who are most likely to improve, those that stay the same, and those who may deteriorate. However, without appropriate matched controls it is still difficult to ascertain how much improvement would have been obtained without the involvement of the therapist, either owing to the passage of time or owing to the interventions of other primary care team members.

Cost-effectiveness

Another argument which can be used to establish psychological therapy within primary care is that it is cost-effective. If therapy is shown to cause an increase in costs, the extra costs need to be shown to be offset by a reduction in the clients' symptoms or improved functioning. Alternatively, if therapy causes a decrease in costs (for example, fewer drugs prescribed, fewer referrals) it will not be necessary to show a symptom reduction or an improvement in functioning. However, the best scenario would be to show an improvement in client outcome with either a reduction or no change in costs.

Just under half the studies in Hemmings's review attempted to measure cost-effectiveness. One study estimated that the counselling service saved £40,000 by the reduction in GP consultation rates. Another three studies, two with controls, found that considerable cost savings were achieved by the reduction in referrals to mental health services. However, another study with controls found no difference in rates of referral to mental health professionals in those practices with a counsellor from those without (Hemmings, 2000).

Cost-effectiveness can also be evaluated by clinical trials, with the costs related to patients in the experimental group being compared with the costs of the controls. Rowland and colleagues' review suggests that the results were not clear-cut regarding whether counselling was cost-effective. The difficulty with measuring cost-effectiveness using single clinical trials is that the sample sizes used to evaluate clinical outcome may be too small to measure cost-effectiveness adequately. It may therefore be more appropriate to measure cost-effectiveness either by a large-scale clinical trial (which is difficult and costly) or by using the technique of meta-analysis with costs derived from several studies.

A meta-analysis of four recent clinical trials (Bower, personal communication, 2001) suggests that there were greater total direct costs and primary care costs associated with counselling in both the short and the long term. These costs were offset but only in the short term by an increased improvement in clinical outcome in those receiving counselling.

Future work on evaluation

There is a considerable amount of work that needs to be done, both at a practice-based level and also for those involved in research trials. In a time of increasing waiting lists, we urgently need to know what is the best use of the therapist's skills within primary care. We need to find out who can benefit most from therapy and who benefits least, as well as the level of skill necessary to treat different patient groups.

There is also the issue of the type of therapy given. At the present time, much research suggests that it is not the methodology that is important but the qualities of the therapist; therapists who offer warmth, genuineness and empathy have been shown to be consistently effective. However, the increasing evidence of the effectiveness of CBT with a range of conditions may challenge these findings (Roth and Fonagy, 1996; Department of Health, 2001).

There is also the need to undertake more long-term follow-up. Previous studies have tended to use only short-term follow up, with contact at one year being the exception rather than the rule. Will improved outcomes be maintained in the long term? Will long-term costs be affected? While it may not be necessary to show improved outcomes over the long term to argue for the provision of therapy (many treatments in primary care have only short-term effects), longer-term evidence of efficacy and effectiveness would provide a convincing case.

Further evaluation is necessary in order to ascertain how best to cope with the large demand for psychological services in primary care. It is essential that the different health professionals, whether they are members of the primary care team, therapists or mental health professionals, are referred the type of patient who can benefit most from their help. Detailed evaluations are therefore crucial in order to ascertain the most appropriate treatment for different populations of clients.

Why counselling psychology?

What does the counselling psychologist have to offer in this context compared with the counsellor or the clinical psychologist? While the majority of the training of clinical psychologists is in secondary care mental health settings, it will be apparent from this chapter that the vast majority of people seen in medical settings are distressed rather than 'mentally ill'. The distress exhibited by the majority of patients in primary and secondary care is a 'normal' reaction to either physical illness or some other problem in their lives. Counselling is an important skill with this group, and although a clinical psychologist will use counselling in their work, the counselling psychologist's training is specifically focused around the development of this skill.

The counselling psychologist, with her or his prior training in psychology, will in most cases have a wider knowledge base than a counsellor without such training. Counselling psychologists bring an understanding of a wide range of psychological theory and research, and this may be valuable in their work in preventive medicine, consultancy, developing protocols and training others. They may also play a major role in providing supervision to other counsellors or other primary care team members. Psychologists have developed an increasing number of targeted, brief interventions which are relevant for different age groups and are both focused and problem-solving.

The scientist-practitioner ideology of psychology professionals will also fit readily into the philosophy of medicine and the recent NHS drive towards an evidence base. Doctors may be more willing to employ counselling psychologists, who are able to evaluate their own work scientifically and be informed consumers of the counselling research literature. They may more readily appoint counselling psychologists who have understanding and knowledge of research and have undertaken a research project as a significant part of their training.

New areas of growth

Primary care counselling and therapy expanded rapidly in the 1990s; however, there may be many other health care settings where counselling psychologists could play an important part. The domain of clinical psychology has itself changed and the focus of clinical psychology intervention is no longer solely the treatment of mental health problems. Clinical psychologists now take on a wide variety of roles apart from client contact, including teaching and training, supervision, consultation and liaison with primary and secondary care staff, training and team building. These roles are also appropriate for the skills and knowledge base of counselling psychologists, who may also start working in areas which were traditionally the domain of clinical psychologists, including working with the elderly and those with learning disabilities.

Another important area is that of health psychology. Counselling psychologists are now working in settings such as pain clinics or on cardiac rehabilitation. Behavioural changes required by participants in such programmes can be improved by practitioners having an understanding of the factors that might influence behaviour change but who also have the skills and training to work with individuals or groups. This may be a relevant role for counselling psychologists, who may start to develop expertise in promoting health-related behaviours such as compliance with medication, the cessation of smoking, or diet control and exercise regimes for patients with chronic illness. The domain of health psychology may provide a number of opportunities for counselling psychologists or for a new hybrid psychologist who has expertise in clinical, counselling and health psychology. New treatment programmes are constantly being developed, creating more opportunities for future growth. The future of counselling psychology in health care settings is very promising indeed.

References

Boot, D., Gillies, P., Fenelon, J., Reubin, R., Wilkins, M. and Gray, P. (1994) 'Evaluation of the short term impact of counselling in general practice', *Patient Education and Counselling*, 24: 79–89.

British Association for Counselling (1993) *Guidelines for the Employment of Counsellors in General Practice*. Rugby: Counselling in Medical Settings Division.

Burton, M. (1998*) Psychotherapy, Counselling and Primary Mental Health Care: Assessment for Brief or Longer-term Treatment*. Chichester: Wiley.

Burton, M. Henderson, P. and Curtis Jenkins, G. (1998) 'Primary care counsellors' experience of supervision', *Counselling*, 9 (2): 122–33.

Chilvers, C., Dewey, M., Fielding, K. et al. (2001) 'Antidepressant drugs and generic counselling for treatment of major depression in primary care: randomised trial with patient preference arms', *British Medical Journal*, 322: 775.

Corney, R. (1992) 'Studies of the effectiveness of counselling in general practice', in R. Corney and R. Jenkins (eds) *Counselling in General Practice*. London: Routledge.

Corney, R. (1999) 'Changes in patient satisfaction and experience in primary and secondary care: the effect of general practice fundholding', *British Journal of General Practice*, 49: 27–30.

Corney, R. and Jenkins, R. (1992) *Counselling in General Practice*. London: Routledge.

Corney, R., Ward, E. and Hammond, J. (1996) 'General Practitioners' Use of Mental Health Services: the Impact of Fundholding', Unpublished report to the Department of Health.

Counselling in Primary Care Trust (1995) *Referral Guidelines for Counselling in General Practice*. Supplement 1. Staines: CPCT.

Department of Health (1998) *A First Class Service: Quality in the New NHS*. London: HMSO.

Department of Health (2001) *Treatment Choice in Psychological Therapies and Counselling*. London: Department of Health.

Eatock, J. (2000) 'Counselling in primary care: past, present and future', *British Journal of Guidance and Counselling*, 28 (2), 161–73.

Foster, J. (2000) 'Counselling in primary care and the new NHS', *British Journal of Guidance and Counselling*, 28 (2): 175–90.

Friedli, K. and King, M. (1996) 'Counselling in general practice: a review', *Primary Care Psychiatry*, 2: 205–16.

Friedli, K., King, M., Lloyd, M. and Horder, J. (1997) 'Randomised controlled assessment of non-directive psychotherapy versus routine general-practitioner care', *Lancet*, 350: 1662–5.

Godber, E. (1996) *Is Counselling in Primary Care Growing too Fast? A Clinical, Economical and Strategic Assessment.* Southampton: Institute for Health Policy Studies.

Goldberg, D. and Huxley, P. (1992) *Common Mental Disorders.* London: Routledge.

Hall, J. (1997) 'Counsellors and psychologists: a subjective experience of working together', *Clinical Psychology Forum*, 101: 18–21.

Harvey, I., Nelson, S., Lyons, R., Unwin, C., Monaghan, S. and Peters, T. (1998) 'A randomized controlled trial and economic evaluation of counselling in primary care', *British Journal of General Practice*, 48: 1043–8.

Hemmings, A. (1997) 'Counselling in primary care: a randomised controlled trial', *Patient Education and Counselling*, 32: 219–30.

Hemmings, A. (2000) 'Counselling in primary care: a review of the practice evidence', *British Journal of Guidance and Counselling*, 28 (2): 233–52.

Hudson-Allez, G. (1997) *Time Limited Therapy in a General Practice Setting.* London: Sage.

Hudson-Allez, G. (2000) 'What makes counsellors working in primary care distinct from counsellors working in other settings?' *British Journal of Guidance and Counselling*, 28 (2): 203–13.

King, M., Sibbald, B., Ward, E. et al. (2000) 'Randomised controlled trial of non-directive counselling, cognitive-behaviour therapy and usual general practitioner care in the management of depression as well as mixed anxiety and depression in primary care', *Health Technology Assessment*, 4: 1–73.

Lyons, J.S., Howard, K.I., O'Mahoney, M.T. and Lish, J.D. (1997) *The Measurement and Management of Clinical Outcomes in Mental Health.* New York: Wiley.

Mearns, D. (1998) *Counselling Workloads: BAC Guidelines.* Rugby: BAC.

Mellor-Clark, J., Simms-Ellis, R. and Burton, M. (2001) *National Survey of Counsellors working in Primary Care: Evidence for Growing Professionalisation.* Occasional Paper 79. London: Royal College of General Practitioners.

Mellor-Clark, J., Connell, J., Barkham, M. and Cummins, P. (2001) 'Counselling outcomes in primary health care: a CORE system data profile', *European Journal of Psychotherapy, Counselling and Health*, 4: 65–86.

Roth, A. and Fonagy, P. (1996) *What Works for Whom? A Critical Review of Psychotherapy Research.* New York: Guilford Press.

Roth, A. and Parry, G. (1997) 'The implications of psychotherapy research for clinical practice and service development: lessons and limitations', *Journal of Mental Health*, 6, 367–80.

Rowland, N., Godfrey, C., Bower, P., Mellor-Clark, J., Heywood, P. and Hardy, R. (2000) 'Counselling in primary care: a systematic review of the research evidence', *British Journal of Guidance and Counselling*, 28 (2): 215–31.

Seligman, M.E. (1995) 'The effectiveness of psychotherapy: the *Consumer Reports* study', *American Psychologist*, 50: 965–74.

Scottish Office Department of Health (1998) *Counselling in Primary Care: a Report by the National Medical Advisory Committee.* Edinburgh: Department of Health.

Sibbald, B., Addington-Hall, J., Brenneman, D. and Freeling, P. (1993) 'Counsellors in English and Welsh general practices', *British Medical Journal*, 306: 29–33.

Sibbald, B., Addington-Hall, J., Brenneman, D. and Freeling, P. (1996) *The Role of Counsellors working in General Practice.* Occasional Paper 74. London: Royal College of General Practitioners.

Simpson, S., Corney, R., Fitzgerald, P. and Beecham, J. (2000) 'A randomized controlled trial to evaluate the effectiveness and cost-effectiveness of counselling patients with chronic depression', *Health Technology Assessment,* 4: 1–74.

Ward, E., King, M., Lloyd, M. et al. (2000) 'Randomised controlled trial of non-directive counselling, cognitive-behaviour therapy and usual GP care for patients with depression' I 'Clinical effectiveness', *British Medical Journal,* 321: 1383–8.

20 Counselling Psychology and Naturally Occuring Systems (Families and Couples)
EDDY STREET

This chapter presents its material in three sections. First the historical and theoretical developments of counselling psychology with families and couples are outlined and some problems of definition are identified. In the second section the theoretical aspects of the interactional/systemic approach are discussed. The final section focuses on the theoretical and empirical evaluation of the field, and this highlights some particular themes that are informative of practice.

Historical overview

In outlining the contributory set of ideas and practices that lead to the formation of any therapeutic approach it is difficult to provide a completely coherent account because such endeavours are typically the product of both disparate and linked developments, involving as they do the activities of single-minded pioneers. Broderick and Schrader (1981) in considering the factors that led to the initial impetus for the delineation of the field have identified two particular strands and themes within this history. First there were those practice strands linked with psychodynamic notions somewhat associated with the social psychiatry of Harry Stack Sullivan (Barton Evans, 1996) and early marital counselling. Among the US pioneers were Bell, Ackerman and Bowen, while in Britain the representative was Skynner. The second thematic strand was that which links the development of family work with research activities principally involved with the investigation of schizophrenia. In the United States a number of projects formulated a conception of psychiatric illness as a developmental process within a distorted familial environment and hence took the focus away from the medical model and intrapsychic concepts. It was particularly Bateson and his group (Bateson, 1973) who developed the application of General Systems Theory (GST) to this field, and it has been this that has had such an organizing impact in later therapeutic and theoretical developments. From a theoretical perspective Dallos and Draper (2000) identified three phases. The first, 1950 to the 1970s, being the development of the basic elements of systemic thinking with the move from the intrapsychic to the interpersonal. The second, from the mid-1970s to the mid-1980s, was characterized by second-order cybernetics, with a move from the mechanistic qualities of systems thinking to a view of families as composed of people actively co-creating meaning. The third phase was the rise of the ideas of social constructionist theory (Anderson, 1996; Gergen, 1991; White and Epston, 1990; Anderson and Goolishan, 1988). Dallos and Draper note that all developments carry with them an emphasis on context and interpersonal processes.

On the basis that there is an attempt to modify the interactions between components of natural systems, it is a common feature of this field to consider couple/marital therapy as a subdivision of family therapy. Wilson and James (1991) have commented on the problems that this can sometimes cause in the research and theoretical arena, as it is not clear whether 'family' and 'marital/couple' are being used synonymously or whether they are being referred to as separate and distinct entities. This is also confused by the clear difference between 'marital' relationships involving heterosexual partners who have subscribed to the institution of marriage and 'couple' relationships, which include homosexual and heterosexual partners who consider themselves as being in relation. At the counselling practice level the additional complicating element is that not all counselling psychologists see themselves as family *and* couples counsellors but as one or the other. Schroder (1991) has made some attempts to address this issue in practical terms but with regard to the general counselling psychology of this area it does remain somewhat ambiguous whether there exists one or two fields. This chapter will present the integrated view, with limitations of space unfortunately precluding continual reference to the arguments that originate from the separate fields view. Neither is it possible to offer an extended discussion of the arguments for and against each position. One of the central tasks that counselling psychology faces in this area is to reconcile the two views: this chapter aims to set some of the parameters that need to be taken into account in this task.

Theoretical considerations

Individuals and interacting systems

The 'systems' view evolved to account for the social interactive nature of the individual. Thus the characteristics of naturally occurring systems are seen as applying directly to the functioning of interacting individuals and are outlined in an earlier chapter. However, as the counselling of families and couples involves individual action as well as the action of the system itself, it is important to begin the discussion of the psychology of the counselling context with a consideration of the self in the interacting system.

The self in the system

The interactional view is distinguished by its attention to processes over time. This is in contrast to those perspectives that have generally sought to identify the fixed traits of a 'normal' individual living in a 'normal' family informed by psychological models of self that operate in terms of metaphors for individual action, for example the individual as machine, the individual as scientist, etc. The interactional focus of interest is on the pattern of connections between individuals that are seen as being complementary or interdependent with respect to some outcome, placing the self within the sphere of social discourse. Individual characteristics are therefore considered as the behaviour illustrating the connection rather than something located within the individual. Hence individuals are described as demonstrating certain behaviour rather than them being labelled as a particular type of person. Therefore to say that a person is 'the possessive type' does not capture the sense of all the interactions around him or her at a particular time; it is more accurate to report that when certain interactions occur the person displays behaviour that may be called 'possessive'. The 'naming' of the behaviour being constructed by those contributing to that particular social context. Human action and activity in this framework are therefore seen as embedded within the connections, the communication and the meanings, between people, for to be involved in a communicating system is at the core of human identity as identity evolves socially. Hence it is within the discussion of the social nature of identity that the process of counselling occurs.

Understanding self and relationship

How then does the 'self' operate in a couple relationship or a family? The psychological notion of a person requires that an individual displays self-awareness and also has the capacity to say what he/she is doing. In human beings the ability to represent oneself to oneself makes it possible for the individual to learn about the connection between bodily states of emotion and the different contextual experiences of identity. This ability of self-reflection and self-representation allows the individual to express his or her own emotions to another and it also permits us to appreciate the intentionality of another through empathy. This is necessary, as a condition for having the concept of oneself as a person is that other people should also recognize one as being a person. For this to happen a group of people must be able to know that each one of them has an idea as to what he/she is doing and is able to communicate that idea to others. As so much of our personal, private view of ourselves evolves out of our communication within our close relationships, interactions within these relationships play the crucial role in the view we have of who we are.

Individual and relationship awareness

In order to be able to maintain communication within relationships individuals need to formulate action ahead of events; they need to create strategies and tactics prior to being involved in situations that are complex and which contain 'information inputs' from a variety of sources. To plan in this way a reflexive withdrawal from on-going events is needed. The individual can then focus on her or his plans for future action. However, momentarily this removes the individual from the consciousness of the moment where the on-going activities of others will have important influences on the interactions occurring. This 'time out' allows the person to work out what he or she is going to do but the period results in the loss of awareness of how the system is operating. A consequence of planning in this way is that the individual relates action to something that is anticipated rather than to the process of the moment. The degree to which any individual indulges in an excessively focused view of his or her own particular conception of events in the system will determine the extent to which that person is removed from appreciating his or her position within the functioning system. Within families and couples this happens continually as individuals focus on 'This is what I need,' or 'This is what others do to me,' rather than considering the process of interaction for the family as a whole or the couple as an entity. Couples and families therefore have the ability to be aware of the social interactive nature of themselves but this awareness requires the individual to subsume his or her identity within that of the system and unfortunately this does not occur at times when problems arise. As Bateson (1973) notes, even though humans are embedded in biological, ecological and social systems, there is a twist in the psychology of the individual person whereby consciousness is almost of necessity blinded to the systemic nature of human beings. Even though we are an element of interacting systems, we somehow forget it.

Because every behaviour is at one and the same time an expression of the person and a communication to others (Watzlawick et al., 1974), there is a strong tendency to experience our communications solely as expressions of the self. We emphasize the 'What I do' to the neglect of 'This is my contribution to what we do.' In order for a couple or family to operate successfully there therefore needs to be a negotiation involving each person's 'contribution'. It is by this process that an agreed 'meaning' of the social context for all evolves. As such meanings are constructed then perceptions, opinions, expressions and actions of the 'self' are also changed. Gergen (1991) has discussed the manner in which self-definition realigns over time as social circumstances change. A person's experience of self is so much a social phenomenon, so much a responsive process, that we cannot imagine it to hold constant as families and couples change and develop.

The self and development in a relationship context

Initially change occurs in families and couples as the outcome of simple developmental pressures. Terkelsen (1980) poses a three-level model of such changes. At the basic level are those relatively short behavioural sequences that characterize day-to-day functions. Some elements of such sequences may change, depending on daily conditions. At the next level is 'first-order change' where individuals alter their own behaviour to accommodate their developing mastery of their situation. The uppermost layer involves 'second-order change', being the system's adaptation to individual changes that results in an alteration of meaning within the system, new meaning then generating new behavioural sequences. Obviously one form of change feeds into the next in a circular fashion, illustrating Hoffman's (1993) assertion that development is not a continuous process but one characterized by transformations, second-order changes and the sudden appearance of functional patterns that simply did not exist before.

The development of 'self' and the behaviour that indicates it cannot therefore be conceived as necessarily a process that follows rigid patterning. Gergen (1982) has criticized standard developmental theories that assume a universal standard by which individuals can measure their functioning. He argues that the whole idea of the 'normal' life-span trajectory is very problematic. The timing and nature of developmental shifts cannot be predicted. A predetermined and optimal path for development cannot be specified. The self can therefore be considered to change through an individual life. Hence counsellors cannot construct their practice on the view that divergence from the optimal path for individuals, couples or families is a failure representing poor adjustment, for indeed there is no optimal path. In this respect counsellors should be aware that it is possible for even the greatest trauma to be overcome developmentally, as the resilience and unpredictability of human beings are enormous.

Models of functioning

Given the social nature of human beings, the scientific needs of a good theory of relationship functioning can readily be linked with the needs of a theory of counselling. A good theory should therefore first offer an adequate means of discussing motivation in the relationship context, given that the system is perceived as being more than a collection of individuals. This will be related to the way individual, couple and family needs are negotiated. Secondly, the theory should offer a means of constructing a notion of psychological reality for everyone in the family. The question 'Whose reality?' is a central one that runs through the family/marital counselling task. Therefore there is a need to understand the way each individual's experience and perception are merged in with a set of common meanings held by the family. Thirdly, the theory should find a way of addressing themes that arise from personal, family and socio-cultural value systems, particularly the issues of gender role, racial questions, autonomy and expression of feeling. This obviously includes those values that are brought to the counselling situation by the counselling psychologist and his or her personal and professional system.

In addition to the points listed above, another foundation for any model of therapeutic activity will be the view held of the notion of the 'normal'. Offer and Sabshin (1974) have synthesized the theoretical and clinical concepts of mental health into four major perspectives on normality:

- *Normality as health*, from a medico-psychiatric model being based on the criterion of absence of pathology.
- *Normality as average*, an approach common in sociological and behavioural studies, uses the statistical norm, or average, to identify typical patterns and traits.
- *Normality as utopia*, an approach embodied in psychoanalytic and humanistic theories, conceives of normality as ideal or optimal functioning, or as 'self-actualization' of potential.
- *Normality as process* attends to developmental processes throughout the life cycle in the context of interactional systems. This perspective based on GST is considered by

Offer and Sabshin to be the most fruitful in that it allows consideration of unique coping styles and multiple routes for adaptation.

Within the field of family and couple counselling, models are now generally subscribing to the view of normality as process. The most obvious common denominator to these models is the concept that families and relationships are patterned and thus repeat time and again the same class of interaction. However, there tends to be a difference in emphasis, with some models focusing on general functioning and others commenting on this via their outline of therapeutic and counselling principles. Some general theories have developed from studies based on self-report, whereas others have arisen from observational methodologies. All these models are discussed by Walsh (1993) and all are constructed on a dimensional basis of varying number, with the types of issues being problem solving, communication and expressiveness, roles allocation, affective responsiveness and involvement (including cohesion), conflict management and behavioural control, whether the family is inwardly orientated or outwardly focused, and the degree of adaptability to change. It is readily apparent that all these models are discussing the same processes with different terminology and much of the difference may just be due to methodological approaches and even semantics. Work in this area is relatively recent and it is noticeable that the dialogue between the researchers is only now beginning, hence the search for communality is only in its infancy. It is beyond the scope of this chapter fully to discuss the evaluation of these particular theories of family functioning.

Those models that focus on the activities of counselling psychology also work on the concept that families and relationships are patterned and thus repeat the same interaction, a corollary of this concept being the idea that symptoms are related to or part of some of the interaction patterns. Any attempt to theorize at this level has the problem of providing a means of describing the moment-to-moment interaction that occurs. To describe a pattern in its entirety for any given system is impossible, because it requires the ability to observe and define a highly complex and continuous stream of behavioural sequences that are connected and persist over time. Despite this difficulty, Breunlin and Schwartz (1986) propose a model that examines the relationships of sequences with the entire pattern of an interpersonal system that is based on time frames. They identify four classes of sequences:

- From seconds to hours.
- A day to a week.
- Several weeks to a year.
- Time that spans at least one generation.

Some sequences are recursive in that in their repetition an element of themselves guarantees the repetition. Some sequences are non-recursive in that they involve sequences of behaviours that do not repeat over time. Within a given generation life-cycle events such as births and marriages are non-recursive in that they do not repeat. However, on taking a frame longer than a generation there may be a recursive element as families repeat similar patterns. As these sequences are interlocking at any one time a small interactive sequence may reflect the past, the present and the expectations of the future. Any problem is embedded in one or more interactional sequences.

The meaning ascribed to any sequence by those involved in it will come to play an important function in how that interaction progresses. Meaning is central to the interaction process in that it constructs the psychological para-meters that enable individuals to co-ordinate their action, manage their relation-ship and hence deal with any problem that emerges. In a manner that builds on the time-frame sequences, Cronen and Pearce (1985) link the different levels of meaning available, suggesting five, which, as with the time frames, are inter-locking. So that the reader appreciates the circularity of short to long and long to short, these levels of meaning are in the opposite order to time frames.

- *Family myth.* Includes general conceptions of how society, personal and family rela-tionships work. This operates over generations, e.g. how men in a family do not assist their partners in some of the daily tasks of living.
- *Life script.* A person's conception of self in interaction. This changes during a lifetime, e.g. How a man is 'unreliable' around the house.
- *Relationship.* The conception of how and on what terms two or more persons engage in interaction. This involves both long and immediate elements of interaction, e.g. how Jane sometimes asks John to help with chores and then gives up.
- *Episode.* A short pattern of reciprocated interaction, being equivalent to the seconds-to-hours time frame, e.g. how Jane asked John to do a task; John says he will do it later. John does not do the task and Jane then does it.
- *Speech act.* The verbal or non-verbal messages that come from one person. This is the individual element of interaction and makes sense only in terms of the analysis of that interaction, e.g. Jane, 'Please take the rubbish out, John'.

Families and couples are faced with the task of organizing these different levels of interactive time and meaning so as to form a wholeness for them. In doing this they have to deal with three essential tasks of social interaction that define who they perceive themselves to be. They need to establish who is involved in their interactions and in what way. They need to experience a sense of control and influence over what happens to themselves. They also need to share the affective elements of those other tasks with other individuals. The construction of an overarching view of these tasks has been elaborated by the Family FIRO Model as outlined by Doherty and his colleagues (Doherty and Colangelo, 1984). This model holds that the themes of inclusion, control and intimacy pre-dominate in human relatedness, determining the framework for understanding the types of interaction that occur within a family.

Having outlined those models that provide an overview of interactive processes, their framework allows us to note the relationship between the different theore-tical formulations of family and couple counselling. Hence, different models of systemic intervention, be they focused on family and/or marital interaction, approach the time frame and thematic dimensions differentially, depending on their theoretical orientation. This is due to inclusion themes being more obvious in the shorter time frames, control themes occurring more readily in the medium-length sequences, whereas the longer sequences are clearly linked with intimacy issues. Thus Minuchin's structural therapy (Minuchin, 1974) emphasizes boundary, role patterns and connectedness within families in which short in-session interactions are addressed. Those models that emphasize control themes, such as strategic approaches (Haley, 1976), the earlier Milan approaches (Palazzoli et al., 1978), brief models (Watzlawick et al., 1974) and behavioural approaches (Jacobson and Margolin, 1979; Crowe and Ridley, 1990) emphasize intermediate time frames. Counselling psychologists with a focus on intimacy tend to be transgenerational in their consideration of time; psychodynamic formulations (Daniell, 1985), the Family Systems Theory of Bowen (Bowen, 1978), Whitaker's Symbolic Experiential Model (Whitaker and Keith, 1981) and the Contextual Therapy of Boszormenyi-Nagy (Boszormenyi-Nagy and Krasner, 1986) are approaches within this category. Some therapeutic theorists such as Pinsof (1995) have constructed models of practice that attempt to integrate elements from different interactional time frames, with the counsellor approaching the themes in a particular manner and order. Carr (2000c) offers a differently based categorization of marital and family counselling theories. His tripartite system identifies those models that focus on behaviour patterns, those that focus on belief systems and those with a focus on contexts. Utilizing this system, he also constructs an integrationalist approach to marital and family counselling. Indeed, the integrationalist trend in this field continues to grow in importance (see Rivett and Street, 2003).

Evaluating theory and practice

There are three broad questions in the evaluation of family and couple counselling that need to be addressed by the counselling psychologist:

*   Is the model/theory used to describe human action adequate? This is a theoretical evaluation and specifically it questions the usefulness of General Systems Theory as an overarching and organizing theory within this area.
*   How can change in the counselling context be maximized? This is a question of practicalities and is typically asked in an empirical manner and hence is an empirical evaluation.
*   Which skills are identified as being necessary for effective practice?

Each question will be examined in turn.

The adequacy of overarching theory: General Systems Theory

Theoretically the systemic approach has been applied at two levels by counselling psychologists. First, at a general level it has been used as a guide to psychological inquiry in the broad sense. Secondly, it has made a contribution to the development of theories of counselling action and therefore as such it is a guide to therapeutic action. Therefore any evaluation of systems theory needs to ask the following questions.

Is the theory a useful guide to psychological inquiry?

There is no doubt that General Systems Theory created an alternative medium for thinking about particular phenomena, but the relationship between its abstract theoretical constructs and empirical facts remains tenuous, especially in the study of human social phenomena (Vetere and Gale, 1987). Indeed, it might be more appropriate to describe this theory as a conceptual framework which spans a wide range of disciplines and links up with less general models; hence one encounters a wide range of other models – for example, psycho-dynamic, cognitive-behavioural – easily being incorporated into explanations based on GST. Unfortunately, as a theory it lacks adequate methods of analysis that spring from its formulations. Consequently when engaged in scientific inquiry it is difficult to establish and apply systems principles. This is particularly so in the investigation of family interactions, where a major problem has been inadequate operationalization of concepts so that data may be collected in a meaningful way. Researchers into the psychology of personal relationships including families require a theory that comprehensively presents concepts that generate testable predictions not only in terms of general behaviour but also with regard to behaviour specific to the counselling situation. Vetere and Gale (1987) list the requirements of such a theory. It should:

- Describe and explain family and couple structure, dynamics, process and change.
- Describe invariant interpersonal structures and emotional dynamics within families and couples, particularly concerning the transmission of distress on to individuals.
- Account for family relationships as the interface between the individual and culture, that is to say, how does the family mediate between external environmental events and individual development, thus acting as a filter through which the child interprets the world?
- Describe the process of individuation and differentiation of the family members.
- Predict health and pathology within the family, that is, provide a source of hypotheses about family function and what causes dysfunction.
- Prescribe therapeutic strategies for dealing with dysfunction.
- Account for the seemingly antithetical functions of stability and change, particularly when viewed within the family's developmental cycle.

Clearly GST has not met these requirements and scientifically the family systems approach has not generated enough empirical research suitable for an evaluation of its methodological sophistication. At present therefore there are still not enough examples of links made between abstract formulations of GST and the reality of everyday interaction. General Systems Theory is therefore not adequate as a general theory but it does provide a framework for describing complex time-related interactional behaviour for which traditional sociological and psychological theories are not conceptually or methodologically suited.

Is GST helpful as a guide to therapeutic action?

The concept of a system as applied to a family or couple relationship carries with it the implication of a set of rules that lead to the organization of structure. In the early development of the field the application of this concept focused on dysfunctional processes presumed to be implicated in the on-going maintenance of individual symptoms, if not in their origins. The family or couple were considered to be unaware of their own rules and their dysfunctional structure. Under these conditions, as Hoffman (1993) has pointed out, the counsellor becomes cast as a person with power who analyses the system, determining the rules in operation, and then moves the system to a position where a more helpful set of rules and structure apply. As a consequence a client–counsellor distance is in-built and the language used to discuss therapeutic processes becomes adversarial. This is linked with a general difficulty of Batesonian descriptions of systems in that it does not include a language to account for experiential events. The focus on the system of the family and couple also leads to the neglect of external social issues that nevertheless affect it; hence for the early systemic therapists issues of race, class and gender were nearly invisible. These formulations developed in this manner because of the separation of the observer from the observed, which as Hoffman (1993) has indicated reflects the dominant masculine value system of Western science. The problems with the systems approach indicate the fundamental difficulty central to all theorizing about human change and behaviour in that any approach that attempts to deal with how individuals function contextually must at one and the same time be interactional whilst addressing the issues of human subjectivity, with the subjectivity being that of both the clients and the counsellor. Rivett and Street (2003) have discussed these issues further.

These criticisms have led Hoffman (1993) to identify the need for a collaborationist stance in which transformation is the goal. Interestingly Anderson (2001) has identified a number of similarities between this approach and the person-centred (Rogerian) approach. The systemic applications of working in a 'person-centred' way with families have been presented in an integrationalist manner by Gaylin (1993), Street (1994) and O'Leary (1999). Anderson (2001) argues that the issue is not so much one of integration as of seeing the collaborationist approach as representing a development of thinking to which Rogers himself would have subscribed.

The centrality of GST to the counselling endeavour is diminishing as the approaches that are informed by social constructionism are coming to the fore. Given the echoes of the person-centred approach in some current practice trends there may be a growing sense in which the systems approach to family and couple counselling in its present development is shifting towards a way of working that it initially saw as being in contradistinction to itself. It is now picking up on those skills and counselling psychology attitudes allied to the person-centred approach which for some time were neglected and taken for granted. The perspective that focused on limitations, deficits and pathology is being overtaken by a paradigm long familiar in the counselling literature that is competence-based and health-orientated, and which recognizes and amplifies strengths and resources. Therefore, as Walsh (1993) notes, there is a clear shift in working with naturally occurring systems from a deficit model informing therapy and counselling to one that emphasizes resources, moving the counsellor from the analysis of what went wrong to being involved in the search for what can be done to enhance family functioning.

Maximizing change in counselling: empirically evaluating effectiveness

The study of interaction raises questions about the nature of science and methodology, for 'systemic thinking' forms the characteristics of 'new' science. This model of scientific inquiry has critiqued the basis on which 'old' science attempts to know and understand the world. The 'old' view holds that cause and effect can be understood, it being possible to make observations that are objective and independent, with those observations being understood as outlining the 'truth'. The critique of the traditional approach has given rise to the question as to the nature of research inquiry into counselling for couples and families. The two principal themes raised by this criticism have been those of objectivity and causality. A systems view challenges the traditional cause-and-effect model, with circular causality implying no distinction between 'independent' ('cause') and 'dependent' ('effect') variables. Thinking systemically requires not merely the investigation of a larger unit of analysis but also the investigation of how the elements that make up the unit are connected and patterned. This view of science holds that knowledge is not something 'out there', nor is it something we process in our heads, it is rather something people do together. It is also argued that the researcher is not able to be objective and the measures, methods and constructs he or she uses are nothing other than the researcher's way of 'punctuating' phenomena. This, then, is a different paradigm for constructing the science of counselling psychology and once again moves towards the social constructionist position (Gergen, 1982).

Notwithstanding these major differences between 'old' and 'new' science in a general and specific sense, the new approaches should incorporate and be incorporated by the more traditional scientific endeavours. Gurman (1983) illustrates this by the numerous ways traditional psychotherapeutic research designs implicitly involve systemic concepts of context, connectedness and interdependence. A historical antagonism between proponents of qualitative methods and quantitative methods has prevented recognition of the benefits to be gained by employing both methods. Increasingly, however, family therapy researchers have begun to recognize the value of a multi-method approach in bridging the current gaps among theory, research and practice. Sells et al. (1995)

show the relative merits of integrating both quantitative and qualitative methods in family therapy research by illustrating how the two methods can iteratively build upon each other to offer information that neither can provide alone. By using such data it may then be possible to construct 'low-level' theories on process research that can set the stage for outcome research. The use of of qualitative methods in family therapy research has only just begun at present; although there are examples of research on activity in sessions (Kogan and Gale, 1993; Kogan, 1998; Burck et al., 1998), most of the work to date focuses on elaboration of client perceptions (Strickland-Clark et al., 1998; Sells et al., 1996; Dallos and Hamilton-Brown, 2000).

Thus it is not appropriate to discard the 'old' simply because the 'new' has appeared, particularly as the new epistemology has not effectively translated its approach into practical research projects. In this respect, however, it should be noted that the more recent development of audit methods within medical and allied activities involves an approach that is essentially systemic.

Frameworks in the field of research

There are two frameworks for considering the research outcomes of any therapeutic practice. The first is the traditional approach that attempts to prove the value of particular strategies to particular problems. This follows the notion, stated most clearly by Bergin in 1971, that the foremost question in the field of psychotherapy research is the specificity question: 'What are the specific effects of specific interventions by specified therapists upon specific symptoms of patient types?' (Bergin, 1971: 45). This is the formulation that underlies the clinical effectiveness model in which the effort is focused on demonstrating the helpfulness or otherwise of particular therapy techniques for particular specified conditions. This approach rests on the assumption that the condition can indeed be specified and that clients 'with' the condition can be treated in similar ways. The second approach takes a different tack and argues that if research demonstrates anything it is that there are core features of any and every therapeutic practice, and these are the factors that should be enhanced and demonstrated by therapists. This position leads to the view that it is the similarities in therapeutic techniques that are important, not the differences in theoretical orientation. With both positions it is important to privilege the perspective of the consumers of counselling. We will consider each of these models in turn.

Clinical effectiveness

It is important to begin discussing this literature by first noting the general areas on which researchers in the field have concentrated. The traditional division has been into outcome and process. Pinsof (1981) queried whether this division is useful and suggested that it is more beneficial to discuss the matter all in terms of outcomes, with some being very close to the more discrete elements of therapist behaviour (proximal) and some being linked with the overall effect of therapy (distal). Here he is clearly pointing to the fact that even process research can be considered in terms of small units of outcome and in the last analysis it has to be linked with whether therapy is beneficial to the clients.

Outcome and effectiveness

There have been a number of excellent reviews of the research literature (Gurman et al., 1986; Pinsof and Wynne, 1995; Freidlander, 1998; Carr, 2000a, b). Pinsof and Wynne (1995) conclude that marital and family therapy 'works' for specific disorders, that it is not harmful, that in particular disorder problems and patients it is more efficacious than standard and/or individual treatments and that there are no data to support the superiority of any particular form of marital and family therapy over another. They also conclude that marital and family therapy is not sufficient in itself to treat effectively a variety of severe disorders and problems, and it may best operate as part of a multimodal service delivery.

Carr (2000a, b) has provided the most through review of the clinical effectiveness of family therapy both with adults and with children and adolescents. He notes the conclusion from meta-analyses of child- and adult-focused problems that family therapy is effective in that the average treated case fares better than 70 per cent of untreated controls and that this underlines the value of family therapy as a viable intervention strategy. The principal conclusions from Carr's review are that:

- Well articulated family-based interventions have been shown to be effective for a wide range of problems (e.g. child abuse and neglect, conduct problems, emotional problems, psychosomatic problems).
- The interventions are brief and may be offered by a wide range of professionals on an out-patient basis.
- For many of the interventions useful treatment manuals have been developed which clinicians in treating individual cases may flexibly use.
- The bulk of interventions for which there is evidence of effectiveness have been developed within the cognitive, structural and strategic models. It must be noted, however, that all outcome research automatically advantages those problems and methods of therapy that can be easily quantified. This may indeed be the reason why cognitive behavioural therapy has been so well researched and psychoanalytic models have not.

To Carr's list we can add a fifth important point:

- A significant proportion of interventions are provided in combination with other treatment types.

Clearly in the 'real' world of work effective counselling for a whole range of problems involves major elements of a treatment context where other varieties of activities are also on-going.

Process research

There is a slow rate of progress in marital and family counselling process research (its essential task being the discovery of how the counsellor system facilitates change), owing to the complexity of the subject (Alexander et al., 1994; Pinsof, 1981, 1986). Marital and family counselling is a particularly complicated form of social interaction compared with the two-person interaction in individual therapy, another hindering factor being the lack of adequate micro-theories about change processes in family counselling. In order to conduct clinically meaningful process research in this area it is necessary to study the progressive exchange of therapists' and clients' verbal behaviours (Gurman et al., 1986) and this has not been undertaken, though developments in qualitative research are being seen (Moon et al., 1990; Kogan, 1998). Sells et al. (1995) show the relative merits of integrating both quantitative and qualitative methods in family therapy research by illustrating how the two methods can iteratively build upon each other to offer information that neither can provide alone. It may then be possible to use the information to create a 'low level' of process that can set the stage for outcome research.

In many ways, such low-level theories provide a form of process research that can set the stage for outcome research. Consistently process research in marital and family counselling has shown evidence that, if the clients do not feel listened to, understood and respected, the likelihood of their dropping out of treatment is high, as is a poor outcome (Reimers and Treacher, 1995; Bischoff and Sprenkle, 1993; Howe, 1989). Equally of interest is evidence from Patterson and Forgatch (1985) that the relationship can undergo 'testing' times in the middle of treatment. Freidlander summarizes this research by suggesting that it implies that families prefer a 'nurturant, authoritative parent' and they want their therapists to be 'both authoritative and collaborative' (Freidlander, 1998).

Investigating the core conditions

It is not surprising that process research leads on to research into the core conditions of therapy, for as one discards assumptions of particular therapeutic orientations the logical conclusion is to discuss what features of therapy are most beneficial to clients. Particularly after the 1980s within individual therapy there was a discernible increase in writing and research on what could be identified as the futures or common factors of psychotherapy (Wineberger, 1995). The central development in the enunciation of common factors in psychotherapy was when Lambert (1992) proposed four therapeutic factors as being the principal elements accounting for improvement in clients. Although they were not derived from a strict statistical analysis, he suggested that these four factors could be seen to be embodied in the findings of empirical studies of psychotherapeutic outcome. The factors have been developed and discussed further by Miller et al. (1997) and Hubble et al. (1999) and are identified as:

- *Extra-therapeutic factors*, such as client characteristics, the hopefully supportive elements of the client's immediate social environment, serendipitous events.

- *Relationship factors*. These represent a wide range of variables focusing on the relationship between the therapist and client (genuineness, empathy, warmth, acceptance, affirmation, encouragement and general caring).
- *Placebo, hope and expectancy*. These are therapeutic factors linked with those features of the client's pre-knowledge, estimation and expectations of therapy.
- *Model or technique factors*. These factors refer to the beliefs and procedures unique to specific therapeutic approaches and treatments. They are the factors of specific theories and they refer to the differences between therapeutic approaches and theories.

Lambert (1992) estimates that these four factors account for approximately 40 per cent, 30 per cent, 15 per cent and 15 per cent of outcome variance respectively.

The four core factors and the family therapy process

At no time has the field of marital and family counselling attended to the common factors *per se*. Sprenkle et al. (1999) consider this to be in large part due to marital and family counselling's interest in itself as different from other psychotherapeutic activities. It is, however, possible to organize research studies with this framework to consider the applicability and outcomes, and Sprenkle et al. (1999) have provided an attempt at this.

Extra-therapeutic change   *Characteristics of individuals*. This relates to client factors such as age, gender, race and sexual orientation. Bischoff and Sprenkle (1993) in their review of variables associated with dropping out of family therapy identify that drop-out rates are higher for clients from lower socio-economic groups and when the ethnic background of the client is different from that of the therapist. In a review of behavioural marital therapy Jacobson and Christiansen (1996) point out that the approach is more effective with younger than with older clients. Although several authors indicate the need to be clear about the effects of gender, race and sexual orientation on the process of therapy from a clinical perspective, these factors have received no consistent attention from researcher' endeavours and one wonders whether clinicians pay enough attention to them. Interestingly, what may be termed the 'non-static characteristics' of couples and families (emotional characteristics, etc.) have not been investigated, except for research into expressed emotion in psycho-educational work with families with major psychiatric illnesses (Goldstein and Miklowitz, 1995; Burbach, 1996; Fadden, 1998). However, the difficulty in researching factors such as cohesion and emotional closeness is the way in which they can be conceptualized. Many of these factors are perceived as being changeable as a direct effect of the therapeutic process and therefore constitute a target for therapeutic change. With a focus on the attempt to change the manifestations of such concepts the effect of the characteristic on outcome tends not to be explored.

Motivational characteristics. The family systems view is that motivation is a feature of the context rather than a characteristic of the individual. The tradition in family counselling is that the counsellor is responsible for the 'motivation' of the session, and much of it derives from Haley's early seminal influence (Haley, 1976). However, variables such as perseverance, willingness to co-operate and other such features do have a bearing on the outcome of therapy. As Sprenkle et al. (1999) note, there is a fine dividing line between motivational characteristics and non-static characteristics. Again this element of the client characteristic has been little explored.

Fortuitous events. It is a feature of the 'egocentricity' of therapists that they always assume the results of therapy to be attributable to therapy – particularly those of a positive nature. What takes place in client lives by happenstance may have more impact on change than therapy itself. Only one marital and family investigation has focused on this characteristic. Jacobson et al. (1987) undertook a two-year follow-up study utilizing telephone interviews to detect differences between 'relapsers' and 'maintainers' from a Behavioural Marital Therapy treatment programme. Neither therapist attributes nor treatment-related skills had any predictive value. Relapsers had experienced more stressful external events in their lives than did maintainers, the external world having more influence on people's lives than the processes internal to therapy.

Social support. There has been no research into the effect of social support for families or couples undergoing therapy and yet the considerable literature from other fields suggests that social support has a major impact on the way crises and difficulties are dealt with. For example, work on resilience particularly in children (see Rutter, 1999) indicates the importance of social factors in dealing with adversity. Similarly the work on divorce adjustment notes that social participation is one of the major factors contributing to divorce recovery for couples as well as for children (Everett and Volgy, 1981; Hetherington, 1989). The developing literature on social support as a resilience factor in coping and managing with chronic illness is also clearly evident (McCubbin et al., 1998). A counsellor using a systemic framework will wish to clinically investigate the role of the social network of the clients and yet the impact of the clients' social support and integration on the outcome of therapy has not been investigated.

Relationship factors The relationship in psychotherapy is the common factor most emphasized in the research literature on individual psychotherapy practices and it is also the most clearly addressed in family therapy research. In their early review of the field Gurman and Kniskern (1978) concluded that the ability of the therapist to establish a positive relationship with his or her clients was the factor that received the most 'consistent' support as an important outcome-related factor in marital and family therapy. Alexander et al. (1977) found that relationship skills accounted for over 40 per cent of the outcome variance in a study with families of delinquents. Among the relationship skill elements that they discussed was that of 'structuring' ability. Similarly Shields et al. (1991) found that, in common with previous results, therapist executive activities involving structuring the interview and joining with all family members were associated with cases going to completion. This skill reported in such studies involves organizing the interaction of several people and it could be said to be one of the skills *par excellence* that marks out the marital and family counsellor from other types of counsellor.

Some studies have investigated the relationship skills of trainees. For example, Stolk and Perlesz (1990) investigated client satisfaction with trainee therapists taking a two-year programme in strategic therapy. They found the clients to be less satisfied with therapy from second-year students as compared with first-year trainees. They interpret this as being due to the decline in the students' relationship skills as they focus more on the strategic techniques. A useful reminder that clients are more able to recognize counsellor relating qualities as opposed to their mastery over techniques.

The question that is often asked is whether or not relationship skills are sufficient in themselves for effective therapy. Gurman and Kniskern (1978) explicitly state that they are not. This statement, however, comes from a time when the main thrust of family and marital therapy was more involved in active interactive techniques, when the contrast between 'mere' relating and the application of interactive techniques was more apparent. Now that marital and family counselling has moved in the direction of narrative, conversational and collaborative approaches the relationship element, and particularly the notion of the 'therapeutic alliance' as discussed by Reimers and Treacher (1995), becomes important. The issue is how one operationalizes therapeutic relationship skills, and in this regard theories of family therapy and counselling psychology have tended to be expressed in terms at a high level of generality, hence they do not provide operational definitions of skills which could aid the construction of notions of counsellor performance that would be available to study. Unfortunately, there is a general lack of refined models for analysing skills so that they can then be reconstructed through the training process. The traditional categorization system of these skills is based on perceptual, conceptual and executive skills. Developing this tripartite division, Tomm and Wright (1979) define the skills within terms of engagement, problem identification, change facilitation and termination. Such means of identifying skills unfortunately fail to place the skills within an appropriate theoretical framework. Street (1994) has presented a structure for considering family counselling skills that rests on attitudes basic to the counselling process. Thus the attitudes of respect, inquiry and action orientation are seen as being hierarchically ordered. Hence the counselling psychologist needs to begin by demonstrating respect before understanding is possible. Understanding then arises through inquiry and its related active listening; once an appropriate understanding is achieved, it then allows interventions to be activated. This approach moves the consideration of skills out of an overemphasis on the cognitive and behavioural aspects of action by counselling psychologists and introduces the counselling psychologist's internal frame of reference.

The identification of any set of relationship factors has to be linked with how they play a part in constructive family systems change. We also need to specify the conditions necessary to initiate that change and sufficient to inaugurate the process. This is obviously related to the question Carl Rogers set himself about the necessary and sufficient conditions to bring about change (Rogers, 1957).

His answer to his own question became a benchmark in the development of counselling practice, and clearly in the field of family and couple counselling an outline of the necessary and sufficient conditions for constructive systems change is required. Street (1994) has attempted this by adding the relational-interactive elements to Rogers's construction. Essentially this involves the counsellor being confident that each individual in the system is being allowed a voice so that he or she can experience empathic understanding of each individual's awareness of his or her own experience. This needs to occur at the same time that the counsellor experiences an understanding of the interactive processes of the system. The communication of this understanding is also at the levels of 'individual' and 'system' in that the counsellor communicates his/her understanding of each individual's experience to them singly and as a group and also communicates his/her understanding of the interaction of the system to its members. In order to be able to meet these conditions another is added that addresses the difference between counselling one person and more than one person at the same time. This condition involves 'setting' the counselling context so that each individual is heard and responded to. As with Rogers's formulation for individual work, the concept being advanced here is that the essential conditions of change exist in a single configuration. Even though counsellors may use them differentially, the implication is that the techniques of various schools are unimportant except to the extent that they serve as channels for fulfilling the conditions. Each counsellor needs to develop a model of practice for him- or herself as a means by which the conditions can be maximized. This approach, of specifying a framework for skills development, not only offers the individual practitioner a means of achieving a *modus operandi* but it also serves the purpose of directing research activity.

Expectation   Unfortunately there are few discussions of client expectation in the marital and family therapy literature, and as one would expect from this state of affairs there is virtually no research devoted to it. Some clinical schools of therapy are built around the prospect of identifying certain client expectations and working within the frame that this offers (e.g. Street and Downey, 1996). Of the studies in this area Adams et al. (1991) attempted to look at expectation in terms of client optimism. Their study compared the impact of a solution-focused versus a problem-focused approach. They found no relationship between client optimism initially and the outcome at the end of ten sessions. Because measurements were made only in the early stages of therapy the authors question whether it is possible that optimism may be stable initially but become more variable later. This type of potential change in client attitudes and perceptions should be central to the understanding of the therapy process and yet it has been given virtually no focus in the development of research in this area. Crane et al. (1986) investigated a group of clients attending MFT clinics and established that when treatment fitted the clients' own view of their problems the fit accounted for 35 per cent of successful outcome variance. In other words the therapist's ability to present therapy as consistent and congruent with client expectations is important.

Model-specific factors and specific techniques   When one considers the research effort in this category some clear conclusions emerge, for the evidence indicates that no orientation has been demonstrably shown to be superior to any other (Pinsof and Wynne, 1995). There are of course numerous difficulties in undertaking research in this area. The best studies of treatment efficacy are randomized, with controlled trials, treatment manuals and strict adherence to treatment protocols. The populations for such research also need to be clearly specified. The demands of research on this topic often make the activity somewhat removed from clinical practice. Not surprisingly, little practice-relevant research has been undertaken. Also, as Gurman and Kniskern (1981) pointed out, it is very difficult to disentangle treatment effects from therapist effects. Untangling the relationship between the actual therapist and the model the therapist is trying to apply undoubtedly causes considerable difficulties for the researcher. To be clear the literature shows that techniques that are the province of any one model have never been proven to be superior.

Within this overarching categorization of the core features of therapy one must ask whether there are unique features for marital and family counselling. Sprenkle et al. (1999) have suggested that, as marital and family counselling is different in form from individual counselling practice, there are other factors which may be unique to family therapy practice. In essence these authors suggest a model of basic theoretical underpinnings of the field and discuss the 'uniqueness' of family therapy factors from this framework. What is of interest is how the discussion of core features leads to the elucidation of 'base level' models, of which Rogers's (1957) 'necessary and sufficient conditions' is the classic and most notable example. Sprenkle and his colleagues suggest that the theoretical basis of family therapy involves a *relational conceptualization*. This leads to the therapist undertaking work with an *expanded direct treatment system*, and this work naturally involves an *expanded therapeutic alliance*. These features, which have been covered in the theoretical section above, can be seen as forming a commonality within the field that should be capable of investigation by research. Needless to say, no research into these areas has been undertaken.

Audit

It can be argued that while research can identify potentially useful interventions and hence should influence the design and strategic direction of services, it says little about how effectively therapy is implemented in any particular setting. To do this local data are needed concerning the effectiveness that occurs in any particular context. The way that this has been approached is via the process of clinical audit. Without an on-going audit the quality of service may actually be poor. Few audits of the family therapy or systems consultations have been reported (Carr et al., 1994; Chase and Holmes, 1990; Frude and Dowling, 1980; Marshal et al., 1989; Manor, 1991). This is unfortunate, as audit studies throw light on patterns of practice that occur in regular clinical settings where multimodal treatment packages are common.

Conclusion

There can be little doubt that theorizing about family and marital counselling has undergone many changes since the field began to organize and define itself. From a position of standing in contradistinction to many of the traditional models of counselling practice aspects of many of those models have become incorporated in the general framework. It is clear, however, that as psychological inquiry moves away from the study of the 'human animal', and begins a more rigorous appraisal of 'ourselves' and the human condition, family and marital counselling is undergoing a fundamental shift of paradigm. The features of this movement noted in the first edition of this volume have continued in the same direction. Counselling psychology has a central role to play in the process, not so much in the answers and solutions it proposes but essentially in the psychological nature of the questions it poses. There are no conclusions for this chapter save that it is continuously necessary to pose such questions in order to enhance the process of assisting individuals, couples and families in distress.

References

Adams, J.F., Piercy, F.P. and Jurich, J.A. (1991) 'Effects of solution-focused therapy's "formula first session task" on compliance and outcome in family therapy', *Journal of Marital and Family Therapy*, 17: 277–90.

Alexander, J.F., Holtzworth-Munroe, A. and Jameson, P. (1994) 'The process and outcome of marital and family therapy: research review and evaluation' in S. Garfield and A. Bergin (eds) *Handbook of Psychotherapy and Behavior Change*. New York: Wiley.

Alexander, J.F., Barton, C., Schiavo, R.S. and Parsons, B.V. (1977) 'Systems-behavioral intervention with families of delinquents: therapist characteristics, family behavior, and outcome', *Journal of Consulting and Clinical Psychology*, 44: 656–64.

Anderson, H. (1996) *Conversation, Language and Possibilities*. New York: Basic Books.

Anderson, H. (2001) 'Postmodern collaboration and person-centred therapies: what would Rogers say?' *Journal of Family Therapy*, 23: 341–58.

Anderson, H. and Goolishan, H. (1988) 'Problem-determined systems: towards transformation in family therapy', *Journal of Strategic and Systemic Therapies*, 5: 1–13.

Barton Evans, F. (1996) *Harry Stack Sullivan: Interpersonal Theory and Psychotherapy*. London: Routledge.

Bateson, G. (1973) *Steps to an Ecology of Mind*. St Albans: Paladin.

Bergin, A.E. (1971) 'The evaluation of therapeutic outcomes' in A.E. Bergin and S.L. Garfield (eds) *Handbook of Psychotherapy and Behavior Change*, second edition. New York: Wiley.

Bischoff, R.J. and Sprenkle, D. H. (1993) 'Dropping out of marriage and family therapy: a critical view of research', *Family Process*, 32: 353–75.

Boszormenyi-Nagy, I. and Krasner, B.R. (1986) *Between Give and Take: a Clinical Guide to Contextual Therapy*. New York: Brunner Mazel.

Bowen, M. (1978) *Family Therapy in Clinical Practice*. New York: Aronson.

Breunlin, D.C. and Schwartz, R.C. (1986) 'Sequences: toward a common denominator of family therapy', *Family Process*, 25: 67–87.

Broderick, C.B. and Schrader, S.S. (1981) 'The history of professional marriage and family therapy' in A.S. Gurman and D.P. Kniskern (eds) *Handbook of Family Therapy*. New York: Brunner Mazel.

Burbach, F.R. (1996) 'Family based interventions in psychosis: an overview of, and comparison between, family therapy and family management approaches', *Journal of Mental Health*, 5: 111–34.

Burck, C., Frosh, S., Strickland-Clark, L. and Morgan, K. (1998) 'The process of enabling change: a study of therapist interventions in family therapy', *Journal of Family Therapy*, 20: 253–68.

Carr, A. (2000a) 'Evidence-based practice in family therapy and systemic consultation' I, *Journal of Family Therapy*, 22: 29–60.

Carr, A. (2000b) 'Evidence-based practice in family therapy and systemic consultation' II, *Journal of Family Therapy*, 22: 250–81.

Carr, A. (2000c) *Family Therapy: Concepts, Process and Practice*. Chichester: Wiley.

Carr, A., McDonnell, D. and Owen, P. (1994) 'Audit and family systems consultation: evaluation of practice at a child and family centre', *Journal of Family Therapy*, 16: 143–57.

Chase, J. and Holmes, J. (1990) 'A two-year audit of a family therapy clinic in adult psychiatry', *Journal of Family Therapy*, 12: 229–42.

Crane, D.R., Griffin, W. and Hill, R.D. (1986) 'Influence of therapist skills on client perceptions of marriage and family therapy outcome: implications for supervision', *Journal of Marital and Family Therapy*, 12: 91–6.

Cronen, V.E. and Pearce, W.B. (1985) 'Towards an explanation of how the Milan method works: an invitation to a systemic epistemology and the evolution of family systems' in D. Campbell and R. Draper (eds) *Applications of Systemic Family Therapy: the Milan Approach*. London: Grune & Stratton.

Crowe, M. and Ridley, J. (1990) *Therapy with Couples: a Behavioural Systems Approach to Marital and Sexual Problems*. Oxford: Blackwell.

Dallos, R. and Draper, R. (2000) *An Introduction to Family Therapy: Systemic Theory and Practice*. Buckingham: Open University Press.

Dallos, R. and Hamilton-Brown, L. (2000) 'Pathways to problems – an exploratory study of how problems evolve vs. dissolve in families', *Journal of Family Therapy*, 22: 375–93.

Daniell, D. (1985) 'Marital therapy: the psychodynamic approach' in W. Dryden (ed.) *Marital Therapy in Britain*. London: Harper & Row.

Doherty, W.J. and Colangelo, N. (1984) 'The Family FIRO Model: a modest proposal for organizing family treatment', *Journal of Marital and Family Therapy*, 10: 19–29.

Everett, C. and Volgy, S. (1981) 'Treating divorce in family therapy practice' in A.S. Gurman and D.P. Kniskern (eds) *Handbook of Family Therapy*. New York: Brunner Mazel.

Fadden, G. (1998) 'Research update: psychoeducational family interventions', *Journal of Family Therapy*, 20: 293–311.

Freidlander, M.L. (1998) 'Family therapy research: science into practice, practice into science' in M.P. Nichols and R.C. Schwartz (eds) *Family Therapy: Concepts and Methods*, fourth edition. Needham Heights MA: Allyn & Bacon.

Frude, N. and Dowling, E. (1980) 'A follow-up analysis of family therapy clients', *Journal of Family Therapy*, 2: 149–56.

Gaylin, N.L. (1993) 'Person-centred family therapy' in D. Brazier (ed.) *Beyond Carl Rogers*. London: Constable.

Gergen, K. (1982) *Toward Transformation in Social Knowledge*. New York: Springer.

Gergen, K. (1991) *The Saturated Self*. New York: Basic Books.

Goldstein, M.J. and Miklowitz, D.J. (1995) 'The effectiveness of psychoeducational family therapy in the treatment of schizophrenic disorders', *Journal of Marital and Family Therapy*, 21: 361–76.

Gurman, A.S. (1983) 'Family therapy research and the new epistemology', *Journal of Marital and Family Therapy*, 9: 227–34.

Gurman, A.S. and Kniskern, D. (1978) 'Research on marital and family therapy: progress, perspective and prospect' in S. Garfield and A. Bergin (eds) *Handbook of Psychotherapy and Behavior Change*, second edition. New York: Wiley.

Gurman, A.S. and Kniskern, D.P. (1981) 'Family therapy outcome research: knowns and unknowns' in A.S. Gurman and D.P. Kniskern (eds) *Handbook of Family Therapy*. New York: Brunner Mazel

Gurman, A.S., Kniskern, D. and Pinsof, W. (1986) 'Research on the process and outcome of marital and family therapy' in S. Garfield and A. Bergin (eds) *Handbook of Psychotherapy and Behavior Change*, third edition. New York: Wiley.

Haley, J. (1976) *Problem Solving Therapy*. New York: Harper & Row.

Hetherington, E.M. (1989) 'Coping with family transitions: winners, losers and survivors', *Child Development*, 60: 1–4.

Hoffman, L. (1993) *Exchanging Voices*. London: Karnac.

Howe, D. (1989) *The Consumers' View of Family Therapy*. London: Gower.

Hubble, M.A., Duncan, B.L. and Miller, S.D. (eds) (1999) *The Heart and Soul of Change: What Works in Therapy*. Washington DC: American Psychological Association.

Jacobson, N.S. and Christiansen, A. (1996) *Integrative Couple Therapy*. New York: Norton.

Jacobson, N.S. and Margolin, G. (1979) *Marital Therapy*. New York: Brunner Mazel.

Jacobson, N.S., Schmailing, K. B. and Holtzworth-Munroe, A. (1987) 'Component analysis of behavioral marital therapy: two-year follow-up and prediction of relapse', *Journal of Marital and Family Therapy*, 13: 187–95.

Kogan, S.M. (1998) 'The politics of making meaning: discourse analysis of a "postmodern" Interview', *Journal of Family Therapy*, 20: 229–52.

Kogan, S.M. and Gale, J.E. (1993) 'Decentering Therapy: textual analysis of a narrative therapy session', *Family Process*, 36: 101–26.

Lambert, M.J. (1992) 'Implications of outcome research for psychotherapy' in J.C. Norcross and M.R. Goldfried (eds) *Handbook of Psychotherapy Integration*. New York: Basic Books.

Manor, O. (1991) 'Assessing the work of a family centre: service offered and referrers' perceptions. A pilot study', *Journal of Family Therapy*, 13: 285–94.

Marshal, M., Feldman, R. and Sigal, J. (1989) 'The unravelling of a treatment paradigm: a follow-up study of the Milan approach to family therapy', *Family Process*, 28: 457–69.

McCubbin, H.I., Thompson, E.A., Thompson, A.I. and Frommer, J.E. (1998) *Stress, Coping, and Health in Families: Sense of Coherence and Resiliency*. London: Sage.

Miller, S.D., Duncan, B.L. and Hubble, M.A. (1997) *Escape from Babel: Towards a Unifying Language for Psychotherapy Practice*. New York: Norton.

Minuchin, S. (1974) *Families and Family Therapy*. London: Tavistock.

Moon, S., Dillon, B. and Sprenkle, D. (1990) 'Family therapy and qualitative research', *Journal of Marital and Family Therapy*, 16: 357–73.

Offer, D. and Sabshin, M. (1974) *Normality: Theoretical and Clinical Concepts of Mental Health*, second edition. New York: Basic Books.

O'Leary, C.J. (1999) *Counselling Couples and Families: a Person-centred Approach*. London: Sage.

Palazzoli, M.S., Cecchin, G., Prata, G. and Boscolo, L. (1978) *Paradox and Counterparadox*. New York: Aronson.

Patterson, G.R. and Forgatch, M.S. (1985) 'Therapist behavior as a determinant for client compliance: a paradox for the behavior modifier', *Journal of Consulting and Clinical Psychology*, 51: 581–6.

Pinsof, W.M. (1981) 'Family therapy process research' in A.S. Gurman and D.P. Kniskern (eds) *Handbook of Family Therapy*. New York: Brunner Mazel.

Pinsof, W.M. (1986) 'The process of family therapy: the development of the Family Therapist Coding System' in L. Greenberg and W.M. Pinsof (eds) *The Psychotherapeutic Process: a Research Handbook*. New York: Guilford Press.

Pinsof, W.M. (1995). *Integrative Problem Centered Therapy*. New York: Basic Books.

Pinsof, W.M. and Wynne, L.C. (1995) 'The efficacy of marital and family therapy: an empirical overview, conclusions and recommendations', *Journal of Marital and Family Therapy*, 21: 585–613.

Reimers, S. and Treacher, A. (1995) *Introducing User-friendly Family Therapy*. London: Routledge.

Rivett, M. and Street, E. (2003) *Family Therapy in Focus*. London: Sage.

Rogers, C. (1951) *Client-centered Therapy*. Boston MA: Houghton Mifflin.

Rogers, C. (1957) 'The necessary and sufficient conditions for therapeutic personality change', *Journal of Consulting Psychology*, 21: 95–103.

Rutter, M. (1999) Resilience concepts and findings: Implications for family therapy', *Journal of Family Therapy*, 21: 119–44.

Schroder, T. (1991) 'Approaches to couple therapy' in D. Hooper and W. Dryden (eds) *Couple Therapy: a Handbook*. Milton Keynes: Open University Press.

Sells, S.P., Smith, T.E. and Sprenkle, D.H. (1995) 'Integrating qualitative and quantitative research methods: a research model', *Family Process*, 34: 199–218.

Sells, S.P., Smith, T.E. and Moon, S. (1996) 'An ethnographic study of client perceptions of therapy effectiveness in a university-based training clinic', *Journal of Marital and Family Therapy*, 22: 331–42.

Shadish, W., Montgomery, L., Wilson, P., Wilson, M., Bright, I. and Okwumabua, T. (1993) 'The effects of family and marital psychotherapies: a meta-analysis', *Journal of Consulting and Clinical Psychology*, 61: 992–1002.

Shields, C.G., Sprenkle, D.H. and Constantine, J.A. (1991) 'Anatomy of an initial interview: the importance of joining and structuring skills', *American Journal of Family Therapy*, 19: 3–18.

Sprenkle, D.H., Blow, A.J. and Dickey, M.H. (1999) 'Common factors and other nontechnique variables in marriage and family therapy' in M.A. Hubble et al. (eds) *The Heart and Soul of Change*. Washington DC: American Psychological Association.

Stolk, Y. and Perlesz, A.J. (1990) 'Do better trainees make worse family therapists? A follow-up study of client families', *Family Process*, 29: 45–58.

Street, E. (1994) *Counselling for Family Problems*. London: Sage.

Street, E. and Downey, J. (1996) *Brief Therapeutic Consultations*. Chichester: Wiley.

Strickland-Clark, L., Campbell, D. and Dallos, R. (1998) 'Children's and adolescents' views on family therapy', *Journal of Family Therapy*, 22: 324–41.

Terkelsen, K.G. (1980) 'Toward a theory of the family life cycle' in E. Carter and M. McGoldrick (eds) *The Family Life Cycle*. New York: Gardner Press.

Tomm, K. and Wright, L.M. (1979) 'Family therapy skills', *Family Process*, 18: 227–50.

Vetere, A. and Gale, A. (1987) *Ecological Studies of Family Life*. Chichester: Wiley.

Walsh, F. (1993) *Normal Family Processes*, second edition. New York: Guilford Press.

Watzlawick, P., Weakland, J. and Fisch, R. (1974) *Change: Principles of Problem Formation and Problem Resolution*. New York: Norton.

Whitaker, C.A. and Keith, D.U. (1981) 'Symbolic-experiential family therapy' in A.S. Gurman and D.P. Kniskern (eds), *Handbook of Family Therapy*. New York: Brunner Mazel.

White, M. and Epston, D. (1990) *Narrative Means to Therapeutic Ends*. Adelaide: Dulwich Center.

Wilson, K. and James, J. (1991) 'Research in therapy with couples: an overview' in D. Hooper and W. Dryden (eds) *Couple Therapy: a Handbook*. Milton Keynes: Open University Press.

Wineberger, J. (1995) 'Common factors aren't so common: the common factors dilemma', *Clinical Psychology: Science and Practice*, 2: 45–69.

21 Psychological Therapy in Groups
MARIA GILBERT AND DIANA SHMUKLER

Theoretical framework

Our central theoretical approach can best be described as an integrative one, both on the level of theory and on the level of interventions into a system such as created in a constructed group. The point is made by Roth and Fonagy (1996) that many group therapists practise in a pluralistic manner, using theories drawn from a wide range of orientations. We see this statement as descriptive of the approach we outline in this chapter. Drawing on a range of concepts within a broad integrative framework, we will develop three major arenas in which change can be effected in a group: an intrapsychic or internal arena, which reflects the person's internal dialogue; an interpersonal or interactional arena which occurs between people in dyads or triads in a group, often in the form of psychological games and the enactment of repetitive patterns of relating; and, finally, the systemic or group arena where the issues of culture, race, class and sex will emerge. At this level the group may be viewed as a microcosm of the world at large, in that universal themes will arise in the life of the group and challenge fixed assumptions on the part of group members.

Such themes invariably include the exploration of intimacy and mutuality, concepts of equality and the recognition of individual difference, the acknowledgement of the darker sides of human nature and achieving a balance between caring for self and caring for others. In our integrative framework we attend to the interface between the subjective internal process, the interactional social process and the unconscious processes that occur as whole-group phenomena. As the life of the group unfolds this process will inevitably reflect many of the norms and tacit assumptions of the prevailing culture or subculture in which the group is located. The presence of a group of people enables such rigid beliefs to be challenged and openly examined, and the premises clearly explored in terms of their origin and their impact. The setting (in-patient or community-based) in which the group therapy is delivered will also exert an impact on the life of the group. The prevailing ethos in a particular care setting (whether statutory, voluntary or private) will inevitably filter into the norms of the group and affect group members' expectations and performance.

In terms of an integrated approach to intervention, we acknowledge the importance of interventions that address the cognitive, affective and behavioural domains of functioning in members of the group who wish to effect change in their lives. In a survey of the mechanisms of group psychotherapy Corsini and Rosenberg (1955) examined 300 articles in the literature of group psychotherapy to locate the expressions used by members in relation to their effect on the dynamics in groups. They finally reduced their categories to three common factors: 'an intellectual one, consisting of universalization, intellectualization, and spectator therapy; an emotional one, consisting of acceptance, altruism, and transference; and an actional factor, consisting of reality testing, interaction and ventilation' (p. 150). This finding supports experience in the field of counselling psychology. For change to be durable and persistent over time, it appears that interventions need to address the cognitive, affective and behavioural domains. We believe that a wide range of interventions which may include confrontation, explanation, the use of metaphor, techniques aimed at emotional release, challenging irrational beliefs as well as interpretation, will be effective in addressing the three categories outlined by Corsini and Rosenberg. Counselling psychology bases its practice in research and promotes a 'research attitude' in its approach to group work.

In summary, we see the task of a group facilitator as assisting group members to effect change cognitively, affectively and behaviourally at the intrapsychic, interpersonal and systemic levels. Each group member addresses the three crucial existential questions, first penned by Berne (1970):

- Who am I? (Intrapsychic.)
- Who are all those others? (Interpersonal.)
- What am I doing in the world? (Systemic or contextual.)

In a well functioning counselling group, members have the opportunity to change and update their schemata and rigid categories for processing reality. They can address non-functional behaviours and learn new, more effective ways of reaching their goals. They can build more rewarding relationships with others and may also address issues of the meaning and relevance of their lives in the larger socio-political context in which they share common concerns with members of the human race. A constructed group experience is geared at its most effective to provide for its members a change in their frame of reference so that they can approach the problems and challenges in their lives in a radically different way. This shift in perspective is generally accompanied by increased awareness of the range of options available to the person in any given context. A counselling group provides a unique opportunity for affective education, for learning about effective communication, for practising a new range of functional behaviours and for acquiring the skills required for maintaining rewarding relationships.

The nature and purpose of a constructed group

A constructed group provides a laboratory for experimentation and a safe context for learning new skills which can be transferred into the person's everyday life. It is both experimental and real in the sense that people's real thoughts, feelings and behaviours in relation to themselves and other people are explored in a context that is structured along very specific parameters for this purpose.

A group is carefully constructed with boundaries around time, place and membership. It is conducted in a place that is protected from intrusion and provides a safe space for the members.

People with a common need are brought together and the opportunity is created for them to experience their reactions in relation to other people and to raise their awareness of the impact of this experience on their view of themselves. This situation allows them to understand and learn about being in relationship and how relating to others influences getting their needs met. The question being addressed is: how can I get what I want in the world and at the same time get on with other people?

The central psychological focus of the learning in a constructed group is for the participants to understand how their internal worlds intersect with the external world. What is implied here is an understanding of how the internal world colours their functioning and experience, particularly with other people, and how this may affect issues concerning work and intimate relationships.

The constructed group provides a bridge between the safety of a therapeutic environment and the client's daily context. In this sense, the constructed group functions as a transitional space or a 'play' space (Winnicott, 1971) where clients can experiment with new ways of expressing themselves. The focus of the group may be on a specific theme, for example 'anger management' (Snyder et al., 1999), reducing a particular behaviour such as achieving more positive drinking patterns in alcohol-dependent patients (Sandahl et al., 1998) or the treatment of specific disorders such as depression (Clarke et al., 1999). Alternatively, the focus may be to provide 'an optimal context within which an active, agentic client can reflect upon the patterns of his or her life' (Bohart et al., 1998). The latter is often the aim of the more humanistically focused group where the purpose is to provide an empathic relationship within which to facilitate the client to re-evaluate his/her life and to implement more satisfying and meaningful personal choices.

Each participant brings into the group their own personal history and their cultural heritage, thus creating a climate or group culture that is reflective of the diversity of all its members. It is therefore inevitable that issues of race, culture, class, sexual identity and group affiliation will emerge and become part of the group content and process (the 'group business'). In this sense each group is unique in its particular constellation and climate, yet on the other hand common themes emerge across groups that appear to reflect shared human concerns. Both the uniqueness and the universality contribute to the learning potential of a group as these reflect the nature of our psychological make-up and the world in which we live.

In line with our integrative approach to group work, we include certain concepts from the general body of psychological theory. These concepts are both consistent with our general approach and have important relevance for group work. Winnicott's (1971) notion of transitional space is one of these. He describes a transitional area as one which is created in an intermediate space between inner and our shared outer reality. When the notion is used to describe a therapeutic space, it denotes a protected area in which the participants (therapist and client/s) share the intimate and internal as well as external aspects of experience. Clients are supported and encouraged to express their internal processes such as the thoughts that inform their schemata, their inner fantasies and their feelings in a safe place. The safety ensures that they will not be criticized, judged or evaluated on the basis of their inner lives.

Winnicott believed that therapy occurs in the overlap of the two transitional areas, that of the therapist and the client. In our description of the tasks of the leader in a counselling psychology group we assume that group leaders have the capacity to create a safe bounded space such that a transitional area is provided for participants. All the qualities that are concomitant with imagination, humour and creativity are linked with this ability. The capacity for metaphor and symbolization and the ability to describe inner experience, feelings and share memories and fantasies are also included.

From a different perspective, the group can be thought of as a transition between the world and people's psychological reality. In this way it is a secure place in which to experiment and 'play with' new ways of being, such as learning assertiveness skills, sharing emotionally with others or practising anger management techniques. Some approaches to counselling actively encourage role playing and rehearsal, and this aspect is also included in our model as a strategy where relevant and helpful. The overarching idea of the group as being a transitional space allows us to consider it as a place for play and experimentation. Early in the life of a group, members will test the boundaries – for example, by coming late or escalating an emotional process close to the end of the group to see how the leader maintains the time boundary. Holding the boundaries firm, providing containment and maintaining confidentiality are crucial to the creation of this safe place.

Summing up this section on our perspective of the psychological environment created in groups, we can do no better than quote Pine in describing factors central to therapeutic change, who writes: 'People will develop if there is a reasonable stability to their environment so that they can develop a reasonable trust in it; if the environment enriches, makes demands and spurs them on, so much the better' (1985: 132).

Assessment process

Assessment involves in part a consideration of the suitability of a particular person for group treatment, but the choice will be mediated by the level of expertise of the proposed group leader and the context in which the group is to be situated.

As a general principle we favour psychological therapy in heterogeneous groups, since these are more likely to resemble in some way the groups we interact with and belong to 'in the world out there' such as family groupings, work contexts or our friendship circles. Such a group offers more scope for the kinds of projections that people carry from the past that may be affecting their current reality testing. Where a safe place is created, the transferential phenomena will occur and allow these metaphors to operate. A heterogeneous group is likely to elicit in members a wide range of transferential phenomena related not only to the early care givers but also to siblings, people in authority positions and to peer experiences in the school playground and the classroom. This offers the opportunity for the exploration of a multiplicity of reactions that may not always emerge in the individual therapeutic relationship.

However, there are certain areas in which a homogeneous group may be of particular benefit to a person, since it offers the unique opportunity of being with a group constructed around a particular theme, experience or human characteristic, e.g. groups for victims of sexual abuse and rape, AIDS groups, groups for clients with alcohol or drug dependence, debriefing groups for people who have jointly experienced a disaster, groups for parents, for adolescents, for men or for women. Where people have shared a common experience, talking with others in a similar dilemma may add to the situation a sense of 'normalizing the experience' so that individuals can accept what has happened to them without guilt, self-punishment and ceaseless remorse. By 'normalizing', in this context we mean the understanding that a person's reaction, for example to an assault or disaster, represents a normal response to an abnormal situation reflecting the organism's adaptive response to extreme stress. It does not constitute anything shameful or a personal failure, as many victims tend to frame it. A homogeneous group offers a unique opportunity for such sharing and contributes the factors of 'universality, altruism and imparting information' (Yalom, 1970) that are particularly important for people who are experiencing themselves as excluded, 'odd and different' or isolated by a devastating experience or trauma.

In the treatment of alcohol-dependent clients group treatment is often the preferred intervention. However, a review of controlled trials from the alcohol literature revealed that approximately 85 per cent of the controlled clinical trials were individually based treatments, whilst within alcohol treatment centres group therapy is the favoured approach (Wilfley et al., 1998). This finding appears to reflect the lack of dialogue between clinicians and researchers, the 'strained alliance' that has been noted by others in the field of outcome research (Goldfried and Wolfe, 1996) who advocate reopening the dialogue between academic researchers and clinicians at the rock face. This would seem particularly pertinent in the field of psychological therapy in groups where many clinicians draw on a wide range of theories and techniques and seldom practise a 'pure form' of therapy. In addition there are few tested group approaches, yet from the above it is clear that the group format is very popular in many clinical settings.

Counselling groups have been conducted in a wide variety of contexts with client populations ranging from patients in psychiatric settings to the inmates of gaols, with students in colleges and universities, the aged, many different special interest groups too innumerable to mention and clients in out-patient settings who wish to improve their social and job-related skills. An impressive longitudinal study conducted with a sizeable random sample of Baltimore residents followed up after a period of fifteen years by Bovasso et al. (1999) is worthy of mention here. The focus was on mental health service use and psychiatric disorders and explored whether those who seek treatment are better off than those who do not, holding level of pathology constant. The results suggest that psychotherapy, particularly group therapy, is effective in producing long-term reductions in distress whereas drug therapy fails to do so (tending to have short-term efficacy only). The mental health services in the area were the suppliers of the treatments, so this study substantially illustrates the effectiveness of various treatments in the everyday context of patients' lives. This raises the interesting question of the influence of the context of delivery on effective outcome combined with how the prospective client may view a particular treatment and its possibilities.

In a study of casualties resulting from encounter groups Yalom and Lieberman (1971) concluded that certain types of group leaders tended to have a higher casualty rate in their groups. Type A leaders, described as 'aggressive stimulators', were reported by participants as having some of the more severe casualties resulting from 'attack by leader'. Participants in groups conducted by more impersonal and *laissez-faire* leaders tended to suffer a type of casualty where 'attack by the group' was responsible for the mode of injury. Rejection played a role in most of the casualties (Yalom and Lieberman, 1971). These findings suggest that the qualities of the leader are at least as important as those of the group participant in the assessment process. It would appear that group leaders who balance acceptance and warmth with setting firm boundaries in a group are most suitable for this type of work. It is also important that confrontation is carefully considered and balanced with support in a holding environment so that group members do not feel under attack by the leader. If a leader is too easy-going or distant and uninvolved, the opposite problem may result and the group may attack or scapegoat a particular individual without the leader's effective intervention to prevent this destructive process. This again underlines the importance of protection and safety for effective work in counselling psychology groups.

Group members do, however, need to be able to withstand frustration and tolerate moderate levels of anxiety without regressing or acting out in ways destructive to the group. We have found that people with severe disorders of the self, particularly where acting out is a strong feature and where adult-to-adult agreement about the purpose of being in the group cannot be mutually maintained, will not benefit from being in a counselling group. The presence of an observing ego, that is, the capacity to maintain adult ego state functioning in the service of adequate reality testing (Berne, 1966), and the ability to be observers of their own process and that of others, are a minimal requirement for group attendance.

However, within these limits people with poor ego functioning may indeed benefit from the structure, the natural atmosphere and the clear boundaries of a constructed group. The setting of clear goals by each group member is a source of security and gives structure to the situation. A shared group goal like 'learning assertiveness skills' or 'learning emotional literacy' will often create solidarity in a group. Glatzer (1978) points out that 'the reassuring presence of other group members decreases dependence on the therapist and reduces initial anxiety about passive submission to an omnipotent figure which, in turn, makes the analyst seem more human and less frightening' (p. 307). In this connection Aaron Stein (1981) suggested that combined group and individual therapy might be suitable for 'narcissistic and borderline patients with defective ego boundaries who are unable to withstand minimal tensions' (p. 335) and need the support of a close dyadic relationship to work through their issues. In our experience, such clients are often best seen in individual psychological therapy for a period of time before moving to a group. In a more recent study of the effects of the therapeutic alliance on outcomes in individual and group psychotherapy with borderline personality disordered patients, Marziali et al. hypothesized on the basis of their findings with this group that 'it may be that the therapeutic alliance in group psychotherapy does not solidify until a later point in therapy' (1999: 433), thus supporting the earlier findings. Clearly further research based on the refinement of therapeutic alliance measures related to effective outcomes in group psychotherapy will be of great benefit to the practising clinician.

Except for the provision discussed above, and in the case of people who are actively psychotic, we consider that most people can benefit from group treatment that is conducted by a competent group leader if they are motivated and come willingly to the group. Enforced attendance is not likely to yield a productive outcome, since people are more likely to resist any intervention if compelled to attend. In such a case, nothing productive will be achieved unless an effective working alliance can be negotiated with group members. A further contra-indication would be the situation where a member was in a deep and early transference with the group leader. Such a participant may not be able to emotionally share the leader's attention and may feel excluded at every transaction not directed to him/her.

We consider that an individual assessment interview is essential before entry into a group. The dynamics that would cause us not to recommend group counselling would be rigid projection of blame, a tendency to rapid regression in a therapeutic situation, acting out of a suicidal or violent nature and incapacity to reflect upon one's own process and the impact of one's behaviour on others.

The nature and facilitation of change in a counselling psychology group

For the purposes of clarity we will consider separately each of the three levels of change listed on p. 443. We recognize that such divisions are artificial, as any interaction in a group could be considered from all these perspectives simultaneously. Most approaches to group therapy focus primarily on one, rather than all, of these dimensions. This of itself does not militate against effectiveness, particularly in symptom reduction, but we are in favour of an holistic approach to the person coming for help.

Intrapsychic change

The intrapsychic level describes the internal process and is the most fundamental level of personality change. Most in-depth and long-term approaches to psychotherapy and counselling aim for intrapsychic change. From this perspective, it is assumed that, once change has occurred in the intrapsychic process, people will effect the external changes that make their lives easier. Furthermore, these changes are long-lasting and usually irreversible. The major disadvantage of this approach is its time-consuming and lengthy nature.

From a group counselling point of view, the model would be that of individual work in the group, or the so-called 'hot seat' approach. By this we mean that the individual therapy is conducted by the facilitator in the group while the rest of the group members observe and participate through identification. The group also forms a backdrop or a chorus to the work, often lending psychic energy to the process. Often members will spontaneously confirm that a person working on an issue not only evokes or reminds them of their situation but they will spontaneously say, 'You were working for me there too', or 'You did that work on my behalf as well.'

In our model we see this as one form of process in a group. There will be occasions when it will be not only appropriate, but also exceedingly useful, to focus on the individual in the group. The intrapsychic work conducted in this format is instructive and interesting to the other members. Work at this level often expedites other members' understanding of their own internal processes by vicarious identification, as well as providing a window into another's inner experience.

Many techniques for doing intrapsychic work in a group context arise from the humanistic approaches to counselling and therapy; in particular Gestalt therapy, interactional therapy and transactional analysis. However, the more recent emphasis in cognitive-behaviour therapy on schema-focused work is also aimed at changes in the person's deep-seated assumptions and beliefs and facilitates intrapsychic change. These approaches have in common an emphasis on the current manifestation of dysfunction in the here-and-now behaviours in the person's life (and hence in the group). The therapist engages with what is immediately presented by the group members, seeing this as a reflection of characteristic patterns of presenting self.

We will describe in some detail an approach central to intrapsychic as well as interpersonal change. Its usefulness and power are contained in the way it integrates cognition, affect and behaviour. The technique developed by Erskine and Zalcman (1979) focuses on cognitive, affective and behavioural aspects of the change process. By looking at the repetitive, non-productive patterns that occur, therapists are able to gain immediate access to people's internal processes. The theory which underpins this technique is that unmet needs, usually dating to early childhood experience, lead to the construction of a faulty belief system in order to contain and understand the deprivation and/or trauma.

The belief system or core (maladaptive) interpersonal schema (Horowitz, 1989) centres around beliefs about the self, others and the quality of life or the larger context of experience. These core beliefs are connected with a set of dysfunctional behaviours which often reinforce the beliefs. Memories of related and similar experiences, fantasies and dreams are used to support the central belief structure and reinforce its circularity. Connected with this cognitive-behavioural system are repressed feelings and needs which were not acceptable in the original scenario/relationships. This interrelated system is formulated in terms of the 'script decisions' in transactional analysis and is akin to the 'core maladaptive schema' of cognitive theory. An example would be a schema of 'unlovability' based on an early conclusion by the child about being 'unwanted and unattractive to others'. These 'script decisions' inform a person's self-narrative and determine how the person frames, colours and understands many experiences in his/her life, based on early conclusions about reality.

The way that change is effected in the group is through intervening in this circular system. This could involve addressing the faulty cognitions (the negative automatic thoughts), looking at the unproductive behaviours or surfacing and identifying the unmet needs. Although working with the script system or core maladaptive schema could be approached on a cognitive-behavioural level (or diagrammed for the client's easier access, as in cognitive-analytic therapy), when in addition the early unmet needs are touched, often deep affective working-through results in a cathartic release and a reversal of the script process. This affective experience will reinforce the change in the frame of reference. The goal of this approach to therapy is to help the individual achieve more constructive ways of solving problems and relating to others in the here-and-now rather than reverting to old patterns developed under stress.

For example, the participant describes how she comes into the group and begins to feel more and more isolated. On tracking her feeling, it emerges that she was often left alone and anxious at night and then might lie awake hearing adults arguing or fighting. The situation in the group triggered her feeling of confusion and pain about what was going on. An inquiry into how that affected her internal process reveals her belief that she is 'helpless, not good enough and stupid', and that others and the world are not 'safe'. Consequently she withdraws and feels isolated. The group counsellor works with the belief system to convey the message that she is 'little' at the time rather than stupid, and adults need to get help if they cannot manage their emotional lives.

In groups the phenomenon often occurs that one person's circular belief system interlocks with that of another, leading to the kind of misunderstanding and confused communication so characteristic of relationship problems. Behaviour on the part of one person triggers the belief system of the other such that the second person behaves in a way that reinforces their own and the other's worst expectations. One person believes 'They're out to get me,' another that 'Others have to be watched in case they make a mistake,' both sets of beliefs clearly based on their early feelings and experiences. Rapidly these interlocking beliefs will lead to projections and acting out on both sides which then need to be addressed in the here-and-now reality of the group experience. This leads us naturally on to the second level of change.

Interpersonal change

The interpersonal aspects are those that are dealt with most powerfully and effectively in constructed systems. It is here that a space is created that allows the replay of habitual patterns of communication between individuals in the group. Group participants will project on to each other features of significant figures in their present or past context as they act out on the basis of entrenched schemata. The conscious and unconscious aspects, overt and covert trans-actions, are revealed for observation and analysis by the facilitator and other group members. Feedback from the group allows the understanding and expli-cation of particular patterns of interacting. Further, the impact of this behaviour on others can be explored in a safe and non-threatening environment. Rehearsal, suggestions and insights into ways of handling conflict and other problems result from this process in the group.

One of Eric Berne's great clinical contributions was his description of the psychological games that people play (Berne, 1964). Unfortunately the pop psychological aspect often obscures the book's profundity and the elegant description of interpersonal dynamics. The analysis of games in a group forms a powerful and central focus. Individual insight gained in this process frees the 'players' of the games to engage in productive interaction. It can also lead to deep emotional insight, in that Berne contends that game playing could be seen as part of the psychological defence system. Games could alternatively be viewed as overt manifestations of a core maladaptive schema. Analysing games, then, often flows into intrapsychic working through of underlying unresolved conflicts. Psychologically unsophisticated group members readily get into a simple 'Yes but ...' game. One player puts a problem to the group and other members propose solutions, all of which are 'Yes butted', supported with 'good' reasons. On analysis it becomes clear that the psychological game, in confirming, 'No one can help me', is a much more powerful motivation than finding a solution to the problem.

On the positive side, a constructed group offers a safe space for experiment-ing with new interactional choices and can lead to the improvement of relation-ship skills. As people check their personal reality against the perceptions of others, their assumptions about their impact may be challenged. The opportu-nity for honest and courageous feedback from peers in the group committed to a common goal of growth is for many people the most valuable aspect of their group membership. Or a group of this kind can offer someone the opportunity of developing skills such as assertiveness or anger management for which there may have been little opportunity to date.

Systemic/communal aspects

The third level or systemic aspect of groups can be classified as therapy for the group as a whole, in that the group rather than the individual is the focus of attention and analysis. A constructed system takes on a life of its own that is larger than the individuals that form it. People become invested in the survival of the group, and work towards group maintenance and cohesion. All members bring to the group their experience of previous systems of which they have been a member; in particular, the formative experiences in the family of origin and at school are brought into and played out in the group. These take the form of psychological roles that people adopt and which influence their projections on others.

On the other hand, psychological roles are also assigned to people by the rest of the group on the basis of their representing a particular class, cultural group or race. Consequently, such a person's interaction with other group members is circumscribed by such a label. It is as though this person is performing a particular function in the system that fits the image that members hold of society and its components. This provides the counselling psychologist with rich material for intervening in the group process.

Another way in which psychological roles operate is represented by the individual who may express anger in a particular manner. Clearly this anger is part of the individual's range of responses to the immediate situation; at the same time, however, if she is expressing anger on behalf of the group, the other members are relieved of experiencing and expressing possibly uncomfortable feelings of their own.

An interpretation such as 'The men are remarkably silent in the group today' can evoke for some members the experience in the constructed system of the men who were absent physically or emotionally in their own families. As the stuck points in the system are addressed and understood, individuals begin to understand how they assume roles and positions in their own lives. Although they are in a constructed system, by its very nature it allows the recreation of the other systems they have experienced, or live in at present. Once roles and positions are brought into awareness, people have a choice about whether they wish to continue to assume or adopt them.

In addition to the unconscious assumptions and processes, analysis of group themes and tasks brings about other important arenas for change. The normalization of problems (Yalom, 1970) is central to acceptance and health. Equally powerful is the instillation of hope; seeing that others can and do change gives great encouragement to group members that change is possible.

Learning to balance one's own needs with the needs of others is another useful and powerful process that occurs in a group. Taking up time in the group, being sure to be heard and at the same time not dominating the conversation are aspects of this process. Group forces monitor and control these aspects. Our experience confirms Bion's (1959) belief that there are powerful forces for healing in a group. In the long run a group will confront reality aspects, curing its members of neurosis by challenging projections and fantasies.

We see as a central task the creation of an environment in which each member can own their own tendencies towards destructiveness and pathology with courage and honesty. It is only through this process that individuals can understand the impact they make and the effect of their projections on others.

The role and tasks of the leader in the counselling psychology group

The leader has a dual role: to create a holding environment that provides safety for clients, whilst at the same time seizing opportunities to facilitate change in maladaptive schemata and non-problem-solving strategies of client interaction. The group needs to provide enough safety for clients to feel supported in reflecting upon and changing patterns of behaviour and interaction that form part of their long-standing defence systems, yet not to become so 'cosy' that members begin to use the group as a haven or alternative to forming external support systems of their own in the wider environment. Maintaining this balance between support and confrontation is the primary task of an effective group facilitator. Facilitating a constructed group involves creating a learning environment for people to confront non-functional patterns and experiment with new options in relationships with others. Group members provide for one another an 'experimental' group situation which closely resembles the groups in their daily lives, yet has the unique dimension that interactions can be halted,'put on hold', so that they can be analysed, explored and understood to provide new learning for the future outside the group. This focus on evaluating effective outcomes for group members is central to what we refer to as the 'research mind-set' in counselling psychology.

It is not unusual for members of a constructed group to utter a sentiment like 'Nowhere else in my life is it possible for me to put my interactions on hold and discuss what lies beneath and behind them – and to get really honest feedback from others that I know I can trust because they have my welfare at heart.' We consider that such a statement reflects the working alliance that exists between the group members and between them and the facilitator. Even when resentment or anger is expressed, if the working alliance is in place, then group members can interact with the understanding that goodwill prevails. If such a working alliance is not in place, members will feel unsafe and there is a chance that the group will disintegrate.

The group leader provides a model for dealing with affect in a direct and non-punitive manner and will accept the anger or dissatisfaction of group members when it is aimed against her. Above all, the group leader needs to be able to withstand provocation without retaliation so that non-productive interaction patterns can emerge in the group and provide material for discussion and change. The group leader needs to emerge intact from this process as a model that negative affect can be tolerated and dealt with in creative ways. For this reason, among others, it is vital that the group leader is well supported in a supervisory context. One of the chief challenges for the group leader is the task of setting limits and maintaining boundaries so that the structure and life of the group are safeguarded and can provide the 'holding environment' essential for the successful attainment of goals.

Another of the leader's tasks is to move the group forward to deal with its primary business of providing a protected space for exploration and change.

The leader will usually keep the group focused on interactions in the group and between its members, the 'here and now' process that is currently occurring in the group. This focus is based on the assumption that people will play out their fixed and rigid defensive patterns of behaviour in the group with the other members and so provide 'live material' for the group facilitator's attention and that of group members. The group context also offers a unique place and opportunity to select new interactional options and try them out for size, judging from the response of other group members how these are likely to be received in the outside world. The group leader needs to be alert to the on-going process in the group, to the 'games' that people play, to the group themes that emerge, and to tendencies to project and scapegoat as a means of avoiding the anxiety associated with change. Group members may be less aware initially of the repetitive patterns that lead them to similar unsatisfactory outcomes as in the past; the group leader's task is to highlight such patterns and support people in the process of learning to achieve more satisfactory outcomes in their lives and relationships.

In summary, the counselling psychologist as group leader provides a context in which affective education can take place, where rigid interpersonal schemata can be changed and where new behaviours can be tried out and chosen as alternatives to inflexible, unproductive modes of operation. The leader's tasks fall into two broad categories: containment, support, facilitation; and confrontation, challenge, interpretation. We do not wish to leave this section without mentioning the importance of humour as a tool of creative change. Laughter and fun can be as powerful in the process of growth and change as the solemn realizations that also form part of the overall canvas.

A group leader's role is demanding of energy and inner resources. We consider it vital that the group leader has regular supervision sessions in which he can explore his own responses in the group, deal with countertransference as it arises and get assistance with interventions and techniques. Berne (1966) drew up a series of questions to guide the group therapist's interventions. We have used these as a basis for our own formulation of the group therapist's tasks

- What is the focus for this client today?
- Has this client said or done something in the group that relates to our shared problem formulation?
- What is my hypothesis about what the client is presenting today?
- How can I best validate this hypothesis?
- How might the client respond to what I say?
- How can I address the client best to ensure that I do not engage his defences?
- What form of intervention is indicated from the above information?
- How might this intervention affect the other group members?
- Whose need am I serving with this intervention, the client's or my own?
- If not the client's, then it is better to drop the endeavour and start anew!

We are not suggesting that the group leader will be able to take the time out before each intervention to go through this list! However, we have found the questions extremely useful as a supervisory tool to assist the group leader to assess interventions that were made in previous sessions and hence to move on to effective and creative planning for future sessions. We also consider that the questions support the development of a 'research mind-set' which focuses on relevant and effective outcomes for the work of counselling psychologists. As group therapists we can all contribute to the research endeavour by observing and documenting carefully processes in our groups and changes in partici- pants' behaviour that may serve to generate research into key clinical issues.

It is important for group leaders to have an awareness of the type of leader- ship stance that they adopt and the impact on participants. Research suggests that the most effective leaders will be flexible and able to adjust their style to suit the needs and characteristics of the individuals in the group. In a group which contains a number of vulnerable people with a fragile sense of self the group leader would be more supportive and would modulate confrontations carefully, while at the same time providing a safe structure. As in individual counselling, so also in group counselling the question 'What type of coun- selling, by whom and for what treatment group, etc.' remains largely unan- swered by the current state of research. The most helpful study remains that of Yalom, in which he identified by means of a factor analysis four basic leader- ship functions: emotional stimulation and confrontation; caring and offering support; providing a cognitive framework for understanding experience; and setting limits and maintaining boundaries (1970: 501).

Research evidence about effectiveness and outcomes in groups

The importance of outcome research for psychological therapy is being increas- ingly stressed with the focus on measurable outcomes and the buying in of 'empirically validated treatments', recently renamed 'empirically supported treatments'.

Most research results in group treatment are, however, closely linked with the common factors research in individual therapy rather than with outcome results relating to differential treatment effects of different forms of group therapy. A survey of group researches by Bergin and Garfield (1994) over a period of fifty years reaches two major conclusions: (1) group treatment has been more effective than no treatment; and in some circumstances more effective than other psychological treatments; and (2) there are certain positive identifiable common factors that are associated with positive outcomes. The study by Bovasso et al. (1999) described above lends support to the enduring effective- ness of group therapy over other forms of intervention, particularly over time.

However, a critical review of psychotherapy research outcome studies by Roth and Fonagy (1996) reveals a paucity of recent studies into group therapy that *in their terms* demonstrate the 'efficacy' of this treatment method. They do mention moderate outcomes for patients with bipolar disorders, for elderly depressed patients and for those seeking therapy for sexual problems. Their conclusions overall suggest that group therapy may be relegated to a back seat: 'It is in the sphere of relapse prevention that groups may prove to be most valuable. Several accounts are available of groups that provide long-term support … ' (p. 328).

Parloff and Dies (1977) in their earlier review of outcomes in groups concentrated on research conducted with clinical categories of clients. Their survey suggests that, for clinical groups, group therapy augments other treatment approaches but may be limited as a sole approach to treatment. Roth and Fonagy's report seems to be in line with this earlier finding.

For the counselling psychologist it becomes important to evaluate such research results and use them as a guide to selecting suitable approaches to treatment for particular clients. How are we to understand these discrepancies in reported results concerning group studies over the past twenty to thirty years?

In this regard, we have asked ourselves whether group therapy outcome research has not perhaps fallen victim to the medical-like research paradigm promoted by a task force of Division 12 of the American Psychological Association in which the focus is on 'empirically validated treatments', recently renamed 'empirically supported treatments'. In this research paradigm the problem or disorder is first specified and then a particular approach to treatment is applied, often in manualized form. The patient is given the recommended 'dose' of a particular form of therapy recommended for the particular problem or disorder. Unfortunately, however, efficacy often speaks more to an approach's privilege in having been researched than as to how such research should be privileged (Hubble et al., 2000). The fact that a particular approach has not been researched does not automatically point to its ineffectiveness!

It is difficult to imagine how any therapy group could ever fit neatly into the task force's research paradigm and how the therapist would be able to respond in a predetermined manner, specified in a manual, to all the possible interactions that arise in a group! This approach would run counter to the immediacy and spontaneity that are the hallmark of much group therapy. In addition, since many group workers tend to be transtheoretical, the question of differential treatment approaches has less validity in this area. We agree with Bohart et al., who maintain 'that empirical support for a therapy should include research based on methods compatible with the assumptions of the therapy, in particular on what it means to say that a given therapy "works"' (1998: 141). Perhaps human science methodology, and in particular qualitative research methods, would suit group therapy outcome research better and be more in keeping with the processes we have described in this chapter.

We consider that the tension between the 'dodo bird verdict' (the finding that there is no difference in effectiveness among the various treatments for psychological distress) and the search for differential treatment effects by client condition underpins the challenges for group psychotherapy outcome research studies as much as for individual work. Will future group outcome research focus on what factors or conditions make for change in psychological therapy in groups or will the major focus be on refining differential group treatments for particular client disorders or conditions? Is it perhaps possible to envisage embracing both these areas of research and maintaining an open dialogue between them and between researchers and clinicians in the field?

Parloff and Dies (1977) issued an interesting challenge to subsequent researchers:

> What kinds of changes are produced by what kinds of interventions provided by what kinds of therapists with what kinds of patients/problems under what kinds of conditions? Such complex questions regarding the effectiveness of group psychotherapy need to be addressed collaboratively by both empirically and clinically oriented professionals. (p. 316)

Their question as it stands embraces both the above strands and could lead to fruitful developments.

Yalom's seminal research, based on careful observation in groups, is a classic reference point. Yalom's curative factors have been consistently recognized in group practice and research as crucial for effective change. He identified eleven primary factors: instillation of hope; universality; imparting of information; altruism; the corrective recapitulation of the primary family group; the development of socializing techniques; imitative behaviour; interpersonal learning; group cohesiveness; catharsis and existential factors. Some of these curative factors consistently emerge as being more crucial than others. Cohesion, interpersonal learning, catharsis and self-understanding have been identified in various researches as the most central and valued by the participants. These fall into the arena of the common factors referred to by Bergin and Garfield.

In 1994 Bednar and Kaul came to the following conclusion:

> We suggest that the underlying problem in the area of definitional adequacy is not a lack of effort by most well-trained group researchers. Rather it is a lack of descriptive data based on truly astute observations about group events that add order, detail and information about the central events in group treatments. (p. 638)

We wish to give our support to the importance of detailed observation of group events and processes with a view to identifying the 'change moments' in groups and those specific factors and leadership behaviours that contribute to successful outcomes for individual members. However, in group outcome research (as in individual therapy research) the role of the client in the process of change has been under-researched and undervalued. The client as an active self-healer has only recently become the focus of renewed research interest. Bohart (2000) argues that the client is the most important common factor in the process of change. Lambert had already in 1992 pointed out that 40 per cent of outcome variance is due to the client and factors in the client's life (Lambert, 1992). Yet even common-factors research has tended to focus more on therapist-supplied factors than on what the client brings to therapy. Duncan and Miller (2000) maintain that respecting the client's theory of change could be a crucial factor in successful therapeutic outcome. This could be a fruitful area for research in group work: an exploration of how an understanding of the client's view of problem formulation and resolution and the client's take on the change process may affect outcome. Duncan and Miller (2000) point out, following Kazdin, that even if a treatment has been demonstrated as efficacious, it may still be rejected by many clients because it is experienced as too intrusive, unfair or unreasonable!

Conclusion and recommendations

In line with the outcome research on groups, we have no doubt that groups are an effective modality for change; overall the results show that participants gain along a number of different dimensions. A well run group is an efficient and economical way of addressing and dealing with a variety of complex psychological issues and processes. In our opinion, groups encompass cognitive, affective and behavioural opportunities that are central to psychological growth and change. This conclusion is supported by our clinical experience and some of the research findings.

As a general recommendation we join the plea for more detailed and careful research into group phenomena as these relate to outcomes for individual members. In particular we believe that looking at the therapeutic alliance in groups, the therapist's style of relating as well as the active healing factors that clients bring to the process may yield fruitful results. Like Pilkonis and Krause (1999) we favour 'the clinical use paradigm' in outcome research – a focus on research that will support the clinician in the field to make the most informed choices for particular clients in an everyday work context. We believe that the combined wisdom emerging from clinical experience and the careful and objective approach of research could enhance both our conceptual understanding and our practice of psychological therapy in groups, thereby strengthening an already powerful approach to addressing psychological distress.

References

Bednar, R.L. and Kaul, T.J. (1994) 'Experiential group research: can the canon fire?' in A.E. Bergin and S.L. Garfield (eds) *Handbook of Psychotherapy and Behavior Change*. Chichester and New York: Wiley.

Bergin, A.E. and Garfield, S.L. (eds) (1994) *Handbook of Psychotherapy and Behavior Change*. Chichester and New York: Wiley.

Berne, E. (1964) *Games People Play*. New York: Grove Press.

Berne, E. (1966) *Principles of Group Treatment*. New York: Grove Press.

Berne, E. (1970) *Sex in Human Loving*. London: Penguin Books.

Bion, W.R. (1959) *Experiences in Groups and other Papers*. New York: Basic Books.

Bohart, Arthur C. (2000) 'The client is the most important common factor: clients' self-healing capacities and psychotherapy', *Journal of Psychotherapy Integration*, 10 (2): 141–57.

Bohart, Arthur C., O'Hara, M. and Leitner, L.M. (1998) 'Empirically violated treatments: disenfranchisement of humanistic and other psychotherapies', *Psychotherapy Research*, 8 (2): 141–57.

Bovasso, G.B., Eaton, W.E. and Armenian, H.K. (1999). 'The long-term outcomes of mental health treatment in a population-based study', *Journal of Consulting and Clinical Psychology*, 67: 529–38.

Clarke, G.N., Rohde, P., Lewinsohn, P.H., Hops, H. and Seeley, J.R. (1999) 'Cognitive-behavioral treatment of adolescent depression: efficacy of acute group treatment and booster sessions', *Journal of the American Academy of Child and Adolescent Psychiatry*, 38: 272–9.

Corsini, R.J. and Rosenberg, B. (1955) 'Mechanisms of group psychotherapy', *Journal of Abnormal and Social Psychology*, 15: 406–11. Also published as 'Mechanisms of group psychotherapy: processes and dynamics' in K.R. MacKenzie (ed.) *Classics in Group Psychotherapy*. New York: Guilford Press (1992).

Duncan, B.L. and Miller, S.D. (2000) 'The client's theory of change: consulting the client in the integrative process,' *Journal of Psychotherapy Integration*, 10 (2): 169–88.

Erskine, R.G. and Zalcman, M.J. (1979) 'The racket system', *Transactional Analysis Journal*, 9 (1): 51–9.

Glatzer, H.T. (1978) 'The working alliance in analytic group psychotherapy', *Journal of Group Psychotherapy*, 28: 147–61. Also published in K.R. MacKenzie (ed.) *Classics in Group Psychotherapy*. New York: Guilford Press (1992).

Goldfried, M. and Wolfe, B.E. (1996) 'Psychotherapy, practice and research: repairing a strained alliance', *Journal of Consulting and Clinical Psychology*, 51: 1007–16.

Horowitz, M. (1989) *Maladaptive Interpersonal Schemas*. New York: Basic Books.

Hubble, M.A., Duncan, B.L. and Miller, S.D. (2000) *The Heart and Soul of Change*. Washington DC : American Psychological Association.

Lambert, M.J. (1992) 'Psychotherapy outcome research: implications for integrative and eclectic therapies', in J.C. Norcross and M.R. Goldfried (eds) *Handbook of Psychotherapy Integration*. New York: Basic Books.

Lieberman, M.A., Yalom, I.D. and Miles, M.B. (1973) *Encounter Groups: First Facts*. New York: Basic Books.

Marziali, E., Munroe-Blum, H. and McCleary, L. (1999) 'The effects of the therapeutic alliance on the outcomes in individual and group psychotherapy with borderline personality disorder', *Psychotherapy Research*, 9 (4): 424–36.

Parloff, M.B. and Dies, R.R. (1977) 'Group psychotherapy outcome research', *International Journal of Group Psychotherapy*, 27: 281-319.

Pilkonis, P.A. and Krause, M.S. (1999) 'Summary: paradigms for psychotherapy outcome research', *Journal of Clinical Psychology*, 55: 201–5.

Pine, F. (1985) *Developmental Theory and Clinical Process*. New Haven CT: Yale University Press.

Roth, A. and Fonagy, P. (1996) *What Works for Whom ?* London: Guilford.

Sandahl, C., Herlitz, K., Ahlin, G. and Ronnberg, S. (1998) 'Time-limited group psychotherapy for moderately alcohol-dependent patients: a randomized controlled clinical trial', *Psychotherapy Research*, 8 (4): 361–78.

Snyder, K.V., Kymissis, M.D. and Kessler, M.D. (1999) 'Anger management for adolescents: efficacy of brief group therapy', *Journal of the American Academy for Child and Adolescent Psychiatry*, 38: 272–9.

Stein, A. (1981) 'Indications for concurrent (combined and conjoint) individual and group psychotherapy' in L.R. Wolberg and M.L. Aronson (eds) *Group and Family Therapy*. New York: Brunner Mazel.

Wilfley, D.E., Frank, M.A., Welch, R., Spurrell, E.B. and Rounsville, B.J. (1998) 'Adapting interpersonal psychotherapy to a group format (IPT-G) for binge eating disorder: towards a model for adapting empirically supported treatments', *Psychotherapy Research*, 8 (4): 379–91.

Winnicott, D.W. (1971) *Playing and Reality*. Harmondsworth: Penguin.

Yalom, I.D. (1970) *The Theory and Practice of Group Psychotherapy*. New York: Basic Books.

Yalom, I.D. and Lieberman, M.A. (1971) 'A study of encounter group casualties', *Archive of General Psychiatry*, 25: 16–30.

22 Career Development Work with Individuals
JENNIFER M. KIDD

Career development work encompasses a range of tasks and activities. The term 'guidance' has come to be used as an umbrella term to describe the various potential elements; these include group work, information giving, teaching, self-help activities and assessment, as well as individual career counselling. Within most of these, of course, basic counselling skills will be essential. This chapter has several objectives: some require a generic perspective on careers work, while others can be addressed only by examining specific activities.

The first objective is to introduce the reader to the field by outlining the kinds of services available to those needing help with career issues and by introducing some of the theoretical perspectives which have informed practice. Here it will be necessary to take a broad view of career development work, which encompasses a range of activities as well as individual career counselling. As we move on to examine the ways in which various theories and conceptual frameworks can inform practice it will be more appropriate to restrict our attention to one-to-one counselling, although many of the issues discussed will also be relevant to those who work with groups, or whose role is primarily to provide information or basic assessment. In the final section of the chapter, which deals with research evaluating the effectiveness of careers work, we return to a broader perspective, so as to do justice to the breadth of the literature.

The range of issues presented in careers work is extremely broad. Examples of some of the concerns which clients bring to the practitioner include:

- I want a job where I don't have to bring work home. Perhaps I should change direction completely.
- I've just been made redundant. What opportunities are there for someone in their fifties?
- I've just left university with an arts degree. What does it qualify me for?
- I would like to work for myself, but it's a big step leaving the security of a monthly salary and a pension scheme.
- I've just left school and my mum wants me to start applying for jobs.
- I've spent fifteen years bringing up a family. How can I build up the confidence to return to work?
- I'm not happy in my job. Should I change my employer or should I contemplate a complete career change?
- My employer is making more and more demands on me. How can I be more assertive, and tell her how *I* see things?
- I've been out of work now for three years and I don't even get job interviews any more. Perhaps I should resign myself to retirement.

What these examples show is that clients can be of any age and at any stage in their careers. Moreover, it is clear that they may need help with decisions about jobs, with managing their work responsibilities in relation to other aspects of their lives, with interpersonal issues, or with finding information about career opportunities. Also, many of these presenting problems may mask deeper emotional issues which will not become apparent until later. The matters discussed in this chapter should be relevant to counselling psychologists working in a range of settings who may be presented with any of these issues.

Provision

Although a wide range of public and private-sector agencies provide career guidance services, the type of service offered varies considerably – from one short interview to two or three days' in-depth assessment and counselling. Guidance provision in the United Kingdom can be grouped into three main categories: education/training-based, employment-based and 'independent' (Watts and Sadler, 2000). Despite increased opportunities for lifelong learning and more job mobility, most state-funded career guidance services operate for young people making the transition from education to work. Very little public money has been invested in providing career counselling and guidance services to adults. The main types of provision are as follows.

Education/training based career guidance

All secondary school and most further education students have access to the Careers Service, which is funded by the Department for Education and Skills. However, services for part-time students are more limited than those for full-timers. Schools and further education colleges also have their own careers specialists. In England, however, the Careers Service is being subsumed within the new 'Connexions' service, which is designed to provide an integrated support service to those between the ages of thirteen and nineteen. Every young person will have access to a 'personal adviser', whose role includes support with a wide range of personal issues, as well as career guidance.

Students in higher education and recent graduates are able to use the careers advisory services in their institutions. The service normally includes individual interviews for those who want them, but there has been some movement towards self-help activities, particularly with the introduction of computer-aided guidance systems, such as PROSPECT (HE), which help students assess their interests, values and skills, retrieve information on opportunities, and learn decision-making skills. Careers advisers in higher education have a wide range of employment and training backgrounds, and this is likely to affect the approach they take to individual interviewing, particularly the amount of emphasis given to advice and information as opposed to counselling.

With regard to provision within vocational training, government-funded schemes for young people and adults have often incorporated guidance, usually emphasizing assessment rather than career counselling.

Employment-based guidance

Partly in response to the need for employees to become more flexible and self-reliant in their career development, many large organizations now offer individuals support in their career planning. Individual career counselling is offered by some organizations, but other initiatives are more common, for example development centres and mentoring schemes. These services are more likely to be offered to professional, technical and managerial staff, although some employers have extended these kinds of interventions to the whole work force, often as part of employee development programmes.

'Independent' guidance

The main types of services provided independently from educational institutions and employers include those offered by the Careers Service, Jobcentre Plus (part of the Department for Work and Pensions) and the private sector. The Careers Service, as well as providing career guidance and placement services to students, is also required to provide these services to young people aged under twenty one who have left education up to two years previously. Most careers services also make their services available to adults. Advice on job search is also available to adults at local job centres.

Perhaps because of limited provision by employers and public-sector providers, many adults seeking career counselling turn to fee-charging services in the private sector. Many of these are staffed by psychologists or professionally trained career counsellors, though since there is no legislation controlling these services' operation there is no guarantee that counsellors have any relevant training or experience. The best agencies offer psychometric testing and feedback, a series of counselling sessions, access to careers information, coaching in job hunting and CV writing, and interview practice.

Outplacement agencies offer help to employees facing redundancy. A comprehensive service will involve activities similar to those offered by independent career counselling services, though often with more emphasis on emotional support to cope with the trauma of redundancy. Few services employ staff with any significant amount of training in counselling, however. Clients are usually companies, rather than individuals, and outplacement is often offered to employees as part of an overall redundancy package to senior staff. Where lower-level staff are offered a service, it may be rather different from the one-to-one programmes offered to executives: it is more likely to be group-based and there will be less in-depth psychometric assessment. An important part of the service, generally, however, is likely to be job search: many services base their marketing on how quickly their 'candidates' become re-employed.

Conceptual frameworks

We turn now to examine some theoretical perspectives relevant to careers work. Over the past fifty years or so, the primary goals of career guidance have shifted, in line with changing views about individual career development and about careers themselves. At the beginning of the twentieth century simple 'matching' models provided the conceptual base for the 'scientific guidance' provided by the Juvenile Employment Bureaux of the 1920s and 1930s where assessments of abilities and interests, sometimes using psychometric test results, led to occupational recommendations. It was not until the 1960s that these approaches began to be augmented and to some extent replaced in Britain by models derived from developmental theories of careers. In this section we summarize some of the most influential career theories and examine their impact on career guidance and counselling practice.

Person–environment fit theories

Perhaps the earliest 'theory' of occupational choice was that of Parsons (1909) who, in the United States, established one of the first vocational guidance agencies. The model which guided his work consisted of three propositions:

- People are different from each other.
- So are jobs.
- It should be possible, by a study of both, to achieve a match between person and job.

From that time, thinking about occupational choice was increasingly dominated by the need to generate verifiable data about individuals and jobs. Psychometric tests of aptitudes and interests were developed to support this task. Parsons's model may seem simplistic, but his matching approach has been accepted and elaborated upon by later writers. In Britain, for example, Rodger's Seven-point Plan (Rodger, 1952) was until recently a commonly used framework for diagnosis, assessment and recommendation, particularly among careers advisers. This is simply a list of questions to deal with in the interview, organized under seven headings. The headings are as follows:

- Physical make-up.
- Attainments.
- General intelligence.
- Special aptitudes.
- Interests.
- Disposition.
- Circumstances.

One of the most widely researched and influential person–environment fit theories of occupational choice is that of John Holland (1997). He proposed that individuals seek occupational environments which are congruent with their interests (or preferences for particular work activities). The theory states that:

- People and occupational environments can be categorized into six interest types: realistic, investigative, artistic, social, enterprising and conventional.
- Occupational choice is the result of attempts to achieve congruence between interests and environment.
- Congruence results in job satisfaction and stability.

Although Holland's main proposition, that individuals make occupational choices that are congruent with their interests, has generally been supported by research (see, for example, Spokane, 1985), other work casts some doubt on his assertion that congruence results in satisfaction and stability (Tinsley, 2000; Tranberg et al., 1993). Nevertheless, Holland's model has provided one theoretical rationale for a diagnostic approach to careers work. A core activity for the career counsellor is the assessment of occupational interests and the identification of occupations which match the client's interest profile. Some of the instruments which might be used are outlined later in this chapter. The theory can also be criticized, however, for its predominantly static approach to occupational choice. Holland also fails to consider social and economic factors as determinants of choice, and we know very little about what happens to employees in 'incongruent' occupations over time. One might ask whether interests and occupations become more congruent as the individual becomes socialized into an organization, and how organizations might facilitate this process. Also, some writers have questioned the validity of Holland's sixfold model of interests. Prediger (2000), for example, has argued for a more parsimonious two-dimensional model of 'people' versus 'things' and 'data' versus 'ideas'. And Hirsh et al. (1998) have questioned the extent to which any one framework can be valid in describing both individual attributes and work environments in the same terms.

Developmental theories

Other writers have taken a developmental view of careers, paying attention to the processes leading up to the initial choice of job and to later developmental tasks.

Donald Super is perhaps the most well known proponent of this type of theory, with his proposition that career development proceeds through stages as the individual seeks to implement the self-concept in an occupation. His original stage theory (Super, 1957) portrayed career development as proceeding through five stages: growth, exploration, establishment, maintenance and decline. A more recent formulation (Super et al., 1988) incorporates four stages and, within each, three sub-stages:

- Exploration: crystallization, specification, implementation.
- Establishment: stabilizing, consolidating, advancing.
- Maintenance: holding, updating, innovating.
- Disengagement: deceleration, retirement planning, retirement living.

This model also has a revised view of the relationship between age and stage, which was previously fairly fixed. Individuals are acknowledged to 'recycle' – those experiencing mid-career change, for example, would be expected to demonstrate some of the concerns of early working life.

Super has also provided us with a framework for viewing careers within the context of the individual's total 'life space' and the various roles within it. His life-span, life-space model (Super, 1980) uses the image of a rainbow with bands that represent the different roles a person assumes during the course of his or her life. Initially the life space contains only one role, that of the child, but during adulthood many people experience seven or eight roles, as when a person is employed in an occupation, studying part-time, being a parent, being a spouse, maintaining a home, supporting ageing parents and pursuing hobbies. Obviously other roles can be identified, too, and not all roles apply to all individuals. Also, the sequencing of roles may vary.

Portraying roles in this way illustrates how the number and nature of activities that we may have to assume in adulthood may be difficult to integrate. On the other hand, roles may enrich each other, as when studying part-time (learner role) enhances performance and satisfaction at work (worker role).

Super's work stimulated a considerable amount of research into the exploration stage of development, particularly into the role of self-concepts in the entry into work. Much less research effort has been directed to issues within later stages, however. This may be because the processes set out as being characteristic of the later stages are discussed in a very general descriptive way. There is little attempt at explanation and it is difficult to formulate testable hypotheses beyond general statements. The model also fails to address the question of what happens to individuals once they become participants in organizations.

The impact of Super's work and other developmental models (see, for example, Ginzberg et al., 1951) on the practice of careers guidance was profound, though. They suggested an educational approach to careers work, which emphasized helping the individual become more aware of self and the world of work and using this knowledge in career decision making. The overarching aim of career guidance became helping individuals make decisions for themselves, rather than persuading them to accept expert recommendations. These models also provided a powerful rationale for the introduction of career education in schools, and their implications for individual career counselling were no less radical. Simple matching approaches and techniques were questioned, and practitioners were encouraged to use client-centred counselling skills in individual and group work.

In essence, then, the earliest models of guidance emphasized *content*, in the form of *gathering information* about the client's abilities, interests and circumstances, and of *giving information* about options. These models have been supplemented by approaches which attend much more to the *process* of career counselling and the *relationship* between the practitioner and the client, and to helping clients develop the skills and knowledge to engage in autonomous decision making.

Opportunity structure theory

In Britain the most robust challenge to psychological theories of career development, whether person–environment fit or developmental, came from Ken Roberts, a sociologist. He castigated psychologists for not taking account of situational variables such as social class and labour market opportunities, and argued that, for many, choice is a myth, since occupational entry is determined largely by the system of social stratification (Roberts, 1968). Roberts's 'opportunity structure' theory operates largely at the societal level of analysis, so it has little to say directly about career interventions at the level of the individual. What it does do, however, is go some way towards defining the structural constraints within which career guidance takes place. If we accept the influence of social and opportunity structures on occupational entry, one obvious role for guidance is to attempt to lubricate the mechanisms through which individuals become 'allocated' to jobs. On the other hand, however, guidance could help individuals explore and question the impact of these structural forces.

Roberts's more recent work shows that while life chances still remain as dependent as ever on social class background and educational attainment, young people's biographies have become more 'individualized' and their future more uncertain as they experience more diversity in their employment patterns (Roberts, 1997). Career guidance, therefore, has to 'trade in possibilities rather than certainties or even probabilities' (Roberts, 1997: 352).

Career management theories

At the risk of over-generalizing, it is probably true to say that, historically, British writers have paid more attention to the impact of economic and social factors on career development, particularly initial occupational choices, than their American counterparts. A more interactive perspective on careers has emerged on both sides of the Atlantic, however. This has been prompted by the need to take account of employees' insecurity and uncertainty in the face of organizational 'downsizing' and delayering, the increase in part-time and fixed-term contracts of employment, and more job changing generally.

In Britain, Herriot and Pemberton (1996), for example, have built on the American work of Argyris (1960) and Rousseau (1990) to propose a model which defines organizational careers as 'the repeated renegotiation of the psychological contract', based on a perceived match between the 'wants' of each party (the individual and the employer) and what the other has to offer (Herriot and Pemberton, 1996: 762). Two kinds of contract result from these negotiations: transactional, where there is simply an instrumental exchange between the parties (for example, performance in exchange for compensation), and relational, where mutual commitment is implied (such as loyalty in exchange for security). The strong emotional reactions experienced by individuals when their relationship with their employer breaks down (for example, where the employee is made redundant or where a promised promotion fails to materialize) are, it is argued, often a consequence of the breaking of a relational contract.

The work of Nicholson and West (1988) is another example of the move towards a more dynamic view of the relationship between individuals and organizations. They portray careers as sequences of 'work-role transitions' where individuals experience recurring states of adjustment to change and preparation for new roles, either within the same organization or after a change of employer.

The main strength of both these models is that they attempt to explain careers as on-going events and experiences which take place in an organizational context where change is a continuous feature. Although they are essentially models of organizational careers and they have relatively little to say about the self-employed, or, indeed, about those in semi- and unskilled work, their central message is that career development is much more than a sequence of occupational decisions; it involves on-going interaction and negotiation with the social environment. The implication for individuals, then, is that, in order to have a base for negotiation with employers, they need to be clear about their work identities and values (that is, how they view work in the context of other aspects of their life, and what they want from it). Furthermore, negotiation skills are important in career management, and individuals need to recognize their negotiating power. This emphasis on work identities and becoming an agent in one's life is consistent with constructivist theories of careers (see, for example, Cochran, 1997) which focus on how work fits into people's lives, rather than assessing 'fit' between individuals and occupations. This approach also emphasizes the importance of individuals gaining understanding of the context in which their careers develop.

Debates about the future of work lead to similar conclusions about the range of career planning and career management skills that will be required. The scenario of labour market opportunities consisting largely of short-term contracts, part-time work and 'portfolio' careers may be overstated, but the moves already apparent towards greater numerical and functional flexibility will demand that individuals will need to be clear about their development needs, more knowledgeable about the labour market generally, and prepared to develop the 'meta-skills' of continuously monitoring self and situation (Kidd and Killeen, 1992). Emotionally, individuals will need the capacity to cope with uncertainty and insecurity, with the likelihood of frequent job moves, and also, of course, with the prospect of periods of unemployment. Those coping well will view the future optimistically, may positively welcome changes of job and employer and the challenge of working with new people, and will have the confidence to challenge exploitative practices in the workplace. This affective component has largely been overlooked in career development theory (Kidd, 1998), though London (1983) has suggested the term 'career resilience' to describe the maintenance or persistence aspect of career development.

This leads to a threefold model of career development, incorporating decision-making skills, career management skills and what might be called, after London, 'career resilience' (though the term is used here more broadly). The main features of each of the three components are set out in Figure 22.1.

Figure 22.1   Components of career development

Career decision-making (Specific knowledge and skills)	Career management (Identity clarification and meta-skills)	Career resilience (Attitudes and emotions)
Relating self- and opportunity-awareness	On-going assessment of values and goals Monitoring and exploring self and situation Negotiating	Confidence Hope Flexibility Self-esteem Self-reliance

It follows, then, that career development work with individuals will need to attend to all these components. It also needs to be recognized, however, that many presenting problems will be ramifications of broader personal and emotional issues, as was suggested at the beginning of this chapter.

As we saw earlier, within most sectors the range of activities encompassed in career development work has become increasingly broad, covering group work and self-help activities as well as individual counselling. It seems likely that these developments will continue, as computer-aided career guidance systems and career resource centres become more sophisticated and practitioners and clients see the value of workshop-type activities, both in employing organizations and elsewhere. However, whilst these types of intervention are well suited to provide opportunities for basic self-assessment activities and for information seeking, they are unlikely to be able to provide adequate support for the angry client facing redundancy, or for someone trying to build the confidence to re-enter the labour market after a period at home bringing up a family. One-to-one work is likely to continue to form the basis of provision for many clients, possibly combined with other activities, and many will also benefit from in-depth psychometric assessment, where individual feedback and interpretation are crucial. The next section of this chapter, therefore, will focus on the individual career counselling process.

The career counselling process

The challenge for counselling psychologists involved in careers work is to be able to work effectively with both career and wider personal issues, attending to the cognitive and affective aspects of both. This task also presents a challenge for career counselling theory. In contrast to career development theory, which attempts to describe and explain development, theories of career counselling aim to prescribe how counsellors might intervene in career development.

As we have seen, new perspectives on careers and on career counselling have emerged over time to meet the needs of individuals in dealing with the tasks of career development. Significantly, though, the role of these new theories has generally been to *supplement* the range of theories available to practitioners, rather than *replace* any of them. Currently, then, there exists a rich and diverse set of models and conceptual frameworks for the counselling psychologist to work with. Few career counsellors take a 'single school' approach: in a survey of careers officers, careers advisers in higher education and educational guidance workers, only 20 per cent reported that they used one model of interviewing (Kidd et al., 1997). For many an 'eclectic' approach will prevail, and practitioners may need to be helped to appreciate how elements from a range of theoretical perspectives can contribute to effective practice (Kidd, 1996). In this section some of the theories and perspectives that have potential in helping us understand the flow of sessions with the client will be outlined.

The career counselling process is characterized as comprising four stages: building the relationship; enabling clients' self-understanding; exploring new perspectives; and forming strategies and plans. This is, of course, an oversimple model of the process – in many cases sessions will move back and forth between these stages – but it will serve to illustrate some of the key activities. Within these stages the aim is to identify the main tasks for client and counsellor and illustrate how certain theoretical perspectives contribute to a fuller understanding of each. Space constraints preclude a comprehensive discussion of the nature of each stage and relevant counsellor skills. For this the reader is referred to one of the key texts on career counselling. Walsh and Osipow (1990), for example, discuss tasks and skills in relation to a range of theoretical orientations, while Nathan and Hill (1992) and Ali and Graham (1996) are more practice-based. The stages and associated main tasks are set out in Table 22.1.

Building the relationship

The image of the career counselling psychologist as 'expert', offering advice and recommendations on suitable careers, is an enduring one. Moreover, many clients expect the counselling sessions to revolve around information about jobs or courses and are disappointed when they do not receive it. It is important, therefore, to help clients understand that career counselling is a collaborative venture, and that they need to be an active participant in the process at every stage.

As Nathan and Hill (1992) have pointed out, it is possible to begin to encourage clients to have realistic expectations of the counselling process even before the two parties meet. Written information about the goals of counselling and how they may be achieved helps to minimize misunderstandings, as can a telephone conversation. Agreeing a client–counsellor contract is crucial in the first session, however. At a basic level, issues of confidentiality and the number, length and frequency of meetings will need to be discussed, but the nature of the counselling process itself will also need to be covered, including the

Table 22.1 Some key tasks within each stage of career counselling

Stages	Key tasks
1 Building the relationship	Establishing the working alliance
2 Enabling clients' self-understanding	Assessment
3 Exploring new perspectives	Information-giving Challenging
4 Forming strategies and plans	Reviewing progress Goal-setting

responsibilities of the counsellor and the client, the techniques that may be used, and the limits of the relationship.

A considerable body of literature confirms the importance of the 'working alliance' to the success of any helping relationship. Among the first to use this term was Bordin (1979), who saw the working alliance as arising out of the transference relationship that the client develops with the counsellor in psycho-analysis, but he also emphasized its importance in other helping settings, including teaching and group work. According to Bordin, the three dimensions of the working alliance are the clarity and strength of the personal *bonds* between the client and the counsellor, and the extent of agreement about first the *goals* of the helping process, and secondly the *tasks* to be carried out.

Egan (1994) also discusses the importance of establishing a contract with the client at the start of the relationship, which may need to be renegotiated several times during the course of the process. This may seem fairly straightforward, but research with careers officers suggests that many were confused about what the contract should consist of and were concerned that the contract could come to dominate the interview, particularly where it was relatively short (Kidd et al., 1997).

Considering the client's cultural origin may be particularly important here. Clients from cultures that emphasize respect for authority may find it difficult to accept that the responsibility for decision making is their own and not the counselling psychologist's. Furthermore, those from cultures where family and group responsibilities take precedence over individual needs may be unused and reluctant to engage in self-reflection and assessment. This will need to be recognized by the counselling psychologist both early on and throughout the counselling process.

Confusion about the working alliance may arise from within the counselling psychologist as well as from the client. Career counsellors who work mainly with young clients facing initial career decisions, perhaps using a predomi-nantly person–environment fit orientation, may feel uncomfortable faced with a middle-aged man who has just been made redundant. The consequence may be that they fail to explore the issue of how much support they can offer the client in coming to terms with his situation, and may want to move too quickly into assessment and information-giving activities.

Enabling clients' self-understanding

During the second stage of the helping process the main task is to help clients deepen their understanding and their insight into their situation. A core activity is likely to be some form of assessment of career-relevant attributes, such as interests, aptitudes and values. Much of the value of assessment at this stage is that it helps clients become familiar with conceptual frameworks to organize their knowledge of self and situation, and simple self-assessment tools, as well as knowledge gained through the interview itself, frequently produce insights which are just as illuminating as those gained by psychometric instruments.

Counselling psychologists working within a person–environment fit orientation emphasize the diagnostic value of tests and inventories. In contrast, those using developmental and person-centred approaches often see test results mainly as a stimulus to discussion. Commonly used occupational interest measures include the Strong Interests Inventory and the SHL Advanced Occupational Interests Inventory. Several self-help devices are also available (see, for example, the interests questionnaire in Hopson and Scally, 1993). Instruments to assess work values, or the satisfactions sought from work, include Pryor's Work Aspect Preference Scale and Super's Work Values Inventory, and most self-help books include checklists of values. Of particular relevance to work with adults are measures based on Schein's concept of career anchors (see, for example, Schein, 1993). Examples of standard tests for the assessment of aptitudes are the Differential Aptitudes Test and the Morrisby Differential Test Battery. Comprehensive reviews of instruments that might be used in career assessment are given in Bartram and Lindley (1997) and Lindley (2000).

It should be noted that many test publishers restrict the supply of their tests to psychologists, those with level A and B testing qualifications from the British Psychological Society or those who have attended the publisher's own course on the use of a particular test.

A less structured way of helping clients assess abilities and skills is to employ a technique known as 'systematic reflection on experience'. This is particularly useful for helping individuals identify 'transferable skills' from previous experience in work and in other settings, such as leisure activities. Clients are asked to reflect on a particular experience, which may be a previous job or some other activity, and the counsellor helps them to:

- *Review the experience* by describing how they carried out the activity and the satisfactions sought and achieved from it.
- *Conclude from the experience* by describing what they feel they learned about their skills and abilities from the activity.
- *Plan the next steps* by identifying other situations in which that learning may be appropriate, and describing how they might generalize that learning to these situations.

It may be helpful to provide a framework for categorizing the skills that emerge. One way of doing this would be to classify them using Prediger's (2000) dimensions:

- *Data*, the skills used to organize and evaluate facts or data.
- *Ideas*, the skills used in creatively using words, concepts, figures and music.
- *People*, the skills used in working with other people, helping, teaching, serving, motivating, or persuading.
- *Things*, the skills used in making, repairing or servicing things.

Systematic reflection on experience is an approach which may be particularly helpful in working with people who are unemployed or have been out of the labour market for some time, or who have few formal qualifications. Because it enables clients to focus on what has been learned from 'informal learning' and on strengths rather than weaknesses, it can be a powerful tool in promoting self-confidence and self-esteem.

Other assessment techniques during this stage of the counselling process are informed by rather different models of careers. As we saw earlier, developmental theories of careers pay more attention to continuous, lifelong processes of career development. They also view career decision making and career management within the context of other life roles. A developmental approach to assessment therefore needs to encourage clients to take a holistic view of career issues, helping them explore the relative importance of work in their lives and potential conflicts between life roles. Constructivist approaches also focus on subjective meanings of work and careers. For example, Cochran (1997) describes a narrative approach to career counselling which focuses on helping clients identify themes and patterns in their careers.

Super's rainbow diagram, or some variation of it, may be helpful in increasing clients' awareness of roles. Also, some feelings and ideas may be hard to verbalize and graphic devices like the rainbow may be helpful for clients who find it easier to express themselves in diagrams rather than words. There are numerous other examples of these sorts of tools, of course, including lifelines and force-field analysis (Hopson and Scally, 1993).

Exploring new perspectives

At the third stage a key task is to help clients develop new perspectives on their problems. The counselling psychologist's active contribution at this point is crucial, especially in challenging the client in various ways and helping him or her 'reality-test' their expectations and aspirations. Egan (1994) defines challenging as 'an invitation to examine internal or external behaviour that seems to be self-defeating, harmful to others, or both, and to change the behaviour if it is found to be so'. So clients may be challenged, for example, to confront inconsistent beliefs about themselves, question strategically unsound plans and recognize mismatches of job ideas with local opportunities. Writers who view challenging as central to the career counselling process include Krumboltz (1981), who emphasizes the role of social learning in career development, and those who have applied rational-emotive therapy to career counselling (see, for example, Dryden, 1979).

Krumboltz's social learning framework highlights the importance of behavioural counselling skills such as reinforcement and modelling. Of particular relevance to this stage, however, are the cognitive strategies which the counselling psychologist may employ to challenge erroneous beliefs. Some of Mitchell and Krumboltz's (1990) guidelines for assessing and changing 'faulty' beliefs are as follows:

- Identify the assumptions and presuppositions behind the expressed belief.
- Examine inconsistencies between words and actions.
- Confront what seem to be simplistic answers.
- Challenge attempts to build illogical arguments.
- Attempt to assess the validity of strongly held beliefs.

It goes without saying that an insensitive use of these kinds of strategies and techniques will be unhelpful or even damaging. Challenging is unlikely to be appropriate early in the career counselling process and it should be attempted only when a trusting relationship has been established.

Labour market information may also be needed at this stage. Most clients will need information about occupational and educational options as well as trends within the labour market generally. A vast amount of career-related information is available, through directories such as the American *Directory of Occupational Titles*, CD-ROMs or the internet (see Offer, 2000, for a review of internet resources). Much careers material, however, is concerned with the characteristics of occupations, such as work activities, skills needed, levels of entry, and types of education and training needed. In contrast, information about organizational environments, in terms of size, structure, culture and human resource strategies, is less readily available. While counselling psychologists working with clients on problems relating to occupational choices are well served with respect to information resources, therefore, those helping individuals with predominantly mid-life career management concerns, such as negotiating career systems and pathways within their organization or contemplating an organizational career move within the same occupational field have very few information resources to refer to. As our earlier discussion of labour market changes and changes in concepts of career showed, clients will increasingly need knowledge of organizations' human resource systems and cultures: for example, the extent to which they operate an internal or external labour market, how much support for employee development is offered, how much emphasis is placed on team as opposed to individual performance, and, crucially, their overall business strategy and plans for the future. Much of this kind of information will be outside the public domain, but some services, outplacement agencies in particular, meet some of these needs through their networks with employers.

Within facilitative, client-centred models of career counselling, where a central goal is to encourage clients to seek out information for themselves, the most appropriate role for the counsellor is that of the supportive 'general practitioner' (Nathan and Hill, 1992). A knowledge of how to access information and where to refer clients who need specialist information is more in line with the values of counselling than specific information giving during the interview. Indeed, as Nathan and Hill point out, using the career counselling session as a vehicle for feeding the client information may confuse the counselling contract and lead the client into a passive role. The counselling psychologist will also need to help clients relate occupational information to their self-assessments, evaluate it and deal with their emotional reactions to it. Challenging will be an important skill here.

Forming strategies and plans

It should be clear that client responsibility lies at the heart of the counselling model proposed here. This means that 'action' will be an integral part of the process at all stages as well as in the final phases. Action does not necessarily imply changes in behaviour: the term is used to denote internal changes in thoughts and feelings, as well as observable actions. A client may, for example, have made progress towards clarifying whether self-employment would really suit her; have become more confident about the transferable skills he possesses; or be nearer to a decision about a career after graduation.

Towards the end of the counselling process, particularly, time will need to be set aside for reviewing progress. Nathan and Hill (1992) suggest that such a review will serve a number of purposes, for example:

- It prepares the client for the end of the relationship.
- It helps the client to see career counselling in perspective.
- Highlighting the progress made will strengthen the client's confidence and resolve.
- It emphasizes the client's continuing responsibility for her or his own development.

In doing this it may be helpful to review the contract made at the beginning of counselling, and recall the agreed objectives.

A central activity in preparing for the end of the counselling relationship will be helping clients set goals and decide on the steps they need to take to achieve them. The literature on goal setting is helpful here (see, for example, Locke and Latham, 1984). To be achievable, goals need to be:

- Clear, specific and expressed in behavioural terms.
- Measurable.
- Realistic.
- Owned by the individual.
- In line with the client's values.
- Realistically scheduled.

The process of goal setting should clearly specify the targets to be reached. A client who, for example, wishes to explore the possibility of self-employment might decide that the first task is to approach acquaintances who work for themselves to explore advantages and disadvantages. This goal might be measurable in terms of the number of people talked to and the range of life-style aspects of self-employment explored.

Goals should be achievable, but not too easy, and within the client's control. A client who sets himself the task of writing six job applications a week may be realistic about what he can achieve in the time, but if part of the goal is to be offered two interviews as a result, failing to achieve it could be harmful to his motivation and self-esteem.

According to Locke and Latham, participation in goal setting and ownership of goals leads to increased performance and feelings of competence. This seems to be because there is an increased likelihood of the individual acting to achieve the goals. Participation will also increase the possibility that goals will be congruent with clients' value systems.

Setting a realistic time plan for the achievement of goals seems to be important for successful accomplishment. This may involve identifying sub-goals which lead individuals to the main goal by making incremental demands on them.

Written action plans are increasingly used to express clients' goals and means of achieving them. This is especially so in the Careers Service, as government funding has begun to depend on numbers of action plans completed. When used simply as evidence that an interview has taken place action plans can be unhelpful and inappropriate, particularly when pre-structured plans are used. However, plans geared to the specific needs of the client are a useful way of clarifying the client's commitment to certain activities, and the act of writing the plan can be a powerful impetus to action.

Evaluation of the effectiveness of careers work

In this final section we move on to consider the effectiveness of career development work, broadly defined. Early evaluation studies were concerned with the effectiveness of career guidance offered in the form of occupational recommendations made to young people by juvenile employment officers. Career outcomes were used as criteria: evaluators assessed whether clients who accepted the recommendations showed greater job satisfaction and success and less occupational mobility than those who did not (see, for example, Burt et al., 1926). Few studies employed control groups to test the hypothesis that those exposed to guidance benefited in comparison with those who were not.

There are considerable methodological problems with these kinds of studies. Among them are the questionable validity and reliability of many of the outcome measures and doubts about their appropriateness. (Job mobility, for example, was viewed as unsatisfactory and indicative of a lack of adjustment to work.) Furthermore, there was no way of knowing whether the occupational recommendations arose from the guidance intervention – they may simply have reflected the pre-existing intentions of the young person.

With moves towards a more developmental approach, evaluators, particularly in the United States, began to attend to assessing the 'learning outcomes' of career guidance and counselling. Learning outcomes can be defined as the 'skills, knowledge and attitudes which facilitate rational occupational and educational decision-making and the effective implementation of occupational and educational decisions' (Kidd and Killeen, 1992). They include awareness of one's own abilities and interests, knowledge of opportunities and options, decision-making skills, transition skills and general attitudes to decision making.

Much of the evidence for these kinds of learning outcomes comes from American studies using controlled trials with pre/post designs. Self-report instruments, such as the Career Factors Inventory (Chartrand et al., 1990) are commonly used to assess outcomes, but tests of career knowledge and skills, for example those within so-called 'career maturity' instruments such as the Career Development Inventory (Super et al., 1981) are also available.

So how effective is careers work in these terms? The clearest evidence for effectiveness comes from meta-analyses, which pool the findings of large numbers of published studies. In one of the most rigorous meta-analyses conducted, Whiston et al. (1998) analysed the findings of 268 studies involving 4,660 participants. The interventions covered a wide range of activities including career education courses, group work, self-help materials (including computer-aided guidance) and individual career counselling. Their overall conclusion was that most kinds of career intervention are moderately effective with most age groups. Individual career counselling was the most effective and efficient intervention, while computer interventions were the most cost-effective. Effect sizes were greatest for the outcomes of career skills (e.g. preparation for interviews and career problem solving) and career maturity.

The evidence also suggests, not surprisingly, that some types of intervention are more helpful to some individuals than others. Kivlighan et al. (1981), for example, showed that 'task-orientated' clients responded more favourably to individual counselling based on problem-solving techniques, while 'people-centred' clients responded better to group counselling.

If most types of intervention are beneficial to some degree, how and why do the effects occur? Holland et al. (1981), examining the interventions employed in hundreds of studies varying widely in sophistication, concluded that four ingredients were essential for success:

- The acquisition of cognitive frameworks for understanding self, opportunities and their relationship.
- Information about self and the world of work, using these frameworks.
- Cognitive rehearsal of aspirations.
- Social support or reinforcement.

It seems to be reasonably clear, then, that career guidance and counselling enhance career-related knowledge and attitudes, at least in the short term. British evidence is scarce, however, as are studies of adult clients. There is also a need for longitudinal research which links immediate learning outcomes with ultimate career or economic outcomes, such as job satisfaction and performance, duration of unemployment and participation in education and training (Killeen et al., 1992).

A further drawback with the evaluation research carried out so far is that, in contrast to career decision making, very little attention has been paid to assessing the career management or career resilience components of career development, such as exploratory behaviour, negotiating skills and a sense of confidence in the future. Among the scant evidence available is an evaluation of a career development programme for women (Kingdon and Bimline, 1987) which produced increases in self-esteem and growth motivation, and a study by Noe et al. (1990) which indicated that encouraging subordinates to set career goals resulted in greater career commitment and increased ability to adapt to changing circumstances.

For the future, then, research will need to address a broader range of outcomes than hitherto. Of equal importance, though, is rigorous examination of the variety of activities practitioners engage in within the realm of careers work. As we have seen, career guidance is a multi-faceted process, and research needs to attend to the relative impact of different approaches and techniques, and the merits of taking an eclectic as opposed to a 'single school' approach.

Conclusion

Comparing career guidance provision at the beginning of the twenty first century with the situation six years ago, when the first edition of this volume was published, this is a time of considerable change as far as young people are concerned. The introduction of the Connexions service is likely to have a major effect on the structures through which guidance is provided. A single national agency will be responsible for meeting all the support needs of young people, and this has raised fears that resources will be aimed primarily at the socially disadvantaged, with others experiencing a reduced level of service (Watts, 2001). As far as adults are concerned, however, the situation has changed little: access to career counselling and guidance is still extremely limited.

One of the aims of this chapter has been to set the practice of careers work within a theoretical context. Given the diversity of settings in which career guidance and counselling takes place, the range of issues it has to address, and the variety of interventions which may be used, it is clear that our understanding of the processes involved can be enhanced by applying paradigms and perspectives from several disciplines within the social sciences. Even in this brief review, we have seen how differentialist psychology, developmental psychology, organizational psychology and functionalist sociology all contribute in their various ways to a more complete understanding of careers, and, furthermore, how a range of perspectives on counselling can inform the career counselling process. Had space permitted, it would have been possible to discuss and debate contributions from other areas of psychology, such as group dynamics, and, indeed, the relevance of other social science disciplines, for example economics and anthropology. We need multiple perspectives on career development, on the social and organizational environments within which careers are experienced, and on career counselling practice. Having practitioners from a wider range of backgrounds working in the field (for example, counselling psychologists, careers advisers and occupational psychologists) would facilitate communication between different disciplines and perspectives. The challenge for counselling psychologists and others working with career issues is to draw on these various perspectives to build a coherent psychological framework for practice and for further research, while remaining open to new ideas from a range of disciplines within the social sciences.

References

Ali, L. and Graham, B. (1996) *The Counselling Approach to Careers Guidance.* London: Routledge.

Argyris, C. (1960) *Understanding Organizational Behavior.* Homewood IL: Dorsey Press.

Bartram, D. and Lindley, P. (1997) *Review of Ability and Aptitude Tests (Level A).* Leicester: British Psychological Society.

Bordin, E.S. (1979) 'The generalizability of the psychoanalytic concept of the working alliance', *Psychotherapy, Research and Practice,* 16: 252–60.

Burt, C., Gaw, F., Ramsey, L., Smith, M. and Spielman, W. (1926) *A Study in Vocational Guidance.* MRC Industrial Fatigue Research Board Report 33. London: HMSO.

Chartrand, J.M., Robbins, S.B., Morrill, W.H. and Boggs, K. (1990) 'Development and validation of the Career Factors Inventory', *Journal of Counseling Psychology,* 37: 191–201.

Cochran, L. (1997) *Career Counseling: a Narrative Approach.* Thousand Oaks CA: Sage.

Dryden, W. (1979) 'Rational-emotive therapy and its contribution to careers counselling', *British Journal of Guidance and Counselling,* 7; 181–7.

Egan, G. (1994) *The Skilled Helper,* fifth edition. Pacific Grove CA: Brooks Cole.

Ginzberg, E., Ginsburg, S.W., Axelrad, S. and Herma, J.L. (1951) *Occupational Choice: an Approach to a General Theory.* New York: Columbia University Press.

Herriot, P. and Pemberton, C. (1996) 'Contracting careers', *Human Relations,* 49: 757–90.

Hirsh, W., Kidd, J.M. and Watts, A.G. (1998) *Constructs of Work used in Career Guidance.* Cambridge: National Institute for Careers Education and Counselling.

Holland, J.L. (1997) *Making Vocational Choices: a Theory of Vocational Personalities and Work Environments,* third edition. Odessa FL: Psychological Assessment Resources.

Holland, J.L., Magoon, T.M. and Spokane, A.R. (1981) 'Counseling psychology: career interventions, research and theory', *Annual Review of Psychology,* 32: 279–305.

Hopson, B. and Scally, M. (1993) *Build your own Rainbow: a Handbook for Career and Life Management.* Leeds: Lifeskills Associates.

Kidd, J.M. (1996) 'The career counselling interview' in A.G. Watts, B. Law, J. Killeen, J.M. Kidd and R. Hawthorn, *Rethinking Careers Education and Guidance: Theory, Policy and Practice.* London: Routledge.

Kidd, J.M. (1998) 'Emotion: an absent presence in career theory', *Journal of Vocational Behavior,* 52: 275–88.

Kidd, J.M. and Killeen, J. (1992) 'Are the effects of careers guidance worth having? Changes in practice and outcomes', *Journal of Occupational and Organizational Psychology,* 65: 219–34.

Kidd, J.M., Killeen, J., Jarvis, J. and Offer, M. (1997) 'Competing schools or stylistic variation in careers guidance interviewing', *British Journal of Guidance and Counselling,* 25: 47–65.

Killeen, J. and Kidd, J.M. (1991) *Learning Outcomes of Guidance: a Review of Recent Research.* Research Paper 85. London: Department of Employment.

Killeen, J., White, M. and Watts, A.G. (1992) *The Economic Value of Careers Guidance.* London: Policy Studies Institute.

Kingdon, M.A. and Bimline, C.A. (1987) 'Evaluating the effectiveness of career develop-ment training for women', *Career Development Quarterly*, 35: 220–7.

Kivlighan, D.M., Hageseth, J.A., Tipton, R.M. and McGovern, T.V. (1981) 'Effects of matching treatment, approaches and personality types in group vocational counsel-ing', *Journal of Counseling Psychology*, 28: 315–20.

Krumboltz, J.D. (1981) 'A social learning theory of career selection', in D.H. Montross and C.J. Shinkman (eds) *Career Development in the 1980s*. Springfield IL: Thomas.

Lindley, P. (ed.) (2000) *Review of Personality Assessment Instruments (Level B) for Use in Occupational Settings*. Leicester: British Psychological Society.

Locke, E.A. and Latham, G.P. (1984) *Goal Setting: a Motivational Technique that Works!* Englewood Cliffs NJ: Prentice Hall.

London, M. (1983) 'Toward a theory of career motivation', *Academy of Management Review*, 8: 620–30.

Mitchell, L.K. and Krumboltz, J.D. (1990) 'Social learning approach to career decision making: Krumboltz's theory', in D. Brown and L. Brooks (eds) *Career Choice and Development: Applying Contemporary Theories to Practice*. San Francisco: Jossey Bass.

Nathan, R. and Hill, L. (1992) *Career Counselling*. London: Sage.

Nicholson, N. and West, M. (1988) *Managerial Job Change: Men and Women in Transition*. Cambridge: Cambridge University Press.

Noe, R.A., Noe, A.W. and Bachhuber, J.A. (1990) 'Correlates of career motivation', *Journal of Vocational Behavior*, 37: 340–56.

Offer, M. (2000) *Careers Professionals' Guide to the Internet*. Richmond: Trotman.

Parsons, F. (1909) *Choosing a Vocation*. Boston MA: Houghton Mifflin.

Prediger, D.J. (2000) 'Holland's hexagon is alive and well – though somewhat out of shape: response to Tinsley', *Journal of Vocational Behavior*, 56: 197–204.

Roberts, K. (1968) 'The entry into employment: an approach towards a general theory', *Sociological Review*, 16: 165–84.

Roberts, K. (1997) 'Prolonged transitions to uncertain destinations: the implications for careers guidance', *British Journal of Guidance and Counselling*, 25: 345–60.

Rodger, A. (1952) *The Seven-point Plan*. London: NIIP.

Rousseau, D.M. (1990) 'New hire perceptions of their own and their employer's obliga-tions: a study of psychological contracts', *Journal of Organizational Behavior*, 11: 389–400.

Schein, E.H. (1993) *Careers Anchors: Discovering your Real Values*. San Diego CA: Pfeiffer.

Spokane, A.R. (1985) 'A review of research on person–environment congruence in Holland's theory of careers', *Journal of Vocational Behavior*, 31: 37–44.

Super, D.E. (1957) *The Psychology of Careers*. New York: Harper.

Super, D.E. (1980) 'A life-span, life-space approach to career development', *Journal of Vocational Behavior*, 16: 282–98.

Super, D.E., Thompson, A.S., Lindeman, R.H., Jordaan, J.P. and Myers, R.A. (1981) *Career Development Inventory*. Palo Alto CA: Consulting Psychologists Press.

Super, D.E., Thompson, A.S., Lindeman, R.H., Myers, R.A. and Jordaan, J.P. (1988) *Adult Career Concerns Inventory*. Palo Alto CA: Consulting Psychologists Press.

Tinsley, H.E.A. (2000) 'The congruence myth: an analysis of the efficacy of the person-environment fit model', *Journal of Vocational Behavior*, 56: 147–79.

Tranberg, M., Slane, S. and Ekeberg, S.E. (1993) 'The relationship between interest con-gruence and satisfaction: a meta-analysis', *Journal of Vocational Behavior*, 42: 253–64.

Walsh, W.B. and Osipow, S.H. (eds) (1990) *Career Counseling*. Hillsdale NJ: Erlbaum.

Watts, A.G. (2001) 'Career guidance and social exclusion: a cautionary tale', *British Journal of Guidance and Counselling*, 29: 157–76.

Watts, A.G. and Sadler, J. (2000) *Quality Guidance: a Sectoral Analysis*. Cambridge: CRAC/GAB.

Whiston, S.C., Sexton, T.L. and Lasoff, D.L. (1998) 'Career-intervention outcome: a repli-cation and extension of Oliver and Spokane (1988)', *Journal of Counseling Psychology*, 45: 150–65.

23 Sexual Identity: Affirmative Practice with Lesbian and Gay Clients

MARTIN MILTON AND ADRIAN COYLE

Although research indicates that lesbians and gay men make substantial use of therapeutic services (Bieschke et al., 2000; Bradford et al., 1994; Hughes et al., 1997; Morgan and Eliason, 1992), the relationship between psychological theory and practice and same-sex sexuality has been troubled – and remains so in some respects (Phillips et al., 2001; Taylor, 2002). Many theorists have constructed same-sex sexuality in terms of pathology, leading therapeutic practitioners to the belief that it is appropriate to try to change the sexuality of lesbian, gay or bisexual clients to something more 'normal' and more 'healthy' – namely, heterosexuality. This tendency is particularly evident in psychodynamic formulations of homosexuality as 'inversion' (Freud, 1977), Jungian interpretations of same-sex sexuality as a problematic over-identification with the contra-sexual (Hopcke, 1989) and behavioural and medical approaches to aversion therapy (Kellett, 1998; Schmidt and Schorsch, 1981; Spencer, 1995). It is manifested both in overtly negative statements (Garnets et al., 1991) and also in the silence on and failure to engage with same-sex sexuality that characterize the responses of some therapeutic domains and practitioners (Coyle et al., 1999). Whilst there have been some developments in recent decades, psychological theory and practice often still struggle to understand sexualities that differ from heterosexuality or that challenge standard assumptions about how sexuality should be structured and organized. This struggle was evident in the responses of some members of the British Psychological Society to the campaign to establish a Lesbian and Gay Psychology Section within the society in the 1990s: although the campaign (which achieved its aim in 1998) produced some reasoned debate and well articulated argument, it also elicited toxic, personalized, anti-lesbian and gay abuse from members (Kitzinger and Coyle, 2002).

This problematic past (and, in some places, still problematic present) poses particular issues for counselling psychology, which has an expressed commitment to recognizing and respecting diversity of experience and the impact of contextual factors in work with clients. This means that ideally counselling psychologists aim to work in ways which empower and which accord with high standards of anti-discriminatory practice (British Psychological Society Division of Counselling Psychology, 2001). One of the aims of this chapter, therefore, is to explore how counselling psychology might fit with these aims and with what is known as 'lesbian and gay affirmative' therapeutic practice.

Lesbian and gay affirmative therapy

In recent decades the topic of lesbian and gay affirmative therapy has become the focus of a relatively substantial literature (for key texts, see Milton and Coyle, 1998a). It has been viewed in a variety of ways, although its core principle is that it 'affirms a lesbian, gay or bisexual identity as an equally positive human experience and expression to heterosexual identity' (Davies, 1996: 25). A minority of authors have understood affirmative therapy as a particular mode of working with a set of stances that must be taken; for example, raising experiences of oppression to consciousness and undoing conditioning associated with negative stereotypes of lesbians and gay men (Clark, 1987). This may or may not be compatible with existing models of therapeutic practice. However, the majority viewpoint has seen affirmative practice as a non-discriminatory, contextually aware attitude when working with lesbian and gay clients that can be incorporated into a range of mainstream psychotherapeutic theories and practices (Davies, 1996; Ellis, 1997; Malyon, 1982; Milton et al., 2002; Shelley, 1998).

In order to review how counselling psychology might lend itself to lesbian and gay affirmative therapeutic practice, this chapter will examine the development of lesbian and gay sexuality and identity in order to contextualize a discussion of psychological distress among lesbians and gay men before examining some specifics of affirmative therapeutic practice with these groups. Note that bisexual sexuality and identity will not be accorded specific consideration because bisexuality is associated with particular developmental and life challenges and it would not be possible to do justice to these within this chapter. Also, much of the research that we draw upon has either not included bisexual men and women or has not accorded them specific and detailed attention (sometimes on the grounds that bisexuality is potentially so complex that it requires separate consideration and should not simply be regarded as analogous to lesbian and gay sexualities). For detailed considerations of bisexual development and of bisexuality and psychology see Firestein (1996), Fox (1991), Fox (1995, 2000) and Paul (1996).

The development of lesbian and gay identity

Before considering the development of lesbian and gay identity, it is necessary to define some key terms. When we refer to lesbian or gay 'sexuality', we primarily mean that which has traditionally been understood as lesbian or gay 'sexual orientation' or 'sexual preference'. These terms have been used to refer to sexualities which, in terms of physical and emotional attraction, are primarily or exclusively directed towards others of the same gender as the individual whose sexuality is under consideration. The use of the terms 'sexual orientation' and 'sexual preference' tends to map on to assumptions about the origins of these sexualities, with the former term tending to reflect biological and essentialist explanations (although some advocates of this term also invoke environmental factors) and the latter being more commonly used in social constructionist accounts.

Lesbian and gay identities are obviously related to sexual orientation/preference but refer specifically to the implications for sense of self. Lesbian or gay identity can be defined as 'the awareness of same-sex sexual attractions and the attempts to acknowledge them as self-relevant and personally meaningful and to fit them into an existing identity' (Coyle, 1992: 189). Thus, there is at least some degree of overlap between lesbian and gay identity and an individual's other identity components and commitments; together these constitute the totality of their identity. This has been recognized by some researchers who have conceptualized lesbian and/or gay identity in terms of more general theories of identity (for example, see Coyle's, 1992, and Markowe's, 1996, use of Breakwell's, 1986, process model of identity). In more specific terms, lesbian or gay identity may be seen as the outcome of efforts by an individual 'to interpret in a meaningful way the experiences that he [or she] has had which are related to his [or her] sexual preference [or orientation] and to impart coherence and purpose to those experiences by forging connections between them and formulating explanations of them' (Coyle, 1992: 189). Lesbian and gay identities can be seen as forms of 'sexual identity', which also includes bisexuality and heterosexuality (among others).

Many writers and researchers have offered descriptions of the experience of developing a lesbian or gay identity. Some have organized the process into stages. However, stage models are fraught with problems, owing to their inflexible and prescriptive nature – or at least the inflexible and prescriptive way in which they tend to be interpreted and used. Furthermore, there is empirical evidence that the gay life course is much less linear and predictable than stage models suggest (Savin-Williams, 1998). It is perhaps better to adopt a more flexible stance and consider the development of lesbian or gay identity as a set of tasks and issues that an individual encounters and addresses, each of which potentially carries developmental implications for sexual identity. What follows is a brief sketch of some key tasks and issues (for a more comprehensive account see D'Augelli and Patterson, 1995; Savin-Williams and Cohen, 1996), with the caveat that no such account can do justice to the diversity and nuances of the process of lesbian and gay identity formation (including differences between forming lesbian identity and gay identity and differences across cultural and ethnic communities): what we highlight here are merely some common, salient developmental tasks.

The nature of the tasks and issues associated with lesbian and gay identity formation is shaped by the attitudes towards homosexuality held by society in general and by the friends and family of an individual who is developing a lesbian or gay identity. Although social attitudes to homosexuality have become somewhat more positive and accepting in recent years, it is important not to generalize about the extent to which negative attitudes have diminished. The construction of same-sex sexuality as pathological and sinful by powerful social institutions – such as the medical profession and the Church – that was accepted for so long is not easily eradicated. Also, shifts in attitude do not seem to be general, with illiberal or at least ambivalent attitudes persisting on such issues as lesbians and gay men working with or raising children (Annesley and Coyle, 1995; Crawford and Solliday, 1996; Ellis, 2002) and in particular community contexts (for example, see Constantine-Simms, 2000; Greene, 1997; Phellas, 2002). Unless they have access to significant and credible others who do not hold negative views, individuals who suspect they may be lesbian or gay may be faced with negative social messages about their sexual feelings which can prove corrosive to self-esteem and psychological well-being. This can lead to a denial of same-sex sexual feelings or at least to a construction of these feelings as indicative of a 'passing phase'. Any experience of same-sex sexual activity may be denied or interpreted in a way that does not carry implications for identity, for example, as 'just experimenting'. Note that, although it is usually assumed that this process occurs in adolescence, research has also outlined how the development of lesbian or gay identity can occur later in life (for example, Kitzinger and Wilkinson, 1995), with potentially highly disruptive consequences (although it may also be the case that an older individual would have more coping strategies and resources at their disposal than would an adolescent).

If denial cannot be maintained (for example, because of the strength and persistence of same-sex feelings), the individual may accept that lesbian or gay sexuality and identity have relevance for them (although sexual attraction, sexual behaviour and sexual identity do not necessarily correspond: see Laumann et al., 1994; Weatherburn et al., 1998) and they may wish to make contact with other lesbian or gay people in order to obtain social support, advice on managing problems and dilemmas associated with sexual identity and/or sexual contact. This can be difficult, although there are many lesbian and gay-run support services which attempt to facilitate the process (for accounts of the establishment and nature of such services, see Birkett, 2001; Devine and Milton, 2000) and it has been recognized that the advent of the internet has made it easier for people to make contact with other lesbians and gay men (Markowe, 2002; McKenna and Bargh, 1998).

Initial contact with other lesbians or gay men may not, however, result in a positive outcome. This can happen if initial contact is made in a purely sexual context where there is no opportunity for social interaction, if the person lacks the social skills needed to engage with others or if they feel they have little in common with those whom they meet. Lesbian and gay communities – like other communities – are not utopian, wholly welcoming and accepting places (for example, see Davidson-Paine and Corbett, 1995, on the rejection experienced by some gay men with learning disabilities). Negative initial experiences with other lesbians or gay men can result in the person experiencing an acute sense of isolation, self-hatred and psychological strain. On the other hand, if initial or subsequent contacts with other lesbian or gay people are validating and supportive, the person can develop a positive sense of what it means to be lesbian or gay (as negative social messages are counteracted) and they may become more committed to a lesbian or gay identity. It is worth noting, however, that when an individual defines themselves as lesbian or gay, this does not mean that they will not redefine themselves at a later stage in response to changing circumstances.

One of the major tasks faced by lesbians and gay men is the management of information about their sexual identity. Individuals may disclose their sexual identity (a process that is sometimes referred to as 'coming out', although the term is also applied more generally to the entire process of developing a lesbian or gay identity) to others whom they believe will be supportive or whom they think need to be told. This can be a difficult, risky and anxiety-provoking task (Cramer and Roach, 1988; D'Augelli et al., 1998; Herdt and Boxer, 1993). However, attempts will also be made to disguise lesbian or gay sexuality from others and 'pass' as heterosexual. Even years after having initially constructed a lesbian or gay identity, many people still hide their sexual identity from at least some others in their social world, most commonly from family members, work colleagues and some friends. For example, whilst under a quarter of the 930 gay men studied by Davies et al. (1993) had disclosed their sexual identity to all their family, friends and workmates, just under a third had disclosed to fewer than half these people. This can lead to feelings of guilt, dishonesty, estrangement from others and from the self and fear of discovery. However, passing may not be as psychologically demanding as is sometimes assumed: over time, passing may become a routine way for an individual to deal with parts of their social world where the disclosure of sexual identity would be risky. For lesbian and gay young people, the social implications of not always managing to pass as heterosexual can be severe. Research on the experiences of young lesbians and gay men (and bisexuals) at school has identified high levels of bullying and victimization, which can have adverse long-term consequences for mental health (Rivers, 2000, 2001; Rivers and D'Augelli, 2001).

Potential mental health implications

The tasks associated with the development of lesbian and gay identity can place significant demands upon the psychological resources of those concerned and – depending on how the tasks are negotiated – can threaten psychological well-being.

To counter the risk of pathologizing lesbian and gay sexualities and identities here, it is important to note that, as long ago as 1982, Gonsiorek conducted a review of studies which had compared heterosexual and lesbian and gay samples on psychological tests. He concluded that 'Homosexuality in and of itself is unrelated to psychological disturbance or maladjustment. Homosexuals as a group are not more psychologically disturbed on account of their homosexuality' (Gonsiorek, 1982: 74). Although we have highlighted some potential problems associated with developing a lesbian or gay identity, many lesbians and gay men cope resourcefully with the challenges of creating a workable and satisfying sexual identity. Indeed, it may be the case that the experience of negotiating the demands associated with this process acts as an opportunity for growth, providing the individual with an increased repertoire of coping resources and strategies for dealing with future life challenges and an increased sense of self-efficacy.

Those who encounter the most serious mental health problems when struggling with a lesbian or gay identity may do so because of other experiences that have already left them psychologically vulnerable. Although dealing with a lesbian or gay sexual identity may not be the fundamental cause of psychological difficulties in these cases, the demands of this process may transform a vulnerability into an actual mental health problem. It is also reasonable to assume that those individuals who are faced with multiple problems and a range of adverse circumstances are at greatest risk of experiencing major psychological difficulties. For example, D'Augelli (1998) has suggested that lesbian, gay and bisexual young people who have experienced victimization on account of their sexuality and who have low self-esteem, little family support and little or no support from lesbian, gay and bisexual community contexts may be at greatest risk of mental health problems.

One particular cause for concern is suicidal ideation and behaviour. Research that has been conducted with lesbian, gay and bisexual youth – largely in the United States and Canada – has consistently found a markedly higher risk of suicidal thoughts and behaviours among these groups than among heterosexual youth (Bagley and Tremblay, 1997; D'Augelli and Hershberger, 1993; Hershberger and D'Augelli, 1995; Rotheram-Borus et al., 1994). To take some specific figures, Bagley and Tremblay (1997) found that, among the 750 males aged eighteen to twenty-seven whom they studied, gay and bisexual males ($n = 115$) accounted for 62.5 per cent of all attempted suicides and self-harming behaviours reported by participants; Hershberger and D'Augelli (1995) found that 42 per cent of the 194 lesbian, gay and bisexual young people whom they studied said they had attempted suicide. In Europe, van Heeringen and Vincke's (2000) study with young people in Belgium found that lesbian, gay and bisexual sexualities were associated with a significantly increased risk of suicidal ideation; lesbian and bisexual females had a significantly increased risk of attempted suicide. There has been limited work on this issue in the United Kingdom but Trenchard and Warren (1984) found that 20 per cent of the lesbian, gay and bisexual teenagers whom they studied had contemplated or attempted suicide because of their sexuality.

This brief review of the process of lesbian and gay identity development and some possible implications for mental health identifies a range of reasons why lesbian and gay clients might seek help from counselling psychologists. However, it is important to remember that lesbian and gay clients may also present with difficulties that are not centrally or obviously related to their sexual identity. In a study which we undertook to explore the meaning of lesbian and gay affirmative therapy (Milton and Coyle, 1999; Milton et al., 2002), lesbian and gay clients reported entering therapy for a range of problems. For example, Ulli said that he had sought therapy because of 'chronic anxiety, recurring depression, panic feelings and social phobia, alcohol abuse and sex addiction'. Another client, Alec, pointed to difficulties that are commonly presented by clients to therapists working in educational settings: 'I was not able to concentrate on my studies properly. [I was] feeling unfocused and chaos [*sic*].' This suggests that the counselling psychologist who is working with lesbian and gay clients has to be a competent broad-based practitioner, able to engage a range of clients successfully and to work with diverse presenting problems – as well as being aware of issues more explicitly related to the client's sexuality. We are not advocating that counselling psychologists who are working with lesbian or gay clients whose presenting problems are not obviously connected to their sexuality should not consider the client's sexuality in their exploration of these presenting problems. To do so may reflect a laudable desire on the part of the therapist to avoid seeming to pathologize the client's sexuality. However, to ignore the client's sexuality would involve participating in the silencing of lesbian and gay sexualities in therapeutic settings (Coyle et al., 1999) and would risk leaving the counselling psychologist with an incomplete understanding of the context within which the client's presenting problems have developed and are experienced.

Affirmative practice: views of practitioners and clients

This chapter began with a reminder that some of the theories and practices underpinning counselling psychology have a difficult history in relation to lesbian and gay sexuality – a situation that persists today in some quarters. The practical implications of this situation became apparent in a study which we undertook to examine the views and practices of clinical and counselling psychologists in working with lesbian and gay clients in the United Kingdom (Milton, 1998; Milton and Coyle, 1998b). Reports of deficient practice centred around psychologists holding problematic and pathologizing views about lesbian and gay sexualities, which led them to over-emphasize the importance of sexuality in the presenting problems of lesbian and gay clients and to view changing clients' sexual orientations/preferences as an appropriate therapeutic aim. In contrast, in their accounts of exemplary, affirmative practice, participants pointed to instances where therapy was conducted within the context of accepting and affirming views of lesbian and gay sexualities, characterized by openmindedness and delivered by therapists who were appropriately knowledgeable about lesbian and gay issues. These qualities overlap with those identified in another British study conducted with lesbian women who had received clinical psychology services (Annesley and Coyle, 1998): these women also valued their therapist having acknowledged and engaged constructively and appropriately with their sexuality.

Subsequently we extended this line of inquiry by undertaking a study (with Charles Legg) – mentioned earlier – in which we interviewed fourteen therapists from various theoretical orientations who described themselves as practising in a lesbian and gay affirmative way and eighteen clients who said they had received affirmative therapy (Milton and Coyle, 1999; Milton et al., 2002).

In light of the diverse accounts of affirmative therapy in the literature on the topic, the aim of this study was to explore what is meant by lesbian and gay affirmative therapy through reflections on practice experiences. In the quotations that follow, the theoretical orientation of therapist participants is made explicit when they are speaking about particular models of therapy; ellipsis points in quotations denote pauses in participants' speech and material in square brackets has been added for clarification.

Evaluation of the affirmative potential of various theoretical models

Participants expressed concern about the manner in which some psychotherapeutic theories (particularly psychoanalytic theory) pathologized or ignored lesbian and gay sexualities. For example, Mark (a client) observed that 'traditional psychoanalytic theory is very homophobic and anti-gay, and people coming from that traditional theoretical training are going to be harder to work with, if not impossible'. It was not only clients who raised this point. Reflecting on his attempt to train as a psychoanalytic psychotherapist, Jon said that his 'first training analysis had to be abandoned after eighteen months … It became apparent that the therapist wasn't going to pass a trainee who was a practising gay man. Only a "cure" to heterosexuality would have passed me.'

Jon's experience was very recent and supports previous research into the denial of psychoanalytic training to lesbians and gay men based on psychoanalytic constructions of homosexuality in terms of pathology (Ellis, 1994). The limitations of other models were also highlighted in terms of affirmative potential. For example, reflecting upon the desirability of including social contextual factors in formulations of lesbian and gay clients' presenting problems, Jack (a cognitive-behavioural therapist) said that cognitive behavioural therapy 'clumsily done, can [ignore] environmental influences … individualize what's going on, blame the stress on the … individual's belief structure'. Maggie (a systemic therapist) saw some systemic perspectives as limited in terms of their difficulties in recognizing those social relationships which may count as 'family' for lesbians and gay men: 'Some kinds of systemic family therapy can be very prescriptive in terms of … ideas about … family in the largest sense.'

Difficulties such as those outlined above are not just theoretical issues; they do, of course, affect the ways in which counselling psychologists will engage with their clients and will therefore have an impact on clients. For example, from some therapists, clients might receive a view of themselves framed in terms of 'perversion or immature sexual development' (Jack, a cognitive-behavioural therapist). Reflecting on how his sexuality had been pathologized, Oliver (a client) said that one experience of therapy had left him feeling 'like a curiosity, a case study. I felt that he [the therapist] attributed all my problems to my sexuality.' Thus it is evident that problematic stances towards same-sex sexuality can create difficulties for the practice of therapy.

However, when asked about the affirmative potential of various theoretical models, the therapist participants were able to identify potential within a wide range of models, including those they had also critiqued. Humanistic therapies were viewed as having a high degree of affirmative potential because it was felt that they explicitly aimed to avoid pathologization (see also Davies, 2000; Perlman, 2000). Reflecting on his own experiences in therapy, Oliver (a client) reckoned that 'humanistic and transactional analysis-influenced therapists have seemed to be more affirmative'. Liam (an integrative and humanistic therapist) suggested that humanistic models might be able to achieve this, as they 'don't hold an illness/sickness view of homosexuality'. The particular qualities and principles of this model were thought to assist in challenging such a view: humanistic therapy was said to have 'a very strong anti-discrimination value embedded in its core philosophy … It's absolutely crystal-clear and so there's a real commitment there' (Anna, an integrative therapist). Jack (a cognitive-behavioural therapist) agreed with this view when he said: 'Rogerian, humanist, existential lend itself very much to a gay affirmative stance … ideas of kind of fulfilling your human potential … being a whole person and getting back to active listening … a fertile ground for gay affirmative practice'. Gestalt therapy was also viewed as respectful of lesbian and gay sexuality, as it was said to allow flexibility and to recognize the value of difference. Mark (a client) suggested that 'It's a way of working. It doesn't have a firm theory of development.' He went on to say: 'Gestalt is very positive to people who are different … [It] would respect people who are in minorities and who view things differently.' Similarly, reflecting on phenomenological psychotherapy, Brad (an integrative/existential-phenomenological therapist) said that 'the whole idea of phenomenology and dialogic relationship is very useful. That the purpose of the therapist is to enter into the phenomenological world of the client … to understand the client – that in itself is extremely curative.'

Several therapists considered the stance that cognitive-behavioural therapy takes towards lesbian and gay sexuality in relation to its potential to be lesbian and gay affirmative. It was generally seen as non-pathologizing but, more specifically, Jack (a cognitive-behavioural therapist) felt that 'it assists because it has pretty much a value-neutral, pragmatic rather than a dogmatic stance … and because it doesn't have much to say about early developmental processes', echoing the above comment on Gestalt therapy. Participants felt that systemic therapy was useful because of the attention that it pays to the relationship between the contexts of the client, the family and the therapist. It was felt that systemic models challenge the blaming of an individual. Maggie (a systemic therapist) expressed the view that 'a systemic orientation is … very useful in assuming that the circumstances of your external world and the circumstances of your internal world are not in fact separate, discrete entities … that they … inevitably … affect each other and are affected by each other'.

The fact that participants were able to identify factors that could facilitate and hinder affirmative practice within the same models may be explained in terms of the emphasis they placed on the relationship between a therapist's values and the affirmative possibilities of the therapy. This means that, for any model of therapy, the therapist may engage creatively with the theory to produce affirmative practice or may use the theory to 'verify' anti-lesbian and anti-gay views. Some participants addressed the question of theory in general terms and identified affirmative therapy with a particular stance towards theory *per se*. For example, Brad (a therapist) felt that lesbian and gay affirmative therapists must be 'open to questioning the theory. They aren't dogmatic and highly opinionated … It is an open-minded examining of theory.' There was also support for affirmative practice moving from a stance of 'theory as truth' to theory as 'frameworks and that's really it … They are quite useful in that respect but to read into them a way of working as being the only way of working is quite dangerous, really' (Hannah, a therapist). Thus, according to these participants, counselling psychologists would be advised to move from a position where theory has the status of an ontological reality to a position where it is seen as one possible understanding among many. Participants suggested that it is important to bring this awareness of a range of theories to bear on one's assessment and formulation of clients' difficulties and to incorporate it into practice. One strategy that participants used to achieve this was to be hesitant about and adopt a questioning approach towards notions of 'truth'. Ross (a therapist) felt that this involved 'something about [being] aware of other models of working and constantly building on that.'

In addition to the importance of psychotherapeutic and psychological theory, findings from this study echo other research which suggests that the therapeutic relationship is a crucial aspect of the process of therapy (Beutler et al., 1986; Gelso and Carter, 1985; Gelso and Hayes, 1998; Safran, 1990a, b) – something which is well recognized in the counselling psychology literature in Britain (British Psychological Society Division of Counselling Psychology, 2001; Clarkson, 1995; du Plock, 1997). Accordingly, we turn now to those findings from the study which relate to the importance of the counselling psychologists' personal resources and qualities when working in relationship with lesbian and gay clients.

Therapists' knowledge of lesbian and gay experiences

Participants felt that affirmative therapists should be highly knowledgeable about the differences between lesbian/gay and heterosexual experiences, including differences in sexual behaviour, sexual and emotional relationships (and the variety of potential relationship structures) and the experience of negotiating a marginalized sexual identity. Natalie (a therapist) identified 'different expectations in a relationship, different role models and things people aspire to … perhaps different norms … the meaning it [the person's sexual identity] has in that person's social circle and the meaning it might have to their commitment to the relationship'. On the topic of lesbian and gay relationships, Adam (a client) said, 'I am not sure that the world is quite the same for a gay couple as it is for a straight couple … polygamy in straight relationships may be more problematic than in gay relationships'. Ewan (a client) felt it was particularly important that the therapist should have 'a good understanding of problems that could face lesbians and gay men', as he thought it would assist the therapist in recognizing the impact of sexuality on the experiences available to the client. Participants believed it was important for the therapist's knowledge to be grounded in experience of some kind rather than being gained through intellectual/academic methods alone. Adam (a client) felt that his therapist had been able to convey experiential understanding because she 'had a brother who was gay and maybe ... that by a process of osmosis she kind of [knew]'.

Some client participants reported negative experiences arising from their therapists' lack of knowledge of lesbian and gay contexts. The most common of these related to therapists seeing 'open' relationships (relationships that were not sexually exclusive) as problematic and as an inevitable source of conflict. Adam (a client) said that he had 'an open relationship and I think I got a vibe that her [the therapist's] feeling was that our relationship was insubstantial, that it was weak, that it needed to be propped up by affairs outside of the relationship ... I had the feeling it had something to do with a ... heterosexual's eye view of what an ideal relationship should be.'

Participants suggested that lesbian and gay therapists have more 'accurate' awareness of their lesbian and gay clients' experiences than heterosexual therapists. However, Ross (a therapist) noted that a shared sexuality does not guarantee similarity of experience and does not automatically confer shared understanding. He said, 'I have had clients say that "You must know what I'm talking about here" and I have ... said, "I kinda know what you're talking about from my own experience but I'm not sure it's exactly the same and I guess some of the questions that I am wondering about in relation to what you're raising are something about the difference between your experience and my experience".'

Creating safety in therapy

Participants linked the conveying of an appropriate understanding of lesbian and gay experiences by therapists to the creation of a sense of safety for clients. Client participants connected a sense of safety with a non-judgemental stance and with therapists attending to experiences of constructing and maintaining lesbian or gay identity. As Greg (a client) put it, 'I wanted to talk about what it was like to be gay. I wanted it to be safe about being gay, to express it.' The topic of 'coming out' is part of the content of many therapeutic encounters with lesbians and gay men. For many client participants, therapy was one of the first places where they had voiced the possibility of a lesbian or gay identity: Grant said that, in therapy, 'I admitted for the very first time to any strangers my sexual orientation ... I must say it was very positive.'

Participants noted that clients (and others) may assume that therapy with a heterosexual therapist will be unsafe. As a heterosexual therapist, Jennifer noted that 'the fact of being straight can set up barriers, whatever my attitude. I may have areas that I am not aware of even though I might try.' These concerns were also voiced by client participants. For example, Mark (a client) said, 'I didn't believe that a straight person would be able to understand my experience of my sexuality and accept it and really understand what is happening for me.' Tania (a client) felt that 'some heterosexual people [therapists] would make judgements'. Similarly, Kyle (a client) suggested that 'if [the therapist] was straight, I'd be assuming that he was automatically against me'. It is important not to suggest that views such as these are purely an aspect of the client's anxiety or projection. Reflecting on their experiences, participants were clear that many heterosexual people do struggle to understand lesbian and gay sexualities and experiences. Oliver (a client) remembered how two previous therapists 'clearly did not understand and it was as though I had to explain everything and check out "Do you know what I mean?"'. One result of such an experience can be that the client pathologizes himself or herself: as Oliver put it, the client may be left wondering 'Are my problems so bad that my counsellor can't understand? I must really be screwed up.'

Therapist flexibility

We noted earlier that some participants advocated a flexible, non-dogmatic, questioning stance towards theoretical models of therapy within affirmative practice. Tom (a therapist) provided a further illustration of this when he said, 'I realized that I didn't accept many of the theories around homosexuality – that I didn't accept theories around perversion.' This suggests that, in order to work affirmatively, counselling psychologists need to be able to think critically and rigorously about their theoretical models, amending them in light of new insights and research. Participants also pointed out that flexibility is required because – as we also noted earlier – affirmative therapists need to assist clients with a wide range of difficulties and not just with issues that are clearly related to sexual identity. Participants stressed the need for affirmative therapists to adopt a stance towards presenting problems that is characterized by a refusal to view sexuality as the necessary cause of the problems. Providing an example of this, Kyle (a client) said of his therapist, 'She'll actually say … whatever but it won't be related to my sexuality – it'll be related to other things … other relationships that may have happened in my past.' Linking back to the need for therapists to be knowledgeable about lesbian and gay experiences, it was felt that, in order to develop a comprehensive analysis of clients' difficulties, therapists require 'a good understanding of problems that could face lesbians and gay men [whether they be] because of … family, religious beliefs … different cultural attitudes to homosexuality [or the] problems that people can have at work because of homophobia' (Ewan, a client). Such flexibility and non-dogmatism in the conceptualization of presenting problems was seen as important because of its perceived potential in facilitating a collaborative working alliance and increased ability to be empathic.

Can heterosexual therapists practise affirmatively?

Various views were expressed by participants on the question of whether lesbian and gay affirmative therapists need to be lesbian or gay themselves.

(We have already noted some opinions on this issue in relation to other themes.) Some participants (both therapists and clients) argued that it is not necessary for a therapist to be lesbian or gay in order to provide affirmative therapy. Indeed, some participants suggested that particular benefits might accrue from working with a heterosexual affirmative therapist who can to some extent represent the heterosexual world within the therapeutic context. As Adam (a client) put it, 'to have a straight person who is on my side – it could actually help with my relationship with the world out there.'

A few participants expressed the view that lesbian and gay affirmative therapy can be provided only by lesbian and gay therapists because of the difficulties faced by heterosexuals in understanding and empathizing with lesbian and gay experiences. Other participants attended to the therapeutic benefits that might flow from having a lesbian or gay therapist working with a lesbian or gay client. For example, affirmative therapists who are themselves lesbian or gay and who are 'out' within the therapeutic context were seen as potentially embodying a challenge to pathologizing stereotypes and providing hope that negative views of lesbian and gay sexualities can be overcome. As Maggie (a lesbian therapist) put it, 'As a therapist you are in a powerful position and you can be a lesbian, which is a not good thing [in the eyes of society and perhaps in the eyes of the client too] – possibly [by being an 'out' lesbian therapist] there's a way to make it a ... slightly gooder thing.' The fact that the therapist is lesbian or gay was also seen as providing them with an authority within affirmative therapy that may not be available to the heterosexual therapist.

Another viewpoint on this issue was that, although there are challenges involved, heterosexual therapists *can* provide lesbian and gay affirmative therapy. This view was accompanied by a discussion of particular issues that heterosexual therapists would need to explore before being able to provide this sort of therapy. For example, Alec (a client) felt that it was important that 'the therapist has spent some time exploring their sexuality and [is] non-judgemental and accepting – then they should be OK whether they are gay or straight'. Liam (a therapist) applied this need for self-reflection and self-exploration to heterosexual *and* lesbian and gay therapists, saying that, in order to practise affirmatively, 'any therapist will need to have explored their own sexuality – probably important for any gay therapist to have explored their heterosexuality and probably for any heterosexual therapist to have found at least a small part of themselves that might loosely be described as gay'.

Contextual considerations in working affirmatively in the National Health Service

As well as examining the theoretical frameworks within which affirmative practice might be located and the resources and qualities needed, it is also important for counselling psychologists to consider the impact of the contexts in which lesbian and gay clients may receive therapy. A survey found that approximately half the chartered counselling psychologists in the United Kingdom held a position within the National Health Service and approximately half worked in other settings such as student counselling services, private practice and the voluntary sector (Bor and Achilleoudes, 1999). With significant numbers of counselling psychologists working in the health service, we need to consider the impact that this context will have on the possibilities of offering affirmative, non-pathologizing therapy to lesbians and gay men. Two contextual issues affecting the practice of counselling psychologists with these client groups are the fact that much practice occurs within multidisciplinary teams and also the nature of the supervision provided for counselling psychologists.

In multidisciplinary teams, counselling psychologists must work closely with a range of professions and professionals (such as psychiatrists, clinical psychologists, nurses, medical psychotherapists, counsellors and social workers), some of which/whom may share the same values and models as the counselling psychologist and some of which/whom may not. In general terms, counselling psychologists may face a range of challenges in attempting to engage in dialogues with other professionals who operate with different sets of assumptions about the conceptualization and treatment of psychological distress. In more specific terms, counselling psychologists who take their profession's commitment to anti-discriminatory practice seriously might find themselves having to take the lead in challenging heterosexist and homo-negative assumptions and practices that may be more firmly embedded in the professional landscape of other long-established professions. Similarly, many therapeutic practitioners working in the National Health Service obtain supervision from a range of professionals. It is therefore important that counselling psychologists identify supervisors who are attuned to the ethos of counselling psychology, its commitment to anti-discriminatory practice and its stance towards working with lesbian and gay clients.

As mentioned above, the National Health Service is not the sole employer of counselling psychologists. We have chosen to focus on this context as it appears to be the most important single work context for practitioners in the United Kingdom and it is the context with which we are most familiar. We recognize that many counselling psychologists with experience in other settings will have useful contributions to make to the debate about appropriate counselling psychology practice with lesbians and gay men in a range of settings.

Conclusion

The material presented in this chapter suggests that it may not always be straightforward for counselling psychologists to work with lesbian and gay clients in ways that empower and that accord with high standards of anti-discriminatory practice. To do so can be a demanding undertaking that is complicated by our immersion within social and professional belief systems that position lesbian and gay sexualities as negative and even pathological; it may involve something much more radical than simply 'adding in' lesbian and gay clients to the range of client groups with which counselling psychologists work. If practitioners are to meet the standards of practice that our profession requires of us, it is necessary that a reflective stance is taken to the assumptions and beliefs that we hold and the way in which these impact on our understandings of sexuality and sexual identity. This is important for us all as individuals but also as supervisors, researchers, trainers and providers of psychological services. Counselling psychologists should not flinch at the potential magnitude of this task as there is much research and practice-related work that has already been undertaken, both in Britain and internationally, to inform and elaborate our reflections on sexuality and sexual identity, some of which has been cited in this chapter. There are also now clear and carefully formulated guidelines – prepared by the American Psychological Association – available to practitioners that describe the outlooks and competences required to work with lesbian and gay (and bisexual) clients (American Psychological Association Division 44/ Committee on Lesbian, Gay, and Bisexual Concerns Joint Task Force on Guidelines for Psychotherapy with Lesbian, Gay, and Bisexual Clients, 2000). These guidelines examine the implicit biases that may be held by practising therapists and the need for practitioners to become more aware of them and to be prepared to address them if they are to work effectively with lesbian and gay (and bisexual) clients. Whilst emanating from US psychological thought and practice, they provide guidance which can readily be applied (sometimes with slight modifications) in many countries. If counselling psychologists are able to rise to the challenge of rethinking old assumptions and integrating new research and knowledge into their practice, counselling psychology may not only challenge outmoded, biased and damaging practices with lesbian and gay clients but could pioneer the development of more thoughtful, ethical and affirmative ways of working with a range of client groups.

References

American Psychological Association Division 44/Committee on Lesbian, Gay, and Bisexual Concerns Joint Task Force on Guidelines for Psychotherapy with Lesbian, Gay, and Bisexual Clients (2000) 'Guidelines for psychotherapy with lesbian, gay, and bisexual clients', *American Psychologist*, 55: 1440–51.

Annesley, P. and Coyle, A. (1995) 'Clinical psychologists' attitudes to lesbians', *Journal of Community & Applied Social Psychology*, 5: 327–31.

Annesley, P. and Coyle, A. (1998) 'Dykes and psychs: lesbian women's experiences of clinical psychology services', *Changes: An International Journal of Psychology and Psychotherapy*, 16: 247–58.

Bagley, C. and Tremblay, P. (1997) 'Suicidal behaviors in homosexual and bisexual males', *Crisis*, 18: 24–34.

Beutler, L.E., Crago, M. and Arizmendi, T.G. (1986) 'Therapist variables in psychotherapy process and outcome' in S.L. Garfield and A.E. Bergin (eds) *Handbook of Psychotherapy and Behavior Change*, third edition. New York: Wiley.

Bieschke, K.J., McClanahan, M., Tozer, E., Grzegorek, J.L. and Park, J. (2000) 'Programmatic research on the treatment of lesbian, gay, and bisexual clients: the past, the present, and the course of the future' in R.M. Perez, K.A. DeBord and K.J. Bieschke (eds) *Handbook of Counseling and Psychotherapy with Lesbian, Gay, and Bisexual Clients*. Washington DC: American Psychological Association.

Birkett, S. (2001) 'Foyle Friend: 21 years of promoting lesbian and gay well-being in the north-west of Ireland', *Lesbian & Gay Psychology Review*, 2: 83–7.

Bor, R. and Achilleoudes, H. (1999) 'Survey of the BPS Division of Counselling Psychology members, 1999', *Counselling Psychology Review*, 14 (4): 35–44.

Bradford, J., Ryan, C. and Rothblum, E.D. (1994) 'National lesbian health care survey: implications for mental health care', *Journal of Consulting and Clinical Psychology*, 62: 228–42.

Breakwell, G.M. (1986) *Coping with Threatened Identities*. London: Methuen.

British Psychological Society Division of Counselling Psychology (2001) *Professional Practice Guidelines*. Leicester: British Psychological Society.

Clark, D. (1987) *The New Loving Someone Gay*. Berkeley CA: Celestial Arts.

Clarkson, P. (1995) *The Therapeutic Relationship in Psychoanalysis, Counselling Psychology and Psychotherapy*. London: Whurr.

Constantine-Simms, D. (ed.) (2000) *The Greatest Taboo: Homosexuality in Black Communities*. Los Angeles CA: Alyson Books.

Coyle, A. (1992) '"My own special creation"? The construction of gay identity' in G.M. Breakwell (ed.) *Social Psychology of Identity and the Self Concept*. London: Surrey University Press/Academic Press.

Coyle, A., Milton, M. and Annesley, P. (1999) 'The silencing of lesbian and gay voices in psychotherapeutic texts and training', *Changes: An International Journal of Psychology and Psychotherapy*, 17: 132-43.

Cramer, D.W. and Roach, A.J. (1988) 'Coming out to mom and dad: a study of gay males and their relationships with their parents', *Journal of Homosexuality*, 15 (3-4): 79–92.

Crawford, I. and Solliday, E. (1996) 'The attitudes of undergraduate college students toward gay parenting', *Journal of Homosexuality*, 30 (4): 63–77.

D'Augelli, A.R. (1998) 'Developmental implications of victimization of lesbian, gay, and bisexual youths' in G.M. Herek (ed.) *Stigma and Sexual Orientation: Understanding Prejudice against Lesbians, Gay Men, and Bisexuals*. Thousand Oaks CA: Sage.

D'Augelli, A.R. and Hershberger, S.L. (1993) 'Lesbian, gay, and bisexual youth in community settings: personal challenges and mental health problems', *American Journal of Community Psychology*, 21: 1-28.

D'Augelli, A.R. and Patterson, C.J. (eds) (1995) *Lesbian, Gay, and Bisexual Identities over the Lifespan: Psychological Perspectives*. New York: Oxford University Press.

D'Augelli, A.R., Hershberger, S.L. and Pilkington, N.W. (1998) 'Lesbian, gay, and bisexual youths and their families: disclosure of sexual orientation and its consequences', *American Journal of Orthopsychiatry*, 68: 361–71.

Davidson-Paine, C. and Corbett, J. (1995) 'A double coming out: gay men with learning disabilities', *British Journal of Learning Disabilities*, 23: 147–51.

Davies, D. (1996) 'Towards a model of gay affirmative therapy' in D. Davies and C. Neal (eds) *Pink Therapy: a Guide for Counsellors and Therapists Working with Lesbian, Gay and Bisexual Clients*. Buckingham: Open University Press.

Davies, D. (2000) 'Person-centred therapy' in D. Davies and C. Neal (eds) *Therapeutic Perspectives on Working with Lesbian, Gay and Bisexual Clients*. Buckingham: Open University Press.

Davies, P.M., Hickson, F.C.I., Weatherburn, P. and Hunt, A.J. (1993) *Sex, Gay Men and AIDS*. London: Taylor & Francis.

Devine, W. and Milton. M. (2000) 'Setting up a youth service for young gay men: a case study', *Lesbian & Gay Psychology Review*, 1: 40–6.

du Plock, S. (1997) 'Sexual misconceptions: a critique of gay affirmative therapy and some thoughts on an existential-phenomenological theory of sexual orientation', *Journal of the Society for Existential Analysis*, 8 (2): 56-71.

Ellis, M.L. (1994) 'Lesbians, gay men and psychoanalytic training', *Free Associations*, 4: 501–17.

Ellis, M.L. (1997) 'Who speaks? Who listens? Different voices and different sexualities', *British Journal of Psychotherapy*, 13: 369–83.

Ellis, S.J. (2002) 'Student support for lesbian and gay human rights: findings from a large-scale questionnaire study' in A. Coyle and C. Kitzinger (eds) *Lesbian and Gay Psychology: New Perspectives*. Oxford: BPS Blackwell.

Firestein, B.A. (ed.) (1996) *Bisexuality: the Psychology and Politics of an Invisible Minority*. Thousand Oaks CA: Sage.

Fox, A. (1991) 'Development of a bisexual identity: understanding the process', in L. Hutchins and L. Ka'ahumanu (eds) *Bi any other Name: Bisexual People Speak Out*. Boston MA: Alyson.

Fox, R.C. (1995) 'Bisexual identities' in A.R. D'Augelli and C.J. Patterson (eds) *Lesbian, Gay, and Bisexual Identities over the Lifespan: Psychological Perspectives*. New York: Oxford University Press.

Fox, R.C. (2000) 'Bisexuality in perspective: a review of theory and research' in B. Greene and G.L. Croom (eds) *Education, Research, and Practice in Lesbian, Gay, Bisexual, and Transgendered Psychology: A Resource Manual*. Thousand Oaks CA: Sage.

Freud, S. (1977) *On Sexuality*. London: Penguin.

Garnets, L., Hancock, K.A., Cochran, S.D., Goodchilds, J. and Peplau, L.A. (1991) 'Issues in psychotherapy with lesbians and gay men: a survey of psychologists', *American Psychologist*, 46: 964–72.

Gelso, C.J. and Carter, J.A. (1985) 'The relationship in counseling and psychotherapy: components, consequences, and theoretical antecedents', *Counseling Psychologist*, 13: 155–243.

Gelso, C.J. and Hayes, J.A. (1998) *The Psychotherapy Relationship: Theory, Research, and Practice*. New York: Wiley.

Gonsiorek, J. (1982) 'Results of psychological testing on homosexual populations' in W. Paul, J.D. Weinrich, J.C. Gonsiorek and M.E. Hotvedt (eds) *Homosexuality: Social, Psychological, and Biological Issues*. Beverly Hills CA: Sage.

Greene, B. (ed.) (1997) *Ethnic and Cultural Diversity among Lesbians and Gay Men*. Thousand Oaks CA: Sage.

Heeringen, C. van and Vincke, J. (2000) 'Suicidal acts and ideation in homosexual and bisexual young people: a study of prevalence and risk factors', *Social Psychiatry and Psychiatric Epidemiology*, 35: 494–9.

Herdt, G.H. and Boxer, A.M. (1993) *Children of Horizons: How Gay and Lesbian Teens are Leading a New Way out of the Closet*. Boston MA: Beacon Press.

Hershberger, S.L. and D'Augelli, A.R. (1995) 'The impact of victimization on the mental health and suicidality of lesbian, gay, and bisexual youths', *Developmental Psychology*, 31: 65–74.

Hopcke, R. (1989) *Jung, Jungians and Homosexuality*. Boston MA: Shambhala.

Hughes, T.L., Haas, A.P. and Avery, L. (1997) 'Lesbians and mental health: preliminary results from the Chicago Women's Health Survey', *Journal of the Gay and Lesbian Medical Association*, 1: 137-48.

Kellett, J.M. (1998) 'The man who did not fancy his fiancée', *Trends in Urology, Gynaecology and Sexual Health*, May–June, pp. 50–1.

Kitzinger, C. and Coyle, A. (2002) 'Introducing lesbian and gay psychology' in A. Coyle and C. Kitzinger (eds) *Lesbian and Gay Psychology: New Perspectives*. Oxford: BPS Blackwell.

Kitzinger. C. and Wilkinson, S. (1995) 'Transitions from heterosexuality to lesbianism: the discursive construction of lesbian identities', *Developmental Psychology*, 31: 95–104.

Laumann, E.O., Gagnon, J.H., Michael, R.T. and Michaels, S. (1994) *The Social Organization of Sexuality: Sexual Practices in the United States*. Chicago: University of Chicago Press.

Malyon, A.K. (1982) 'Psychotherapeutic implications of internalized homophobia in gay men' in J. Gonsiorek (ed.) *Homosexuality and Psychotherapy: A Practitioner's Handbook of Affirmative Models*. Binghamton NY: Haworth Press.

Markowe, L.A. (1996) *Redefining the Self: Coming Out as Lesbian*. Cambridge: Polity Press.

Markowe, L.A. (2002) 'Coming out as lesbian' in A. Coyle and C. Kitzinger (eds) *Lesbian and Gay Psychology: New Perspectives*. Oxford: BPS Blackwell.

McKenna, K.Y.A. and Bargh, J.A. (1998) 'Coming out in the age of the internet: identity "demarginalization" through virtual group participation', *Journal of Personality and Social Psychology*, 75: 681–94.

Milton, M. (1998) *Issues in Psychotherapy with Lesbians and Gay Men: A Survey of British Psychologists*. Leicester: British Psychological Society.

Milton, M. and Coyle, A. (1998a) 'Reference library on counselling psychology: lesbian and gay affirmative therapy', *Counselling Psychology Review*, 13 (4): 36–40.

Milton, M. and Coyle, A. (1998b) 'Psychotherapy with lesbian and gay clients', *The Psychologist*, 11: 73–6.

Milton, M. and Coyle, A. (1999) 'Lesbian and gay affirmative psychotherapy: issues in theory and practice', *Sexual and Marital Therapy*, 14: 41–57.

Milton, M., Coyle, A. and Legg, C. (2002) 'Lesbian and gay affirmative psychotherapy: defining the domain' in A. Coyle and C. Kitzinger (eds) *Lesbian and Gay Psychology: New Perspectives*. Oxford: BPS Blackwell.

Morgan, K.S. and Eliason, M.J. (1992) 'The role of psychotherapy in Caucasian lesbians' lives', *Women and Therapy*, 13 (4): 27–52.

Paul, J.P. (1996) 'Bisexuality: exploring/exploding the boundaries' in R.C. Savin-Williams and K.M. Cohen (eds) *The Lives of Lesbians, Gays, and Bisexuals: Children to Adults*. Fort Worth TX: Harcourt Brace.

Perlman, G. (2000) 'Transactional analysis' in D. Davies and C. Neal (eds) *Therapeutic Perspectives on Working with Lesbian, Gay and Bisexual Clients*. Buckingham: Open University Press.

Phellas, C.N. (2002) *The Construction of Sexual and Cultural Identities: Greek-Cypriot Men in Britain*. Aldershot: Ashgate.

Phillips, P., Bartlett, A. and King, M. (2001) 'Psychotherapists' approaches to gay and lesbian patients/clients: a qualitative study', *British Journal of Medical Psychology*, 74: 73–84.

Rivers, I. (2000) 'Long-term consequences of bullying' in C. Neal and D. Davies (eds) *Issues in Therapy with Lesbian, Gay, Bisexual and Transgender Clients*. Buckingham: Open University Press.

Rivers, I. (2001) 'The bullying of sexual minorities at school: its nature and long-term correlates', *Educational and Child Psychology*, 18: 32–46.

Rivers, I. and D'Augelli, A.R. (2001) 'The victimization of lesbian, gay, and bisexual youths: implications for intervention' in A.R. D'Augelli and C.J. Patterson (eds) *Lesbian, Gay, and Bisexual Identities and Youth: Psychological Perspectives*. New York: Oxford University Press.

Rotheram-Borus, M.J., Hunter, J. and Rosario, M. (1994) 'Suicidal behavior and gay-related stress among gay and bisexual male adolescents', *Journal of Adolescent Research*, 9: 498–508.

Safran, J.D. (1990a) 'Towards a refinement of cognitive therapy in light of interpersonal theory I, Theory', *Clinical Psychology Review*, 10: 87–105.

Safran, J.D. (1990b) 'Towards a refinement of cognitive therapy in light of interpersonal theory II, Practice', *Clinical Psychology Review*, 10: 107–21.

Savin-Williams, R.C. (1998) *And then I became Gay: Young Men's Stories*. New York: Routledge.

Savin-Williams, R.C. and Cohen, K.M. (eds) (1996) *The Lives of Lesbians, Gays, and Bisexuals: Children to Adults*. Fort Worth TX: Harcourt Brace.

Schmidt, G. and Schorsch, E. (1981) 'Psychosurgery of sexually deviant patients', *Archives of Sexual Behavior*, 10: 301–21.

Shelley, C. (ed.) (1998) *Contemporary Perspectives on Psychotherapy and Homosexualities*. London: Free Association Books.

Spencer, C. (1995) *Homosexuality: A History.* London: Fourth Estate.

Taylor, G. (2002) 'Psychopathology and the social and historical construction of gay male identities' in A. Coyle and C. Kitzinger (eds) *Lesbian and Gay Psychology: New Perspectives*. Oxford: BPS Blackwell.

Trenchard, L. and Warren, H. (1984) *Something to Tell You … The Experiences and Needs of Young Lesbians and Gay Men in London*. London: London Gay Teenage Group.

Weatherburn, P., Hickson, F.C.I., Reid, D.S., Davies, P.M. and Crosier, A. (1998) 'Sexual HIV risk behaviour among men who have sex with both men and women', *AIDS Care*, 10: 463–71.

24 Cross-cultural Counselling Psychology
ZACK ELEFTHERIADOU

The main focus of this chapter will be to outline the changes within psychology and the implications for counselling psychology practice. It will begin with an exploration of some commonly held notions surrounding cross-cultural therapy, including an exploration of the concepts of race, culture and identity. Experiences from cross-cultural therapeutic relationships will be used to illustrate the realities of cross-cultural counselling and to challenge existing stereotypes. Issues such as racial/cultural matching of client and counselling psychologist, and how racial and cultural issues filter into the counselling psychology relationship, will be explored. Case material will be used to illustrate the dynamics at play when the client and counselling psychologist share a culture and when they have different cultural and racial backgrounds.

Background

In today's international community cross-cultural issues filter into all aspects of our lives and inevitably have a significant role to play in therapeutic work. The whole area of cross-cultural counselling psychology has been investigated significantly less than other areas of counselling psychology. There has also been an increase in the number of therapists from different cultural/racial groups training in counselling psychology, although many more are required. To some extent, this has had an impact on the numbers from ethnic minorities seeking support. Centres such as the Intercultural Therapy Centre, called NAFSIYAT, and the Medical Foundation for the Care of Victims of Torture (both based in north London) have demonstrated that people of all cultures not only require, but will use, appropriate therapeutic support. Counselling organizations such as the British Association for Counselling's subdivision, RACE (Race and Cultural Education in Counselling), and a special interest group on race and culture within clinical psychology, formed in the 1990s, acknowledging (1) the need to consider the implications for clinical practice and (2) the need for further professional training, in order to work effectively within cross-cultural relationships.

The intellectual debates have recently began to filter into the mechanics of clinical practice. Numerous academic journals, such as the American publications entitled *The Journal of Cross-cultural Psychology and Multicultural Counseling and Development* and the *Journal of Cross-cultural Psychology*, and an increasing number of books, are being published every year in cross-cultural work. The huge expansion of literature in the cross-cultural field in the United

Kingdom (and indeed around the world) has been a result of the growing evidence that clients are being misdiagnosed, largely owing to the misunderstanding of cultural factors and existing racism. Through vast clinical and research evidence, Littlewood and Lipsedge (1989) have concluded that the psychiatrist:

> has less clear expectations of how the patient is likely to behave and what, in different societies, the limits of normality and abnormality are. In addition to his background and training, the psychiatrist's attitude to the minority patient will be formed by his own personal problems, concious and unconscious racist assumptions and the particular setting in which the two meet. (pp. 13–14)

Although the above observations apply more to psychiatric assessments, as counselling psychologists we also need to be aware of how we understand another culture's norms and practices, and hence the danger of labelling something as pathological because it is 'different'. Of course the area of psychiatric assessment is complex and rather vast, so for the purposes of this chapter the focus will remain on psychological work. Nonetheless, as a result of these factors (among others), there has been considerably less use of the mental health services by ethnic minority clients. Even when people use the existing services there is still a higher drop-out rate from ethnic minorities (Fernando, 1991). These are issues which require much consideration.

Psychological research is still new and much more is required in order to really begin to understand the impact of race and culture in clinical practice. Thus far, the notion that if you have trained in one theoretical framework you can work with people from all cultures, however, has been challenged. Undoubtedly, cultural issues cut across every approach of therapeutic work. The cross-cultural counselling psychologist has to keep these debates in mind and keep up to date with the research findings. Most important, though, we need to understand the impact of culture in our clients' lives as well as the meaning culture has in our own lives. For a long time cultural and racial issues have been viewed as the client's 'issues', implying something that we are disconnected from and even problematic.

Psychology, cross-cultural psychology and cultural psychology

The relationship between culture and psychology has been of interest for over a century and yet it is only recently that psychology has been able to take a formal part in the academic debates and research (Berry et al., 1992). There are broadly two schools of thought within psychology which deal with cultural issues; 'cross-cultural psychology' (Berry et al., 1992) and the more recent field which has been called 'cultural psychology' (Shweder, 1991).

The field of cross-cultural psychology compares concepts and events between different cultures, based on the premise that there is one inherent universal aspect across cultures. Cultural psychology takes a more anthropo-logical view; that is, to examine a culture within itself. It takes the view that everything can be understood within its context, and if the framework is removed it becomes senseless. An example of cross-cultural psychology research might be to take a concept such as adolescence and to explore it across cultures. In the latter approach there would not be a preconceived notion of 'adolescence'. In fact many would argue that it does not even exist as a concept, as it is not seen as a distinct 'stage' of development. The other difference is that cross-cultural psychology has generally used Western measuring research tools, and researchers may have not belonged to that culture. This is changing, however, through the involvement of more countries in formulating research and assessment tools (see Suzuki et al., 1996). The latter approach uses 'insiders' or researchers who are part of the culture or at least understand and speak the language and will observe the process as such. Cultural psychology also comes from a different philosophical base where the observer is in interaction with the subject, hence the influence on each other, observer and subject, needs to be considered. Applied to clinical work, the philosophy of cultural psychology implies that there would be no use of concepts which are considered to be universal, for example asking a client to talk about their 'adolescent years'. Both approaches, cross-cultural and cultural psychology, are necessary if we are to have any type of comparison across cultures. Furthermore, if we are to work across cultures we also need to understand the object within its context (demonstrated numerous times in the research of visual illusions where there is more than one image. The longer that one observes the picture alternates between one image and the other. Therefore at all times both images are present, it is never one or the other). Cultural psychology has challenged the notion that all thinking mechanisms are fixed or that there is a central inherent mechanism across cultures which is universal. In fact, this *is* the main debate in this field; that is, whether deep down we are all the same and any variations are masked by culture. And if this is the case and we are all the same, then how can we can really translate these thinking mechanisms across cultures? This will be examined throughout the chapter, but perhaps the most crucial element in cross-cultural work is accepting that there are differences and not all are bridgeable. This can be explored further by finding ways of opening up a dialogue about the meaning of culture.

Issues of race, culture and identity

The concept 'race' is generally used to refer to unchangeable characteristics such as skin colour, hair, eye colour, facial characteristics, which are shared by a group of people who have the same ancestral origins. It does not refer to genetic differences between races although, sadly, many still hold these views. We live in a society which is racist and prejudiced and this has a profound impact on the psyche. Ethnic minority groups continue to face discrimination, social, political, educational and economic disadvantage. We hear from our clients accounts of racism and culture-blindness. As Thomas states:

> Racism, however, is not just a hatred of, or a conscious belief in the inferiority of, black people. Nor is it just physical violence. Disavowal of a person's 'different' existence is in itself a way of not recognising the degree to which this pervasive system operates in groups and in the individual. Inevitably, racism has a detrimental effect on social and personal relationships. Not only is this evident in relationships between black and white people but between black people themselves. (1992: 135)

So we need to be able to take into account the reality of racism and the impact it has on people, at both conscious and unconscious levels. If we are open to it, then stories of race and racism will undoubtedly be recounted by our clients. The counselling psychologist needs to take responsibility to address this with the clients, who are often unsure whether it is safe enough to do so. Hence it often emerges in unconscious ways or disguised ways (Vannoy Adams, 1996), unless triggered by a media event such as the September 11 2001 attacks on America and then people somehow feel there is the 'permission' to discuss it and to be passionate about the issues.

Race is often extended to include cultural elements, implying that somehow people's behaviours or values are rigid and unchangeable. Sadly, not only in time of war, among people of the same race there is strong prejudice and even torture due to cultural factors such as religion or political beliefs; these differences become perceived, like race, as 'unbridgeable'. Although race and culture are often used interchangeably, in this context culture is defined as something psycho-social and therefore changeable.

Culture can be defined as 'a way of creating shared ways of functioning in order to communicate effectively ... we create shared events, practices, roles, values, myths, rules, beliefs, habits, symbols, illusions and realities' (Eleftheriadou: 1994: 1–2). Culture includes the visible aspects, such as dress code, as well as all the invisible aspects such as the way we relate, think and even 'culturally appropriate' ways of expressing emotions. Culture is such a part of us that it becomes incredibly difficult to convey. In fact clients can often feel a sense of being overwhelmed when they have to try to do this in counselling psychology. This is because much of what constitutes culture is around us, we are part of it and require it, but it is not directly observable. The individual and culture have a dynamic relationship. This can change through time and with the arrival of newcomers or people returning to their culture after exposure to new cultures and ways of living. Therefore it is always the *relationship* that we are interested in, not just the culture or only the individual. If we concentrated on the culture we would be in danger of viewing the person within a stereotypical box and, likewise, if we concentrated on the self only we would be trying to understand a person without a context. In other words, we would not be viewing the whole, only parts of it. At all times, the relationship between the triad – that is, the person, the familial system and the cultural context – needs to be considered. If this framework can be kept in mind it will enable the counselling psychologist to keep a balance between the different aspects which contribute to people's way of being.

The distinction between various cultures is usually made in relation to dramatic and obvious differences, but of course there are endless, often less marked distinctions. These can be observed in everyday behaviours, for example the way of relating to others such as patterns of greeting, comfortable distance when in conversation with others, child-rearing values, dependence and independence, and all the ways one interacts with one's social community. The challenge of cross-cultural work is to have the sensitivity and the ability to enter a different world, or at least its significant components, and not only understand it, but feel comfortable to challenge it.

Racial and cultural factors, together, form what we call our identity or the way we define ourselves, psychologically and socially, in terms of our sense of belongingness or rootedness. Although there is a level of constancy in terms of identity, it is not formed through adherence to one single culture. As Pedersen (1997) states:

> Culture's complexity is illustrated by the hundreds or perhaps even thousands of culturally learned identities, affiliations, and roles we each assume at one time or another. Culture is dynamic as each one of these alternative cultural identities replaces another in salience. (p. 177)

Since it is a constellation of more than one culture, the counselling psychologist has to be aware of which is the client's salient cultural identity, depending on the cultural framework at the time. This idea of multiple identities is increasingly supported by client accounts (see the case of Alessandro at the end of this chapter) and research. For example, research conducted in the Intercultural Therapy Centre, Nafsiyat, found that over over 20 per cent of clients were British-born and their parents or grandparents had migrated (Moorhouse, 1992). They may be seen as 'foreign' owing to their racial appearance, but his group have grown up biculturally. For example, many clients talk about how they feel about constantly being asked where they were born when in fact they have been born in the majority culture. One client talked about how it 'throws her into feeling different again just when she was beginning to fit in'.

Ethnic minorities define their identity through the images and expectations of their own culture, but also by how they are perceived by the majority culture. If the cultural context and its influences are ignored, and indeed if the cross-cultural relationship is not mentioned, it dilutes the richness of the client and therapist relationship.

Clinical Issues

Challenging stereotypes

Working cross-culturally means raising and challenging awareness of some of the commonly held stereotypes around race and culture such as:

- *The distinction between 'them' and 'us'*. The label 'they' is given to the racial/cultural grouping which is different from 'ours' as if one is the norm. Also neither 'they' nor 'ours' are a homogeneous group. There is great diversity among any ethnic group, in terms of numerous factors, such as socio-economic status, among many others. Cultural groups themselves can also use this as a defence, especially at times where defences are high, such as when abroad. This can result in groups holding on to cultural practices rigidly.

- *Hierarchies*. There is often a 'poor them' attitude of pity for people of other races/cultures, which ignores the richness of their lives, and becomes limiting. Interestingly, a hierarchy is created, where the 'other' is seen as being 'less than', in terms of different factors such as education and social background. This is a common occurrence with minority groups, particularly with refugees. Somehow being a refugee is often perceived as *now having nothing, but also having had nothing in one's past*. This makes it difficult to remember that people had their own support networks and resources, perhaps a certain educational and professional status. For example, one particular client, Omar, who had been a judge in his own country, during sessions would constantly relay everyday situations where he would end up having disagreements with others. We explored this at length, as it was difficult for him to see what he communicated to people and in turn how he was perceived as a refugee with nothing to offer. It was hardly surprising how the loss of so much in his life, including his high status, was unbearable in the new country. Additionally, owing to his poor English he was unable to take part in professional activities until he gained proficiency in English. His anger was getting in the way of relationships as well as preventing him from mastering the new language.

- *Negative images*. The fear of the 'other' is portrayed in all kinds of media forms. The results are images of ethnic minorities who are often described as impulsive, irresponsible, dangerous and not to be trusted. Growing up among these images, they may be taken on board as if they belong to that particular cultural group.

- *Client seen as the racial/cultural group*: This refers to the danger of seeing the individual client as representing the 'race' and 'culture'. This is common when anxieties are high and in order to strengthen one's beliefs the client is seen to represent the whole group's behaviours and thinking. It is much more difficult for their individuality to be taken into account.

- *Suitability for therapy*: Clients from different cultural backgrounds have often been seen as so different that they are 'untreatable' or as if 'they' require specialist services. Of course, therapists communicate, both consciously and unconsciously, to their clients about their 'suitability' for therapeutic treatment.

All the stereotypes result from our anxieties about working with difference and an often rather ethnocentric view of the world. *Ethnos* is the Greek word for 'nation', and the last part comes from 'centre', meaning that one's own group is the centre of what is the norm and correct. Furthermore, there is the hierarchical judgement that one group is superior, since what it carries represents the norm. Shifting ethnocentrism means reflecting on our behaviours, but challenging them can take place only with the right type of facilitation within a safe context. Although, in today's international community, cross-cultural interaction is inevitable, it can result in extremely powerful dynamics: it can significantly raise people's anxiety and increase defensiveness; raised anxiety can influence people's clarity of thinking and ability to understand others' behaviour, as well as to have insight into their own. As a result, people often do not reflect on their behaviour and simply do not understand how behaviours vary cross-culturally. In fact, sometimes issues of difference, namely racism, are so difficult to understand or to relate to that if they have not had personal experiences, people may choose to become emotionally detached from them. Another way of coping may be to feel that they are so unreal and overwhelming that one can not take on board societal issues. Often, if expectations are more reality-based (perhaps by being more informed about another culture) there will be less disappointment or upset (Pedersen, 1997). Cross-cultural interactions can create these extremely complicated dynamics when people lose their familiar framework and do not feel safe.

Ethnocentrism also means shifting from the individualistic position of Western psychology and its clinical implications. 'Individualistic' refers to cultures which value, as stated, individualism, or the person developing independently from the group. The individualism–collectivism distinction can be witnessed in every aspect of our life-style; for example, the degree of movement around the world for jobs is going to be largely guided by life-styles and family expectations. For example, an individualist is more likely to travel in order to take a job many miles away, whilst a collectivist will remain closer to the family or community group. There will be a greater feeling of obligation to remain linked and near the collective.

Another example of different value systems across cultures can be seen in the structure of cultural naming systems. For example, among the collectivist Balinese culture personal names are rarely used. Personal and birth order names are used mainly to refer to children and adolescents. Balinese use tekonyms, or words which describe the relationship between two people, especially that between older and younger family members. Also when a child is born the parents are known as the 'mother of' and 'father of' that particular child. In a more individualistic culture the person will be known and there may be little mention of the connections with the rest of the cultural/familial group. These show that other cultures have different ways of relating (Gardiner et al., 1988), which have implications for cross-cultural psychology and counselling. Similarly, a South East Asian Muslim man will have a different name from his wife. For example, he may be called Mohammed Isha; the first name is his religious name and the latter his personal name. Female Muslims also have two names, but there is a different structure. For example, in the name Fatima Bibi the first name is the personal one and the second one means 'Miss' or 'Madam'. In English, therefore, it would be meaningless to call someone 'Bibi' only (Eleftheriadou, 1996). However, this is not to state that every individualist or collectivist will behave in the same way, and indeed there are many variations within one culture. It is perhaps more helpful to view it as a spectrum where some cultures show a greater degree of collectivism than others, and in different areas of life.

The counselling psychologist does not need to have information about all cultures – indeed, this would be an impossible task. The cross-cultural therapeutic process is about finding a way to work with the similarities and differences *at the same time*. There needs to be enough openness to challenge one's views and to consider diverse value systems.

Therapeutic goals

The therapeutic goals of cross-cultural counselling psychology work are:

- To have a clear awareness and challenge our ethnocentricism and any stereotypes evoked when coming into contact with other cultural groups.
- To take into account the role of race and culture(s) in the client's life.
- To explore the client's relationship with the majority culture.
- To understand their choice of therapist and the meaning it holds.
- To be open to how the client presents their culture, rather than the societal or media images of the culture.
- To have some understanding of the client's journey, voluntary or involuntary, to the new culture.

Non-verbal communication and language

A large part of cross-cultural work involves an awareness of cultural variation in non-verbal and verbal communication. In terms of the non-verbal aspects, for example, there are differences in the 'desirable' spatial distance across cultures, including the ideal conversational distance. In terms of kinesics, it has been found that people can decode body behaviour and facial expression more accurately when it is exhibited by those who share a common language, culture and race. Paralanguage, which involves tone, loudness of voice, pauses, hesitations, pitch and rate of speech, also differs across cultures. Similarly, it has been found that paralanguage is easier to comprehend by those who belong to the same culture. Paralanguage, kinesics and proxemics are so much part of everyday communication that they can provide stronger messages than the verbal. If the therapist is attentive they can pick up a great deal of information from the body language of the client. Non-verbal behaviour is also more unconscious, hence more primitive, than words; therefore it can be more revealing than the verbal.

In all therapeutic work, we need some awareness of the client's historical background. Recalling something which was experienced at a younger age may be extremely difficult, especially if it is the first time it is being talked about and in another language.

Generally, it is unrealistic to expect the counselling psychologist to find out exactly what the client would have said in their mother tongue. However, there may be times when meanings become too unclear owing to language difficulties. It may be important to pause and ask the client to think/say the words in their own language. Even when there is confusion over finding the exact words or frustration at not being able to 'say it in English' at that point, this might still access the emotional experience. One client described the emotion attached to her story in such a way that it did not seem congruent with the content. When asked how she would say it in her own language she said 'she would then sound really sad'. This enabled her to discuss the frustration of having to convey these feelings in another language, but also how (although perhaps in a rather more long-winded way in this case) she got in touch with the sadness, which was avoided when she was speaking in English. Cross-cultural communication may require a great deal of explanation, needing to be made more explicit, than if people shared a cultural background with the other.

Where there are language barriers it may mean that therapeutic work can only remain at a particular level and not progress. However, when clients have mastered the 'new' language they may be able to relate their emotional life well, and sometimes even more explicitly than in their own language. This is because they may not have as rich a vocabulary and cannot intellectualize; they just have to use the first word which comes to mind. Using another language than one's 'mother tongue' in psychotherapy is complicated and can be a help or become a hindrance to the client, depending on the meaning attached to it.

Building the therapeutic relationship

Any relationship needs time to develop and seeking help from a stranger is not to be underestimated. However, the added component of speaking to a stranger who belongs to a different culture/race needs careful consideration. During the initial meeting the therapist can gain insight into the reasons why they need support at that particular time of their life. The counselling psychologist can gain significant information through exploration of their journey to that particular therapist/therapy centre.

Counselling psychology is a delicate process because clients have to be understood within their cultural context. However, inquiry about cultural issues should not be the focus, unless it is the problem itself. A client can sense how the cultural information is asked and why. Counselling psychologists need to be clear that they are able to work with particular issues and certain cultural groups. This is because conscious and unconscious meanings and assumptions, such as strongly held religious or political beliefs, will be communicated to the client. This is where cross-cultural training, supervision and personal development are crucial. If a therapist has not explored his or her own prejudices and feelings about certain cultural groups and practices, then this can result in distancing the client and intensifying feelings of difference. I remember a client of mine who was talking about a relative's struggle with the veil. Although I had said very little she paused, saying, 'I feel that you understand what I am saying by the way you have looked at me.' I had indeed understood and had lived in a country which required the veil but had not disclosed this to my client at the time.

Anyone engaged in cross-cultural work would need to have some familiarity with the socio-cultural context of our clients. Cross-cultural clients may fall into one of the following categories; first-generation immigrant, second or more generation immigrant, refugee, student, temporary worker or traveller/tourist.

Each group will bring their own issues and these need to be understood in order to separate what is internal in the client and what is external (and perhaps) group experience and probably out of the client's control (see Eleftheriadou, 1996). For example, working with refugees the counselling psychologist needs to have some sense of what it is like to be persecuted, to flee and to experience severe loss. Allowing clients room to convey the context means that they can bring in the aspects which *they* consider of importance. For example, a particular cultural element may not be brought into the session until there is an event back 'home' and then this will be on their mind. This process will include their assumptions of what the counselling psychologist is familiar with or not. If the sessions become an information giving of socio-political events without affect then the counselling psychologist needs to explore what is going on which is leaving the emotional attachments out.

These aspects are not unique to cross-cultural counselling work, but we know from research that the anxieties are usually intensified in cross-cultural contact (Ward et al., 2001). This is due to far too many uncertainties about the 'other'. Taking time and creating the space to understand, and allow for, difference is crucial to understanding the client's construction of the meaning of the world.

Choice of therapist: racial or cultural matching

There is a long history of debate in counselling and psychology whether there should be racial matching of client and therapist. All clients have ideas on who they feel they can trust to work with. This can be discussed from the beginning of the counselling psychology relationship when anxieties are heightened. The client's qualitative accounts and hence preference reflect more accurately who they think (and trust) would support them best. This would be useful information to find out where their identifications lie. That is, they may identify with the culture, the religion, the language, or gender might be the most crucial factor. For example, the most important factor for one client was to work with a black female whilst for another working with a Lingala-speaking counselling psychologist was of greatest importance.

There is controversy as to when and how the differences should be addressed. After all, when a man and woman are working together, or adult and child, this will need to be addressed. Why should two people from different races/cultures avoid it? As Kareem (1992) states, 'a psychotherapeutic process that does not take into account the person's whole life experience, or that denies consideration of their race, culture, gender or social values can only fragment the person' (p. 16). For those whose race has been reflected as negative, it may be useful to work with someone from the same racial background. However, matching on racial background does not necessarily mean that the client and therapist are going to have exactly the same racial, cultural or psychological experience. In fact they are likely to give a rather different subjective meaning to their experience.

The research in this area is vast, but there are some consistent findings. For example, Ewing (1974) showed that preference for a culturally similar counselling psychologist does not apply to all cultural groups. Acosta and Sheehan (1976) and Atkinson (1983) found that with different ethnic groups there was little support for the same ethnicity counsellor. There is also research to show that some people choose to go to a different ethnicity counsellor (Gambosa et al., 1976). This may be precisely because they wish to have someone who is not part of the in-group to ensure confidentiality and/or because they can identify with the host culture more than their own cultural background. For example, a Moroccan client wished to see a female therapist who spoke either Arabic or French, but felt she could not work with someone from the same country. The fear was both about being known and consequently that it would somehow inhibit what she wanted to discuss in confidence. In later sessions it emerged that her father was Moroccan and her mother was French. She had had a hierarchy in her mind about the superior culture being French which she was rather surprised and rather embarrassed to find herself talking about.

Generally a decision has to be made as to whether the client and therapist match should be made taking into account a shared racial, cultural, language or gender background. Whether the client and the therapist are from the same culture or not, we need to explore what it means to be perceived by the client as being 'different' or 'the same as'.

This raises the crucial question of whether clients can be helped in culturally different systems. For some clients, a cross-cultural relationship may be a more facilitating relationship, which will support change of some kind. However, if the cultural distance between the two is too great, the outcome will not only be unfavourable, but it is unlikely that clients will remain in the therapeutic relationship. Communities are also very close and if there is no trust in a particular service it quickly becomes known among the community.

Understanding life stages across cultures

An interesting area to explore cross-culturally has been the whole notion of life stage expectations. In this context, the concept of life stages is not used to mean strict guidelines on what is supposed to happen at each stage, but some idea of what cultures/communities' expectations may be of their members. We know that expectations about development vary enormously across cultures (Segall et al., 1990; Gardiner et al., 1998).

In counselling psychology practice we will get to know how our clients' expectations during a particular life age/phase are informed by the cultural context. Similarly, couple/marital relationships which are common and the norm in one country may be seen as inappropriate in another context (Buss et al., 1990). Another area which has been researched widely in cross-cultural work is the whole area of child rearing and how parental expectations vary significantly across contexts (Luthar and Quinlan, 1993). In family work, for example, meanings have to be constructed taking into account the client's expectations, their familial as well as their cultural norms. This is a delicate area, and as stated earlier, the information has to stem from the client, in order to avoid gross generalizations taking place to the cost of the individual meaning for that particular client.

Working with interpreters

To some extent, language barriers can also be overcome when working with interpreters. This is also particularly useful if one is working with young children who are not fully aware of all the socio-political facts. An intercultural organization for the support of refugees who have experienced violence and torture, the Medical Foundation for the Care of Victims of Torture, works alongside interpreters where necessary. This provides an interesting scenario, as in some cases it may provide the necessary socio-economic context. As stated earlier, it is important as therapists to have some factual information and awareness of our clients' countries of origin. If, for example, we are working with a client who has experienced torture and is unable to return to his or her home country, part of the work will be to understand their social reality.

The interpreter in the room can also complicate dynamics when they see themselves as inferior/superior to the client. It is interesting to observe who identifies with whom in the session. Identifications are also interesting because they can provide useful information in the setting; that is, the therapist might feel as if they have a co-therapist in the room or that they are dealing with two clients who need support. Interpreters often have emotional difficulties around certain issues, especially when working with someone who shares a socio-political background, so it is something to be aware of. This was the case working with one client who seemed to be experiencing a psychotic episode, and it took a long time to assess, as she had very little English and the interpreter was being extremely protective. The interpreter blamed housing and other external issues for the 'distress', ending up in the position of justifying rather than directly translating the content of the client's material. Of course what the interpreter was pointing out was that there were many contributing factors to the client's distress, but it was difficult to formulate a clear impression of how distressed the client was and whether they needed further (psychiatric) input. Overall, however, working with a good interpreter does provide additional information which can help the process, such as asking about how a word is pronounced and picking up the emotional nuances of language. Often, working with refugees or asylum seekers who may be quite (understandably) suspicious of disclosing difficulties to strangers, an interpreter may help them feel at ease.

Clinical vignette

The following case material illustrates the themes and the challenges faced in therapeutic work involving two individuals. There is not one homogeneous community or culture, therefore the clinical vignette will serve to illustrate specific dynamics of cross-cultural work with a particular person within a particular relationship.

Alessandro

Alessandro was a thirty-year-old man who came to see a counselling psychologist after taking time off work for ill health. When I asked him about his background he looked extremely surprised and described himself rather uncomfortably as coming from 'mixed parentage'. His mother was British and his father was originally from Africa and had settled in Brazil. Alessandro was brought up in South America, where his parents had met and lived together in Brazil until he was five years old. He had then moved with his mother to the United States and remained there until he was twenty-two years old. Alessandro had come over to Britain to study but later, as he said rather passively, 'just ended up staying', as many immigrants do, for another year and then another which ended up being eight years in total. He has been in a series of short-term relationships and after the last relationship broke up he felt utterly hopeless that he could maintain anything long-term. He had been prescribed anti-depressants by his doctor and he had reluctantly agreed. He told me that it had made him feel even more of a failure for not coping, but that he was finding it hard to hold on to any motivation in his life. For example, there were many decisions that had been abandoned for some time, such as his returning back to work. I met a man whom I can only describe as 'lost' in every way, personally, socially and professionally. His tone was flat and hollow.

Initially, although he had requested to work with someone from another culture than his own, he did not really think it was important to discuss this. In fact I was interested in what words he used to define his culture. (His English was perfect, but he thought in Spanish.) He found it difficult to do and said he had never really had the space to think about it. Unconsciously he related to me as if I was the key to British culture, and commented on how good my English was. (By saying this, of course, he was acknowledging that I was also from another culture.) If he visited a new place in the United Kingdom he would assume I had been there and, if not, that 'I knew all about it'. It was as if I was the one who had completely embraced the host culture, very much as he had tried to do for the time he had been in the U.K. When his relationship with a British woman had finished he had to review his life. One aspect that he considered was that in his relationships he sought to be with women who were also slightly 'lost' culturally. His last relationship epitomized this: he chose to be with someone who worked for the Red Cross, frequently travelled abroad and suddenly felt rather an outsider in her own culture.

During those times he described how difficult it had been for him to hold on to any continuity in their relationship. He realized that there was an element in him that he had not quite acknowledged and therefore, unconsciously, he chose people who were similar and slightly nomadic, and sadly emotionally uncommitted. In a way he did not know how to keep a relationship, especially a cross-cultural one, as he had never had a model of this. Now we were in a cross-cultural therapeutic relationship and it was a good starting point.

I slowly understood how much he wanted to fit in and have a home. Back 'home' in the United States he felt torn between his father's culture and race and his mother's. When he felt safe enough to discuss his childhood and family relationships, I learnt that the parental relationship had been looked down upon by his maternal grandparents and in fact there had not been much contact with them. He realized how furious he was that he knew so little about his mother's background and that she had never really introduced him to her family. He felt she had found a refuge in another country, just like his own reasons for coming to Britain. Most of his contact had been with his father's relatives, but that stopped a few years after his parents separated. He had taken on board the parental values placed on race and culture to such an extent that it became impossible to feel that he could be himself – that is, a man of mixed parentage.

For many people of mixed parentage when the parents are seen not to be able to hold the diversity, there is no model for the young person in how to engage in their most intimate relationships. Alessandro attempted to do this by being on his own 'neutral ground', as he called it, although of course he had returned to his mother's home culture. Initially, being in London made him feel very different and he was desperate to fit in. But later he began to like the fact that London was multicultural and enjoyed not being placed into a slot automatically. At the beginning of the therapy, one of the obstacles had been that he wanted to travel, but he postponed obtaining a new passport. This was due to his wish to change his surname and take on his mother's British name. He later gave up this wish and said it meant that he could hold on to his identity and did not have to fulfil her wish to belong. Like so many clients he felt he was not only seen as but inside he felt more 'Spanish' in the United Kingdom, more British in South America and more 'black' in the United States. This is quite common where people hold on to more than one identity, determined by the different environments.

At first Alessandro needed to put aside our cultural differences and see me as fitting into the British culture completely. It was too painful for him not to belong, so he had to feel I had managed it. Of course this pretence could not last as he began to be in touch with the emotional cost of fitting in and rejecting his diverse background. Also it was impossible to do as he was constantly asked about his origin. Later he asked me whether I was also of 'mixed' background. In his eyes this meant we could understand each other. He felt it enabled us to work with his material, and at times I think he hoped because of the commonalities we would not have to discuss certain areas which were best left undiscussed. During this phase of the therapy he seemed to take note of objects in the consulting room that he assumed I had obtained from abroad. I reflected this back to him and how he had let go of the image of me as belonging to the majority culture. We linked it with the parallel in his life where, rather than 'fitting in', it became more meaningful to him to integrate all the cultural components of his diverse background.

I have chosen this case because it illustrates some poignant cross-cultural themes. We had to address both the similarities and the differences between us and both of us being part of a different context. As stated earlier, each culture has a different view of the developmental stages and the goals expected at each stage. In Alessandro's case he was reaching thirty and was struggling with his own cultural expectations as well as the majority culture expectations of what he 'ought to be doing with his life'. To his surprise many of the internally imposed expectations were in line with Spanish cultural expectations. The case also illustrates that the experience of 'culture shock' (Littlewood and Lipsedge, 1989), which includes sadness, fear and anger about being in a different context, is not necessarily triggered on entry to the new culture and it does not always have to be a negative experience. For Alessandro coming to the United Kingdom had been a turbulent journey, but it was not explored until some years later. Once he entered the exploration process, he felt there was so much that had been pushed aside and it was time to review his identity and be proud of his roots.

It is interesting that when asked about significant attachments at the beginning, he had said humorously about a potential therapist that 'it didn't matter who they were as long as they liked South Americans' and did not think 'they all were into drugs'. It was a revelation to him that he had devalued himself to such an extent and was fearful of being judged. Clients will often bring stereotypical images before the therapist does so, as this is part of their experience through societal images. The stereotype was brought into our consulting room as a way of testing my stereotypes. It was my responsibility to open it up for exploration with him. Emotionally Alessandro was at a stage of his life where he was open to change. Since he had grown up multiculturally he was also more at ease in a cross-cultural therapeutic relationship.

Conclusion

This chapter has highlighted the key reasons why cross-cultural issues need to be taken on board by counselling psychologists. Although the cross-cultural work process is relatively new territory for counselling psychologists, there has been more thinking about the issues. This is reflected in the number of publications and events about the subject.

Since psychology has considered the issues relatively recently and the cross-cultural issues are about our private, psychological, as well as interpersonal group lives, we may need to step out of psychology and draw on the work of anthropologists, sociologists and many others who have observed the plethora of interpersonal interactions, particularly on a group/community level. The field of social psychology may need to be incorporated much more also, as it has dedicated itself to understand and to take into account the power of the group on the individual. It has provided useful information about the dynamics of groups and has brought a balance to the often rather individualistic Western view of general psychology. Issues of race and culture need to be taken into account, but it is, at all times, a delicate balance. That is, if we focus too much on race we make it into something concrete and unchangeable. We need to redefine our observations of cultural communications and meanings and to translate these into clinical practice guidelines.

We can take many good practice examples from the fast-growing literature, from cross-culturalist practitioners mentioned, such as Sue and Sue, Pedersen, Ponterotto, among many others (see references). They have provided us with good practice guidelines and ethics for clinical practice, and have also outlined research guidelines for cross-cultural work. The process is complex, but by no means impossible. Transcultural work has generally been portrayed as filled with barriers and yet many clients who have engaged in a cross-cultural therapeutic relationship seem to find it a useful and creative process, but, and perhaps predictably, only when their culture is truly taken into consideration and respected.

The counselling psychologist and client match does not have to be identical, but:

> Intervention or treatment is more likely to be effective when it matches or fits the cognitive map, life-style, or cultural background of clients. That is, ideally the intervention strategy is culturally consistent with the expectations and background of the clients. (Sue et al., 1987: 275–6)

For some clients cross-cultural work can be creative precisely because it takes the person out of the familiar context, where it is taken for granted that all is understood. In fact the person can find the space to explore their cultural milieu, understand its influences, review them and as a result accept or reject them. This does not mean that every client will be willing to or should do this.

As stated earlier, cross-cultural work is not about a specific theory, but about being open to people's different ways of thinking and behaving as a result of different socio-cultural experiences. As counselling psychologists we need to be able to take on board the differences and similarities at the same time. Taking culture on board does not imply that it is problematic, only that it needs to be taken into account if we are to have a good enough understanding of our clients' way of being.

First and foremost, the purpose of this chapter is to emphasize that cross-cultural therapy is not a list of skills to be learnt. It is a way of thinking and relating in cross-cultural encounters that can take place only when we have undergone our own conscious and unconscious exploration of the issues.

References

Acosta, F. and Sheehan, J. (1976) 'Preferences toward Mexican American and Anglo-American psychotherapists', *Journal of Consulting and Clinical Psychology*, 44: 272–9.

Atkinson, D.R. (1983) 'Ethnic similarity in counseling: a review of research', *Counseling Psychologist*, 11 (3): 79–92.

Berry, J.W., Poortinga, Y.H., Segall, M.H. and Dasen, P.R. (1992) *Cross-cultural Psychology*. Cambridge: Cambridge University Press.

Best, D., House, A.S., Barnard, A.E. and Spicker, B.S. (1994) 'Parent–child interactions in France, Germany and Italy', *Journal of Cross-cultural Psychology*, 25 (2): 181–93.

Buss et al. (1990) 'International preferences in selecting mates: a study of thirty-seven cultures', *Journal of Cross-cultural Psychology*, 21 (1): 5–47.

Casas, J.M. and Pytluk, S.D. (1995) 'Hispanic identity development: implications for research and practice', in J.G. Ponterotto, J.M. Casa, L.A. Suzuki and C.M. Alexander (eds) *Handbook of Multicultural Counseling*. Thousand Oaks CA: Sage.

Eleftheriadou, Z. (1992) 'Multi-cultural counselling and psychotherapy: a philosophical framework', *Psychologos: an International Review of Psychology*, 3: 21–9.

Eleftheriadou, Z. (1993) 'Application of a philosophical framework to transcultural counselling', *Journal of the Society for Existential Analysis*, 4: 116–23.

Eleftheriadou, Z. (1994). *Transcultural Counselling*. London: Central Publishing House.

Eleftheriadou, Z. (1996a) 'Skills for communicating with patients from different cultural backgrounds', in R. Bor and M. Lloyd (eds) *Communication Skills for Medicine*. Edinburgh: Churchill Livingstone.

Eleftheriadou, Z. (1996b) 'Notions of culture: the impact of culture on international students', in S. Sharples (ed.) *Changing Cultures: Developments in Cross-cultural Theory and Practice*. London: United Kingdom Council for Overseas Student Affairs.

Eleftheriadou, Z. (1997) 'Cultural differences in the therapeutic relationship', in I. Horton, and V. Varma (eds) *The Needs of Counsellors and Psychotherapists*. London: Sage.

Ewing, T.N. (1974) 'Racial similarity of client and counselor and client satisfaction with counselling', *Journal of Counseling Psychology*, 21: 446–9.

Fernando, S. (1991) *Mental Health, Race and Culture*. London: Macmillan/MIND.

Fernando, S. (ed.) (1995) *Mental Health in a Multi-ethnic Society*. London: Routledge.

Gambosa, A.M., Tosi, D.J. and Roccio, A.C. (1976) 'Race and counselor climate in the counselor preference of delinquent girls', *Journal of Counseling Psychology*, 23: 160–2.

Gardiner, H.W. Mutter, J.D. and Kosmitzki, C. (1998) *Lives across Cultures: Cross-cultural Human Development*. Boston MA: Allyn & Bacon.

Grieger, I. and Ponterotto, J.G. (1995) 'A framework for assessment in multicultural counselling' In J.G. Ponterotto et al. (eds) *Handbook of Multicultural Counseling*. Thousand Oaks CA: Sage.

Kareem, J. (1992). 'The Nafsiyat Intercultural Therapy Centre: ideas and experience in intercultural therapy', In J. Kareem and R. Littlewood (eds) *Intercultural Therapy*. Oxford: Blackwell.

Keitel, M.A., Kopala, M. and Adamson, W.S. (1996) 'Ethical issues in multicultural assessment' in L.A. Suzuki, P.J. Meller and J.G. Ponterotto (eds) *Handbook of Multicultural Assessment*. San Francisco: Jossey Bass.

Littlewood, R. and Lipsedge, M. (1989) *Aliens and Alienists*. London: Unwin Hyman.

Luthar, S.S. and Quinlan, D.M. (1993) 'Parental images in two cultures', *Journal of Cross-cultural Psychology*, 24 (2): 186–202.

Minsel, B., Becker, P. and Korchin, S.J. (1991) 'A cross-cultural view of positive mental health', *Journal of Cross-cultural Psychology*, 22 (2): 157–81.

Moorhouse, S. (1992) 'Quantitative research in intercultural therapy' in J. Kareem and R. Littlewood (eds) *Intercultural Therapy*. Oxford: Blackwell.

Moreland, K.L. (1996) 'Persistent issues in multicultural assessment of social and emotional functioning', In L.A. Suzuki, P.J. Meller and J.G. Ponterotto (eds) *Handbook of Multicultural Assessment*. San Francisco: Jossey Bass.

Pedersen, P. (ed.) (1987) *Handbook of Cross-cultural Counselling and Therapy*, London: Praeger.

Pedersen, P. (1997) *Culture-centered Counseling Interventions*. London: Sage.

Pedersen, P.B., Draguns, J.G., Lonner, W.J. and Trimble, J.E. (eds) (1989) *Counselling across Cultures*, third edition. Honolulu: University of Hawaii Press.

Ponterotto, J.G., Casas, J.M., Suzuki, L.A. and Alexander, C.M. (1995) *Handbook of Multicultural Counseling*. Thousand Oaks CA: Sage.

Segall, M.H., Dasen, P.R., Berry, J.W. and Poortinga, Y.H. (1990) *Human Behaviour in a Global Perspective*. Oxford: Pergamon Press.

Shweder, R.A. (1991) *Thinking through Cultures: Expeditions in Cultural Psychology*. London: Harvard University Press.

Stigler, J.W., Shweder, R.A. and Herdt, G. (1990) *Cultural Psychology*. Cambridge: Cambridge University Press.

Sue, S., Akutsu, P.D. and Higashi, C. (1987) 'Training issues in conducting therapy with ethnic minoritiy-group clients' in P. Pedersen (ed.) *Handbook of Cultural Counseling and Therapy*. New York: Praeger.

Suzuki, L.A., Meller, P.J. and Ponterotto, J.G. (eds) (1996) *Handbook of Multicultural Assessment*. San Francisco: Jossey Bass.

Thomas, L. (1992) 'Racism and psychotherapy' in J. Kareem and R. Littlewood (eds) *Intercultural Therapy*. Oxford: Blackwell.

Vannoy Adams, M. (1996). *The Multicultural Imagination: 'Race', Colour, and the Unconscious*. London: Routledge.

Ward, C., Bochner, S. and Furnham, A. (2001) *The Psychology of Culture Shock*. London: Routledge.

25 Time-limited Practice
DAVID PURVES

A chapter that considers arguments on the use of time in therapy can exist only in a field where there are differing views of human development and the genesis of psychological problems. Psychological understanding does not remain static; the subjective nature of our business means that at any time there will be competing perspectives on any given human problem. Indeed, all therapeutic endeavours, Counselling, Counselling Psychology or Psychotherapy, can be characterized by variety (Caro, 1996). Yet alternative viewpoints also give rise to alternative therapeutic strategies. Pre-existing and alternative treatments can then be subjected to the rigours of research. In this way, rational treatments evolve. Time-limited practice provides an interesting illustration of all of these processes.

Interest in time-limited practice has increased over the last four decades. There have been combinations of pragmatic, financial, theoretical and clinical forces that have influenced this movement. The combination of these forces has meant that therapy is getting shorter and shorter. In looking at these developments it is possible to see some attempts at brief work that have been miniaturizations of standard long-term work, whereas others have been perhaps more novel and innovative. Research, however, has demonstrated that good time-limited psychotherapy is an entity in its own right (Koss and Shiang, 1994). It is not merely a superficial or cost-cutting means of rationing fuller treatment. In many settings time-limited psychological therapies are often considered the treatment of choice for most patients. Even so, there are different versions of time-limited practice, there are resistances to working in this way and there are assumptions about what kinds of client are suitable for time-limited work. Time has the potential to be used therapeutically in many ways, for the benefit of the client, and therefore a proper consideration of time is likely to be helpful. This chapter will address the variety in the therapeutic use of time, and will suggest practical considerations for planned, time-limited practice.

What is time-limited practice?

Time-limited practice spans the whole diversity of therapeutic approaches. Hence there are many terms to describe this type of work. Some of these are: brief therapy, strategic therapy, time-limited therapy, focal therapy or short-term therapy. Whatever the terms used, all of these approaches have many practical similarities, while retaining important theoretical differences.

Budman and Gurman (1988) suggest that the key to success in treating clients effectively in a time-limited way is to develop sensitivity to time, to make the most of each session. However, even within time-limited practice there is considerable variation in how many sessions 'time-limited' means. It has generally been agreed that time-limited work would not normally last more than twenty to twenty-five sessions (Koss and Shiang, 1994) but can be as short as one session (Talmon, 1990; see Bloom, 2001, for a review). In short, there is a considerable range in the number of sessions defined by time-limited practice and it furthermore covers most types of psychological work. There is, however, the assumption that time-limited work automatically means short-term involvement. I do not consider that this view best serves the client or the therapist. I have therefore used a definition of time-limited practice that reflects the drive to be efficient but still recognizes the importance of clinical judgement. I shall consider the following a definition of time-limited practice: 'Time-limited practice is specified not by a fixed number of sessions, but by an intention to help clients move towards their goals as time-efficiently as possible.'

How is the length of therapy decided?

When a client and a therapist come together for the first time, there are likely to be only a few issues that are uppermost in the client's mind, and of these 'Can this person help me?' and 'How long will it take?' are liable to be paramount. Yet the length of therapy initially offered by a therapist often relies upon at least six important factors:

- How the therapist views time.
- What the client presents as a problem.
- The problem theory held by the therapist.
- The expectations of therapy held by the client.
- The outcome of the assessment process.
- The training of the therapist.

All of these aspects of a clinical decision need to be teased out in order to clarify the debate over the use of time.

Time-limited practice: planned and unplanned

There is a paradox inherent in considering time-unlimited and time-limited psychotherapy. This is that planned time-limited work can take longer than time-unlimited (open-ended) work. This paradox arises from the fact that clients remain in therapy for only as long as they wish to do so, and not for the length of time a therapist might consider to be appropriate. For numerous reasons, which include the notion of sufficient change being achieved as defined by the client, clients seem to expect and adhere to very short contracts. A considerable amount of research has demonstrated this fact. Koss (1979) investigated the average length of attendance of clients in a private clinic. The median number of therapy sessions was eight, with 80 per cent discontinuing treatment before twenty sessions. Goleman (1993) identified the average number of psychotherapy sessions in the American population as being fourteen. Brech and Agulnik (1996) in a study of a British counselling service found that 40 per cent of clients received one to four sessions and another 40 per cent between five and twenty sessions, with only 20 per cent having contracts beyond six months. Interestingly, these figures do not simply represent a new phenomenon that reflects a drive for economy or accountability, rather they demonstrate the reality of short therapeutic contracts for most clients. Garfield (1986) reviewed the data on the length of psychotherapy contracts between the years 1948 and 1970. He found the median number of sessions to be five or six, with most clients terminating before twenty sessions. The inescapable fact is that clients seem to take what they need from therapy and then leave. Clients who actually adhere to a time-limited contract could have more psychotherapy than many open-ended psychotherapy clients, who have the option of a potentially unlimited number of sessions. This is an important point because it helps to define the debate on time-limited practice. Short-term work, as opposed to long-term work, would seem to be the norm. This suggests that the discussion about whether short or long-term work is better or more effective may be of only marginal interest. The important debate should focus on how to increase the rational and effective design of time-limited therapy within the constraints and expectations placed upon us by our clients.

This perspective becomes clearer when one considers the parameters of time-limited work. The consensus in the literature would seem to suggest that brief, short-term or time-limited work lasts up to a maximum of twenty to twenty five sessions. In light of this research, we can see that anyone adhering to this maximum time limit would actually be in the minority for psychotherapy clients. Is it sufficient, however, to suggest that all clients be limited to a short fixed number of sessions? It is important to recognize that time-limited practice does not automatically mean brief, rather that time-limited practice reflects sensitivity to time. From this viewpoint the client is provided with what he/she needs to effect sufficient change. Neither too much time nor too little, the process is limited only by sufficiency. Therefore we need to be open to the client experience and flexible in our approach. This can mean loosening rigid views of time and becoming more focused on ways of helping the client move forward. A concept allied to this time-limited viewpoint is that not every client issue or problem can be adequately worked through in one long contract. This was never likely to be the case anyway, even in what was thought of as open-ended or long-term work. Evidence suggests that when clients present for therapy they have specific problems they feel unable to overcome and, having lived with them for what is likely to be a considerable period of time, they expect that help will be forthcoming and that it will be of shorter, rather than longer, duration (Garfield, 1986; Lambert et al., 1986).

What is a session?

In any consideration of time-limited work we need to establish some common metric by which we can consider how much is more, or how little is less. Budman and Gurman (1988) suggest that most therapies have applied a very low level of creativity to the problem of time. For instance, most therapies specify one session per week of one hour (or so) until resolution. Would then a thirty-minute session also be considered a session? Or would fortnightly or monthly sessions also warrant the same counting system? Would twelve monthly sessions equal in some way twelve weekly sessions? In the development of time-limited practice the most notable innovation in the use of time in the last eighty years has probably been the introduction of a fixed time limit set at the outset of therapy (Malan, 1963).

Yet some workers have attempted to use time in a more flexible way. Notably Milton Erickson, who would reputedly see some clients for as little as a few minutes, and others for sessions lasting hours (Haley, 1986). Similarly, clients might be seen daily or weekly, or with months between visits. This type of therapeutic practice may seem innovative to some practitioners but, to others, unprofessional and counterproductive. Perhaps the key to understanding Erickson's approach resides in his understanding of the client's problem, and the likely solution to that problem.

In their research on the use of time in psychotherapy Johnson and Gelso (1980) considered that a minimum amount of time with a therapist was needed to start the process of change; after such time, while the total number of sessions was not predictive of change, the total amount of time in counselling was predictive of change. Further research has also revealed that change continues after termination. In one study Gelso and Johnson (1983) demonstrated that college students continued to expand their therapeutic gains eight to fourteen months post termination of brief therapy. This demonstrates that brief work mobilizes resources and starts a change-in-motion process that continues after the work has finished; in general, suggesting that we do not always need to have sessions fixed by duration. Nor do we need to have sessions spaced on a weekly basis. These more radical views may suggest creative or innovative ways of delivering psychological therapy.

Very brief therapy

It is often thought that, if a patient does not return after the initial session, they have made the decision that therapy is not for them. However, research has demonstrated that psychotherapy contracts as short as one session can be beneficial (Talmon, 1990). In a review of the literature on single-session therapy Bloom (2001) presented evidence that demonstrated equivalent levels of effectiveness between groups of clients seen for one session or more than one session. I shall give two examples to illustrate this effect. Askevold (1983) described a study of three matched groups of women suffering from anorexia nervosa. One group received one session of therapy, a second group received a brief therapy programme and the third group received an open-ended contract therapy. Follow-up data collected between four and fourteen years after the conclusion of treatment found no difference between the groups. Suggesting that one session equals in treatment efficacy both brief and open-ended therapy.

Talmon (1990) described a programme where three therapists attempted single-session therapy with sixty randomly assigned clients presenting with heterogeneous complaints and levels of severity. Altogether, 58 per cent of the clients were actually seen for only one session. At follow-up 88 per cent of that group reported being either improved or much improved. These and other studies provide provocative evidence that a single session of focused therapy can be effective for some people.

Indeed, Malan et al. (1975) in an early retrospective view of assessment found that some patients who had received one assessment session and followed up, while on the waiting list experienced spontaneous recovery from their previously diagnosed neurotic state. This research seems to suggest, as Aveline (1995) asserts, that assessment is also therapy and can therefore be therapeutic. Some newer specific therapies have taken the view that sufficient client change can be achieved in very few sessions. Indeed, Barkham and Shapiro (1990) have developed a two-plus-one method where a client receives two sessions followed by one follow-up session three months later. Using this approach, with an original diagnosis of mild depression, between 42 per cent and 67 per cent of clients showed improvement after two sessions. At the very least, these kinds of data tell us that our traditional view of the nature of human problems and what constitutes a curative Psychotherapy and Counselling Psychology need not remain static. Later work by Barkham et al. (1999) supports the efficacy of this approach, particularly for less severe cases.

Perhaps one of the most important considerations in planning session length or frequency should be what we want to achieve with a client. As an example from my own practice, I often mix hourly and two-hourly sessions. Hourly sessions seem adequate for most therapeutic activities, but where there is likely to be significant client re-experiencing or exposure to traumatic or very distressing material, a longer session is often necessary to allow for sufficient processing and resolution. The longer session provides the opportunity for more time if needed. Finally, it is also worth considering how much our own diary scheduling constraints determine how we treat a client. There are undoubtedly times when the client gets what we can give, irrespective of what they may ideally need!

Therapist attitudes to time

The values and attitudes of the therapist to time have been shown to be of importance in determining what kind of therapy they offer (Feltham, 1997; Budman and Gurman, 1988). Four factors would seem to be important in differentiating those who favour long and those who favour time-limited work. It is worth noting that many time-limited therapists believe that clients can be helped relatively quickly regardless of diagnosis or problem severity (Bloom, 2001).

Therapeutic time is valuable

Time-limited workers value an awareness of limited time while longer-term workers value 'timelessness' in their work. Research has shown that time limits can increase client motivation (Johnson and Gelso, 1980). Because time is limited the sessions must be more structured, with mutually agreed upon goals. This process seems to help engage clients, and there is often a lower drop-out rate, with clients developing positive expectations of the therapy.

The developmental stance

Time-limited therapists tend to take a developmental view with their patients. They incorporate ideas of lifelong change and growth, where one or more periods of time-limited therapy may play a role. They de-emphasize structural personality change, while longer-term workers may place more emphasis on static aspects of personality, where the presenting problem is viewed simply as a manifestation of an underlying pathology. Therefore, character change is often assumed by the long-term worker to be synonymous with treatment. Implicit in the time-limited approach is the implausibility of treating all of a client's ills in one long contract; rather the client opts for working on the foremost or current problem. When this piece of work is completed they leave therapy and continue with their life, knowing that at some point in the future they can, if they wish, return to work on other problems.

Any piece of psychological work has the potential to alter other aspects of the client's life. It is possible for small changes in thinking or behaving to have far-reaching effects that are often unpredictable. This means that a small piece of work could remove the necessity for later work altogether, suggesting that a parsimonious way forward for many clients is to engage in a discrete contract, then disengage and take some time to see how things settle.

Supporting the client as they change

A further key difference between the time-limited and longer-term workers is that by definition the latter feel that it is necessary to be with the client during the 'working through' process. There can be a de-emphasis on the client 'being in the world' and an emphasis on the client 'being in therapy'. In contrast the time-limited worker accepts that a client can do things on their own and in doing so may learn the additional lessons of self-reliance and self-confidence. Often an essential component of time-limited practice is the use of out of session tasks. Once a therapist is freed from believing that the client therapy session is the most important hour of the week the possibility of psychological change throughout the week can be encouraged, thereby multiplying opportunities for progress.

Apprenticeship may be the wrong model

Finally, many therapists have themselves experienced long-term or on-going therapy. They have been taught that deeper work requires longer time, and that necessarily anything quick is not lasting (Feltham, 1997). Yet ultimately, when the therapist moves from the position of client to practitioner, their responsibility lies in the provision of what the client needs, and not what they have experienced themselves. Indeed, the purpose of therapy may actually be different for a trainee therapist than for a client not anticipating the job of therapist. The client may simply require help to solve a problem. The problem may often not require a serious process of personality restructuring. Nor are they likely to need the level of therapeutic insight one would hope comes from prolonged personal therapy. Naturally, the client is entitled to these objectives should they make an informed choice from all of the alternatives. However, my personal view is that clients should not be subjected to psychotherapeutic goals by default.

The theoretical perspective of the therapist

We might assume that serious psychological problems require more treatment time than less serious ones; however, research does not seem to support this assumption. There appears to be little relationship between psychological severity and differences between brief and long-term therapy to achieve an improvement (Steenbarger, 1992; Howard et al., 1986). It would seem to be the case that the human response to psychological distress captures such wide variation that it is virtually impossible to predict with much accuracy how long healing should take (Feltham, 1997). Research has demonstrated that brief approaches can be used successfully with the full variety of patients, even those who are very disturbed, including personality disorders (Pollack et al., 1990).

Koss and Butcher (1986), reviewing the literature on brief psychotherapy, concluded that there was very little difference in outcome between brief treatments and those of time-unlimited therapy. When follow-up data were included, there remained no significant differences (Johnson and Gelso, 1980). Indeed, studies that have included long-term follow-up periods similarly support a lack of difference between time-limited or time-unlimited approaches (Johnson and Gelso, 1980; Bloom, 1992). An interesting insight into why there appear to be no differences between long and short-term therapies is given by Howard et al. (1986) in a meta-analysis of outcomes in psychotherapy. This study investigated a total of 2,400 patients and demonstrated that when drop-outs were controlled 29–38 per cent of psychotherapy clients improved in the first three sessions, 48–58 per cent improved by the first four to seven sessions, and 56-68 per cent improved by the first eight to sixteen sessions, thereafter 85 per cent of clients had improved by the first fifty-three to 100 sessions. It was concluded that there was a clear dose-response relationship such that the maximum change occurred during the first few sessions and thereafter the amount of change diminished over time. These data suggest that for many people relatively little psychological intervention was required to effect change. The research also suggested that many clients leave psychotherapy after relatively few sessions. It appears that clients feel better before they appear better on clinical scores. Therefore any improvement is less likely to be apparent to the clinician. This finding may account, in part, for why clinicians and clients have differential views of the efficacy of time-limited therapy. Johnson and Gelso (1980) also concluded that therapists tend to be biased towards longer-term work, whereas observers, clients and standardized measures rated time-limited work as effective as longer work. It seems clients assume that change can occur over short periods, whereas some therapists are more sceptical (Garfield, 1986).

In terms of treatment planning, up to 38 per cent of clients could potentially suit a very time-limited approach and nearly 60 per cent of patients a slightly longer one of up to eight sessions. Allowing for a more traditional view of time-limited practice (twenty to twenty-five sessions), 85 per cent of clients would improve with this level of treatment. This suggests that only 15 per cent of clients need be referred for very long-term work. Even then, longer-term work results in smaller and smaller changes, leaving open the possibility that long-term work *per se* may not be much more helpful. Perhaps an alternative approach would be a series of time-limited interventions as and when client need arises over the life span.

An important trial of time-limited practice was conducted in the Sheffield study by Shapiro et al. (1995). They used a time-limited dynamic psychotherapy that integrates many of the characteristics of other brief dynamic approaches. These included an emphasis on the client-therapist relationship, and the concept of the corrective emotional experience (Fonagy, 1998). They assessed 117 patients for differential outcomes in a randomized controlled trial of time-limited dynamic psychotherapy versus cognitive behavioural psychotherapy. The study also attempted to evaluate any distinctions between two treatment lengths (eight sessions or sixteen sessions). The data suggested that both therapies were effective overall. There was no significant interaction between severity of presenting symptom and duration of therapy. At one-year follow-up the cognitive behavioural approach appeared to be more efficacious than the psychodynamic therapy. A further interesting early analysis of these data combined Eysenck's (1952) percentage spontaneous improvement estimates, and concluded that fifteen sessions of psychotherapy accomplish what spontaneous remission accomplishes in two years (McNeilly and Howard, 1991).

Elton Wilson (1996) has proposed a structure for time-limited intervention whereby different time contracts are arranged depending upon the needs of the client. Elton Wilson conceived of five different options: a holding contract of one to three sessions, a mini-commitment of four to six sessions, a time-focused commitment of ten to thirteen sessions, a time-extended commitment of twelve-plus sessions with a four-session notice of termination, and a time-expanded commitment of virtually unlimited time with two months' notice of termination. Perhaps this approach captures the full range of time-limited options and allows for successive time commitments as required by the client. The model put forward by Elton Wilson represents a rational and evidence-based approach to integrating the reality of client therapy needs within the structure of time-limited practice.

The therapist's understanding of the client problem

Psychodynamic therapy

An important determinant of what the client is offered stems from the understanding of problem formation held by the therapist. The longest form of therapy is probably classical psychoanalysis. As originally devised by Freud, it is an investigation of unconscious mental processes through the development by the patient of a regressive transference neurosis with resolution through interpretation (Davanloo, 1978). Paradoxically, in Freud's earlier treatments, and even in training analysis, he was not averse to brief work. Freud treated the composer Gustav Mahler in one four-hour session, and the conductor Bruno Walter for psychosomatic paralysis in his arm in six sessions. The training analysis of Sandor Ferenczi was conducted in six weeks between 1914 and 1916 (Jones, 1955). Freud, it seems, had accepted what is now regarded as self-evident by many practitioners: psychotherapy does not have to be long-term. However, as his theorizing about personality became more complex, Freud focused more on the construction of theory and less on clinical outcome and efficacy. The consequence was that psychoanalysis became longer and more costly, but not necessarily more effective. Psychoanalytic treatment became predicated upon, and inextricably linked with, the psychoanalytic understanding of normal and abnormal development.

Innovative followers of Freud, such as Ferenczi and Rank, had tried to focus on the development of useful treatment strategies within the traditional interpretation of psychoanalytic theory. These were not well received by Freud, and one by one the master rejected innovative followers. The prevailing view became: if psychotherapy is good for you, then more must be better! The continued psychoanalytic alienation of the client led Davanloo to comment:

> In the early 1960s some of my observations in the out-patient psychiatric clinic of the Montreal General Hospital were that there was a very long waiting list, a small number of clinical patients were in long-term psychotherapy and, generally speaking, the number of patients treated with long-term psychotherapy was extremely limited compared to the number of patients seeking treatment. (Davanloo, 1978: preface)

Psychodynamic brief therapy

By the 1960s a number of innovative psychoanalysts had attempted to find briefer methods of working within a psychodynamic framework. Reflecting the divergence of psychodynamic thinking, four main approaches emerged; these can be partitioned into those that emphasized the interpersonal aspects of the relationship (Alexander and French, 1946), those that attempted a truncated version of the standard psychoanalytic method (Malan, 1963) and, in America, those that placed emphasis on session-induced anxiety and patient confrontation as a means of overcoming psychic defence and resistance (Davanloo, 1978; Sifneos, 1992).

In Britain the important early attempt to develop brief psychoanalytic therapy was conceived by Malan (1963). Malan worked to develop and test a modification of the standard psychoanalytic method known as Brief Intensive Psychotherapy (BIP). BIP typically was designed to last for around twenty sessions. Although the session number varied depending on the experience of the therapist (for example, thirty sessions for trainees), BIP introduced the concept of working on a focal problem. Initial sessions were used to identify conflicts, which would then become the focus of future work. The job of the therapist was to maintain this problem-based focus, ignoring other material. Clearly, the skill was to identify the conflict that was fundamental to the problematic symptoms.

Treatment was through interpretation and encouragement of insight by the client. Follow-up sessions encouraged the continuation of client insight. Termination is always an important aspect of psychodynamic work and Malan experimented with different permutations of the time limit. In the end, he opted for using a fixed future date for termination as an alternative to a fixed number of sessions. If a client needed further psychotherapy, then they had to change therapist. There never could be continuation with the same therapist, thereby undermining possible dependence. Although Malan found effective brief methods of working psychoanalytically he still accepted the psychoanalytic understanding of the origins of client problems (Fonagy, 1998).

Cognitive and behavioural models of therapy

Cognitive and behavioural psychotherapies may be practised with more or less brevity. There is, however, a widespread tendency to consider these psychotherapies as inherently brief. Cognitive psychotherapy is based on an information processing theory (Beck, 1976). In their interaction with the environment, people develop beliefs about themselves and the world. All information is filtered through the cognitive system, often before we become actively aware of it, and core beliefs have the ability to select and de-select information to bring into awareness, leaving the potential for cognitive bias. In cognitive theory the bedrock of our understanding of the world in terms of schemas or core beliefs leads to assumptions about the self and the world, and hence to automatic thoughts about the same. Treatment uses a variety of structured interactions to reverse the effects of cognitive bias. In general, it would seem that for time-limited work to be practical a psychologist should develop the ability to determine a focal problem and ignore other material, even though it might be interesting. The key consideration for the psychologist is the relevance of the material to the agreed goals of the therapy. Cognitive behavioural psychotherapy for many reasons seems able to fit well into this more constrained framework.

Integrative, eclectic and strategic approaches

Integrative and eclectic approaches also appear to fit well into time-limited practice, since they assume that no single theoretical approach is the repository of all clinical truth, and that some psychological problems are best treated through the use of techniques from a variety of sources. This view is usually supported with data demonstrating equivalent outcomes from a variety of therapeutic approaches (Elkin et al., 1989; Elkin, 1995; Smith et al., 1980). Interestingly, research into the practice orientation of Counselling Psychologists in the British Psychological Society Division conducted by Bor and Achilleoudes (1999) determined that 38 per cent of respondents identified one of their approaches as integrative and 11 per cent as eclectic. Research from the United States suggests that as many as 30–40 per cent of psychotherapists describe eclecticism as their primary orientation (Norcross, 1986).

Ryle has developed an interesting synthesis of aspects of cognitive theory and object relations. Cognitive Analytic Therapy (CAT) (Ryle, 1991) is an innovative therapy that utilizes a highly structured approach for the treatment of a wide range of problems, some previously thought intractable. Whereas most of the extant brief psychodynamic therapies remain insight-based and interpretive, CAT would seem to be descriptive and collaborative, providing both the client and the therapist with a common language in which to understand patterns of behaviour in ways that also suggest a solution. Of particular interest is the work on a Borderline Personality disorder group of clients (Ryle and Golynkina, 2001). The data suggest that an average of twenty-four sessions plus follow-up meetings, for the purpose of on-going therapy outcome assessment, were sufficient to remove 52 per cent of the sample from the Borderline Personality diagnostic category. Cognitive Analytic Theory also seems to offer the promise that client groups, traditionally thought of as difficult, may be able to benefit from time-limited structured sessions, apparently severing the link between difficult problems and longer-term therapy. One reason CAT may work well as a time-limited approach is because it follows what are understood to be some of the rules for successful time-limited practice, such as: clients are selected carefully; there is a clear conceptualization of the problem that is shared with the client; and there are a clear structure and clarity of purpose for sessions. In combination, the above few important points can be very powerful therapeutic tools in time-limited work.

The solution-focused approach

A different way of understanding how knowledge is created and understood may sometimes lead to more effective therapeutic ends. This is the basis of the solution-focused therapy (SFT) approach. Solution-focused therapy is centred on the epistemology that knowledge is socially constructed and people co-construct their meanings through the medium of language. De Shazer and colleagues, at the Milwaukee Brief Family Therapy Center, found that their clients were helped just as much by talking about the future as by talking about the past (O'Connell, 1998). This led to further discussions about the solution to the problem and a de-emphasis on the problem itself. Ultimately this resulted in the clients viewing themselves as active implementers of a solution, as an alternative to simply becoming symptom or problem-free. One of the most significant features of the SFT approach is the apparent creative freedom it gives practitioners to help a client develop means of solving problems without necessarily spending much time understanding the client's background.

The success of SFT suggests that we can be wrong about the inevitability of psychological causality, and we must be prepared to experiment and to test the theory we hold, such that we are always looking to find a better way to help our clients.

There is growing evidence to suggest that only a proportion of cases require longer-term work, and as research develops it would seem that this proportion is getting smaller. Shapiro et al. (1995) demonstrated that time-limited work (either eight or sixteen sessions) had the ability to return participants, diagnosed as suffering from a major depressive disorder, to levels compatible with those of the general population as assessed on Beck Depression Inventory scores. Perhaps the view of Hoyt captures the future of time-limited practice:

> Most patients come to therapy because they hope that working with a psychotherapist will soon relieve some state of unhappiness, distress or dysfunction that has become so troublesome that professional consultation appears preferable to continuing the *status quo*. (Hoyt, 1995: 287)

The problem and the ideal solution

Most therapies adhere to the view that events can be causally related to one another, in that one event necessarily precedes another. The traditional therapeutic understanding is that a client's problem needs to be understood, at least in part, before a solution can be found. The solution therefore depends upon the problem in an obvious way. Such strict adherence to a causal view of psychological phenomena could, however, act to inhibit creative thinking about time-limited opportunities in practice.

Because many of the main approaches to time-limited work make very different assumptions of the origins of psychological problems, and hence how to remedy them, one might expect to find outcomes in the research literature that differentiate them. This does not appear to be the case (Steenbarger, 1992; Elkin, 1995). Indeed, most brief therapies seem to produce comparable changes across interpersonal, behavioural, cognitive and affective dimensions (Koss and Butcher, 1986). Indeed, Imber et al. (1990), in an analysis of the data from the National Institute of Mental Health Treatment of Depression Collaborative Research Program, concluded that none of the three active strategies (CBT, interpersonal therapy and imipramine + clinical management) used in the outcome studies of the treatment of depression showed differences in treatment process, or consistent effects related to their theoretical origins. There was only a marginal interaction between severity of depression and clinical outcome, with imipramine showing slight effects over other treatments. It was suggested that common core processes may be more responsible for treatment than any special characteristics of the particular school.

What are the resistances to time-limited work?

Time-limited practice has been met with varying levels of resistance, since it challenges many traditional ways of thinking and understanding. In the current climate of financial accountability it may appear to be simply a way of cutting costs. Karasu (1992) has suggested that, in order to reach inner recesses of the mind, psychotherapy must take as long as it takes. While this may be true for some clients, treating all clients to this open-ended contract would seem inappropriate. The most cogent argument against Karasu's view comes from the behaviour of clients themselves. In one study of a counselling agency, clients who were offered an initial contract of six sessions only took up a mean of three and a half to three and three-quarter sessions (Goss, 1995). This might suggest that a structured time-limited approach could be a more rational choice for this group. Yet there is still resistance to time-limited practice. Hoyt (1995) has considered some of the sources of resistance to the use of brief therapy:

- The belief that more therapy is better.
- Overvaluation of insight and exploration and less on other possibilities such as skills training and practical problem solving.
- The confusion of therapist's and patient's interests, with therapists tending to want to move in broad strokes and the client seeking a solution of their particular problem.
- Theoretical obligations such as a belief that alliances develop slowly and unconscious material must be deeply probed.
- In private practice, there may be no incentive to work briefly.
- A therapist may have countertransference issues, such as difficulties in saying goodbye.

This list undoubtedly captures many aspects of some therapists' resistance to time-limited practice, but remember that in fact all therapy is time-limited.

Assessment for time-limited practice

Client expectations

All psychotherapy starts before the client and the psychologist meet. Indeed, the client's expectations will help provide a context for what happens during the first session and certainly the client will have some expectations of therapy informed by popular understanding. However, if the relationship between client and therapist is not to fail, then during the first assessment/engagement process the psychologist should attempt to make something happen that is possibly surprising, novel or encourages change.

At the first meeting a client will be somewhere along his or her own journey between illness and wellness. For time-limited practice a fundamental purpose of assessment is to determine where the client currently is in this process: getting better, getting worse, or just stuck somewhere in between. Where a client is on this journey will have a bearing on how much psychological input they may need to reach their desired level of functioning. For a proportion of clients the journey to recovery will already have started before they meet the therapist. Barkham and Shapiro (1990) found that for clients with mild depression 20 per cent showed improvement before the first session. Therefore the more we know about the client's journey the greater the precision in treatment planning.

Focal issues for time-limited assessment

It must be recognized that while assessments for different therapeutic approaches will have aspects in common, there will be fundamental differences that clearly separate the different approaches. In terms of treatment, for example, a time-limited insight-oriented therapy, which clearly has insight as its goal, will assess a client for their capacity for self-reflection, and will consider this as a primary inclusion factor. Other relevant factors in time-limited assessment are:

- *Level of psychological mindedness*. It is necessary that the client's current problems can be formulated in psychological terms that they can accept. If a client does not accept that there is a psychological facet to their troubles they will be less likely to accept a psychological solution.
- *Willingness to face unpleasant feelings*. A client requires the ability to self-sooth and to face potentially powerful negative emotions without recourse to regressive or primitive defence mechanisms, such as splitting or dissociation.
- *Motivation to change*. It is important to explore the actual motivation for change, and what the client is willing to do and endure in order to achieve their goals.
- *Ability to form an adult relationship with the psychologist*. All forms of time-limited work require that regressive phenomena be kept to an absolute minimum. Regression is fostered by dependence and powerlessness in the therapeutic relationship, and so the client can be tested for their willingness to accept some responsibility for their own treatment.
- *Capacity to form a working alliance*. Can the client make a rational decision to engage in the process of change, and will they be able to stick to it if things get tough? Are they able to attend regularly, pay the required fee, if any, and do they have any history of sporadic or punitive non-attendance?
- Does the psychological formulation specify a key focal point that the client will agree to work on, such that when solved other things will automatically follow?

As described earlier (Malan et al., 1975; Bloom, 2001) clients can benefit so significantly from one assessment session that they require no further input. Therefore, a creative assessment process can also be an opportunity for creative time-limited therapy. Bearing this in mind subtly changes the process from one of decisions about inclusion to one of starting the process of change – that may or may not require further therapeutic work.

Training in time-limited practice

The importance of effective and reliable training in brief therapy has become increasingly emphasized (Koss and Shiang, 1994; Garfield, 1995, Burlingame et al., 1989). Doing time-limited practice is not a short cut, or easier route through training. In fact a competent time-limited worker should be able to work in the longer term. However, it would be incorrect to assume that a competent long-term worker can simply shorten their practice and call it time-limited work without specific training in their selected approach. Indeed, Budman (1981) has concluded that a longer-term worker may lack the specific competences for brief work. Longer-term workers may fall into the trap of simply offering truncated versions of their habitual longer practice, with the possibility of incorporating practices that are generally considered not conducive to efficacious time-limited work and in so doing fail to offer a well planned time-limited therapy.

Research from the United States has shown that in one large-scale survey 80 per cent of licensed psychologists were practising some form of brief work for about 40 per cent of their time (Levenson et al., 1992, cited in Koss and Shiang 1994: 675). About one-third of this sample claimed no training in brief work. Complementary research has demonstrated that competence in time-limited work increases after formal training (Burlingame et al., 1989). As little as twelve hours of training significantly reduced client attrition, recidivism and resulted in significant positive change for clients.

Recall that by default the median length of long-term psychotherapy is about six sessions. Therefore *de facto* long-term psychotherapists are often giving short-term psychotherapy in a long-term setting. The research of Howard et al. (1986) would suggest that a more rational approach to time-limited practice could foster therapeutic goals and could paradoxically increase a client's commitment to the process of therapy.

Conclusion

Time-limited practice requires increased psychologist activity, the ability to develop an early working alliance, and the ability to elicit and maintain a clear therapeutic focus. These are not competences for the beginner in therapeutic work. Time-limited practice done badly is probably worse than longer-term work done badly. The time-limited practitioner has only the moment to facilitate change, and may not have the time to recover from technical mistakes that is available to longer-term workers.

In time-limited practice we have fundamentally only one goal: to help the client to change. Research has demonstrated that this can usually be accomplished in much fewer sessions than traditional long-term therapy has suggested, and probably less than we might initially think possible. The fact remains, however, that by intention or default most therapy delivered today is time-limited. One important variable that separates the intentional time-limited psychologist from the default time-limited psychologist is the explicit recognition of the importance of time, and indeed this explicit recognition is likely to make a difference for some clients. This suggests that we could enhance our practice if we were to make more use of time as a therapeutic tool.

References

Alexander, F. and French, T.M. (1946) *Psychoanalytic Therapy: Principles and Applications.* New York: Ronald Press.

Askevold, F. (1983) 'What are the helpful factors in psychotherapy for anorexia nervosa?' *International Journal of Eating Disorders,* 3: 193–7.

Aveline, M. (1995) 'How I assess for focal psychotherapy' in C. Mace (ed.) *The Art and Science of Assessment in Psychotherapy.* London and New York: Routledge.

Barkham, M. and Shapiro, D.A. (1990) 'Brief psychotherapeutic interventions for job-related distress: a pilot study of prescriptive and exploratory therapy', *Counselling Psychology Quarterly,* 3: 133–47.

Barkham, M., Shapiro, D.A., Hardy, G.E. and Rees, A. (1999) 'Psychotherapy in two-plus-one sessions: outcomes of a randomized controlled trial of cognitive-behavioural and psychodynamic-interpersonal therapy for subsyndromal depression', *Journal of Consulting and Clinical Psychology,* 67: 201–11.

Beck, A.T. (1976) *Cognitive Therapy and the Emotional Disorders.* London: Penguin Books.

Bloom, B.L. (1992) *Planned Short Term Psychotherapy.* Boston MA: Allyn & Bacon.

Bloom, B.L. (2001) 'Focused single session psychotherapy: a review of the clinical and research literature', *Brief Treatment and Crisis Intervention,* 1: 75–86.

Bor, R. and Achilleoudes, H. (1999) 'BPS Division of Counselling Psychology Survey of Members 1999', *Counselling Psychology Review,* 14: 35–45.

Brech, J. and Agulnik, P. (1996) 'Do brief interventions reduce waiting time for counselling?' *Counselling,* 7 (4): 322–6.

Budman, S.H. (1981) *Forms of Brief Therapy.* New York: Guilford Press.

Budman, S.H. and Gurman, A.S. (1988) *Theory and Practice of Brief Therapy.* New York: Guilford Press.

Burlingame, G., Fuhriman, A., Paul, S. and Ogles, B.M. (1989) 'Implementing a time-limited therapy program: differential effects of training and experience', *Psychotherapy,* 26: 303–13.

Caro, I. (1996) 'A walk through time: what you should have read by now or will read soon about psychotherapy', *Counselling Psychology Quarterly,* 9: 399–418.

Davanloo, H. (1978/1994) *Basic Principles and Techniques in Short-term Dynamic Psychotherapy.* New York: Aronson.

Elkin, I. (1995) 'The NIMH treatment of depression collaborative research program: major results and clinical implications', *Changes,* 13: 178–86.

Elkin, I., Shea, T.M., Watkins, J.T., Imber, S.D., Sotsky, S.M., Collins, J.F., Glass, D.R., Pilkonis, P.A., Leber, W.R., Docherty, J.P., Fiester, S.J. and Parloff, M.B. (1989) 'National Institute of Mental Health treatment of depression collaborative research program: general effectiveness of treatment', *Archives of General Psychiatry,* 46: 971–82.

Elton Wilson, J. (1996) *Time-conscious Psychological Therapy.* London: Routledge.

Eysenck, H.J. (1952) 'The effects of psychotherapy: an evaluation', *Journal of Counselling,* 16: 319–24.

Feltham, C. (1997) *Time-limited Counselling.* London: Sage.

Fonagy, P. (1998) 'Psychodynamic approaches', in A.S. Bellack and M. Hersen (eds) *Comprehensive Clinical Psychology,* 6, 107–29.

Garfield, S.L. (1986) 'Research on client variables in psychotherapy', in S.L. Garfield and A.E. Bergin (eds) *Handbook of Psychotherapy and Behavior Change,* third edition. New York: Wiley.

Garfield, S.L. (1995) *Psychotherapy: an Eclectic-integrative Approach*, second edition. New York: Wiley.

Gelso, C.J. and Johnson, D.H. (1983) *Explorations in Time-limited Counselling and Psychotherapy*. New York: Teachers' College Press.

Goleman, D. (1993) 'When a long therapy goes a little way', *New York Times*, 18 April, sect. 4, p. 6.

Goss, S. (1995) 'The Value of Listening: The Final Evaluative Report on Effectiveness of the Advice, Support and Counselling Unit of Lothian Regional Council Education Department'. Glasgow: Strathclyde University Counselling Unit.

Haley, J. (1986) *Uncommon Therapy*. New York: Norton.

Howard, I.K., Kopta, S.M., Krause, M.S. and Orlinsky, D.E. (1986) 'The dose–effect relationship in psychotherapy', *American Psychologist*, 41 (2): 159–64.

Hoyt, M.F. (1995) *Brief Therapy and Managed Care*. San Francisco: Jossey Bass.

Imber, S.D., Pilkonis, P.A., Sotsky, S.M., Elkin, I., Watkins, J.T., Collins, J.F., Shea, M.T., Lever, W.R. and Class, D.R. (1990) 'Mode-specific effects among three treatments for depression', *Journal of Consulting and Clinical Psychology*, 58: 352–9.

Johnson, D.H. and Gelso, C.J. (1980) 'The effectiveness of time limits in counselling and psychotherapy: a critical review', *Counselling Psychologist*, 9: 70–83.

Jones, E. (1955) *The Life and Works of Sigmund Freud* II. New York: Basic Books.

Karasu, T.B. (1992) *Wisdom in the Practice of Psychotherapy*. New York: Basic Books.

Koss, M.P. (1979) 'Length of psychotherapy for clients seen in private practice', *Journal of Consulting and Clinical Psychology*, 47: 210–12.

Koss, M.P. and Butcher, J.W. (1986) 'Research on brief psychotherapy', in A.E. Bergin and S.L. Garfield (eds) *Handbook of Psychotherapy and Behavior Change* third edition. New York: Wiley.

Koss, M.P. and Shiang, J. (1994) 'Research on brief psychotherapy' in A.E. Bergin and S. L. Garfield (eds) *Handbook of Psychotherapy and Behavior Change* fourth edition. New York: Wiley.

Lambert, M.J., Shapiro, D.A. and Bergin, A.E. (1986) 'The effectiveness of psychotherapy' in A.E. Bergin and S.L. Garfield (eds) *Handbook of Psychotherapy and Behavior Change* third edition. New York: Wiley.

Levenson, H., Speed, J.L. and Budman, S.H. (1992) 'Therapists' Training and Skill in Brief Therapy: A Survey of Massachusetts and California Psychologists', paper presented to the Society for Psychotherapy Research, Berkeley CA. Cited in M.P. Koss and J. Shiang 'Research on brief psychotherapy' in A.E. Bergin and S.L. Garfield (eds) *Handbook of Psychotherapy and Behavior Change* (1994) fourth edition. New York: Wiley.

Malan, D.H. (1963) *A Study of Brief Psychotherapy*. New York: Plenum.

Malan, D., Heath, E., Bacal, H. and Balfour, F. (1975) 'Psychodynamic changes in apparently untreated neurotic patients' II, 'Apparently genuine improvements', *Archives of General Psychiatry*, 32: 110–26.

McNeilly, C.L. and Howard, K.L. (1991) 'The effects of psychotherapy: a reevaluation based on dosage', *Psychotherapy Research*, 1: 74–8.

Norcross, J.C. (1986) *Handbook of Eclectic Psychotherapy*. New York: Brunner Mazel.

O'Connell, B. (1998) *Solution Focused Therapy*. London: Sage.

Pollack , J., Winston, A., Mcullough, L. and Flegenheimer, W. (1990) 'Efficacy of brief adaptational psychotherapy', *Journal of Personality Disorders*, 4: 244–50.

Ryle, A. (1982) *Psychotherapy: a Cognitive Integration of Theory and Practice*. London: Academic Press.

Ryle, A. (1991) 'Object relations theory and activity theory: a proposed link by way of the procedural sequence model', *British Journal of Medical Psychology*, 64: 307–16.

Ryle, A. and Golynkina, K. (2000) 'Effectiveness of time-limited cognitive analytic therapy on borderline personality disorder: factors associated with outcome', *British Journal of Medical Psychology*, 73: 197–211.

Shapiro, D., Rees, A., Barkham, M., Hardy, G., Reynolds, S. and Startup, M. (1995) 'Effects of treatment duration and severity of depression on maintenance of gains after cognitive-behavioural and psychodynamic-interpersonal psychotherapy', *Journal of Consulting and Clinical Psychology*, 63: 378–87.

Sifneos, P.E. (1992) *Short-term Psychotherapy and Emotional Crisis*. Cambridge MA: Harvard University Press.

Smith, M.L., Glass, G.V. and Miller, T.I. (1980) *The Benefits of Psychotherapy*. Baltimore MD: Johns Hopkins University Press.

Steenbarger, B.N. (1992) 'Toward science-practice integration in brief counseling and therapy', *Counseling Psychologist*, 20: 403–50.

Talmon, M. (1990) *Single Session Therapy*. San Francisco: Jossey Bass.

26 Counselling Psychology in the Workplace
VANJA ORLANS

Updating this chapter for the second edition gave me an opportunity to reassess developments in the field of counselling psychology in terms of its application to the workplace. What has most surprised me has been my perception of time – although it is only five years since the original publication, the field as a whole seems to have done more than five years' worth of developing. The Division of Counselling Psychology within the British Psychological Society is now well established; a number of accredited courses offer programmes of study for psychology graduates to train in this specialty, and there is also an active and established independent route to chartered status. Chartered counselling psychologists have a greater presence in a number of practice settings, including increasingly in the workplace.

The practice of psychological counselling in the work setting has also continued to grow in popularity with both practitioners and organizations. The British Association for Counselling and Psychotherapy (BACP) has an active and well established professional section concerned with counselling at work, and its journal *Counselling at Work* continues to reflect a range of workplace issues and challenges that are relevant both to counselling professionals and to organizational decision makers. Employee Assistance Programmes (EAPs) continue to be widely marketed, and managers are becoming more acceptant of psychological counselling as a useful resource both to individuals and to the organization as a whole. The issue seems to revolve not so much around *whether* psychological counselling has a relevance to the workplace, but rather *what form* it is likely to take. In terms of the latter focus, especially, it would appear that there is still scope for the further development of 'a legitimate body of psychological knowledge' and a 'professional field of psychological activity' (British Psychological Society, 1999). Although this chapter is concerned primarily with counselling psychology practitioners, I do not wish to exclude the large number of counsellors who are interested in, and involved with, workplace counselling programmes. Much of what I have to say is also relevant to those professionals. I do have a particular interest, however, in considering the ways in which workplace counselling issues appear to mirror some of the processes which may be regarded as key to an underlying philosophy of counselling psychology, and its manifestations in theory and practice.

Defining our terms

In the first edition I referred to the activity denoted by the term 'counselling' as being most often concerned both with a set of values as well as particular intervention practices, and I expressed the view that 'counselling psychology' extended *beyond* a consideration of a helping relationship *per se*, incorporating a psychological ground to the counselling activity. While this is pragmatically true, I now view the two components of 'counselling' and 'psychology' as potentially more challenging as bed partners than I had previously understood to be the case. In the following sections I review a number of issues concerned with both historical factors and basic terminology, in order to point to a clearer role which counselling psychology might play in relation to workplace challenges and difficulties.

The origins of the field of counselling psychology in the United Kingdom lay in the interest that a group of psychologists had in the activity referred to as 'counselling', and in the acquisition and development of a set of clinical skills within a new professional framework. Training in counselling, that is, without the addition of the 'psychology', tended historically to take place within one particular frame of reference, i.e. Rogerian, Gestalt, Transactional Analysis, often with relatively little attention to a research-based approach. The bringing of 'psychology' together with 'counselling' made an evaluative stance more central, and has been a key and required component of training courses in counselling psychology. The inclusion of different models in training settings was also a key feature. This new relationship, between 'involved doing' in the form of counselling, and 'evaluation through research' as held by the psychology end of the polarity, brings with it a tension of a kind already in evidence in the broader field of psychology and its application to a number of different fields. While the scientist-practitioner model has been strongly promoted, in particular within clinical psychology in the United Kingdom, the assumption of the correspondence of the aims of 'scientists' and 'practitioners' has been called into question by a number of writers. Roth et al. (1996), for example, suggest that practitioners and scientists are concerned with different lines of inquiry, and each field is constructed to answer different questions. There are valid arguments that research participants are often not representative of clients seen in practice settings, and that the concern of many researchers to hone their methodology to ensure a clear pattern of results can mean that presenting problems may be simplified and lack applicability in many settings. In the psychological therapies in general the research/practice issue is becoming more important and is likely to remain so at a time when counsellor competence is being more closely scrutinized and controlled, where the climate of clinical governance is having a profound effect on the evaluation of practice, and where the development of training standards and professional recognition is being so widely debated and developed.

This tension between research and practice has dogged the broader field of applied psychology, and presents a particular challenge to counselling psychologists to develop research paradigms which do not polarize research and practice, and which take subjectivity for granted. A response to this challenge which is recognized and accepted by the wider research community is still at a very early stage. The historical traditions prevail in many settings and manifest also in counselling psychology. 'Counselling' focuses us not only on a field of practice but on something that speaks of relationship and the co-creation of meaning, and also on a process over time. Alongside this we have 'psychology' – long dogged by over-reliance on a model of research derived from the physical sciences, open to valid criticisms of reductionism and reifying of the positivist philosophy and method, and more often concerned with structure than process. These then are the bed partners of 'counselling' and 'psychology' – a potentially uneasy alliance. On reflecting on my thoughts for the update of this chapter, and more generally in terms of a coherent philosophy for counselling psychology, I began to see that I had perhaps spent too much time, together with other colleagues, on trying to effect a kind of artificial denouement between the two. How would it be, I thought, if we held off looking for integration and accepted *the holding of the two polarities* as the task of counselling psychology? In general terms, this poses potentially a challenging and interesting position for practitioners in this field. If we are successful in holding this kind of tension in ourselves in a creative way, we should be in a better position to help others do so. It would leave us well disposed both to understand, and to work with, a range of presenting difficulties which emanate from settings with a similar tension. From this point of view, the potential for conflict between 'counselling' and 'the workplace', where personal values and subjectivity interface with fixed organizational structures and a value base of objectivity, is likely to carry a sense of familiarity for the counselling psychologist.

The relevance of counselling psychology to workplace issues

The 'bridging' nature of the field of counselling psychology, in terms of the demand to attend to different values and traditions, is one reason for its potential usefulness to the work setting. Relevant also are the counselling psychologist's training and experience in the therapeutic process coupled with the increasing trend for organizations to make some form of counselling available to employees, whether as an in-house scheme or as an external resource. Since the first edition, however, there have been some significant developments in the field of workplace counselling which are worthy of review. While there is on-going debate as to how 'stress in the workplace' can be measured and responded to (see, for example, Briner, 2000), there is increasing interest in the provision of resources which take account of the emotional functioning of employees. Although such interest is based to a large extent on cost-effective considerations, researchers in the field tend to agree that there is much more acceptance of the emotional as well as the physical demands of work settings. Indeed, it is argued that being 'stressed' may even have become fashionable in some settings (Berridge and Cooper, 1994). This greater awareness of the potential effects of our jobs, and the willingness of a number of employers to take action as a result, is one reason why more programmes for the management of stress are now available to employees in the United Kingdom.

The legislative environment puts added pressure on organizations to attend to emotional factors at work. The Health and Safety at Work Act 1974 already places a 'duty of care' on employers for the health of employees, which includes both physical and mental health. Further legislative developments in 1992 have required 'health surveillance' of employees, a development with a proactive preventative steer. In a report by the Health and Safety Executive (1995) there is an emphasis on the requirement of employers to address the issue of 'excessive stress'; the report also provides suggestions as to how this might be done, and highlights the importance of such difficulties being seen not as purely personal problems, but as issues which are relevant at the level of management thinking and strategy. At the time of writing the Health and Safety Executive has some thirty publications listed which relate to the topic of stress in the workplace.

The recent trend among employees to take a 'litigious' approach to the issue of the 'duty of care' appears to be impacting psychological counselling in a general way and resulting in more publications designed to support counselling professionals both to make sense of, and to take account of, this trend (Jenkins, 1997). Between 1995 and 2000 there were four cases of litigation concerned with workplace stress – three involved an out-of-court settlement, and in two cases the employer in question admitted liability (Jenkins and Pollecoff, 2000). Partly as a result of such pressures, organizations are now much more concerned to have a broad-ranging policy in place for the management of employee problems, to include those of an emotional kind. The fear of litigation and resulting compensation at high levels are clearly a strong incentive for change.

The issue of employee claims for stress-related problems which arise from workplace issues continues to be debated in the courts. In one appeal court ruling the judges concerned overturned three compensation claims for stress-related difficulties, and put forward some new guidelines for employers and employees. These state that the onus is on the employee to make any 'failure to cope' or stress-related concerns known to the employer in the first instance. Employees cannot simply go off sick and then put in a claim. The onus will then be on the employer to respond to the reported difficulties. The specific point made is that where an employer makes confidential counselling available to the employee it will be extremely unlikely that they will be held in breach of their responsibilities. This ruling is likely to add impetus to the provision of counselling facilities in workplace settings, even though developments are likely to be driven more by a desire to avoid litigation than by a desire to take the emotional life of employees actively into account. Nevertheless, there is a clear role here for the counselling psychologist, both in terms of research on the effectiveness of different provisions, and as clinicians involved with the counselling of employees, and many counsellors and counselling psychologists are already involved in such services.

Alongside this, counselling professionals may find themselves under more scrutiny as the focus shifts from the provision of a service as a structural entity to the details of the service itself. As Jenkins (1999) points out, it is increasingly the case that counselling professionals cannot rely on certain issues being dealt with by 'the legal department'. The effectiveness of the particular counselling provision is likely to be a focus in future cases where 'counsellors, and their organizations, may well need to be prepared to defend their interventions through a sound knowledge of the research findings, under the searching cross-examination of the courts' (p. 4). The wider cultural trend, led by developments in the NHS, towards 'evidence-based practice' also has a part to play in encouraging clients to expect that standards can be demonstrated, and impacts on counselling psychologists in promoting an attitude of research in service provision. There is a clear role here for counselling psychologists who already have experience of conducting research as part of their training, as well as being in a position to grapple with the issue of what may constitute 'evidence' in terms of both counselling effectiveness and the overall effectiveness of a workplace programme.

Although the 'brief therapy' contract is part and parcel of the structure of an Employee Assistance Programme, since the first edition we have seen a mushrooming of interest in brief therapy in general, a development which lends significant support to the programmes in workplace settings. The interest in brief therapy has been driven partly by economic considerations in the provision of mental health services, as well as by a managerial perspective with regard to the broadest possible provision for large numbers of clients. Many of the developments within the field of brief therapy also mirror the trend for 'the consumer to be in charge'. Preston et al., (2000) suggest that seeking therapeutic help is simply another way of using consultancy time when all is not well, or when guidance is needed. They equate the use of a 'mental health consultant' with the services of an accountant or fitness trainer – someone who 'will listen objectively and help guide you toward the results that *you* choose' (p. 11). The picture presented is of an informed and aware client who is in charge of the contract and looking for a quality service, and although this publication emanates from the service culture of the United States, the trend appears to be similar in the United Kingdom, and has been supported by organizations such as BACP which have been pursuing an active policy of client education.

In many ways the level of interest in brief therapy is a useful support to workplace counselling services in that it enables practitioners in those settings, where the number of sessions available to clients is, for the most part, extremely limited, to feel that there is a growing body of theory and research which supports what they do. Most counselling training courses that take an interest in brief work provide only small amounts of training in this area of practice. While this is understandable in terms of the wider curriculum in general counselling courses, it can leave counselling professionals unsupported if their primary context for practice is in a setting where only short-term therapeutic help is available. At the same time, there is increasing evidence of the effectiveness of short-term therapeutic work with clients, regardless of the orientation of the particular clinician (see, for example, Barkham, 1990; Barkham and Shapiro, 1990). Recent publications also raise a number of issues which are challenging some of the assumptions of longer-term approaches and are forcing all of us to consider the issues of time and effectiveness in our clinical endeavours. Elton Wilson (1996) makes the point that even where the qualities of short-term therapeutic work are recognized, there is still often an implication that the choice is based on cost-effective considerations rather than on quality, and that a longer-term solution would be the treatment of choice. Yet the research evidence, based both on therapeutic outcomes and on the preferences of clients, suggests that we should take seriously the potential for a quality service in short-term work (see, for example, Smith, et al., 1980; Koss and Butcher, 1986; Garfield, 1989, 1995). According to Feltham (1997) it is at our peril that we ignore the research findings in this area of practice. These developments are likely to be impacting counselling psychologists in their work generally, promoting greater awareness, and possibly greater skill, in the effective management of short-term clinical contracts, and providing appropriate support for involvement with workplace schemes.

Counselling facilities and the workplace setting: an overview

Early approaches concerned with bringing counselling into the work setting revolved around the alcohol programmes developed in the United States in the 1940s. Although originally conceived of as a way of dealing with the problems of alcohol-dependent employees amid growing awareness of the greater cost-effective potential of getting people 'cured' and back to safe and productive working as quickly as possible, there was increasing emphasis also on the families of these 'patients' and on the range of needs which they brought. This trend led, in time, to the development of the 'broad brush' programmes which dealt with a range of emotional and practical difficulties experienced by employees and their families. The evolvement of a wide-ranging programme of responsive help is increasingly widely utilized by organizations, and Employee Assistance Programmes are now available to a far greater number of employees, either as in-house programmes or as an external provision. In 1988 Whitbread established what was believed to be the first EAP in a British company. Less than a decade later it was estimated that over one million employees and their families in the United Kingdom would have had access to EAP support (Reddy, 1994). Employees have access to financial and legal help and advice, as well as to counselling for emotional problems. The extent to which the organization concerned involves itself directly with the EAP and its running varies, depending on the values and strategic thinking of the organization concerned. Some companies insist on certain kinds of feedback from employed counsellors and occasionally become involved in the monitoring of problems and risk, a position which can present a particular challenge to counselling professionals with regard to the management of confidentiality within the counselling contract. Employee Assistance Programmes have their own professional body (the EAPA) designed to support quality control in the design and implementation of programmes. Typically, an EAP deals with a range of employee problems, either on the telephone or face-to-face, and access to the service is most often on a twenty-four-hour basis.

It is worth noting that a counselling facility need not take the form of a full-blown EAP. More restricted facilities are also available to employees, which offer primarily emotional support in the form of telephone or face-to-face counselling. Such a service might also be on offer at only limited times, and supplemented by the use of the voluntary sector (e.g. the Samaritans) as a way of handling emergencies. Carroll (1997) distinguishes between the two main ways in which a counselling facility might be provided, that is, as an *internal* facility which is part of the organizational structure, or as an *external* facility brought in by the company. Either form can range from a full EAP service to a smaller facility with a limited focus, and some companies may also utilize a combination of both internal and external provision which has been put forward as the optimum solution (Summerfield and Van Oudtshoorn, 1995). Carroll highlights a number of strengths and weaknesses of each facility. In terms of internal provision, it is suggested that counsellors have a greater possibility of being more in touch with the culture of the organization; that it is easier to get feedback into the wider system as the internal provision already has an in-built structural connection; and that the work of the counsellors can be more easily adapted to organizational needs. On the minus side, counsellors may be more swept up in the culture of the organization and therefore take a more subjective stance; the provision is more vulnerable to any reorganization within that setting; and there may be greater challenges to the holding of confidentiality within the system concerned.

In relation to external counselling provision, Carroll makes the point that counsellors may feel more protected from the politics of the organization, can offer a potentially wider skills service, and can maintain an easier independence in professional terms. Drawbacks highlighted include a potential lack of flexibility on the part of the counsellor, a lack of understanding about the organizational culture and the nuances of the politics, and the potential perception of the counsellor as an 'outsider'. Megranahan (1995), writing from the perspective of service effectiveness, highlights a number of factors relevant to the overall functioning of an EAP, and the need for the EAP provision to be tailored to a specified range of organizational needs. He advocates the inclusion of procedures for evaluation built in at the start so that the effectiveness of the provision in meeting those needs can be monitored. Berridge and Cooper (1994) describe the underlying rationale as to why an organization might include an EAP provision for employees. Their view is that an EAP provision highlights the employer's recognition that stress is a normal response to certain life challenges, and that the response can emanate from a variety of sources (e.g. work, family, professional role), which are generally interlinked. The onus is on employees to take responsibility for their own stress reactions, and to seek appropriate help via the service provision.

Bull (1997) charts the development of workplace counselling through a number of different phases. He suggests that the early initiatives were conceived in the context of a disease model along the lines of Alcoholics Anonymous. This progressed through a more client-centred phase, exemplified by the development of a broad-brush approach to EAPs, to a period where the environment is acknowledged as having a potentially significant impact on the employee. The current position identified is one where the company is a potential 'client' for the counselling professional, alongside the individual client. This latter view challenges individual counselling professionals who deal with workplace issues to view their role more broadly than might have been reflected in their clinical training context. Although training programmes for counselling psychologists will tend to include a review of issues relevant to organization-based work, the overriding frame of reference is still a 'clinical' one which pays more attention to contact in a specific therapeutic setting. It is most often left to individual counselling professionals to work out for themselves how to apply their clinical skill to 'the organization' as a potential client.

The effectiveness of workplace counselling

Evaluation studies cited in a review of workplace counselling (McLeod, 2001) fall into two categories, those concerned with psychosocial outcomes, and those concerned with 'value for money'. The former group of studies reviewed point to the overall effectiveness of brief-term counselling in terms of beneficial effects on psychological symptoms. The effects more widely, in terms, for example, of changes in work attitude and commitment, were more varied. Also, the emphasis in the studies reviewed was largely on individual-level outcome, with little attention paid to factors such as culture or management style. In terms of cost-effectiveness, research studies are fewer and more complex in terms of the analyses. However, the evidence according to McLeod appears to be that workplace counselling schemes at the very least cover their costs, even though there were very wide variations across companies and schemes. He concludes that two-thirds of studies reviewed suggest that counselling interventions are generally effective in alleviating symptoms of anxiety, stress and depression, and that there is some evidence that counselling interventions have a positive impact on job commitment, work functioning, job satisfaction and the reduction of substance abuse. These studies may, however, tell us more about the *accommodation* of employees to existing environments than about investment in any attempts to improve environmental conditions. Carroll (1996) also takes a contextual approach to the evaluation of workplace counselling, highlighting the importance of clearly identified therapeutic goals for particular settings, and the use of a range of perspectives – from clients, counsellors and the organization concerned – in the evaluation of the service.

A few evaluation studies have focused on a range of techniques rather than only on psychological counselling *per se*. In a review of the evaluation of stress management techniques in the work setting, Murphy (1984) highlights the problem of non-specific effects. Outcomes may, for example, relate more to the enthusiasm of the worker in taking part in a programme than to a specific technique or strategy. He points out that 'significant decreases in physiological measures observed in control groups may be a function of taking time out of the workday and sitting in a comfortable chair for forty minutes or more' (1984: 8).

Bruning and Frew (1985) compared the effects of management skills training (including time management, conflict management and goalsetting) with meditation, physical exercise and combinations of these. While all techniques brought about a reduction in pulse rate and systolic blood pressure, the largest reductions were observed for management skills training! Such studies underpin the importance of looking beyond the individual level of analysis and 'problem' management to strategies which are more broadly preventative and which have the potential for producing a greater generalizable effect, both perhaps for the individual and for the company as a whole.

Firth and Shapiro (1986) highlight the effectiveness of brief psychotherapy for the alleviation of job-related distress. They also suggest that it is more productive to identify and offer help to those individuals who are recognized as currently distressed than to offer more general programmes to all workers. Barkham and Shapiro (1990) review a number of different interventions for dealing with job-related distress, and present some of the findings of a pilot study implementing brief psychotherapeutic models. Their results demonstrate the effectiveness of short-term psychological counselling interventions for presenting problems, both in terms of improvement in client functioning and in terms of cost-effectiveness to the organization. Cooper et al. (1990) have outlined a programme of short-term psychological counselling which has been implemented in the Post Office, and present evaluation data on the effectiveness of this scheme. Results from an initial sample of seventy eight questionnaires, and the analysis of 155 sickness absence records, indicate significant improvements in mental well-being and a reduction of days lost at work. This early programme has been refined and extended over the years, and Tehrani (1997) presents some of the details of these developments, and highlights this service as being in line with the findings of Highley and Cooper (1996) that internal provision of counselling has been more successful than external provision in meeting the needs of employees and the organization.

Highley and Cooper (1994) take the view that although organizations in the United Kingdom are increasingly seeing EAPs as a potential investment for the company, there are no *conclusive* evaluations available in the United Kingdom on such a service. Their view is that researchers in this field still seem to be undecided about methodological approaches, as well as the best information to use in undertaking research. They put this down to the mix of 'hard' and 'soft' benefits which are derived from EAPs, making a clear outcomes model difficult to identify. Overall, there are a number of factors which have been identified as contributing to the shortage of adequate evaluation studies in relation to workplace counselling and EAPs. These include: the time-consuming and costly nature of evaluation research; the fact that counsellors who work in these programmes are often more interested in treatment than in research; the extent to which organizations are not welcoming of outside evaluators; the virtual impossibility of producing a tight research design, given the complexity of interrelating factors; the irresistible temptation for EAP providers to make their own programmes look good; lack of interest in evaluation where the adoption of a scheme is concerned more with the public relations exercise of conveying 'care'; issues of client confidentiality or even organization confidentiality where the company concerned does not want to be seen as 'a stressed organization' or be highlighted as providing a less than effective service; the difficulty of gaining access to data from company records, either because the records are incomplete or because access to individual records is not seen as ethical by the organization concerned; the absence of control groups; and the fact that symptoms of stress tend to fluctuate, leading to spontaneous recovery without the help of counselling (Holosko, 1988; Shapiro et al., 1993; Sonnenstuhl and Trice, 1986).

The challenges in evaluating employee counselling services involve us in consideration of a range of issues and leave us with the sense that there is much interesting evidence which we can reflect on, but no definitive statement overall. It makes sense also to approach individually orientated strategies from a critical perspective, for to offer such a solution as a way of avoiding addressing wider concerns raises certain ethical dimensions. We need to bear in mind the fact that individuals who come for psychological counselling may be carrying the problems of a wider context with them. Postmodernist writers such as Gergen and Kaye (1992) approach the issue in a slightly different way, drawing attention to the implicit field in the therapeutic relationship itself. In highlighting the therapist's 'narrative' as an abstract formulation, artificially divorced from particular cultural or historical circumstances, they make the point that 'None of the modernist narratives deal with the specific conditions of living in ghetto poverty, with a brother who has AIDS, with a child who has Down's Syndrome, with a boss who is sexually abusive, and so on' (1992: 172). At the same time, there does seem to be some convincing evidence from a range of clinical settings of the usefulness of professional counselling help for short periods of time, and that this may be helpful in alleviating both individual and organizational 'distress'.

How an EAP programme actually works in practice may also depend on the extent to which the scheme is a fully integrated part of the organizational structure as a whole, the availability of suitably trained professionals who can handle the role of being a counsellor or counselling psychologist in that setting, and the extent to which senior management is committed to the implementation of primary prevention strategies. Most EAPs and stress management activities within organizations appear to be more concerned with the secondary and tertiary stages of prevention (that is, the detection of early problems and the subsequent alleviation of the distress) than with the longer-term reduction in relevant risk factors within the system as a whole. This may relate partly to concern about costs, partly to the limitations of counsellors' skills in dealing with the complexisties of organizational dynamics, and partly to a fear on the part of senior management that a commitment to primary prevention might open Pandora's box.

Issues and challenges in the provision of workplace counselling facilities

A number of factors may be identified which influence the nature of the provision of counselling for workplace problems. One consideration is the extent to which 'context' is included in any design or analysis, a factor which may be either theoretical or practical. The issue of context is also highlighted in the *Guidelines for the Professional Practice of Counselling Psychology* (BPS, 1998): 'Practitioners will consider the contexts that affect clients experiences and incorporate these into assessment, formulation and intervention' (p. 8). Some theoretical and training perspectives more than others include context as a part of their schematic approach, and those that do are likely to produce professionals more suited to an organizational setting. Current developments suggest that context is being taken more seriously in a range of approaches to therapeutic work, for example Brazier (1993) illustrates the ways in which the person-centred approach is highlighting the relevance of contextual factors. These developments may also be affected by the general trend towards integration in the fields of both psychological counselling and psychotherapy (see, for example, Norcross and Arkowitz, 1992).

An additional way of approaching the issue of context is to consider the positioning of a counselling activity in relation to a particular organization. For instance, a psychological counselling scheme might be organized in a form which renders it separate from the rest of the organization, or it might be designed in a way which integrates this activity with broader aspects of organizational functioning. Whatever the structural aspects of a particular scheme, the organization will nevertheless be present as 'the ground' to that scheme – whether it is explicit or tacit. A more explicitly linked scheme can potentially be more useful in the organization as a whole, since it encourages 'systemic thinking', and may enable the counselling psychologist to distinguish more readily between 'pathological individual conditions' and 'environmentally induced reactions'. Bott (1988), in relation to family therapy work, refers to the distinction made in systems thinking between 'first-order change' within the system and 'second-order change' *of* the system, and demonstrates the implications of such thinking for diagnosis in that context. In the workplace setting, however, it is more difficult to escape the idea that 'counselling' is potentially an intervention into an on-going system, rather than a separate activity. Fisher (1997) provides us with a powerful analysis of the interface between an employee counselling facility and the NHS, the range of issues and challenges which are presented in this setting, and the crucial importance of careful consideration of context to the effective provision of that service. Not all organizations are willing to commit to a more wide-ranging analysis of that kind, possibly because of lack of funds and relevant human resources, or because such a process could be viewed as more threatening and more likely to throw up additional issues such as confusion about, for example, individual versus organizational responsibility, and resource allocation, which would then require further discussion and working through. The study does, however, serve to highlight the centrality of the organization in the process, and the importance of the counselling component retaining an explicit link with the system as a whole.

A second issue relates to the presence or absence of certain attitudes or values. Even a cursory look at the literature on psychological counselling highlights the potential for discrepancies between many values promoted in that context and those to be found in most organizational settings. Carl Rogers (e.g. 1951, 1959) emphasizes a number of key conditions which he regards as both necessary and sufficient for client change and development to occur. These 'core' conditions, which are created by a combination of both skill and attitude on the part of the counsellor, are empathic understanding, respect for the client in the deepest sense, and congruence or genuineness. While there is substantial debate as to what might constitute 'core' conditions and how these might be pursued, most approaches to psychological counselling highlight the importance of empathic attunement in the counsellor-client relationship, as well as respect for the client's world-view and recognition of a client's capacity, and ultimate right, to choose his or her own destiny as far as possible.

In the organizational domain by comparison we find a world where judgement and decision making are valued and actively developed among employees; where the emphasis is largely on objective experience and the pursuit of objective facts; where rational choice takes priority over feeling states; and where the system demands conformity to a set of rules and procedures, and exercises relevant controls within a hierarchical system to ensure that they are adhered to. Such values and approaches may, of course, be present to varying degrees in the counselling relationship. Behavioural approaches to psychological counselling, for example, have as their keystone an objective, cause-and-effect model; cognitive approaches emphasize the importance of rational thinking, goal setting and decision making; and the person-centred approach has been criticized for its covert exercise of power. At the same time, we know from the research literature that a crucial factor which underpins client change is the quality of the relationship between counsellor and client, whatever the counsellor's therapeutic orientation (see, for example, *inter alia*, reviews by Truax and Mitchell, 1971; Rogers, 1975; McLeod, 2001; Batchelor and Horvath, 1999). Organizations, however, do not generally tend to see themselves as being in business to form relationships – their task is to produce the 'widgets', or sell a service, with the key indicator of 'success' so often being financial return. 'Morale' and 'relationships' are important to the extent that they support this process – they are not ends in themselves.

All of this highlights the potential for conflict between the two sets of values. If such potential tensions are not taken seriously, the result can be a waste of valuable resources, including time, money, creativity and commitment on the part of counselling practitioners, clients, and managers, and an increase in the risk that any counselling facility introduced will proceed on the margins of organizational functioning. Introducing a psychological counselling scheme into the work setting can also throw up contradictions within the system which have continuously been present under the surface, but which have not been openly acknowledged. I am thinking predominantly of the tension in many organizational settings between 'helping' and 'controlling' employees. There can often be confusion on this issue, as well as a fear that to discuss the matter openly is likely to promote greater awareness of 'us and them', the opening of a Pandora's box, or possibly even the encouragement of trade union involvement and the prospect of additional negotiating factors being placed on the table. For these reasons, there may be a tendency to steer clear of this debate.

It can be helpful if both parties can understand and explore these differences in ways that enable them to feel challenged rather than threatened. Both managers and professional counsellors are likely to gain substantially from an exploration of their own assumptions, values and goals, and to identify ways in which they might engage with each other as 'reflective practitioners' (Schön, 1983). Positive outcomes could include: greater understanding on the part of both counsellors and managers of important issues in the other person's world; better communication as a support to an on-going programme; a psychological counselling service which does not operate on the margins of organizational functioning; the integration of counselling activities with other organizational support functions; and a potentially wider use of the service. We could envisage counselling professionals, particularly those responsible for the running of a workplace counselling programme, being interested actively to engage with the organization as client, and in having a creative interest in the development of an effective contract between a counselling provision and senior managers (Orlans and Edwards, 2001). Such an interface would also offer considerable scope for innovative research, of potential benefit to both counselling psychologists and to organizations.

A further issue centres on the skills of counselling professionals who work in an organizational setting. There would seem to be a need for an attitude of openness to a range of value systems, a willingness to understand different perspectives and to actively engage with them. While there are debates here as to whether we are dealing with a 'skill' or a 'disposition', I have found in training settings a real need for more discussion and exploration of such issues, and a willingness on the part of counselling professionals to explore their own prejudices and to identify useful ways forward. In that context we have frequently talked about such skills as being in the region of 'the capacity to translate' – that is, to talk about therapeutic endeavour and change in terms that can be understood by different professionals in a range of settings.

A second 'skill' or, perhaps, more precisely, an area of knowledge of relevance to clinical work in the organizational context, relates to the range of dynamics which are operating in that setting. A key dynamic for the organizational counsellor lies in the fact that they are being paid for their services by the organization concerned, and therefore do not potentially have the same freedom as they would have in private practice. In other words, there is a three-way contract operating, with the requirement for a continuing balancing of the needs of both the organization and the client or clients concerned. This is a continual reality for the organizational counsellor. Additional skills which have a bearing on this issue are the capacity to clarify boundaries in a meaningful and articulate way, a capacity to hold the trust of different parties to a therapeutic contract, the capacity to be self-supported and assertive in the face of 'unreasonable' demands, and the capacity to negotiate a clear and meaningful contract with organizational decision makers. In terms of the demands of short-term therapeutic work, counselling professionals will need to be skilled in the assessment of clients, and be knowledgeable about the demands of short-term contracts. There is likely also to be a need to be both knowledgeable about, and able to engage in, a range of procedures and processes relevant to organizational functioning such as, for example, the management of absence and policies for stress management, redundancy procedures, issues of disability or discrimination, career development, and policies concerned with bullying or harassment.

Ethical considerations present yet another challenge, in terms of the demands to maintain adequate boundaries, and to manage the requirements of three-party contracts in an effective and professional way. This involves debates concerning who should be told about what difficulty, about where adequate support might be mustered for difficulties that go beyond the individual level of analysis and intervention, about what should be done when organizational issues are reduced to the individual level, and how serious suicide risk should best be managed. Relatively little has been written about the more 'macro' considerations in terms of ethical issues, a notable exception being the work of Shea and Bond (1997) on the subject of the match between organizational ethos and counsellor attitude.

Conclusion

In this chapter I have reviewed a range of issues relevant to the practice of psychological counselling in the workplace setting. While this field of practice is not limited to counselling psychologists it could potentially be of special interest to that group of practitioners, given the broad-ranging values and skills which are a part of this profession, and the need to be able to bridge different value bases and approaches when working in the organizational setting. Workplace counselling is a complex yet challenging field of theory and practice, demanding as it does a wide range of perspectives and skills. There is, I believe, a need for on-going training, education and debate in this area among researchers, professional counsellors and managers, a need which may partly be addressed through the developing trend towards interdisciplinary work. In that way we may be able to support a higher quality service to clients, be they individuals or organizations, learn more about the most useful ways forward in the application of psychological counselling to workplace settings, and ultimately contribute to the development of more effective and supportive working environments.

References

Barkham, M. (1990) 'Research in individual therapy' in Dryden, W. (ed.) *Individual Therapy: a Handbook*. Milton Keynes: Open University Press.

Barkham, M. and Shapiro, D.A. (1990) 'Brief psychotherapeutic interventions for job-related distress: a pilot study of prescriptive and exploratory therapy', *Counselling Psychology Quarterly*, 3 (2): 133–47.

Batchelor, A. and Horvath, A. (1999) 'The therapeutic relationship' in M.A. Hubble, B.L. Duncan and S.D. Miller (eds) *The Heart and Soul of Change: What Works in Therapy*. Washington DC: American Psychological Association.

Berridge, J.R. and Cooper, C.L. (1994) 'The employee assistance programme: its role in organizational coping and excellence', *Personnel Review*, 23 (7): 1–20.

Bott, D. (1988) 'The relevance of systemic thinking to student counselling', *Counselling Psychology Quarterly*, 1 (4): 367–75.

Brazier, D. (ed.) (1993) *Beyond Carl Rogers*. London: Constable.

Briner, R. (2000) 'Do EAPs work? A complex answer to a simple question', *Counselling at Work*, 29: 1–3.

British Psychological Society (1998) *Guidelines for the Professional Practice of Counselling Psychology*. Leicester: Division of Counselling Psychology.

British Psychological Society (1999) *Division of Counselling Psychology: Rules*. Leicester: BPS.

Bruning, N.S. and Frew, D.R. (1985) 'The impact of various stress management training strategies: a longitudinal experiment' in R.B. Robinson and J.A. Pearce (eds) *Academy of Management Proceedings*. San Diego CA: Academy of Management.

Bull, A. (1997) 'Models of counselling in organizations' in M. Carroll and M. Walton (eds) *Handbook of Counselling in Organizations*. London: Sage.

Carroll, M. (1996) *Workplace Counselling*. London: Sage.

Carroll, M. (1997) 'Counselling in Organizations: an overview', in M. Carroll and M. Walton (eds) *Handbook of Counselling in Organizations*. London: Sage.

Cooper, C.L., Sadri, G., Allison, T. and Reynolds, P. (1990) 'Stress counselling in the Post Office', *Counselling Psychology Quarterly*, 3 (1): 3–11.

Elton Wilson, J. (1996) *Time-conscious Psychological Therapy*. London: Routledge.

Feltham, C. (1997) *Time-limited Counselling*. London: Sage.

Firth, J. and Shapiro, D.A. (1986) 'An evaluation of psychotherapy for job-related distress', *Journal of Occupational Psychology*, 59: 111–19.

Fisher, H. (1997) 'Plastering over the cracks? A study of employee counselling in the NHS', in M. Carroll and M. Walton (eds) *Handbook of Counselling in Organizations*. London: Sage.

Garfield, S.L. (1989) *The Practice of Brief Psychotherapy*. Oxford: Pergamon.

Garfield, S.L. (1995) *Psychotherapy: an Eclectic-Integrative Approach*, second edition. New York: Wiley.

Gergen, K.J. and Kaye, J. (1992) 'Beyond narrative in the negotiation of therapeutic meaning' in S. McNamee and K.J. Gergen (eds) *Therapy as Social Construction*. London: Sage.

Health and Safety Executive (1995) *Stress at Work: a Guide for Employers*. London: HSE.

Highley, C. and Cooper, C. (1994) 'Evaluating EAPs', *Personnel Review*, 27 (7): 46–59.

Highley, J.C. and Cooper, C.L. (1996) 'An Evaluation of Employee Assistance and Workplace Counselling Programmes in British Organizations', paper delivered at the January 1996 Occupational Psychology Conference, Eastbourne.

Holosko, M.J. (1988) 'Perspectives for employee assistance program evaluations: a case for more thoughtful evaluation planning', *Employee Assistance Quarterly*, special Issue 'Evaluation of Employee Assistance Programs', 3 (3–4): 59–68.

Jenkins, P. (1997) *Counselling, Psychotherapy and the Law*. London: Sage.

Jenkins. P. (1999) 'Stress at work: the creaking of floodgates', *Counselling at Work*, 26: 3–4.

Jenkins, P. and Pollecoff, P. (2000) 'Opportunities for workplace counselling to minimize the threat of litigation', *Counselling at Work*, 30: 4–6.

Koss, M.P. and Butcher, J.N. (1986) 'Research on brief psychotherapy', in S.L. Garfield and A.E. Bergin (eds) *Handbook of Psychotherapy and Behavior Change*, (third edition.) New York: Wiley.

McLeod, J. (2001) *Counselling in the Workplace: the facts. A Systematic Study of the Research Evidence*. Rugby: British Association for Counselling and Psychotherapy.

Megranahan, M. (1995) 'Quality control for an EAP', *Personnel Review*, 24 (7): 54–64.

Murphy (1984) 'Occupational stress management: a review and appraisal', *Journal of Occupational Psychology*, 57: 1–15.

Norcross, J.C. and Arkowitz, H. (1992) 'The evolution and current status of psychotherapy integration' in W. Dryden (ed.) *Integrative and Eclectic Therapy: a Handbook*. Buckingham: Open University Press.

Orlans, V. and Edwards, D. (2001) 'Counselling the organization', *Counselling at Work*, 33: 5–7.

Preston, P., Varzos, N. and Liebert, D.S. (2000) *Make Every Session Count: Getting the Most out of your Brief Therapy*. Oakland CA: New Harbinger.

Reddy, M. (1994) 'EAPs and their future in the UK: history repeating itself?' *Personnel Review*, 23 (7): 60–78.

Rogers, C.R. (1951) *Client-centered Therapy: its Current Practice, Implications, and Theory*. Boston MA: Houghton Mifflin.

Rogers, C.R. (1959) 'A theory of therapy, personality, and interpersonal relationships, as developed in the client-centered framework' in S. Koch (ed.) *Psychology: a Study of Science*. New York: McGraw-Hill.

Rogers, C. (1975) 'Empathic: an unappreciated way of being', *Counseling Psychologist*, 5 (2): 2–10.

Roth, A., Fonagy, P. and Parry, G. (1996) 'Psychotherapy research, finding, and evidence-based practice' in A. Roth and P. Fonagy (eds) *What Works for Whom? A Critical Review of Psychotherapy Research*. New York: Guilford Press.

Schön, D.A. (1983) *The Reflective Practitioner: How Professionals think in Action*. London: Temple Smith.

Shapiro, D.A., Cheesman, M. and Wall, T.D. (1993) 'Secondary Prevention: Review of Counselling and EAPs', Paper presented at the Royal College of Physicians Conference on Mental Health at Work, London, January.

Shea, C. and Bond, T. (1997) 'Ethical issues for counselling in organizations' in M. Carroll and M. Walton (eds) *Handbook of Counselling in Organizations*. London: Sage.

Smith, M.L., Glass, G.V. and Miller, T.I. (1980) *The Benefits of Psychotherapy*. Baltimore MD: Johns Hopkins University Press.

Sonnenstuhl, W.J. and Trice, H.M. (1986) *Strategies for Employee Assistance Programs: the Crucial Balance*, Key Issues, 30. New York: New York State School of Industrial and Labor Relations, Cornell University.

Summerfield, J. and Van Oudtshoorn, L. (1995) *Counselling in the Workplace*. London: Institute of Personnel and Development.

Tehrani, N. (1997) 'Internal counselling provision for organizations' in M. Carroll and M. Walton (eds) *Handbook of Counselling in Organizations*. London: Sage.

Truax, C. and Mitchell, K. (1971) 'Research on certain therapist interpersonal skills in relation to process and outcome' in A. Bergin and S. Garfield (eds) *Handbook of Psychotherapy*. New York: Wiley.

27 Enhancing Learning Skills
PETER J. ROSS AND ANGELA M. TAYLOR

This chapter examines the experience of learning at university and the work of the counselling psychologist in supporting the process. Many university students find that the emotional hurdles can be more challenging than the academic ones. Just as possessing social skills does not make an individual socially adept, so the mere possession of learning skills is often not sufficient to enable learning to take place. Students need motivation. They need to be able to manage their anxieties so they do not inhibit their skills. The material must resonate with elements of their values and identity if they are to connect with it and make it their own. They must be able to relate their learning style with the teaching style of the staff. In other words a student's emotional resources and intellectual resources constantly interact, enhancing or inhibiting academic performance.

For this reason most British universities provide counselling services for students. These provide clinical support for clients whose severity of problem is comparable to that found in NHS settings (CORE System Group, 1998). Developmental work may include focus on homesickness, cultural adjustment, bereavement, self-esteem, and relationship difficulties. Academic support may target motivation, concentration, and performance anxiety. Many provide assessment for specific learning difficulties and subsequent individual support. Workshop programmes may vary from how to avoid test anxiety to presentation skills, assertion, social skills, personal confidence, overcoming procrastination.

Within these services counselling psychologists are ideally placed to make a major contribution because they can draw upon their counselling expertise, their knowledge of psychology, and the theoretical bases of both disciplines. At the University of Reading, where six of the eight core staff are chartered psychologists, the practitioners can value and share different theoretical approaches. Responding to clients, they work within therapeutic relationships underpinned by the fundamental counselling requirements of self-awareness, gained through personal therapy, and independent clinical supervision. Cross-cultural counselling training is also invaluable for working within this multicultural environment. However, in common with others, university services are required to increase productivity and be accountable. Short-term, focused individual work and group work are needed to cope with the growing demand, and in this the psychologists' skills in assessing and managing need, risk and priorities become essential. In addition, the research skills of the psychologist as scientist-practitioner are invaluable for auditing and evaluating the work in relation to both individual and institutional needs and for promoting evidence-based practice.

What are the learning problems which engage counselling psychologists in these settings? We begin this chapter by considering the 'inheritance' that the student brings to the task of learning, such as past experiences of success and failure at school and the continuing influence of parental relationships. For individuals with specific learning difficulties, such as dyslexia, the increasing demands of academic rigour can exacerbate hitherto unrecognized problems. Gender and age differences are explored. While male and female students may approach their studies and the accompanying challenges in different ways, mature students may adopt different learning styles and can also shift their life perspectives and their concept of self at a time when such transitions would be unexpected.

With widening access to higher education an increasing number of students arrive with a history of failure in other spheres and with mental health difficulties. We examine the range of emotional difficulties which may block learning, by looking at homesickness and culture shock, which some students experience at entry, through perfectionism and procrastination to examination anxiety and panic. Different counselling and practical approaches are discussed. The final section reports on recent studies evaluating the effectiveness of university counselling services and suggests further areas for development.

Prior experience

As Wankowski (1991) points out, learning is part of the on-going dynamics of the life process and it is not an activity which can occur independently from the rest of life. From past educational experience the student has developed feelings of self-confidence (or lack of them) regarding academic ability and this is one of the foremost qualities associated with success at university.

Feelings of academic confidence and competence develop during years of schooling, marked with successes and/or failures. There are unconscious responses to judgements by teachers and to competition, whether real or implied, with fellow students. Supportive teachers and peers may have encouraged the introverted student to put forward innovative academic arguments that would not have been volunteered otherwise. On the other hand the ability to think creatively and to apply theories to practical questions may have been suppressed in an individual who has been intimidated by a sarcastic teacher or by peers who sneered at 'teacher's pet'. Old anxieties, reawakened before giving a seminar presentation to college peers, may cause a student to avoid a class or module or even leave a course rather than risk being seen as academically unworthy or otherwise incompetent.

Family dynamics, expectations and inhibitions also affect feelings of competence. Some individuals bear the burden of fulfilling parental aspirations and are only too aware of the financial sacrifices that have been made for them to achieve. Others feel they have to emulate high-achieving parents or siblings who have perhaps gone to Oxbridge or studied subjects more valued by the family than their own. Less obvious early influences of family relationships may also undermine self-esteem, general psychological well-being and the necessary ability to adjust to independent living. Drawing on attachment theory, Kenny (1987) proposed a parallel between the adolescent leaving home and facing the unknown university environment and the well known paradigm of the toddler facing the 'strange situation'. Confident of the availability of parental support back home, the student with secure parental attachment would thrive, whereas the adolescent with insecure attachment would adjust less well. Students with secure parental relationships have greater self-confidence and better social adjustment (Kobak and Sceery, 1988; Rice and Cummins, 1996) and are generally better adjusted at college (Rice et al., 1995; Taylor, 1997). Kobak and Sceery (1988) also found that undergraduates classified as having secure attachment were more ego-resilient than others. This probably enabled them to cope better with the inevitable difficulties, disappointments and frustration involved in study and research. Counselling psychologists working with students suffering from low self-confidence, or from difficulties using social support, find exploring past and present parental relationships can be helpful (Kenny and Donaldson, 1991; Mallinckrodt, 1992; Kenny and Rice, 1995).

Early experiences can inhibit learning, even in mature students after they have enjoyed many successful years in the workplace. For example, fifty-year-old Margaret was fully able to understand her chosen subject but was inexplicably anxious. Although she asked for practical help, the psychologist used a counselling approach and found that she had been an adopted child who was brighter than the natural children of the family. As a schoolgirl she had always fallen ill at important examinations. It appeared this was her way of ensuring that she would not be singled out to go to a higher class or a better school and so again be different from her siblings. Margaret was unable to risk success in her current studies until she could understand her 'past' fears.

In a contrasting example, Bob always missed his coursework deadlines because he needed to check and recheck his work for mistakes. When he received the marked work back he only glanced at the mark and hid it ashamedly away. He never learned from the marker's helpful comments, because he was convinced that, as at school, any writing by the marker would be critical and a sign of his academic unworthiness. By contrasting past and present, the counselling psychologist and client could work on present interactions with lecturers, peers and family so that emotional and academic understanding could develop together.

Specific learning difficulties

Although the effects of specific learning difficulties such as dyslexia and dyspraxia are thought to inhibit the learning of schoolchildren, there is now increasing recognition that these neurologically based difficulties also affect learning in higher education. *Dyslexia*, which is the most prevalent, affects some or all literacy skills (reading, writing or spelling) in that the formally measured standards of these skills, together with working memory, are significantly poorer than other cognitive abilities (Turner, 1997; Beech and Singleton, 1997). The National Working Party on Dyslexia in Higher Education (HEFCE, 1999) survey of 1995–96 found that between 1.2 per cent and 1.5 per cent of students in higher education had declared dyslexia on entry. This proportion has been growing and will continue to do so as more children with dyslexia are identified and given support which will eventually enable them to gain the qualifications for university entry. If students have managed to cope with their early learning difficulties, why do specific learning difficulties become a problem again at university?

While at secondary school students may have learned to compensate by, for example, relying on context to read unfamiliar words, or writing in short sentences or choosing only words that they can reliably spell. On reaching university students are frequently confronted by subjects with completely new vocabularies and more complex concepts, which will slow down their reading considerably. If the competent reader has to reread material to fully comprehend it, then the student with dyslexia may have real difficulties and lose confidence in his general academic ability. Weak working memory also affects essay writing and, in attempting to write complex sentences, the student may lapse into grammatical inconsistencies or lose the thread of an argument. Dyslexic students may grow particularly frustrated when they find that their weeks of work do not produce higher marks than the two nights of effort put in by non-dyslexic peers. Explaining solutions to problems can also be a difficulty. The bright student with dyslexia might move from point A to solution D without consciously going in a linear direction through steps B and C. However, for others to follow his solution or replicate his research he has to learn to describe his processing as A–B–C–D. Thus academic work may be an on-going struggle for the student with dyslexia. Having to learn a new range of compensatory skills may be doubly frustrating if the student believes that by getting to university he has already conquered all the dyslexia stumbling blocks. When reassessing the student to permit additional provision in test and examination marking, or to give grounds for a Disabled Student's Allowance to fund computer equipment, the psychologist should also be aware of the possible need for additional emotional support.

A HEFCE (1999) survey showed that although 57 per cent of students with dyslexia knew of this on entry to university the remaining 43 per cent were identified only during their course. These students may be struggling with much of their work and losing confidence in their abilities. Some may have been vaguely aware of long-term problems with reading or writing but put it down to laziness or stupidity. Teachers may have misconstrued poor spelling and grammatical errors as rushed work. The student who painstakingly produced good course work may have been predicted good grades for AS and A level but failed to get them when under time constraint in examinations. These students can be disappointed in their achievement and may well arrive at a university or on a course which was not their first choice. This colours initial perceptions and expectations and can generally detract from the university experience.

When choosing subjects at school, students are likely to opt for those in which they can excel. Thus a student who has difficulty with words may well choose maths or science subjects and so avoid reading and essay-writing problems. However, once at university many scientific, engineering or medical subjects eventually require lengthy reports or dissertations and old problems suddenly reappear. An astute lecturer may recognize what could be a dyslexic difficulty while marking work and refer for assessment.

A diagnosis of dyslexia can be received with a range of emotions from disbelief to anger or shame. For the student long aware of difficulties, receiving an explanation may be a relief. One is not stupid, after all, and, with some support and compensatory marking provision, may even begin to achieve higher marks. However, the long-term struggle with dyslexia has often been high in emotional expense. One significant population of students with undiagnosed difficulty are the mature students returning to education. Frequently these individuals failed at school, their difficulties attributed to low intelligence or poor behaviour. Routes to university differ. Some have slowly worked their way up through a career such as nursing or youth work and suddenly find that a degree is required if they are to have career advancement. Others have been made redundant and when offered retraining suddenly discover that higher education is open to them after all. Difficulty with written work is usually the catalyst for referral but when first meeting the psychologist the student is quite sure that dyslexia will not be diagnosed. The student may well believe that the condition is stigmatizing and implies stupidity and inability to read. When testing proves positive and they are found to be of normal or higher intelligence but with reading, writing or spelling skills significantly below the level expected from their other good abilities, the emotional response is frequently one of loss. The unhappiness of schooldays and the loss of earlier opportunities must be mourned. Some are angry with parents or teachers for not recognizing their dyslexia. They need to grieve and to come to terms with the disability before they can start work on developing new compensatory skills and benefiting from their course.

The specific disorder encompassing difficulty with motor control and coordination is known as *dyspraxia*. Far fewer students are diagnosed as having this as the substantive difficulty. No formal figures for university students are available but males are more frequently diagnosed. However, as dyspraxia gains a larger media profile, more students with this difficulty may enter higher education. Some are ill prepared. Typically the disorganized adolescent schoolboy who cannot participate effectively in ball games, who misplaces his property and who turns up late or misses appointments can be supported by indulgent parents and teachers, particularly if he still manages to produce some good academic work. His eccentricities may be smiled upon and not recognized as difficulties to be overcome. However, once in the strange environment of university his inability to follow a seminar timetable that changes on alternate weeks or cope with three essay deadlines that fall on the same day is judged to be slapdash and lacking commitment. He may be surprised to find that the majority of his peers are much better organized than himself even if they will not admit to it. Portwood (2000) explains that coping with the difficulties of dyspraxia frequently leads to low self-esteem. Some dyspraxic students also have difficulty reading social cues and relating to others. They need help to both understand and compensate for underlying psychological difficulties.

Practical strategies have to be introduced alongside emotional support. For the disorganized student, just keeping a diary, using an alarm clock and written reminders stuck on the door can all make a difference. However, the greatest help can be derived by using computer technology. Apart from word-processing packages with spell checkers and grammar checkers there are specialist packages such as Inspiration to organize the structuring of material for essays and dissertations together with Texthelp! which reads out material. Occasionally a student with dyspraxia chooses to pursue a new area of interest but finds the course wholly unsuitable. For example, the individual with a moderate degree of dyspraxia, who has difficulty following instructions precisely and who has a tendency to be heavyhanded, will not be very welcome in a laboratory full of delicate equipment.

Dyscalculia, difficulty with numbers, presents less frequently. Nowadays even the historian, archaeologist and classicist may need to use statistics or computer modelling. For the severely dyscalculic student dates and even centuries can be muddled. A non-numerical scale must be devised, perhaps using colour. The counselling psychologist may need to dig deep into seldom used resources of creativity and work alongside the student to develop innovative learning strategies.

International students can have special difficulty with a diagnosis of dyslexia. Some do not permit the psychologist to report the matter to their tutor for well deserved allowances. They fear it would have to be noted in any reference subsequently provided for an employer or sponsor back home and consequently they may be disbarred from employment.

Most studies of specific learning difficulties in children suggest that there is a marked gender difference, with the female:male ratios of between 1:3 and 1:5. However, HEFCE (1999) reported the dyslexic student population as consisting of 39 per cent females and 61 per cent males, a ratio of only 1:1.6. This is in line with our findings at the University of Reading. The report suggested that 'females with dyslexia stand a better chance of entering higher education than males with dyslexia, possibly because males tend to be more seriously affected and/or females are better able to compensate for the disabling effects of the condition' (p. 18). Another explanation is that schoolgirls are better at networking with their friends, supporting one another as they work in tandem, not actually copying but taking the lead from one another. That way the girl with dyslexia can get peer support and can mask the extent of her difficulties. Boys on the other hand are more likely to work alone and, when stuck, are more likely to give up than ask for help. This gender difference in study behaviour may be reflected generally across the school population and may partly explain why girls are tending to outperform boys in GCSE examinations and even at A level.

Gender differences

In the elite UK universities it has long been of concern that men significantly outperform women in obtaining first-class degrees. The Universities' Statistical Record from approximately 1985 to 1995 showed that women obtained fewer first-class degrees than men even in traditionally female subjects such as English, Psychology and Nursing. However, men also significantly under-achieve, with about 9 per cent of men gaining third-class degrees in comparison with only 4 per cent of women. Various explanations have been put forward, including the suggestion that the men are more likely to take risks, such as proposing more original academic arguments, which may be more valued by an examiner. However, a self-report survey of 1,500 students at the University of Cambridge (Surtees et al., 2000) suggested that the gender difference was partly due to the different ways the male and female students dealt with stress. Focusing on 3,155 undergraduate students who entered the university in 1995, 24.6 per cent of the men obtained first-class degrees and 3.6 of them obtained third-class degrees. In contrast only 15.5 per cent of the women obtained first-class degrees and only 1.3 per cent obtained third-class degrees. The researchers concluded that about half the difference could be accounted for by course selection. In the Science Faculty, where 26.4 per cent of students were awarded first-class degrees, only 33.1 per cent of the student body were female, whereas in the Arts Faculty, which awarded only 14.9 per cent first-class degrees, 57.6 per cent of the students were female. Adjusting their statistical analysis for this, for prior academic qualifications and for school type, they found that the remainder of the gender difference could be accounted for by 'a reduced capacity to cope with social problems'. This was supported by some of the findings of the self-assessment questionnaires which were repeated over three years as follows:

- Of the 20 per cent of students who reported at least one problem causing substantial worry at each of the three assessments, women reported one and a half times as many problems as men.
- Over twice as many women as men reported their degree course to be extremely stressful on each assessment.
- About one in five women reported an episode of either depression or anxiety during each assessment period, in contrast to one in ten men.
- About 10 per cent of students reported seeking help in each of the three assessment years, with women's rates twice those of the men.

However, they also found that about 10 per cent of students recognized personal emotional problems which they felt required professional help but they did not seek that help. Perhaps the female students are just more willing to acknowledge their emotional difficulties and seek support, while males prefer to manage alone. The question arises as to whether the greater proportion of emotional difficulties for females really affect their ability to achieve first-class degrees but not increase their proportion of third-class degrees.

Perhaps for many women the need to be an equal member in a social group is of greater importance than individual success. Gilligan (1982) proposed a gender-based difference in emotional development, with masculinity being defined as learning to separate and femininity as learning to attach to others. Based on studies of schoolchildren and adolescents, she suggested that males perceive relationships as hierarchies and view success as reaching the top of the hierarchy, whereas females understand relationships as a web and view success as being at the centre. The female student will use the network of available female support to ensure that she achieves more than a third-class degree. However, she may remain satisfied and emotionally comfortable by setting her sights at an upper second-class degree and remaining within her network, unless she can be sure that a good number of her group would keep her company with a first-class degree.

Mature students

Those entering university after the age of twenty-one are considered to be mature students. Many are considerably older, and there are increasing numbers in their sixties and even seventies. Those with broad life experience or a successful career history may exude self-confidence, and feel comfortable asking questions in lectures or expounding their own ideas. They may be less concerned about exposing their lack of understanding than their younger peers. However, other mature students worry that their study skills are rusty and that they are in competition with the younger students, whom they believe have 'better' academic bases to their learning. However, Zeegers (2001) compared the learning styles of recent school leavers and older students on a chemistry course. He used the Student Process Questionnaire which measured individual learning styles as three distinct approaches: the 'deep' approach (discussing and questioning material), the 'surface' approach (e.g. rote learning) and the 'achieving' approach (e.g. choosing a strategy specifically to get high grades.) Of the three the deep approach was the one most associated with high grades. The investigation showed that the older students were significantly more likely to adopt the deep approach and that they received higher grades and completed more units of their courses. Perhaps the counselling psychologists and tutors who support mature students can encourage them to recognize their strengths and not think in terms of competition. If they can relax sufficiently to enjoy engaging with the academic material they may naturally find the 'deep' approach which will help them to succeed.

While we can readily acknowledge that school-leaving students are still working through a late adolescent stage of transition to adulthood, it is easy to forget that mature students are also negotiating change. The process of life change may be recognized when the mature individual mirrors the *Educating Rita* stereotype, but it may be missed in a middle-aged family man or a middle-class businesswoman. Some positively choose education to make a change, to get out of a rut or to prove themselves but others are reacting to circumstances such as divorce, bereavement or redundancy. They may not recognize the effects of the learning experience on their own concepts of self. Investigating the mature students' experience, Walters (2000) developed a 'three Rs' framework, standing for Redundancy, Recognition and Regeneration, to explain the maturational process. Alongside the new learning, the student's old frames of reference and perspectives become redundant, as do some roles and skills and, with them, the concept of self. As these are relinquished the student has to recognize the need for changing role models, changing perspectives and new directions which are consistent with and relevant to the new learning. Regeneration is the outcome of the process, and with it the student may develop greater self-confidence and higher self-esteem and may take on new roles to go with newly developed skills. However, this emotional impact is frequently overlooked. While education can bring improved self-esteem and new opportunities it will also bring higher expectations, new responsibilities and challenges (Walters, 2000). Tutors and psychologists supporting mature students may find the three Rs a useful way of discussing emotional change alongside academic development.

Homesickness

The first hurdle for many students is the transition from home to university life. Homesickness has attracted much theoretical speculation over the centuries. When Napoleon's armies roamed Europe it was thought that perhaps it was due to change of atmospheric pressure – farmers coming down from the hills to fight, whales beaching themselves on arising from the depths, and so on. The remedy tried was being spun around in a high tower. Nowadays, homesickness continues to debilitate, although the remedies have changed. Fisher (1989) found that about 60 per cent of first-year university students reported symptoms, but less than 1 per cent of that 60 per cent required serious counselling time. Each year, a small number at any university will return home, some eschewing all help, some unable to cope even with intensive support. Attempts are made to skill new students in dealing with the problem by sending them written information in advance. Many university counselling services assist with welcome programmes and encourage students to resist the temptation to isolate themselves with academic work immediately. Instead, putting time into making friends and joining clubs, societies and sports teams can be much more important in preventing premature drop-out.

Culture shock

The culture shock experienced by international students can be severe (Furnham and Bochner, 1986). It is comprised of three elements: the 'bereavement' of loss of home, the sense of inadequacy resulting from confounded expectations in a new culture, and having to take responsibility for organizing oneself academically rather than being told what to do by authority. Much of the distress is expressed somatically, so initial presentation is often to a physician, with subsequent referral to a counsellor. The notion of counselling is in itself foreign to many cultures. Stresses therefore predominate in the early days after arrival, not only from the above, but from the idea that grants may have to be repaid if the student fails to complete their studies.

The counselling psychology of homesickness and of culture shock overlaps a good deal. Bowlby (1969, 1973, 1980) has described in detail the effects of, and processes involved in, separation from, and loss of, people and familiar places. The many theories of bereavement, involving high levels of shock, panic, anxiety, disbelief, reminiscing and preoccupation with home (Fisher, 1989) are relevant here too. However, unlike the situation in bereavement, when the death of a loved one is imposed, the student has chosen to deprive herself of the valued home. The evidence shows that students sent by their governments to study overseas 'for their country', as opposed to having actively chosen to do so largely for their own benefit, have more emotional problems. For the same reasons, students who have suddenly been given a visa or scarce currency against all expectation and previous refusal, and who arrive without a period of psychological preparation, usually show more distress than others. The most important theoretical literature is on 'learned helplessness' and 'hopelessness in depression' (Seligman and Seligman, 1975). This approach is crucial, not only because it provides counsellors with strategies, but because the ideas appeal intuitively to students on induction programmes and can therefore be used to empower them with the skills of prevention. It is easy to give students examples of how, in coming from one culture (including a British subculture) to another, predictions of how others will react when we do something familiar to us are quite simply confounded. One can describe the sense of frustration and then mounting anger which accompanies further attempts to influence and change which are, in turn, confounded. Finally, one can describe the mounting sense of helplessness and finally hopelessness which follows and undermines our whole sense of identity. Encouraging positive cognitions and continuity of competence (continue playing ping-pong if that is a sport enjoyed at home) is of far greater importance in transition than attempting to reduce negative cognitions. This is because it promotes a continuity of self-concept. Also, pleasurable physical activity reduces stress.

Student mental health

There is growing interest in student mental health. The early twenties are a classic time for the onset of psychiatric disorders. Subclinical problems are frequent in those attending university following failure in other walks of life and who are encouraged to enter university on the basis that university education might well be good therapy. However, there is increasing recognition of the negative impact which emotional problems can have on academic achievement as well as the impact which academic demands can have in destabilizing vulnerable personalities. For example, depression can reduce concentration; poor social skills can inhibit participation in group activities, both academic and social; anxiety can prevent existing social skills being deployed to make class presentations; low self-esteem can inhibit a student from approaching others for help.

There are numerous research studies showing that student mental health is worse than that of the general population (Stuart-Brown et al., 2000). Numerous reports show that the degree of disturbance being dealt with at university counselling services is increasing (HUCS, 1999). University authorities have hastened to issue guidelines on policy and procedures to be adopted across higher education (CVCP, 2000) and those charged with reflecting on what such issues imply for the duty of care towards all students have consulted widely (AMOSSHE, 2001).

Emotional problems, help seeking and achievement

The earlier discussion of gender differences noted that a reduced capacity to cope with social problems impacted to reduce academic achievement. But Surtees et al. (2000) showed some 10 per cent of all students recognized they needed professional help but did not seek it. Ciarrouchi and Deane (2001) show that it is the emotionally competent who are most likely to seek help from family, friends and professionals. This holds true even for those seeking help from professionals for suicidal ideation. It is in fact those who need help the most, those low in emotion management skills, who are least likely to respond to invitations to access available support. This is not just a matter of poor management of their own emotions but of them predicting they will be poor at managing the emotions of others too.

We have already drawn upon attachment theory (Bowlby, 1988) to illuminate homesickness. In an important application of attachment theory Lopez et al. (1998) explore help seeking, or the lack of it. A very basic assumption of attachment theory is that variations in the quality of one's early experiences of care givers shape internal models used to deal with current care givers and authority. In effect we are said to have a *self-model* regarding our perception of our own worth, competence, lovability, etc., and an *other model* incorporating assumptions about the trustworthiness, dependability, patience, goodness, etc., of other 'important' people such as tutors, counsellors, etc. Lopez et al. found that individuals with positive self-models acknowledged fewer current problems than their peers with negative self-models. They also found that among students reporting high levels of problems, those with positive models of others were more willing to seek counselling than student peers with negative models of others. This fits nicely with the prior finding that such individuals who do eventually find the counselling service evaluate their relationship with the counsellor negatively (Satterfield and Lyddon, 1995) and often terminate counselling early (Mallinckrodt et al., 1995). In addition, Wankowski (1991) exploring the relationship between personality (as measured by the Eysenck Personality Inventory) and academic success found stable introverts did better than unstable introverts or extroverts. Wankowski notes that the vulnerable student tends to be impulsive and is thrown by the need for rapid adjustment to the new environment. Such a student needs emotional support, feedback and stimulation in large quantities but is reluctant to ask for it, especially from authority. Work patterns rapidly become haphazard, and tenacity and resilience quickly dissipate. The student is often 'sent' for counselling, too late, as opposed to seeking help himself.

The successful student tends to be relatively independent already, and has the confidence to be resilient to pressure and inconsistencies. Such a student enjoys the idiosyncrasies of staff rather than being thrown by them, does not fear authority, makes friends easily, enjoys long hours alone in the library, and is not addicted to constant social stimulation. Meeting a problem, it is discussed early with others rather than allowed to become a crisis. Being rewarding to be with, staff and other students tend to give such a student more attention than perhaps is merited, so leading them to become even more resilient and independent.

Perfectionism and procrastination

It is no surprise that idealists and high achievers are attracted to enter universities. Academic staff have higher rates of obsessive-compulsive disorder than normal populations. Perfectionism, though seldom presented as such, is a frequent problem brought by students to university counselling services.

Chang (2000) distinguishes between those who expect themselves to be perfect (self-oriented perfectionists) and those who expect others to be perfect (other-oriented perfectionists). He identifies advantages in self-oriented perfectionism: high standards, pleasure in order and organization, persistence of effort, unwillingness to procrastinate and willingness to pay opportunity costs to achieve. Chang and Rand (2000) explored maladaptive self-oriented perfectionism. Such behaviour included excessive self-criticism and concern about mistakes, doubts about the effectiveness of actions, concern regarding expectation of others, and a tendency to procrastinate from fear of proceeding. These were associated with stress, worry, low satisfaction and a sense of inadequacy. Most important of all, they highlight the low self-esteem frequently found among such students. Self-esteem is, of course, a buffer between perception and mood. The constant inadequacy and failure experienced by perfectionists, combined with worry and doubt, lead to hopelessness and depressive mood if a good self-esteem buffer does not exist.

Understanding the cause of a problem is commonly thought to be essential to overcoming it. Cook (2000) explored whether students suffering from procrastination would overcome the problem more quickly if they agreed with counsellors' aetiology and attributions or disagreed – or indeed were told attribution regarding cause did not matter, they just needed techniques to sort it out. The latter got better quicker. This reminds us of the crucial CBT distinction between cause and maintenance.

In dealing with procrastination it is important to begin with the recognition that it is not so much a problem with a cause as an attempted 'cure' for fear of inadequacy, boredom, etc. The evidence is that, for about one-third of procrastinators, simple techniques (such as the standard sandwich of work/reward/ work system) work well. About one-third appear to be relapsed procrastinators – work-avoiding and pleasure-seeking but actually reality-avoiding: like the alcoholic they need to be faced with or face themselves with a crisis in order to reform. About a third are anxiety-filled procrastinators, their anxieties maintained by negative self-talk (I 'insist' I do really well!).

Suicide and despair

However good university counselling services may be (Stone et al., 2000) they can be good only with those they see. Experience shows very few who are seen commit suicide, despite huge numbers of the despairing and suicidal attending. Few of those who do commit suicide appear to their peers to be unduly depressed or disturbed. Our understanding of suicide in general (O'Connor and Sheehy, 2000; Shneidman, 2001) has greatly increased in recent years, leading to important clinical strategies: for example, to a focus on increasing positive cognitions rather than attempting to reduce negative ones in the suicidal. Our understanding of risk assessment in general (Bongar et al., 1998) and of students in particular (Gutierpez et al., 2000) has likewise increased. For example, with students we know that even strong suicidal ideation is unlikely to lead to suicide if the student is embedded in good relationships with family, friends, etc., as a sense of responsibility to them will prevent it. Equally, we know negative self-evaluation, among other factors, to be crucial. But the question remains as to how we get students who need help to identify themselves and seek help. Preparation for help seeking may have an important contribution to offer.

Positive psychology

The authors are involved in piloting a series of 'self-management' workshops for students at the University of Reading as part of the Study Advisers' Workshop programme (not, it should be noted, 'Personal Development' as part of any Counselling Service programme). These workshops – enhancing motivation, overcoming procrastination, developing confidence, etc. – all focus on identity narrative and positive self-concept, the core issues highlighted as crucial in this chapter. They are designed to appeal to students who would not normally approach a counsellor. It remains to be seen whether this implementation will prove effective. Counselling psychologists can be greatly encouraged by the development of theoretical underpinnings for prevention and preparedness rather than cure. The Positive Psychology movement (Seligman and Csikszentmihalyi, 2000) point out the very ordinary processes which enhance resilience, but which need to be kept in working order (Masten, 2001).

Examination anxiety and stress

Academic performance in course work and examinations is the means by which a student can communicate the depth and breadth of what is known and provide evidence of ability to apply it appropriately. For some courses, the continuous assessment of written assignments and seminar presentations contributes substantially to the class of the final degree. With modular courses or semesters there is a rising trend for tests or examinations to be set at the end of each module or semester. However, in most universities some final examinations have been retained, whether all at the end of the course or split between the final two years. For many students the impending examinations are a source of anxiety and stress which has to be managed effectively if academic ability is to be fully demonstrated.

While some courses prepare their students for examinations by suggesting different revision techniques and exam strategies, the majority of students are left to their own devices. This can be particularly stressful for international students, who may be unused to examinations requiring creative thinking, and to mature students whose past exam experiences have been linked with under-achievement. Even British students tend to forget that their A-level techniques can be transferred and adapted to meet new challenges. As an educational psychologist working with university students, Smith (1999) described two groups requiring particular support. First, the traditional age mainly male undergraduate who had not worked particularly hard to achieve GCSE grades, and who, despite only scraping through A levels, continued to put in the minimum of effort in the face of the real possibility of exam failure. Intervention from the psychologist was acceptable and enabled some of them to obtain their final degree, even if they did not fulfil their potential. A second, mainly female, group considered 'fourteen hours-plus of work a day as insufficient. They so disabled themselves that they could achieve only mediocre results at best' (Smith, 1999: 511). Such debilitating anxiety and defensive disorders are not always easy for academic staff to discern.

Exam preparation support may be delivered individually or as group workshops. Naming the fear of failure or, even more often, the concern about not achieving the acceptable benchmark of the upper second-class degree, and putting this into perspective, can be a helpful start. For some discussing the basic physiological symptoms of examination anxiety in terms of both its inhibitory effects and its positive functions is worth while. Some are relieved to hear that they are not expected to learn 'everything' and that selection of what to learn is about taking calculated risks. With a strategy of how to select and how to balance studying with rest and relaxation, some understanding of the psychology of learning can also enhance the process. For example, the use of short-term memory can be useful for just a limited amount, such as key formulas, spellings of key terms or names, and perhaps a set of mnemonic memory triggers. Most academic learning, like other learning, is about connecting new information with meaningful material that has been previously acquired and established as knowledge in long-term or semantic memory. Conway et al. (1997) asked first-year undergraduates sitting a multiple-choice examination whether they 'remembered' the information or whether they 'knew' it. On the first test correct answers came from those who 'remembered', which could have been their short-term or 'episodic' memory. When retested half an academic year later the correct answers came from students who 'knew' the answer, that is, they had the information stored as long-term or 'semantic' memory. It is the long-term knowledge that will remain of value.

An understanding of information processing can also enhance study skills. When encouraged to consider whether they absorb information more easily in visual or auditory form students are usually quick to identify their preference. From there they can maximize their strengths by enhancing the distinctiveness of the material to be learned, for example by using colour and shape for the visualizers and tape recordings with bullet points for the auditory learners. As failure to answer the actual question is the cause of much exam failure, a timely warning about misperceiving the question can also be helpful. On first reading the anxious examinee can often see what he hopes or expects to see but rereading and underlining key words will ensure that the actual question is fully analysed.

Panic

However, for the student who suffers from panic attacks and other debilitating symptoms, which strike in the examination hall or undermine the revision process, the underlying anxieties must be addressed. If a simple explanation of the physiology is insufficient, then an understanding of the negative feelings attached to the symptoms is required. Is the anxiety about evaluation by others and/or failing them or of failing to meet one's own unrealistic expectations? Individual counselling can help, although it is usually time-limited.

Clark (1994) shows that in the person-centred approach the focus is on getting the client to trust and put down roots into personal values, rather than be controlled by those of others. In gaining awareness through the relationship with the counsellor the student not only learns to shift the focus of evaluation from the 'other, outside' to the 'self, inside' but to self-appreciation too.

Psychodynamic approaches depend on a combination of insight and the transference relationship. For example, a student who produced good course work and was predicted good grades had a history of fainting and even vomiting in the exam halls. She always performed poorly in tests and exams. She described a settled life with a boyfriend and a close relationship with her mother and sibling but she dismissed an inquiry about her father, who had left home when she was fourteen. However, in talking she came to realize that her father had been her main mentor and motivator, particularly in competitive situations. As she spoke of her disappointment and anger at his present lack of interest she also realized that she was rejecting his current approaches. This insight enabled her to renew the relationship and also to sit the exams successfully just four weeks later. It was a dramatic and sustained change, although for most clients the unpacking is more gentle and progress is slower.

The cognitive-behavioural approach is probably the most common, however. It certainly has the most evidenced-based foundation in applications to stress, anxiety and panic (Barlow and Cerny, 1988; Roth and Fonagy, 1996). For example, consider a student with a history of chronic panic attacks sufficient to absorb much time from support staff, sheltered examination conditions to reduce disruption to other students and parents in attendance 'to give support'. Assessment revealed a core belief: '*I must always* do as well as I can'. (In everything, because it's the only way to be secure: a version of 'love is conditional on performance'.) The cognitive rule which emerged from this was '*If* I do an exam, *then* I have to fulfil all my potential' (and if I don't it's awful). The automatic thinking which occurs as 'froth' on the surface of this is 'How can I *show* myself now I'm at complete potential, maybe I'm not, how could I know … ' The display of panic, sometimes hysteria, had a clear function: to show significant others that she was trying so hard she could not have tried any harder and therefore should not be blamed in any way for any result short of perfection.

It takes a lot of careful listening to isolate such thinking, the process of which conveys complete acceptance of the person, even if not of their thinking. Humour can help to highlight the core issues: 'Well, I am so relieved to hear you suffer all these distressing symptoms! Given what you say to yourself, there would be something really seriously wrong with you if you did not!'

CBT focuses, within the 'core belief/cognitive rule/automatic thought' framework above, on identifying cognitions which maintain problems, disclosing their significance to the client, and of course encouraging change so that more realistic cognitions become equally automatic.

Evidence of effectiveness

Aware of the need for accountability and recognizing the value of evidence-based practice, university counselling services have been conducting research into their own practices. The University of Cambridge Counselling Service (Surtees et al., 2000) was involved in a cohort study investigating the mental health of a 25 per cent sample of the 1995 undergraduate intake, tracking them through their university careers. Eight per cent of the sample consulted the counselling service, and this group reported a greater number of problems, compared with the general student population. In addition to academic problems they demonstrated increased prevalence of anxiety, major depressive episodes and suicidal tendencies. Seventy-five per cent of these students reported subjectively that the service had helped them to resolve their problems.

At the University of Birmingham, Rickinson (1997) investigated the effectiveness of counselling intervention for final-year undergraduates. In addition to self-assessment questionnaires she used the symptoms checklist SCL-90-R pre- and post-counselling to measure the level of psychological distress. She compared a quasi-control group of students with a similar profile of psychological distress to a group of students who attended at least four sessions of psychodynamic counselling. The results showed a significant reduction in the level of stress for the students who received counselling, with a dramatic fall in distress for thirty six of the forty three students in the group. In contrast the change in the level of distress for the control group over the same period of time was marginal. This was, however, just one student group at one institution. Other university services are now monitoring their client population, and the University of Reading among others has used CORE (Clinical Outcome Routine Evaluation) (CORE System Group, 1998), a questionnaire which has been used in primary care counselling services to measure symptoms pre- and post-counselling. Our own initial results show on a small sample that before counselling the majority of clients scored within the clinical range in terms of well-being, symptoms and day-to-day functioning. After counselling 72.3 per cent of clients showed statistically reliable improvement, with a further 22.2 per cent showing some improvement. However, we await a collation of results from different universities to give an overall view of effectiveness.

Rickinson (1998) reported the effect of intervention on first-year students who were at high risk of withdrawing from the university. Fifteen out of forty four students accepted an invitation which included attending a counselling session to explore their difficulties, liaison with their personal tutor, attendance on an introductory workshop programme and a review counselling session. Of these students two accepted additional counselling. All these undergraduates remained at the university and completed their degrees, and none of them requested further counselling support from the university service after that first year. Thus the research testifies to the efficacy of this sort of intervention. It is likely that similar good practice occurs in many other institutions but there is a dearth of published studies. In a major research review conducted by the Association for University and College Counselling (1998) few studies actually focused on outcome.

Integration

While this chapter has focused on the breadth of difficulties facing university students and the different ways that counselling psychologists may address them, it has not looked at the role of the latter in relation to academic and pastoral staff. This area of work involves education and training so that staff know how to recognize students with difficulties, make timely referrals and encourage students with difficulties to be organized and responsible for their own learning. Overall the work of counselling psychologists in universities will be most effective when it is fully integrated with teaching and support from academic staff.

References

AMOSSHE (Association of Managers of Student Services in Higher Education) (2001) *Responding to Student Mental Health Issues: 'Duty of Care' Responsibilities for Student Services in Higher Education.* Winchester: AMOSSHE.

Association for University and College Counselling (1998) *Review of Research relevant to Counselling in UK Colleges and Universities.* Rugby: British Association for Counselling and Psychotherapy.

Barlow, D.H. and Cerny, J.A. (1988) *Psychological Treatment of Panic.* New York: Guilford Press.

Beech, J.R. and Singleton, C.H. (1997) *The Psychological Assessment of Reading.* London: Routledge.

Bongar, B., Berman, A.L., Maris, R.W., Silverman, M.M., Harris, E.A. and Packman, W.L. (eds) (1998) *Risk Management with Suicidal Patients.* London: Guilford Press.

Bowlby, J. (1969, 1973, 1980) *Attachment and Loss* I–III. New York: Basic Books.

Bowlby, J. (1988) *A Secure Base: Parent–Child Attachment and Healthy Human Development.* New York: Basic Books.

Chang, E.C. (2000) 'Perfectionism is a predictor of positive and negative psychological outcomes: examining a mediation model in younger and older adults', *Journal of Counseling Psychology*, 47 (1): 18–26.

Chang, E.C. and Rand, K.L. (2000) 'Perfectionism as a predictor of subsequent adjustment: evidence for a diathesis–stress mechanism among college students', *Journal of Counseling Psychology*, 47 (1): 129–37.

Ciarrouchi, J.V. and Deane, F.P. (2001) 'Emotional competence and willingness to seek help from professional and non-professional sources', *British Journal of Guidance and Counselling*, 29 (2): 233–46.

Clark, P. (1994) 'A person-centred approach to stress management', *British Journal of Guidance and Counselling*, 22 (1): 27–37.

Conway, M.A., Gardiner, J., Perfect, T.J., Anderson, S.J. and Cohen, G.M. (1997) 'Changes in memory awareness during learning: the acquisition of knowledge by psychology undergraduates', *Journal of Experimental Psychology: General*, 126: 393–413.

Cook, R.F. (2000) 'Effects of counselors' etiology attributions on college students' procrastination', *Journal of Counseling Psychology*, 47 (3): 352–61.

CORE System Group (1998) *CORE System (Information Management) Handbook.* Leeds: CORE System Group, University of Leeds.

CVCP (Committee of Vice-chancellors and Principals of the Universities of the United Kingdom) (2000) *Guidelines on Student Mental Health: Policies and Procedures for Higher Education.* London CVCP.

Fisher, S. (1989) *Homesickness, Cognition and Health.* Hove: Erlbaum.

Furnham, A. and Bochner, S. (1986) *Culture Shock.* London: Methuen.

Gilligan, C. (1982) *In a Different Voice.* Cambridge MA: Harvard University Press.

Gutierpez, P.M., Osman, A., Kopler, B.A., Barrios, F.X. and Bagge, C.L. (2000) 'Suicide risk assessment in a college student population', *Journal of Counseling Psychology*, 47 (4): 403–13.

HEFCE National Working Party on Dyslexia in Higher Education (1999) *Dyslexia in Higher Education: Policy, Provision and Practice*. Hull: University of Hull.

HUCS (Heads of University Counselling Services) (1999) *Degrees of Disturbance: the New Agenda*. Rugby: British Association for Counselling and Psychotherapy.

Kenny, M.E. (1987) 'The extent and function of parental attachment among first-year college students', *Journal of Youth and Adolescence*, 16: 17–29.

Kenny, M.E. and Donaldson, G.A. (1991) 'Contributions of parental attachment and family structure to the social and psychological functioning of first-year college students', *Journal of Counseling Psychology*, 38: 479–86.

Kenny, M.E. and Rice, K.G. (1995) 'Attachment to parents and adjustment in late adolescent college students: current status, applications, and future considerations', *Counseling Psychologist*, 23: 433–56.

Kobak, R.R. and Sceery, A. (1988) 'Attachment in late adolescence: working models, affect regulation and representations of self and others', *Child Development*, 59: 135–46.

Lopez, F.G., Melendez, M.C., Sauer, E.M., Berger, E. and Wyssmann, J. (1998) 'Internal working models, self-reported problems, and help-seeking attitudes among college students', *Journal of Counseling Psychology*, 45 (1): 79–83.

Mallinckrodt, B. (1992) 'Childhood emotional bonds with parents, development of adult social competencies and availability of social support', *Journal of Counseling Psychology*, 39: 453–61.

Mallinckrodt, B., Gantt, D. and Coble, H.L. (1995) 'Attachment patterns in the psychotherapy relationship: development of the client attachment to therapist scale', *Journal of Counseling Psychology*, 42 (3): 307–17.

Masten, A.S. (2001) 'Ordinary magic: resilience processes in development', *American Psychologist*, 56 (3): 227–38.

O'Connor, R. and Sheehy, N. (2000) *Understanding Suicidal Behaviour*. Leicester: British Psychological Society.

Portwood, M. (2000) *Understanding Developmental Dyspraxia*. London: David Fulton.

Rice, K.G. and Cummins, P.N. (1996) 'Late adolescent and parent perceptions of attachment: an exploratory study of personal and social well-being', *Journal of Counseling and Development*, 75: 50–7.

Rice, K.G., FitzGerald, D.P., Whaley, T.J. and Gibbs, C.L. (1995) 'Cross-sectional and longitudinal examination of attachment, separation-individuation and college student adjustment', *Journal of Counseling and Development*, 73: 463–74.

Rickinson, B. (1997) 'Evaluating the effectiveness of counselling intervention with final year undergraduates', *Counselling Psychology Quarterly*, 10: 271–85.

Rickinson, B. (1998) 'The relationship between undergraduate student counselling and successful degree completion', *Studies in Higher Education*, 25: 95–102.

Roth, A. and Fonagy, P. (1996) *What Works for Whom?* London: Guilford Press.

Satterfield, W.A. and Lyddon, W.J. (1995) 'Client attachment and perceptions of the working alliance with counselor trainees', *Journal of Counseling Psychology*, 42 (2): 187–9.

Seligman, M. and Seligman, P. (1975) *Helplessness*. San Francisco: Freeman.

Seligman, M.E.P. and Csikszentmihalyi, M. (eds) (2000) *Positive Psychology*, special issue of *American Psychologist*, 55 (1).

Shneidman, E.S. (2001) *Comprehending Suicide*. Washington DC: American Psychological Association.

Smith, G. (1999) 'Universities need educational psychologists', *Psychologist*, 12: 510–11.

Stone, G.L., Vespia, K.M. and Kanz, J.E. (2000) 'How good is mental health care on college campuses?' *Journal of Counseling Psychology*, 47 (4): 498–510.

Stuart-Brown, S., Evans, J., Patterson, J., Peterson, S., Doll, H., Balding, J. and Regis, D. (2000) 'The health of students in institutes of higher education: an important and neglected public health problem', *Journal of Public Health Medicine*, 22 (4): 492–9.

Suanum, S. and Zody, Z.B. (2001) 'Psychopathology and college grades', *Journal of Counseling Psychology*, 48 (1): 72–6.

Surtees, P., Wainwright, N. and Pharoah, P. (2000) 'Student Mental Health, Use of Services and Academic Attainment: a Report to the Review Committee of the University of Cambridge Counselling Service'. Cambridge: UCCS.

Taylor, A.M. (1997) 'Parental Attachment and Adjustment to College for Adolescent Students in Further Education', unpublished Ph.D. thesis, University of London.

Turner, M. (1997) *Psychological Assessment of Dyslexia*. London: Whurr.

Walters, M. (2000) 'The mature students' three Rs', *British Journal of Guidance and Counselling*, 28: 267–78.

Wankowski, J. (1991) 'Success and failure at university', in K. Raaheim, J. Wankowski and J. Radford (eds), *Helping Students to Learn*. Buckingham: Open University Press.

Zeegers, P. (2001) 'Approaches to learning in science: a longitudinal study', *British Journal of Educational Psychology*, 71: 115–32.

28   Stress Management and Prevention Programmes
STEPHEN PALMER

Since the mid-1990s, in the United Kingdom, there has been a steady increase in the media coverage given to stress. This has been partially due to employees successfully suing their employers in the courts for occupational stress and the associated clinical disorders that accompany it. With the Health and Safety Executive (e.g. HSE, 2001) recommending stress prevention programmes at work, employers are under mounting pressure to take action. The opportunities for skilled counselling psychologists to help in organizations have never been so great. This chapter will focus on the major issues and problem areas involved in stress, stress management and the development of stress management or stress prevention programmes rather than concentrating on how to set up a programme.

History and theories of stress

In this section we will focus on the various ways in which stress has been conceptualized, taking a historical perspective. As no one theory has gained universal acceptance, it is important for the practitioner to decide which approach best fits the individual or organization, as this may shape the type of intervention undertaken.

The word 'stress' was originally derived from *stringere*, a Latin word used three centuries ago to describe hardships. Subsequently it denoted strain or effort. At the beginning of the twentieth century the relationship between illness and 'busy' individuals was observed. In 1908 Yerkes and Dodson concluded from their research that, up to a certain optimum point, performance improved as pressure or stress increased. However, beyond this optimum point, performance was reduced. Later Walter Cannon in 1935 developed the concept of homeostasis, which basically reasserted the earlier views of Claude Bernard from the previous century, who suggested that regardless of external changes an individual's internal systems should ideally remain unaltered. This could almost be likened to a modern central heating system which is thermostatically controlled.

The basic theories of stress can be summarized under three headings: stimulus, response and interactive variables, which will now be examined.

The *stimulus* variable or engineering approach conceptualizes stress as a noxious stimulus or demand that is externally imposed upon an individual which can lead to ill health. In this model stress can also be caused by too much or too little external stimulation.

The *response* variable or physiological approach is based on Selye's (1956) triphasic model involving the initial alarm reaction (sympathetic adrenal-medullary activation), the stage of resistance (adrenal-cortical activation) and the stage of exhaustion (final reactivation of the sympathetic adrenal-medullary system). This response process is known as the *general adaptation syndrome*, where an individual will eventually suffer from physiological 'diseases of adaptation' to stress caused by aversive or noxious external stimuli if the last stage of exhaustion is reached. However, the model does not take into account that some noxious external stimuli (such as heat) do not necessarily trigger the stress response.

Both the stimulus variable and response model are based on the stimulus–response paradigm (SR) and disregard the importance of cognitions and perceptions which may exacerbate, moderate or inhibit the activation of the stress response in any given situation. In applying the SR paradigm, much research has been undertaken into the possible effect of specific life events upon individuals. A number of life event scales (e.g. Holmes and Rahe, 1967) have been developed which were based on averaging procedures which totally ignored the personal meaning of life events for each individual and subsequently only weakly predict stress-related illness episodes. However, the research did indicate that as some individuals experienced an increasing number of life changes/events this increased their chances of developing more serious diseases. It is recommended that the *interaction* of the external and internal worlds of the individual needs to be included in any practice-based theory of stress.

The interactive variable or psychological approach to stress attempts to overcome the deficiencies of the earlier models. There have been a number of proposed psychological theories: the interactional and the transactional. The interactional theories centre on the fit between the person and their environment, often known as the 'person–environment fit' theory. Others focused on the interactive nature of job demands and decision latitude, but later studies have indicated that there is only weak evidence to support real interactions between specific demands leading to disease (Warr, 1990). If anything, research discovered that the additive nature of different demands increased ill health.

Transactional theories of stress focus on the cognitive and affective aspects of an individual's interactions with their environment and the behavioural coping styles they may adopt or lack. One of the most well known theories is that of Richard Lazarus (Lazarus, 1976; Lazarus and Folkman, 1984), who defined stress as resulting from an imbalance between demands and resources. Lazarus asserts that a person evaluates a particular incident, demand or on-going situation. This initial evaluation, known as primary appraisal, involves continuous monitoring of the environment and analysis of whether a problem exists. If a problem is recognized the stress response may be activated and unpleasant feelings and emotions may be experienced. The next stage, secondary appraisal, follows when the person evaluates his or her resources and options. Unlike the earlier models of stress, the important issue is whether the person recognizes that a problem exists. Once recognized, if the demands are greater than the resources only then does stress occur. If the resources are greater than the demands the person may view the situation as a challenge and not a stress scenario. If the person is too inexperienced to recognize that a particular problem exists it would not be considered as a stress scenario. This is an important distinction as, ironically, it is the subjective and not the objective assessment of any scenario that may trigger the stress response.

Tom Cox (see Cox, 1978; Cox and Mackay, 1981) developed a five-stage transactional model of occupational stress. It was later developed into a general multimodal transactional theory of stress to help counselling psychologists and other professionals underpin stress counselling/management practice with a 'guiding' theory, thereby enabling the appropriate selection of psychotherapeutic, psychoeducational, emotion- and skills-focused interventions (Palmer and Dryden, 1995, later modified in Palmer, 1997). This general model of stress is applicable to both occupational and non-occupational settings. According to Palmer (1997), assuming a situation is perceived as stressful and has personal significance, attempts are usually made by individuals to deal and cope with the problem by making a combination of behavioural, affective, sensory, imaginal, cognitive, interpersonal and physiological changes. However, if the problem remains, eventually the person's health may be negatively affected. (See Gregson and Looker, 1996, for information about the physiology of stress and health.)

In the literature the concepts of 'stress' and 'strain' are often confused. In physics stress is externally imposed upon a substance and the strain is the substance's reaction to the stress. This can be equated to the loss of a job being a stressor and the psychophysiological reaction being the strain.

Spielberger and Reheiser (1994: 204), concluding the debate about the occupational theories of stress, stated: 'In summary, [Richard] Lazarus' conception of occupational stress and Person–Environment Fit theory both have merit and limitations, and can be construed as complementary rather than contradictory in providing a meaningful conceptual framework for understanding stress in the workplace.'

The next section will focus on a number of issues that need to be considered when developing stress management programmes for individuals, families or organizations.

General issues

Coping

Coping is a key part of the relationship between stressors and strain, although it is an area that is not well understood (Cooper et al., 2001; Oakland and Ostell, 1996). It has three main properties:

- It is a process involving what the person thinks and how the person behaves in a stressful situation.

- It is context-dependent, as it is affected by the specific situation or initial appraisal of it, and then by any resources the individual has to deal with the situation.
- Coping as a process is 'independent of outcome', that is, it does not depend upon whether it does or does not lead to a successful result (also see Lazarus and Folkman, 1984).

Coping can be divided into emotion-focused and task-focused strategies which include rationalizing/reappraisal of the problem, de-awfulizing a problem, seeking social support, denial, information-seeking, delaying action by using distraction/relaxation, developing better skills and competence to deal with the specific problem, and symptom management. In addition, coping has been described as a problem-solving strategy which starts with 'recognition and diagnosis (analysis) followed by actions and evaluation through to reanalysis' (Cox, 1993: 21; see this reference for an overview of the subject). However, this cycle of action may actually exacerbate a stress scenario if an unhelpful approach is chosen. Helpful or adaptive behaviour is considered as developmental, whereas unhelpful or maladaptive behaviour is defensive in nature and includes problem denial, procrastination and substance abuse. Research indicates that if individuals on balance use more maladaptive coping strategies, in contrast to adaptive ones, they increase their chances of suffering from negative health outcomes.

Social support

One major coping strategy that can reduce stress or help reframe stressful situations is appropriate social support. A spouse, a member of the family, a work colleague or friend may provide a stressed individual with somebody who appears to care and listen. This helper may enable the individual to use problem-solving skills or reframe the importance of specific events. The Whitehall II Study (HSE, 2000) found that low social support at work was associated with increased sickness absence, poor mental health and poor health functioning. In another study unemployed workers who were able to obtain social support from the community, family and friends had significantly fewer symptoms of stress than those who had less support. In addition, those who had less support also had a higher serum cholesterol level and suffered more depression. A family's belief system helps an individual to interpret and understand the way the world works, and family members may offer practical assistance. It can also provide a rest place and support when a member suffers disappointment or failure. However, a family that does not offer support, or is itself a stressor, may leave its members more susceptible to stress. In the workplace, co-workers can act as a surrogate family providing support, constructive feedback and friendship which helps buffer the individual from stress. In work and non-work situations social support that helps an individual to assess and resolve a problem is preferable to colluding support that prevents a person from accurately appraising the stress scenario.

Few researchers have manipulated social support and have generally used correlational or descriptive designs, focusing on client groups with particular problems. Also there has been a tendency to use white middle-class adult samples, selected by convenience, although this is beginning to change (see Underwood, 2000).

Locus of control

This concept emerged from social learning theory and was developed by Julian Rotter (1966) and focuses on the amount of control individuals believe they have over situations. Individuals with an external locus of control believe that they have limited or no influence over events whilst internals believe that they do have influence. This construct can be viewed as a continuum and not bipolar. Perceptions of control increase the ability to deal with frustrating situations and thereby reduce anxiety and stress, whereas little or no perceived control can increase anxiety and depression, and negatively affect psychological health. Paradoxically, when individuals with an internal locus of control perceive that they are unable to influence the outcome of a stress problem, their level of anxiety is inclined to rise higher than that of a person who has an external locus of control. There is a possibility that, when given a choice, 'internals' choose occupations where they can exert control over their work environment, thereby reducing stress.

Wallston and associates (1978) expanded the theory and developed the Health Locus of Control. This is a multidimensional construct which has become popular in health psychology research. Recent research (HSE, 2000) has found an association between having little input in how work is undertaken with a higher risk of alcohol dependence and poor mental health.

The coping construct could be viewed as individuals attempting to exercise control over their stressful environment, and perhaps the control construct is the most relevant issue, and not coping. Therefore stress management programmes that help individuals to believe they have control over situations or control over their responses to different situations, whether realistic or otherwise, may ameliorate the effects of stress.

Type A behaviour

In the late 1950s two cardiologists, Meyer Friedman and Ray Rosenman (1959), asserted that specific overt behaviours were associated with increases in blood cholesterol, blood clotting time, and the incidence of arcus senilis and clinical coronary artery disease. They developed methods of assessment and later labelled the particular behaviour pattern Type A for descriptive purposes. The specific overt behaviours included a chronic sense of time urgency, impatience, polyphasic activity, explosive speech patterns, aggressiveness, free-floating hostility, being extremely competitive, high-achieving and very strongly committed and involved in work. One of the mainstays of Type A assessment is a mildly challenging structured interview (SI) method (Rosenman, 1978), although self-report instruments such as the Bortner Rating Scale (BRS),

Framingham Type A Scale (FTAS) and the Jenkins Activity Survey (JAS) are often used, as they are less time-consuming and easy to apply. However, the validity of the JAS self-report instrument has been questioned, as its classificatory agreement with the SI is low and the JAS has sometimes led to negative outcomes in studies.

In 1975 the Western Collaborative Group Study found that Type A males are twice as likely to experience coronary heart disease (CHD) as non-Type A males (known as Type B). Studies that have not used the JAS as a measure tend to support this conclusion in population studies.

Type A behaviour has been described as a coping pattern, a learnt style of behaviour, and as a personality trait by various researchers. Research has found that 'anger-in' and 'potential for hostility' were the two main predictors of atherosclerosis (Dembroski et al., 1985). Individuals with both problems increased their chances of developing atherosclerosis. This research indicates that the most relevant issue that needs to be focused on in cardiac counselling or preventative stress management training may be these areas and not other so-called indicators of Type A behaviour such as impatience. Fortunately, research shows that the three main CHD risk factors, that is, Type A behaviour, hypertension and serum cholesterol, can be reduced by using a range of stress management techniques (Bennett and Carroll, 1996; Friedman, 1996). Although one stress management intervention may lower the three risk factors for CHD, the best efficacy is achieved from comprehensive treatment programmes. Interestingly, just reducing the rate of speech of Type A individuals can lower their cardiovascular responses. It is worth noting that there are some differences in outcome between the research studies undertaken in Europe and those of North America. Perhaps the self-report instruments are not valid for the different cultures, and counselling psychologists may need to take these issues into consideration when developing programmes.

The 'hardy personality'

One of the problems with the Type A construct is that it does not adequately explain why some individuals do not suffer from stress-related illness even though they are in stressful situations or occupations. Suzanne Kobasa (1979) developed the 'hardy personality' theory to account for this inconsistency. She suggested that 'hardy individuals' shared three major beliefs, summarized below:

- *Commitment:* belief in oneself and what one is doing, including involvement in many life situations, such as work, family, relationships and social institutions and thereby maintaining a balance.
- *Control:* belief in oneself having influence over the course of events. Also seeking explanations for why something is happening, with a focus on one's own responsibility.
- *Challenge:* belief that change is the normative mode of living.

Hardy individuals would tend to perceive difficult situations as challenges and not as stressful by using cognitive coping skills to keep stressors in perspective. Unpleasant events would be interpreted as new opportunities instead of threatening situations. This may explain why some Type A individuals do not suffer from ill health or cardiovascular disease, as they also have beliefs similar to those of hardy individuals. Owing to hardy individuals being committed to many life situations they are more likely to be able to obtain social support, which is an additional buffer against stressors. The hardy individual theory goes a stage further than Rotter's locus of control theory, as it includes additional constructs. The belief that change is the normative mode of living would help hardy individuals to cope with the change that is occurring in industry, with downsizing and redundancies.

However, Kobasa's research and hardiness construct has been criticized: the research participants were primarily male executives; hardiness could be one of three distinct constructs; various measurement and analysis problems. Later work into a Health-related Hardiness Scale has overcome some of these issues.

Other factors

There are a range of other different factors that counselling psychologists need to consider when developing stress management programmes: age, ethnicity, cultural background and gender.

An individual's biological *age* may influence how the stress response is activated and whether the individual perceives a particular situation as stressful. At different stages in life an individual may have different goals and objectives, which can be thwarted by life events. For example, a job redundancy at twenty-five years may be seen in a different light from redundancy at fifty-five years by the same person, especially if there are financial and familial responsibilities at a particular age. A young manager may respond to a stressful situation by feeling slightly anxious and with a minute rise in blood pressure. The same manager in a similar situation twenty years later might suffer from panic attacks and angina due to long-term stress, smoking and poor diet. If an individual's self-esteem has been heavily dependent on work-related achievement, on retirement the person can develop reduced self-esteem, leading to depression or psychosomatic symptoms of depression. Preventative programmes can focus on these issues, depending upon the age of the individuals.

Self-efficacy appears to influence the impact of job demands and control on blood pressure. Thus 'when people are confident in their abilities, having control mitigates the stress consequences of demanding jobs' (Schaubroek and Merritt, 1997: 750). Jex and Gudanowski (1992) found that that collective self-efficacy (of a group of employees) moderated the effects of a stressor whereas individual self-efficacy did not.

Minority groups in work and social settings can experience both overt and covert racial prejudice which may lead to heightened levels of stress. Racist attitudes and behaviour can exacerbate low self-esteem that minority group members may have owing to their social setting and previous life experience. They may also have a reduced social support network which can exacerbate stress. American studies have consistently shown that black employees have less job satisfaction than whites, although this may reflect the type of work black employees are given and their relative socio-economic status. Often the belief systems and behaviours of members of cultural subgroups may be in conflict with those from the predominant culture. Unfortunately the Eurocentric bias in counselling approaches and the fact that most counselling psychologists and trainers are white, educated, middle-class, possibly possessing different values and communication styles, could lead to inadvertent cultural oppression by the imposition of Western values on their ethnic minority clients (see Alladin, 1993). This raises issues for counselling psychologists developing stress management programmes for minority groups or mixed groups in counselling, clinical, family or industrial settings.

Gender. Life expectancy of men is lower than women by about eight years. This could be due to a number of factors, including Type A behaviour, alcohol intake and smoking as well as genetic and hormonal reasons. With the changing role of women in society and, in particular, the dual-career couple, women may experience additional stressors. Women may have a career and still have a home to maintain, as studies have shown that many men are still not prepared to assist their female partners. In addition the Equal Pay Act has been in existence for over three decades, yet according to the Structure of Earnings Survey, the United Kingdom has the worst gender gap in the European Union, as women are paid 66 per cent of male earnings. (The UK government statistics exclude public-sector earnings and therefore provide a slightly 'healthier' pay differential of 82 per cent.) The Equal Opportunities Commission has estimated that up to 50 per cent of the differential could be caused by discrimination. In addition, a career ceiling still exists for women in the United Kingdom.

Some of the main issues relating to stress and its management have now been covered. The next section focuses on the stress management programmes for the individual, the family and for organizations, still with reference to the available research.

Stress management programmes

Stress management programmes for the individual

When developing stress management programmes for the individual the counselling psychologist will be influenced by the needs of the client, who may require stress counselling/management for a current problem or preventative stress management to help cope with daily hassles and general stress reduction, or a combination of both. If the individual is stressed by a current problem then interventions based on cognitive-behavioural and problem-solving methods are generally effective. Although relaxation and distraction techniques may have some benefit for symptom management, they may not necessarily help the individual to reappraise or resolve the problem or stress scenario. If the problem will resolve itself over the course of time then non-directive counselling may appear to be just as effective as more prescriptive or focused approaches. However, cognitive behavioural therapy is the psychological therapy of choice for the majority of stress-related symptoms and conditions such as phobias, obsessive compulsive disorder, panic disorder and somatic complaints (see Department of Health, 2001). Surviving a difficult life event may in itself lead to an increase in self-efficacy, which will help the person adaptively appraise and thereby manage similar events in the future.

In counselling, a thorough assessment of the problem and the client's symptoms may guide the counsellor towards the appropriate interventions to use. Palmer and Dryden (1995) have found the multimodal assessment procedure developed by Lazarus helpful. This involves close examination of the seven modalities that Lazarus believes comprise the entire range of personality: Behaviour, Affect, Sensation, Imagery, Cognition, Interpersonal, Drugs/biology. A questionnaire can be used to assist the process (Lazarus and Lazarus, 1991). By assessing each modality, it may become apparent that an individual, for example, avoids doing certain useful behaviours, feels anxious, has physical tension, catastrophic imagery, unhelpful thoughts, passive-aggressive behaviour, and is taking medication for headaches. Once the assessment of each modality is finished a series of research-based techniques and interventions could be discussed and the rationale explained to the client and the most useful interventions applied. Technique selection may depend upon which modality the client may be more sensitive to. Therefore, in the previous example, if a client's catastrophic imagery appears to trigger high levels of anxiety then coping imagery may become the desired intervention. Furthermore, individuals suffering from specific stressors such as financial problems do not necessarily find the interpersonal and emotional strategies as helpful as those individuals with relationship difficulties. These factors need to be considered when developing stress management programmes.

Taking into account the stress research and interactional theories of stress there could be a variety of objectives in an intervention, for example to:

- Solve the problem.
- Alter the way the client responds.
- Help the client reappraise the stressor.
- Help the client change the nature of the stressor.

To attain these objectives an individual may need to acquire or use a range of cognitive and behavioural skills. Consequently, to be effective, the counselling psychologist also needs to be competent in these skills in order to teach or demonstrate them. As research suggests that stress management programmes are effective when applied in group sessions, counselling psychologists working in under-resourced organizations may need seriously to consider running groups (White et al., 1992). This requires additional skills, such as facilitation.

Effectiveness of interventions

The important ethical issue for the counselling psychologist is to design an intervention that is based on research and has face validity with the client. For example, there is limited research that points to psychodynamic interventions helping individuals to overcome situation-specific phobias and panic attacks. Yet there is an interesting paradox in the field of psychotherapy and stress management, that however compelling the published research is for a particular approach, different forms of psychotherapy generally 'appear' to have similar outcomes (Shapiro and Shapiro, 1982). This 'equivalence paradox' is still being researched to find the specific mechanisms that lead to change during psychotherapy and stress management training (Reynolds et al., 1993). However, cognitive behavioural therapy is generally considered as the psychological therapy of choice for the majority of stress-related symptoms and conditions such as phobias, obsessive compulsive disorder, panic disorder and somatic complaints (see Department of Health, 2001).

If the client wants to receive preventive stress management training then a psycho-educational approach could be applied. Some examples are stress inoculation training, cognitive-behavioural skills training, rational emotive behaviour training, multimodal skills training, assertion training, Type A modification, relaxation training, life-style management and physical outlets. From the initial assessment, skill deficits such as cognitive skills or relaxation skills may become apparent and these could be the focus of the intervention. These methods have also been used successfully in group stress management training. What is not so clear from the published research is which is the best approach or technique to use for a particular individual. Furthermore, most research has been undertaken with subjects suffering from clinical disorders such as generalized anxiety. There is still a lack of research with non-clinical populations and evidence that preventive stress management programmes actually help such individuals manage future stress scenarios.

Considering that the research indicates that a wide range of interventions may help reduce stress and the risk factors involved in coronary heart disease, the most important aspect of a stress management programme may be to help clients increase their subjective belief of control over a particular stressful situation or their psychophysiological response to it. This may help to explain why even placebo interventions such as 'bogus' subconscious retraining (White et al., 1992) can help to reduce stress and anxiety if a convincing rationale is provided. White et al. found that didactic psycho-educational cognitive, behavioural, or cognitive-behavioural 'stress control' training for large groups enhanced post-therapy improvement whilst even the placebo group maintained progress compared with the waiting list. In this study the cognitive and the behavioural training groups were slightly more effective than the cognitive-behavioural group. White has suggested that more training may be required to teach both cognitive and behavioural techniques to the subjects. This could possibly account for the cognitive-behavioural group being less effective. Butler et al. (1991) found cognitive-behavioural therapy superior to behaviour therapy. Powell (1987) found that clients rated 'the experience of being in a group and meeting people with similar problems' and 'information about anxiety and stress' higher than learning any active coping skills. This may indicate that counselling psychologists running stress management programmes should see their role as facilitators, educators and organizers of self-help services rather than just individual therapists.

Stress management programmes for the family

Stress and strain in families or households is common. This poses a problem for the counselling psychologist in that sometimes family-orientated interventions may be more effective than individual counselling for a member of a family. Stress in families and households has been measured by a variety of indices, including 'expressed emotion'. Family-based interventions have usually focused on the enhancement of constructive communication, thereby reducing 'high expressed emotion', that is, discussions in preference to rows. However, when the underlying causes of conflicts were mainly due to a family member suffering from severe physical or mental disorder, improved communication alone did not always reduce stress. This led to the inclusion of additional problem-solving strategies into the approach (see Falloon et al., 1993).

Falloon and associates listed the problems most likely to benefit from behavioural family therapy strategies: children's conduct disorders, learning disabilities and autism, adolescent behavioural disturbance, marital and family conflict, sexual dysfunction, drug and alcohol misuse, family violence and child abuse, pre-marital counselling, divorce mediation, eating disorders, suicide prevention, residential care, criminal offending problems, depression, bipolar disorders, schizophrenia, anxiety disorders, relapse prevention, chronic physical health problems, dementias, prevention of stress-related disorders in high-risk groups. The main steps in a time-limited family-based stress management intervention as described by Falloon et al. (1993: 223) are:

- Assessment of current ways of dealing with stress, and current personal goals.
- Education about specific disorders.
- Enhancing communication about problems and goals.
- Enhancing problem solving as a household group.
- Specific strategies for dealing with difficult problems.

A thorough assessment will help the design of the stress management programme whereby the individual and group needs and skills deficits are ascertained. The emphasis on communication skills training is to ensure that group members learn how to communicate and listen actively to each other. This is essential if the household or family members are going to use a six-step group problem-solving approach to any problems or stress scenarios as they arise.

The six steps are as follows.

- Identify the problem (or goal).
- List all possible solutions.
- Highlight probable consequences.
- Agree on the 'best' strategy.
- Plan and implement.
- Review results.

One of the long-term goals is to train the family to be able to cope with stressful problems without the constant aid of a counsellor. The problem-solving approach has also been used in couples counselling, adolescent conflict and dementias. Controlled studies demonstrate the effectiveness of the problem-solving approach in a variety of different settings. The challenge for the counselling psychologist is to make an accurate assessment, teach the necessary skills and encourage the participants to use their skills to resolve a crisis in the most efficient way. The stress management intervention is considered effective if it is able to avert the impact of a stressful event within seven days of its occurrence (Falloon et al., 1993).

Stress management programmes for organizations

The Health and Safety Executive (HSE, 2001) estimated that in 1995–96 work-related stress cost employers and society £4.12 billion in sickness absence alone, with an average of sixteen days off work for each person suffering from a stress-related condition. This is a total of approximately 6.5 million working days lost in 1995. This section will focus on the main causes of organizational stress and stress management interventions undertaken in organizations.

Figure 28.1   The relation between stress factors, the individual and the symptoms

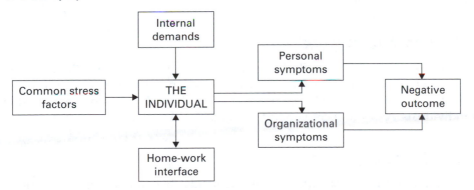

Figure 28.1 illustrates diagrammatically the organizational stress process and highlights the relationship between stress factors, the individual and the

symptoms. There are a number of common stress factors which include those intrinsic to the job, relationships at work, role in the organization, career development, organizational structure and climate. In addition, the individual may place internal demands upon him or herself which may exacerbate a seemingly innocuous event into a stressful situation. The home–work interface may also be a cause of stress.

According to the research, the organizational indicators or symptoms of stress include: high staff turnover, high absenteeism, increased health care claims, increased industrial accidents, industrial relations difficulties, lowered efficiency, low morale, poor quality control, poor job performance, staff burn-out and suicide. However, these symptoms need to be seen in a wider socio-economic context, as during worldwide recession employees may be reluctant to change jobs or take time off work for illness, especially if such action would put their income in jeopardy. The symptoms of stress that the individual may suffer range from hypertension, anxiety, depression and alcohol abuse to serious conditions such as coronary heart disease.

To understand occupational stress it is useful to look at the common factors, home–work interface and the internal demands.

Factors intrinsic to the job

The more common environmental workplace stressors include air pollution, dust/fibres, heat, humidity, lighting, noise, noxious chemicals/nicotine, sick building syndrome, static electricity, uncomfortable chairs/work stations and visual display unit glare. These stressors may come under the remit of health and safety regulations, and unlike other workplace stressors employers can be obligated to rectify the problems. Studies have found other factors intrinsic to the job, including boring repetitive tasks, dangerous work, deadlines, excessive travel, isolated working conditions, long hours culture, shift work, work underload/overload, and the work too difficult for the individual. E-mail overload arose in the 1990s.

Relationships at work

Interpersonal relationship difficulties can be a major cause of stress in the workplace. Problems can arise for a variety of reasons, which can include office politics, competition, bullying, peer pressure, Type A behaviour and hostile individuals. A lack of social support and high social density can also be stressful.

Role in the organization

There are a number of different role demands that can contribute to stress: ambiguity, conflict, definition, expectations, incompatibility, overload, underload and sign. The long-term effects can be very detrimental to the individual's health; for example, research indicates that employees who supervise others are more likely to suffer from coronary heart disease compared with those who are responsible for machinery. Often employees are unaware of the source of their role stress and therefore are unable to change or manage it.

Career development

Career development can cause stress at different stages of an employee's progress or lack of progress through a company. Promotion prospects can become increasingly difficult to achieve as an employee moves higher up an organization, and in addition, older employees may need to retrain to be able to use new technology. This can lead to stress in some individuals. Older employees tend to share a number of fears: demotion, obsolescence, redundancy, job insecurity and forced early retirement. In some 'high-tech' industries – computing software, for example – the income earned at the bottom of the career ladder can sometimes be the same as or higher than in management.

Organizational structure and climate

Some organizations have a structure and climate that may restrict the autonomy of employees whereby they do not believe that they have much control or influence over their workload. Research has highlighted how this may lead to an increased risk of alcohol dependence and poor mental health (HSE, 2000). They may find the work unchallenging and boring, and this can contribute to job dissatisfaction, resentment, apathy and reduced self-esteem. Ageism, racism and/or sexism can also be prevalent in some organizations, with management not taking a proactive approach to deal with these issues. Some organizations are reluctant to involve staff over redundancies, thereby increasing uncertainty and lack of control. In addition, company restructuring has brought an increase in the use of technology and reduced staffing levels, with those remaining doing more work. This has contributed to UK employees working the longest hours in the European Union.

Internal demands

If it is assumed that transactional theories offer the most useful models for the practitioner to conceptualize the stress process, then an important factor in the equation is the internal demands employees place upon themselves (and others) in any given situation. This may help to create stress in a situation unnecessarily. A good example is a person who has strong perfectionist beliefs not being able to achieve a work deadline. This may seem like a 'catastrophe' for the individual, whereas another person with less demanding beliefs may not become stressed. Taking this one step further, Abrams and Ellis (1996: 62) adopt a radical cognitive view and assert that 'stress does not exist in itself. Stress is like good and evil: it exists only in its perceptions and reactions [*sic*] of the beholder (or the stressee)'.

A number of unhelpful beliefs seem to exacerbate work-related stress, and are regularly raised by participants attending multimodal stress management workshops:

- I/others must perform well at all times.
- I/others must always reach deadlines.
- The organization and others must treat me fairly at all times.
- I should get what I want, otherwise I can't stand it.
- Significant others must appreciate my work, otherwise I am worthless.
- If I fail at an important task, then I'm a failure.
- I must be in control of the situation, otherwise it would be awful and I couldn't stand it.

A school study has highlighted how absolutist and all-or-nothing thinking styles lead to a greater number of stress-related symptoms in head teachers (Ostell and Oaklands, 1999). Models of occupational stress that overlook the importance of internal demands in creating stress scenarios do not aid the practitioner in the development of stress management programmes.

Home–work interface

If employees are suffering from stress due to problems at home, in some cases it can reduce their performance and effectiveness at work owing, for example, to lack of concentration. Conversely, if employees are suffering from occupational stress it may affect their home life as they literally take their worries home and become, for example, irritable with the family. Sometimes a negative stress cycle can be created whereby a problem in one domain can cause stress in the other domain which subsequently adds stress to the original domain. This compounds the individual's initial problem.

When assessing the types of problems employees brought to occupational stress counsellors in the Post Office, Cooper and Cartwright (1996) found that 46 per cent were related to mental health and stress issues, and 24 per cent were about relationship problems, 'with the majority focusing on marital difficulties' (1996: 94). As predicted, counselling substantially reduced absenteeism among those employees who received it. Some research has found that women are more prone than men to bring their 'work stress' home, and this may be due to incompatible demands.

Managing workplace stress

The individual and organizational methods for either managing or reducing workplace stress have focused on interventions at three different levels:

- Primary prevention (stressor-directed).
- Secondary prevention (response-directed).
- Tertiary prevention (symptom-directed).

We will briefly look at individual-focused interventions. At the primary prevention level the employee can attempt to manage his or her personal perceptions of stressors by changing their internal demands, reducing Type A behaviour, reappraising situations more realistically, disputing cognitive distortions, etc. The employee can manage the personal work environment by using time management, assertion and communication skills, overload/underload avoidance, social support, task variation, etc., and manage their life-style by appropriate leisure time use, maintaining a balance, suitable diet, etc.

At the secondary prevention level, the employee can attempt to alter the ways in which he or she responds to stressors by using relaxation methods such as meditation, Benson relaxation response, progressive relaxation, hypnosis, biofeedback, etc. Physical outlets such as muscle strength and endurance training, yoga, aerobic exercise, jogging, walking, sports, etc., can also be employed. Emotional outlets such as talking and writing about their stressors can be beneficial.

Finally, at the tertiary prevention level the main aim is to help the employee once he or she is suffering from the symptoms of stress by attending symptom-specific programmes (for example, anxiety management), individual or group psychotherapy, or by receiving medical care. This would include staff with post-traumatic stress disorder.

Organization-focused interventions at the primary level attempt to remove or reduce the employee's exposure to the stressor (or hazard). If this is not possible then the impact of the stressor upon the employee is reduced. This can include focusing on work redesign, organizational and role restructuring (see Cooper et al., 2001). At the secondary level, methods are used to improve the ability of the organization to recognize and subsequently deal with stress-related problems as they arise. Examples include communication and information sharing, stress management training and 'wellness' programmes. Tertiary interventions focus on helping employees deal with, and recover from, work-related problems and include stress counselling and employee assistance programmes.

The new HSE guidelines (2001) recommend a five-step stress risk assessment, focusing on assessing and then addressing seven major hazards: culture; demands; control; relationships; change; role; support, training and factors unique to the individual. The HSE (2001) asserts that a proactive approach as opposed to the more usual reactive approach is undertaken to tackle work-related stress. The focus should be on stress prevention and not stress management, pressure training or stress counselling. Employers are expected to remove hazards. Qualitative assessment methods to find out whether work-related stress is a problem can include performance appraisals, informal discussions with staff, focus groups, and return-to-work interviews. Quantitative methods include productivity data, sickness/absence data, staff turnover and questionnaires. However, the HSE does not recommend commercially available stress audit questionnaires, as they may not be reliable or valid tests for work-related stress.

Effectiveness of organizational interventions

Occupational stress is a compelling and powerful notion. This power is embedded in the belief that occupational stress is a causal factor in the development and mainte- nance of ill-health. Although the notion of the stress concept has been repeatedly criticized and the evidence to support the relationship between stress and ill-health is conflicting and inconclusive, even the mere suspicion that stress may cause ill-health has apparently been sufficient to raise concerns about individual well-being and its social, financial and commercial implications. (Reynolds and Briner, 1996: 142–3).

These authors' concern about organizational stress management programmes is based on reviewing the relevant literature and needs further examination. Essentially, the majority of workplace interventions are focused on the indivi- dual and based on multimodal cognitive-behaviour therapy, theory and methods. In clinical settings these methods have been comprehensively evaluated on individuals with clinical disorders, for example depression and anxiety, and have been shown to be effective. In contrast, when the methods are applied to a non-clinical population not suffering from stress, there is less evidence to sug- gest that positive gains are achieved and maintained. In addition, most studies do not include a long-term follow-up to assess whether the interventions 'inoculate' the employees against future stress scenarios. However, there are notable exceptions (e.g. Kushnir and Malkinson, 1993). Some studies have con- firmed the efficacy of work-site stress management in reducing anxiety, urinary catecholamines and blood pressure. One important study by Bruning and Frew (1985) compared the effects of meditation, exercise and management skills training and a combination of these interventions on galvanic skin response, blood pressure and pulse rate. Interestingly, the study indicated that manage- ment skills training consisting of conflict resolution, goal setting and time man- agement had the best effect on reducing blood pressure and pulse rate. Although stress management training is useful for tackling some stressors or sources of strain (Dewe, 1994), studies that have assessed organizational out- comes, such as work performance, job satisfaction, accidents and absenteeism rates, have found inconsistent results (Ganster, 1995). This may reflect the type of intervention and/or the selection of the participants. More convincingly, one often quoted study (Jones et al., 1988) found that workplace stress levels in a group of hospitals correlated with the frequency of malpractice claims. Hospitals in the group that implemented a stress management programme significantly reduced the number of claims.

Research has found that distressed employees who receive cognitive- behavioural stress counselling as part of a company programme do benefit (see Cooper and Cartwright, 1996). Even these studies can only be 'quasi- experimental', as there are many factors that could affect their validity. This criti- cism also applies to studies that appear to support the effectiveness of employee assistance programmes. Another major problem in the field of occupational stress research is that there are few well designed evaluated studies which focus on the elimination or reduction of the sources of stress in the workplace. In addition, the majority of studies have targeted managerial or administrative workers for the focus of intervention. So what research has been evaluated has not usually included all levels of workers.

Organizational stress management interventions are inherently difficult to evaluate, owing to the many factors involved that could affect the outcome. In addition, organizations tend to resist organization-focused interventions, preferring employee-focused interventions such as stress management workshops or counselling. In future, research strategies should avoid measurement overlap and clearly distinguish between dependent and independent variables (Dewe, 2000). The field of organizational stress management needs more research to evaluate the methods used, and practitioners need to develop stress prevention programmes based on careful examination of the literature and subsequent application of theory to practice. Will the HSE recommended stress risk assessment procedure be seen as the gold standard for organizational interventions? More research is required to answer this question.

Conclusion

Stress management programmes have been undertaken in a variety of counselling, clinical, family and occupational settings. Where distressed individuals have received stress counselling or group training/therapy, there has generally been substantial improvement in their condition. When non-clinical populations have received stress management, there is less evidence of long-term benefit. However, this could reflect the limitations of the studies or the skills of the practitioners teaching the relevant components. Tackling work-related stress is now on the agenda of an increasing number of UK companies, and this is a possible area of work for counselling psychologists, who can offer a range of skills when working with individuals and groups. With additional continuing professional development, counselling psychologists may be in a position to offer stress risk assessment too.

References

Abrams, M. and Ellis, A. (1996) 'Rational emotive behaviour therapy in the treatment of stress' in S. Palmer and W. Dryden (eds) *Stress Management and Counselling: Theory, Practice, Research and Methodology*. London: Cassell.

Alladin, W.J. (1993) 'Ethnic matching in counselling: how important is it to ethnically match clients and counsellors?' in W. Dryden (ed.) *Questions and Answers on Counselling in Action*. London: Sage.

Bennett, P. and Carroll, D. (1996) 'Stress management approaches to the prevention of coronary heart disease' in S. Palmer and W. Dryden (eds) *Stress Management and Counselling: Theory, Practice, Research and Methodology*. London: Cassell.

Bruning, N.S. and Frew, D.R. (1985) 'The impact of various stress management training strategies: a longitudinal experiment' in R.B. Robinson and J.A. Pearce (eds) *Academy of Management Proceedings*. San Diego CA: Academy of Management.

Butler, G., Fennell, M., Robson, P. and Gelder, M. (1991) 'A comparison of behavior therapy and cognitive-behavior therapy in the treatment of Generalized Anxiety Disorder', *Journal of Consulting and Clinical Psychology*, 59: 167–75.

Cannon, W.B. (1935) 'Stresses and strains of homeostasis', *American Journal of Medical Science*, 189 (1): 1–14.

Cooper, C.L. and Cartwright, S. (1996) 'Stress management interventions in the workplace: stress counselling and stress audits' in S. Palmer and W. Dryden (eds) *Stress Management and Counselling: Theory, Practice, Research and Methodology*. London: Cassell.

Cooper, C.L., Dewe, P.J. and O'Driscoll, M.P. (2001) *Organizational Stress: a Review and Critique of Theory, Research, and Applications*. Thousand Oaks CA: Sage.

Cox, T. (1978) *Stress*. London: Macmillan.

Cox, T. (1993) *Stress Research and Stress Management: Putting Theory to Work*. London: Health and Safety Executive.

Cox, T. and Mackay, C.J. (1981) 'A transactional approach to occupational stress' in E.N. Corlett and J.Richardson (eds) *Stress, Work Design and Productivity*. Chichester: Wiley.

Dembroski, T.M., MacDougall, J.M., Williams, R.B., Haney, T.L. and Blumenthal, J.A. (1985) 'Components of Type A, hostility, and anger-in: relationship to angiographic findings', *Psychosomatic Medicine*, 47: 219–33.

Department of Health (2001) *Treatment Choice in Psychological Therapies and Counselling: Evidence Based Clinical Practice Guideline. Brief Version*. London: Department of Health.

Dewe, P. (1994) 'EAPs and stress management: from theory to practice to comprehensiveness', *Personnel Review*, 23: 21–32.

Dewe, P. (2000) Measures of coping with stress at work: a review and critique' in P. Dewe, M. Leiter and T. Cox (eds) *Coping, Health and Organizations*. New York: Taylor & Francis.

Falloon, R.H., Laporta, M., Fadden, G. and Graham-Hole, V. (1993) *Managing Stress in Families: Cognitive and Behavioural Strategies for Enhancing Coping Skills*. London: Routledge.

Friedman, M. (1996) *Type A Behavior: its Diagnosis and Treatment*. New York: Plenum Press.

Friedman, M. and Rosenman, R.H. (1959) 'Association of a specific overt behavior pattern with increases in blood cholesterol, blood clotting time, incidence of arcus senilis and clinical coronary artery disease', *Journal of the American Medical Association*, 2169: 1286–96.

Ganster, D. (1995) 'Interventions for building healthy organizations: suggestions from stress research literature' in L. Murphy, J. Hurrell, S. Sauter and G. Keita (eds) *Job Stress Interventions*. Washington DC: American Psychological Association.

Gregson, O. and Looker, T. (1996) 'The biological basis of stress management', in S. Palmer and W. Dryden (eds) *Stress Management and Counselling: Theory, Practice, Research and Methodology*. London: Cassell.

Holmes, T.H. and Rahe, R.H. (1967) 'The Social Readjustment Rating Scale', *Journal of Psychosomatic Research*, 11: 213–18.

HSE (2000) *Work-related Factors and Ill Health: the Whitehall II Study, CRR266*. Sudbury: Health and Safety Executive.

HSE (2001) *Tackling Work-related Stress: a Managers' Guide to Improving and Maintaining Employee Health and Well-being*. Sudbury: Health and Safety Executive.

Jex, S. and Gudanowski, D. (1992) 'Efficacy beliefs and work stress: an exploratory study', *Journal of Organizational Behavior*, 13: 509–17.

Jones, R.L., Barge, B.N., Steffy, B.D., Fay, L.M., Kunz, L.K. and Wuebker, L.J. (1988) 'Stress and medical malpractice: organisational risk assessment and intervention', *Journal of Applied Psychology*, 73: 727–35.

Kobasa, S. (1979) 'Stressful life events, personality and health: an inquiry into hardiness', *Journal of Personality and Social Psychology*, 45: 1–13.

Kushnir, T. and Malkinson, R. (1993) 'A rational-emotive group intervention for preventing and coping with stress among safety officers', *Journal of Rational-emotive and Cognitive Behavior Therapy*, 11 (4): 195–206.

Lazarus, A.A. and Lazarus, C.N. (1991) *Multimodal Life History Inventory*. Champaign IL: Research Press.

Lazarus, R.S. (1976) *Patterns of Adjustment*. New York: McGraw-Hill.

Lazarus, R.S. and Folkman, R. (1984) *Stress, Appraisal, and Coping*. New York: Springer.

Oakland, S. and Ostell, A. (1996) 'Measuring coping: a review and critique', *Human Relations*, 38: 107–26.

Ostell, A. and Oaklands, S. (1999) 'Absolutist thinking and health', *British Journal of Medical Psychology*, 72 (2): 239–50.

Palmer, S. (1993) 'Organisational stress: symptoms, causes and reduction', *Newsletter of the Society of Public Health*, 2: 7–8.

Palmer, S. (1997) 'Stress counselling and management: past, present and future' in S. Palmer and V. Varma (eds) *The Future of Counselling and Psychotherapy*. London: Sage.

Palmer, S. and Dryden, W. (1995) *Counselling for Stress Problems*. London: Sage.

Powell, T.J. (1987) 'Anxiety management groups in clinical practice: a preliminary report', *Behavioural Psychotherapy*, 15: 181–7.

Price, V. (1982) *Type A Behavior Pattern: a Model for Research and Practice*. New York: Academic Press.

Reynolds, S. and Briner, R.B. (1996) 'Stress management at work: with whom, for whom and to what ends?' in S. Palmer and W. Dryden (eds) *Stress Management and Counselling: Theory, Practice, Research and Methodology*. London: Cassell.

Reynolds, S., Taylor, E. and Shapiro, D.A. (1993) 'Session impact in stress management training', *Journal of Occupational and Organisational Psychology*, 66: 99–113.

Rosenman, R.H. (1978) 'The interview method of assessment of the coronary-prone behavior pattern' in T.M. Dembroski, S.G. Haynes and M. Feinleib (eds) *Coronary-prone Behavior*. New York: Springer.

Rotter, J.B. (1966) 'Generalized expectancies for internal versus external control of reinforcement', *Psychological Monographs: General and Applied*, 80: 1–26.

Schaubroeck, J. and Merritt, D. (1997) 'Divergent effects of job control on coping with work stressors: the key role of self-efficacy', *Academy of Management Journal*, 40: 783–54.

Selye, H. (1956) *Stress of Life*. New York: McGraw-Hill.

Shapiro, D.A. and Shapiro, D. (1982) 'Meta-analysis of comparative therapy outcome research: a replication and refinement', *Psychological Bulletin*, 92: 581–604.

Sloane, S.J. and Cooper, C.L. (1986) *Pilots under Stress*. London: Routledge.

Spielberger, C.D. and Reheiser, E.C. (1994) 'The Job Stress Survey: measuring gender differences in occupational stress', *Journal of Social Behaviour and Personality*, 9 (2): 199–218.

Underwood, P. W. (2000) 'Social support: the promise and the reality' in V.H. Rice (ed.) *Handbook of Stress, Coping, and Health: Implications for Nursing Research, Theory and Practice*. Thousand Oaks CA: Sage.

Wallston, K.A., Wallston, B.S. and DeVellis, R. (1978) 'Development of the multidimensional health locus of control (MHLC) scales', *Health Education Monographs*, 6: 161–70.

Warr, P.B. (1990) 'Decision latitude, job demands and employee well-being', *Work and Stress*, 4: 285–94.

White, J., Keenan, M. and Brookes, N. (1992) 'Stress control: a controlled comparative investigation of large group therapy for generalised anxiety disorder', *Behavioural Psychotherapy*, 20: 97–114.

Yerkes, R.M. and Dodson, J.D. (1908) 'The relation of strength of stimulus to rapidity of habit formation', *Journal of Comparative Neurology and Psychology*, 18: 459–82.

29 Counselling Psychology and the Body
BILL WAHL

> The body has been invisible, for years unaddressed and ignored, left in the waiting room of the therapist's office. (Conger, 1994: 211)

I am very pleased at the inclusion of this chapter in the second edition for the following reasons. First, the importance of the body is minimized or overlooked altogether in virtually all introductory texts related to psychological therapy, psychotherapy and counselling. Second (and related to point one), those models of therapy which have given most consideration to the topic of the body in therapeutic practice (i.e. the psychological body therapies) are normally relegated to 'oddball status' and are currently well outside mainstream therapy. As a result, many students and even seasoned practitioners may have little exposure to such therapies. Third, the topic of the body in therapeutic practice often incites unease and raises certain challenging ethical issues (e.g. touch in therapeutic practice). While this may help to explain why the body is so often ignored, without exposure to such issues students and qualified practitioners alike may encounter confusion and indecision concerning body-related clinical experiences. This chapter aims to offer the reader an enhanced understanding of the theory of the body in therapy as well as a variety of body-oriented therapeutic skills which may be integrated into current practice.

Background

The body in therapeutic practice: a brief overview

A discussion concerning the body in twentieth-century therapeutic models requires some historical context, in large part because any contemporary view of the body exists in relation to a history of Western philosophy that extends back at least 2,500 years. Clearly, this chapter is not the place for a comprehensive review of the history of the body in Western philosophy, but it seems important to make two general points: (1) Western models of philosophy have frequently ascribed an inferior status to the body in relation to the mind, soul or spirit, and (2) philosophers have struggled with the 'mind–body problem' in ways that are consequential in terms of how we view this issue today.

A review of Russell's seminal text *A History of Western Philosophy* (1945) would indicate that a less than favourable view of the body dominated much of Greek, ecclesiastical and modern philosophy. For Socrates the soul was seen as distinct from the body and was thought to be unchanging, immortal, pure and equated with wisdom. The body, however, was a problem. Given that perception occurs through the body (i.e. the senses), everything necessarily becomes distorted and confused. A similar view is put forth by Plato, for whom the body was seen as a source of desire that prevented the perception of truth:

> And thus having got rid of the foolishness of the body we shall be pure and have converse with the pure, and know of ourselves the clear light everywhere, which is no other than the light of truth. (Plato, quoted in Russell, 1945: 137)

St Augustine is a typical representative of ecclesiastical philosophy. His essential view concerning the body was that the need for lust in sexual intercourse was a punishment for Adam's sin in the Garden of Eden. The body, being the site of physical desire, therefore becomes equated with sin and fallenness.

Descartes's radical scepticism eventually led him to the conclusion that one can place trust in or have a chance of knowing truth only through one's own thoughts, and that sensory/bodily experience was likely to be misleading. This conclusion had the unfortunate side effect of devaluing sensory/bodily experience.

The relationship of the mind to the body has perplexed Western philosophy tremendously from ancient to contemporary times, leading Schopenhauer to refer to the problem as 'the world-knot'. There have been, generally speaking, three major attempts to solve this problem (Priest, 1991), all of which are open to criticism. Solution one, espoused by the *materialist* (e.g. Democritus, Epicurus, Hobbes, Davison, Honderich), suggests the monistic view that only matter exists (the body and brain being a form of matter). In this solution there is no problem concerning how the mind and body interact simply because there is no mind as such. The materialist position is problematic, however, simply because it flies in the face of direct human experience, i.e. I experience myself to have consciousness. This is the main argument of *dualism* or interactionism (e.g. Plato, Descartes, Locke, Leibniz, Popper, Swinburg). This position states that both mind/consciousness and matter exist, that they are comprised of two totally different substances and that they interact with one another. The big headache for the dualist, however, has always been the inability to explain how consciousness (i.e. mind) and matter (i.e. body) communicate. *Idealism* (e.g. Plotinus, Hegel, Berkeley) is a monistic view which holds that only minds or, in some views, Spirit exists. Idealism is the attack on physical reality as we normally understand it. Idealism represents the exact opposite position of materialism but suffers from the same problem, i.e. the notion that physical reality does not really exist flies in the face of direct human experience in the same manner as the notion that consciousness does not exist.

Neither the materialist, dualist nor idealist perspective has proven its case, yet therapists cannot wait for philosophy to sort the problem out prior to assisting human beings. It is perhaps important, however, to acknowledge how these philosophic perspectives impact and express themselves through practice. For example, certain orthodox applications of psychiatry or behaviourism assume (perhaps unconsciously) the materialist position in the manner they apply psychoactive medication to the brain or schedules of conditioning to an individual, or in the way they ignore features of consciousness such as will or choice. Many models assume the dualist position in the manner they take for granted the interaction of mind and body. Some transpersonal models of psychology and psychotherapy espouse views of Mind or Spirit which are consistent with idealism.

Whatever view of the mind-body problem one takes, professionally the Western world has had a strong tendency to separate body, mind, soul and spirit into relatively isolated fields of inquiry and practice. The body has largely been the province of medical practice; the mind, emotion and behaviour have principally been the province of philosophy and later psychology; the soul has been the province of religion and Spirit the province of mysticism. While these fields have independently amassed a huge amount of information and often made indispensable discoveries, they frequently have failed to integrate their discoveries with each other (Wilber, 2000). In short, what much of Western medical science, psychology, philosophy and religion did not acknowledge was the possibility that body, mind and soul/Spirit may be seen to represent a unified and interactive field.

Concerning the historical relationship between the body and therapeutic practice, Sigmund Freud played an important role, at least at the level of theory. Smith's (1985) illustration of Freud's view of the body is illuminating. In his historical review we are reminded that Freud gave the body a significant place in the development of personality, indicating in 1923 that the ego is 'first and foremost a body-ego' (Freud, 1960: 17). 'The ego is ultimately derived from bodily sensations, chiefly from those springing from the surface of the body. It [the ego] may thus be regarded as a mental projection of the surface of the body' (p. 16). What Freud was in essence saying was that the development of the ego is dependent on and grows out of the quality of physical nurturance the baby/child receives. The implication here is that a lack of physical nurturance will result in a corresponding lack of ego development. For example, 'if the child does not receive enough experience in being supported against gravity by the parenting figures, then the ego would develop with a deficiency in the self-support function' (Smith, 1985: 3).

Historically, psychoanalysis has expressed both interest and concern regarding the potential uses and abuses of touch occurring within the therapeutic relationship. On the one hand, some analysts indicate that consciously using touch (e.g. holding a hand, sitting a client on the therapist's lap, etc.) can incite a regression which can be used therapeutically. Alternatively, withholding touch that is requested can also invoke regression. The most significant areas of concern cited are that the therapist, through touching, may unwittingly recreate traumatic circumstances or simply abuse their role as therapist. This is a big area which cannot be done justice here (see Holder, 2000).

More recently, and especially in Germany, some analytic therapists have integrated psychoanalysis and psychological body therapy to produce a hybrid referred to as *analytic body therapy* (Geissler, 1995). Analytic body therapy has often represented a blend of psychoanalytic and bioenergetic technique, and these practitioners have, in addition to analytic training, usually undergone a training in one or more of the psychological body therapies.

While Freud's view of personality development and pathology placed a strong *theoretical* emphasis on the role of the body, his technical approach nevertheless remained almost entirely analytic. It was left to Wilhelm Reich to make the leap from body-oriented theory to body-oriented practice. Reich (1949) developed the first truly body-focused therapy and the development of most, if not all, subsequent psychological body therapies are descendants from his theorizing and practice. Reich retained much of classical psychoanalytic theory but indicated that difficulties in personality development or 'character structure' (to use his term) exist on a somatic level in the form of chronic muscular rigidities. These muscular rigidities, referred to as muscular armour, serve as defences against free-floating anxiety. Reich was therefore indicating that characterilogical defences reside not only within psychic structures, but on a somatic level as well. Reich also took the logical and courageous step (given the professional norms of his day) of working directly on the client's body for both diagnostic and therapeutic purposes. Smith (1985) writes: 'First, by feeling the patient's body, Reich would assess the muscular armouring, locating the focal points of bound energy. Second, release of the [bound] energy sometimes could be facilitated by exerting pressure on these points of tension' (p. 6). Towards the latter part of his career Reich focused less on therapeutic practice and more on researching orgone, a substance he saw as the life energy which either flows freely or is blocked through muscular armouring. The ideas and practices he developed in this area led him to fall into disrepute, and to some extent, psychological body therapy was rescued by students of Reich – Alexander Lowen and John Pierrakos – who created bioenergetic analysis. Over time, bioenergetics was developed by Lowen (1975), and Pierrakos (1987) went on to develop core energetics, a psychological body therapy with a spiritual emphasis.

Lowen retained many of Reich's original ideas, but extended Reich's notion of 'character' through the creation of five basic pathological types and by extending the range of methods used for direct body work. More than anything else, bioenergetics has popularized psychological body therapy and is today the best known and most widely practised therapy of its type. A number of more contemporary psychological body therapies have grown out of the original work of Reich and Lowen, many of which will be mentioned later.

While many therapies focus largely on interpersonal history, intrapsychic structures or behaviour, the humanistic and experiential paradigm allows a focus on broader topics, including authenticity, growth and autonomy. This broader focus frequently serves to give the therapist permission to experiment with a wide range of practices, and such practices have frequently included the body:

One of the distinctive features of the humanistic approach is its friendliness to human touch ... in a humanistic group devoted to growth there will almost always be some touch, for reassurance, for sensual pleasure, for parental comforting, for support, as a form of meditation or in any other of the many ways in which touch is used in normal human interaction. (Rowan, 1988: 68)

A significant body focus also appears within individual humanistic therapy as well. Prime examples include Perls's (1969) development of Gestalt therapy, Gendling's focusing therapy (1981) and Mahrer's therapeutic experiencing (1986). More will be said of these approaches later, so I will here mention a humanistic therapy that offers a body-centred theoretical orientation which is often overlooked: Carl Rogers' person-centred therapy. A central, if not the most central, feature of Rogers' approach was his conception of 'organismic experiencing', which refers to all sensory and bodily experience, both conscious and unconscious (Fernald, 2000). 'Big boys don't cry' is a condition of worth that clearly marks not only self-development but the entire organism of the individual. The creation of a therapeutic environment is in many ways about enabling the client to more directly experience and trust in the whole organism, bodily experience comprising a significant feature of such experience.

The body and helping professions

The body is so basic to human existence and being that virtually all helping professions focus upon it to some extent. However, various Western professions have a tendency to relate to the body from either a psychological or a medical vantage point. Generally speaking, counselling/clinical psychology, psychotherapy and counselling tend towards a psychological stance, focusing largely on the topics of behaviour, cognition, emotion, interpersonal relations, meaning construction, etc. On the other hand, medical practice (e.g. general practice, surgery, pathology, etc.) tends to focus largely on the body, but from the perspective of biology/physiology. In addition to these two groups, there is a rather interesting class of professions that take up a middle ground that sits somewhere within the psychological-medical spectrum. Consideration of the interaction of psychology and physiology represents a core feature of these fields, which include health psychology, psychoneuroimmunology (Newman and Reed, 1996), behavioural medicine, clinical psychophysiology (Pearce and Wardle, 1989), psychiatry (Clarkson, 1994) and Naturopathy. See Figure 29.1.

Three traditions of therapeutic practice

For the purposes of discussing the body it is helpful to distinguish between three therapeutic traditions: psychological therapies, psychological body therapies and bodywork therapies. Most *psychological therapies* attend to the body in some manner, but rarely is the body a core feature of practice. Main areas of focus are more likely to constitute behavioural analysis and skills, as in behavioural therapy (O'Sullivan, 1990), the relationship of behaviour and emotion to cognitive processing, as in cognitive therapy (Dryden and Yankura, 1993; Beck et al., 1985), or transference and intrapsychic structures, as in psychodynamic therapy (Bateman and Holmes, 1995). The above areas of focus tend to occupy 'centre stage', and, when it occurs at all, a body focus often emerges as a by-product of these areas.

Figure 29.1   How various professions view the body

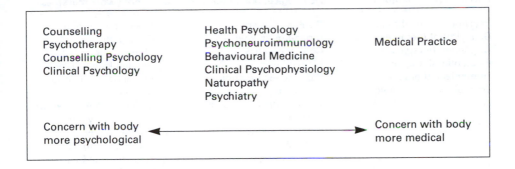

Historically, however, there are a group of therapies that have seen the body as *central* to therapeutic understanding and practice. These therapies have received a number of descriptors, including body psychotherapy (Smith, 1985; Guimon, 1997), psychological body therapy or somatic therapy (Conger, 1994), body-mediated therapy or corporeal psychotherapy (Fortini and Tissot, 1997), mind–body therapy (Whitfield, 1988) and even somatic education (Keleman, 1985). Cadwell (1997) uses the term somatic psychology to describe a somewhat broader field of interest in this area.

For the purposes of this chapter I will use the term *psychological body therapy*. All such therapies are derived originally from the work of Wilhelm Reich (1949), and include bioenergetic analysis (Lowen, 1975), core energetics (Pierrakos, 1987), biosynthesis (Boadella, 1988), biodynamic psychology (Boyesen, 1985), focusing (Gendling, 1981), hakomi (Kurtz, 1990), as well as the approaches of Mahrer (1986), Keleman (1985), Smith, (1985) and Conger (1994). Despite the potential importance of these approaches, psychological body therapies are well outside 'mainstream' therapy. Virtually all popular textbooks which offer general overviews of various therapies (e.g. Dryden, 1990; Prochaska and Norcross, 1994; Palmer, 2000; Feltham and Horton, 2000) ignore these practices, though Rowan and Dryden (1988) represents an exception. It is also curious that important psychological body therapy texts such as Boadella (1986) and (until recently) Smith (1985) are out of print and that the Society of Bioenergetic Analysis, while active on the Continent and in the United States, has no training centre in Britain.

Bodywork therapies concern themselves with mind–body issues (Lawrence and Harrison, 1983), but treatment often bypasses psychological/interpersonal methods and goes straight for direct physical manipulation, contact or movement. These approaches will not be considered here but are mentioned in order to offer a broader context. An overview of many psychological, psychological body and bodywork therapies is offered in Table 29.1.

The columns into which the three therapeutic approaches are divided in Table 29.1 represent, admittedly, an oversimplification. For example, Gestalt therapy is usually considered a humanistic or existential therapy. However,

Table 29.1   Therapies summarized

Psychological therapies	Psychological body therapies	Bodywork therapies
Psychodynamic therapies	Reichian therapy	Swedish massage
Behavioural therapies	Bioenergetic analysis	Osteopathy
Cognitive therapies	Core energetics	Chiropractic
Existential therapies	Biosynthesis	Applied kinesiology
Humanistic therapies	Biodynamic psychology	Alexander technique
Transpersonal therapies	Focusing	Rolfing
etc.	Therapeutic experiencing	Shiatsu and Acupressure
	Hakomi	Zone Therapy and
	Stanley Keleman	Reflexology
	Edward W.L. Smith	Therapeutic touch
	John P. Conger	Yoga and T'ai Ch'i
	etc.	Feldenkrais
		Aromatherapy
		Physiotherapy
		etc.

given Gestalt's insistence on the mind–body link, its focus on non-verbal processes and its use of body movement and awareness techniques, a case could easily be made for considering Gestalt a psychological body therapy. A similar case could be made for a number of the transpersonally oriented therapies, given their focus on the body and silence; notable examples include Vaughan (1985), Houstin (1982), Mindell (1985) and especially Grof (1985). It is also difficult to know where to place the phenomenological-existential therapies. Phenomenology certainly is body-focused, for 'it was the phenomenological tradition that most insisted on the body as primary experience, a pre-representational and ante-predicative experience' (Barale, 1997: 167). However, phenomenological practice has often been blended with existential approaches, some of which (e.g. Yalom, 1980), while valuable, have a tendency to dilute a body focus in favour of a more conceptual approach. Mahrer's therapeutic experiencing (1986) and Gendling's focusing (1981) are often seen as humanistic or experiential therapies, but have been placed into the psychological body therapy camp, given my perception that the body here constitutes a core feature of practice.

The body in counselling psychology practice

As a profession, counselling psychology tends to emphasize an integrative or eclectic theoretical orientation, an emphasis consistent with the notions of methodological diversity or pluralism (Woolfe, 1996). This can be seen in the finding that 49 per cent of counselling psychologists describe their orientation as either integrative or eclectic (Bor and Achilleoudes, 1999). Therefore, I will discuss the body-oriented perspectives and practices which seem most meaningful, and will leave it to the reader to *integrate* this information into their on-going practice in a manner which fits with their orientation, personhood and professional development. This makes more sense than trying to convey *how counselling psychology views the body in practice*, simply because there is no consistent view on this topic within our field.

The perspective of body-oriented therapists

Sigmund Freud was to psychoanalysis what Wilhelm Reich was to psychological body therapy. In the same way that Freud's model spawned a number of related models (e.g. analytic psychology, object relations, self-psychology, etc.) Reich's publications, teaching and practice encouraged (and continue to encourage) the development of innovative and yet related psychological body therapies. These models (see Table 29.1) are each unique and yet share a perspective which contains a number of significant features.

Cadwell (1997) summarizes the basic premises of the psychological body therapy perspective. First, there is a strong emphasis on seeing and working with the client holistically. In practice, this means that 'any event that occurs impacts our whole being ... healthy functioning is a physical as well as emotional, cognitive, and behavioural experience, and dysfunction in any part of the organismic continuum will effect the whole system' (1997: 9). Second, although the implications are often different, psychological body therapies share with psychoanalysis a particular interest in the notion of energy. Human beings are seen as energy systems, and the experience of energy and our exchange of energy interpersonally determine our experience of self and well-being. The experience of depression, anxiety, joy, apathy, etc., are not fundamentally conceptual experiences – they are energetic in nature. 'When someone compliments me, blood rushes to my cheeks and makes them hot. My stomach feels fluttery, and I label this energetic event embarrassment' (Cadwell, 1997: 8). Third, while the roles of behaviour and cognition are not ignored, symptomology is often viewed in terms of energy either being blocked (overbound) or given impulsive and usually destructive release (underbound). Fourth, and consistent with the humanistic perspective, a strong emphasis is placed on well-being. Again, energy is emphasized, and the healthy person experiences themself and life in an energetic, expressive manner, being in contact with wishes, emotions and other persons.

The body and the development of human suffering or symptomology

Various models of therapy have focused on a remarkably wide range of developmental issues that are meant to explain current symptomology. Such issues include trauma, adequacy of attachment, introjection or fixation (psychodynamic therapy), conditioning (behavioural therapy), the acquisition of maladaptive cognitive schemas (cognitive therapy), conditions of worth (person-centred therapy), toxic introjects (transactional analysis), the denial of being (existential therapy), maladaptive interpersonal relations (interpersonal and systemic approaches), oppression and cultural indoctrination (feminist and multicultural approaches) and identification with ego or self (transpersonal approaches).

Virtually all developmental models indicate that current symptomology is based in historical circumstances of trauma, disturbance or neglect. The impact of these circumstances is most often presented as emotional, behavioural or relational. While recognizing these areas of impact, *psychological body therapies* indicate that the body or soma also absorbs and retains the 'psychological blows' that the developing individual encounters. Speaking from the bio-energetic perspective, Whitfield (1988) explains that when the infant or child experiences trauma or neglect, it uses the 'body to cut off from the pain by tensing of the muscles ... the result is a body that is shaped by the misuse of the muscles to absorb hurt and to control the responses which would be unacceptable if expressed' (p. 137). Lowen (1975) offers an example of this process;

> Consider what happens to an infant who is weaned from the breast at a very early time. Most infants do not accept the loss of their first love object willingly. They cry and reach out for the breast with mouth and hands. This is their way of expressing love. Since they will be frustrated in this attempt, they will become restless and fitful and cry in anger. This behaviour on the part of the infant often evokes a hostile reaction from the mother and the infant or child soon realizes it must restrain the desire. It does so by choking off the impulse to reach out and the impulse to cry. The muscles of the neck and throat become contracted to constrict the opening and block the impulse. Now the breathing is affected, for the constricted throat also blocks the impulse to reach out and suck in air. (p. 132)

The results of such childhood experiences are seen to continue into adulthood, becoming embodied in ways that remain largely unconscious:

> Often in response to stress and trauma, our body tenses and muscles contract. We hold our breath in momentary fright, but afterward we do not always relax completely. Our shoulders tighten with rage, but we dare not strike our parents. Our shoulders continue to hold the rage through the years as our muscles, once contracted, refuse to extend ... [as adults] we have no way of 'knowing' that our immobilized thick shoulders have warded off psychic blows and held back rage. (Conger, 1994: 92–3)

The effects of both physical and sexual abuse are certainly traumatic (Etherington, 1995; Dubner and Motta, 1999) and here it is especially important not to ignore the impact on the body – the manner in which the body has become the repository of such assaults against one's being.

It is important to also point out that trauma may occur prior to an infant or child developing language that can be used to encode and store such experiences. These pre-verbal experiences may only be encoded in the body and are therefore unavailable to forms of therapy which operate on verbal levels alone:

Many people have traumatic experiences when very young for which there are no words ... for example, children exposed to uncomfortable abuse by a parent or other adult on whom the small person depends for love ... Talking cannot penetrate many areas until certain tensions in the body have been released. (Ladas, 1998: 1–2)

The body as expression of self

Therapists seek to understand their clients, for it is through understanding that we have some basis for providing a therapeutic or healing relationship. Most models of psychological therapy have a tendency to *minimize* the role of the body in this respect, focusing instead on behavioural analysis (O'Sullivan, 1990; Curwen and Ruddell, 2000), cognitive processing and schemas in relationship to affect and behaviour (Beck et al., 1985; Dryden and Yankura, 1993), transferential material and historical circumstances (Blank and Blank, 1994; Bateman and Holmes, 1995) or diagnostic categories (Perry et al., 1990).

Just why the body receives relatively less attention is not entirely clear, but Conger (1994) tells us, 'The body is ruled out of therapy because of the fears of sexual invasion, but also the body is absent because culturally the body is divorced from our spiritual salvation, divorced from our psychological and interpersonal development' (p. 211). Ladas (1998) suggests that 'Most psychotherapists are well trained in relational, cognitive, or analytic psychotherapy but have little training in working directly with the body' (p. 1). This lack of training seems unfortunate, particularly because bodily expression may be a more reliable source of information than verbal reports.

More consciousness is invested in the ego than in any other function. Correspondingly, we are more conscious of our thoughts than our feelings and least conscious of our bodily processes [p. 148] ... The language of the body cannot be used to deceive, if one knows how to read it. (Lowen, 1975: 99)

Rowan (2001) has indicated that people can indeed use the body to create a false impression (as in theatre, for example), so perhaps it is more realistic to say that the body is *less likely* to deceive.

While not making it into most introductory texts, there does exist a literature and tradition which include an appreciation of the body in terms of understanding or 'framing' the self of the client. Biosynthesis (Boadella, 1988) is particularly strong in this area, seeing somatic expression as a significant facet of self-development. In this approach a framework for the assessment of health includes a consideration of the quality of breathing, muscle tonus, the capacity of muscle to move easily between states of relaxation and tension, the appearance of the skin, facial expression, the appearance and use of the eyes, quality of the voice and the client's sexual feelings and experiences (e.g. the quality of orgasm). The client is seen to express poor levels of general well-being through three different forms of 'armouring': visceral, muscular and cerebral. In visceral armouring, there is a breakdown or dysfunction in the peristalsis or the breathing, usually expressed through hyperventilation (overbreathing) or hypoventilation (underbreathing). In muscular armouring the muscle tone is disturbed, as expressed by either hypotonus (weakness, lack of energetic charge) or hypertonus (tightness, overcharge). In cerebral armouring there is evidence of disturbances of the bioelectric charge processes in the brain that can show up as difficulties with vision or thought processes such as obsessive thinking.

Keleman (1985) employs the concept of 'shape' in understanding the self-development of the client:

> The study of the human shape reveals its genetic and emotional history. Shape reflects the nature of individual challenges and how they effect the human organism. Have we stiffened with pride or shrunk with shame? Are we hardened because of deprivation or have we kept safe by collapsing? Does our form indicate a failure to convert feelings into action? [p. 57] ... Shape is imprinted by the challenges and stresses of existence. Human shape is marked by love and disappointment. [p. xi]

Bioenergetics pays a great deal of attention to the body when trying to understand the client.

> If my client really feels fine, his body should reflect that state of being. I would expect his countenance to be bright, his eyes to have a shine, his voice to have resonance, and his movements to be animated. In the absence of these physical signs, I would question his statement [i.e. that he feels fine]. (Lowen, 1975: 99)

In both Gendling's focusing (1981) and Mahrer's therapeutic experiencing (1986), the sensations emanating from within the client's body are believed to be loaded with information, and usually constitute the starting point of therapy. Speaking from the standpoint of focusing, Leijssen (1998) tells us:

> By carefully dwelling on one's bodily experience, which often is quite vague at first, one can get in touch with the whole felt sense of an issue. Through interaction with symbols, the felt experience can become more precise, it can move and change, it can achieve a felt shift: the experience of real change or bodily resolution of the issue. (p. 121)

Mahrer (1986) emphasizes bodily sensations to such an extent that he suggests that the therapeutic focus must be accompanied by 'at least moderate sensations' (p. 27). Such sensations, often experienced and shared by therapist and client, serve as a basis through which understanding and meaning may arise.

Perhaps part of the problem with many psychological therapies is that they contain the tacit assumption that cognitive, behavioural or emotional components can be understood adequately in isolation from the soma. Gestalt is free from any such assumption, stipulating that mind, body, behaviour and emotion ideally act together as a unitive process. Awareness of the body can be 'split off' or dissociated in just the same fashion as awareness of insight, emotion or behaviour. Therefore, Gestalt therapists insist that bodily expression *must* be taken into account when seeking to understand the client:

> A person who habitually walks with a caved-in chest and rounded shoulders continues to enact in the present the beaten-up little boy of the past, while at the same time signalling to the environment that he is the kind of person who 'gets beaten up'. (Clarkson, 1989: 22)

Somatic approaches are often mistrustful of the client's capacity to give a comprehensive *verbal* account, and Gestalt often shares this view. Students who watch Fritz Perls's performance in the *Gloria* film are often shocked at his capacity to ignore Gloria's verbal presentation in favour of noticing and naming what she does through bodily expression. While Perls's behaviour is rather rude in terms of conventional interpersonal etiquette, his bodily focus nevertheless gets to significant therapeutic material with remarkable speed.

Among many psychological body therapies, the historical use of the body to absorb or ward off stress/trauma is seen to result in particular personality-based patterns, often referred to as *character structure*. Various models emphasize sometimes different typologies of character, e.g. bioenergetics suggests five basic character types (Lowen, 1975), hakomi suggests eight types (Kurtz, 1990) and Keleman (1985) presents four types. While such typologies may be thought-provoking, they are based almost entirely on the clinical experience and personal reflections of a handful of theorists and their followers and are without any significant body of research evidence. However, the system of character type employed (or whether a 'system' is employed at all) is perhaps less important than Reich's (1949) original ideas on the topic of character. Boadella (1988) explains that Reich felt that a person could be understood at three levels of existential depth. On the surface we can see the defensive character structure (or the mask), serving to hide the true self which was threatened in infancy or childhood. This defensive character structure is revealed not only through what the client tells us but also through the body (e.g. the way the body is held, body movement, muscle tone, skin colour, voice quality, the eyes, etc.). In therapy, when the defensive character structure begins to soften, painful feelings emerge, often including rage, anxiety and despair. Beneath this layer exist core feelings of well-being, love and basic self-confidence. This deep, healthy layer has been referred to variously as the 'core self', 'first nature' or Reich's unfortunate term 'genital nature'. Lowen (1975) describes this image of health articulately, making a distinction between 'second nature' (i.e. character structure) and 'first nature':

> The expression 'second nature' is often used to describe psychological and physical attitudes that, though 'unnatural', have become so much a part of the person they seem natural to him. The term implies that there is a 'first nature', one freed of these structured attitudes. (p. 104).

Body-oriented therapeutic interventions

The heading 'body-oriented therapeutic interventions' is somewhat misleading, because it implies that we are talking about interventions meant to exclusively impact the body. However, as mentioned earlier, body-oriented therapists see body, mind, cognition, and spirit as intimately related, as a holistic process; so in working with the body we are also working to impact change throughout the person, on every level.

The body as teacher

In the West we equate the mind with knowledge or wisdom, and most models of therapy are consistent with this bias, given the extent they focus on conceptual exchanges. The body, however, can be said to possess its own intelligence. The immune system can identify a particular virus from thousands and design a response custom-tailored to destroy it. Without any conscious input from the mind, the body regulates temperature, controls heart and respiration rates, extracts nutrients from food and expels waste. Some therapeutic approaches see the body as capable of communicating meaningfully within the therapeutic relationship.

In both focusing (Gendling, 1981) and therapeutic experiencing (Mahrer, 1986) the client is encouraged to slow down and listen to/experience their body, as it is felt that bodily sensations are pregnant with meaning. The following example, taken from the practice of focusing, illustrates:

> A 32 year-old woman has been depressed since the birth of her child three years ago. She has read a great deal about post-natal depression, but the explanations don't touch her … The therapist invites her to stop looking for explanations, to direct her attention to the centre of her body and remain with the question 'What is really the matter with me?' Tears well up in her eyes. She wants to give an explanation for it but the therapist encourages her to wait and remain silently attentive to her body … suddenly an image appears of her daughter being carried away immediately after birth. 'I don't want them to take away my daughter!' she shouts. (Leijssen, 1998: 121–2)

Psychological body therapies indicate that conceptual understanding that occurs without the experiencing of the body is stillborn. Therefore, these approaches often encourage the client to slow down and experience their body and related emotions before any attempt at meaning creation occurs. Developed by Ron Kurtz (1990), hakomi is an impressive example of this sort of approach. Therapeutic process involves progressive stages: creation of a therapeutic relationship, helping the client establish mindfulness (the capacity to turn inward and focus on present experience), the evocation of direct experience (sensations, feelings, images, thoughts, memories, unconscious material), deepening such experience and *eventually* looking for meaningful or core material. Typical of the body therapy stance, hakomi begins with present awareness and the need to 'get with the body and feeling' prior to even contemplating the evocation of meaning.

Breathwork

The moment-to-moment quality of our breathing is indicative of our well-being. When depressed we sigh, when anxious our breathing is shallow, when panicked we hyperventilate, when frightened we hold our breath. Disturbed or unnatural patterns of breathing can also become an unconscious and chronic part of our character. Noticing the common tendency of clients to hold their breath and inhibit exhalation as a means of controlling feelings, Reich's first therapeutic task was to help clients experience and change habitual and patho-logical patterns of breathing. Virtually all psychological body therapies practise breathwork in some manner and cognitive behavioural therapy deserves recog-nition for the emphasis placed on this area.

Breathwork can be particularly therapeutic with clients exhibiting any of the anxiety disorders. In my work with such clients I explain the manner I am intending to work, and after receiving the client's permission to proceed I place my chair next to them so they will not need to worry about me watching them during the work. I first ask the client to sit up straight in their chair, place one hand over their upper chest and the other over their diaphragm, and notice the process of their breathing for a few minutes. I then ask them to explain what they noticed. Almost without exception, anxious persons breathe up in the chest (i.e. shallow breathing), use the lungs to force air in and out rather than the diaphragm and actively push air out of the lungs rather than simply relax-ing and allowing the air to expire on its own. I then teach my client what healthy breathing looks and feels like, demonstrating for them how my diaphragm rises and falls (i.e. deeper breathing) and how the air expires natu-rally by simply relaxing the diaphragm/lungs (see Smith, 1985, for a detailed description of healthy breathing). While demonstrating, I also put one hand on my chest and the other over my diaphragm to illustrate in a more dramatic manner. My client is then invited to experiment with healthier breathing while I offer feedback or answer their questions. Normally clients are quite surprised to discover the extent to which their breathing has become unnatural. I also point out that such patterns are habitual and unconscious and that the client will need to become more aware in noticing and correcting anxious breathing patterns between sessions. There are a number of ways to practise breathwork and Grof (1985) deserves special recognition in this area.

Body awareness techniques

As mentioned earlier, people are often most aware of their behaviour, less aware of their thoughts and feelings and least aware of their body. By helping our clients become more aware of their body we encourage integration and, in the process, open up creative possibilities within the therapeutic process. Gestalt is particularly strong in this area, with phenomenological description and intensi-fication of body movements representing two powerful techniques. In *phenome-nological description* the therapist simply describes what they see or experience (e.g. 'I noticed your fists clenched when you said that,' 'Your voice seems small, like it struggles to come out'). The therapist can also ask the client to describe their verbal accounts further (e.g. 'What is it like to have a hard stone in your chest?' 'What is it like when your body goes cold?'). Clients often prefer to keep the dialogue on a conceptual level in order to defend against threatening emotions and sensations. However, their bodily/emotional experience often 'slips out' through gestures, posture, a flushed neck or face, eye contact, body movements, etc. A client speaks in a rather detached manner about her ex-husband while her eyes become moist and she places her right hand on her chest. Noticing and describing the tears in her eyes or the position of her hand may well lead to a more impactful interchange than simply responding to the content of her verbal expression.

Emotion, meaning, well-being, self-concept, etc., are encoded in the manner our body moves or fails to move. By asking clients to *intensify body movements/tensions or speech*, new meaning can be invoked: 'By deliberately intensifying the tension, Daisy discovered that the "pain in [her] neck" is a physiological enactment of her daughter "being a pain in her neck". (Clarkson, 1989: 21–2)

Facing and sounding

Facing (eye contact) and sounding (voice) are common areas of focus in psychological body therapy and are particularly strong in biosynthesis (Boadella, 1988). Our client's eye contact and the quality of their voice speak volumes about their character structure as well as personal and interpersonal difficulties. As with body movement, we seek to enhance the client's awareness of their eye contact and voice quality and help them explore the meaning behind their use of eyes and voice. The use of the eyes can be contactful and at ease, defensive, evasive and anxious or glaring. The voice can resonate clearly, can be overpowering and aggressive or timid and 'stuck in the throat'. Though sensitivity is required, there are many opportunities here for phenomenological description, feedback, exploration and the practising of new ways of looking and sounding.

Body-image work

Body image can be a significant facet of certain clients' difficulties and of course is especially important when working with persons suffering with anorexia/bulimia nervosa or obesity. Cognitive therapy is often effective at digging through the various layers of confusion which serve to prop up body image and related eating difficulties. Here the therapist helps the client to look for deeper explanations behind their difficulties, a process that produces a chain of explanations eventually leading to deeper and more meaningful explanations. In working with one woman with anorexia, this chain looked like: (1) 'I can't eat,' (2) 'I can't eat because I would get fat,' (3) 'If I got fat, no one would love me,' (4) 'If no one loved me, I would just die.' On exploration, there was little evidence that eating would lead to getting fat or that getting fat would lead to either being unlovable or dying. In fact, the best evidence we could find was for self-starvation leading to dying.

Muscular relaxation and bio-feedback

Behavioural therapies certainly appreciate the role that physiological arousal and particularly muscle contraction play in generalized anxiety, phobias and post-traumatic stress disorder, and several methods of muscular relaxation have been developed for therapeutic use (Goldfried and Davison, 1976; Ost, 1987). Bio-feedback has also been shown to be successful in the treatment of hypertension, migraine headache and stress-related problems (Hollandsworth, 1986).

Touch-oriented techniques

Psychological body therapists often receive specialist training/supervision in techniques that extend to working directly on the client's body. Character structure includes muscular armouring, that is, the use of the musculature to absorb psychological hurt and trauma. The result is chronic muscular tensions that contain trapped emotional and physical reserves of energy. Direct body manipulation or orgonomic massage is employed to break up muscular armouring. When the muscular armour and defensive character begin to soften under the hands of the therapist, the client may be able to experience feelings and sensations that had previously been repressed. Space does not permit a discussion of the range of touch-oriented interventions available, but the reader may refer to Smith (1985), Lowen (1975) and Boadella (1988), or to the websites at the end of the chapter.

Outcome research evidence and the body

Empirical research methodologies have largely focused on the efficacy of particular models of therapy rather than specific body-oriented techniques, so aside from some support for behavioural techniques such as relaxation training and bio-feedback (Hollandsworth, 1986) there is little base of information on the range of techniques mentioned above. However, psychological body therapies extend back seventy years to Reich, so we might ask what outcome evidence there is for these therapeutic approaches. Aside from West (1994), who suggests that a majority of clients are 'highly satisfied' or 'satisfied' with post-Reichian therapy, there is, despite a considerable base of case studies, very little empirical outcome evidence for individual psychological body therapy approaches. This is most likely down to three reasons:

- Individuals with a substantial psychological body therapy training are relatively few in number and they are not likely to receive a significant training in quantitative research methodologies.
- Many psychological body therapists share the commonly held view of humanistic therapists that quantitative science is demeaning to research subjects or fails to produce meaningful results.
- Given the historical status of psychological body therapy within scientific circles, these approaches have received little funding for research.

However, a visit to the European Association for Body Psychotherapists' Web site (see below) suggests that Europe-based therapists are beginning to take outcome research evidence seriously and are actively encouraging and engaging in on-going outcome studies.

Touch in therapeutic practice

Many counselling psychologists, owing to the nature and extent of their current training/supervision, will probably not feel that it is appropriate to use direct body-contact therapeutic interventions. However, it is possible and foreseeable that counselling psychologists may seek out training/supervision that incorporates such interventions. To my knowledge, there is nothing in the counselling psychology training regulations that would prevent this sort of training for students, nor can I see any reason why qualified counselling psychologists cannot seek such training as part of their on-going professional development. However, while body-contact therapeutic interventions may be of significant therapeutic value, such interventions also raise serious ethical issues. The potential for therapist touch to become abusive is a serious issue. We know that between 5 per cent and 11 per cent of therapists engage in sexual contact with their clients, that 80 per cent of all cases involve male therapists as the perpetrator and that 80 per cent of perpetrators engage in sexual relations beyond a single instance (Spinelli, 1994). I therefore conclude by offering some ethical guidelines concerning the use of direct bodywork interventions within the therapeutic relationship.

- The BPS *Code of Conduct, Ethical Principles and Guidelines* (1996) indicates that psychologists must be *competent* to deliver any given form of practice. This would include therapeutic interventions involving touch. Psychologists using touch as a formal intervention must therefore have training and supervision that provides an adequate level of competence concerning this form of intervention.
- *Clear contracting* is essential. The client must understand exactly what the body-contact interventions involve prior to use.
- *Informed consent*. The client must not only fully understand what is involved, but must clearly consent to the use of body-contact interventions.
- *Adequate boundaries*. Touch must be used for psychological or therapeutic purposes alone, and the therapist–client relationship must be clear on this point. The purposes of touch must never overstep this mark (e.g. for sexual purposes).
- The use of touch must be *consistent* with the therapist's overall therapeutic approach, e.g. conducting three sessions of cognitive therapy and then switching to the use of body-contact interventions is likely to be misleading and confusing.

References

Barale, F. (1997) 'Body and psychopathology' in J. Guimon (ed.) *The Body in Psychotherapy*. Basel: Karger.

Bateman, A. and Holmes, J. (1995). *Introduction to Psychoanalysis: Contemporary Theory and Practice*. London: Routledge.

Beck, A.T., Emery, G. and Greenburg, R.L. (1985) *Anxiety Disorders and Phobias: a Cognitive Perspective*. New York: Basic Books.

Blank, G. and Blank, R. (1994) *Ego Psychology: Theory and Practice*, second edition. New York: Columbia University Press.

Boadella, D. (1986) *Lifestreams*. London: Routledge.

Boadella, D. (1988) 'Biosynthesis', in J. Rowan and W. Dryden (eds) *Innovative Therapy in Britain*. Milton Keynes: Open University Press.

Bor, R. and Achilleoudes, H. (1999) *British Psychological Society, Division of Counselling Psychology, Survey of Members, 1999*. Handout for paper presentation at 1999 Counselling Psychology Annual Conference.

Boyesen, G. (1985) *Entre Psyche et Soma*. Paris: Payot.

British Psychological Society (1996). *Code of Conduct, Ethical Principles and Guidelines*. Leicester: BPS.

Cadwell, C. (1997) 'The somatic umbrella' in C. Cadwell (ed.) *Getting in Touch: the Guide to New Body-centred Therapies*. Wheaton IL: Quest.

Clarkson, P. (1989) *Gestalt Counselling in Action*. London: Sage.

Clarkson, P. (1994) 'The nature and range of psychotherapy' in P. Clarkson and M. Pokorny (eds) *The Handbook of Psychotherapy*. London: Routledge.

Conger, J.P. (1994) *The Body in Recovery: Somatic Psychotherapy and the Self*. Berkeley CA: Frog.

Curwen, B. and Ruddell, P. (2000) 'Behaviour counselling and psychotherapy' in S. Palmer (ed.) *Introduction to Counselling and Psychotherapy: the Essential Guide*, London: Sage.

Dryden, W. (1990) *Individual Therapy: a Handbook*. Milton Keynes: Open University Press.

Dryden, W. and Yankura, J. (1993) *Counselling Individuals: a Rational-Emotive Handbook*, second edition. London: Whurr.

Dubner, A.E. and Motta, R.W. (1999) 'Sexually and physically abused foster care children and posttraumatic stress disorder', *Journal of Consulting and Clinical Psychology*, 67: 367–73.

Etherington, K. (1995) 'Adult male survivors of childhood sexual abuse', *Counselling Psychology Quarterly*, 8: 233–41

Feltham, C. and Horton, I. (2000) *Handbook of Counselling and Psychotherapy*. London: Sage.

Fernald, P.S. (2000) 'Carl Rogers: body-centred counsellor', *Journal of Counselling and Development*, 78: 172–79.

Fortini, K. and Tissot, S. (1997) 'For a typology of body-mediated therapies', in J. Guimon (ed.) *The Body in Psychotherapy*. Basel: Karger.

Freud, S. (1960) *The Ego and the Id*. New York: Norton.

Geissler, P. (1995) *Psychoanalyse und Bioenergetische*. Frankfurt: Lang.

Gendling, E.T. (1981) *Focusing*, revised edition. New York: Bantam Books.

Goldfried, M.R. and Davison, G.C. (1976) *Clinical Behavior Therapy*. New York: Holt Rinehart & Winston.

Grof, S. (1985) *Beyond the Brain: Birth, Death and Transcendance in Psychotherapy*. Albany NY: SUNY.

Guimon, J. (1997) 'Corporeity and psychotherapy: some preliminary concepts' in J. Guimon (ed.) *The Body in Psychotherapy*. Basel: Karger.

Holder, A. (2000) 'To touch or not to touch: that is the question', *Psychoanalytic Inquiry*, 20 (1): 44–64.

Hollandsworth, J.G. (1986). *Physiology and Behavior Therapy: Conceptual Guidelines for the Clinician*. New York: Plenum Press.

Houstin, J. (1982) *The Possible Human*. Los Angeles: Tarcher.

Johnson, D. and Steptoe, A. (1989) 'Hypertension' in S. Pearce and J. Wardel (eds) *The Practice of Behavioural Medicine*. Oxford: Oxford University Press.

Keleman, S. (1985) *Emotional Anatomy: the Structure of Experience*. Berkeley CA: Center Press.

Kurtz, R. (1990) *Body-centered Psychotherapy: the Hakomi Method*. Mendocino CA: LifeRythem.

Ladas, A.K. (1998) 'What is Bioenergetic Analysis?' Internet site: http://www. bioenergetic-therapy.com/content/Ladas_bioenergetics.htm.

Lawrence, D.B. and Harrison, L. (1983). *Massageworks: a Practical Encyclopedia of Massage Techniques*. New York: Perigee Books.

Leijssen, M. (1998) 'Focusing microprocesses' in L.S. Greenburg, J.C. Watson and G. Lietaer (eds) *Handbook of Experiential Psychotherapy*. New York: Guilford Press.

Lowen, A. (1975) *Bioenergetics: the Revolutionary Therapy that uses the Language of the Body to heal the Problems of the Mind*. New York: Penguin.

Mahrer, A.R. (1986) *Therapeutic Experiencing: the Process of Change*. New York: Norton.

Mindell, A. (1985) *Working with the Dreaming Body*. London: Routledge.

Newman, R. and Reed, G.M. (1996) 'Psychology as a health care profession: its evolution and future directions', in R.J. Resnik and R.H. Rozensky (eds) *Health Psychology throughout the Lifespan: Practice and Research Opportunities*. Washington DC: American Psychological Society.

Ost, L.G. (1987) 'Applied relaxation: description of a coping technique and review of controlled studies', *Behaviour Research and Therapy*, 25: 397–410.

O'Sullivan, G. (1990) 'Behaviour therapy', in W. Dryden (ed.) *Individual Therapy: a Handbook*. Milton Keynes: Open University Press.

Palmer, S. (2000). *Introduction to Counselling and Psychotherapy: the Essential Guide*. London: Sage.

Pearce, S. and Wardle, J. (1989) 'Introduction' in S. Pearce and J. Wardle (eds) *The Practice of Behavioural Medicine*. Oxford: Oxford University Press.

Perls, F.S. (1969) *Gestalt Therapy Verbatim*. Moab UT: Real People Press.

Perry, S., Frances, A. and Clarkin, J. (1990). *A DSM III-R Casebook of Treatment Selection*. New York: Brunner Mazel.

Pierrakos, J. (1987) *Core Energetics*. New York: Synthesis Press.

Priest, S. (1991) *Theories of the Mind*. London: Penguin Books.

Prochaska, J.O. and Norcross, J.C. (1994) *Systems of Psychotherapy*. Pacific Grove CA: Brooks Cole.

Reich, W. (1949) *Character Analysis*. London: Vision Press.

Rowan, J. (1988) *Ordinary Ecstasy: Humanistic Psychology in Action*. London: Routledge.

Rowan, J. (2001) Personal communication to the author.

Rowan, J. and Dryden, W. (1988) *Innovative Therapy in Britian*. Milton Keynes: Open University Press.

Russell, B. (1945) *A History of Western Philosophy*. New York: Simon & Schuster.

Smith, E.W.L. (1985) *The Body in Psychotherapy*. Jefferson NC: McFarland.

Spinelli, E. (1994) *Demystifying Therapy*. London: Constable.

Vaughan, F. (1985) *The Inward Arc: Healing and Wholeness in Psychotherapy and Spirituality*. Boston MA: New Science Library.

West, W. (1994) 'Clients' experience of bodywork psychotherapy', *Counselling Psychology Quarterly*, 7 (3): 287–303.

Whitfield, G. (1988) 'Bioenergetics', in J. Rowan and W. Dryden (eds) *Innovative Therapy in Britain*. Milton Keynes: Open University Press.

Wilber, K. (2000) *Integral Psychology: Consciousness, Spirit, Psychology, Therapy*. Boston MA: Shambhala.

Woolfe, R. (1996) 'The nature of counselling psychology' in R. Woolfe and W. Dryden (eds) *Handbook of Counselling Psychology*. London: Sage.

Yalom, I.D. (1980) *Existential Psychotherapy*. New York: Basic Books.

Useful web sites

European Association for Body Psychotherapy www.eabp.org/
United States Association for Body Psychotherapy www.usabp.org/
Public Orgonic Research Exchange www.orgone.org/
American College of Orgonomy www.acoreich.org/
International Institute for Bioenergetic Analysis www.bioenergetic-therapy.com
David Boadella's biosynthesis http://orgon.org/therpy00-biosyn.htm
Gerda Boyesen's Institute of Biodynamic Psychology www.biodynamic.org/
Stanley Keleman's site www.holonet.net/centerpress/sk.html
Pierrakos' core energetics www.core-energeticsintl.org/Main.htm
Gendling's focusing www.focusing.org/
Grof's holotropic breathwork www.breathwork.com/
Ron Kurtz's hakomi www.nas.com/~richf/hakomi.htm
Naropa Institute (major training institute) www.naropa.edu/somatic/index.html

Part VI
Social, Professional and Ethical Issues

30 Ethical Issues in Counselling Psychology
CAROL SHILLITO-CLARKE

Ethics, or moral philosophy, seeks to establish guidelines by which human character, relations and actions may be judged as good or bad, right or wrong. What is considered 'ethical' practice varies between professions and cultures and changes over time. Francis (1999) refines the definition of ethics in relation to psychologists as 'a codified set of value principles which have application to a nominated subset of people (professional practitioners)'. All psychologists who are members of the British Psychological Society (BPS) are bound by the society's *Code of Conduct, Ethical Principles and Guidelines* (BPS 2000).

Counselling psychology is a relatively new branch of psychology in Britain, which combines the requirements of good psychological and therapeutic practice. At the heart of counselling psychology lies the relationship between the practitioner and the client – the person, or persons, for whom the practitioner is working. Because the quality of the relationship carries with it an expression of its values, a good understanding of ethical behaviour and practice is of fundamental importance. This applies equally to the relationship with therapy clients, supervisees, trainees, employees, colleagues, other professionals or employing organizations. The aim of this chapter is to draw attention to the kinds of ethical issues that arise in our profession and to encourage counselling psychologists to ask questions of themselves, of their practice and of their professional relationships.

Despite the guidance offered by the BPS and other professional bodies, there are few simple answers to the ethical questions which arise in counselling psychology. An ethical dilemma exists whenever there are 'good, but contradictory ethical reasons to take conflicting and incompatible courses of action' (Kitchener, 1984: 43). However, ethics is about more than resolving dilemmas; it is about a way of being, of interrelating and of practising.

This chapter clarifies what ethics is about and its relation to personal and socio-cultural values. A model of ethical reasoning is described. The person of the counselling psychologist, and their ethical relationships with others, are then explored. The chapter ends with a consideration of some of the ways in which practitioners may avoid major pitfalls and resolve ethical dilemmas.

Ethics in counselling psychology

The nature of ethics and ethical principles is neither simple nor static. They vary between professions and evolve over time, reflecting developments in thought and practice. Developments in medicine, and more recently sociobiology and bioethics, have heavily influenced the way we think about ethics in psychology. Other socio-political developments such as the feminist movement have also challenged our conception of ethical practice (Francis, 1999; Rave and Larsen, 1995; Tjeltveit, 1999). Tjeltveit argues that ethical reasoning is broader than scientific reasoning and must account for six 'distinguishable but inter-twined dimensions' (Tjeltveit, 1999: 18):

- *Professional ethics:* the obligations and ideal behaviours expected of practitioners within a profession as exemplified by their codes of practice.
- *Theoretical ethics:* the intellectual foundations of ethical thought.
- *Clinical ethics:* the practical, ethical decisions made in respect of individual cases by practitioners, usually around therapeutic practice and goals.
- *Virtue ethics:* the values, characteristics and ways of being, above and beyond a specific situation. Values may include prudence and integrity, respectfulness and benevolence.
- *Social ethics:* emphasizing the relationship between individuals and their communities, professional institutions and society.
- *Cultural ethics:* the ways in which ethical issues, values and principles are perceived by different cultures. For instance, the relative importance assigned to individual autonomy as against family or community needs.

Thus ethics involves more than just resolving moral dilemmas. It requires awareness and consideration of all the dimensions in order to offer a reasoned and defensible conclusion.

A model for moral and ethical reasoning

A model of moral justification devised by Beauchamp and Childress (1989) is useful in describing the relationship between individual conscience, rules, principles and philosophical theories. Beauchamp and Childress propose two levels of ethical reasoning (see Figure 30.1). The *intuitive level* represents the immediate response of the individual's moral conscience. This is based on their moral upbringing and experience. While this is often a sound guide for ethical behaviour under simple circumstances, it may not be sufficiently well articulated to cope with more complex and challenging circumstances. For example, under time pressure or when subjected to special pleading, the intuitive level may not be a sound enough guide to ethical behaviour. This may require a *critical-evaluative* level in order to illuminate, refine and guide moral reasoning.

The critical-evaluative level comprises three hierarchically related sub-levels.

- *Rules,* specific laws and codes of conduct.
- *Principles,* or universally applicable values of equal merit.
- *Theories,* or philosophical ideas about the nature and meaning of human existence. This may be extended to include the values of such theories.

The hierarchical structure of the critical-evaluative level is important for moral reasoning and problem solving. It proposes that, because the levels are

Figure 30.1   Model of moral and ethical reasoning

Critical-evaluative level	Theories	
	Principles	Autonomy Beneficence Non-maleficence Justice Fidelity
	Rules	
Intuitive level	Individual conscience	

interrelated, the solution to an ethical problem, which is difficult at one level, may be clearer at a higher and more abstract level. For example the legal right to abortion (rule) may be influenced by the moral principle of respect for autonomy or by the principle of non-maleficence. These principles, in turn, reflect different philosophical approaches to the meaning and sanctity of life.

Rules: codes of conduct

The codes of conduct of professional bodies such as the BPS provide a regulatory framework for the protection of clients. They identify standards of ethical practice that are acceptable to the majority of members and with which all members must comply. Those whose practice is shown, on evidence, to fall below the required standards may be sanctioned by their professional body although not necessarily by the law. Such codes are not fixed for all time and may be renegotiated in the light of experience.

A code of conduct can provide only a broad framework for ethical behaviour and is unlikely to be able to provide detailed guidance when subtle ethical conflicts of interests arise. For example, 'whistle blowing' may be considered unethical if, by publicizing unacceptable practice, it brings an organization into disrepute (Szymanska and Palmer, 1993). Similarly, codes of conduct rarely provide guidance on how ethical dilemmas may be prioritized and resolved. In our own field, the responsibility for resolving any ethical dilemma rests with the counselling psychologist and not with the client. The BPS code makes it clear that 'taking account of their obligations under the law, [members] shall hold the interest and welfare of those in receipt of their services to be paramount at all times and ensure that the interests of participants in research shall be safeguarded' (BPS, 2000: 1).

Codes of conduct resolve some ethical issues but may themselves be the source of ethical dilemmas. 'Conformity to a code is not necessarily the same thing as acting ethically in the broad philosophical sense. Indeed, if conformity is uncritical it may actually be unethical' (Pattinson, 1999). It has been argued that codes are devised primarily not to protect the public but to enhance professional elitism (Holmes and Lindley, 1991). On the other hand, an exploitative, vengeful or disturbed client may seek to use the code unfairly against the counselling psychologist (Holmes et al., 2000).

Principles

Beauchamp and Childress consider that there are four moral principles which have *prima facie* validity. That is, each principle is binding unless, in a given situation, there is a more significant principle that overrides it. The principles are: respect for autonomy, beneficence, non-maleficence and justice. To these we can add the principle of fidelity, which is considered by Kitchener (1984) to be of particular importance for psychologists.

Autonomy incorporates two fundamental freedoms: the freedom of the individual to make their own choices and to decide their own actions. Within counselling psychology, the principle of autonomy implies unconditional regard for the client; the maximization of the client's informed choice and their right to choose their own destiny; the intrinsic worth of each person and the right to self-fulfilment. The concept of free choice and action is not unlimited; it is axiomatically bounded by respect for others' freedom and autonomy. For instance, the client's right to confidentiality in respect of their stated desire to harm another must be weighed against the rights of that other person to avoid being harmed. Following the ideas of the philosopher Levinas, some ethicists argue that heteronomy (putting the other before oneself) should be a more important principle (Gordon, 1999; Loewenthal and Snell, 2001).

The concept of free choice also raises theoretical questions about the individual's ability to know, and distinguish between, their conscious and unconscious desires. The concepts of limited and intermittent competence to make decisions are important aspects of autonomy and will be discussed further in the section on informed consent.

Beneficence involves working to promote the greatest good of others. Counselling psychologists, as members of a 'caring profession', have an obligation (a 'duty of care') to benefit their clients through their interventions. This obligation may not comfortably accord with the therapeutic experience of 'things getting worse before they get better' as the client faces the difficulties he or she has hitherto tried to ignore. It also requires that the practitioner respect the client's autonomy when considering what is beneficial.

Non-maleficence, the principle of 'do no harm', or 'do the least harm', involves the responsible use of power and ability and the avoidance of exploitation. The principle is important when facing the problem of encouraging the therapy client to experience distress and discomfort in order to effect change. The principle is also important in research, where the possible benefit of the many must be weighed against the possibly negative experience of a few. The practitioner's competence is an important contributor to avoiding harm, as is their awareness of the differences between themselves and their clients. These issues will be explored later in the chapter.

Justice incorporates fairness and an appropriate balance between costs and benefits. In counselling psychology, fairness is particularly important in ensuring equality of access to training and services, particularly for people from minority groups. For instance, justice must be considered when arguing the case for short or long-term therapy, or publicly funded versus private practice. The relationship between costs and benefits is also a key issue in research. How can the researcher compensate clients for their contribution?

Fidelity is especially important for counselling psychologists and is implied in the previous four principles (Kitchener, 1984). It is fundamental to the therapeutic relationship, which depends on trustworthy and unpretentious communication, clear boundaries and respect for the individual's autonomy. Good contracting, informed consent and confidentiality are relevant not only to the therapeutic work of counselling psychologists but also to the domains of training, consultancy and research.

Theories and values

Ethical theories are underpinned by systems of values. As with ethics, there is no single definition of 'value'. Definitions vary according to the theoretical perspective of the individual and the time and culture within which they operate (Tjeltveit, 1999). Value systems are built up by an individual through cultural socialization processes and experience, mediated by history and environment. Many values are introjected or accepted without question in childhood. Where values are questioned and reflected upon they may be affirmed or they may be rejected and different values substituted. In an increasingly plural society, values vary widely, even within a single community. Neighbourliness may be perceived as nosiness; individuality may be construed as abdication of social responsibility.

The values of therapy

Counselling psychology practitioners differ from one another, from their clients and from other professionals in how they conceive and value psychological health and dysfunction. The values inherent in preferred theoretical models determine the kinds of therapeutic interventions made, such as promoting rationality or spontaneity, emotional expression or impulse control, subjectivity or objectivity. Therapy cannot be value-free. The key issue thus becomes: who determines what is desirable and against which criteria?

The promotion of personal values and beliefs as generally accepted counselling psychology practice is unethical. Any action or attitude that discriminates on the grounds of race, gender, disability, class, religion, is contrary to the core values of counselling psychology. However, Cooper (1992) reminds us that the individual is also subject to primitive needs of which she or he may be unconscious but which may affect, or conflict with, the values expressed. The ethical imperative for all counselling psychologists should therefore be self-awareness (Lakin, 1991).

An additional ethical problem faced by counselling psychologists today is the divergence in the value systems of scientific psychology and practice-based psychotherapy; what Meara et al. (1996) call the 'language of evidence'. Science values objectivity, accuracy, quantification and predictability – a validation of what is. Therapy values subjectivity, description and the consequences of actions – what ought to be. The situation is further complicated by the value systems of politics and commerce. Increasingly, health-care providers are preferring therapies which can demonstrate statistically significant evidence of their outcomes over those which judge results from a more subjective, clinical perspective. Insurance companies are requiring an evaluation of every client's mental health against diagnostic systems devised by psychiatrists. Such preferences and demands will raise ethical issues for counselling psychologists who hold different value systems, especially those working in or for health-related services.

The importance of context

All values are set in a context of culture and history. It may be difficult to judge the extent to which our values and our positive or negative perceptions of others' values are shaped by our individual context. It may also be difficult to gauge the extent to which enacting our value systems contributes to those of the cultures in which we practise.

Counselling psychology upholds anti-oppressive practice, that is, practice which addresses 'interconnections between issues of power within the therapeutic relationship and the cultural and socio-political contexts' (Strawbridge, 1994: 6). Tjeltveit's model of ethics is useful here because it emphasizes the social and cultural dimensions. It recognizes that, despite a predominantly theoretical emphasis on the therapist/client dyad, many other people may be implicated in the work of the counselling psychologist. Partners, family members, employers of the client and the practitioner, supervisor, health-care referrers, insurance companies, training institutions and accrediting bodies such as the BPS may also be 'stakeholders' in the outcome, exerting overt or covert pressure on the counselling psychologist (Carroll, 1996). Different domains and occupations have different codes of ethics, different expectations and value different outcomes. A 'good outcome' for one party may not be considered 'good' by another. For instance:

> Monica is referred by her GP for therapy for anxiety and depression. Her partner's insurance scheme agrees to fund six sessions of therapy. In the course of therapy it becomes clear that Monica's problems are located in her relationship but her partner refuses to accept any responsibility, blaming her work. Monica's parents are also concerned about the outcome. At the end of the six sessions, Monica has techniques for managing the anxiety and some insight into the aetiology of the depression. She believes she can return to work but feels she needs to continue taking medication. Her GP agrees. Although Monica says she would like to continue, she refuses further therapy because her partner will not support private fees.

Although the counselling psychologist has behaved ethically throughout, such a case raises a number of ethical issues. Monica is enabled to return to work after the contracted number of sessions, has a better awareness of her difficulty, is better able to manage her symptoms and is apparently making a choice about her relationship. But has Monica's therapy done more harm than good by: questioning and potentially destabilizing the nature of the relationship; giving her means to manage her symptoms without facilitating their removal; and colluding with a model of therapy provision that is driven by economics, emphasizes brief intervention and seeks to individualize the problem?

Power and ethics

Whenever there are differences of values and beliefs, and differences in perceived power, there is the opportunity for one person to abuse or exploit another. Hence the fundamental importance of the principles of fidelity and justice in all counselling psychology practice. In therapeutic practice, as in all branches of the 'caring' professions, the counselling psychologist is in a position of power relative to the client. The client is psychologically vulnerable by virtue of having a problem or difficulty which he or she feels cannot be resolved unaided. The client who wishes to be helped must give the counselling psychologist personal information about him or herself. Such knowledge, often about something of which the client is afraid or ashamed, gives further power to the counselling psychologist. It is therefore important that the client can trust the practitioner to use that knowledge to help or empower them rather than use it against them. There is a parallel position of vulnerability for the supervisee in relation to the supervisor, especially whilst in training.

A practitioner also holds power by claiming experience, expertise and the right to be paid. Counselling psychologists whose values are rooted in the humanistic tradition may wish to argue for a position of equality with their clients. However, it must be remembered that the client may have a different perception of the relationship, particularly at the beginning of the work and depending on the context of the referral. The label 'psychologist' itself carries numerous fearful connotations, and may be confused with the label of 'psychiatrist' or 'psychoanalyst' by lay people. This confusion may be compounded if the counselling psychologist makes unnecessary use of psychometric tests or medical language.

Counselling psychologists who work as managers and trainers may have particular ethical concerns about balancing the needs of the clients, trainees or supervisees against those of the institution or organization. For example, should a trainee be expected to take on extra work when there are staff shortages and long waiting lists, and how should a supervisor respond if a manager with a different theoretical orientation countermands their direction? Sugarman (1992) argued for the creation of policy documents to cover such issues if resources are scarce and confidentiality is in danger of being compromised. In the absence of such policy documents, individual counselling psychologists need to take responsibility for clarifying conditions of employment and related issues.

A further point to be considered here is that of *responsibility to* or *responsibility for* the client. The desire to assume some responsibility for the client and 'make it better' is one way, common among helping professionals, of construing the 'duty of care'. However, taking such responsibility may conflict with respecting the client's autonomy. Many counselling psychologists will struggle with the finer distinctions between their professional responsibility, their personal desire to take control for the client and trusting the client to know what is best for him or her self.

Virtue ethics and the person of the counselling psychologist

Meara et al. (1996) propose that 'principle ethics' should be integrated with 'virtue ethics' to provide a more comprehensive ethical system to guide the actions of individuals, particularly in multicultural settings. Virtue ethics are concerned with ideals to which practitioners may aspire rather than rules to which they are obligated. The virtuous agent is one:

who

- is motivated to do good;
- possesses vision and discernment;
- realises the role of affect or emotion in assessing and judging proper conduct;
- has a high degree of self-understanding and awareness;
- and, perhaps most importantly, is connected with and understands the mores of his or her community and the importance of community in moral decision making, policy setting and character development and is alert to the legitimacy of client diversity in these respects. (Meara et al., 1996: 28)

Meara et al. (1996) also propose four key virtues for psychologists. These are prudence, integrity, respectfulness and benevolence. The first two are reflected in the behaviour and attitudes of the counselling psychologist. The second two are evidenced in the practitioner's relationships with others.

Counselling psychologists have taken a strong position within the BPS over the importance of the person of the practitioner and the practice of working reflexively within the relationship. Personal psychological therapy during training, and on-going supervision post-qualification are considered to be essential requirements for ethical practice (BPS DoCP, 1998). Given the importance that virtue ethics places on the person of the practitioner and their context, it is suggested that complementing principle ethics with virtue ethics is particularly relevant to counselling psychology. It also accords with the dimensions of ethics proposed by Tjeltveit.

Competence

The BPS emphasizes that it is the psychologist's duty to 'maintain and develop their professional competence, to recognize and work within its limits and to identify and ameliorate factors which restrict it' (BPS, 2000: 1). Throughout practice, unexpected issues may arise that challenge the competence of the practitioner. These in turn pose questions about the amount and kind of training in counselling psychology and related specialisms, including supervision, needed to claim 'competence'. Similar questions arise concerning the competence of those involved in the management, education and training of counselling psychologists. For example:

> Tony is a trainee counselling psychologist who has been working with a client who unexpectedly discloses her deep desire for gender reassignment. Tony feels he is not yet adequately trained to work with the client and would prefer to refer her to a specialist. However, the client feels that she has, for the first time, established a therapeutic relationship which can be trusted. Tony's manager is not aware of any local facilities to which the client could be referred and is happy for Tony to continue to work with her. Tony's supervisor is personally and theoretically unsympathetic to gender reassignment and has reservations about Tony's competence.

In this example, a referral to someone with more specialized knowledge and experience might be prudent and accord with the principle of beneficence but might negatively affect the fidelity of the established relationship and the therapeutic benefits which have accrued from that relationship. Respect for the client's autonomy might lead to support for her right to choose to stay with the less competent practitioner. Practitioners with different theoretical orientations may argue the importance, or lack of importance, of 'specialist' knowledge in helping with this kind of life experience. How much should Tony, his supervisor and his manager know about gender identity and reassignment in order to claim the competence to help this client? In this instance the principle of non-maleficence may provide a valuable guideline.

Fitness to practise

Fitness to practise is an intrinsic part of competence. Because the counselling psychologist is a tool in the therapeutic process, any impairment in his or her psychological, emotional and physical well-being will affect the effectiveness of therapy. The client may be put at risk if the therapist's ability to perceive and respond appropriately is reduced. Further, the practitioner who fails to treat her or himself with due care and respect provides a poor model for the client.

A practitioner's fitness to practise may decline slowly, for personal or medical reasons, or it may suddenly decline owing to an unforeseen change in external circumstances. For example:

Amanda's mother dies unexpectedly. Amanda immediately cancels her work, leaving messages where she can't speak to clients directly. Unfortunately Henry, whose mother has also just died, does not get the message and turns up, in considerable distress, at Amanda's house for his regular appointment.

Ethical practice requires recognition of personal states and honesty in acknowledging impairment, albeit temporary. In such a position, it is an ethical requirement for the counselling psychologist to consult his or her supervisor and to find as much personal support outside the work relationship as possible (BPS DoCP, 1998). Counselling psychologists who work as managers have a responsibility to balance the competing interests of the organization and those of the people working under them.

The development of a personal ethical system helps the practitioner to avoid being drawn into unethically poor practice. Lack of awareness of, or disregard for, the shadow aspects of any personality or personal limitation increases the practitioner's vulnerability. He or she risks sliding or being coerced into unethical behaviour to protect personal self-image or esteem (Page, 1999).

Ethical relationships in counselling psychology

As has been emphasized above, the quality of the relationship between the counselling psychologist and the client is a key factor in determining the success of the work (Elton Wilson and Barkham, 1994; Meara et al., 1996). Aspects of the relationship relating directly to ethical practice will be explored further under the following headings: respect for the client's autonomy; clear contracting; the obtaining of informed consent; respect for confidentiality; avoidance of inappropriate sexual relations; sensitivity to dual and multiple relationships; and proper regard for personal safety.

Respect for the client's autonomy

Respect for the client's autonomy may challenge beliefs about the professional's duty of care and responsibility, particularly when an employing organization is also involved. For example:

You work in a rehabilitation unit's group home. Zara, who is recuperating from a serious head injury, has formed a close friendship with another patient and they want to become lovers. Neither patient has been sectioned and the ethos of the home is about normalization. Should the staff attempt to dissuade them? Should the staff tell Zara's husband?

When clients' beliefs, values, morals, needs, goals and understanding of their situation are at odds with those of the counselling psychologist and/or an organization an ethical dilemma may easily arise. Differences of opinion may be exacerbated if practitioners are not aware of, and respectful towards, the clients' historically determined construction of their world and their racial and cultural beliefs. This is particularly significant in the case of the Western theoretical emphasis on the self, which undervalues the importance of self in relation to family, community and culture (d'Ardenne and Mahtani, 1989; Strawbridge, 1994; Rave and Larsen, 1995; Meara et al., 1996). While benevolence may be considered a virtue, it is frequently contaminated with arrogance. The questions 'Am I really acting in my client's best interests?' and 'Would I work differently if the client was of a different race/culture/gender?' are crucial here.

Ethical issues relating to autonomy may arise as a result of the practitioner's theoretical approach to the client (Spinelli, 1994). For example, a counselling psychologist trained in psychodynamic psychotherapy may believe that she or he is in a better position to interpret the client's unconscious processes than the client. To what extent is the client free to challenge or reject the interpretation? To what extent is a client receiving cognitive-behaviour therapy in a position to reject the concept of rational thought and choose what the therapist considers 'irrational' behaviour? The humanistic models place particular emphasis on respecting the client's autonomy. However, do all clients necessarily want or know how to use the responsibility of defining their needs? Such questions may be easy to answer theoretically but the answers may be difficult to incorporate into practice. Ethics become important when the client challenges the perceived wisdom of the theory, or the authority of the counselling psychologist, or when the client does not respond to treatment or precipitates an unexpected outcome.

Contracts

A contract is a written or spoken agreement intended to be enforceable by law (*Concise Oxford English Dictionary*, 2000). Good ethical practice requires that a clear contract should be negotiated with the client which respects their autonomy and promotes the principles of fidelity and benevolence. Such a contract recognizes that the parties involved have needs to be met and it draws a firm boundary around those needs. However clear the initial contract may be, unexpected circumstances can challenge the boundaries agreed. For instance:

> Mary is in therapy with Martha when she is made redundant. She can no longer afford Martha's fees and dreads the loss of her relationship with Martha. Martha herself is struggling financially and is dependent on clients for her income.

As well as respecting the needs of the client, counselling psychologists have a duty to respect their own needs and not do harm to themselves. Situations in which the needs of the practitioner conflict with those of the client need careful consideration and discussion both with a supervisor and the client, in order to promote the client's learning and autonomy without harming the psychologist. Apart from financial considerations, the desire to have a client remain in therapy or leave may be affected by pressure from employing organizations. The length of the waiting lists, outcome statistics and other indicators of effective management may all play a part. Such pressures need to be acknowledged by the counselling psychologist while trying to find a solution that honours, as far as possible, the original contract with the client.

Informed consent

For a contract to be meaningful the client must be able to give 'valid consent' that they have 'adequately understood the nature of the investigation or intervention and its anticipated consequences' (BPS, 2000: 2). The concept of obtaining consent may be clear in theory but less clear in practice. There is a need to balance the client's right to free choice against their ability to understand the arguments. Some of the questions which need to be considered are: how general or specific should the counselling psychologist be in explaining the process or procedure? To what extent is it possible to anticipate immediate or future consequences of the intervention? How will the emotional and psychological state of the client affect their ability to comprehend the offer and the possibility of refusing it? Children, the elderly and those with learning difficulties may require special consideration. In such cases it is important to include the concepts of limited and intermittent competence in decision making (Kitchener, 1984). Limited competence usually refers to those, such as children and impaired adults, who have a limited capacity for making rational decisions. Intermittent competence refers to a fluctuating state of rationality, as in cases of Alzheimer's disease or psychosis. In both cases the individual's choice should be respected when possible and supported by responsible others.

The counselling psychologist has the responsibility for identifying and eliminating or minimizing risks to the client in therapy, supervision and research (Heppner et al., 1992). Such risks may include the risk of actual physical or mental harm when working with clients who may be abusive of themselves or others. They may also include the risk of emotional distress such as embarrassment, stress and loss of self-esteem or personal dignity. Because such risks depend largely on the individual's construction of the situation, they may change over time. What, to the client, seemed a good idea at the start of therapy may subsequently be regarded very differently.

Making clear contracts and gaining informed consent are important in all the relationships in which counselling psychologists engage. Having made the parameters of the work clear and negotiated a contract for that work with the client, the ethical responsibility of the practitioner is the maintenance of the agreed boundaries. The personal and professional relationships between the practitioner, the client and other parties must be skilfully managed in order to avoid ethical problems arising from conflicts of interest and dual relationships.

Confidentiality

The success of all 'talking' therapies rests on the premise that what one person says to another will be treated with respect and kept private. However, promising total confidentiality to the client is unethical because it denies the practitioner's requirement for supervision, contractual obligations to team colleagues or to an employer, intra-agency support systems and some legal requirements. While a policy of confidentiality appears to uphold the client's autonomy, it does not ensure the principle of non-maleficence and threatens the principle of fidelity. If total confidentiality is an impossibility, a number of questions arise. Who draws the boundaries to protect the client and facilitate practice? Where are they drawn? What happens if they change over time?

Confidentiality and the law

Practitioners have an ethical responsibility to avoid illegal activities (Bond, 2000; Cohen, 1992). The relationship between ethics and the law is complex and subject to change. In Britain today there is a legal obligation for practitioners to disclose information concerning terrorism (Prevention of Terrorism (Temporary Provision) Act 1989) and drug trafficking (Drug Trafficking Offences Act 1986). Under the Children Act (1989) the obligation to disclose information concerning child abuse is regarded somewhat differently unless one is working for one of the public authorities (Bond, 2000; Jones, 2000).

Practitioners are also legally obliged to disclose information when summoned as a witness or subpoenaed by a court of law. The Data Protection Act 1998 and the Human Rights Act 1998 have both affected the interpretation of the laws concerning confidential information, with significant implications for practitioners. For instance, authorities such as the police, the Crown Prosecution Service or the Health and Safety Executive have the right to subpoena all forms of notes held by therapists and supervisors that identify a specific client. Such 'unused material' may be interpreted in a different light from that in which it was recorded for therapeutic purposes. For example:

> Three years ago, James was referred to you following a car accident for which he was not responsible. In talking about the trauma that he experienced, James worked through a significant earlier experience, the emotional impact of which he had hitherto denied. Now James's solicitors require you to release his case notes for a legal hearing. Your notes contain information about the earlier experience, which could be used to weaken James's current claim for compensation, and which could identify and compromise others.

The ethical dilemmas that arise in such a case relate, in part, to the information that James was given in the original therapeutic contract about the limits of confidentiality. There are also broader questions about the rights of individuals to decide what personal information to withhold or to make public, and to whom.

Counselling psychologists are advised by the BPS to be aware of the specific legal and ethical context of their work and the general legal requirements concerning giving and withholding information and to inform their clients appropriately. The Divisions of Clinical Psychology and Counselling Psychology, and the BACP, have all prepared guidelines on confidentiality and case notes. But because legal requirements change, organization members are strongly advised to seek professional support and guidance as necessary. All psychologists are also advised, by the BPS, to carry personal indemnity insurance, over and above any provision made by an employer.

Holding confidentiality in exceptional circumstances

One of the most difficult ethical questions is when to break a client's confidentiality when there is no legal imperative and the client wants it upheld. The most obvious examples are the threat of suicide or physical/sexual abuse. The principle of non-maleficence towards self (suicide) or another has to be weighed against the client's autonomy, the other's autonomy and the fidelity of the relationship. It is particularly difficult, in highly charged emotional situations, to know whether one is under or over-reacting. Codes seem to agree that breaching confidentiality is acceptable if the practitioner has tried, and failed, to get the client's consent and if there has been consultation with an experienced colleague. Counselling psychologists accountable to others for their work need to be aware of any discrepancy between their own values and attitudes and those of their employers.

Confidentiality and other relationships

Different contexts, cultural values and expectations concerning privacy of information also need to be taken into account in considering where the boundaries of confidentiality should be drawn. When the counselling psychologist and the client have more than one role in respect to one another (a dual relationship), such as working for the same organization or moving in the same social circles, the issue becomes more complicated. As the boundaries become more complex, so the likelihood of accidentally breaching confidentiality becomes greater.

During training, use of client material is needed to demonstrate the student's developing competence. Similarly client material may be used in research or in publications. In each circumstance the counselling psychologist takes on a dual role in relation to the client. An ethical conflict of interest may develop between the needs of the client and those of the practitioner. If material is used without the client's informed consent the fidelity of the relationship is jeopardized. This applies as much to a student's 'client study' as to a thesis or research project (Shillito-Clarke, 2000). As in the case of James above, it is not always possible to know how specific the consent negotiated with the client at the outset should be. It is also impossible to predict whether a client, or other person mentioned in material placed in the public domain, will be recognized.

Care to preserve anonymity needs to be taken, not only in the recording of information about clients but also in its transmission, transportation and storage. This is particularly important with audio and video tapes. As with case notes, the ethical tension is between protecting the clients' confidentiality and holding evidence to validate one's work. The falsification or suppression of information about clients to protect the practitioner is, of course, unethical.

Confidentiality after death

The client's confidentiality continues after their death 'unless legal and ethical considerations demand otherwise' (BPS DoCP, 1998). Counselling psychologists are also expected to make provision for emergency disclosure of information in the event of their own death or prolonged, involuntary absence, perhaps owing to a serious accident. Respecting confidentiality, the client's autonomy and the fidelity of the former relationship are all important. Dealing with an unexpected end to therapy is not a matter that is usually discussed in the initial contract. How practitioners choose to plan for such eventualities will vary but they do have an ethical responsibility to make appropriate arrangements.

Sexual relationships

Sex, sexuality, gender and erotic desire are all aspects of being human. Counselling psychologists have to be able to work with issues relating to sexuality, both heterosexuality and homosexuality, whether or not they are the main focus of the work. This applies not only to the practitioner's relationship with the client but also to relationships with supervisees, trainees and colleagues. What is considered acceptable for discussion, let alone expression, is influenced by an individual's socialization, culture, religion and politics. It is often difficult to predict. Because sexuality is such a fundamental and emotionally powerful element in any relationship, it is one that is open to misinterpretation, exploitation and abuse. The transition from acceptable therapeutic practice to gross malpractice has been referred to as a 'slippery slope' down which the unwary practitioner can slide (Gutheil and Gabbard, 1993). The Prevention of Professional Abuse Network (POPAN) suggests that warning signs may include: the therapist talking more than the client, close physical contact without consent, inappropriate questions about sex life, ignoring agreed boundaries around time, fees and social contact (POPAN, 1998).

There is little disagreement about what constitutes the rocks at the bottom of the 'slippery slope'. Sexual harassment is not only deemed unethical by the BPS and the major therapeutic bodies (BPS, 2000; BACP, 1997; UKCP, 1998), it is also illegal under British law and contrary to the Human Rights Act 1998. Similarly, it is considered unethical for psychologists to enter into a dual relationship that is 'a personal loving and/or sexual relationship with someone to whom they also have professional responsibilities' (BPS, 2000: 40). Books such as Rutter's *Sex in the Forbidden Zone* (1990) and Russell's *Out of Bounds* (1993) publicized the issue of sexual abuse by professionals. Pope and associated writers (Pope and Bouhoutsos, 1986; Pope, 1989; Pope et al., 1987) and Seto (1995) also considered the prevalence of abuse by therapists in the United States and the damage done by the abuse of trust in the therapeutic relationship. In Britain the percentage of reported cases of professional abuse by psychologists has varied between 4 per cent and 7 per cent over the years 1997-2000 (POPAN, 2001).

Fearing accusations of unethical practice, some practitioners may avoid even exploring issues of sexuality and present sexual attraction. Their fears may be justified. It is not unknown for a client to believe, incorrectly, that they have been the subject of sexual interest and involvement with their therapist. It is argued that acknowledging any feelings of sexual attraction towards the client may enable the practitioner to define clear boundaries and minimize the possibility of misunderstanding or abuse (Spinelli, 1994). It is important to distinguish between sexual attraction *towards* a client and sexual feelings *with* the client resulting from an exploration of their material (Woskett, 1999). The starting point for the counselling psychologist's assessment of the benefits and dangers of addressing sexual issues in any working relationship is training (Webb, 1997). This should include awareness of their own sexual values, desires and boundaries, and addressing others' possible perceptions and constructions (Hunter and Struve, 1998).

Dual and multiple relationships

Dual relationships arise when the counselling psychologist or their client hold more than one role with respect to each other. Not all dual relationships are avoidable, sexually exploitative and unethical. Woskett (1999) cites other writers' good arguments for holding them. In some communities it may be difficult to avoid meeting clients or supervisees in another capacity. Indeed, in some cultures it would be considered strange or even antisocial to refuse to work with a colleague's friend or relative. While Pearson and Piazza (1997) suggest that most dual and multiple relationships can be managed, some arise unexpectedly and may give rise to an ethical dilemma. For example:

> Your partner has an accident and is admitted to hospital. The senior ward nurse that night turns out to be a client of yours. Among the issues you have focused on with her are her concerns about the competence of the consultant whom you now recognize as having responsibility for your partner's care.

Some personal relationships may pre-date the professional relationship. For example, partners, one or both of whom are counselling psychologists, may be involved in the same course or may elect to work or do research together. However, it is important to recognize that dual relationships may call into play subtle and not always conscious forces, not only between the two people directly involved but also involving others such as colleagues and course participants. When boundaries get blurred or confused, mistakes and ethical difficulties become more likely. In every case, it is the counselling psychologist who must take responsibility for the relationship. Good supervision and further training may give confidence in handling difficult situations.

Personal safety

Counselling psychologists have an ethical responsibility to their clients as well as to themselves to safeguard their physical state. This includes being clear about the boundaries around personal availability and about behaviour towards oneself. For instance, Holmes et al. (2000) suggest that stalking of therapists is an underreported problem. Training in assessment of the client's psychological state in order to avoid taking on dangerous clients or provoking physical or psychological attack is therefore essential.

Avoiding unethical practice

Lakin suggested that 'whereas ethical dilemmas in the practice of psychotherapy are inevitable, unethical actions and behaviours are not' (1991: 11). But is it possible to avoid unethical practice completely? Palmer Barnes (1998) considers there to be four levels of unethical behaviour:

- *Mistakes* in otherwise good practice.
- *Poor practice* in which the overall standard of work is inadequate.
- *Negligence* or wanton lack of care.
- *Malpractice* which is intentionally exploitative and abusive.

Anyone, regardless of their training and experience, can, and probably will, make mistakes during their career. Hopefully most will not be serious. However, every mistake should be taken seriously. An opportunity to apologize, and change the offending behaviour in the light of feedback, may accord more closely with the principle of justice and be a more reparative process for all concerned. Repeated mistakes herald decline into poor practice. Recognizing and dealing with them requires a high level of self-awareness and personal integrity, sensitivity to declining standards and humility in consultation. It also requires being able to make reasoned decisions based on evidence and being able to reflect on and review those decisions in the light of new information.

Ethics as a part of training and continuing professional development

If, as has been proposed, behaving ethically as a counselling psychologist involves more than unquestioning adherence to the latest codes or guidelines, ethics needs to be an integral part of the training programme. Frequent questioning and reflection on the ethical implications of ideas and actions, both conscious and unconscious, are crucial. The implicit and explicit roles of values and ethics need to be considered in every aspect of personal and professional development throughout practice. Discussions provide important recognition of the diversity of others' understanding and values. They also encourage the challenge, articulation, elaboration and review of previously held values and beliefs. The roles of trainers, supervisors, managers and personal therapists are also important in modelling ethical behaviours and attitudes as well as drawing the interconnections between personal experience, theory and practice. Challenging perceived impairment and providing good remedial support are essential for trainees (Forrest et al., 1999; Lamb, 1999). The same could be said of supervisees and employees.

Systematic investigation into the outcomes of ethical decisions may help clarify and define future decision making under similar circumstances (Forrest et al., 1999; Bond, 2000). Published research could also encourage awareness and debate (Heppner et al., 1992; Szymanska and Palmer, 1993). Above all we need to foster a climate in which acknowledgement of, and involvement in, the resolution of ethical dilemmas is regarded without prejudice.

Working through ethical decisions and dilemmas

As has been suggested, part of the difficulty in dealing with ethical dilemmas is that different people react to the same problem in very different ways. Professional guidelines and codes may be helpful but ultimately inadequate. The pressure to act quickly may be strong. The key is to be able to make well reasoned decisions based on the evidence available. A number of models for making ethical decisions have been suggested (Bond, 2000; Carroll, 1996; Francis, 1999; LeBon, 2001; Shillito-Clarke, 1996). The common elements would appear to be:

- Take time to clarify the elements of the dilemma from several different, and preferably opposing, perspectives.
- Consult as widely as possible in the time available; study professional codes and seek the views of supervisors, managers (if relevant) and legal advisers, giving information on a need-to-know or in-principle basis.
- Consider alternative courses of action and their consequences not only for the people immediately concerned but also for those close to them.

- Choose what appears to be the best option, but be prepared to review it in the light of new evidence.
- Check the outcome and review the process for further learning.

While stressing the importance of consulting, Francis (1999) further suggests two quick tests for urgent decisions:

- Could you defend your decision in a court of law?
- Would your family still be proud of you after you had explained your reasoning?

Conclusion

This chapter has identified the moral principles of autonomy, beneficence, non-maleficence, justice and fidelity that underlie the ethical decisions that must be taken by the counselling psychologist in their daily life and work. It has suggested that these principles could be complemented with the virtues of prudence and integrity, respectfulness and benevolence. It has emphasized that different ethical interpretations are inevitable because of the different values held by clients and counselling psychologists alike – our different upbringings, cultures, experiences, understanding and working contexts. Different theoretical approaches to counselling psychology also embody different values, which need to be taken into account. All such differences must be recognized and respected. The codes of ethics and practice of relevant professional bodies such as the BPS offer sound guidelines but may not be able to account for the subtle nature of many ethical dilemmas.

It is suggested that in order to work through, if not pre-empt, ethical difficulties, counselling psychologists should be trained and encouraged to develop their personal awareness of ethical issues and boundaries, both within themselves and between themselves and those with whom they work. Use of professional consultation, careful analysis and informed reflection are all-important. Above all, it is urged that the profession should foster a climate in which ethics are regarded as an intrinsic part of the daily life and work of the practitioner, that debate about ethical dilemmas should be encouraged and that more investigation and research should be conducted into the process and outcomes of their resolution.

Note

Although the examples of ethical dilemmas have a basis in reality they do not refer to specific people and incidents.

References

Beauchamp, T.L. and Childress, J.F. (1989) *Principles of Biomedical Ethics*, third edition. New York: Oxford University Press.

Bond, T. (2000) *Standards and Ethics for Counselling in Action*. London: Sage.

British Association for Counselling and Psychotherapy (1997) *Code of Ethics and Practice for Counsellors*. Rugby: BACP.

British Psychological Society (2000) *Code of Conduct, Ethical Principles and Guidelines*. Leicester: BPS.

British Psychological Society: Division of Counselling Psychology (1998) *Guidelines for the Professional Practice of Counselling Psychology*. Leicester: BPS.

Carroll, M. (1996) *Workplace Counselling*. London: Sage.

Cohen, K. (1992) 'Some legal issues in counselling and psychotherapy', *British Journal of Guidance and Counselling*, 20 (1): 10.

Cooper, G.F. (1992) 'Ethical issues in counselling and psychotherapy: the background', *British Journal of Guidance and Counselling*, 20 (1): 1.

d'Ardenne, P. and Mahtani, A. (1989) *Transcultural Counselling in Action*. London: Sage.

Elton Wilson, J. and Barkham, M. (1994) 'A practitioner-scientist approach to psychotherapy process and outcome research' in P. Clarkson and M. Pokorny (eds) *A Handbook of Psychotherapy*. London: Routledge.

Forrest, L., Elman, N., Gizara S. and Vacha-Haase, T. (1999) 'Trainee impairment: a review of identification, remediation, dismissal and legal issues', *Counselling Psychologist*, 27 (5): 627–86.

Francis, R.D. (1999) *Ethics for Psychologists: a Handbook*. Leicester: BPS.

Glaser, R.D. and Thorpe, J.S. (1986) 'Unethical intimacy: a survey of sexual contact between psychology educators and women graduate students', *American Psychologist*, 41: 43—51.

Gordon, P. (1999) *Face to Face: Therapy as Ethics*. London: Constable.

Gutheil, T.G. and Gabbard, G.O. (1993) 'The concept of boundaries in clinical practice: theoretical and risk management dimensions', *American Journal of Psychiatry*, 150 (2): 188–96.

Heppner, P.P., Kivlighan, D.M. and Wampold, B.E. (1992) *Research Design in Counselling*. Pacific Grove CA: Brooks Cole.

Holmes, D.A., Taylor, M. and Saeed, A. (2000) 'Stalking and the therapeutic relationship: on-going research', *Forensic Update*, 60. Leicester: Division of Forensic Psychology, British Psychological Society.

Holmes, J. and Lindley, R. (1991) *The Values of Psychotherapy*. Oxford: Oxford University Press.

Hunter, M. and Struve, J. (1998) *The Ethical Use of Touch in Psychotherapy*. London: Sage.

Jones, C. (2000a) 'Ethical counselling is properly described as highly confidential. What are some of the limits to complete confidentiality within a counselling relationship?' in C. Jones, C.M. Shillito-Clarke, G., Syme et al. *Questions of Ethics in Counselling and Therapy*. Buckingham: Open University Press.

Jones, C. (2000b) 'What should counsellors consider when contacted by persons such as solicitors or the police and other authorities in connection with client work or when clients request such assistance on their behalf?' in C. Jones, C.M. Shillito-Clarke, G. Syme et al. *Questions of Ethics in Counselling and Therapy*. Buckingham: Open University Press.

Kitchener, K.S. (1984) 'Intuition, critical evaluation and ethical principles', *Counseling Psychologist*, 21 (3): 43–55.

Lakin, M. (1991) *Coping with Ethical Dilemmas in Psychotherapy*. New York: Pergamon Press.

Lamb, D.H. (1999) 'Addressing impairment and its relationship to professional boundary issues', *Counseling Psychologist*, 27 (5): 702–11.

LeBon, T. (2001) *Wise Therapy*. London: Continuum.

Loewenthal, D. and Snell, R. (2001) 'Psychotherapy as the practice of ethics' in F. Palmer Barnes and L. Murdin (eds) *Values and Ethics in the Practice of Psychotherapy and Counselling*. Buckingham: Open University Press.

Meara, N.M. and Schmidt, L.D. (1991) 'The ethics of researching counselling/therapy processes' in C.E. Watkins and L.J. Schneider (eds) *Research in Counselling*. Hillsdale NJ: Erlbaum.

Meara, N.M., Schmidt, L.D. and Day, J.D. (1996) 'Principles and virtues: a foundation for ethical decisions, policies, and character', *Counseling Psychologist'*, 24 (1): 4–77.

Page, S. (1999) *The Shadow and the Counsellor: Working with Darker Aspects of the Person, Role and Profession*. London: Routledge.

Palmer Barnes, F. (1998) *Complaints and Grievances in Psychotherapy: A Handbook of Ethical Practice*. London: Routledge.

Pattinson, S. (1999) 'Are professional codes ethical?' *Counselling*, 10 (5): 374–80.

Pearsall J. (ed.) *The Concise Oxford Dictionary*, tenth edition. Oxford: Oxford University Press.

Pearson, B. and Piazza, N. (1997) 'Classification of dual relationships in the helping professions', *Counsellor Education and Supervision*, 37 (2): 89–99.

Pilgrim, D. (1991) 'Psychotherapy and social blinkers', *Psychologist*, 14 (2): 56–60.

Pope, K.S. (1989) 'Therapists who become sexually intimate with a patient: classifications, dynamics, recidivism, and rehabilitation', *Independent Practitioner*, 9 (3): 28–34.

Pope, K.S. and Bouhoutsos, J.C. (1986) *Sexual Intimacy between Therapist and Patients*. New York: Praeger.

Pope, K.S., Tabachnik, B.G. and Kieth-Spiegel, P. (1987) 'Ethics of practice: the beliefs and behaviors of psychologists as therapists', *American Psychologist*, 42 (11): 993–1006.

POPAN (1998) *What to Look for when you Go into Therapy*. London: POPAN.

Rave, E.J. and Larsen, C.C. (1995) *Ethical Decision Making in Therapy: Feminist Perspectives*. New York: Guilford Press.

Russell, J. (1993) *Out of Bounds: Sexual Exploitation in Counselling and Therapy*. London: Sage.

Rutter, P. (1990) *Sex in the Forbidden Zone: When Men in Power abuse Women's Trust*. Glasgow: Aquarian.

Seto, M.C. (1995) 'Sex with therapy clients: its prevalence, potential consequences, and implications for psychology', *Canadian Psychology* 36 (1): 70–86.

Shillito-Clarke, C.M. (1996) 'Ethical issues in counselling psychology' in R. Woolfe and W. Dryden (eds) *Handbook of Counselling Psychology*. London: Sage

Shillito-Clarke, C.M. (2000) 'What ethical considerations need to be taken into account when writing up client work for training, CPD, research and publication?' in C. Jones, C.M. Shillito-Clarke, G. Syme et al. *Questions of Ethics in Counselling and Therapy*. Buckingham: Open University Press.

Spinelli, E. (1994) *Demystifying Therapy*. London: Constable.

Strawbridge, S. (1994) 'Towards anti-oppressive practice in counselling psychology', *Counselling Psychology Review*, 9 (1): 5.

Sugarman, L. (1992) 'Ethical issues in counselling at work', *British Journal of Guidance and Counselling*, 20 (1): 64.

Szymanska, K. and Palmer, S. (1993) 'Therapist–client sexual contact', *Counselling Psychology Review*, 8 (4): 22.

Tjeltveit, A.C. (1999) *Ethics and Values in Psychotherapy*. London: Routledge.

United Kingdom Council for Psychotherapy (1998) *Ethical Requirements for Member Organisations*. London: United Kingdom Council for Psychotherapy.

Vasquez, M.J.T. (1991) 'Sexual intimacies with clients after termination: should a prohibition be explicit?' *Ethics and Behaviour*, 1: 45–61.

Webb, S.B. (1997) 'Training for maintaining boundaries in counselling', *British Journal of Guidance and Counselling*, 25 (2): 175–88.

Woolfe, R. (1983) 'Counselling in a world of crisis: towards a sociology of counselling', *International Journal for the Advancement of Counselling*, 6: 167–76.

Woskett, V. (1999) *The Therapeutic Use of Self: Counselling Practice, Research and Supervision*. London: Routledge.

31 Training and Professional Development in the Context of Counselling Psychology
DIANE HAMMERSLEY

Background

When the Division of Counselling Psychology was established in 1994 the chartered membership was composed of people who had been granted a statement of equivalence to the diploma in counselling psychology, which was the newly established independent route to chartered status. Some were in academic posts or had appropriate training and experience or sought lateral transfer from other divisions. The diploma provided a route for those members who were partially qualified and wanted to be accredited and provided a means for graduate psychologists to be trained as chartered counselling psychologists. The development of the Syllabus and Regulations for the Diploma in Counselling Psychology guided the process of the independent route as well as acting as a standard for the evolution of accredited courses. These early developments in training have been described by Farrell (1996) and this chapter follows on from there.

Training and practitioners

There has been a desire to move away from a mechanistic approach to training towards a process in which personal reflection and development feature more strongly. However, the drive towards competence-based models and performance criteria with its emphasis more on technical skill than personal qualities has highlighted once again the inevitable tension between them. This is not a problem that can be solved but rather an issue that will need to be constantly readdressed in order to find a balance. In addition, the British Psychological Society has made significant moves to prepare for the statutory regulation of psychologists, emphasizing the need for ethical issues to feature strongly throughout training and for professional development to be recognized as a lifelong commitment. This is the contextual background against which some of these key issues are explored.

What kind of practitioner are we training?

The objectives of training centre around the evolving ideas about what kind of applied professional psychologists are being trained. Clearly the practitioner needs to be technically competent as a counselling psychologist, and this part of the training has to be integrated with the development of the person as well as drawing on the scientific roots in psychology developed in the first degree. The links with counselling have meant acknowledging the humanistic tradition of valuing the person and their subjective experience and the wider context of the person's cultural and social life. Links with psychotherapy have led to the inclusion of theories and approaches from other disciplines such as art, literature, medicine and psychiatry. Working alongside clinical psychologists whose roots are in the scientist-practitioner model has brought ideas about evidence-based approaches and outcome research (Kennedy and Llewelyn, 2001).

Emerging professional identity

Over the past few years there has been a debate about the title of the Division, and this has highlighted some of the issues of beliefs, language and power which both unite us with and separate us from similar professions of counselling and psychotherapy (Tholstrup, 2000). Spinelli (2001) suggests that this search for a unique professional identity goes beyond being just a hybrid of others, perhaps into an innovative position where being a researcher and practitioner of psychotherapy are combined. While the differences in language must not be allowed to obscure the similarities in practice, neither must differences in practice be obscured by similarities of language. The training of counselling psychologists draws on similarities with comparable professions both in psychology and therapy but has a unique quality of its own which must constantly be renewed and rediscovered.

Furthermore, the philosophical assumptions and ethical principles upon which our practice is based need to be part of the postgraduate study required of the practitioner. This must be combined with both quantitative and qualitative research training in order to develop the skills of scholarship that are a necessary part of a practitioner's academic development. As well as being a scientist, philosopher and researcher, the counselling psychology practitioner needs also to be an artist in order to be creative and innovative to produce the particular 'moments of change' or internal shift which should result from the deep engagement with the client in a therapeutic relationship. The concept of the reflective practitioner (Schön, 1983) and the principles of action research (McNiff, 1988) seem to me to be essential elements in the professional identity and practice of counselling psychologists.

Reflection

Theory and practice are inextricably linked by reflection, since if a word is deprived of its dimension of action, reflection suffers and it becomes idle chatter (verbalism) and if action is emphasized exclusively to the detriment of reflection, it becomes action for action's sake (activism). 'Men are not built in silence, but in word, in work, in action-reflection' (Freire, 1972: 76). Boyd and Fales (1983) see reflection as 'a process of internally examining ... an issue of concern, triggered by experience, which creates and clarifies meaning in terms of self, and which results in a changed conceptual perspective' (p. 100).

Bond et al. (1985) draw attention to the 'intellectual and affective activities in which individuals engage to explore their experiences in order to lead to new understandings and appreciation' (p. 3). Mezirow (1991) sees reflection as a 'process of critically assessing the content, process, or premise of our efforts to interpret and give meaning to an experience' (p. 104), the 'what, how and why'. Schön (1991) states that reflective practice is not a sufficient condition for wise or moral practice but it is a necessary one, for practitioners learn wisdom by reflection on practice dilemmas.

The reflective practitioner

Schön (1983) describes professionalism as traditionally associated with technical rationality, which emphasizes problem solving by the application of scientific theory and technique. He challenges this and a claim to a monopoly of knowledge because he says it is ineffective and that professionals do not always live up to the values and norms they espouse. He reminds us that each patient is a universe of one, a unique case which calls for an art of practice which might be taught if it were constant and known but it is not constant. Reflection-in-Action involves tacit knowing, know-how, surprise, spontaneity, trial and error, thinking on your feet, developing a feel for something, being intuitive and inquiring. But because professionalism is mainly identified with technical rationality, reflection-in-action is not generally accepted as a legitimate form of knowing even by those who practise it.

Schön warned that many professionals find nothing in the world of practice to occasion reflection because they have become too skilful at techniques of selective inattention, 'junk categories' as labels of convenience and situational control, and use their techniques to preserve the constancy of their knowledge. Moving away from this may make the reflective practitioner profoundly uneasy because they cannot say what they know how to do and therefore cannot easily justify it, its quality and rigour. It is not that technical competence is unnecessary, rather that the professional–client relationship is transformed when such expertise is embedded in a context of meanings – the professional recognizing that they and the client may have different meanings to explore and make accessible to each other.

The process of reflection-in-action is essentially artistic, there being no explicit rationale, but the practitioner has an intuitive sense of confidence in it (Brookfield, 1986). Thinking on one's feet must be followed by reflection in order to produce 'a new theory of the unique case' (Schön, 1983: 68). It involves contextuality and individual creativity in the process of playing hunches, using intuition, inspired guesswork and improvisation, since being creative must be seen as useful, legitimate and valued professional behaviour. Programmes of adult learning can take into account contextual features, and the ability to improvise should be seen as crucial to professional practice.

The crucial element in Schön's (1983) argument is that professional people think on their feet and therefore learn from their own practice. Similarly, Kolb's (1984) theory of the learning cycle is that concrete experience is followed by observation/reflection, from which generalization/abstract conceptualization of theory develops, which is tested through active experimentation before being implemented in practice. Professionals do not merely apply theory to a situation, they use the situation as a place where they can learn and create new procedures and knowledge.

This is important to allow for individual differences and situations that may have changed slightly, which could be dangerous and unethical if the practitioner were not aware of it. This is similar to a condition described by Mezirow (1981) where the first stage of what he calls perspective transformation is a 'disorientating dilemma', an awareness that the current situation is not exactly like any other but subtly different. Reflection is therefore something that is both personal and individual, in which feelings play a part, and which should also be a purposeful process.

Training the reflective practitioner

In the training of adults, the notion of 'praxis' (Freire, 1972), that is, the alternating and continuous engagement in exploration, action and reflection, is central, being similar to double-loop learning (Argyris and Schön, 1974) and critical reflectivity (Mezirow, 1981). Effective practice, according to Argyris and Schön (1974), has three governing variables that inform it. They are that practice is based upon valid information from people who are also participating in the activity (the client), secondly that they exercise free and informed choice over practice activities (not relying on predetermined techniques) and thirdly that they show an internal commitment to the chosen course of action and constantly monitor its implementation (reflection). It follows that educators must structure training programmes to foster such self-direction and reflection and recognize that reflection is socially conditioned and affective in nature, not just an intellectual activity.

Schön (1991) in considering the implications for professional education states that learners need to be involved in real-life situations, doing rather than observing, intuitively reacting to events and subsequently reflecting on them in a practicum or practice placement. Critical self-reflection requires the learner to feel empowered not just as a product of it but also as a prerequisite of it, because pain, fear, frustration and humiliation are conditions which repel adult learners. Support for the trainee is a crucial element in developing the confidence necessary to take the risks inherent in developing and trusting an intuitive process within the therapeutic relationship, which goes beyond the skilled application of theory and technique.

Transformative learning

Transformative learning is defined by Mezirow (1990a) as the process of learning through critical self-reflection to allow a more inclusive, discriminating and integrative understanding of one's experience, which includes acting upon these insights. Critical reflection involves examining one's assumptions and presuppositions, the sources, consequences and validity of those assumptions, for the distortions that may be present in the meaning perspective. This implies a view that reality is not fixed and entirely knowable but rather a socially con-structed interpretation. Distortions may be *epistemic, sociocultural* or *psychic* and have occurred through the uncritical acceptance of another's values. Training must provide an opportunity to explore these assumptions.

Epistemic distortions have to do with the nature of knowledge and how people know what they know. A belief that every problem has a correct solu-tion if only we could find the right expert or treatment, seeing some problems as immutable, or that only propositions which are empirically verifiable are meaningful, are examples of such distortions. Counselling psychologists acknowledge the need to view the problem from the client's perspective in order to explore possible solutions with the client, and trainees therefore need to explore their own and others' subjectivity.

Socio-cultural distortions are about power and social relationships, which might include self-fulfilling prophecies, particularly about minority subgroups. Examples of these distortions might include the beliefs that gender, sexual orientation, ethnic origin or social class, make people behave in a certain way and thereby bring the expectation to fulfilment. This may occur either through the behaviour being interpreted to clients overtly as explanations or because people are inclined to do what is expected of them in certain situations where they are less powerful. Similarly, assuming that a particular ideology, because it is widely held or belongs to the host community, belongs to all is an example of such a distortion. Trainees need to learn about social and cultural similarities and differences that may lead them to make such assumptions.

Psychic distortions have to do with presuppositions about an individual's psychological make-up such as where parental prohibitions might limit or impede action in adulthood. An example might be in believing that some adults have a nervous disposition whereas an anxious parent might have dis-couraged risk taking. Similarly, ideas from medicine about the organic or genetic cause of psychological distress need to be critically evaluated for their philosophical assumptions.

A number of Mezirow's (1990a) contributors suggest ways in which trans-formative learning may be fostered. Hart (1990) discusses how consciousness raising is subversive and deals with the internal and external effects of power, using the example of the women's liberation movement, which came together to talk, and shows how that transformed what was thought to be a personal problem into a problem with a social cause and a political solution. Uniting around a theme of oppression, assuming knowledge is constructed and subjective, empowering the individual, linking theory and practice leads towards emancipatory action.

Roth (1990) discusses how we come to be who we are and describes the role of the facilitator of personal development as providing guidance to the trainee evolving from one identity to another. One way of helping the trainee reflect on his/her assumptions and become aware of them is through the use of experiential workshops. Kitchener and King (1990) describe a 'Reflective Judgement Model' which encourages epistemological development and describe a workshop which develops understanding that different people may provide discrepant accounts of the same event, which makes it difficult to know what to believe.

To be an educator in this context means to be an 'empathic provocateur' (Mezirow, 1990b: 360), combining sensitive understanding with timely challenge. It also means to serve as a role model for critical reflection and the ethical idea of caring, to serve as a committed co-learner and occasional guide. Educators are to encourage multiple reading of texts, make a wider range of symbols of meaning available and create reflective dialogic communities. This has implications for all the educators involved in the training of counselling psychologists, as tutors, individual therapists, practice supervisors and co-ordinators of training. It will have applications in the processes of therapy and supervision both one-to-one and group, in personal development groups and experiential workshops.

The place of personal development

> Instead of needing to be in control and become an expert in decision-making, supervisees benefit in the longer term from being open in revealing and clarifying some of the helplessness and disillusion they experience in their work. Understanding personal vulnerabilities can lead to increased understanding of the vulnerabilities of others ... (Jennings, 1996: 41)

The experience of personal development and therapy, by whatever name, is a significant part of training, providing the chance to explore and strengthen personal vulnerabilities and wounds which might resurface with clients if they have gone unrecognized previously. The practitioner will require resilience to survive being exposed to considerable emotional distress, and an attitude of tolerance towards people who are angry, critical or dismissive.

There has been some discussion in a number of journals by counsellors, psychotherapists and accrediting organizations about the requirement of a minimum of forty hours of personal therapy, which is specified for becoming a chartered counselling psychologist as well as for other professions. It may be seen as expensive, time-consuming, and, since it is applied universally regardless of whether the trainee wants to engage in it or not, it is not entered into voluntarily. On the other hand it provides an experience of what it may be like to be a client, allows the trainee to learn by experience from a skilled practitioner and provides containment for issues that may arise during training as well as an opportunity to address unresolved personal issues.

Courses can provide a personal development group with an external facilitator where trainees can discuss issues about work, training and personal matters and experience feedback from other group members and learn about group dynamics. Trainees preparing for the Diploma in Counselling Psychology, the professional qualifying examination, on their own do not have this built in and may find belonging to a group for supervision or counsellors' support provides some of this experience. While experiential workshops at conferences or training courses can help trainees learn about themselves, attitudes and presuppositions, the short-term nature of them may limit the depth of self-reflection and personal discovery.

Training the researcher

One of the earliest qualitative research methods applied in therapeutic work was the case study, and the application of quantitative methods for evaluating outcomes of psychological therapies is a more recent development. This latter methodology is better when the issue can be based upon statistical analysis or comparative studies where human unpredictability is not involved. It is a significant part of the undergraduate studies that trainees will have successfully completed in order to obtain the Graduate Basis for Registration before postgraduate training. However, it encourages the researcher to stand apart from the field of investigation rather than recognizing the impact of the researcher on the researched, and vice versa, which qualitative methodology acknowledges.

Counselling psychologists need training not only to conduct inquiry from outside but also to be able to open up an issue from inside for exploration outside, which requires the researcher to be a praxis-orientated researcher, what Lieberman (1986) calls 'scholars of practice'. The benefits are that by interacting in the research process, the action-researcher increases awareness of the contradictions hidden or distorted by everyday understandings (O'Hanlon, 1996). Edwards (1996), discussing the preparation for lifelong reflective practice and critical inquiry required for training teachers, sees action research as relevant to trainees, particularly in defending reflective practitioners from the onslaught of competence-based models of teaching.

For exploring interpersonal issues such as the establishment of a therapeutic relationship, action research is a very useful strategy, with its broadly based liberal approach conducted in a human fashion, where the one-to-one relationship is at the centre of the inquiry (McNiff, 1988). It is not just a more sloppy approach, because the philosophical base is an overarching awareness and respect for the integrity of individuals. Reason and Rowan (1981) see new paradigm research as softer and having validity in the personal and interpersonal skills of the inquirer rather than in the methodology. It is primarily the insights and understandings of the inquirer that are moved forward by his/her own involvement in the inquiry. Any proposed application affects the lives of real people, and in this way becomes political and ethical focusing on issues of social justice.

Zuber-Skerritt (1992) defines action research in higher education as critical and self-critical collaborative inquiry by reflective practitioners being account able by making the results of their inquiry public. They are self-evaluating of their practice and engaged in participative problem solving and continuous professional development. That seems like a description that is very close to the sort of practitioner that is being trained to be a counselling psychologist. It is not the panacea for all problems because it can be time-consuming, and other methods may be faster and more certain. However, it is an appropriate approach in an uncertain environment, for exploring complex situations where there are no simple answers.

The commitment to lifelong learning and continuous professional development (CPD) reminds practitioners that action research as a living practice is not just something that one does. Our knowledge is grounded in our experiences, so insistence on a responsive, contextually embedded scholarship lies at the heart of action-research, as it should at the heart of counselling psychology practice. Carson and Sumara (1997) in discussing action-research as a living practice, state that when who one is becomes caught up with what one knows and does, then the theory and practice problem is eliminated. What one knows and does cannot be separated from lived experience and the lived experience of others, always changing and not fitting predetermined categories.

McLeod (2001) discusses the reasons why counsellors and psychotherapists seem to have little interest in research and have low expectations that it will help them in their work with clients. Much research has focused on verification rather than discovery, has been dominated by hypothesis-testing experimental designs and has not been emphasized in their training. This is an area where the training of counselling psychologists is different, because being a psychologist means being encouraged to take research seriously as a professional activity, which counsellors and psychotherapists are not obliged to do. The shift towards pluralism in psychotherapy research, encompassing both quantitative and qualitative methodologies, encourages counselling psychologists to engage in forms of research which may be seen as more relevant to their practice and more consistent with their world-views. Postgraduate training needs to enhance qualitative research skills to match trainees' previous undergraduate training in experimental design and statistics.

Occupational standards

As a result of requests from a variety of sources, the BPS decided to develop its occupational standards in applied psychology, originally published in 1998, and these are likely to become an accepted benchmark against which to judge the competence of practising applied psychologists, including of course counselling psychologists. The statements of competence will detail the standard of performance required, the knowledge and skills that must be learned in order to achieve it and how competence should be assessed. Implicit in these statements will be the values and ethical principles to which the profession gives high priority, and the divisions will be closely involved in these developments. This will have an impact on training and continuing professional development.

Employers and people who commission counselling psychologists have a right to know what counselling psychologists can do, in which contexts and with whom (Division of Counselling Psychology, 2001a). There is much demand for evidence of outcomes, flexibility of approach, diversity in applications, multiple skills and being client-focused. In addition employers may look for teamworking skills as well as assessment, evaluative and management skills. It has become clear that counselling psychologists need to be broadly trained practitioners of psychological therapies in a wide range of settings and contexts in order to meet these requirements. However, there is a danger inherent in being too closely defined by employers, since it may limit training objectives and bring security at the cost of the profession's independence and freedom to constructively challenge employers.

Within a core-competences framework for applied psychologists, to complement the scientist-practitioner approach, there is a need for interpersonal effectiveness and an emphasis on the development of the self as a reflective practitioner, Schön's (1983) model of professional artistry. Drawing upon concepts of scientist-practitioner, scholar, reflective practitioner and action researcher defines what a counselling psychologist is as well as does. A competence model is not an attempt to define a different type of practitioner, but rather a language in which to describe the practitioner in terms of outcome rather than input.

Competence models that emphasize what practitioners can do and with whom, and in which contexts, encourage changes in the methods of providing training and assessment rather than fundamental changes to the nature of the practitioner. Employers are making similar demands on the profession and it is important that the profession is confident of its identity as professionally valid, and finds ways to express it in a language that is easily understood by the employer. Moves towards accreditation of prior learning, modular courses, portfolios of training, self-directed learning and so forth have already been developed by the Division in its independent route to qualification.

Training routes

A counselling psychologist can qualify by either completing a course accredited by the Training Committee in Counselling Psychology, or by being awarded a diploma in counselling psychology by the Board of Examiners in Counselling Psychology, sometimes known as the independent route because trainees construct their own portfolios. Either of these awards permits the trainee to apply for Chartered Counselling Psychologist status with the BPS. It is possible to combine these routes either by being granted part one of the diploma and joining an accredited course for part two, or by achieving part one on a course and applying to complete training for the diploma under the supervision of a co-ordinator of training.

Both accredited courses and the diploma syllabus include theoretical studies covering the three main therapeutic traditions, supervised counselling psychology practice with a range of clients and settings, experiential training to develop therapeutic skills and an understanding of diversity. Personal development training may be included in experiential groups but will also include a minimum period of forty hours of personal therapy. Training in a variety of research methodologies, conducting a research project and presenting findings are also included. Ethical issues are integrated throughout the programme of study. Both academic and professional practice are assessed.

The Graduate Basis for Registration (GBR) is a precondition for training, and new trainees are now required to be conditionally registered by the BPS throughout their training (British Psychological Society, 2001). The candidate's personal qualities of maturity, resilience and suitability may be assessed by selectors for courses (Wilkinson et al., 1997) and may also be discussed by potential co-ordinators of training for those choosing the independent route. Candidates may be required to demonstrate an interest in or experience of working with people using interpersonal skills or to have already completed an introductory course in counselling skills. Relevant experience in another sphere or voluntary work may benefit candidates.

Accredited courses

The number of accredited courses is growing but most have been concentrated in London and the south-east of England, posing problems of cost, and disruption to home life and work for some trainees. Some courses have been accredited by universities to award practitioner doctorates in counselling psychology, and that may be a growing trend. Each course is encouraged to develop its own core purpose and philosophy (British Psychological Society, 1993), specialization or approach. Some are able and increasingly expected to offer supervised practice placements in the locality or with local NHS psychology departments, but trainees from outside the area may not be able to benefit from them.

The key aims of counselling psychology courses (BPS, 1993) reflect the objective of training a particular kind of practitioner, who is competent, reflective, resourceful and informed, and who can critically evaluate the practice, research and theory of counselling psychology. There is to be respect for subjective experience and values and the way practitioner and client interpret the world, as well as a commitment to personal development for the practitioner. Ethical principles of respect for autonomy, responsible professional conduct, accountability and sensitivity to issues of social justice are fundamental to the development of the trainee.

Trainees should be able to demonstrate their competence in both academic and professional work. They must show they possess the personal qualities and sensitivity to engage in helping relationships, that they understand a broad range of theoretical frameworks, and that they demonstrate in their practice high standards of professional and ethical conduct (BPS, 1993). The ability to reflect and analyse aspects of the work, particularly to be able to distinguish what the client brings from issues which stem from trainees' own involvement, echoes Mezirow's (1990a) definition of transformative learning through critical self-reflection. He makes the point that training must provide an opportunity and a safe environment within which the trainee can explore assumptions and presuppositions.

Diploma in Counselling Psychology

Candidates who wish to enrol for the diploma in counselling psychology must do so before starting training, submitting a training plan for approval by the Registrar of the Examination Board. Although prior learning may be subsequently approved and accredited, there is no guarantee. Counselling psychology training is different from both counselling and psychotherapy training because of its emphasis on psychological knowledge and research. The plan will be individually structured to reflect the interests and needs of each candidate in order for them to be able to satisfy the Diploma requirements. The plan must include a range of theoretical courses and experiential workshops. Practice placements will normally be supervised by a qualified chartered counselling psychologist, likewise research training and personal therapy. Where no chartered counselling psychologist is available to fill these roles, equivalently experienced therapists or psychologists may be approved.

Trainees are expected to keep a log of training events and client work and are assessed by the presentation of client studies, process reports and written examination. The co-ordinator of training receives regular reports from supervisors and confirmation from the personal therapist and is responsible for advising and guiding the trainee (Didsbury, 1997).

Comparing routes

University courses in counselling psychology normally take three years full-time or an equivalent period of part-time study to complete. The independent route to the diploma may be taken full-time or part-time, and the trainee may choose to take longer to complete the training. Training is inevitably costly in terms of the time and effort required, particularly when studied part-time, and the financial commitment. The independent route may be more suitable for candidates already practising as counsellors or in academic posts, but a number of trainees by both routes have been successful in obtaining assistant psychologist posts in the NHS and some financial support for training costs.

There are other considerations apart from the time required and cost comparisons. Wilkinson et al. (1997) draw attention to the fact that trainees who are contracted to an employer or the NHS may find that it limits the variety of practice experience available to them. They may be reluctant or unable to leave a job, to gain experience with clients without health problems or in a different mode of therapy. Finding placements outside statutory authorities raises questions about the criteria for the suitability of the organization for a placement, and both statutory and voluntary settings may not be able to provide suitably qualified and experienced supervisors who are willing or able to act as training supervisors.

Courses which are based in universities have their own priorities which usually centre around theory and research and are less concerned about the clients with whom trainees are working, because their clients are the postgraduate students (O'Brien, 1977). Some trainees in the past have struggled to find their own placements but universities have recognized that taking responsibility for organizing placements assists them in quality control. In the assessment process, universities may favour written and oral examinations, course work and case studies, while self-awareness and the ability to critically reflect, which are cherished characteristics among professional practitioners, may have been seen as less important or inadmissible evidence by the university.

The bulk of practitioner training was formerly provided by voluntary, statutory and independent training organizations before the universities became more involved, and O'Brien (1997) suggests there may be a move back towards more courses being provided by training organizations which can compete with higher education institutions. Training organizations may be more able to accommodate the requirements for developing reflective practitioners with their emphasis on skilled and experienced practitioners as trainers and potential for links with counselling services. On the other hand, universities have the resources to provide access to libraries and computing expertise and a diverse research community, which the training organization probably cannot match.

The independent route is sometimes more suited to trainees who want to stay in a job, who have completed some counselling or psychotherapy training, or whose location or family commitments would not fit in with a course. It also allows trainees more flexibility to decide when they are ready to register for one component to be examined, rather than having to keep up with the rest of the training cohort and meet course deadlines. Trainees who choose this route are often mature candidates with relevant experience who are able to accept responsibility for their training and can find support elsewhere to combat the sense of isolation this route may involve. It is a part-time route but can be just as demanding of time, effort and cost as the course route.

Accreditation

It is becoming clear that at some time the government will require chartered psychologists and psychotherapists to be statutorily registered. In addition to being registered as psychologists, some chartered psychologists also identify themselves as psychotherapists. This has led the BPS to explore the development of a sub-register of chartered psychologists who are also recognized as psychotherapists by the Society. The requirements for accreditation are not likely to diminish, as the government and the Society demand that psychologists should be accountable to the public. Employers are also concerned to demonstrate how they audit and assure the quality of the services that they provide to their clients.

Employment opportunities

Some counselling psychology trainees have been successful in gaining employment as assistant psychologists within the National Health Service and substantive posts have been available on chartering as counselling psychologists. NHS employers may focus more on what the psychologist can do, with whom and in which settings rather than the particular route to chartering that they took (Division of Counselling Psychology, 2001a). The NHS offers many openings, and because many trainees have experience in primary care, general practice, psychology departments, mental health teams and hospitals, it is often the first avenue for seeking employment.

Counselling psychologists are also involved in the workplace through the growing movement to provide counselling to employees through external companies (EAPs). Medical insurance-based counselling schemes may require assessment and treatment by a psychologist, and counselling psychologists are well placed to provide both. Schools, colleges and universities also require staff not only to work with children and students, but also to develop services or supervise and manage the work of others. The charitable sector, social care services and independent consortia also provide a wide range of posts for counselling psychologists. Many practitioners combine salaried employment with self-employment or work entirely independently.

Trainee issues

The Division allocates places for trainees on the Division Committee (Division of Counselling Psychology, 2001b), its subcommittees on practice and research, conference planning, on the Training Committee in Counselling Psychology and others. In this way the views of trainees are taken into consideration formally. In addition, there are arrangements via the internet for trainees to be in contact with each other, and where they can find therapists, supervisors, co-ordinators of training, and support in regional groups and networks. These measures have evolved in order to address some of the difficulties that were highlighted by independent route trainees (Gaskins, 1997; Bartlett, 1999).

There are still concerns about how some other professional groups, particularly in the NHS, view the training of counselling psychologists and what it equips them to do. Some of these may relate to identifying counselling psychologists as counsellors rather than psychotherapists or psychologists and therefore not having the same status. This is particularly important where trainees do not have senior members of the profession working in their practice placement.

Another major concern is the funding of training places in the NHS, where counselling psychology trainees, unlike clinical trainees do not receive mandatory support. There may be scope for many more individual approaches, particularly where the trainee is already employed but also where counselling psychologists may be welcomed. The prison and probation services, social services, human resource managers, and many other employers might be willing to assist the cost of training in part, but it is still a major concern of trainees who may have outstanding debts from their undergraduate courses.

Demands by employers for staff to have the same competence as clinical psychologists in testing, using diagnostic manuals, assessing and writing reports may relegate to the background the counselling psychologist's special competence in using a therapeutic relationship and the personal self-awareness they bring to the process. There are various views on the function of supervision but counselling psychologists place greater emphasis on supervision for qualified practitioners, which has implications for both cost and professional accountability. Rather than extending training requirements, some of these other skills, when they are relevant might be left to the professional development of the counselling psychologist after qualification.

Supervision

In practice-based learning, supervision provides the context for learning about professional practice in the following ways that are important to trainee counselling psychologists (Jennings, 1996):

- Modelling and learning by identification.
- Interviewing techniques.
- Setting personal and professional boundaries.
- Confidentiality.
- Ethical concerns and the protection of clients.
- Attitudes of tolerance and acceptance of mistakes.
- Learning not to be punitive or patronizing to clients.
- Learning from mistakes.

In supervision, process dynamics between client and supervisee, which may parallel the relationship between supervisee and supervisor, can be explored (Hawkins and Shohut, 1991), and contextual factors can be considered (Carroll and Holloway, 1998). O'Hanlon (1996) comments on the trainee's response to the clinical gaze of the facilitator–supervisor relationship as paralleling what occurs in the client–practitioner relationship. It is not so much that the supervisor does not want to impose expert knowledge as a realization that where knowledge is being produced, there are always also dynamics of power and assumptions about reality.

Integration of theory, research and practice is facilitated through the supervisory relationship, which is in itself a modelling of the centrality of the therapeutic relationship. It may be a place to hold uncertainty ethically, a place to discover new knowledge, a place to explore the wider context of the work, a place which encourages the trainee to recognize the importance of their own personal development.

In selecting a supervisor, counselling psychologists need to consider issues of therapeutic orientation, professional identity, differences of ethics or moral values, finding a balance between sufficient similarity to make working together compatible and sufficient difference to provide some objectivity and challenge. The relationship must be mutually respectful in order for there to be a good working alliance, should provide an ethical basis for the protection of clients, and should facilitate the psychologist's further learning. The functions of training supervision are evaluating practice, advising, modelling, consulting and supporting, with elements of tutoring, coaching and instructing.

With qualified practitioners, the emphasis changes towards a more consultative, sharing and collaborative style that is more equal. The supervisor clearly has a crucial role to play in advising the practitioner about issues of competence, effectiveness, fitness to practise, conflicts of interest, ethical principles, legal issues and boundaries. Furthermore the supervisor can help the practitioner identify areas of professional development, prioritise the goals, plan a range of activities and monitor and review those activities.

Continuing professional development

A commitment to lifelong learning needs to encompass all that the practitioner is and knows and does. Once a practitioner is qualified, there is an obligation to engage in worthwhile professional development activities. The trained practitioner needs to have developed skills for self-directed learning, which will fulfil the duty to self, clients, colleagues and society.

Candy (1991: 459–66) in describing self-direction for lifelong learning has identified the elements that make up a profile of the autonomous learner, including the following. They provide one way of looking at the kind of practitioner who will be capable of undertaking autonomous professional development.

- Be methodical and disciplined.
- Be logical and analytical.
- Be reflective and self-aware.
- Demonstrate curiosity, openness and motivation.
- Be flexible.
- Be interdependent and interpersonally competent.
- Be persistent and responsible.
- Be venturesome and creative.
- Show confidence and have a positive self-regard.
- Be independent and self-sufficient.

- Have information seeking and retrieval skills.
- Have knowledge about and skill at the learning process.
- Develop and use criteria for evaluating.

When psychologists begin to offer services to the public on becoming chartered, they take responsibility for their future professional development (British
Psychological Society, 1999). Continuing professional development is seen as
obligatory at present but prepares members for the mandatory requirements
that statutory registration may place on psychologists (Sharrock, 2000). The
Society's policy (BPS, 1999) outlines the requirements of the Society and the
Divisions and types of CPD activity, both directed and self-directed. Members
are urged to keep records of CPD activities so that a sample of members can be
monitored each year.

The Division of Counselling Psychology expects members to log seventy
hours of CPD activities a year, forty of which comprise the Society's basic
requirement; thirty hours is the additional amount specified by the Division
(Division of Counselling Psychology, 2001c). The Society suggests that CPD
activities could include:

> Training courses, supervision, attending or presenting at conferences, research, learn-
> ing skills or information, preparing material for teaching, training or publication, short
> courses, peer discussion, professional committee work, reading, personal coun-
> selling, systematic reflection on practice, as well as maintaining the log. (BPS, 1999)

Within the Division's guidelines on supervision of a minimum expectation
of an hour and a half per month (Division of Counselling Psychology, 1998),
and if reflective and systematic case notes are written following every one of
400 sessions a year, taking on average fifteen minutes each, it is clear that this
requirement of seventy hours is not difficult to meet. However, in the spirit of
undertaking an obligation to engage in CPD, chartered members will want to
do more than meet the minimum and will also consider how CPD can be of
benefit to themselves. The Division's Guidelines for CPD (2001c) set out in
greater detail areas for professional development and point to the need for self-
appraisal and CPD planning. Supervision is again the key to this.

It is part of CPD activities for the practitioner to keep up to date with developments in psychology, counselling and psychotherapy, ethical, legal and professional issues, by attending conferences and short courses. However, it may be
too easy to pay lip service to professional development requirements by attending what is cheap, accessible and not too demanding. This is the reason for a
plan that goes beyond accumulating hours or attending what the employer
provides, to meet the need for stimulus, challenge and growth.

If the work of the practitioner requires new expertise that will allow work
with client groups or psychological difficulties beyond the experience of the
practitioner, it should be possible to include that as CPD activity. Practitioners
may train to fill other roles that require experience, such as supervisor, training
therapist, co-ordinator of training and examiner, for example. Professional

work on committees of the Division and the Society is valuable because it widens the practitioner's perspective.

Academic work could lead to higher qualifications such as practitioner and research doctorates, and some courses now provide top-up courses for chartered counselling psychologists. Such academic work may lead to lecturing, research, presenting and writing. Senior practitioners now occupy management positions in the NHS and training organizations, so management training may be part of professional development to enable practitioners to fill these roles. The Society has the means for practitioners to establish test competence and there are guidelines on being an expert witness and civil proceedings. These are a few of the many areas that practitioners may wish to explore in order to keep themselves involved in lifelong learning and development.

Conclusion

I have outlined my perspective on the aims and processes of training, how competence may be assessed, and how our unique professional identity has evolved and is evolving. I propose that there is a convergence of theory and practice which finds expression in the concept of the critical reflective practitioner, who is also engaged in scholarship and lifelong learning. I foresee the development of more modules within courses that can be used flexibly, the development of common assessment criteria in line with occupational standards and a review of the ways in which training may be financially supported.

The counselling psychologist needs to be an artist, creative, innovative and imaginative in addition to being technically competent. There is little room in courses for more to be added to the curriculum, and the pressure to train for competence may eliminate space for artistry and creativity. It is all too easy to focus exclusively and conservatively on meeting assessment criteria. This is the culture of expediency, where the 'need to know' takes over from 'the desire to learn more about' (Tomlinson, 2001). With literature and the wider culture, time spent on sport, cinema, theatre, concerts, novels, poetry, and in art galleries, feeds the imagination.

[The imagination] is at work in our everyday perception of the world, and is also at work in our thoughts about what is absent; [it] enables us to see the world, whether present or absent, as significant, and also to present this vision to others, for them to share or reject. And this power, though it gives us 'thought-imbued' perception, is not only intellectual. Its impetus comes from the emotions as much as from reason, from the heart as much as from the head. (Warnock, 1976: 196)

References

Argyris, C. and Schön, D.A. (1974) *Theory in Practice: Increasing Professional Effectiveness*. San Francisco: Jossey Bass.
Bartlett, S. (1999) 'The Diploma in Counselling Psychology by the independent route: thoughts from a candidate in free-fall', *Counselling Psychology Review*, 14 (4): 19–21.

Bond, D., Keogh, R. and Walker, D. (eds) (1985) *Reflection: Turning Experience into Learning*. London: Kogan Page.

Boyd, E. and Fales, A. (1983) 'Reflective learning: key to learning from experience', *Journal of Humanistic Psychology*, 23 (2): 99–117.

British Psychological Society (1993) *Guidelines for the Assessment of Postgraduate Training Courses in Counselling Psychology*. MQB Training Committee in Counselling Psychology, Leicester: BPS.

British Psychological Society (1999) 'Policy statement on CPD', *Psychologist*, 12 (6): 310.

British Psychological Society (2001) *Regulations and Syllabus for the Diploma in Counselling Psychology*. Leicester: BPS.

Brookfield, S.D. (1986) *Understanding and Facilitating Adult Learning*. Milton Keynes: Open University Press.

Candy, P.C. (1991) *Self-direction for Lifelong Learning*. San Francisco and Oxford: Jossey Bass.

Carroll, M. and Holloway, E. (eds) (1998) *Counselling Supervision in Context*. London: Sage.

Carson, T.R. and Sumara, D.J. (1997) *Action Research as a Living Practice*. New York: Peter Long.

Didsbury, P. (1997) 'Some thoughts on the role of Co-ordinator of Training', *Counselling Psychology Review*, 12 (2): 63–5.

Division of Counselling Psychology (1998) *Guidelines for the Professional Practice of Counselling Psychology*. Leicester: British Psychological Society.

Division of Counselling Psychology (2001a) 'Chartered Counselling Psychologists' training and areas of competence', *Counselling Psychology Review*, 16 (4): 41–3.

Division of Counselling Psychology (2001b) *Rules*. Leicester: British Psychological Society.

Division of Counselling Psychology (2001c) *Guidelines for Continuing Professional Development*. Leicester: British Psychological Society.

Edwards, A. (1996) 'Can action research give coherence to the school-based learning of experiences of students?' in C. O'Hanlon (ed.) *Professional Development through Action Research in Educational Settings*. London: Falmer Press.

Farrell, W. (1996) 'Training and professional development in the context of counselling psychology' in R. Woolfe and W. Dryden (Eds) *Handbook of Counselling Psychology*, London: Sage.

Freire, P. (1972) *Pedagogy of the Oppressed*. New York: Herder & Herder.

Gaskins, S. (1997) 'A tale of excitement and confusion', *Counselling Psychology Review*, 12 (2): 66–9.

Hart, M.U. (1990) 'Liberation through consciousness raising' in J. Mezirow (ed.) *Fostering Critical Reflection in Adulthood*. San Francisco: Jossey Bass.

Hawkins, P. and Shohut, R. (1991) *Supervision in the Helping Professions*. Buckingham: Open University Press.

Jennings, C. (1996) 'Training the reflective professional: the practice of supervision' in C. Jennings and E. Kennedy (eds) *The Reflective Professional in Education*, London: Jessica Kingsley.

Kennedy, P. and Llewelyn, S. (2001) 'Does the future belong to the scientist practitioner?' *Psychologist*, 14 (2): 74–8.

Kitchener, K.S. and King, P.M. (1990) 'The reflective judgement model: transforming assumptions about knowing' in J. Mezirow (ed.) *Fostering Critical Reflection in Adulthood*. San Francisco: Jossey Bass.

Kolb, D.A. (1984) *Experiential Learning*. Englewood Cliffs NJ: Prentice Hall.

Lieberman, A. (1986) 'Collaborative research: working with, not working on', *Educational Leadership*, 43 (5): 28–32.

McLeod, J. (2001) *Qualitative Research in Counselling and Psychotherapy*. London: Sage.

McNiff, J. (1988) *Action Research: Principles and Practice*. London: Routledge.

Mezirow, J. (1981) 'A critical theory of adult learning and education', *Adult Education*, 32 (1): 3–24.

Mezirow, J. (1990a) 'How critical reflection triggers transformative learning' in J. Mezirow (ed.) *Fostering Critical Reflection in Adulthood*. San Francisco: Jossey Bass.

Mezirow, J. (1990b) 'Towards transformative learning and emancipatory education' in J. Mezirow (ed.) *Fostering Critical Reflection in Adulthood*. San Francisco: Jossey Bass.

Mezirow, J. (1991) *Transformative Dimensions of Adult Learning*. San Francisco: Jossey Bass.

O'Brien, M. (1997) 'Training in higher education', *Counselling Psychology Review*, 12 (3): 127–32.

O'Hanlon, C. (ed.) (1996) *Professional Development through Action Research in Educational Settings*, London: Falmer Press.

Reason, P. and Rowan, J. (1981) *Human Inquiry*. Chichester: Wiley.

Roth, I. (1990) 'Challenging habits of expectation' in J. Mezirow (ed.) *Fostering Critical Reflection in Adulthood*. San Francisco: Jossey Bass.

Schön, D.A. (1983) *The Reflective Practitioner*: New York: Basic Books.

Schön, D.A. (1991) *Educating the Reflective Practitioner*. San Francisco: Jossey-Bass.

Sharrock, S. (2000) 'Continuing professional development', *Psychologist*, 13 (9): 450–2.

Spinelli, E. (2001) 'Counselling psychology: a hesitant hybrid or a tantalising innovation?' *Counselling Psychology Review*, 16 (3): 3–12.

Tholstrup, M. (2000) 'Division title round table', *Counselling Psychology Review*, 15 (4): 27–30.

Tomlinson, A.L. (2001) *Training God's Spies*. Contact Pastoral Monographs 11, Edinburgh: Contact Pastoral Trust.

Warnock, M. (1976) *Imagination*. London: Faber & Faber.

Wilkinson, J.D., Campbell, E.A., Coyle, A., Jordan, R. and Milton, M. (1997) 'Trials, tribulations and tentative triumphs', *Counselling Psychology Review*, 12 (2): 79–89.

Zuber-Skerritt, O. (1992) *Action Research in Higher Education*. London: Kogan Page.

32 Counselling Psychology: the Next Ten Years
ALAN FRANKLAND

Since the future of Counselling Psychology is inevitably tied up with the development of Psychology in general I shall commence this chapter with some thoughts about the future of the discipline as a whole, and the place of Counselling Psychology within it. Then I shall turn to a more detailed consideration of this particular area of thinking and practice before finally turning to Counselling Psychology as an organized body within the framework of the British Psychological Society and its relation to other psychotherapeutic organizations. I have considered a number of ways of setting out what I have to say here. As I re-read Hooper's (1996) parallel chapter in the first edition of this book I played with the possibility of organizing my ideas within the same framework as he had used, but felt uncomfortable with that (although I would dearly have liked to use his initial quote from Sam Goldwyn: 'Never prophesy, especially about the future'). In the end I think the structure that has emerged for this piece simply reflects me and where I am in my professional life, as a working therapist, a Counselling Psychologist who has been active in the affairs of the Division of Counselling Psychology and the British Psychological Society as a whole for some years but who also maintains a loyalty and identity as a counsellor, as a Fellow of the British Association for Counselling and Psychotherapy. I still contribute to a BACP Accredited Counsellor training programme.

I include this autobiographical note, as I would in a qualitative research enquiry, so that the potential biases in this speculation can be understood. Although I shall base my thoughts both on some quite well developed research and on the more limited empirical base of my own experience I am well aware that the formal evidence is slight so that my understanding of the future is as much shaped by feelings derived from my experience as by more objective data. I think the enterprise we are engaged in here together may be human science; it is also fallible speculation.

Almost fifty years ago Carl Rogers wrote to the editor of the (American) *Journal of Counseling Psychology*, who had questioned his decision to submit an article substantially written in the first person, as follows: 'The fact that it is in quite personal form is not accidental nor intended to make it a letter ... I believe that putting an article in personal form makes it communicate more directly and, even more important, keeps us from sounding like oracles' (Rogers, 1957, in Kirschenbaum and Henderson, 1989). This chapter is in similar vein.

The future of the discipline of Psychology, and the place of Counselling Psychology within it

As part of the British Psychological Society's celebration of its centenary, Helen Haste and her collaborators undertook a Delphi study (which certainly sounds oracular despite my protestations above) on the future of Psychology as a whole (Haste et al., 2001). Such studies seldom produce a clear unidirectional set of predictions and this is no exception. Haste and her associates identified twenty-four possible trends or themes for the future, divided into four main areas: Fragmentation, the Biological base of Psychology, Reputation, and Optimism.

Under the fragmentation heading I was not surprised to see that the risk of a split between academics and practitioners is not expected to diminish significantly, for this has been a constant in British psychology all my working life. I would expect the tension to ebb and flow in the next decade as it did in the last. However, in Counselling Psychology (as seen in the structures of the BPS Division – and echoed elsewhere in the Society) we have seen some attempt to create a more unified model of science and practice, for, in this branch of the discipline, most academics and researchers are also practitioners and many practitioners maintain at least a critical research base to their practice and in some cases continue to see themselves as active researchers. I have a sense that this is more than window dressing for us and will hold to some degree over the next decade, even if the tensions elsewhere generally increase.

The study strongly suggests that within Psychology as a whole there will be further development of psychobiology, evolutionary factors and neuropsychological understanding. However, at the same time we may expect an increased emphasis on issues to do with everyday life, on the quality of life and on the whole person. Haste et al. point out 'there is no *necessary* divide between context-based, qualitative approaches, and approaches that pay attention to evolutionary and biological perspectives' (emphasis original), and it seems likely that the on-going redefinition of psychological science to embrace more qualitative analyses and methodologies will become even more salient.

Haste and her associates seem to suggest that such developments will help psychologists to increase their perceived usefulness. Since psychologists will increasingly be trained in skills applicable across a wide range of enterprises outside the laboratory and academia, it is suggested that they will be increasingly effective in influencing public policy and so will increasingly replace the medical profession as advisers to governments on social well-being and mental health. In part this perceived usefulness will be a response to psychologists being understood as very well qualified (with a doctorate as the norm for practitioner status). It may also stem from greater familiarity with psychologists on the part of the general public, as they see more members of the profession in the media and have more workaday contact with psychologists, for example in the Health Service, where they are predicted to acquire the same status as medical practitioners in areas like primary care. Psychologists are expected to become generally more available in health settings – sometimes replacing medical practitioners.

Counselling Psychologists need have no fears in such a scenario, indeed it seems to me very likely that we shall share with academic and clinical colleagues in pushing forward a number of these developments. For example, many Counselling Psychologists are already very active in areas of health care (and not only primary care). They have moved into a sphere in which Counsellors and some Clinical Psychologists had previously been the dominant non-medical personnel and now offer ways of working which draw on a wide range of psychological models and research (both scientific and humanistic) as well as ideas drawn from medicine, physiology and neuro-psychology, for example in their work with individuals suffering from depressive conditions (Hammersley, 1995) and in areas like post-traumatic stress. It would be my view that the shift towards qualitative understanding identified by Haste and her collaborators is already strongly established and will continue to grow within psychology as a whole. As therapeutic practice becomes ever more strongly (re-)established as a keystone of the discipline (a factor which may be further enhanced if the statutory registration of psychologists goes ahead under the Health Act) this kind of practice will have an increased impact on the way the discipline is defined and the ways in which it conducts research and develops its focus and epistemology. Counselling Psychology has clearly played a strong part in the existing shift and will continue to do so.

The future of undergraduate Psychology is important to us all because a steady stream of undergraduate psychology students assures funding and employment for academic psychologists and continuing pressure for post-graduate training programmes. Psychology as an undergraduate discipline has grown apace in the last decade, and is now the fourth most popular subject for applicants to university. It may well be that this growth and level of popularity cannot be sustained in the next decade, but it seems to me very unlikely that there will be a complete reversal of our fortunes in this regard, particularly if Psychology education and training encompass the new psychology that the Delphi study (ibid.) envisaged. Such courses are likely to attract students for their breadth and marketability. A wide variety of employers will be attracted to new staff with a range of ideas about human behaviour and social interactions, pragmatic and empirical intellectual habits and (if courses here follow some of their US counterparts) some practical interactive skills too, in areas like effective listening and negotiation. It may incidentally be this area in which Counselling Psychologists have their greatest impact on the undergraduate curriculum.

Haste and her associates noted (with some disappointment, I thought) that their study had not thrown up any 'knight's move' predictions, and this may be because of the 'curious omission' of the effects of developments in techno-logy and communications by their respondents. I am very conscious of this issue as I switch between laptop and desktop computers as I write, and contact a client going through a particularly lonely time through her mobile. I know technology will change a number of issues that surround Counselling Psychology, from how we make appointments or keep secure records to the possibilities of face-to-face work through web cameras and other sophisticated video links. The technology is already there for all this and the practice of counselling through the keyboard in real time or through e-mail has already begun. And there are so many other possible developments. However, the phenomenon of messaging/texting (which caused considerable surprise in the telecommunications industry both in the way that it took off and subsequently by the fact that it has not been superseded by WAP phones and portable access to e-mail and the web) is salutary here. It would seem to indicate a need to be extremely circumspect in making predictions in this area. We know that technology will change aspects of the ways we work; we do not know how, or how profoundly. Nevertheless I would be very surprised if a great proportion of therapeutic work in the next ten to twenty years shifted away from the personal setting of the consulting room, because human contact (and not simply virtual contact) will remain, in my view, a vital ingredient in the therapeutic enterprise. However, for a longer future who knows how technology may lead us to redefine our sense of real contact, and hence of what becomes possible and acceptable in therapeutic encounters?

Developments in Counselling Psychology

Continuing growth

It seems to me highly likely that current trends towards expansion in training and recruitment into Counselling Psychology will continue, and I will make some suggestions later, which might allow us to increase that trend. I am confident that there will be employment opportunities for these new entrants to the profession and in particular I can envisage a general increase in opportunities for Counselling Psychologists in the Health Service in the coming decade. I would be surprised if my experience of developments in a small city in the East Midlands were not replicated elsewhere in the United Kingdom. Here I am already in touch with Counselling Psychologists (in practice and in training) who work in a number of different areas in the Health Service. These include Rehabilitation and Pain Management, Occupational Health, Genetics and Assisted Reproduction, and I know of others working in General Practice settings, in work with AIDS and HIV, and in Psychiatric settings. To the best of my knowledge none of this existed as little as five years ago. The rate of growth of work in these areas will inevitably be influenced by the relative affluence of the country and by policy decisions at governmental level. However, I cannot see that these developments will now be reversed, and it seems to me that the influence of Psychology, and Counselling Psychology in particular, in these areas is assured.

Evidence-based practice

Another Delphi study (also stimulated by the BPS centenary: Kennedy and Llewellyn, 2001) may throw some light on the reasons for this. These writers note the current and developing expectation that practice in Health Service settings will be evidence-based. Although the authors question the easy assumption that all psychologists working with clients are going to be 'scientist-practitioners' (in the sense that they will be actively engaged in both practice and research) they do uphold the view that psychologists as practitioners will expect to base their practice on scientific evidence when it is available and will have developed the habits of assessing research findings alongside seeking logical and pragmatically effective outcomes for their clients. The training of Counselling Psychologists certainly includes the expectation that they will learn about research and indeed has some expectation that they will prove themselves capable researchers. Nevertheless, like other practitioners I think many will find it difficult to maintain an active research profile when fully immersed in therapeutic work. What they will bring, however, is that appreciation of the value of evidence, which the Health Service (and indeed other employers) will increasingly require. It may be this, more than anything else, that gives Counselling Psychologists an edge over non-psychologist counsellors and therapists in the Health Service of the future. Counselling Psychologists are already using psychological expertise in Health Service settings, not just for therapeutic work and research but in organization and management, occupational assessment and clinical audit as well, and it seems to me that this is a trend that will continue steadily over the next decade.

Although there is a risk that evidence-based practice is used as an excuse for imposing manualized care strategies on therapy (Norcross, 2002) there can be little doubt of its growing importance to all psychotherapeutic workers. Libby Wattis (2001) in a recent speculation of her own about the future of counselling put it like this:

> health professionals can no longer get away with offering treatments which are not supported by clear evidence of their effectiveness ... if counsellors wish to be seen as professionals we shall have to grasp the nettle of research into the effectiveness of counselling, and once effective research tools are developed we shall have to audit our practice accordingly. Evidence-based practice is coming and if we do not engage with its implications we shall become as outmoded as medical treatments with leeches ...

The question has then to be asked about where the evidence is going to come from, and who is going to develop the research tools? The answer is pretty obvious to me: from psychology, because whether counsellors and psychotherapists like to acknowledge it or not the academic traditions of their disciplines on the whole rely on psychological theory and research. So many of those who have made positive contributions to the theory and practice of counselling and psychotherapy have been psychologists that it is not excessive to claim that in reality counselling and psychotherapy are branches of applied psychology and that when we want to strengthen the empirical and evidential roots of the 'talking therapies' we will once again be looking to psychological understanding and methodologies to do so. This is not to deny all the important insights that have been brought into our work by counsellors and therapists who are not (or were not) psychologists. Nor is it intended to be petty intellectual colonialism. The point I am trying to make is that the need for evidence-based practice will bring us all back to psychological research, and to make sense of that all counsellors and psychotherapists will have to become more like psychologists. (This echoes a point made by Hooper, 1996, who wondered whether 'all counsellors will become counselling psychologists because employers will require this kind of grounding for every counselling service'. He suggests that the sheer size of non-psychologist counselling organizations would ensure this did not happen, whilst it is my view that it is not so much the power of numbers that will make the difference as the need to have a research base for evidence-led practice that will gradually turn us all into psychologists.)

The Health Service

Counselling Psychologists are already expanding into areas of practice which until recently might have been seen as the domain of other professional groups. Although we have seen considerable expansion into the Health Service, which may occasionally be because there are not enough trained Clinical Psychologists, it is not other psychologists whose job opportunities may be constrained by the employment of Counselling Psychologists. The main pressure is falling and will fall on Counsellors (and possibly some Psychotherapists) who could be seen as having a less developed pragmatic and evidential base for their practice. In primary care and in other areas of the Health Service (as well as in EAPs) Counselling Psychologists are already taking jobs that might otherwise have gone to well established counsellors. In my view counsellors and psychotherapists will be increasingly subject to a double squeeze, having to become more formally engaged with psychology in order to provide themselves with an evidential base and yet at the same time finding themselves losing out to those with recognized qualifications in psychology who are seen by employers as the real McCoy. This tendency may be strengthened if the Haste Delphi prediction (2001) about a doctorate becoming the norm for psychological practitioners also comes to pass.

Had I been asked a few years ago to predict growth areas for Counselling Psychology I would not have started with the Health Service at all. It was simply not apparent to me, even in the late 1990s, that Counselling Psychologists would make such a rapid breakthrough into this service, not least because I believed that other branches of psychology (clinical, health and the neuropsychologists) held sway in this area and would continue to do so. It may be mainly the failure of government to train sufficient Clinical Psychologists to meet the demand for psychological services which has given Counselling

Psychologists (who mostly pay for their own training) their original foothold in health spheres, but there can now be little doubt that they are there to stay, and their contributions (particularly, but not exclusively, as therapists) are valuable and valid. Indeed, it seems to me that employers who initially took on Counselling Psychologists because of a shortage of trained Clinical Psychologists have now discovered that in certain areas of their work the skills and attributes of Counselling Psychologists are more precisely what is needed and they will, in future, look for such practitioners when new employment opportunities arise. The specific attributes that Health Service employers have brought to my attention include developed capacities in a broad spectrum of psychotherapeutic work (where Counselling Psychologists have a considerable edge over initially trained Clinical Psychologists) and engagement in a more rigorous philosophical and research tradition (where Counselling Psychologists will have the edge over most Counsellors, even well trained ones.) As Chartered Counselling Psychologists have now virtually assured that they have financial parity with Clinical Psychologists in the Health Service, we can no longer explain away the growth of this work force simply in terms of cost savings!

Employment Assistance Programmes

A few years ago I would have expected, like Hooper (1996), that the major growth area for Counselling Psychologists would be work-based psychological services, initially through Employee Assistance Programmes but subsequently through consultation at lots of different levels, including coaching and mentoring and some significant aspects of the organizational and group dynamics of industrial and commercial institutions. It still seems to me likely that this is an area that will see considerable expansion in the next decade. Employment Assistance Programmes themselves will undoubtedly continue to grow as businesses seek the means to get expensively trained staff back into the work force when they might otherwise have long periods of stress-related sick leave or even leave jobs for which they have been expensively trained. Since there have now been a number of decisions in the courts against employers related to both work stress and reactive depression, many more employers are likely to consider using EAPs (or making similar provision in-house) to avoid the accusation of insufficient care which could lead them towards escalating settlements. Already a number of employment-based counselling organizations are actively seeking to utilize Counselling Psychologists to help them to provide appropriate therapeutic services for their clients and customers (the individuals who approach them for help and the organizations they work for). There can be little doubt that the pragmatic approach to counselling and therapy and a tendency towards evidence-based practice that is characteristic of Counselling Psychology appeals to business somewhat more than the (supposed) woolly idealism of counsellors or the abstract intellectualism of psychotherapy. Counselling Psychologists here are (perhaps unwittingly) trading on the image of a technological scientific discipline, even though their own preferences may be humanistic and relational. Michael Carroll (2000) has argued most persuasively that Counselling Psychologists may have a unique contribution to make to commercial and bureaucratic organizations, having an entrée on the basis of their therapeutic and consulting expertise and a role to play in helping them become more satisfying and humane establishments for all their staff.

Both evidence-led practice and the growth of work in and for large organizations (through EAPs and in the Health Service) creates a fairly serious challenge for many Counselling Psychologists who value their roots in a radical, even subversive, tradition that puts the unique value of the person as their first consideration. This tradition, which stresses a phenomenological humanistic perspective and values the human, subjective responses of the Counselling Psychologist as much as their objective knowledge and capacities, may seem to sit uncomfortably with the aims of profit-led organizations. It is not at all clear to me how this potential disjunction can be resolved, and there is clearly some risk of division between those psychologists who are not uncomfortable with the values of such organizations and their more radically inclined colleagues. However, I suspect that most Counselling Psychologists find themselves in the middle ground, a grey area which accepts both the need for objective evidence at times whilst holding on to largely humane and broadly client-centred principles. Surely it is the balancing of these vectors within individuals that will determine the developing value base of Counselling Psychology as a whole. I am not sure that we currently have the evidence on which we can base an assessment of whether or not psychologists can work humanistically and developmentally in large organizations without finding many of their principles disregarded or devalued. It is certainly possible that both profits and the satisfaction of a work force can be improved together (even if there is no altruistic intention on the part of the employer). It seems that at least some organizations have economic evidence to justify their continuing investment in psychological services. I remain hopeful of the possibility of 'working from within' although increasingly aware, at a personal level, that large organizations of any kind seem rather hostile to aspects of our essential humanity.

Independent practice

Although the proportion of all Counselling Psychologists working independently may drop in the forthcoming years (as a greater proportion find employment opportunities in the Health Service and in business) I think it likely that the absolute number of Counselling Psychologists working independently or in small group practices may well rise substantially. I see no evidence in the literature or from supervisees or other colleagues that this is related to a rise in a specific demand for the services of Counselling Psychologists (as opposed to other subsets of therapists) by the paying public. In my view, it results simply from the gentle, steady growth in demand for therapeutic services as a whole, and possibly more significantly the attraction of flexible self-employment.

I think there can be little doubt that there *is* an increasing demand for therapeutic services in both the public and the private sectors. In the 1990s the number of GP surgeries offering at least some counselling services rose from under one-third to over a half (Rice, 2000), and although the increase may be less dramatic in the independent/fee-paying sector it seems unlikely to have declined in this time. Some clients given a taste of therapeutic work in a primary care setting then seek the therapy they feel they need from independent practitioners. Although there are some signs that our clients are interested to know whether potential therapists are qualified and registered in some way, they do not seem particularly interested in whether their therapist is accredited by UKRC, UKCP, BACP, BPS or whatever, seeming to value personal recommendations and their own experience of the therapist much more than formal theoretical orientation or professional sub-groupings. This may be something of a surprise to new therapists and something of a disappointment to those who believe that only one brand of therapy or therapists can provide what clients really need, but it is currently a fact of life and seems likely to remain so. Our internal disputes about the relative merits of different approaches and styles of therapy and training must seem arcane and unnecessary to our clients when their principal concern is to find someone who will be welcoming and helpful (Howe, 1993).

The other factor (quite possibly the main factor), which I think will lead to modest growth in the area of independent practice, reflecting my earlier comment on the potentially dehumanizing effects of working in large organizations, is the attraction of flexible self-employment. In a number of areas of commercial and professional enterprise the last two decades have seen the rise of the 'portfolio professional' and it may well be that ours is a trade that is philosophically and practically suited to this pattern of working. Portfolio professionals are those workers who generate their income from a number of sources, with different combinations of remunerative frameworks, including partial employment, hourly fees, outcome payment, etc. Some portfolio professionals are engaged in radically different activities at different times whilst others do similar work within different contracts for different organizations. Thus we may have a worker whose main occupation is providing therapy but who does so for three different part-time employers and on spare days works as a supervisor and trainer on an independent, hourly fee, basis. Whilst some people would clearly prefer to have the security of full-time employment, it seems to me that more and more of my colleagues are wanting to be free of institutions and the constraints of full-time contracts and thus be more able to respond to their own needs, and to plan their work as it suits them.

The reasons for preferring self-employment and a portfolio of commitments may be very varied. They will undoubtedly reflect broad demographic trends such as increasing carer responsibilities for all of us (both for children and elders) as well as specific aspects of a therapeutic career which makes significant demands on the emotional lives of its workers so that such flexibility may be particularly attractive. Independent practice also gives rise to the possibility of working from home, which for some is really difficult but for others (and I am one) a delight, allowing a flexibility of work patterns that at times can be responsive to my moment-to-moment experiencing. It even ensures that I have to spend relatively little time commuting. No wonder it's set to become ever more popular.

Insurance work

One other issue that links both commercial work and independent practice is the growth of therapeutic work funded by insurance. This comes in three forms. It may come through EAPs working to protect employers on an insurance basis, as already discussed. It may be available to people who have specific health insurance policies that cover psychotherapeutic work. It also arises from more general insurance cover as the result of a claim following an accident, frequently referred by the solicitors pursuing the claim. In 1997–2002 there was a noticeable rise in these areas of work. Counselling Psychologists have attained parity as therapy providers with Clinical Psychologists with many health insurers (e.g. BUPA) and are also seen as viable providers of service by solicitors seeking a therapeutic resource for their clients. As we become a better insured and more litigious society there can be little doubt that such work will grow. Some colleagues may be resistant to aspects of this work, because it often seems to call for an expert-centred, assessment-based style of working which is not the primary therapeutic mode of many Counselling Psychologists, but the work will be there, and if Counselling Psychologists are slow to take it on other subgroups will undoubtedly do so. In my experience once one has negotiated the foothills of tendering for work, explaining the basis on which an assessment might be made (which does not have to be based on objective testing and *DSM* IV, but see Sequeira and Van Scoyoc, 2001, for an interesting exploration of this topic) the work itself is valid, interesting and usually well paid, which are all important considerations in job satisfaction.

I think that all these potential areas of growth will increase the pressure on Counselling Psychologists (along with all other service psychologists) to be effective, as rounded professionals. By this I mean that:

- We will increasingly need to be able to deal with colleagues who may not always share our understanding of the world and have the capacity to work in teams.
- We will be potentially developing business acumen and need to have a sense of the legal and financial responsibilities of professionals.
- We will have an active concern for ethics and values, and skills in resolving ethical dilemmas.

All this must complement, not replace, our skills in the therapeutic relationship, and our capacity to justify, and make sense of what we do with clients, to all those we work with, clients and colleagues alike. Clearly there are a number of issues that are problematic or challenging but it seems to me that Counselling Psychologists are used to confronting many of them already and are well placed to continue to do so.

Counselling Psychology and the British Psychological Society

I have been a Counsellor much longer than I have been a Counselling Psychologist. I have been proud to hold office in both counselling and psychological organizations, so it gives me no pleasure to predict that jobs for counsellors will increasingly be pressurized by practitioners who hold qualifications in Counselling Psychology. I think it would be wasteful for these two groups to get engaged in turf wars or occupational protectionism, so I would like to see an unprecedented opening up of opportunities for mutual recognition of qualifications, and the rapid expansion of opportunities for counsellors who want it to gain the qualifications and accreditations that would allow them to become mature and respected members of the British Psychological Society, and chartered as Counselling Psychologists.

This is not the place to try to work out the details of such lateral transfers but there are a number of ways in which the BPS could move on this, especially for those who started life with first degrees in Psychology or who have acquired them through the Open University or other avenues whilst training and working as counsellors. At the moment only experience gained after acquiring the graduate basis for registration can count towards professional qualifications in Psychology, and there is no straightforward route for psychotherapeutic professionals who are not psychologists to establish professional credentials in Psychology without going back virtually to square one. This seems to me to be overly protectionist and exclusive, and could lead to conflictual relations with such groups, which seems to me to be in no one's best interests. The BPS is moving towards the development of an approach to qualifications based on occupational standards, which recognize task-specific knowledge and skills, rather than relying on a particular pattern of training and qualifications. I would hope that this route (or one parallel to it) could be developed quite rapidly to enable the lateral transfer of appropriate counsellors and psychotherapists into the Division of Counselling Psychology as chartered members. If the Division can move on this soon the BPS might well be able to significantly boost the numbers of Chartered Counselling Psychologists, taking in well qualified and experienced colleagues who would help to develop the Division and the overall enterprise of the psychological therapies rather than wasting energy in unnecessary competition. I have no great confidence that this will happen, but it *could* happen, if we chose it as part of our future for the next decade.

Related to the issue of competition between different subsets of the 'talking therapies' is the issue of their statutory regulation and the continuing desire of Psychology as a whole to achieve such regulation as a single professional group. At the time of writing the details of the government's intentions are unclear. Although we shall undoubtedly see some kind of national registration of all the 'talking therapies', within a relatively short time scale, quite how it will happen and the position of Psychology is unclear. The BPS is still seeking an independent registration council for Psychology as a whole (on the grounds of the size, organization, competence and diversity of the profession). This would lead to statutory recognition of all professional psychologists (including, but not exclusively, those engaged in therapy) and regulation of the use of the title Psychologist. The government wants to set up a unified register for the whole range of the 'talking therapies', and might wish to include Psychology in such a grouping. However, the majority of psychologists are not therapists or even engaged in therapeutic work, so the BPS takes the view that this would be an anomalous and unhelpful position for Psychology as a profession. The compromise position might be that the government seeks to regulate all psychologists through the Health Professions Council (alongside other professions formerly regulated as Professions Allied to Medicine) and then creates a new body covering all practitioners of 'talking therapies' apart from those regulated as medical practitioners or psychologists.

From the point of view of clients seeking some kind of therapeutic service it might be simplest if *all* therapists were required to meet certain minimum standards and to register with a single authority. The separation of therapists who also are psychologists (or medical practitioners) from other counsellors and psychotherapists may be unhelpful, but since Psychology (even in just its applied forms) covers much more than therapeutic work it seems unlikely that the BPS will easily concur with joining a registration body that is essentially about the 'talking therapies'. I have a sense that we are still a long way from achieving a measure of consensus between the various groups of practitioners who offer the 'talking therapies'. Although statutory registration may bring some groups together on the basis of a modest assessment of what effective therapists have in common, for the most part the new register or registers that include such practitioners will tend to enshrine the differences between the competing therapeutic subgroups (or tribes, as they have been described by Proctor and Inskipp, 1999), which will probably reduce its value to the potential consumer and may make professional coherence and co-operation more difficult than they really need to be.

There is another element adding complexity to this situation: the decision by the BPS (shortly to become a reality) to recognize the qualifications of psychologists who are psychotherapists. This recognition has been a long time coming and has had rather a tortuous history within the Society but it is clear that it will now happen; what is less clear is what implications it may have for Counselling Psychology and the whole field in which we work. The highest probability is that all Chartered Counselling Psychologists will be able to obtain registration as accredited Psychotherapists, as will the great majority of Clinical Psychologists who want this recognition, as well as other Society members who have undertaken formal psychotherapeutic training. It is just possible that with careful thought the Society could also use this recognition to make an entry route to qualified professional status in the Society for some of those other practitioners identified above.

The major impact could be much wider than that. Psychotherapy registration explicitly recognizes common ground between applied psychologists with quite different kinds of professional training. It is just possible that this change could be an important trigger that leads to the deconstruction of the professional groups within Psychology which currently undertake work in the fields of mental health and the psychological therapies. I have heard this view advocated by some and criticized by others over many years now. Where currently we have Clinical Psychologists, Counselling Psychologists, Neuropsychologists, Health Psychologists and psychological technicians of various kinds it seems to be possible that these groups may come together to form a new (super) Division (or College) of Mental Health Psychology. One of the risks of such a development would be that (like the current Division of Clinical Psychology) this grouping would be easily dominated by the concerns of members employed by the National Health Service, and although that itself is not the monolith it was, I cannot help feeling that a grouping dominated in this way would lose more than it gained.

Conclusion

I wrote the first draft of this chapter in the summer of 2001 when white supremacists were intent on stirring up racial tension in our northern cities. At that time I was wondering whether Psychology as a whole or Counselling Psychology in particular had any role to play in relation to such difficulties. I returned to work on this piece immediately after the events of 11 September and I concluded editing it just prior to the fall of Kandahar in the American war in Afghanistan. As a result of these events and the responses of some of my colleagues in Psychology around the world I have become convinced that as a discipline we *must* follow the lead of seminal Counselling Psychologists (like Rogers) and attend more to these issues of communal tension and national and international conflict. I hope that as a result of these events and the feelings they have evoked Psychology will become increasingly aware of the wider dimensions of the world in which we operate.

Along with many colleagues I have experienced these issues entering my professional space as a therapist and as a teacher. We have faced, with our clients and students, issues of grief and loss, concerns about racism and oppression, the anxiety and depression that may be to do with the current politics of aggression and spin or the sense of alienation from the political process that this seems to have triggered in so many people. As individuals and as therapists we may have had to dig deep to bring humane and sensitive responses to all these issues, but I have some confidence that we will have been able to do that reasonably well. Where I fear we have been found wanting is in offering a contribution from theory or research to the wider debate. The BPS has not felt able to make any kind of authoritative statement related to all this based on psychological research or theory and so has made no statement at all. I understand that reticence, although my heart cries out for something to be said, and I hope that a decade from now we will not still be found wanting. In ten years' time I hope that Psychology as a discipline and the BPS as an organization will have drawn together more thoroughly and shared more widely a reasonably coherent (initial) understanding of the processes that turn alienation into 'fanaticism' and grief into retaliation; that allow us to identify with one set of unknown victims of violence and weep for them and their loved ones when we have managed for years to avoid any feelings at all for so many other victims of violence whose deaths, we are told, were 'a price worth paying'. Since Counselling Psychologists frequently work with individuals and groups in areas concerned with emotional communications and conflict resolution I am hopeful that working on these issues in a wider context will become part of the future of this group of colleagues in the next decade.

In October 2001 the British Psychological Society celebrated the centenary of its foundation. Psychologists have a substantial history to stand on to look forward. Counselling Psychology is still very much a new grouping that barely registers in this context (see Bunn et al., 2001) but it does have roots in the work and traditions of many who are recognized as pioneers of the discipline. I am sure that our interests lie in making links with other psychologists both academic and professional within BPS, and one of the things I look forward to is seeing more Counselling Psychologists in positions of leadership in the society as one indication that we are truly coming of age as a professional group.

As I review the potential situation of Counselling Psychology in the next decade many issues seem to me to be important, from the minutiae of registration and inter-professional recognition to issues concerned with evidence-based practice and opportunities for expansion, and the vital task of developing psychological insight into wider political processes and events. Each of these can be seen to present some kind of challenge to aspects of the way we work and the way we think and theorize. On the one hand Counselling Psychology may be pushed back towards modernist formulations and manualized interventions and on the other there is the risk that the discipline may drift towards aspirational philosophy or individualized sentiment. However, what is most salient for me is the sense that as Counselling Psychologists we have already forged quite a robust way of holding together some quite traditional aspects of scientific psychology and a more personal and radical sense of the importance of feelings and experience. If we continue to maintain and value this heterogeneous history I feel confident that Counselling Psychology can respond positively to all the challenges and opportunities that may arise in the next ten years.

References

Bunn, G.C., Lovie, A.D. and Richards, G.D. (eds) (2001) *Psychology in Britain: Historical Essays and Personal Reflections*. Leicester: BPS Books.

Carroll, M. (2000) Keynote address to the Division of Counselling Psychology Conference, York.

Hammersley, D. (1995) *Counselling People on Prescribed Drugs*. London: Sage.

Haste, H., Hogan, A. and Yiannis, Z. (2001) 'Back (again) to the future', *Psychologist*, 14 (1): 30–3.

Hooper, D. (1996) 'Counselling psychology: into the new millennium' in R. Woolfe and W. Dryden (eds) *Handbook of Counselling Psychology*. London: Sage.

Howe, D. (1993) *On being a Client*. London: Sage.

Kennedy, P. and Llewellyn, S. (2001) 'Does the future belong to the scientist-practitioner?' *Psychologist*, 14 (2): 74–8.

Kirschenbaum, H. and Henderson, V.L. (1989) *The Carl Rogers Reader*. London: Constable.

Norcross, J.C. (2002) 'Empirically supported therapy relationships' in J.C. Norcross (ed.) *Psychotherapy Relationships that Work: Therapist contributions and responsiveness to patient need*. New York: Oxford University Press.

Proctor, B. and Inskipp, F. (1999) '*Post-tribalism: our Millennium Gift to our Clients'*, keynote speech to BAC annual conference, Warwick.

Rice, M. (2000) 'Britain on the couch', *Observer Magazine*, 13 February, pp. 16–21.

Rogers, C.R. (1957) 'A Note on the "Nature of Man"', *Journal of Counseling Psychology*, 4 (3): 199–203.

Sequeira, H. and Van Scoyoc, S. (2001) Divisional round table 2001, 'Should counselling psychologists oppose the use of *DSM* IV and testing?' *Counselling Psychology Review*, 16 (4): 44–8.

Wattis, E. (2001) Unpublished keynote address '*The Future of Counselling'*, Compass Counselling Services annual general meeting. March.

Index

Compiled by INDEXING SPECIALISTS (UK)
LIMITED, 202 Church Road, Hove, East Sussex
BN3 2DJ. Tel: 01273 738299.
Email: richardr@indexing.co.uk
Website: www.indexing.co.uk